EAST ANGLIAN ARCHAEOLOGY

Frontispiece: The defence of islands — the Wardy Hill-top pillbox
Photo J. Akerman

Power and Island Communities: Excavations at the Wardy Hill Ringwork, Coveney, Ely

by Christopher Evans

with contributions from
A. Bayliss, C. Bronk Ramsey, A. Clarke, S. Davis, A. Dickens, N. Dodwell, M. Edmonds, C. Ellis, C.A.I. French, K. Gdaniec, C. Gleed-Owen, D. Hall, J.D. Hill, L. Horne, G. Lucas, N. James, D. Mackay, F.G. McCormac, P. Murphy, K. Robbins, M. Robinson, D. Serjeantson, C. Stevens, D. Williams and P. Wiltshire

principal illustrations by
C. Begg, M. Berger and A. Hall

and photographs by
C. Evans, K. Gdaniec, G. Owen, R. Palmer, C. Price and B. Robinson

artwork contributions by
Jeremy Akerman and Cornelia Parker

East Anglian Archaeology
Report No.103, 2003

Cambridge Archaeological Unit

EAST ANGLIAN ARCHAEOLOGY
REPORT NO.103

Published by
Cambridge Archaeological Unit
Department of Archaeology
University of Cambridge
Downing Street
Cambridge CB2 3DZ

in conjunction with
ALGAO East

Editor: Stewart Bryant
Managing Editor: Jenny Glazebrook

Scole Editorial Sub-committee:
Brian Ayers, Archaeology and Environment Officer, Norfolk Museums and Archaeology Service
David Buckley, County Archaeologist, Essex Planning Department
Keith Wade, Archaeological Service Manager, Suffolk County Council
Peter Wade-Martins
Stanley West

Set in Times New Roman by Trevor Ashwin using Corel Ventura™
Printed by Geerings of Ashford Ltd., Kent

© CAMBRIDGE ARCHAEOLOGICAL UNIT

ISBN 0 9544824 0 9

For details of *East Anglian Archaeology*, see last page

This volume is published with the aid of a grant from English Heritage

Cover illustration
Excavations in progress at the Ringwork. Aerial photograph taken by Ben Robinson

Contents

List of Plates iv
List of Figures iv
List of Tables vi
Contributors viii
Preface and Acknowledgements ix
Summary x

Chapter 1. Introduction: Islands and Context
I. Coveney and the Isle of Ely 1
   Wardy Hill and the larger enclosure system 6
II. The Coveney environs 7
   The provision of context 7
   Survey and environmental reconstruction (with C. Ellis) 10
III. Methodologies
   Survey and excavation 15
   Finds and dating 18
IV. Report structure
   Process and history 18
   First and last things 21
   'Place' and landscape values 21
   An excavation aesthetic (with M. Edmonds) 21

Chapter 2. Structure and Sequence
I. Period I (Bronze Age): Pre-Ringwork usage 23
   The lithic assemblage, by M. Edmonds 23
   Pottery 24
   Discussion 26
II. Period II (Iron Age): Ringwork components 26
   The ditch circuits 26
   Entrance access 31
   Buildings and structures 39
   Pits and 'troughs' 44
   Pre-/Early Ringwork enclosure 45
III. Phasing dynamics and structuring principles 54
   Circles and diagonals: spatial determinants 56
   Linkages and embankment 56
   Phasing outline 57
   Phasing alternatives and ambiguities 63
IV. Period III: historical usage 64
   Features 64
   Pottery, by D. Hall 64
   Tobacco pipes, by D. Mackay 65
   Metalwork 65
   Artefact distributions 65
   Discussion: lost from history 67
   Local attitudes to the landscape's history, by N. James 67

Chapter 3. Environmental Setting, Land-Use and Economic Practices
I. Soil micromorphological analysis, by C. French 69
II. Palynology, by P. Wiltshire 71
III. Plant macrofossils and molluscs, by P. Murphy 84
IV. Insects, by M. Robinson 114
V. Wood, by P. Murphy 121
VI. Animal bone, by S. Davis 122
VII. Surface bone, sieved fraction and herpetofauna (with A. Clarke, C.P. Gleed-Owen and D. Serjeantson) 131
VIII. Discussion 132
   Situating and denying 'the Wet' 132
   Agricultural processing: an overview, by C. Stevens 138
   Carrying capacities and land-use modelling 143

Chapter 4. Material Culture
I. Iron Age and Early Roman pottery, by J.D. Hill with L. Horne, and contributions by G. Lucas and D.F. Williams 145
   Phasing and dating 145
   Period I (pre-Iron Age) 161
   Period II (Iron Age) 161
   Fabric types 166
   Petrology 169
   Production and exchange 170
   Forms, surface treatment and decoration 171
   Use 181
   Sieved fraction 184
II. Metals (with A. Dickens) 184
   Fieldwalking 184
   Machining 184
   Excavation 184
III. Metalworking debris, by K. Robbins 185
   Analytical methods and definition of terms 185
   Results 186
   Interpretation and conclusions 189
IV. Worked stone, by G. Lucas 189
   Quernstones and rubbers 189
   Whetstones/grindstones 190
   Spindle whorls 190
   Beads 190
   Others 190
   Discussion 190
V. Fired clay, by K. Gdaniec and G. Lucas 190
   Loomweights 194
   Spindle whorl 194
   Oven fragments 194
VI. Worked bone 194
VII. Other finds 194
   Decorated stave 197
   A red mineral 197
VIII. Discussion 197
   Situating activities 197
   Decorative styles 199
   Trade and importation 200

COLOUR INSERT: 'Fieldworks'

Chapter 5. Articulating Settlement Structure and Re-addressing Sequence
I. Ploughsoil distributions 203
   Iron Age pottery 203
   Roman pottery 203
   Bone 203

	Phosphate	203
	Magnetic susceptibility	206
	Discussion	206
II.	Test-pit densities	206
III.	Feature patterning	208
	Buildings and eaves-gullies	208
	The Ringwork catchment: feature densities and depositional processes	212
	Relative frequencies: modelling abandonment	215
	Reduction dynamics and cubic capacity	216
	Modelling artefact populations	216
IV.	Chemical signatures	218
V.	Transgressing circuits	222
	Artefactual paths	222
	Occupation dynamics	223
VI.	Building types and inter-relationships	223
VII.	Human bone, by N. Dodwell	232
VIII.	The 'rhythm' of buildings	232
	Phase 1	233
	Phases 2/3	233
	Phase 4	233
	Phase 5	233
IX.	Enclosure categorisation	233
X.	Absolute chronology, by A. Bayliss, C. Evans, F.G. McCormac and C. Bronk Ramsey	238
	General approach	238
	Objectives and sampling	238

	Radiocarbon analysis and quality assurance	239
	Results and calibration	239
	Analysis and interpretation	239
XI.	Sequence and chronology	242
XII.	The Cove Environs/Ely excavations	243
	West Fen Road, Ely: 'decorative assemblages' and status	245
	Watson's Lane, Little Thetford: the calculation of buildings	248
	Hurst Lane Reservoir: houses and bodies	248

Chapter 6. Discussion: Violence, Power and Place

I.	Bronze Age: an embanked landscape	250
II.	Iron Age	253
	Assembly and the translation of space	253
	Defensive architectures, status and the labour of others	258
	Causeway approaches and marshland networks	263
III.	Roman(isation): 'archaic' communities?	270
IV.	Post-medieval: naming and ends	272

Appendix: Bone measurements 273

Bibliography 279

Index, by Sue Vaughan 289

List of Plates

Frontispiece	The Wardy Hill-top pill box (photo by J. Akerman)	ii
Plate I	*The Ringwork as crop-mark*	4
Plate II	Excavations in progress, aerial view	4
Plate III	Excavations in progress, general view looking west	15
Plate IV	Ringwork interior with Structures I, III and IV	17
Plate V	Excavations in progress with ditch F.2	19
Plate VI	F. 2 ditch terminal with F.58 cobbled surface in middle ground	19
Plate VII	Looking north, Structure IV under excavation	20
Plate VIII	The Watergate	33
Plate IX	Structure I	41
Plate X	Structure IV	41
Plate XI	Mistletoe remains	113
Plate XII	Herpetofanual remains	195
Plate XIII	A: *'Ceramic Appearances'*: the range of pottery	195
	B: the decorated stave	
Plate XIV	A 'blue' cold morning (K. Gdaniec)	201
Plate XV	C. Parker 'experiments'	202
Plate XVI	*The Spoon that Excavated Itself* (C. Parker)	202
Plate XVII	Human bone	231

List of Figures

Fig. 1	The Isle of Ely: Fenland location map	xii
Fig. 2	The Isle of Ely: location map	1
Fig. 3	'Great islands'	2
Fig. 4	*The Camp of Refuge*	3
Fig. 5	Location map, showing crop-mark, topsoil contours and geophysical survey area	5
Fig. 6	The Ringwork: topsoil contours	6
Fig. 7	The Wardy Hill-top: magnetometer survey plot	7
Fig. 8	*The Cove*: location of Iron Age and Roman sites	8
Fig. 9	Surface and geological deposits	11
Fig. 10	Fenland geological succession 5000–1800 BP	12
Fig. 11	Wardy Hill: subsoil contours with environmental core positions	13

Fig. 12	Environmental transects	14	Fig. 54	Frequency of herb taxa (Period II)	107
Fig. 13	Wardy Hill: area of excavation; fieldwalking grid, test pit points and location of original trial trenches and test stations	16	Fig. 55	Grains and chaff fragments (Period II)	108
			Fig. 56	Grains and fruits/seeds (Period II)	108
			Fig. 57	Overall density of macrofossils	110
Fig. 14	Section illustration conventions	18	Fig. 58	Densities of charred plant macrofossils (Structures I–VI)	110
Fig. 15	Surface collection: burnt and worked flint	24	Fig. 59	Plant macrofossils (F. 1)	111
			Fig. 60	Species groups of Coleoptera	115
Fig. 16	Lithic distributions and the burnt flint mound	25	Fig. 61	Sheep size in England: log ratio of mean widths	123
Fig. 17	The radial grid	27	Fig. 62	Sheep size in England: log ratio of mean lengths	123
Fig. 18	Section locations	28			
Fig. 19	Sections: the Main Circuit (F. 1, 4 and 64)	29	Fig. 63	Sheep size in England: log ratio of mean depths	124
Fig. 20	Sections: the Main and Inner Circuits (F. 1 and 2)	30	Fig. 64	Wardy Hill pig bone measurements compared with Durrington Walls	124
Fig. 21	Sections: the Outworks (F. 10, 11, 28, 42, 96, 144 and 152)	32	Fig. 65	Bone distribution plots	135
			Fig. 66	Ely Environs: ratio of hulled wheats	140
Fig. 22	The Watergate	33	Fig. 67	Ely Environs: cereal grains and weed seeds	142
Fig. 23	The Landward Entrance	35			
Fig. 24	Cobbled surface F. 58	36	Fig. 68	Land-use model	143
Fig. 25	The Landward Entrance: phased development	36	Fig. 69	Schematic elevation of Wardy Hill and Coveney Islands	144
Fig. 26	Entrance profiles	37	Fig. 70	Pottery: vessel types	147
Fig. 27	The West Central Entrance troughs (F. 76, 80 and 107)	37	Fig. 71	Pottery: size of handmade pots	147
			Fig. 72	Pottery: size of wheelmade pots	147
Fig. 28	Development of West Central Entrance and Structure IV	38	Fig. 73	HAD V pottery sizes	148
			Fig. 74	Pottery: ditches F. 1 and F. 2	149
Fig. 29	Main buildings: Structure I and Structure IV	40	Fig. 75	Pottery: ditch F. 2 and Structure I	150
			Fig. 76	Pottery: Structure I	151
Fig. 30	Minor buildings: Structure III and Structure V	42	Fig. 77	Pottery: Structure I and Outworks Ditches F. 11 and F. 12	152
Fig. 31	Ancillary buildings: Structure II and Structure VI	43	Fig. 78	Pottery: ditch F. 13	153
			Fig. 79	Pottery: Structures III and IV	154
Fig. 32	Plotting of pit/trough dimensions	45	Fig. 80	Pottery: Structure IV	155
Fig. 33	Pit/trough sections (F. 31–33, 47, 48, 79, 94, 107 and 108)	46	Fig. 81	Pottery: Structure IV	156
			Fig. 82	Pottery: Structure IV	157
Fig. 34	The north-west double-ditch system and the Outworks junction	47	Fig. 83	Pottery: Structure IV	158
			Fig. 84	Pottery: Structure IV and ditch F. 27	159
Fig. 35	Sections: ditches in north-western quarter (F. 11, 14, 73 and 82)	48	Fig. 85	Pottery: ditches F. 27 and F. 37; pit F. 32	160
Fig. 36	Sections: North Circuit features (F. 1, 15, 29, 30 and 93)	49	Fig. 86	Pottery: Phase 2, 'inner' western ditch, F. 37	161
Fig. 37	The South-East Rectilinear System	50	Fig. 87	Distribution of flint-tempered and wheelmade Iron Age wares	163
Fig. 38	Sections: Interior Western Circuits (F 37, 38, 46, 76 and 148)	51	Fig. 88	Frequency of wheelmade and burnished Iron Age pottery	164
Fig. 39	Sections: Southern Interior Circuit (F. 2, 27, 45, 52, 57 and 101)	52	Fig. 89	Metalwork	185
			Fig. 90	Crucible fragments	188
Fig. 40	Sections: Southern Exterior Circuit (F. 1, 106, 110 and 145)	53	Fig. 91	Worked stone	191
			Fig. 92	Spindle whorls	192
Fig. 41	*Circles and Diagonals:* main spatial axes	55	Fig. 93	Loomweights	193
			Fig. 94	The decorated stave	196
Fig. 42	Ringwork banks: reconstructed transect sections	58	Fig. 95	Distribution: metalwork and metal-working debris	198
Fig. 43	Ringwork banks: reconstruction plan	59	Fig. 96	Distributions: worked stone, loomweights, spindle whorls, worked bone	199
Fig. 44	Phase plans (Phases 1 and 2)	60			
Fig. 45	Phase plans (Phases 3 and 4)	61			
Fig. 46	Phase plan (Phase 5)	62	Fig. 97	Decorative styles	199
Fig. 47	Post-medieval surface distributions	65	Fig. 98	Ringwork-related surface finds densities	204
Fig. 48	Historical usage (Period III)	66			
Fig. 49	Location of environmental samples	70	Fig. 99	Iron Age pottery surface distributions	205
Fig. 50	Pollen diagram (1/37)	72	Fig. 100	Surface survey results: phosphate and magnetic susceptibility	205
Fig. 51	Summary pollen diagram (1/37)	73			
Fig. 52	Pollen diagram (2/63)	76	Fig. 101	Test-pit finds densities	207
Fig. 53	Summary pollen diagram (2/63)	78	Fig. 102	Excavated finds densities	209

Fig. 103	Inner circuit and test-pit finds densities	210
Fig. 104	Frequency of pottery and bone by Structure	211
Fig. 105	Main Structure finds densities	211
Fig. 106	Mean segment finds densities from main Ditch Circuits and Structures	213
Fig. 107	Total finds estimates by Ringwork component	213
Fig. 108	Magnetic susceptibility survey results	219
Fig. 109	'Chained' phosphate and magnetic susceptibility values	220
Fig. 110	Plotting of Structures by mean bone/sherd weight and phosphate/magnetic susceptibility values	221
Fig. 111	Distribution of wheelmade Iron Age wares and Roman pottery	224
Fig. 112	Ringwork interior: constraints upon building location	225
Fig. 113	Building forms	226
Fig. 114	Frequency of roundhouse diameters	228
Fig. 115	Building inter-relationship models	229
Fig. 116	Human bone distribution	230
Fig. 117	Building sequence phasing	234
Fig. 118	Controlled access: the Phase 4 entrances	234
Fig. 119	Ringwork phasing sequence	235
Fig. 120	Enclosure sequence (Phase 1)	236
Fig. 121	Enclosure sequence (Phases 2–5)	237
Fig. 122	Probability distributions of radiocarbon dates	240
Fig. 123	Probability distributions of simulated dates	240
Fig. 124	Probability distribution of duration of Iron Age activity	242
Fig. 125	West Fen Road, Ely: plan of Iron Age and Roman features	244
Fig. 126	West Fen Road, Ely: impressed clay plaque	244
Fig. 127	Watson's Lane, Little Thetford: location of roundhouses	246
Fig. 128	Frequency of finds by structure size at Wardy Hill and Little Thetford	246
Fig. 129	Hurst Lane: Iron Age features with distribution of human skull fragments	247
Fig. 130	The Bronze Age landscape	250
Fig. 131	*Landscape axes*	251
Fig. 132	Broom Quarry, Bedfordshire: later prehistoric landscape and settlement	251
Fig. 133	*Ringwork dynamics*	254
Fig. 134	*A gradient of 'control'*: reconstruction of the ditch and bank system	254
Fig. 135	Comparative plans of Iron Age 'forts'	256
Fig. 136	'Elaborated' concentric enclosures	257
Fig. 137	Comparable Iron Age enclosures and components	259
Fig. 138	Comparable Iron Age 'great' houses	261
Fig. 139	Plot of ditch capacity against area of both domestic-scale and 'great' regional enclosures	264
Fig. 140	*A spectrum of ambiguity:* concentricity and enclosure	265
Fig. 141	Iron Age and Roman distributions in the south-western Fenlands	265
Fig. 142	The Cove settlement system	267
Fig. 143	*Compounded enclosure:* The Cove network sites	267
Fig. 144	*Landscape polities:* the Isle of Ely, Danebury and Stonea territories compared	269
Fig. 145	*The cumulative imprint:* the long-term structure of surface finds distributions at Wardy Hill	270

List of Tables

Table 1	'Trough-like' features	44
Table 2	Visitor Survey: when did the fens first become marsh?	68
Table 3	Visitor Survey: what caused 'bog oaks'?	68
Table 4	Visitor Survey: how will the fens look a century from now?	68
Table 5	Visitor Survey: would you prefer the fens to be dry or wet?	68
Table 6	Pollen assemblage zones (Core 1/37)	75
Table 7	Pollen assemblage zones (Core 2/63)	77
Table 8	Charred macrofossils, Period I and II.1 contexts	85
Table 9	Charred macrofossils, Period II, Phase 2 contexts	87
Table 10	Charred macrofossils, Structure I	89
Table 11	Charred macrofossils, Structures II and III	90
Table 12	Charred macrofossils, Structures V and VI	93
Table 13	Charred macrofossils from pits and other contexts	96
Table 14	Charred macrofossils, Outer and Inner Ringwork Circuits and Outworks	99
Table 15	Charred macrofossils, Structure IV	101
Table 16	Summary of frequencies of charred cereal and other plants remains	102
Table 17	Summary of assemblage composition	103
Table 18	Plant assemblages from Structures I–VI	103
Table 19	Plant macrofossils from F. 1 sections	105
Table 20	Summary of plant macrofossils from F. 1	105
Table 21	Molluscs from F. 1	106
Table 22	Coleoptera from F. 1	119
Table 23	Other insects from F. 1	120
Table 24	The wood assemblage	121
Table 25	Numbers of mammal teeth and bones	125
Table 26	Animal bones and teeth	126
Table 27	Main animal species compared to other Iron Age sites	126
Table 28	Cattle measurements: Wardy Hill and Barrington	128
Table 29	Butchered and gnawed bones	128

Table 30	Dental wear stages of sheep/goats	129
Table 31	Distribution of animal bones and mandibles	128
Table 32	Distribution of main animal limb-bones and phalanges	128
Table 33	Fish remains	132
Table 34	'Midden core' animal bones	134
Table 35	Estimates of annual kill-off rates	134
Table 36	Identifiable bones and teeth by Structure	134
Table 37	Faunal remains from the Ely sites	134
Table 38	Ely Environs: weed seeds, cereal grains and chaff counts	139
Table 39	Ely Environs: weed/cereal percentages	139
Table 40	Characteristics of pottery assemblage	146
Table 41	Comparative pottery assemblage sizes	146
Table 42	Ten main features producing pottery	146
Table 43	Fabrics by weight from phased features	165
Table 44	Fabrics selected for petrological analysis	168
Table 45	Fabric, surface treatment and rim decoration by Eves	172
Table 46	Fabric and surface treatment	173
Table 47	Vessel form characteristics	173
Table 48	Rim diameter by Eves	175
Table 49	Rim diameter by vessel type	179
Table 50	Rim ornamentation by vessel type	181
Table 51	Rims with residues	182
Table 52	Metalworking debris from flotation residues	186
Table 53	Metalworking debris: XRF analysis	187
Table 54	Grind-/whetstones	190
Table 55	'Other' stone	190
Table 56	Fired clay fabrics	192
Table 57	Summary data on complete loomweights	192
Table 58	Test-pit finds densities	204
Table 59	Artefacts by Structure	212
Table 60	Main Circuit densities	214
Table 61	Mean finds densities from main buildings and ditches	214
Table 62	Finds capacity estimates from metre-segment densities	215
Table 63	Artefact population estimates	217
Table 64	Factoring of the site's estimated 'total' assemblages	218
Table 65	Mean phosphate and magnetic susceptibility values	221
Table 66	Frequency of pottery assemblages by structure	227
Table 67	Radiocarbon age determinations	241
Table 68	Watson's Lane, Little Thetford: pairing of roundhouses	245
Table 69	Watson's Lane, Little Thetford: total finds densities compared with house size	245
Table 70	Cubic capacity/labour estimates for enclosure perimeters	262
Table 71	Cubic capacity/labour estimates for Wardy Hill Ringwork and its larger system and the other 'great' fenland enclosures	262
Table 72	Cubic capacity/labour estimates for Wardy Hill and 'medium-scale' enclosures	264
Table 73	Bone measurements (pig teeth)	273
Table 74	Bone measurements (cattle teeth)	274
Table 75	Bone measurements (humerus)	275
Table 76	Bone measurements (tibia)	275
Table 77	Bone measurements (astragalus)	276
Table 78	Bone measurements (calcaneum)	276
Table 79	Bone measurements (proximal phalanx)	276
Table 80	Bone measurements (metacarpal)	276
Table 81	Bone measurements (metatarsal)	277
Table 82	Bone measurements (carnivores mandibles/teeth)	278
Table 83	Bone measurements (bird bones)	278

Contributors

Miss Alex Bayliss, BA
Centre for Archaeology, English Heritage, 23 Savile Row, London W1X 1AB

Dr Christopher Bronk Ramsey, MA, DPhil
Oxford Radiocarbon Accelerator Unit, 6 Keble Road, Oxford OX1 3QJ

Andrew Clarke, BA, MA
Cambridge Archaeological Unit, Dept of Archaeology, University of Cambridge, Downing St, Cambridge CB2 3DZ

Dr Simon J.M. Davis, BA, PhD
(Formerly English Heritage) Instituto Português de Arqueologia, Avenida da India 136, P-1300 Lisboa, Portugal

Alison Dickens, BA, MIFA
Cambridge Archaeological Unit, Dept of Archaeology, University of Cambridge, Downing St, Cambridge CB2 3DZ

Natasha Dodwell, BA, MSc
Cambridge Archaeological Unit, Dept of Archaeology, University of Cambridge, Downing St, Cambridge CB2 3DZ

Dr Mark Edmonds, BA, PhD
Reader in Landscape Archaeology, Dept of Archaeology and Prehistory, University of Sheffield, Northgate House, West Street, Sheffield S1 4ET

Dr Clare Ellis, BA, PhD
AOC Scotland Ltd, The Schoolhouse, 4 Lochend, Leith, Edinburgh EH6 8BR

Christopher Evans, BA, MA, MIFA, FSA
Cambridge Archaeological Unit, Dept of Archaeology, University of Cambridge, Downing St, Cambridge CB2 3DZ

Dr. Charles A.I. French, BA, MA, PhD
Dept of Archaeology, University of Cambridge, Downing St, Cambridge CB2 3DZ

Kasia Gdaniec, BA
Bradford Cottages, 1 Lode Road, Bottisham, Cambs, CB5 9DJ

Dr Christopher Gleed-Owen, BA, PhD
Dept. of Geography, Coventry University, Priory Street, Coventry

David Hall, MA, FSA
The Gables, Raunds Road, Hargrave, Wellingborough, Northants NN9 6BW

Dr J.D. Hill, BA, MPhil, PhD, FSA
Dept. of Prehistory and Early Europe, British Museum, Great Russell St, London WC1B 3DG

Laclan Horne
Former student at Dept. of Archaeology, University of Southampton, Highfield, Southampton S017 1BJ

Dr Gavin Lucas, BA, PhD
Cambridge Archaeological Unit, Dept of Archaeology, University of Cambridge, Downing St, Cambridge CB2 3DZ

Dr Nicholas James, DipEA, MA, PhD
59 Mawson Road, Cambridge

Duncan Mackay, BA
Cambridge Archaeological Unit, Dept of Archaeology, University of Cambridge, Downing St, Cambridge CB2 3DZ

Prof. F. Gerry McCormac, FSA, FRSA
The Queen's University, Belfast BT7 1NN

Peter Murphy BSc, MPhil
Regional Advisor for Archaeological Science, English Heritage, 24 Brooklands Ave., Cambridge CB2 2BU

Keith Robbins
Former Bradford University placement student at Ancient Monuments Laboratory, English Heritage, 23 Savile Row, London W1X 1AB

Dr Mark Robinson, MA, PhD
University Museum, Parks Road, Oxford OX1 3PW

Dale Serjeantson, MA, MIFA
Honorary Research Fellow, Dept. of Archaeology, University of Southampton, Highfield, Southampton S017 1BJ

Dr Christopher Stevens, BSc, PhD
Institute of Archaeology, Unversity College London, 31–34 Gordon Square, London

Dr David Williams, BA, PhD, FSA
Dept. of Archaeology, University of Southampton, Highfield, Southampton S017 1BJ

Dr Patricia Wiltshire, BSc
Milford, The Mead, Ashtead, Surrey KT21 2LZ

Preface and Acknowledgements

Since the time of the excavations a striking aerial photograph of the site by Ben Robinson has already twice been published, and even adorns the cover of the region's official research agenda (Brown and Glazebrook 2000; see also Bewley 1994, plate 9). Reproduce something enough times, however, and it becomes tame. In the course of this text, whatever analogies are drawn, this must not be allowed to happen. This site — this *thing* — is unparalleled, and should not be too readily subsumed by a desire to fit it to pattern. Nevertheless, in the almost ten years since the fieldwork occurred the writing of this report has necessitated the assembly of as full a picture of the Ringwork's context as possible. Certainly, the report's long gestation has benefited from subsequent Cambridge Archaeological Unit (CAU) fieldwork on the Isle of Ely, and the relevant sites are variously discussed within this text. Equally important has been that production of the text has followed the writing of the Haddenham volumes, and many of the themes rehearsed here owe much to the working-through of the second volume of that series (Evans and Hodder forthcoming). Much as the Haddenham fieldwork programme proved a unique formative experience, so too did grappling with writing the report.

Appropriate to the intangible nature of inspiration (and the vagaries of personal history), distant sources and 'displacement' have also been influential. Substantial portions of the text were written, penned up in hotel rooms, during enforced delays during the course of more ethno-historically related fieldwork abroad. The most recent of these, allowing for the drawing together of the final chapter, was in Hohhot (the capital of Inner Mongolia) following a season spent recording, amongst other monuments, a portion of the Great Wall of China. Whilst obviously greatly removed from the problems of Ely's sequence, both there and otherwise in Nepal (where Chapter 3 saw fruition) the question of the constitution of cultural identity within landscapes finds resonance in the text that follows. Equally, in the case of the Mongolian fieldwork and particularly 'The Wall', exploring the multi-faceted character of defence provided distant parallels.

Behind the Wardy Hill programme lies a sense of archaeological sites hosting a range of appropriate activities, and as places of experiment. Not only does this pertain to student dissertation work (Ellis and Roberts, see below), public surveys and specific techniques (*e.g.* the many topsoil surveys and the radial sampling grid), but also an artist-in-residence programme sponsored by the Kettle's Yard Gallery, Cambridge. Arising from a gallery initiative undertaken with Mark Edmonds, we remain grateful for the inspirational support of its curator, Charles Erche, and also to the participating artists, Cornelia Parker, Jeremy Akerman and Elspeth Owen. Now that it is complete, the balance of analysis/discourse and science/art that this volume has become appropriately conveys something of what I hold to be the diverse character of *the project of archaeology*.

I would like to thank many at English Heritage and the Fenland Management Committee for their tolerance for these asides and their support throughout: J. Coles, D. Hall, C. de Rouffingac, T. Williams and P. Walker, and more recently K. Buxton. For their sterling efforts over what proved a most harsh winter the CAU project staff are heartily thanked: R. Boast, A. Dickens, D. Hart, J. Hunter, K. Gdaniec, J. Miller, K. Miller, A. Oswald, R. Taylor-Wilson and G. Wait. The finds were dealt with most efficiently by J. Boast, L. McFadyen and N. Challands. The formidable graphic and computing skills of C. Begg, R. Boast, M. Berger and A. Hall have been crucial to post-excavation analyses and the production of this volume, and S. Smith proofed the text. I am also grateful to G. Owen of the Faculty of Archaeology and Anthropology, University of Cambridge, for studio photography. The farmer, Mr B. Dix of Coveney, proved most tolerant and gracious in the face of our exposure of his land, and is here sincerely thanked.

Apart from the specialists directly contributing to this text, the participation of A. Challands (magnetic susceptibility), M. Cole and A. David (AM Lab, geophysics), G. Edwards (AM Lab, conservation), and Z. Sanigar (phosphates) proved invaluable. I am equally grateful to Paul Craddock of the British Museum for his expertise concerning the find of arsenic; R. West of the Godwin Institute for Quaternary Research, University of Cambridge concerning the site's immediately geology; S. Laurie, of the University's Sedgwick Museum for his identification of stone; and M. Taylor's insights concerning the decorated wood fragment. Both N. Dodwell and I would like to thank P. Miracle of the Dept. of Archaeology, University of Cambridge for his identification of the alterations to the human bone. L. Stazicker of Cambridgeshire County Council's Libraries and Heritage Section first drew my attention to Richard Taylor's post-Coveney renown, and P. Saunders of the County Records Office supplied further details; N. Redfern's briefings concerning pill box typologies were equally insightful. Long practised in our routines, R. Palmer variously entertained and (thankfully) grounded a barrage of my aerial photographic queries.

Simon Davis would like to thank U. Albarella and D. Serjeantson for advice concerning Iron Age England; P. Baker confirmed identification of the pike bones. U. Albarella and S. Payne commented upon an earlier version of his report, and K. Clark arranged for the electronic despatch of measurements of Iron Age sheep bones from the Southampton University ABMAP data base.

For discussions about Ely and its now numerous assemblages, I am particularly grateful to M. Alexander, A. Dickens, D. Gibson, L. Higbee, M. Knight, R. Mortimer, A. Mudd, R. Regan and C. Stevens; and for matters relating to later prehistory in general to R. Bradley, M. Edmonds, I. Hodder, T. Lane, M. Parker Pearson, F. Pryor, N. Sharples and M.L.S. Sørensen. Finally, beyond the debts of generic inspiration, a now long-standing and still challenging interaction with J.D. Hill and Gavin Lucas in the 'sounding' of pertinent issues must — with pleasure — be acknowledged.

Cambridge, Kathmandu and Hohhot, 1999–2000

Summary

The Wardy Hill site occupied a prominent spur dominating a former marsh embayment on the north side of the Isle of Ely, and was delineated by a complex ditch network during the Middle/Later Iron Age. An occupied bivallate ringwork that arose from an enclosed farmstead was totally excavated in 1991–92. Issues relating to character of 'defence' and to social hierarchies (*i.e.* the command of labour and territory) are central to the research. An overview considers other major enclosures within the region, and summarises the results of recent Iron Age/Roman excavations nearby.

The locale saw later Mesolithic/Neolithic visitation and more substantive Bronze Age occupation, the latter possibly involving a series of embanked land boundaries. The question of pre-Iron Age utilisation of Ely's heavy clay lands is explored. The ringwork system fell from use in the late 1st century AD (there was no evidence of the Boudiccan Rebellion of AD 60). Early Roman ceramics occurred within its interior (including Samian within its roundhouses); the research considers the issue of archaic communities (*i.e.* a 'lingering' Iron Age) and processes of Romanization, aided by a Bayesian radiocarbon chronology.

Full environmental and palaeo-economic analyses allow reconstruction of Iron Age land-use. The dynamics of roundhouse settlement models are addressed, and depositional practices are considered in detail. When combined with the results of surface investigation (fieldwalking and test-pitting), the latter research permits estimation of the enclosure's total artefact populations. The site produced substantial finds assemblages: among the finds were a decorated La Tène pot and, uniquely, a rivet-decorated stave from a small wooden container. Iron Age pottery analysis was supported by pottery thin-sectioning.

The results of artefactual and chemical ploughsoil surveys are integrated with excavation data. Methodological issues are highlighted, as are the practices of a *contextual archaeology*. The character of cultural landscapes is explored, particularly in relation to 'island identities' (the Isle of Ely only having become a great marsh-locked fenland island during later prehistory). The volume concludes on the theme of marginalisation and the impossibility of recovering 'totalities' — these communities, no matter how 'remote', were linked to networks that led outwards.

The volume is interspersed with 'fieldwork' pieces arising from an artist-in-residence programme. Variously relating to the loss and distinction of 'place'/monuments, also included are the results of a survey concerning local attitudes towards the fenland past.

Résumé

Le site de Wardy Hill occupe un large éperon dominant une ancienne baie marécageuse au nord de l'île d'Ely. Ce site était délimité par un réseau complexe de fossés pendant le Moyen Âge et la fin de l'âge du fer. Des fouilles exécutées en 1991-92 ont permis de mettre à jour une forteresse circulaire qui se trouvait dans une ferme close et était entourée d'une double ligne de remparts. Les questions relatives au caractère « défensif » du site et aux hiérarchies sociales (impliquant le contrôle du travail et du territoire) sont au coeur des recherches entreprises. Les principales enclosures de la région font l'objet d'un examen général résumant les résultats de fouilles récentes, qui ont été menées aux alentours et qui portent sur la période romaine et sur l'âge du fer.

L'endroit a également connu une occupation comprise entre le mésolithique tardif et le néolithique, suivie d'une assez longue présence humaine à l'âge du bronze, cette dernière période pouvant impliquer l'existence de limites territoriales marquées par des talus. Par ailleurs, le thème d'une utilisation des lourdes terres argileuses d'Ely avant l'âge du fer fait l'objet d'investigations. Le système de la forteresse circulaire a été abandonné à la fin du premier siècle ap. J-C (on n'a relevé aucune trace de la rébellion de Boudicca en 60 ap. J.-C.). On a également découvert sur le site des céramiques de la première période romaine qui étaient de type samien au niveau des rotondes. En s'appuyant sur une chronologie établie à l'aide du carbone 14 selon le théorème de Bayes, il a été possible d'avancer l'hypothèse de communautés archaïques (une persistance de l'âge du fer en quelque sorte) et de processus de romanisation.

Des études environnementales et paléo-économiques approfondies permettent de mieux connaître l'usage de la terre à l'époque de l'âge du fer. L'installation des rotondes est examinée dans son évolution et les formes de dépôts sont analysées avec précision. Cette dernière recherche, menée conjointement à des investigations en surface (en arpentant le terrain et en effectuant quelques sondages) a permis d'évaluer le nombre total des artefacts présents dans les enclosures. On a ainsi découvert des ensembles d'objets en grand nombre, parmi lesquels se trouvait un pot décoré de la période de La Tène ainsi qu'une exceptionnelle douelle ornée d'un rivet et provenant d'un petit coffre en bois. La poterie de l'age du fer a été analysée en sectionnant finement les pièces découvertes.

Les fouilles entreprises ont permis d'obtenir des résultats qui tenaient compte de l'analyse chimique de la terre et de l'examen des objets découverts. L'accent a été mis sur les questions méthodologiques et sur les pratiques d'une archéologie contextuelle. L'idée de paysage culturel a été examinée, en particulier dans sa relation avec la notion d'« identité insulaire » (l'Ile d'Ely est devenue une grande île ceinturée de marécages uniquement à la fin de la préhistoire). Le volume conclut sur le thème de la marginalisation et sur l'impossibilité de reconstituer des « totalités ». Les communautés étudiées, quel que soit leur caractère « éloigné », étaient liées à des réseaux tournés vers l'extérieur.

Le volume comprend également « un travail sur le terrain » exécuté par un artiste invité dans le cadre d'un programme de résidence. La façon dont les monuments et les « lieux » ont tantôt été perdus tantôt mis en valeur est traitée par l'artiste qui s'est également attaché à rendre l'attitude des habitants sensibles à l'origine de leurs terres autrefois marécageuses.
(Traduction: Didier Don)

Zusammenfassung

Wardy Hill, einst auf einem markanten Vorsprung gelegen, der die frühere marschige Ausbuchtung an der Nordseite der Insel Ely dominierte, war in der mittleren/späten Eisenzeit durch ein komplexes Grabennetz markiert. 1991/92 wurde eine bewohnte Ringwallanlage mit zwei Festungswällen, die aus einem eingefriedeten Gehöft hervorging, vollständig ausgegraben. Zu den zentralen Forschungsfragen zählten die Art der Verteidigung und die sozialen Hierarchien (d. h. die Befehligung von Arbeit und Territorium). In einer Übersicht werden weitere größere Einhegungen in der Region betrachtet sowie die Ergebnisse der kürzlich in der Nähe durchgeführten Grabungen zur Eisenzeit/Römerzeit zusammengefasst.

Der Ort wurde in der Mittel-/Jungsteinzeit aufgesucht und in der Bronzezeit recht stark besiedelt. In dieser Zeit entstand wahrscheinlich eine Reihe von Feld- und Flurgrenzen aus Erdaufhäufungen. Es wird untersucht, ob eine voreisenzeitliche Nutzung der schweren Lehmböden Elys stattfand. Das Ringwallsystem wurde gegen Ende des 1. Jahrhunderts n. Chr. aufgegeben. (Es fanden sich keine Hinweise auf den von Königin Boudicca angeführten Aufstand im Jahr 60 n. Chr.) In seinem Inneren wurde frührömische Keramik gefunden (darunter Terrasigillata in den Rundhäusern). Mithilfe der Bayes'schen Methode zur Kalibrierung von C14-Daten wird die Frage erörtert, ob archaische Gemeindestrukturen (d. h. eine verlängerte Eisenzeit) und Romanisierungsprozesse stattfanden.

Die eisenzeitliche Landnutzung lässt sich mithilfe umfassender ökologischer und paläoökonomischer Analysen rekonstruieren. Außerdem werden detaillierte Betrachtungen zur Dynamik von Rundhaussiedlungsmodellen und Deponierungspraktiken angestellt. In Verbindung mit den Ergebnissen von Oberflächenuntersuchungen (Feldbegehungen und Testgrabungen) ist damit eine Schätzung des gesamten Artefaktbestands in den Einhegungen möglich. Die Stätte förderte beachtliche Fundkomplexe zutage, darunter ein verziertes Gefäß aus der La-Tène-Zeit und eine einzigartige, mit Nieten verzierte Daube eines kleinen Holzbehälters. Die Analyse der eisenzeitlichen Töpferwaren wurde durch Dünnschliffuntersuchungen unterstützt.

Die Ergebnisse der Artefakt- sowie der chemischen Untersuchungen des Ackerbodens sind mit den Grabungsdaten abgeglichen. Neben methodischen Fragen werden auch die Praktiken einer kontextbezogenen Archäologie erörtert. Daneben wird der Charakter von Kulturlandschaften erforscht, und zwar besonders im Hinblick auf »Inselidentitäten«. (Die Insel Ely entwickelte sich erst in der Spätzeit der Ur- und Frühgeschichte zu einer großen, von Marschland eingeschlossenen Insel.) Der Band schließt mit den Themen der Marginalisierung und der Unmöglichkeit, »Ganzheiten« zu erschließen – selbst die entferntesten Gemeinden waren an Netze angeschlossen, die sie mit der Außenwelt verbanden.

Außerdem werden »Geländearbeiten« beschrieben, die sich aus einem Artist-in-Residence-Programm ergaben und die die Unterscheidung und den Verlust von Monumenten und des »Ortsgefühls« behandeln, sowie die Resultate einer Studie zu den vor Ort vertretenen Ansichten über die Vergangenheit der Gegend.
(Übersetzung: Gerlinde Krug)

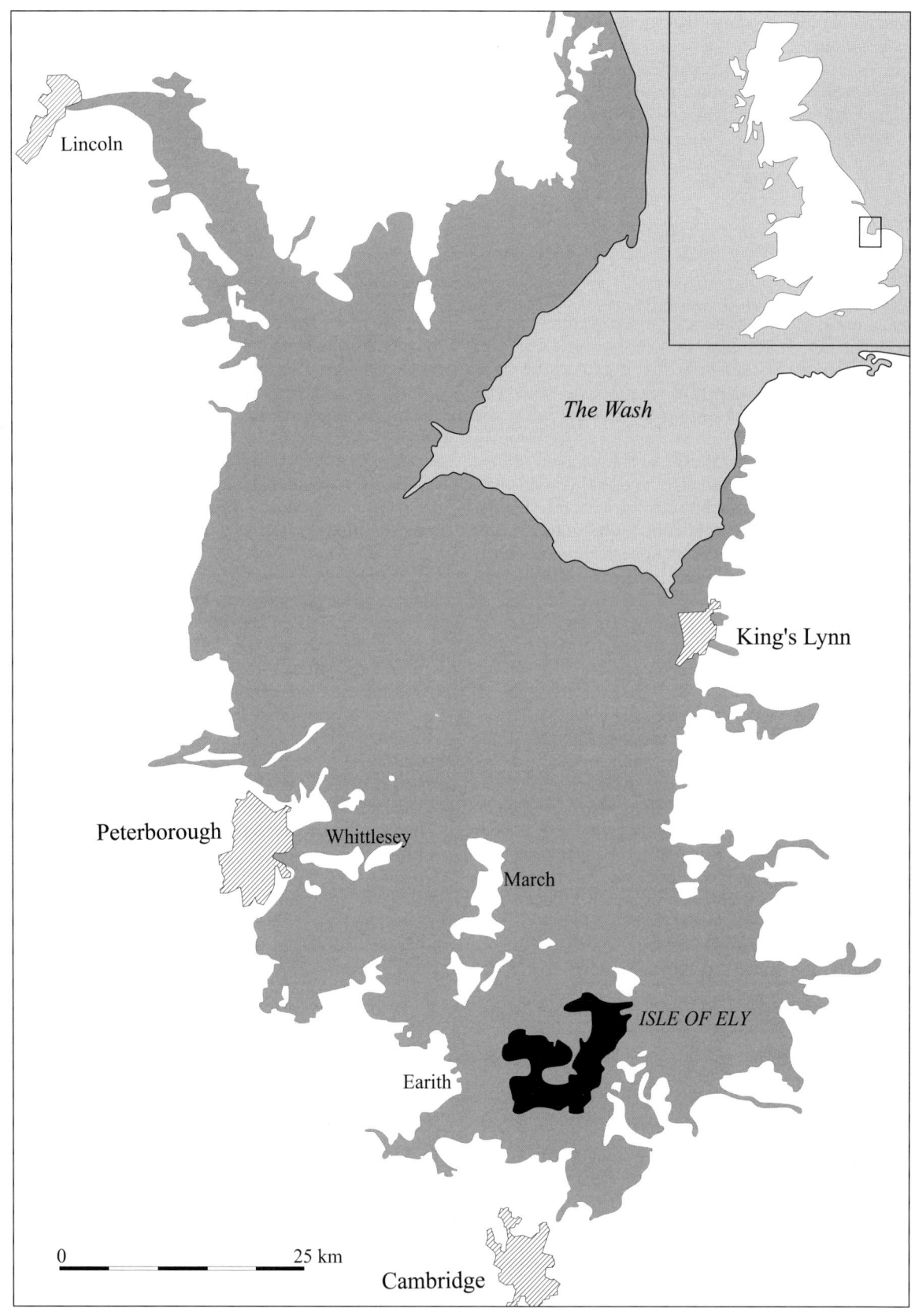

Figure 1 The Isle of Ely: Fenland location map

1. Introduction: Islands and Context

I. Coveney and the Isle of Ely
(Figs 1–4)

At a certain point, things disintegrate into muck, or dust, or scraps, and what you have is something new, some particle or agglomeration of matter that cannot be identified. It is a clump, a mote, a fragment of the world that has no place: a cipher of it-ness ... Everything falls apart, but not every part of every thing, at least not at the same time. *The job is to zero in on these little islands of intactness, to imagine them joined to other islands, and those islands to still others, and thus create new archipelagos of matter.*

Paul Auster, *In the Country of Last Things* (emphasis added by writer; quoted in Parker and Corrin 1998)

Coveney, 'The Island in the Cove', refers to a large, formerly marsh embayment — *The Cove* — in the north side of the Isle of Ely ('The Island of Eels'; Figs 1 and 2). Wardy Hill, a spur of Ampthill clay jutting into the peat fen, commands the northern approach into this basin. Although rising to only 6–10.00m OD, it is a strategic locale in relation to the subtle 'off-island' topography (Fig. 5). Emphasised by the World War II pill box that today still stands on its crown (Plate IV), the hill's name is thought to derive from 'warning' and in 1251 it is recorded as *Wardeye* — an 'island where there is a look-out' (Reaney 1943, 230–1; *Witchford*, situated 4km to the south-east on the stream/drain joining Grunty Fen to the Cove, denotes 'The Watch on the Ford'). As part of English Heritage's Fenland Management Project (FMP), the Cambridge Archaeological Unit's brief was to excavate a major crop-mark enclosure located on the north-eastern fenward slope of Wardy Hill where later Iron Age material had been recovered during the Fenland Survey (COY 1: TL 478820; Hall 1996). The investigations occurred over a period of four and a half months during the autumn of 1991 and late winter 1992 (see Evans

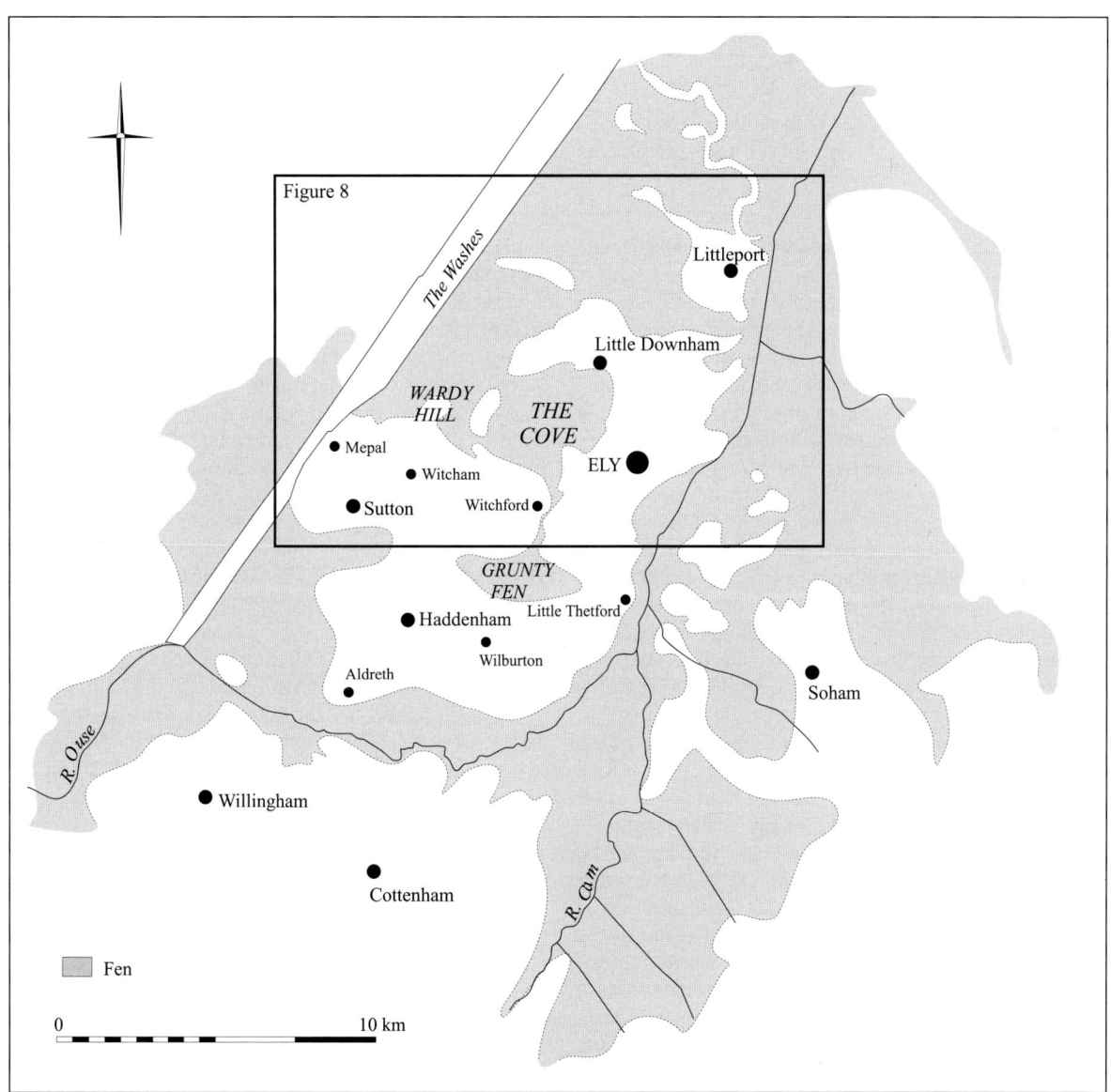

Figure 2 The Isle of Ely: location map

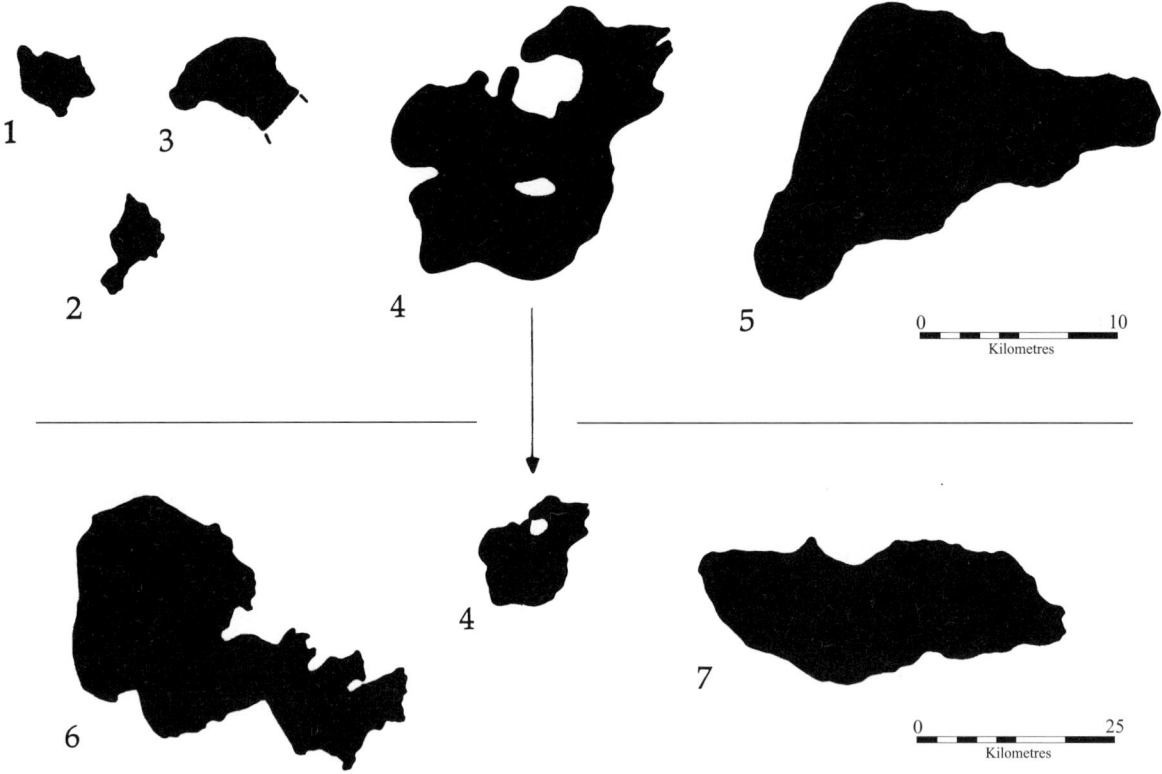

Figure 3 'Great islands': (1) St Kilda; (2) Sark; (3) Glastonbury Peninsula; (4) Isle of Ely; (5) Easter Island; (6) Orkney Mainland; (7) St Cristobel, Galapagos

1992 and 2000b; Hall and Coles 1994, 98–9 for earlier site summaries).

The site proved to be a defended Iron Age enclosure complex — arguably a fort — probably strategically located to command a causeway crossing the Cove. With this as its focus the character of later prehistoric social hierarchy, and the expression of power in landscape, are issues that must lie at the heart of this volume. These are currently unfashionable themes. Recently much emphasis has been given to the symbolic attributes of later prehistoric defensive systems (*e.g.* Bowden and McOmish 1987; Hill 1986), and the ritual components of the period's settlements have been emphasized (*e.g.* Wait 1995; Hill 1995; Parker Pearson 1996 and 1999). Important though these approaches are to balance the gameboard-like Thiessen polygon analyses that characterised so much earlier Iron Age hillfort study (*e.g.* Cunliffe 1971; Collis 1997), it is argued that they represent a 'levelling-off' of prehistory and advocate, if tacitly, a picture of 'static continuities'. Given the character of the Wardy Hill complex, here *social dynamics* must be at the fore.

Another central theme is that of Ely's island status — evocatively conjured up as a marshland fortress and/or refuge — and the emergence of fenland islands in later prehistory in relationship to the cultural construction of landscape 'place'. From St Kilda and St Helena to the Galapagos, Hawaii and Easter Island, the world's 'great' islands display cultural impacts disproportionate to their size and resident populations (Fig. 3). They feature in history due (variously) to exile, the death of James Cook, the origins of evolutionary theory, ecological awareness and the spice trade, and are a particular environmental and cultural phenomenon. Most geographic zones have blurred boundaries: their edges are not hard, and the criteria by which they are distinguished are often not appreciable to 'lay' observers. Island communities, by contrast, tend to know themselves. It is because of their ready definition and finite borders that they can be envisaged as 'closed laboratories' where the impact and transmission of specific practices, types or species can be readily charted (*e.g.* resource depletion: Grove 1995). Because of their physical isolation, island communities are equally associated with socio-cultural archaism, expressed through their resistance to mainland developments. Whilst trying to avoid mechanistic environmental determinism, the extent to which physical geography contributes to the construction of cultural landscapes is certainly relevant here.

Extending over 91km (excluding its low embayments), Ely is a great land-locked island, rising up to 30m OD amid the flat lowlands of the southern peat fens. Surrounded by marsh, it is isolated by 3–4km from the fen-edge villages to the south and by 5–10km from those in the east. It is a place that has a remarkably strong sense of identity. Largely based upon Saxon and medieval associations, this hinges variously upon a series of near-legendary characters and the Island's resistance to mainland authority (*cf.* Darby 1940, 144–6). Focussing upon the exploits of Hereward the Wake, this ethos permeates, for example, Kingsley's *Hereward the Wake* of 1866, and MacFarlane's earlier *The Camp of Refuge* (Fig. 4):

In all times it had been a land of refuge against invaders. In the days of Rome the ancient Britons rallied here, and made good stand after all the rest of England had been subdued. Again, when Rome was falling fast to ruin, and the legions of the empire had left the Britons to take care of themselves, that people assembled here in great numbers to resist the

fierce Saxon invaders. Again, when the Saxons were assailed by the Danes and Norwegians, and the whole host of Scandinavian rovers and pirates, the indwellers of the Isle of Ely, after enjoying a long exemption from the havoc of war and invasion, defied the bloody Dane, and maintained a long contest with him ... The saints and martyrs of the district were chiefly brave Saxons who had fought the Danes in many battles, and who had fallen at last under the swords of the unconverted heathen. The miracles that were wrought in the land of many waters were for the most part wrought at the tombs of these Saxon warriors. *The legends of patriotism were blended with the legends and rites of religion.*
(MacFarlane 1844, ed. 1897, 36–7; emphasis added).

While clearly bound up with 19th-century concepts of Anglo-Saxon nationalism (*e.g.* Curtis 1968), it also reflects upon the 'folk' and landscape sentimentality that became particularly acute in the region as the effects of stream-driven drainage became apparent (see Evans 1997b concerning the region's equally 'sentimental prehistories'). Nevertheless, parallels can be drawn between this type of historical projection and the Celtic 'warrior spirit' that has underlain so much of Iron Age studies, and which will be here further discussed in the concluding chapter of this volume.

While attempting to avoid any sense of a 'sided' prehistory, this volume will consider how far back the Island's regional distinction can be traced. While its elevation relative to the low fen would seem to recommend it as a locale, its heavy clay sub-soils inhibited early settlement, and accordingly its sequence varies from that of its lighter terrace gravel skirtlands (Evans forthcoming a). The theme of islands' isolations and, effectively, 'backwaterness' equally raises its corollary — colonisation. This has particular relevance for Ely as the marked later Iron Age horizon in its settlement record (common with other claylands in the region) could suggest 'arrival', and incursion by off-island communities. Following from this is the impact of Romanisation, and to what degree there is evidence of the survival of Iron Age practices that

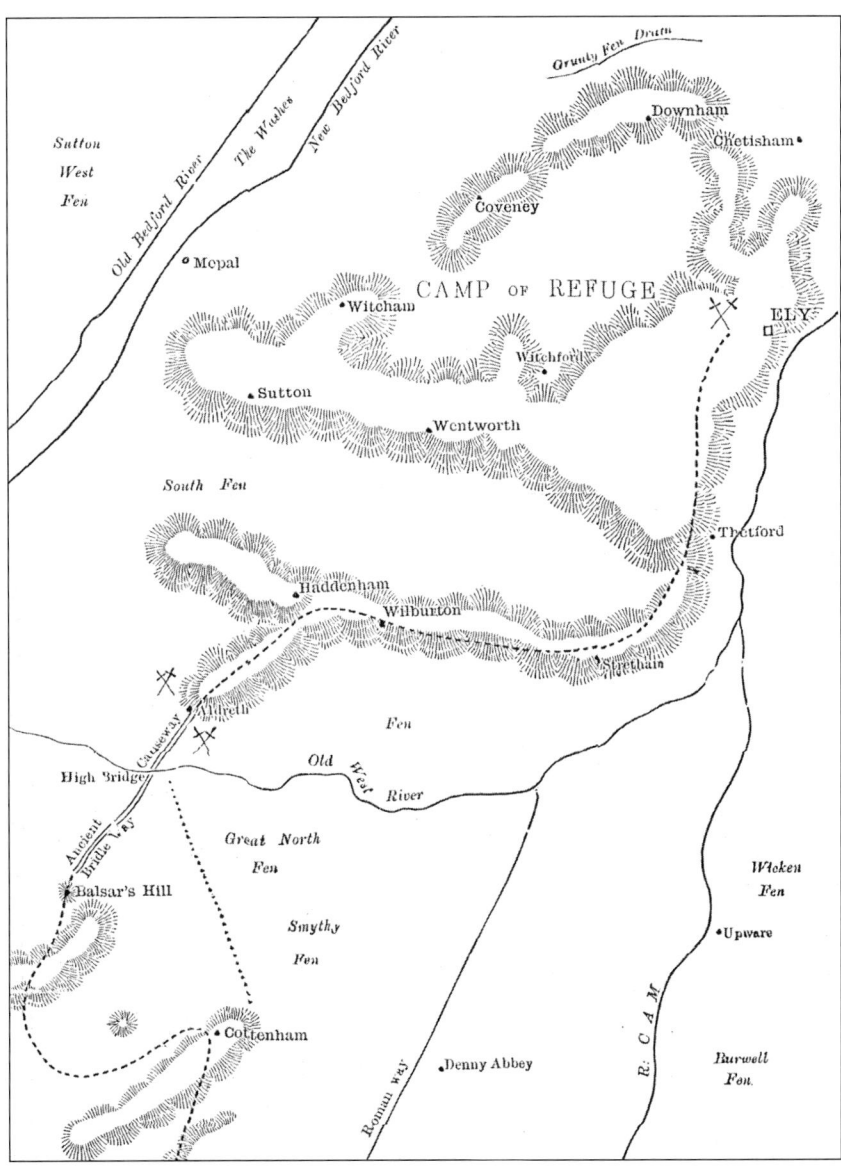

Figure 4 *The Camp of Refuge*

Islands made by the sea, and yet more islands, inland by rivers, lakes and meres, have in many places ceased to be islands in everything save only in name ... in some future age, men may find it hard to conceive, from that which they see in their day, the manner of country the Fen country was when the Normans first came among us. Then, I wist, the Isle of Ely was to all intents an inland island, being surrounded on every side by lakes, meres and broad rivers ...

MacFarlane 1844 (ed. 1897), 34.

Plate I *The Ringwork as crop-mark.* Looking north with hilltop pill box in lower left corner; note the linear crop-marks extending north from the perimeter of the enclosure's Outworks, one of them curving to the east beyond the central field division

Plate II The Ringwork excavations in progress, aerial view looking north-west (photo by R. Palmer)

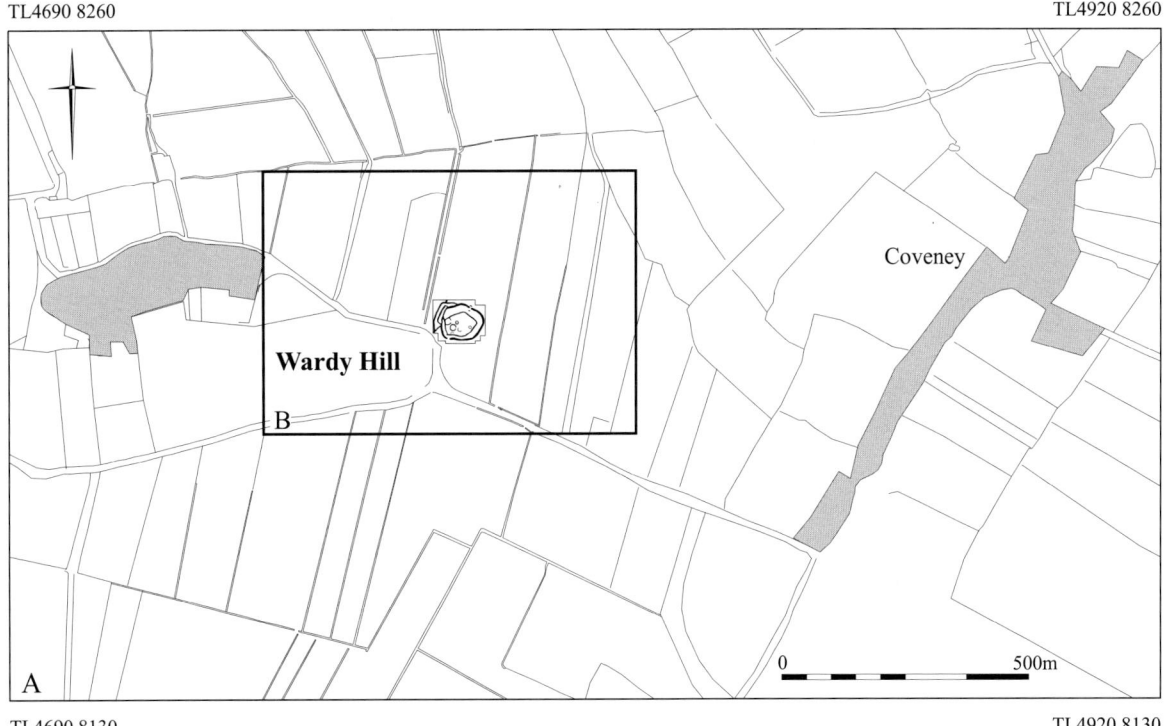
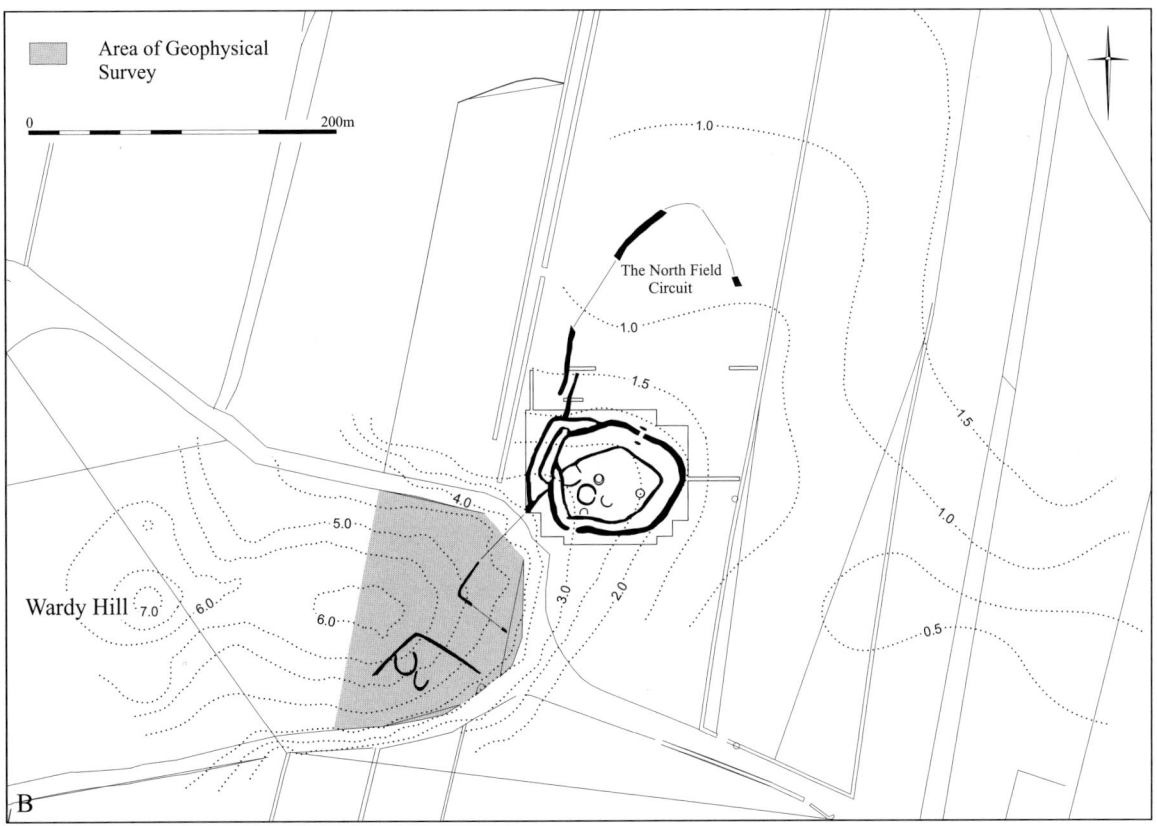

Figure 5 Location map: **B** showing crop-mark, topsoil contours and geophysical survey area

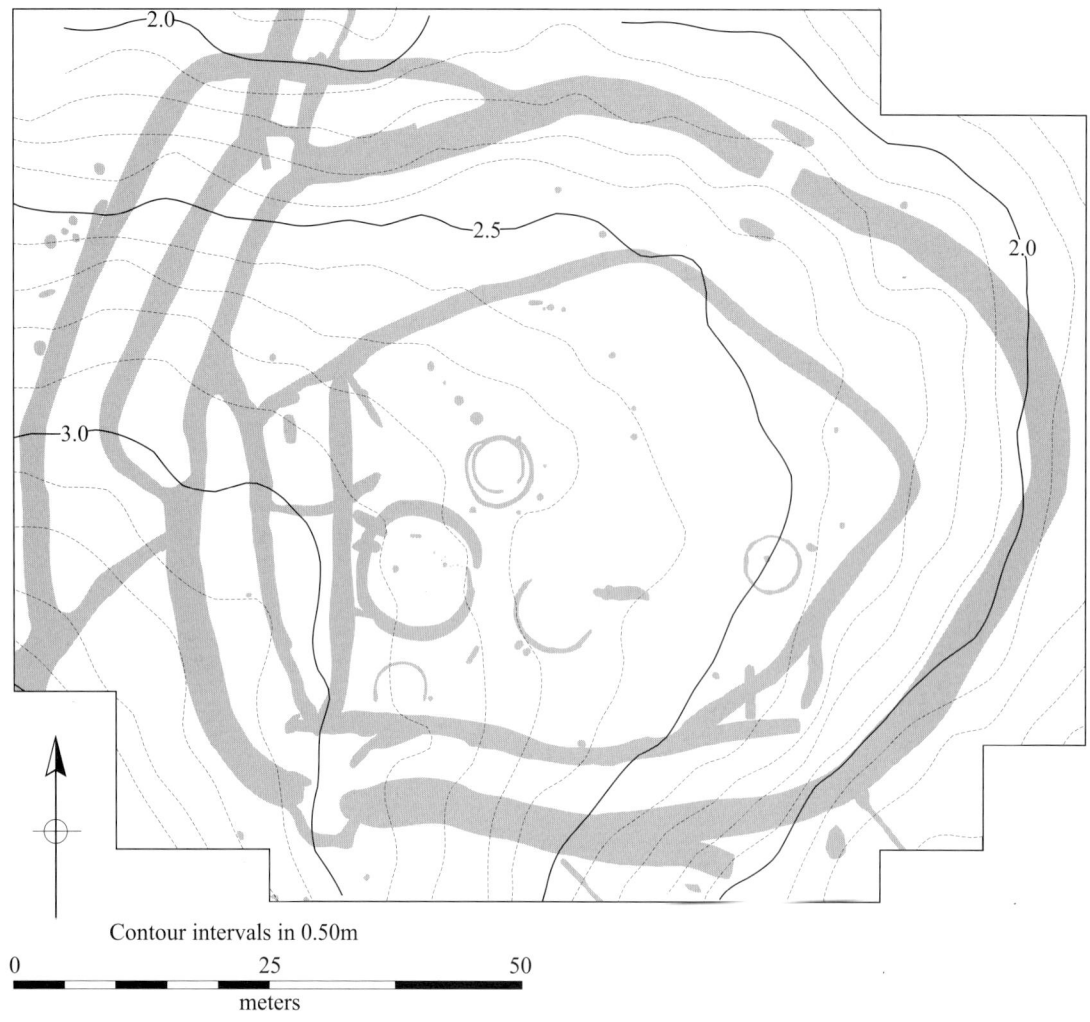

Figure 6 The Ringwork: topsoil contours

appear archaic in relationship to mainland developments. Ultimately, of course, no island is simply that: 'an island'. They interact with mainlands and 'others', and what must be charted is the inter-relationship of local structure/sequence with 'the world' and broader histories (see Boon 1982 and Sahlins 1987 on these themes, and Kirch 1986 concerning the archaeology of islands). Finally comes the issue of earthwork survival. Although the Wardy Hill Ringwork was evidently still visible in post-medieval times, that it was neither recognised nor named tells of discontinuities (and, arguably, 'insensitivities') in the historical constitution of landscape identity.

Wardy Hill and the larger enclosure system
(Pls I and II; Figs 5–7)
The Wardy Hill enclosure, as plotted from aerial photographs, was in part double-ditched (Plate I). Radiating from the north-western terminal of its 'C'-shaped outer circuit was a network of linear features. Even if obviously incomplete, its crop-mark plan suggested that this complex was extraordinary — either incorporating a series of defensive outworks or comprising a palimpsest of multi-phased enclosures. The main aim of the programme was to excavate the Ringwork according to its manifestation as a crop-mark. During the course of fieldwork, major ditch lines were found to extend both north and south from its perimeter. This led to the realisation that the enclosure was evidently not discrete, and that the designated 'site' was only one element in a much more extensive system.

Accordingly, following the excavations, the Ancient Monuments Laboratory, English Heritage, undertook geophysical survey over a 1.2ha area at the eastern end of the Wardy Hill spur proper in 1993 (Fig. 5; Cole 1993). Whilst the resistivity survey proved ineffective, the magnetometer results were successful. They show two ditches *c.* 30m apart, running parallel north-west to south-east for *c.* 50m up the eastern slope of the spur (Fig. 7). At that point they return south-west and north-east respectively; the latter is probably continuous with a ditch leading up the spur on the axis from the Ringwork's Outworks (as excavated, see F. 10/28). Although no definite interior features can be identified within the north-east 'corner' of the survey-defined system, within the southern corner a parallel north-west to south-east oriented ditch and what are probably the eaves-gullies of two roundhouses are visible. The location of this settlement component correlates with the discovery of a scatter of Iron Age material (Middle/later Iron Age handmade sherds) in the bordering field during the course of CAU fieldwork.

It is the pair of ditches running parallel north-west to south-east up the eastern slope that probably provides the *raison d'être* for the Wardy Hill complex as a whole. They

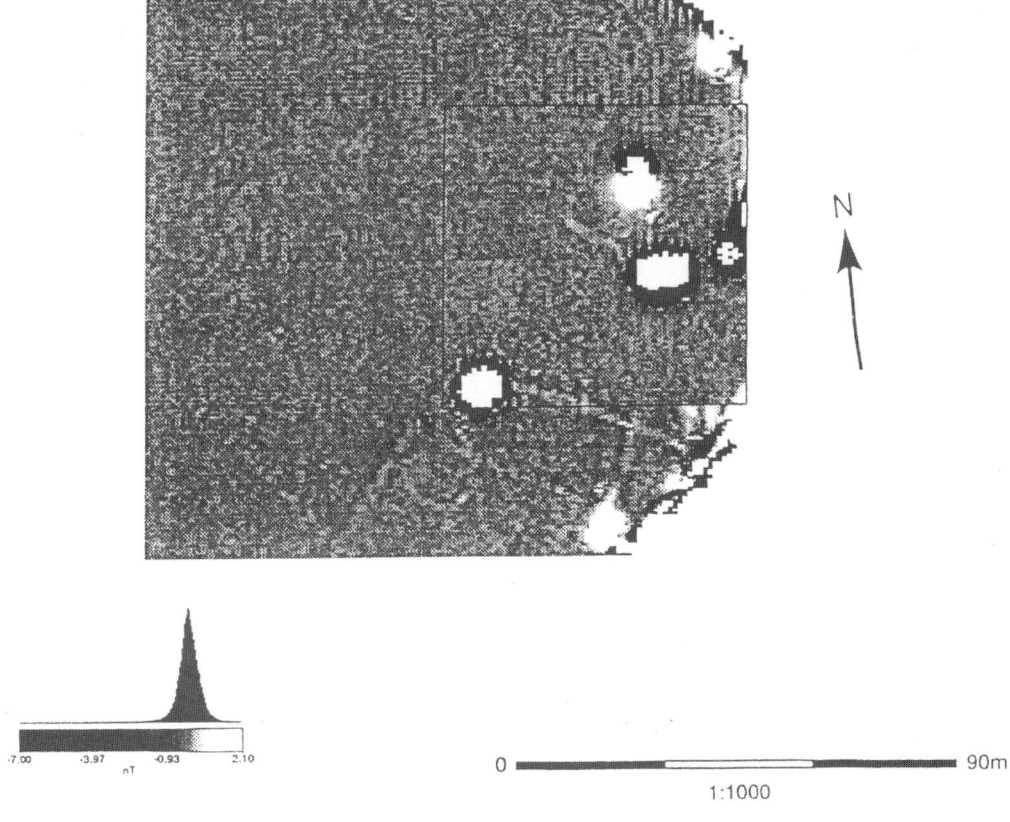

Figure 7 The Wardy Hill-top: magnetometer survey plot

appear to define a great droveway sharing the same approximate alignment as the 'Short Causeway' which today leads from Wardy Hill to Coveney, and suggest that the Ringwork may have commanded the approach to an earlier trans-marsh causeway. Incorporation of the Wardy Hill spur-top geophysical survey results is also important in terms of 'framing' or understanding the Ringwork itself. It is not a 'un-oriented' circular enclosure but one with a 'front' — the north-west side, whose south-west–north-east line is the dominant axis (facade) of the broader complex as a whole — from which the quasi-Ringwork projects. (During the course of graduate fieldwork Kate Roberts, then of the Dept. of Archaeology of the University of Cambridge, also undertook geophysical trials across the hilltop. Although her surveys over the latter were more limited than those of the Ancient Monuments Laboratory, they essentially confirmed the same layout.)

During the course of excavation a major ditch line, of obvious Iron Age attribution and directly associated with the Ringwork, was found to project from its north-western perimeter (F. 14: see Fig. 17). This is clearly visible on aerial photographs, where it is seen to extend for some 30m north beyond the line of the Ringwork. Only on one aerial photographs do other possible crop-mark features register to the north of the Ringwork (Plate I; CUCAP BFH-34). After long scrutiny, and not without some doubt, this was presented to R. Palmer and subsequently plotted (Fig. 5). The crop-marks only register strongly on the north-western side where they are confused by tractor lines; those to the north are fainter and less distinct. A ditch, slightly overlapping with the line of F. 14 and continuing to run parallel to the north, can be distinguished. Angularly returning north-eastwards, part of a larger circuit which extends some 140m north of the Ringwork can be made out. On this photograph alone, other possible crop-mark features may also be present along the eastern edge of the field within the vicinity of the Ringwork (including at least one possible house-ring).

Due to the reconnaissance techniques employed, details of this larger Wardy Hill complex remain ambiguous. Nevertheless, there can be no doubt that the Ringwork related to a much more extensive enclosure system, essentially cutting off the eastern end of the spur through a dyke-like boundary. In total, it is now known to extend for over some 350m from north to south, and across an area or at least 3.5ha (see Fig. 13).

II. The Coveney environs

The provision of context
(Fig. 8)

Coveney is noted for its stray finds of bronze metalwork. Including both Middle and Late Bronze Age rapiers and leaf-blade swords, the most renowned of these is the pair of bronze shields found below the peat in Coveney Fen in 1846 (Evans 1881, figs 313 and 430; Fox 1923, 56, 59, 60, pls VIII and IX). To this could be added the hoards of Early and Middle Bronze Age metalwork from Grunty Fen, especially the gold armilla and bracelet found with a broken rapier in 1850 (Fox 1923, 57, 63). Given their character and location, these must attest to votive deposition within 'watery' places and, as such, reflect the existence of

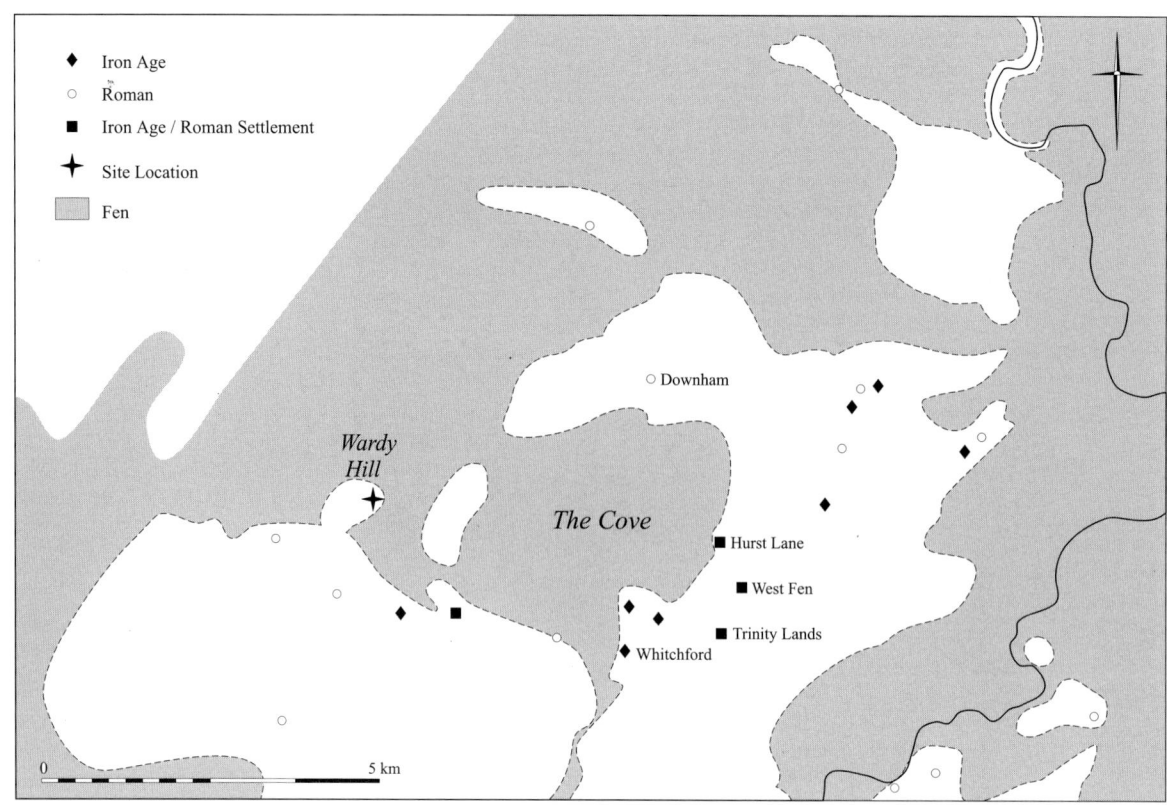

Figure 8 *The Cove:* location of Iron Age and Roman sites

locally 'wet' marshland conditions by the mid-2nd millennium BC (see Evans forthcoming a. for overview).

Another equally outstanding find from the vicinity — bracketing the other end of the site's occupation — is the Roman helmet found just north of Wardy Hill at Witcham Gravel early last century, which has since been displayed in the British Museum (Fox 1923, 215; British Museum 1922, plate IV; Russell Robinson 1975, 89, plate 250). An iron currency bar is reported from the Island (Hall 1996), and high-status later Iron Age metalwork has been found only a little further afield: the boar-stamped swords from Isleham, Cambs and West Fen Row, Suffolk (Stead 1985).

Substantive traces of 'early' occupation were recovered from the Wardy Hill area during the course of the Fenland Survey (Hall 1996, 46–50, fig. 25). Apart, however, from a minor scatter of probable Neolithic flintwork found on a small sand rise west of Wardy Hill (Coveney Site 5), a few flints reported from near Wilbey Holes Farm (TL 481807) and chance finds of axes, these are from small sand islands amid the low skirtland on the northern side of the Island. Some 1km north-west of Wardy Hill, near the Bedford Level, both a small later Mesolithic/Early Neolithic flint scatter (Witcham Site 1) and a large Neolithic spread (Site 2) were found. At the end of the low peninsula on which the Ringwork lies, *c.* 2.5km north-east of Wardy Hill, discrete Mesolithic/Neolithic, Neolithic and later Bronze Age scatters (respectively Coveney Sites 4, 3 and 2) have been found.

Against this background, prior to the Wardy Hill excavations there had been little evidence of pre-Iron Age activity *per se* on the Ely clays proper. The Island's heavy sub-soils obviously discouraged sustained occupation prior to the later 1st millennium BC; in keeping with the results of subsequent investigations on the claylands elsewhere in the region, this suggests 'arrival' and colonisation during the Iron Age. Since the excavation, however, development-led fieldwork on the west side of Ely has produced evidence indicating low-level usage — probably reflective of seasonal visitation — during the Neolithic and Bronze Age. The relevant excavations are fully summarised below (Fig. 8). On the Trinity Lands a large pond and pit-well associated with later Bronze Age material were found, in association with much burnt flint, suggesting processing activities (Masser and Evans 1999). The recovery of lithics and some pottery in direct association with a few minor pits on the nearby West Fen Road site would attest to Neolithic and Bronze Age activity (Mortimer 2000; Regan 2001). While finds were again only of low intensity, remarkably enough the hilt of a bronze rapier was recovered during topsoil survey at the site, which provides some degree of context for the wealth of Bronze Age metalwork known from the area (Evans forthcoming a.). Also significant is the fact that, during the course of the Trinity Lands investigations, colluvium was found to seal both Iron Age and Roman features that may represent clearance at the end of the 1st millennium BC and in Roman times. This concealment may help to explain why so little evidence of pre-Iron Age occupation has previously been detected upon Ely's claylands.

During the course of the Fenland Survey, relatively high densities of both Iron Age and Roman sites were identified across the northern half of the Isle of Ely, especially along the southern side of the Cove (Hall 1996, fig. 88). Four of these fall within the Wardy Hill environs (*ibid,* 50–1):

Coveney 6 (TL 487806): A broad ditched, square crop-mark enclosure (sides 50m) from which both Iron Age and Romano-British material has been recovered.

Witcham 5 (TL 478806): This square crop-mark enclosure lies just 800m west of Coveney 6, and mirrors it apart from the fact that it has a possible annexe on its western side; Iron Age occupation evidence was recovered in association with it.

Witcham 4 (TL 46208140): A Late Roman occupation scatter probably associated with a sub-rectangular crop-mark (SMR 9501; TL 46208158).

Witcham 6 (SMR 9499; TL 469807): A complex crop-mark enclosure consisting of an internally subdivided double-ditched square (sides *c.* 100m) with an annexe on its north-eastern side. A few Roman sherds (in poor condition) were recovered when it was surveyed.

The cluster of two small, square crop-mark enclosures and at least three ring-ditches immediately west of Wardy Hill may also be of relevance (Coveney Site 5, TL 46648210: Hall 1996, fig. 25; CUCAP XS 27-32, BRY 17-18, RC8-EC 50-51). Other than those lithics described above (which were localised to a small sand rise), when these sites were fieldwalked no associated material was recovered. Given their location on the hill's low skirtland they are obviously of pre-medieval date. The much larger northern 'circle' is probably a later Neolithic/Bronze Age ritual monument (*i.e.* a ploughed-out barrow or ring-ditch). Although it is conceivable that the smaller circles are contemporary ring-ditches, they may alternatively relate to the square enclosures and be of Iron Age/Romano-British date. This latter date would be surprising, however, given the paucity of surface finds and local recovery patterns elsewhere on the Island, certainly if they were settlement-associated. Some kind of later Iron Age cemetery, therefore, remains a possibility (*cf.* Hill *et al.* 1999).

Another cluster of apparent Late Iron Age sites has been found near the head of the Witchford Inlet (WID 1, TL 51688051; WID 3, TL 51168000; WID U2, TL 51428057). Of these, WID 3 (SMR 7879) is of particular interest. Both Early and Late Iron Age material (including Romanised pot forms and Puddingstone querns) has been recovered from within the area of a large, possibly double-ditched rectangular enclosure. (Portions of two sides and a rounded corner are just visible on an RAF photo: F21/558/1337.) If this is of Iron Age date this might be a major site. (Alternatively, they could relate to the 'Roman Camp' said by Walker to have been destroyed during the construction of Ely's airfield: Phillips 1970, 227.) Commanding or 'watching' *The Ford* (*i.e.* Watch-/Witchford) into Grunty Fen, this site is also strategically located.

Against this survey background, the excavations at Wardy Hill remained in relative 'limbo', and without immediate context, until the latter half of the 1990s and the impact of house construction around Ely's fringes. Since then the following sites have been discovered through development-led fieldwork, leading to date to three major excavations:

Watson's Lane, Little Thetford (TL 520770): Discovered beneath ridge-and-furrow, *c.* 0.4ha of this later Iron Age and Roman settlement was fully excavated in 1995 (Lucas and Hinman 1996; Lucas 1998). It lies on a narrow peninsula of high ground (at *c.* 6.00m OD) that extends into the floodplain of the River Great Ouse south-east of Ely. Interpreting the excavation results was impeded by the limited scale of exposure. Although portions of eight later Iron Age round buildings were excavated, it proved impossible to disentangle any associated paddocks adequately from the subsequent Roman system; the only mid-1st century 'Conquest Period' wares recovered came from this system, and not the buildings themselves. Although involving later Roman components, including a tile kiln and cemetery, with hindsight this settlement has clear affinities with those described below: unfortunately too little of the system was exposed to make sense of it. Nevertheless, given its dating and the density of roundhouses, this site does provide contextual parallels for the Wardy Hill buildings.

West Fen Road, Ely (TL 530808): The construction of a pipeline along the northern side of West Fen Road on the western fenward side of Ely in 1996 led to discovery by the CAU of a substantial later Iron Age settlement (Gibson 1996). Subsequent housing construction on both sides of the road in the course of 1999 resulted in the excavation of a major multi-period complex — largely of Saxon date — that was presumably determined by the route of a causeway heading either north to Downham or west to Coveney (Mortimer 2000; Regan 2001). While only limited Iron Age occupation was recorded (two sub-square compounds) across the south fields, more extensive Roman systems were recovered; the core of the Iron Age complex instead lay to the north (there excavated by Northamptonshire Archaeology: Mudd 2000). To date, evaluation within fields to the south has revealed another later Iron Age and Early Roman settlement on the 'Trinity Lands' (TL 526804; Masser and Evans 1999). Lying *c.* 400m south of the West Fen Road complex and extending over 1ha, full excavation is anticipated shortly.

Hurst Lane, Ely (TL 524814): Located at the fen-edge only some 0.5km north-west of the West Fen Road complex (at 2–4.00m OD), this major settlement was only discovered during casual inspection by the CAU during the construction of a reservoir in the late summer of 1999 (Evans and Knight 2000a). Having, for various reasons, escaped planning notice, application was duly made to English Heritage for emergency funding which eventually allowed for its summary excavation over 2.85ha. In the course of this work 29 later Iron Age round structures, set both within and around a series of quasi-polygonal/sub-rectangular compounds (*i.e.* laid out 'organically'), were exposed. These were overlain by an Early Roman field- and paddock system associated with four contemporary structures, both circular and sub-square. Given the fieldwork's pressing timetable, a decision was made to opt for wide-scale plan exposure, while concentrating excavation resources upon a distinct sub-circular/horseshoe-shaped Iron Age compound in the south end of the field (A). With five roundhouses within the interior of the latter, this choice was prompted by two factors. First, because this compound appeared to represent the origin of the Iron Age system and, secondly, due to its marked affinity to the interior circuit of the Wardy Hill Ringwork. The relevance of this site to the present volume is obvious. This being said, another major factor must be considered: the nature of the excavated assemblages and the broad scale of exposure (in contrast, for example, to the Watson's Lane site) has led to the Hurst Lane complex providing a remarkably clear example of Late Iron Age to Early Roman continuity. The layout of its later 1st century AD linear systems was clearly determined by the line of the Late Iron Age paddocks, while the pottery sequence (including, for example, butt beaker) seems to continue uninterrupted throughout the mid 1st century AD.

More recently, later Iron Age settlement remains have been discovered during evaluation fieldwork on the higher western margins of Ely proper (Abrams 2000). Traces of Iron Age occupation have also been exposed in the City itself in the area of the Cathedral and Market (Hunter 1992a and b).

The subsequent excavation of the above-listed sites reflects the nature of archaeological process and its 'spiralling' logic. Having excavated Wardy Hill, in order to provide a fuller background context application was made for a subsidiary Isle of Ely Project to investigate specifically the character of its settlement hierarchies, and the impact of Romanisation upon the island. This bid was unsuccessful: the main thrust of this initiative lay in the study of potentially archaic communities, and exploration of a hypothetical lingering Iron Age which saw only limited Roman 'inroads' prior to the 2nd century AD. In terms of detailing the mixed character of 1st century AD pottery assemblages, this interpretative thrust remains justified. In the case of the central fenland sequences as typified by Stonea (Jackson and Potter 1996; see also Evans forthcoming b.), however, the reverse now seems equally to hold true: there is evidence of Romanisation in the 1st century AD, probably fostered through Ely's south- and south-westward trade connections and cultural affiliations. What this attests to now seems commonplace in fenland studies — the fragmentation of grand schemes of pan-regional development underpinned by notions of environmental determinism. It would seem that Iron Age communities on the Isle of Ely maintained broader cultural ties that may have conditioned their immediate response to early Romanisation. To what degree this included the adoption of a complete 'package', and/or was a matter of trade and the negotiation of material cultural identities, must be considered crucial.

Another major issue arising from the discovery of these sites is an appreciation of the density of settlement of this period around the fringes of the Cove. That the Hurst Lane, West Fen and Trinity sites fall within 4–500m of each other complements Hall's distribution of Iron Age/Roman sites along its southern side. The issue to address here is whether densities of this order are considered typical of the region as a whole, or if they should be seen as reflecting the specific 'historical' circumstance of this area's occupation.

Survey and environmental reconstruction
(with C. Ellis)
(Figs 9–12)

The crown of Wardy Hill is capped with Kimmeridge Clay; as a northern outlier of the main extent of these beds, it is surrounded by Ampthill Clays (Fig. 9; Gallois 1988, figs 12 and 17). In contrast to these heavy clays, a deposit of Pleistocene river gravels is known to border the south-eastern side of the spur (Gallois 1988, fig. 25).

There have been no dated environmental columns collected within the Cove embayment, which has only a shallow deposit sequence. The nearest, at Pymore north-east of Little Downham, is from considerably deeper fen deposits and has little immediate relevance (Waller 1994, 137–41). Instead, the site's palaeo-topography can only be considered in relationship to Waller's large-scale fenland sequence maps (1994, figs 5.18–5.23) and Gallois' study of Ely's geology (1988). Only in the mid-2nd millennium did Ely became isolated as a fen-fast island, at the maximum extent of the Fen Clay marine incursion and the resultant back-up of freshwater drainage and rising marshland conditions (the southern extent of the marine sediments lies 2.5km north of the site: Figs 9 and 10). While the marshland embayment surrounding Coveney would appear to date to the later 1st millennium BC a deeper channel, running from Little Downham and west of Coveney to Witchford and Grunty Fen in the south, was probably open to freshwater conditions throughout this time. Previous to the establishment of the Cove as such, Coveney Island would have been joined to Wardy Hill and the main body of the Isle of Ely. This correlates with the fact that most of the embayment only carries 0.90m or less depth of peat cover (the Nordelph Upper Peat), though between Coveney and Downham, and along the West Fen channel (the line of Grunty Fen Drain) it locally drops to as much as 1.80–3.65m depth (Gallois 1988, fig. 35; Seale 1975).

On Ellis's map of 1768 Wardy Hill itself is shown as a distinct island detached from the main bulk of the Isle of Ely, with marsh extending around the low skirtland of its southern side. When this separation occurred is obviously an issue of significance for the interpretation of the site. Unfortunately, the low 'bridge/spit' connecting Wardy Hill to the Island has not been auger-investigated, and therefore this must be a matter of speculation. Waller indicates that Coveney became isolated as an island between 2500–1800 BP and dates the separation of Wardy Hill to a time post-1800 BP (1994, figs 5.22 and 5.23). Hall (1996, *cf.* figs 25 and 26) also suggests Wardy Hill's isolation dates to historical times. Therefore, pending further investigation, it will be taken that Wardy Hill was still linked to the main (is)land during the Iron Age.

During the excavations Clare Ellis, then of the University of Leicester, undertook transect coring across the basin north and east of the Ringwork. To assist in reconstruction of the area's palaeo-topography (Figs 11 and 12), nine depositional horizons were identified:

> **Unit 1:** Aop ploughsoil. A brownish black peat loam/silt peat loam; Adventurer's Series (Nordelph or Upper Peat; Seale 1975). The date of this amorphous, well humified and friable peat is Bronze Age at the earliest, but could be Early Iron Age in the Block Moor. The peat was formed under eutrophic, wet conditions, with a high watertable and in an environment that was possibly fed by shallow channels.

> **Unit 2:** Bo horizon. Black to dark brown peat loam (Adventurer's Series). This survives only as deposits a few centimetres thick. It is

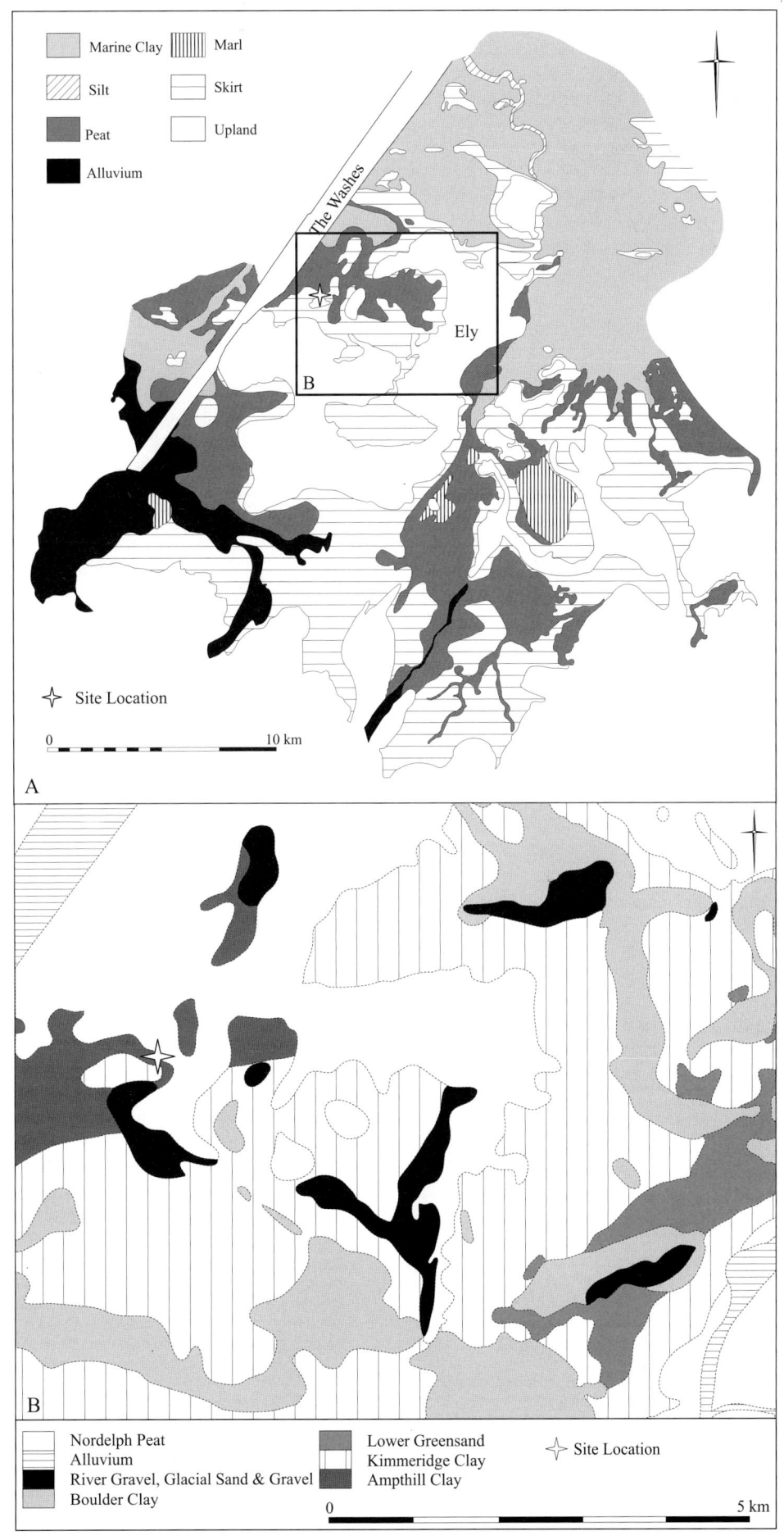

Figure 9 Surface and geological deposits: **A** the Isle of Ely environs; **B** the geology of *The Cove*

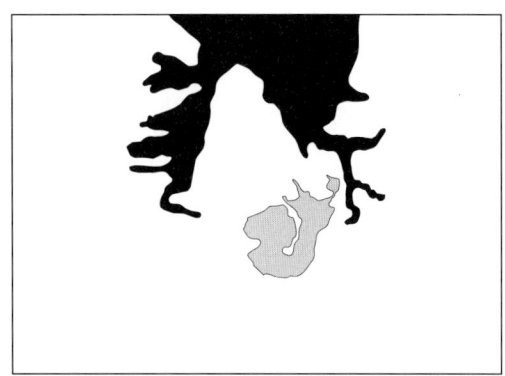

*C.*5000 BP

*C.*2600 BP

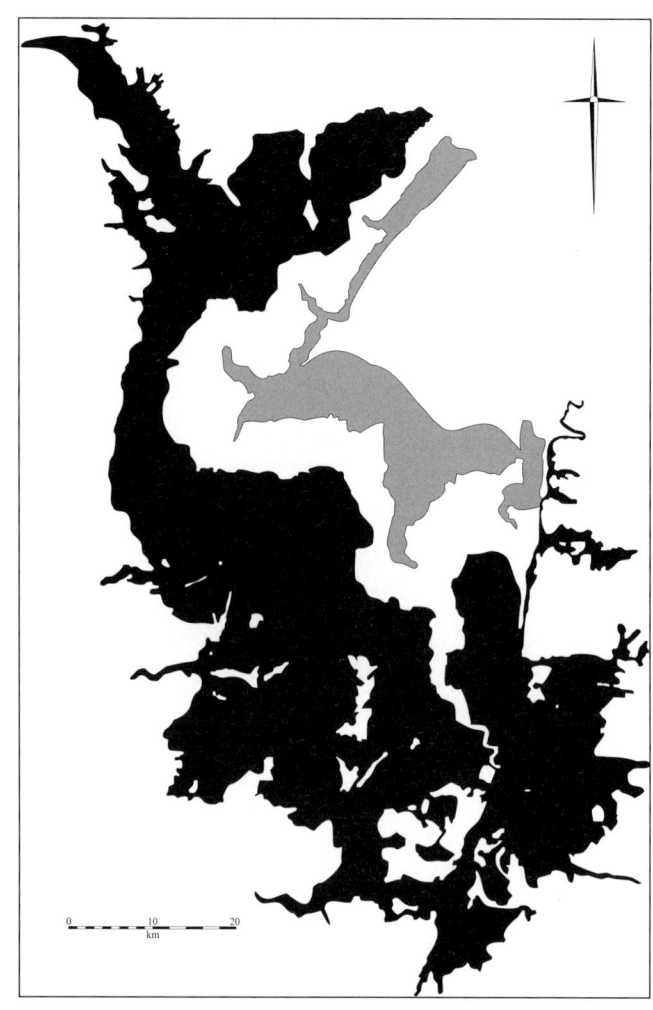

Post *C.* 1800 BP

Figure 10 Fenland geological succession 5000–1800 BP, showing loss of skirtland around the Chatteris/Ely Peninsula. Marshland blackened; on the 5000 BP map, the later location of the Isle of Ely is in grey tone; after Waller 1994)

a highly organic material with a granular, crumb-like structure. Wood fragments in some samples indicate the presence of Fen Carr; a high charcoal content suggests fire. It evidently formed under fairly wet, eutrophic conditions with a high watertable.

Unit 5: A reddish brown to dark brown/black sandy peat loam (Nordelph Peat, Adventurer's Series). There are occasional wood fragments; small stones, and medium to coarse bleached sand grains possibly forming laminae. The sand may be of local aeolian origin, deposited penecontemporaneously with the peat (Seale 1975).

Unit 5 and 6 display a reversal in stratigraphy.

Unit 6: Wood Peat; Fen Carr, Adventurer's Series. Very dark reddish brown, eutrophic and formed under high watertable conditions. The greatest depth occurs in areas of low relief, the palaeochannels or natural depressions, indicating either that the Fen Carr first started forming in these areas or that it survived subsequent erosion and wasting there. Since drainage this material has become extremely acid due to the deposition of iron translocated in acid conditions, and forms a dry hard barrier to roots; it is known locally as Drummy Peat. There are occasional small gypsum crystals, formed by sulphuric acid partially neutralised by calcium carbonate.

Unit 8: A greyish brown peaty silt with small sand component; contains pale lemon-coloured jarosite flecks (formed by the oxidation of iron sulphide after drainage and indicative of acid soils). This deposit represents the silting-up of the shallow palaeochannels and/or natural depressions and the first growth of peat. Containing some charcoal, it has a shelly component and clay-rich patches.

Unit 7: White/grey to greyish yellow/brown sandy silt, with clay component near base. Non-calcareous, it contains jarosite flecks and has possible laminae of silt, sand and charcoal; occasionally shows ancient roots now replaced by iron oxide, charcoal and sulphur. This deposit probably represents either fluvially reworked, sorted and deposited Ampthill Clay with detrital charcoal or (less likely) fine colluvium from Coveney and Wardy Hill 'Islands' which collected in the depressions in the Ampthill Clay surface.

Unit 3: Weathered Ampthill Clay. This is difficult to identify and distinguish from Unit 7 in some areas; its composition varies from clay through to medium sand. Iron has been leached, though a small amount of oxidized iron occurs as red flecks: lepidocrocite and limonite (yellow brown). In auger holes located on the edge of Hale Fen the basal deposit is gravelly; this has been interpreted as the top of the River Terraces 1–2 (Gallois 1988). Yellow/orange brown with fine to medium sand, this material is composed of fine to medium gravel, Cretaceous flint and chalk, and Jurassic rocks derived from local glacial deposits.

Unit 9: A dull yellowish brown silty clay. Possibly laminated, with sub-millimeter laminae of silt/clay and detrital charcoal; fossil oyster shells were observed. Possibly represents weathered, disturbed Ampthill clay. (The Ampthill clay is weathered to a considerable depth below the surface. Chemical, and to a lesser

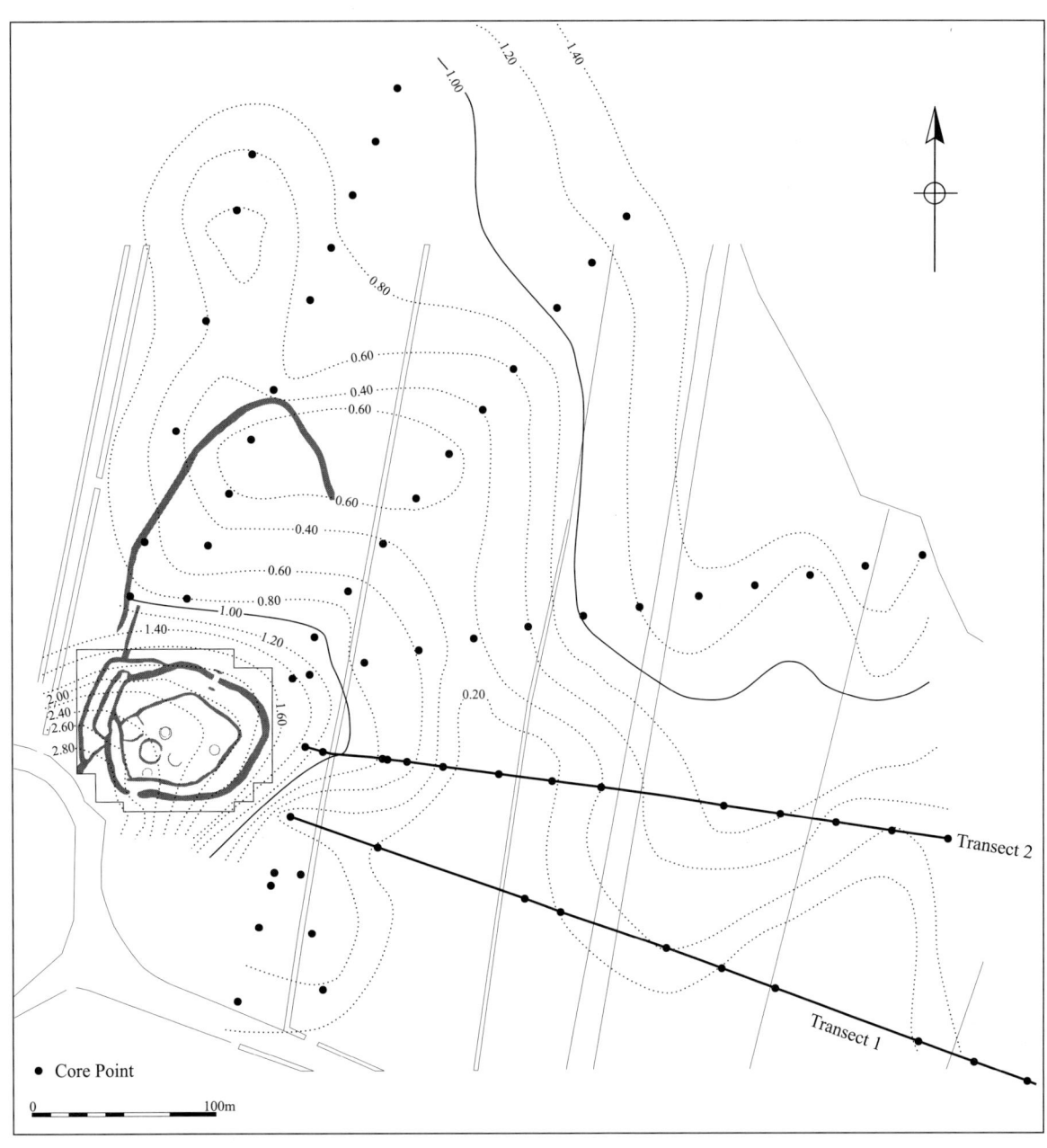

Figure 11 Wardy Hill: subsoil contours with environmental core positions indicated

extent physical, weathering transforms the mudstones of the Ampthill clay to a sticky silt-clay of a dull yellowish brown colour; Gallois 1988.) This material was then eroded and transported from the site and Wardy Hill, being deposited at the break of the slope. Low calcium carbonate levels are due to its dissolution and leaching during weathering.

The results of the transect plotting indicates that the Ringwork sits on (and largely 'fills') a low peninsular spur on the north-east side of Wardy Hill. Lying between *c.* 0.80–2.80m OD, beyond this the buried topography undulates and carries up to 0.40–1.00m of peat and topsoil cover.

The auger hole data demonstrates that there are shallow depressions in the weathered Ampthill clay surface (0.40–0.60m deep). These appear to be linear, semi-continuous features that sweep around the eastern and northern edges of the spur; the base of the former lies at *c.* 0.10–0.20m OD. One interpretation of these is that they represent shallow, but relatively wide, palaeochannels. These would have been cut into the soft Ampthill Clay either by fluvial water derived from the south or perhaps, though less likely, by water from the estuarine system approximately 1.5km to the north. As seen in Units 7 and 8 sandy silt was then deposited in the palaeochannels, as they gradually received less water from the south or silted up because of greater sediment input. Both these sediments are locally derived – Unit 7 perhaps from the weathered Ampthill clay, like Unit 8 – and relate to the start of the Upper Peat formation. The Adventurer's Series n1 is described as a eutrophic peat, fed by a high watertable rather than by precipitation. Unit 6, found in many points overlying Unit 7 or 8, is formed under high watertable conditions induced by greater precipitation. The Drummy Peat first formed in the silted-up palaeochannels, spreading onto the slightly higher inter-channel areas with time. Sandy peat formed

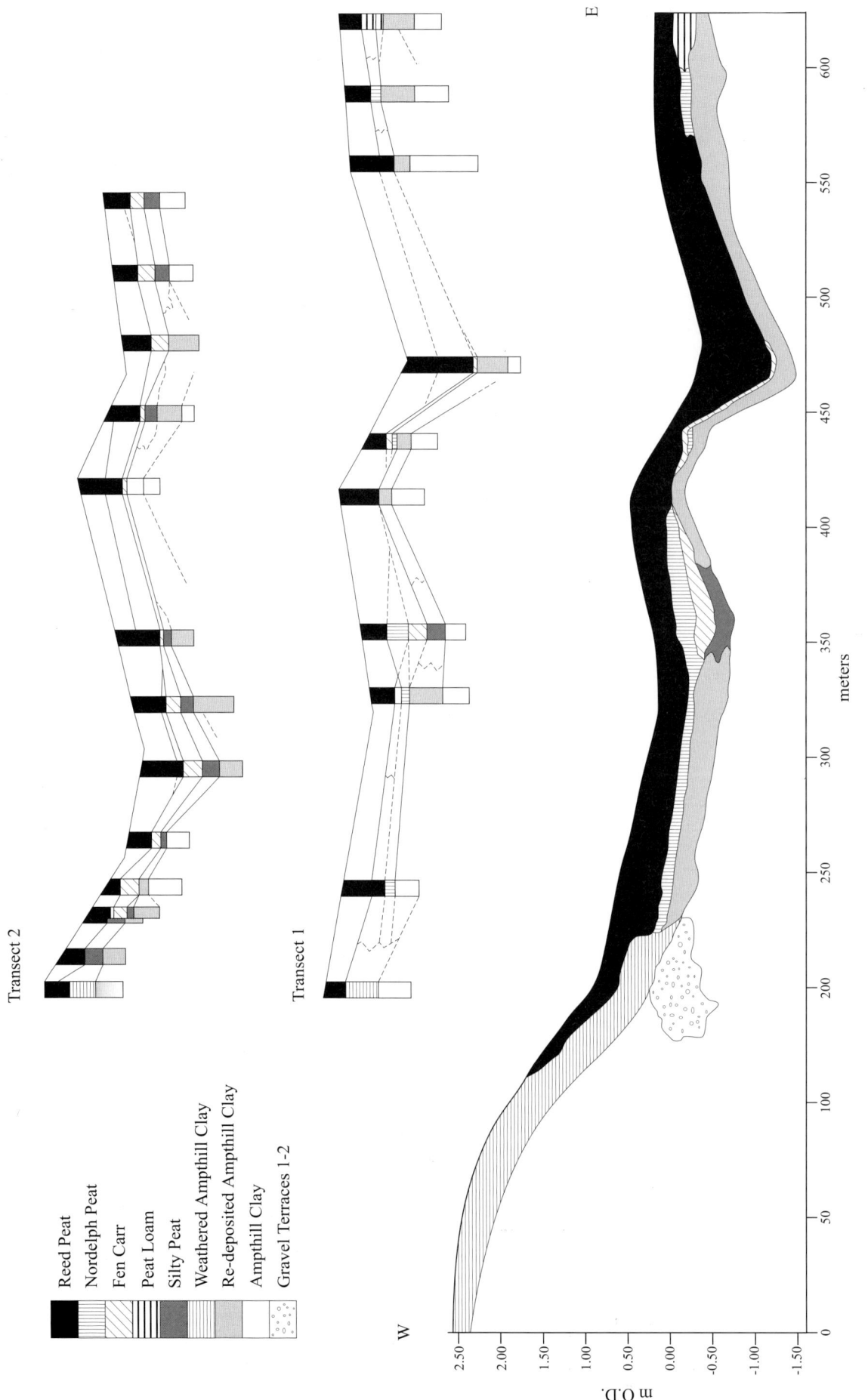

Figure 12 Environmental transects (see Fig. 10 for location)

in some locations (Unit 5), the sand being blown in from a local source. Unit 1, sealing the various deposits identified, is a reed peat which would obviously have been much thicker before the impact of drainage.

Aside from being sealed by the Unit 1 peat, there is no sedimentological evidence to correlate off-site and on-site sediments in terms of depositional environment, and certainly no distinct off-site flood deposit can be identified. Waterlain sediments within the Ringwork's main ditch can be explained in terms of gradual deposition of 'site'-derived material in a water/sediment trap; the Block Moor environs seem gradually to have become wetter during the Bronze/Iron Ages, with greater precipitation, occasional low-magnitude floods and continuous growth of peat. This, and a wetter climate, may have gradually affected the locale, making it less attractive to the site's inhabitants. It is not possible, however, to link the abandonment of the site directly with rising marsh levels.

In the absence of local environmental data, determination of where 'the wet' lay in any one period must be extrapolated from other sequences in the south-western fenlands. Due to differential rates of shrinkage, perched watertables and sub-soil geology, this is notoriously difficult. These caveats aside, on the basis of regional precedent the site obviously lay immediately adjacent to the contemporary fen-edge during the later 1st millennium BC. Generally placed at *c.* 2–3.00m OD, no Middle/Late Iron Age settlements are known below this height in the region. The depth of waterlogging within the main Ringwork circuit — to 1.00m OD — may not directly reflect this level as the clays into which it was cut may have supported a raised watertable. This being said, since the site's shallower circuits showed no such evidence of standing water there must have been some degree of groundwater movement.

During the Bronze Age marsh levels would have lain *c.* 2.00m lower, from sea level (0m OD) to upwards of 1–1.50m OD. While 'dryland' would therefore have been much more extensive prior to the 1st millennium BC, the poorly-drained clays in the area would have probably still then been quite wet, and have discouraged settlement. Over the course of later prehistory and early historical times, the immediate area saw the emergence of marsh-bounded islands: Ely itself and, within its northern embayment, Coveney and eventually Wardy Hill. Ely's clays are themselves pocketed with sub-surface deposits of lighter gravels, supporting local micro-environments. All this would have contributed to an increasingly differentiated landscape, characterised by distinct 'places' (*i.e.* 'this' island or 'that' marsh).

III. Methodologies
(Pls III–VII; Figs 13 and 14)

Survey and excavation
Registering both as a crop-mark and a surface scatter, from the outset a staged excavation policy was adopted at the site. This was to proceed in such a way as to test the surface survey techniques to be employed on other non-crop-mark/artefact-scatter-only sites in the then-current Fenland Management Programme fieldwork (see Evans 2000a for FMP sampling procedures). Appropriate to the larger project's survey background, this approach also enables the interrogation of surface and 'in-depth' distributional data. Moreover, when coupled with the site's quite strict feature and ploughsoil sampling programme, they allow for estimations of total artefact populations.

Following the contour survey, the interior of the enclosure was sub-divided into quadrants, with metre-square

Plate III Excavations in progress, general view looking west; note the pattern of plough scarring (photo by C. Price)

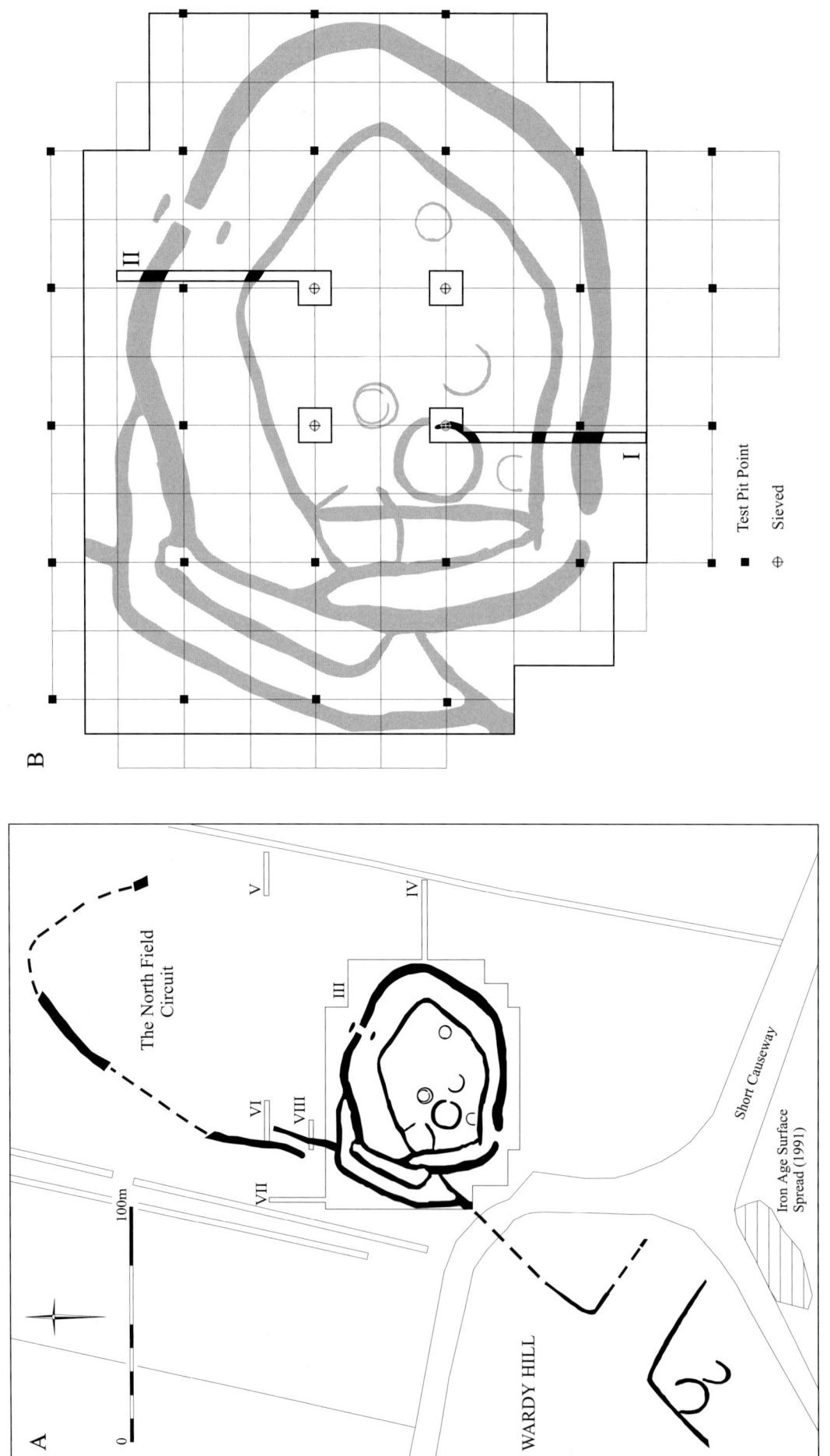

Figure 13 Wardy Hill: **A** Area of excavation and trench locations; **B** site plan showing fieldwalking grid, test pit points and location of original trial trenches and test stations.

test-pits hand-dug through the ploughsoil in each; laid out on the corners of a 20m square, their spoil was sieved using 5mm mesh (Fig. 13). These were then machine-expanded into 5 x 5m test stations (in one of which the eaves-gully of a roundhouse was exposed), and trenches were extended from two across the line of the main ditch circuit (Trenches I and II). These assessment procedures not only confirmed the Iron Age date of the enclosure and provided evidence of interior settlement, but also demonstrated that the fills of its deep ditches were still partially waterlogged. While the site was shown to be entirely ploughed-out, with neither horizontal occupation strata nor buried soil horizons surviving, high artefact densities were present within the ploughsoil. Surface phosphate samples were also taken from along two transects bisecting the enclosure. Rapidly processed, these indicated that phosphate levels varied directly in relation to the main ditch lines and that the readings from within the innermost circuit were dramatically high. This, along with the high test-pit artefact densities, showed that a great deal of information lay locked within the site's heavy clay-based ploughsoil. Prior to machining, phosphate samples were therefore taken across the entire area on a 5m grid, which was also magnetic-susceptibility surveyed. The stubble field was ploughed and grid fieldwalked, after weathering, using 10m units. Metre-square ploughsoil test pits were sited on a 20m grid to evaluate total artefact populations and complement surface distributions. Only once these sample tests were completed was the site stripped down to the surface of 'natural', which proved to be extensively plough-scarred.

The entire c. 8000m area of the Ringwork was machine-stripped (Fig. 13). In addition, trenches were extended from the north-western corner and eastern side (VII and IV respectively), and three were cut north of the main area to trace individual features (V, VI and VIII; a metre-square test-pit was also sunk in the extreme south-eastern corner of the field to determine the depth of overburden at that point). Upon machining, prior to the excavation *per se*, further magnetic susceptibility trials were undertaken by A. Challands. This included a 1350m zone within the western central part of the enclosure (corresponding with the area of the main roundhouses), and 'chained' metre-interval readings were taken from around all building eaves-gullies and the inner Ringwork circuit.

In the light of its size and plan complexity, and the resourcing available, the Ringwork itself could only be sample-excavated. To control artefact distributions, all linear features (including building eaves-gullies) were excavated in standard metre-long segments. While all discrete features (*i.e.* pits) were dug, and the eaves-gullies completely emptied, only c. 20% of the length of the main ditches were excavated. To permit comparisons between artefact and ecofact distributions across adjacent areas of its circuit, the Ringwork was laid out in a concentrically radial sample grid (approximately 10% fraction: see Fig. 17). Beyond this, a further 10% was excavated according to judgemental criteria (critical ditch junctions, entranceways and house-proximity *etc.*: see Chapter 5 for detailed discussion of the sampling ratios). A comprehensive environmental sampling programme was implemented, with bulk samples taken from all features

Plate IV The Ringwork interior looking south-west, with the Wardy Hill-top (and pill box) in the background. Across the middle of the scene Structure IV lies to the right; Structure I is central, with III to the left; excavation of Structure V, in the foreground, is yet to commence (photo by C. Price).

(and from all the radial sample units of the Ringwork ditches), for the analysis of plant macrofossils and to control small artefact densities. In addition to soil micromorphology profiles, five column samples were taken from the deeper ditch deposits for the detailed study of macro-fossils and pollen (LS 1–5: see Chapter 3 and Fig. 49). Upon completion of the excavations, in order to ensure recovery-control of 'indistinct' (*i.e.* backfilled) features, large swathes of the site were further machine-reduced by 0.10–0.20m down to 'clean' natural.

Finds and dating
The finds density was high with more than 31,000 artefacts recovered (273.892kg), including substantial pottery and bone assemblages (6895 and 17,228 sherds/pieces respectively). If the 'prehistoric' (*i.e.* pre-Iron Age) and post-medieval material is subtracted from this total it still leaves more than 28,000 finds of Iron Age date, including some 6000 pieces of pottery. This density should not so much be considered in relationship to the area of the site as to its six (*and only*) structures. Perhaps the best way to appreciate the Ringwork's densities is to compare them with the similarly ploughed-out, broadly contemporary settlement at Cats Water, Fengate, which produced only 11,600 sherds from 57 structures (Pryor 1984, 133). Yet the Wardy Hill total pales in comparison to the more than 40,000 finds recovered from the contemporary HAD V enclosure (*c.* 15,000 sherds from seven round structures: Evans and Hodder forthcoming). However, this is attributable to the extraordinary survival of that settlement compound. As demonstrated by extrapolation from the Wardy Hill sampling, a much greater total artefact population could be postulated for the Ringwork had its preservation been comparable (Chapter 5).

The presence of both wheel- and handmade pottery is important in relation to problems of later Iron Age dating in the region, and in considering the possibility that some places or areas experienced 'archaicisation' in the early Roman period. It is particularly important that the assemblage includes 'imports' and/or potentially high-status items. These include two Samian vessels and a handful of early Roman sherds, and also two La Tène-style decorated vessels.

One extraordinary find was made, a metal decorated piece from either a small wooden bucket or a tankard. This is all the more noteworthy given the poor survival of wood from the site. Its quality may well indicate the status of the Ringwork inhabitants. As an object, it is broadly comparable to the Glastonbury buckets/tubs (Earwood 1988) and resonates with tankard fittings from rich Iron Age burials (Corcoran 1952).

Due to technological mishaps, this report had to be written without the benefit of radiocarbon dates, which were only received after it had gone through its readership. Without their benefit the sequence, not illogically, had to hinge upon its final phase usage involving Late Iron Age wheelmade wares occurring with Early Roman ceramics. Based on the succession of the site's main buildings (*i.e.* two major roundhouses replacing each other), it was envisaged to have a short, 100–300 year long span. Upon receipt of the absolute dates this view has changed. The dates do not so much alter its sequence as require additional 'space' between its components. Their implications will be fully considered in the final section of Chapter 5. It

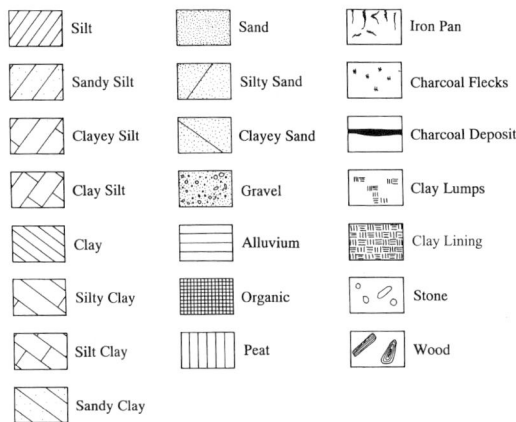

Figure 14 Section conventions

is, however, worth noting the trap that we fell into by adopting this *relative* temporal structure. While recognising that the 'rhythms' of enclosure circuit and house sequences need not have interrelated, it still inadvertently embraced the idea that excavation could be sensitive enough to detect a 'moment' of change. This was thought to be represented by the predominance of wheelmade wares in the final 'great' house (Structure IV), as opposed to the handmade ceramics of the primary main building (I), thereby relating building succession to changes in pottery manufacture. Having received the radiocarbon dating greater distance must be introduced between these phases, with the site's final usage representing an 'after-life' and not the finale of uninterrupted occupation. What, of course, this also does is give greater emphasis to the Ringwork as a significant earthwork 'place' within the Iron Age itself.

IV. Report structure

Process and history
The 'grammar' of the Ringwork's interior settlement — essentially eaves-gully defined roundhouses and shallow pits — is typical of Iron Age occupation within the region. Variously pertaining to the drainage of houses and the definition of domestic space (Evans 1997a), it relates to the 'manifestation' of settlement at the time and to contemporary processes of occupation.

Although a need for defence may have become widespread by then (*e.g.* Evans and Hodder forthcoming), it is difficult to see the establishment of the defensive enclosure at Wardy Hill as representing anything other than an act of historical specificity and 'opportunism'. Pocketed by marshes, the fenlands of the period certainly do not represent any kind of uniform landscape comparable, for example, to portions of the Wessex downlands. Instead this would have been a much more diverse environment, with elevated in-fen drylands amid wetlands crossed by lines of causeway access. Yet, given this basic distinction in terms of land-use analysis, is Wardy Hill entirely unique? Its situation is, for example, comparable to that of Belsar's Hill commanding the landward approach to the Aldreth causeway on the southern side of the Isle of Ely (Hall 1996; Evans and Hodder forthcoming); similarly, an

Plate V Excavations in progress looking south, with south-west terminal of inner circuit F. 2 in foreground (photo by J. Akerman)

Plate VI Looking east down the line of the F. 2 terminal (with F. 58 cobbled surface visible in middle ground); the rise of Coveney Island is visible in the background (photo by J. Akerman)

Plate VII Looking north with excavation in progress around the circuit of Structure IV (photo by J. Akerman)

Iron Age precursor has also been argued for Ely Castle itself (Baggs n.d.). Therefore, we find principles of historical specificity and more general processes operating at both levels of this site's study. Firstly, interpretation has involved adopting a more general Iron Age settlement 'model' to the remarkable defensive architecture of the enclosure. Secondly, despite the relative uniqueness of the enclosure system within the region, is the more general phenomenon of defence during the period, and with it the implication of threat.

First and last things
Bound as it is in context, and determined by the assembly of sources and delineation of fields of enquiry, there can be no simple exposition of site data. In the course of excavation, sites are 'untangled' and during this process — often involving reversals and teasing out of logics — results, hopefully, coalesce. Yet our reports are usually structured as if interpretation somehow builds cumulatively and regularly, saving the 'punch line' of discursive explanation to the end. Here, appropriate to a more *contextual archaeology*, it is held that the ends should determine the ordering. This approach admittedly owes something to Hawkes' concept of viewing archaeology 'backwards' from history (Evans 1998a; forthcoming b). Where it differs is that it is not primarily concerned with distance from (proto-)history, but rather with intelligibility.

A similar ethos also usually extends to the presentation of the results of site methodologies — particularly the incorporation of surface survey data early in a report, as if the sequence of a site's unearthing must be replicated in the structuring of the text. Here we will try to avoid a facile concern with appropriate 'first and last' things. The results of the surface surveys will only appear 'deep' in the text. Otherwise, presented in relative isolation and without the context of the underlying Ringwork's settlement framework, they would 'float' with little immediate resonance.

Having few overlapping relations, the Ringwork's structural sequence is not itself an absolute that exists independently of interpretation. The phasing, as such, is the 'story' of the site and cannot be decontextualised. Whilst trying to avoid circularity and unnecessary repetition, a 'staged' approach will be employed here. Initially a basic periodisation of the site's Bronze Age occupation (I), the Iron Age Ringwork and its enclosure precursors (II), and then post-Ringwork utilisation (III) will be presented. Even this is not simple; the first and last of these relate primarily to finds distributions and have few structural correlates. Having outlined the Ringwork's structural components, a phasing sequence for its development will be outlined within the latter part of Chapter 2. Thereafter, only following full specialist environmental and artefactual reportage, the phasing will be 're-visited' in Chapter 5 with particular emphasis given to the inter-relationship between the site's buildings and the enclosure sequence. Even this cannot be finalised in its entirety, and phasing alterations must be considered.

Given the nature of the site — extensive, but relatively 'simple' in terms of feature density — much emphasis will be paid to distribution and depositional studies. It is only by this that access can be gained into the daily operations — the routines and structures — of the enclosure system. It is here advocated that such depositional study allows for insight into facets of site activities going beyond what must be considered the essentially construction-focused framework of feature-based 'logic' alone. Since Bersu's establishment of what amounts to an Iron Age settlement model at Little Woodbury (Bersu 1940; Evans 1989c) settlement studies of the period have come to over-rely on the recovery of 'building blocks' of settlement architecture — as if fulfilling a standard check-list of roundhouses and various pit and post-hole configurations — although this approach is now challenged by ritual/structuralist precepts. Subsequently, due to the sheer frequency of settlements of this type, no matter how seemingly once 'alien' their basic parameters (*e.g.* roundhouse form and pit storage), it has become a 'captured' settlement form. It is here understood that finds and distributional analyses offer the greatest potential to challenge this now-normative reasoning and advance the period's settlement studies. In the immediate context of the site, this emphasis requires analysis of depositional patterning between the Ringwork's many circuits and buildings. This effectively involves 'unwinding' the site, and innovative modelling and graphic approaches are necessary to conceptualise and portray these complex interrelations adequately.

'Place' and landscape values
As will be demonstrated, the Iron Age Ringwork continued to exist as an earthwork into the first decades of the 20th century. Therefore, the site's long-term definition as a 'place' (*i.e.* a recognised landscape feature) becomes relevant and, equally, the reason why it was not 'named' as such. During a site open day Dr N. James, enlisting Cultural Heritage students from the University of Cambridge, undertook a survey of the 'archaeological attitudes' of the local populace. Attended by some 550 visitors (the event was only advertised on the Isle of Ely!), this resulted in almost a hundred completed questionnaires. Their prompts ranged from 'when was the last time you visited a local museum?' to 'when do you think the fens got wet?' and (if local to the Coveney area) 'did you know about the site?'. Concerning the issue of place cognition, it is the last question which is the most important — how do people know about their immediate past? The few respondents who were familiar with the site all participated in the local farming network.

An 'extra' to site study, and certainly not a final statement on this complex issue, the survey is an initial attempt to understand contemporary fenlanders' attitudes towards their past, and build upon studies of 19th-century, academically-inspired 'folkloric' knowledge (Evans 1997b). Its results are outlined and discussed in Chapter 2 below.

An excavation aesthetic
(with M. Edmonds)
Largely due to the strong contrast between its sub-soil and dark peaty feature fills — and the very concentricity of the Ringwork's layout — Robinson's aerial photograph well conveys the enclosure's striking visual quality. At the time of fieldwork, we were involved in the organisation of an exhibition at Kettle's Yard Gallery in Cambridge concerned with the concept of excavation as metaphor, *Excavating the Present* (Edmonds and Evans 1991). Co-organised by Charles Erche, then of the Gallery, some of the artists involved with this show briefly participated in the excavations. The nature of this involvement relates to the inclusion of other languages of 'documentation', and a belief that excavation can serve as a vehicle for diverse agendas and voices. Equally, akin to Paul Nash's

earlier primitive/surrealist appreciation of archaeology (and in contrast to the monumental constructions of much recent 'Land Art'), it is held that excavation can generate startling imagery precisely because it is literally *un-earthed* and previously unviewed (*i.e.* 'new').

Of those artists participating, the photographs of Jeremy Akerman (only a few of which are reproduced here: cover and Pls V–VII) are starkly atmospheric and well capture the bleakness of deep-fen winter work. The involvement of Elspeth Owen, the Cambridge potter and artist, was somewhat belated. She was not 'resident' at the excavations but instead, after experimentation with ceramics made from the site's clays, produced a hollow spheroid inspired by the notion of excavation and what lies hidden.

The most renowned of those taking part was Cornelia Parker, who has since been a nominee for the Turner Prize. She has work in the collection of Tate Modern and, recently, a permanent installation in the Victoria and Albert Museum, and is an artist deeply concerned with process (Parker and Corrin 1998). This is apparent in her small-scale site experiments involving weathering/decay (the flag-surrounded pieces: Plate XV) and the inter-relationship between excavation and burial; a large silver spoon which 'dug itself' was subsequently buried on site with the date of its interment inscribed (Plate XVI; a print of this hangs in the collection of New Hall, Cambridge). No claim is here made that these are great works of art in themselves. In fact, the inclusion in the 'Fieldworks' section of Kasia Gdaniec's early-morning portrayal of the excavations (Plate XIV), like Ben Robinson's aerial photographs — both the 'work' of archaeologists — touches upon the issue of where site-related documentation ends and 'art' begins.

Since the time of the fieldwork, such artistic ventures have become more commonplace and the entire issue of the aesthetics and aesthetic experience of excavation is now much explored (*e.g.* Molyneaux (ed.) 1997; Shanks 1992). While sympathetic to these efforts, the approach here is rather more conservative, or at least understated. It is not a matter of artistic experience somehow 'problematising' excavation as such or having a significant impact on interpretation, but rather highlighting similar concerns relating to process and documentation.

2. Structure and Sequence

The Ringwork appears so striking in photographs of the excavation largely because the upper profiles of its major circuits were filled with dark peats (Plate II; cover). Not only does this tell of the long earthwork survival of the enclosure after its Iron Age usage, but also the cumulative nature of its organic plan. Eventually all of its quasi-circular ditch circuits were open and functioned together. That new circuits were evidently added while previous ones were maintained implies that much of its construction sequence must be inferred by plan 'logic'. There are few direct stratigraphic relations to assist analysis; as a result, much ambiguity pervades the sequence.

Bracketed by the site's pre- and post-Iron Age usage — respectively Period I (Bronze Age) and Period III (its 'employment' in post-medieval times) — the emphasis of the text will obviously lie with the intervening Iron Age enclosure systems (Period II). While issues relating to longer term patterns of land-use and 'place' reference will be a theme of the final discussion, in order to maintain a sense of focus here the evidence for Period I and III will be presented in its entirety, including the results of appropriate artefact studies. The ensuing chapters, variously concerned with specialist reportage and distributional patterning, will essentially only concern the site's Iron Age phases. This being said, more can be teased out of the remnant framework of the preceding Period I occupation through analysis of the Ringwork's spatial structure. These elements will only be presented as they 'emerge' in the context of the study of the Iron Age occupation, and will be summarised in Chapter 6.

I. Period I (Bronze Age): Pre-Ringwork usage
(Figs 15 and 16)

The traces of a 'lithic site' were largely confined to the ploughsoil, and to residual artefacts within later contexts; only a few features are attributable to this phase, and their dating is highly suspect. The ploughsoil density of worked flint varied from 0–12 pieces per collection unit (2.9 pieces per 10 x 10m mean; 2.2 st. dev.: Fig. 15). At first there seems little obvious sense of any patterning, or even of a 'site' as such, aside from the fact that higher densities (5+ pieces) tend to occur in a *c.* 40m-wide east-to-west band across the middle of the collection grid. Even this swathe is punctuated with nil values, however, and the more consistent pattern could be read as attesting only to a distinct western-central 'high'. While definition of the latter perhaps acquires greater credibility through the occurrence of locally higher burnt flint values in the same area (though these seem to have a more southward 'pull'), this immediate spread also corresponds with the main peak in Iron Age pottery and bone distribution (Fig. 98). As will be discussed below, this may well mark the location of enclosure-contemporary middens, and therefore high flint values could equally well relate to material scraped up and re-deposited during its Iron Age occupation. (The eaves-gully of Structure I — an Iron Age building thought to become the site of a midden in the later phase of enclosure usage — produced 88 worked and 105 burnt flints, as opposed to the totals from the comparably-sized gully of Structure IV which yielded only 38 and 30 pieces in each of these respective categories.)

Yet the distribution of this material continues south-westwards beyond what is argued to be the main extent of these midden spreads. It correlates clearly with an increase in worked flint re-deposited within Iron Age cut features (>2 flints per metre segment) that does not directly correspond with the main focus of Ringwork-associated deposition (Fig. 16). Therefore, taken as a whole, the evidence suggests a distinct distributional 'high' in the south-western/central quarter of the grid.

Across the collection grid as a whole, the density of burnt flint ranged from 0–612 pieces per 10m unit or 0–5020g (22.6 pieces/283.4g mean; 79/638.8g st. dev.: Fig. 15). Apart from a local swathe of increased values in the western-central of the grid which fringes the worked flint 'high' there, it is the concentration in the north-eastern sector that is most obvious. There, over an area of *c.* 30 x 30m, values greater than 500g consistently occurred (0.57–5.02kg), averaging 1.68kg per 10m unit. Given these densities and their extent, this must reflect the former location of a burnt flint mound comparable to other 'pot boiler' sites in the region (Edmonds *et al.* 1999, table 5).

A test-pit dug in the approximate centre of this spread (producing more than 5kg of burnt lithics) indicated that the postulated mound had been ploughed out (*i.e.* its soil sequence was 'structureless'). Upon machine stripping, a number of shallow burnt-flint-filled 'features' were found scattered over a 5 x 5.00m extent within the area of the 'core' densities; traces of burnt flint lay impressed in the surface of the natural over an area of 12 x 14.00m (Fig. 16). These proved to be irregular hollows — probably natural ground surface depressions and the impressions of tree-rooting. These were filled with a black soil matrix of the kind characteristic of pot boiler mounds, which seemed largely to be derived from reduced charred material. The flot from a bulk sample taken from one of these features consisted of fine charcoal and charred fragments of indeterminate stems and rhizomes; no other macrofossils were noted (Murphy, Chapter 3). A soil micromorphology sample was also taken from one of these hollows (French, Chapter 3).

The lithic assemblage
by M. Edmonds

The fieldwork resulted in the recovery of a total of 676 pieces of worked flint, of which 258 were collected during fieldwalking and test-pitting. In addition, 2685 pieces of burnt flint were recovered; 1627 in the course of the survey (20.4kg) and 1058 during excavation (12.7kg). A full discussion of the nature and context of this material will not be presented here, but a series of broad observations regarding the chronology and character of the assemblage will be offered.

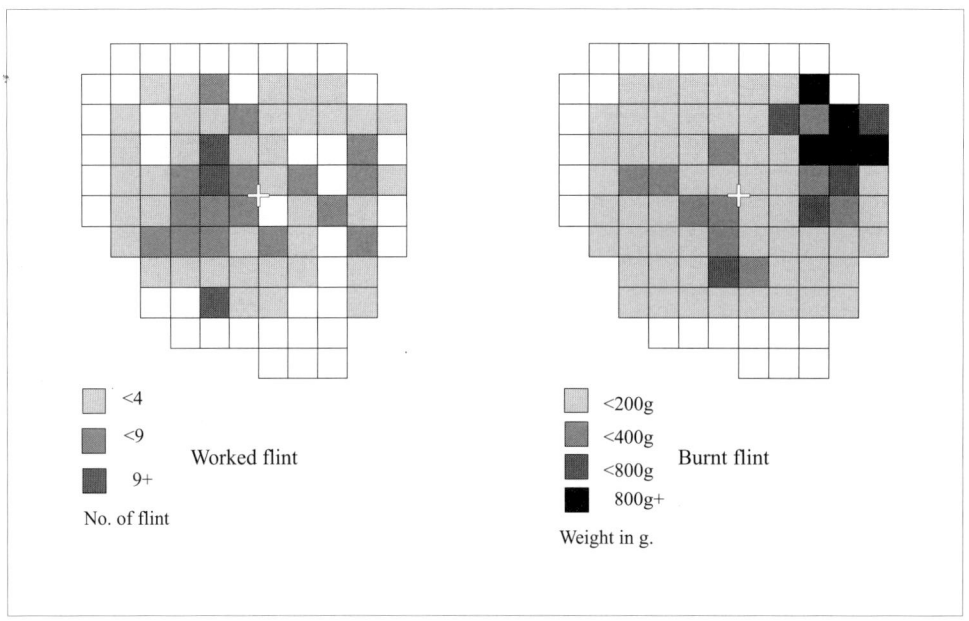

Figure 15 Surface collection: burnt and worked flint

For a variety of reasons, inferences concerning the chronology of the lithic materials require caution. In addition to the limitations that accompany the use of surface survey data, it is clear that much of the material recovered in the course of the excavation is residual. Under these circumstances, diagnostic artefacts provide the only reliable indicators of chronology. At the most general level, artefacts reflecting a number of different periods can be recognised within the assemblage. These include two microliths — from *561* (F. 99) and *644* (a tree-throw in the north-western corner of the site) — which probably date to the later Mesolithic. A similar date may also apply to one of the cores recovered during fieldwalking, although it should be stressed that similar forms were also produced during the earlier Neolithic. Neolithic artefacts are also present. These include a particularly fine leaf-shaped arrowhead from the surface of the clay natural, and a burnt end scraper from tree-throw *644*, both of which are probably of earlier Neolithic date. Other artefacts of the period include a flake with a polished dorsal surface that is likely to have been detached from an axe, and an end scraper with invasive retouch along both sides.

Artefacts attributable to the Bronze Age form the largest component of the assemblage as a whole. A small number, such as the multi-platform core from ditch F. 37, probably date to the Early Bronze Age: a crude thumbnail scraper can be assigned to the period during which Beaker pottery was in use. However, many of the crude notches, scrapers and retouched flakes are likely to belong to a later phase of the period. This may also apply to the crude cores and worked pebbles which show no signs of consistent platform preparation and maintenance. In addition, a number of pieces display evidence for the reworking of discarded tools and waste through the patina upon the original flaked surfaces. Whilst this does not in itself provide a reliable means of dating, this pattern of re-use after a considerable interval is a trend which can be seen in many Bronze Age assemblages.

Given the residual nature of much of the data, and in the absence of detailed technological analyses, inferences concerning the character of the material must remain at a relatively general level. In broad terms, the relatively small number of Mesolithic and earlier Neolithic pieces represent little more than the usual 'background noise' encountered when survey and excavation are conducted on this scale. Microliths and projectile points do not in themselves provide reliable indicators of settlement activity *per se*, and here it can be suggested that they reflect little more than a human presence in the immediate area. By contrast, the scale and general character of Bronze Age lithics suggest that the area witnessed some form of settlement activity prior to the establishment of the Iron Age enclosure. Given that raw material does not occur naturally in the immediate area, it is difficult to interpret the densities of crude flakes and cores as a simple product of 'off-site' discard. This impression is reinforced by the overall density of burnt flint, *c.* 30–40% of which appears to have been worked, and by the presence of a possible burnt mound. Having said that, the generally low densities of Bronze Age ceramics raises the possibility that the area examined during survey and excavation actually lies on the margins of the main focus of Bronze Age activity here. With regard to Iron Age lithics issues recently raised by Young and Humphrey (1999), on the basis of present evidence it is difficult to establish whether any of the material reflects the continued use of flint during the Iron Age.

Pottery
Aside from a few scraps of probable Beaker found in the tree-throws in the north-western corner of the site, a quantity of burnt-flint tempered pottery was recovered in the course of the excavation (only one sherd was found during fieldwalking). Occurring residually within later features, their distribution is dispersed and displays no obvious patterning. Hill assigns this material to the Late Bronze Age (*c.* 1200 – 800 BC: Chapter 4) and this, along with the vast majority of the site's lithics, probably dates the 'pot boiler' activity.

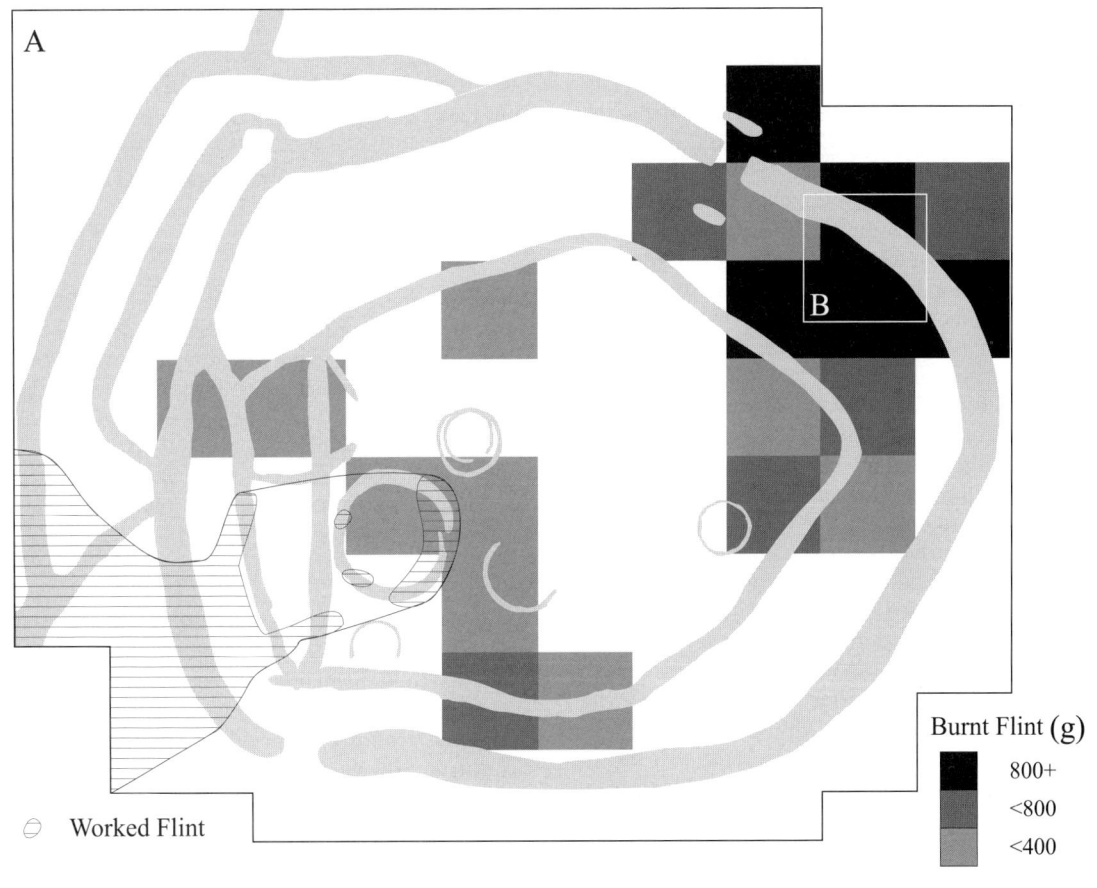

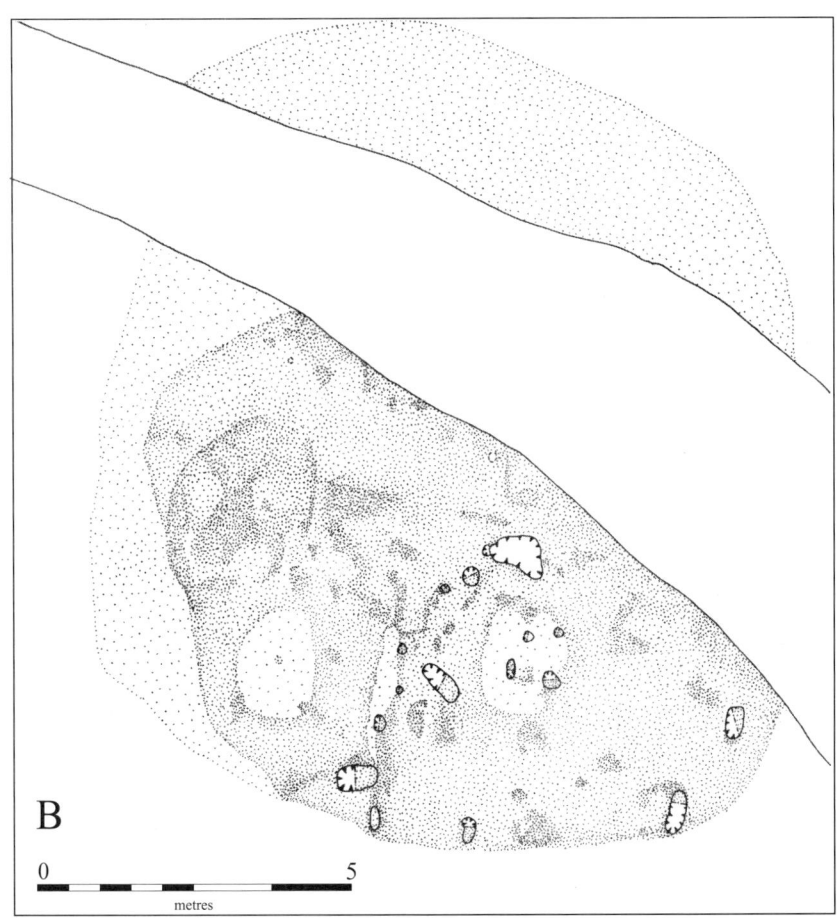

Figure 16 **A** lithic distributions: 2+ worked flints per segment in Iron Age features; burnt flint, surface 'highs'; **B** the burnt flint mound, density of flint exposed in surface of subsoil (stippling indicates extent and density of burnt flint.

Discussion
As outlined by Edmonds, the lithic assemblage suggests a palimpsest of episodic usage from the later Mesolithic, earlier Neolithic and the Late Neolithic/Early Bronze Age eras, but with the vast majority of the material of later Bronze Age attribution. Despite the site's relatively low overall lithic densities compared, for example, with those from the generally contemporary complex at Eye Hill Farm, Soham (Edmonds *et al*. 1999), a basic structure can be detected when the evidence is viewed as a whole. The main spread of worked flint, extending from the slope of the Wardy Hill spur, lies in the south-western quarter of the grid. This is fringed by a swathe of burnt flint 'waste', with the possible pot boiler mound lying some 20–30m to the north-east. Site-marginal burnt flint deposition was also identified in the Eye Hill Farm collections.

Although by any measure only a low-density lithics site this must be qualified, as at Soham, by the quantities of worked flint that had evidently been burnt later and subsequently re-deposited in the pot boiler mound. With 30–40% of the burnt material having been previously worked, and extrapolating from the test-pit-to-fieldwalking densities assuming an average weight of 10g per flint, then upwards of 15–20,000 worked flints must be bound up in its matrix. If so, this effectively represents a considerable 'erasure' of the original lithics site. Of course, one cannot be certain that all this material was generated at the immediate site itself and some, if not most, of it may derive from the larger Wardy Hill complex. The crucial issue is that this activity occurred on clay sub-soils and all the flint had to be imported into the site, the nearest gravel terrace deposits lying *c.* 100m to the south-east.

While burnt flint mounds like that evidenced on the site were not an uncommon feature of the cultural landscape of the 2nd millennium BC along the southern and south-eastern fen-edge, none have previously been found on the region's clays. Concerning their character and inter-relationship with monuments, it has been argued that it is wrong to view them strictly in a context of quasi-industrial refuse (Edmonds *et al* 1999). Formal 'enmoundment' of this material – on a scale comparable to barrow construction – would not have been a 'natural' way to dispose of such mineral waste. Whatever their functional derivation, given this mounded form and what would have been (previous to plough dispersion) their brilliant white matrix they probably served as cairns of some type, marking settlement and/or seasonal territory. This demarcation of the spur suggests its early distinction as a locale. That the Iron Age outer Ringwork circuit cut through the mound (which would presumably still then have been without plough damage, and therefore prominent) without deflection could be read as indicating a lack of respect. Nevertheless, the possibility exists that the site saw continuity between its Bronze and Iron Age usage. This complex issue will be addressed further below.

Substantive Neolithic and Bronze Age sites are known around Ely's lighter skirtlands, and the area is renowned for its Bronze Age metalwork (*e.g.* Hall 1996). Yet, despite extensive development-led fieldwork in recent years, there has been little evidence to date of pre-Iron Age settlement on the Island's clays (Evans forthcoming a). However, the landscape was clearly 'visited' in this period. Amongst the most intriguing recent discoveries has been on the western side of Ely overlooking West Fen, where a large natural hollow was evidently utilised during the Bronze Age for processing activities involving burnt flint (Masser and Evans 1999).

II. Period II (Iron Age): Ringwork components
(Pls VIII–X; Figs 17–46)

Based on the premise that the site's 'totality' must be appreciated before its fractured phase-divided expression can be understood, in this section the 'basics' of the Iron Age enclosure system — both the Ringwork's elements and its precursors — will be presented. A 'trajectory' or growth model of the development of its form follows (Phasing outline, below), but here it is imperative to bear in mind the 'final' interaction of its diverse parts — the sense of the enclosure *as a whole*.

The ditch circuits
Aside from their eventual contemporaneity, two points must be stressed concerning the Ringwork's boundaries. First, that only the main outer circuit (F. 1) and the line of F. 14, continuing north from the Ringwork's northern perimeter, are truly major ditches (though F. 28, coming off the south-western corner of the outworks, also approaches this scale: Fig. 17). Secondly, despite the overall 'organic' layout there is a degree of regularity between its circuits — a sense of ripple-like 'echo'. This is apparent in the interval maintained between the outwork ditches (F. 10–12) and the inner circuit and main perimeter in the southern and south-western sectors of the Ringwork (F. 1 to F. 2/13/38): all had a *c.* 5.00m space between them. Moreover, despite variability in the width of the berm between the main inner and outer circuits around the rest of the perimeter (10.00m in the south-east; 13.00m in the north half), the arrangement of the two mirrored each other sector-by-sector and they were clearly related. These inter-relationships were obviously determined, at least in part, by the situation of their intervening banks — arguably 'ramparts' — whose status is further discussed below.

The main circuit
(F. 1: Figs 17, 18, 19, 20, 36 and 40)
F. 1 was of a reversed 'C'-shaped configuration, there being a 30m wide gap on its north-western side that was spanned by ditch F. 12. The latter ditch re-cut what may have been an earlier version of the main circuit (F. 144: see below), suggesting that F. 1 was once continuous and that it had been re-cut into this 'C'- pattern. There was considerable variability in the profile and size of ditch F. 1, which ranged between 3.40 and 4.50m in width and 1.35–1.80m deep. For the most part, it was 1.50–1.70m deep and 3.60–4.50m across with a broadly angular 'V'-shaped profile (*i.e.* a round, tight base). Two major entrance crossings were identified — a 'Watergate' to the north-east and the main 'Landward' Entrance in the south-west. Described below, these will be referred to here when describing lengths of its circuit.

The ditch was deepest adjacent to the south-western entrance — 1.80m on the west side and 1.65m to the east. Around the south-eastern, eastern and western sectors it was 1.45–1.55m deep. It neither deepened adjacent to the 'Watergate' nor at the north-western terminal (*i.e.* the 'top' of the 'C'), and at the latter point it was actually relatively shallow at 1.35m depth. This contrasts with the western terminal (where it conjoins F. 12/144), where it was markedly different from the rest of the adjoining circuit on that side. There, over a distance of some 9.00m, it was *c.* 1.75m deep and had a distinct waterlogged trough in its base. Coring indicated that 0.75m south of that point there was a distinct butt/shelf, beyond which the base was only 1.35–1.40m deep. The profile also differed along this length (up to the main south-western entrance), having a broad base *c.* 0.90–1.20m across and a flat, broad concave profile. The deepening of the profile adjacent to the western side of the main entrance (to

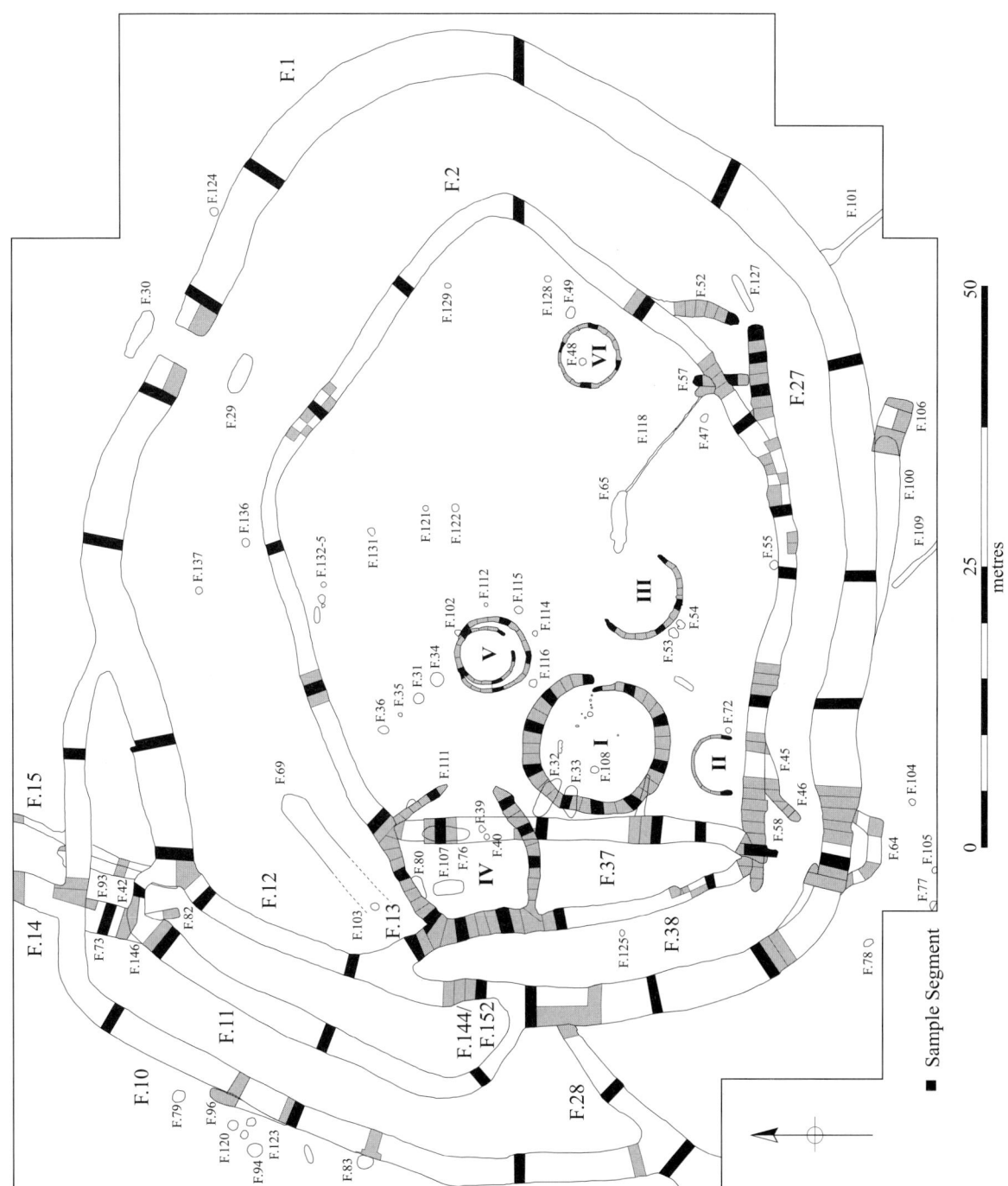

Figure 17 The radial grid: locations of metre-segment excavation units around main circuits and structures, and sample segments (black)

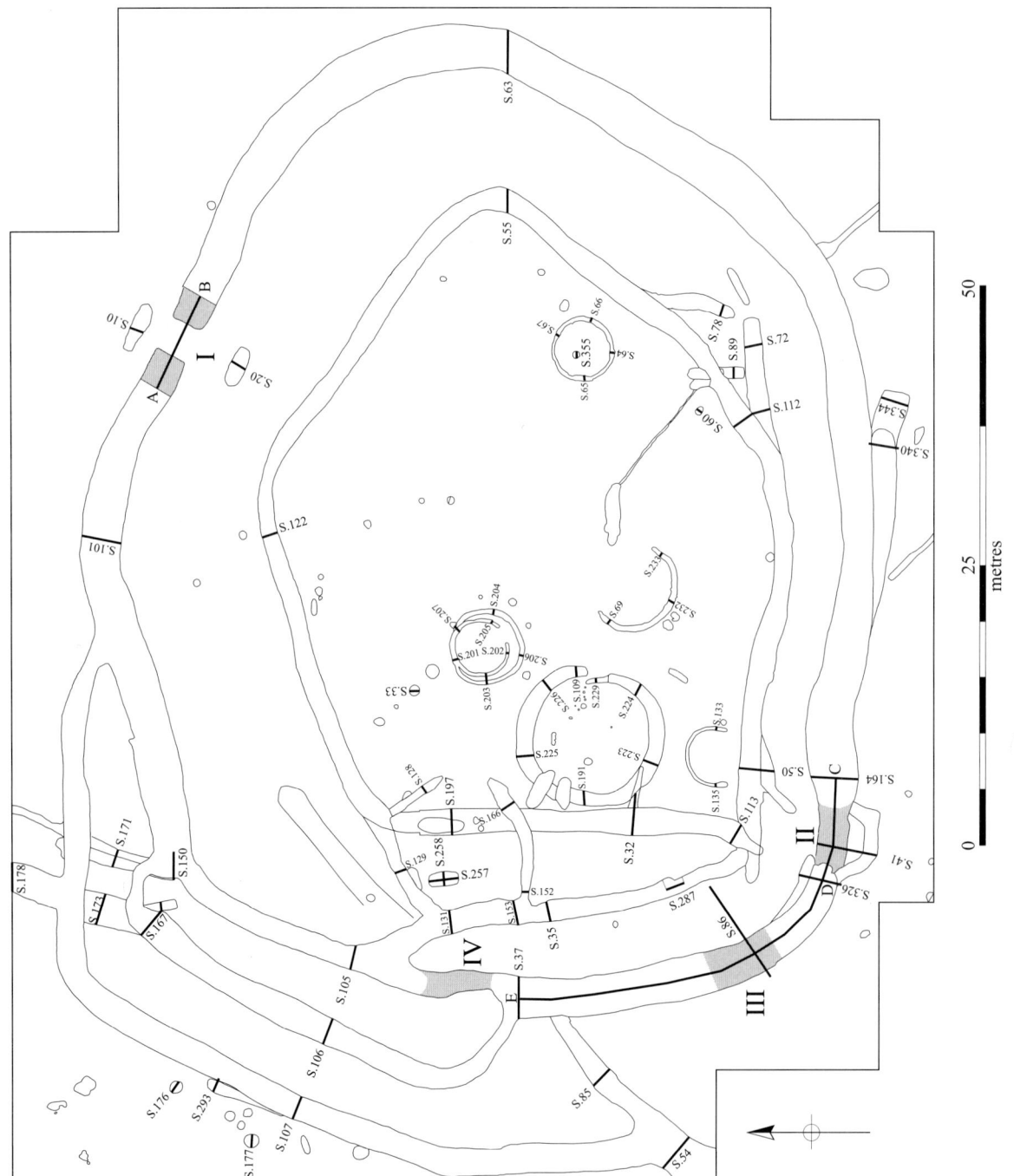

Figure 18 Section locations (I–IV: entrances)

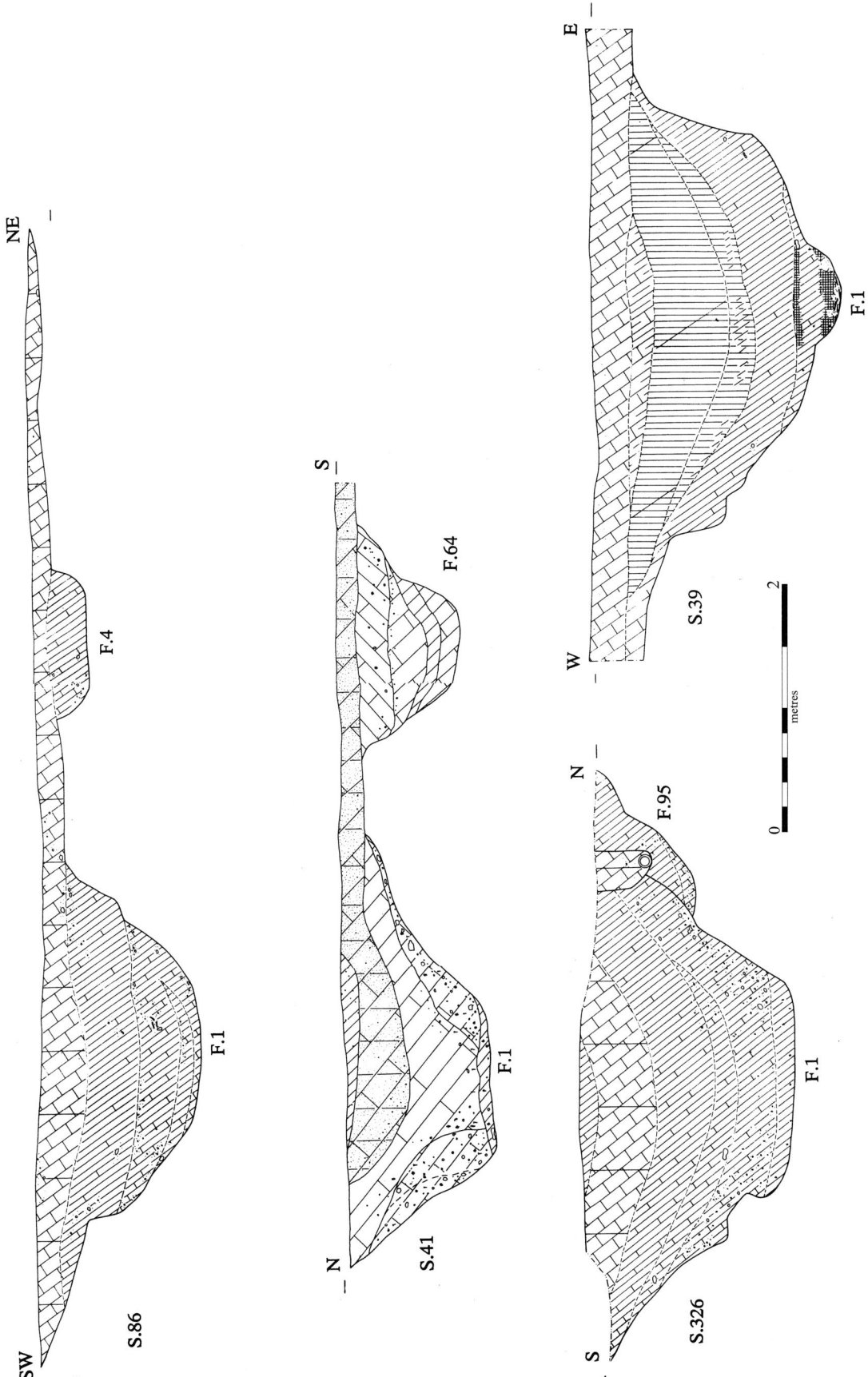

Figure 19 Sections: the Main Circuit (F. 1, 4 and 64)

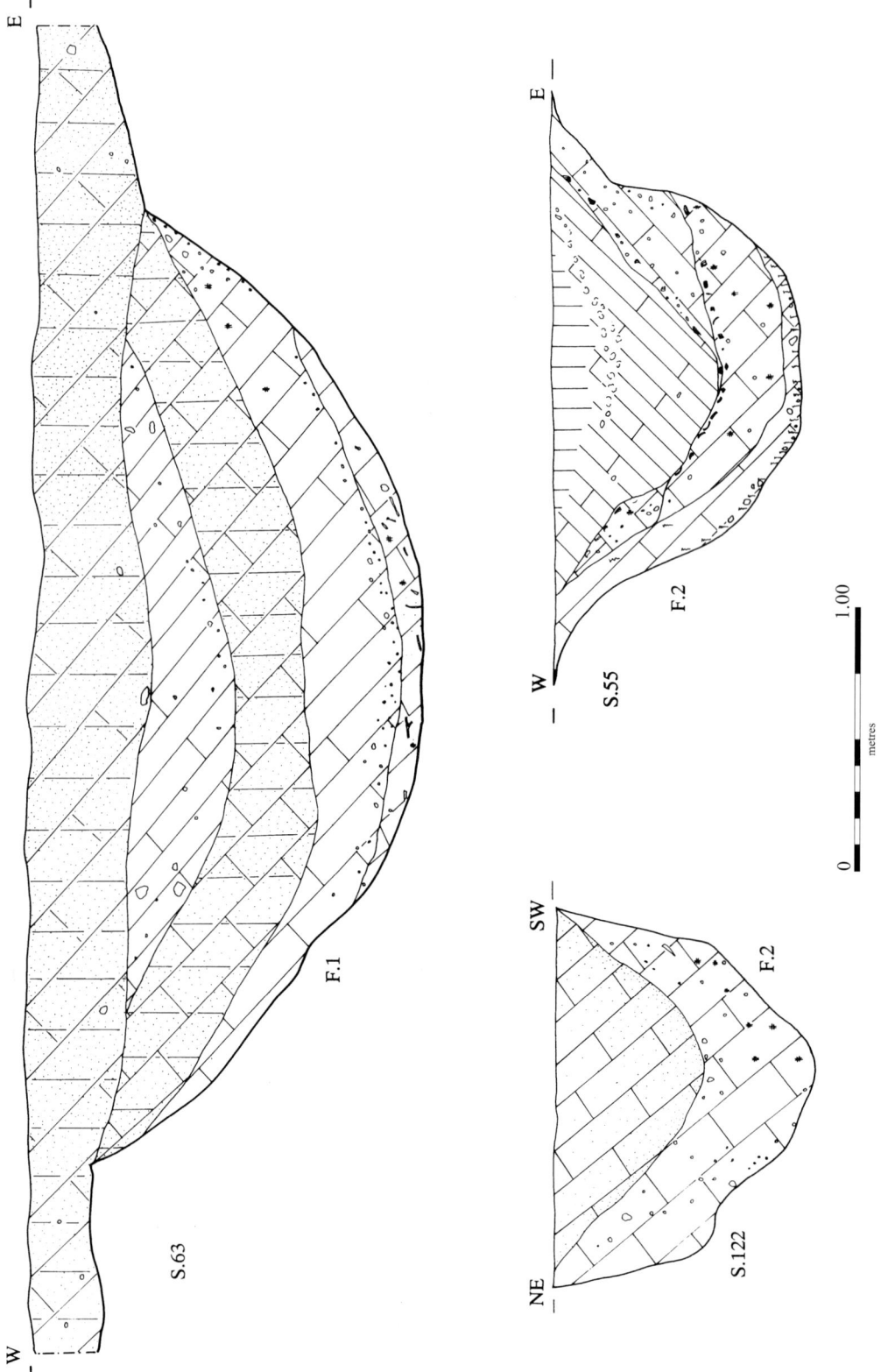

Figure 20 Sections: the Main and Inner Circuits (F. 1 and 2)

30

1.80m depth) was shown by coring to be localised. Whilst those portions with the greatest depth probably reflect key points of re-cut maintenance (*e.g.* the main entranceway), the very deep, 'sump-like' profile immediately west of the entrance and at the western terminal might relate to water provision — effectively forming 'wells' within the circuit — as otherwise the site would lack such supply (see below concerning discussion of Iron Age segmented ditch form).

It warrants notice that evidence was found in the area of the south-western entrance to indicate that the primary construction of this circuit involved the cutting of segmented pit-like lengths (see *The main entrance*, below).

The inner circuit
(F. 2/38/45: Figs 17, 18, 20, 28, 38 and 39)

Generally 1.80–1.90m wide and 0.80–1.00m deep, the profile of this ditch varied from a 'V'-shape to a tight or broad 'U'. It was at its smallest along the north-central/eastern circuit (1.40m wide; 0.80–0.95m deep), and most substantial along its south-western length where it was some 2.00m wide and up to 1.20m deep; it diminished to 1.25m width and 0.55m depth before terminating in a sub-circular butt. At its north-western end F. 2 may have originally conjoined with Ditch F. 37, the junction between the two being truncated by the eaves-gully of Structure IV.

Within the south-west part of the circuit the western sub-circular terminal of an east-to-west oriented ditch (F. 45) was truncated by the main F. 2 ditch-line, so that the southern side and full base (and lower northern edge) only locally survived truncation (it having truncated/re-cut the F. 46 terminal of the previous phase: see below). Ditch F. 45 was *c.* 1.10m deep, with a steep 'U'-shaped profile 1.20m across (as truncated: *c.* 1.60m full estimated width). The profile of this ditch was exposed in another excavation segment 2.00–3.00m east of the terminal, beyond which its line had been entirely cut away by the main (inner) Ringwork circuit. The F. 45 'end' probably represents the original south-western terminal of F. 2; as such, it defines the eastern side of an entranceway whose western edge would have been determined by the southern end of F. 38 (*i.e.* F. 2 west of this point is a later extension).

The extended south-western terminal of F. 2 apparently truncated ditch F. 38. Superseding an earlier north-to-south boundary (F. 37), this latter feature continued north as the 'secondary' inner circuit on the western side of the Ringwork. Over its southern 6.00m length this was generally 1.20–1.25m wide and 0.60m deep, with a concave 'U'-shaped profile. Adjacent to its southern end it broadened (to 1.60m width), and displayed a 'double' concave base indicative of re-cutting. At the northern end of this length it was only *c.* 0.45m deep, and the impression of a 0.15m deep sub-circular terminal was recorded in its base. This portion had been backfilled with re-deposited natural clays. North of this point it had been re-cut to 0.70m depth, the southern terminal being broader and very distinct (1.50m width). Where sectioned further north, this ditch was 1.45m wide, its profile changing to a deep 'V' (1.00m deep) with a flat base 0.45m across. This northern length of F. 38 had not been backfilled, and represented an 'open' feature.

Adjacent to Structure IV (there dug as F. 13) this ditch was continuously excavated over a length of 13.00m. Despite kinking north-eastwards, its profile remained unchanged for some 7.00m (2.30m wide and 0.90–1.10m deep; 'V'-shaped with a flat base 0.40m across). While beyond this point its depth remained consistent (0.80–0.90m: *c.* 1.60m OD) and its width comparable (*c.* 2.10m), its profile changed to a broad 'U' with a flattish base 0.75–1.00m across, and here it had a broadly splaying upper eastern edge. Whilst there is no absolute evidence for its re-cutting, it is possible that this change of alignment and profile related to an early southern terminal, perhaps corroborated by the initial base-plan plotting of the ditch's upper peat fill. (A terminal in this area might correlate to the north-western end of F. 1 — the southern side of the West Central Entrance.)

The outworks
(F. 10–14, 28, 42, 144: Figs 17, 18 and 21)

A *c.* 4.00m-wide ditch (F. 10/28) 'entered' the extreme south-western corner of the site from Wardy Hill, where it must continue as the boundary distinguished in the hilltop geophysical plots. With a broadly splaying western exterior edge (1.20m deep), its east side dropped to meet a distinct basal profile 0.25m deep conjoining a flat base 0.80m wide. Oriented south-west to north-east, this ditch divided *c.* 7.00m beyond entering the area of excavation. Its eastern arm F. 28 had a tight 'U'-shaped profile 1.40–1.55m wide and 0.70–1.05m deep; it was shallowest at its northern end where it conjoined the main Ringwork perimeter F. 1. The western arm (F. 10) continued north to define the outermost perimeter of the Ringwork, turning sharply eastwards to conjoin with the line of the main circuit one-third of the way along its northern side. Along its western side F. 10 was *c.* 2.50–3.20m wide and 1.00–1.30m deep, deepening towards the south. Whereas midway along this side it had a broad 'U'-shaped profile with a flattish base, along the southern length this varied. The upper third of its profile splayed broadly, below which it dropped in a tight 'U'-shaped profile 1.70–1.90m wide and 0.80–0.90m deep. Along the northern length it was generally slighter, *c.* 1.90–2.00m across and 0.75–0.80m deep, and there was no indication that it deepened adjacent to its junction with F. 1. It was, however, partly interrupted upon the line of ditch F. 14. At that point, sub-square butts were seen in the base of F. 10 on either side of a slight, *c.* 0.60m wide causeway (this did not extend up to the stripped surface, but was reduced by 0.50m along the line of F. 14).

Ditch F. 14, re-cutting the projected line of ditch F. 73 (see below), ran north from ditch F. 10 and shared the same peat upper fill. In the section recorded along the edge of excavation, its 'U'-shaped profile was 3.60m across and 1.25m deep. At its junction with F. 10, although its upper profile was continuous just beyond the line of F. 10 it had a distinct sub-square butt 0.95m deep (in total), from which point it must slope down to the north. This ditch was also exposed in Trench VIII, 7.5m to the north; left unexcavated there, it was 2.20m wide.

Running north from the south-western butt end of ditch F. 1, ditch F. 11 lay *c.* 5.00m concentrically within the line of F. 10. Its profile varied from a 'U' to a broad 'V'-shape, 2.15–2.90m across and 1.00–1.25m deep. At its northern end, where it truncated ditches F. 73/82, this ditch terminated in a sub-circular butt 0.95m deep. (At a point 2.50m further to the south the east edge of this ditch narrowed by 0.75m, suggesting the presence of another terminal: unfortunately this was not excavated.) Its fills were, however, continuous with those of F. 42 to the east, which conjoined the north-western terminal of F. 1. F. 42 was 1.25m wide and 0.50m deep, and was clearly a distinct ditch length and not just a return of F. 11; that its base deepened just east of F. 11 suggested a distinct 'butt' arrangement, not unlike that of F. 10/14 to the north.

Extending south from the north-western terminal of F. 1, F. 12 ran concentrically within the line of ditch F. 11, preserving the same *c.* 5.00m interval seen between F. 10 and F. 11. Along its northern length it was 1.75–2.30m across and 0.70–0.83m deep. Distinct changes in its profile (from a regular concave to wide flat base) would confirm the evidence of the 'double concave' base of its northern section adjacent to the F. 1 junction that it had been re-cut. This was most apparent over its southern length, where an evidently flat-based primary ditch (F. 144: 1.60–2.30m wide and 0.85–0.90m deep; base 0.70–1.30m across) had been re-cut in a steep 'U'-shaped profile 0.80–1.10m wide and 0.70–0.80m deep (F. 152). It was the peaty fills of the steep secondary profile that so clearly defined the re-cut in relationship to the clay fills of the primary ditch (F. 144, probably equating with F. 1).

A shallow, 'path-like' trough F. 69 (1.50–2.50m wide, with a flat base 0.10–1.15m deep) had been truncated by the northern circuit of Structure IV. Generally running parallel with the arc of F. 12 and the north-western end of F. 1 (though turning more sharply westward over its southern end), and filled with charcoal-flecked greenish-grey silty clay fills, the status of this feature is ambiguous. However, after much deliberation it has been interpreted as a path worn around the interior eastern side of an F. 1/12-related bank.

Entrance access

Set on a diagonal north-east to south-west axis across the Ringwork, two main points of crossing were evident in the main F. 1 circuit (Fig. 17). Whilst that facing up-slope to the south-west (the 'Landward Entrance') was complicated, having often been re-defined, that opening onto the fen to the north-east — the 'Watergate' — was relatively simple. Apart from these, upon the eventual closure of the south-western entrance another entrance was later established nearby on the Ringwork's western side (the 'Western Crossing'). Finally, evidence of another possible line of access was detected extending south-west from the area of Structure IV and continuing across the southern end of the Outworks system. Largely recognised through finds distributions, the evidence for this 'West Central Entrance' is more tenuous. Identification in the latter instance is not helped by the absence of any accompanying ground surface reduction. Such broad reduction swathes, evidently wrought by sustained movement at these points, were apparent on the exterior side of the Landward Entrance, at the interior approach to the Western Crossing and throughout the Watergate

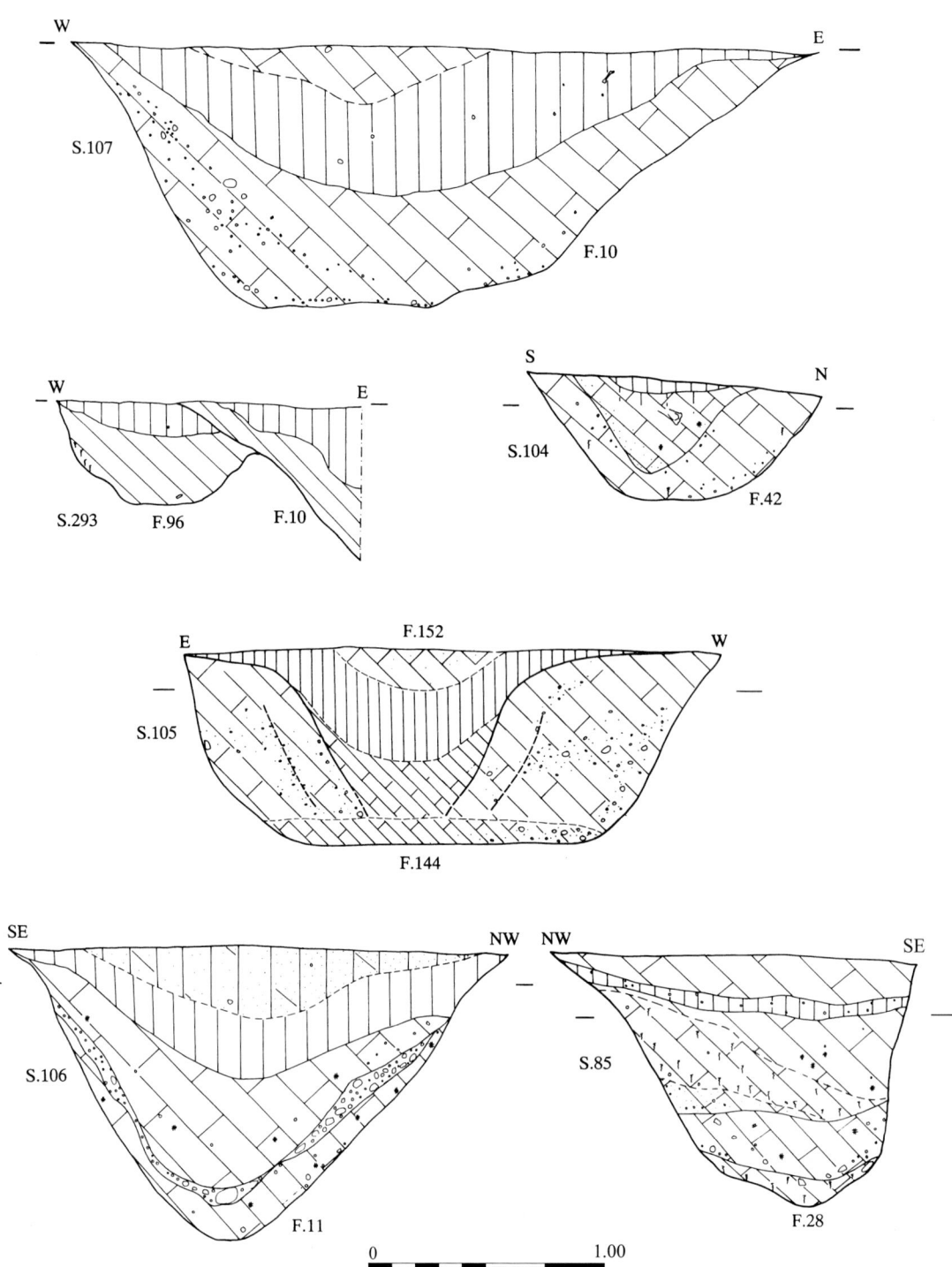

Figure 21 Sections: the Outworks

causeway. (A similarly peat-filled hollow extended beyond the Ringwork's outer circuit in the south-eastern corner of the site. This, however, would seem to relate to 'late' access around the perimeter as it survived as an earthwork in post-medieval times.)

The Watergate
(F. 29, 30: Plate VIII; Figs 17, 18, 22, 26 and 36)
Flanked by the squared terminals of F. 1, this consisted of a 3.10m-wide interruption in the outer circuit. Across its intervening causeway the ground surface had been reduced by up to 0.30m, presumably through sustained trampling action. Sharing the axis of the causeway were two roughly symmetrical square-butted blocking trenches. The exterior of these, F. 30, lay 1.80m beyond the main ditch circuit; the other, F. 29, fell 3.60m inside its line. Both had flat-based 'U'-shaped profiles 0.90–1.30m wide and were respectively 4.60 and 3.60m long and 0.40 and 0.60m deep. Obviously placed to deflect entrance access, neither seems to have been a post-setting trench, nor had they been backfilled. Therefore, any entrance-related timber defensive component may have been set atop upcast banks presumably resulting from their excavation. If these inferred banks lay exterior to their respective trenches — a bank could not have lain behind the exterior feature without completely blocking the causeway — then the access between the F. 29 bank and trench F. 30 would have been roughly comparable, with entrance-related movement restricted to c. 2.00m-wide corridors upon entering and exiting the causeway.

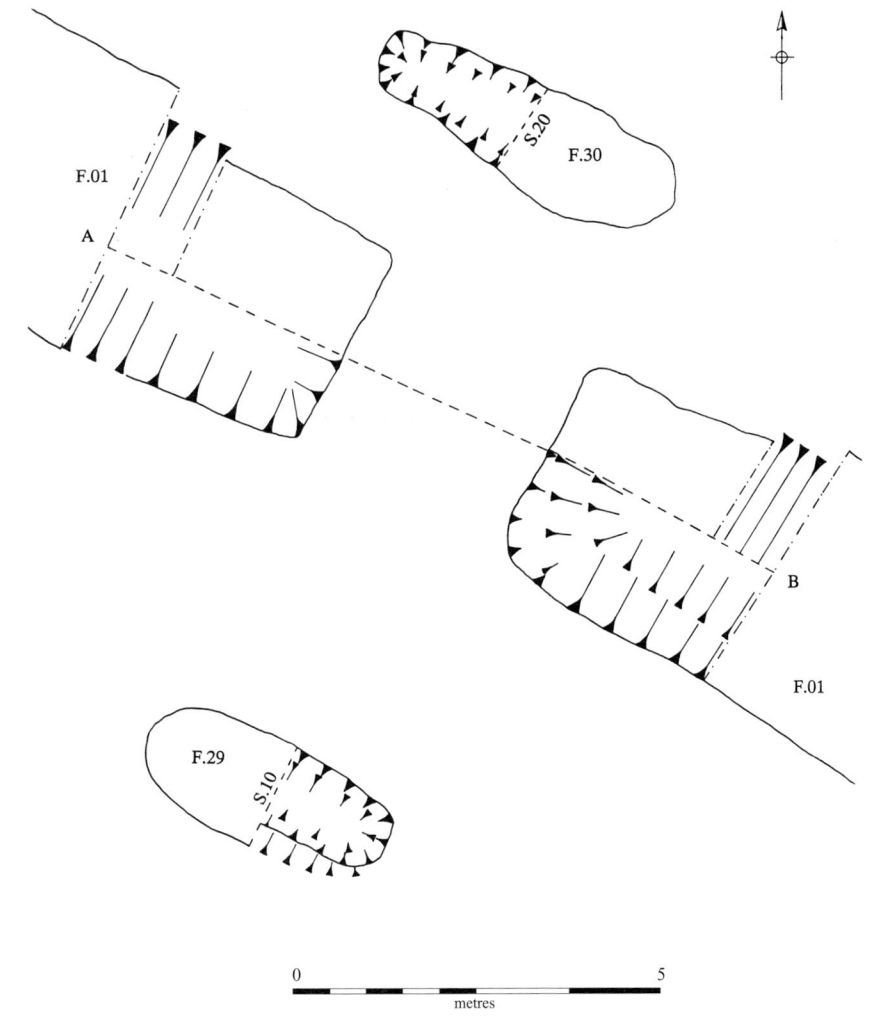

Figure 22 The Watergate

Plate VIII The Watergate, looking north-west across the entrance (photo by C. Price)

Little material was recovered from either of the ditch terminals in this configuration. Evidently a point of crossing removed from the interior house-zone, it did not see significant deposition. This may reflect the nature of the Ringwork interior which this crossing accessed: although the interior circuit was investigated intensively at this point no evidence of a corresponding entrance was recovered.

The main Landward Entrance
(F. 41, 46, 56, 58–60 and 149–51: Figs 17, 18, 23 and 24–6)
Situated along the south-western perimeter, this was an extraordinary 'work'. The ditch gave way to a 4.20m(+) wide causeway, 0.90m deep (F. 151). The sunken causeway was itself complicated, as its interior was reduced by *c.* 0.30m within a sub-rectangular depression 3.40m long and 1.50m wide (F. 149). This was very regular and 'box-like', with a flat base. On the west side of the causeway the resultant ridge was only *c.* 0.10m wide, from which point the 'bulbously' re-cut ditch-butt proper dropped away by *c.* 1.00m. To the east the causeway ridge was 0.60m across. There the ditch butt was stepped, indicating at least two phases of termination. The westernmost butt was a sub-rectangular, flat-based shelf *c.* 0.30–0.35m deep which survived over a length of *c.* 1.20m (F. 150), from where another sub-circular terminal dropped a further 0.50m to the level of the main ditch circuit.

It is extremely difficult to disentangle the sequence of this entrance configuration, especially the reduced F. 149 'box' within the causeway. The crossing itself was probably bridged somehow; hence the deeper ditch terminals on either side of the causeway. Here, however, it is worth stressing how similar the F. 150 'impression' was to that of F. 149. Moreover, the scale of the overall ditch profile at the point of F. 150 was of the same narrow width as beside F. 149 — 2.80m across, and not the full *c.* 4.00m span west of the crossing. These factors could suggest that F. 149 and F. 150 were related, and that both had been 'protected' by the bridge structure. There may, therefore, be two explanations for the reduced causeway 'box' (F. 149). The first would have it relate to the earlier F. 64 ditch configuration, which roughly encircled it (*i.e.* assigning it a pre-F. 1 date: see below). The second would instead stress its affinities to the F. 150 profile, and see it together with F. 149 as reflecting a primary, quasi-segmented form of ditch. The circuit must have been dug originally as a series of elongated box-like pits that were only subsequently joined up into a continuous circuit. (By extension, this ditch was originally only *c.* 0.90m deep: see Gwilt 1997 concerning segmented ditch construction.) With hindsight, the latter interpretation is the more plausible: therefore, the survival of F. 150 would also be attributable to its bridged protection, and thereby indicate that the point of crossing was actually *c.* 5.00m wide.

Behind the entrance, in the berm between the Ringwork circuits, a coarse cobble spread consisting of medium-large pieces of unworked flint and river pebbles (F. 58) was found over an area of 1.70 x 2.40m. (In the north it had been truncated by the extended length of the inner Ringwork circuit, F. 2; Plate VI.) Clusters of animal bones were embedded within this surface, which was sealed by a layer of mid/dark greyish-brown silty clay. Whilst the latter may possibly represent some kind of occupation spread it did not seem sufficiently dirty for this attribution, and is more likely to have been derived from later ditch upcast (*i.e.* bank material).

Given the manner of its excavation and the general homogeneity of the site's feature fills, phasing of the entrance-related configuration of the inner circuit's ditches cannot be precise, and to some degree must operate at the level of general principles. The main reference point for this is the western extension of F. 2, which truncates all of the ditch features described below. As previously discussed, the original western terminal of the inner Ringwork circuit was identified and excavated at this point (F. 45). This clearly corresponds with the southern end of ditch F. 38 (whose southern terminal probably equates with F. 44 recorded in the side of F. 2). Together they would have defined an entrance gap *c.* 5.00m across, whose size and location would correspond with the combined width of the F. 151 causeway within the outer circuit, and presumably correlate also with the use of the F. 58 cobbled surface.

Symmetrically situated between the F. 38/45 entrance terminals, and midway between the line of the inner and outer circuits, were two large ovoid pits, F. 56 and F. 59 (respectively 1.20 x 1.80m and 1.50 x 1.60m across, and 0.45m and 0.40m deep). Although no post-pipes were recognised within their homogenous clay fills, these flat-based features can only be assumed to have held substantial posts up to *c.* 0.50m in diameter; they must relate to some kind of gate structure *c.* 2.50m wide. (The eastern of the pair — F. 59 — was actually recorded as being truncated by a ditch pre-dating the F. 45 terminal. It was so difficult to distinguish features in this area, however, that in this case broader spatial relations and plan formality will be taken as paramount, and the features have been phased accordingly.)

An earlier entrance configuration was also distinguished at this point. Its eastern side was defined by F. 46, which was truncated by the original terminal of the main inner circuit (F. 45). Extending south-west from that point for some 3.50m, this clay-backfilled ditch length was 0.80–1.00m wide and 0.70m deep with a 'V'-shaped profile. By its alignment it would directly correspond with the southern terminal of F. 37, and together they would have defined an entranceway 4.00m across. Situated midway between these two terminals was F. 60. This ovoid post-hole (0.25 x 0.30m; 0.17m deep) probably relates to some kind of central blocking post. The suggested association between the F. 46 and F. 37 terminals is based entirely upon their shared north-east to south-west alignment. (No stratigraphic relationship between F. 37 and F. 38 was demonstrated as such; that the latter post-dates F. 37 *seems*, however, a reasonable inference.) Note, however, that the line of access if projected on this orientation would not match the F. 151 crossing in the outer circuit, but would have passed to the west of it. This suggests either that it relates to an undetected earlier crossing of the outer circuit (subsequently eradicated through re-cutting) or, more probably, that it pre-dated the outer F. 1 perimeter. If so, it may well relate to the F. 64 ditch configuration (see below).

A backfilled north-to-south oriented ditch (F. 41), probably truncated by F. 37, was found to extend for an estimated distance of at least 1.80m south of the line of F. 2. The feature was 0.80m wide and 0.40m deep, with proportions reminiscent of F. 46. Although much ambiguity remains concerning its status, there would appear be two ways of interpreting its associations: either it must relate to an earlier system, or it was an earlier version of ditch F. 37. These two options will be further explored below.

The Western Crossing
(Figs 17, 19 and 26)
A number of factors contributed to the recognition of this entranceway. Though individually none of them are unequivocal, given the weight of collective evidence its existence must be regarded as conclusive. The first relates to the western extension of the south-western terminal of the inner circuit cutting off the F. 38/45 entrance, and the backfilling of the southernmost 6.00m of the F. 38 circuit to give a more westward point of access. This in itself would not necessarily entail the abandonment of the main outer perimeter access of the Landward Entrance, as its approach could always have been staggered. This seems unlikely, however, given that the southern F. 38 crossing directly corresponds with a reduced swathe leading down to F. 1 at this point and that a range of primary 'tossed' refuse (*e.g.* large bone and a decorated wooden stave) was recovered there in the primary fills of the outer circuit. The base of the main ditch lies relatively high within this area, but so it was along the 25m of the circuit's south-western sector as a whole (as determined by deeper, flanking 'pit-pool' points), and this length is unlikely to have all been bridged. Nevertheless, the evidence suggests a 'late' line of crossing of both circuits in this location; and to this may also be added the localised distribution of wheelmade ceramics (see below).

West Central Crossing
(F. 76, 80, 107; Figs 17, 27, 28, 33 and 38)
There is less certainty as to the existence of this entranceway than of any other. Not recognised as such during the course of the excavation, its identification is based on the direct correspondence of a number of factors:

1. The very high finds density (and magnetic susceptibility values) immediately beyond the north-western corner of Structure IV's circuit south of the junction of F. 12 and F. 13. Also the fact that the artefact densities and key 'type' distributions have a distinct westward axis across the line of the Outworks beyond Structure IV.
2. The 'pinching' of the southernmost *c.* 6.00m of F. 12 before its junction with the large south-western terminal of F. 1. This length appears to have been dug (F. 144), subsequently backfilled, and later re-established through a relatively minor re-cut (F. 152).
3. The westward turning of the southern end of the F. 69 trough: if demarcating the backside of a bank, this configuration suggests its termination.
4. The very distinct turn in the alignment of the inner circuit at this point — effectively the junction of F. 13 and F. 38 — suggests a northern terminal of the latter.
5. The existence of the pair of trough-like pits F. 76 and F. 107 (and possibly F. 80), similar to the Watergate's blocking trenches, which also seem structurally related.
6. Although not symmetrical with the layout of the F. 2 circuit, an entrance in this position would complement the overall plan of the western side of the outer perimeter (F.1/12), since it would fall approximately midway along its length. Without it, moreover, it

34

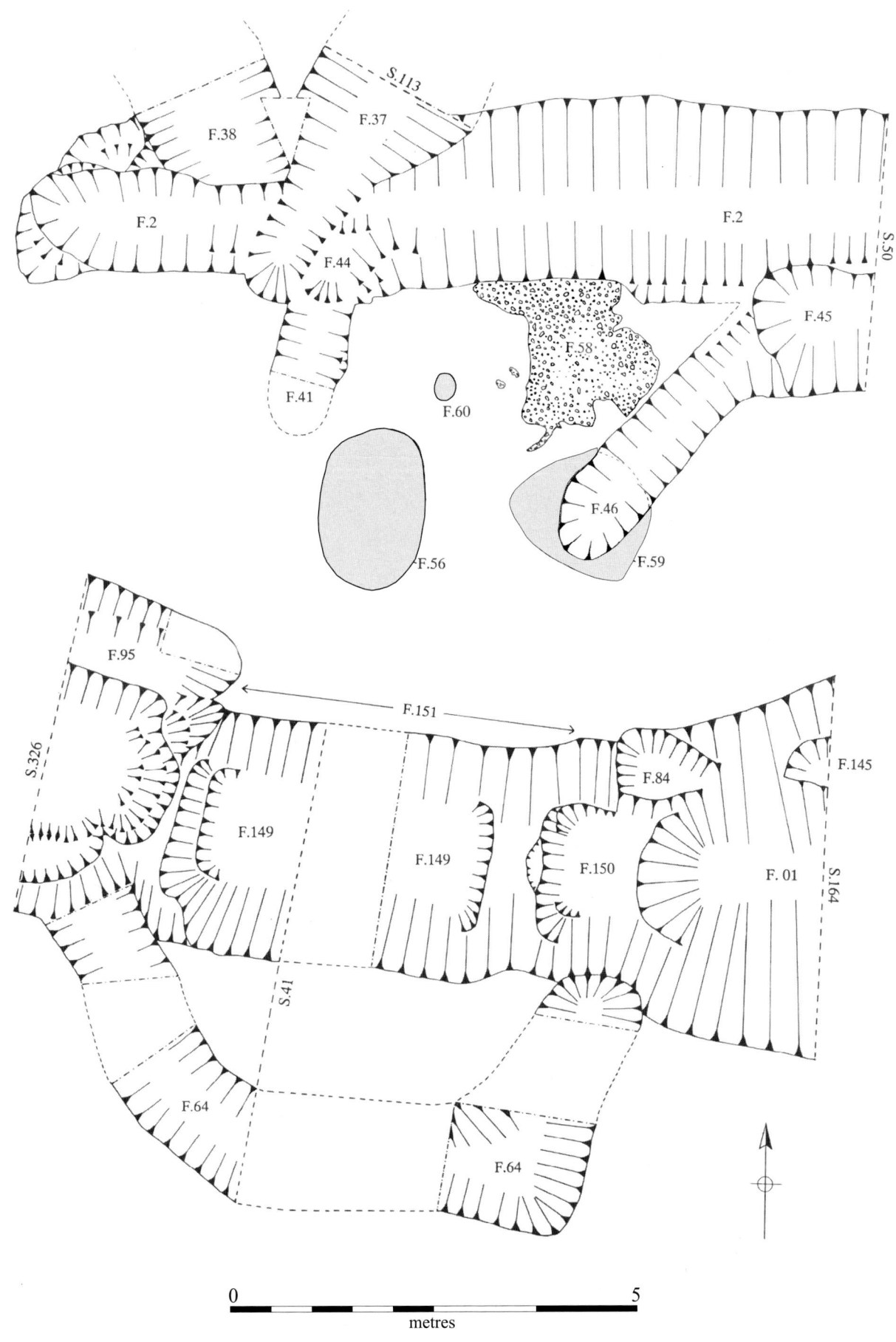

Figure 23 The Landward Entrance

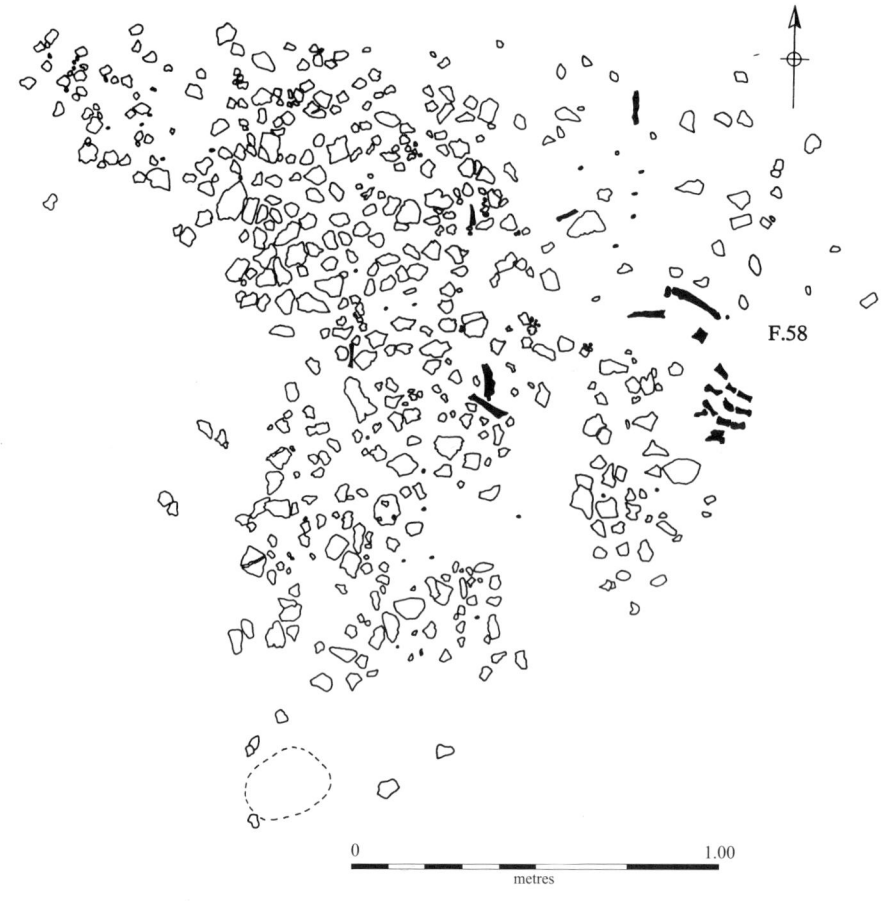

Figure 24 The Cobbled Surface (F. 58: bones in black)

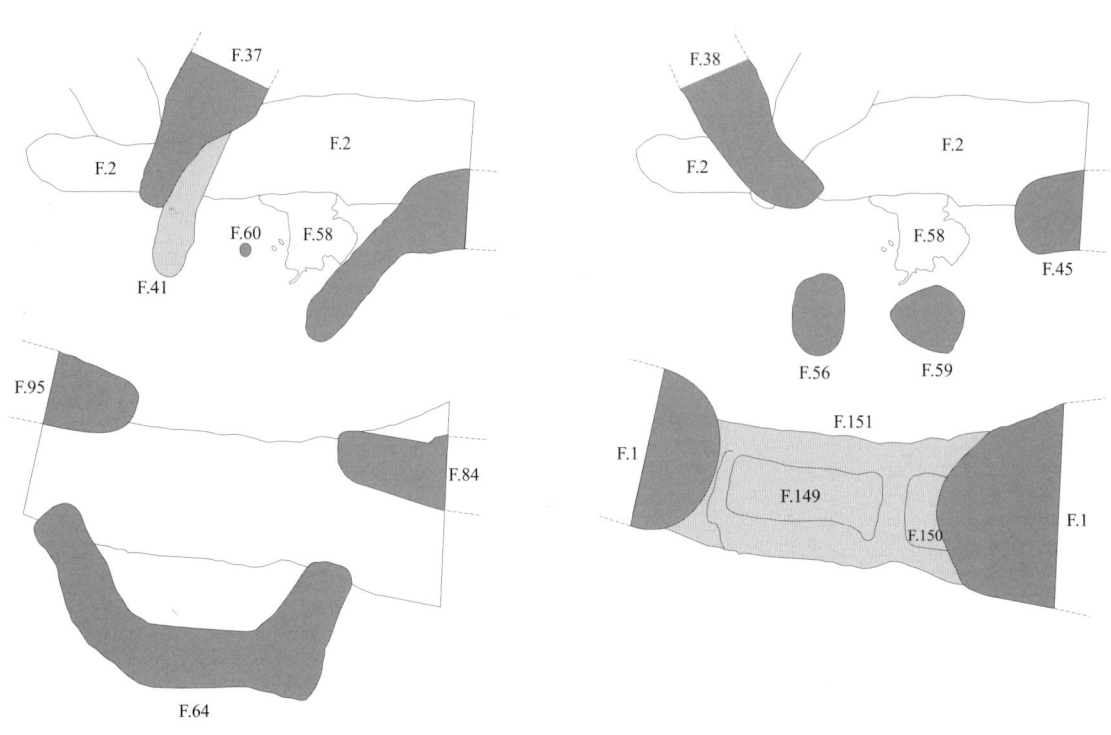

Phases 2 & 3   *Phase 4*

Figure 25 The Landward Entrance: phased development

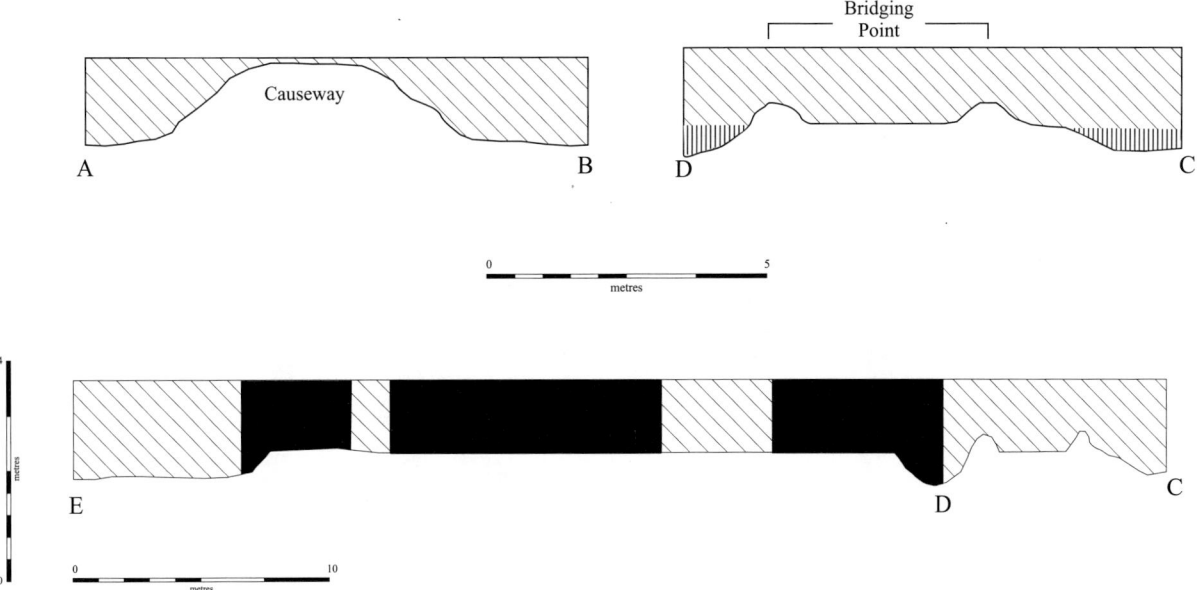

Figure 26 Entrance profiles: A–B the Watergate; C–D the Landward Entrance; C–E (lower) across Landward Entrance north-west across secondary Western Crossing
(see Fig. 18 for location)

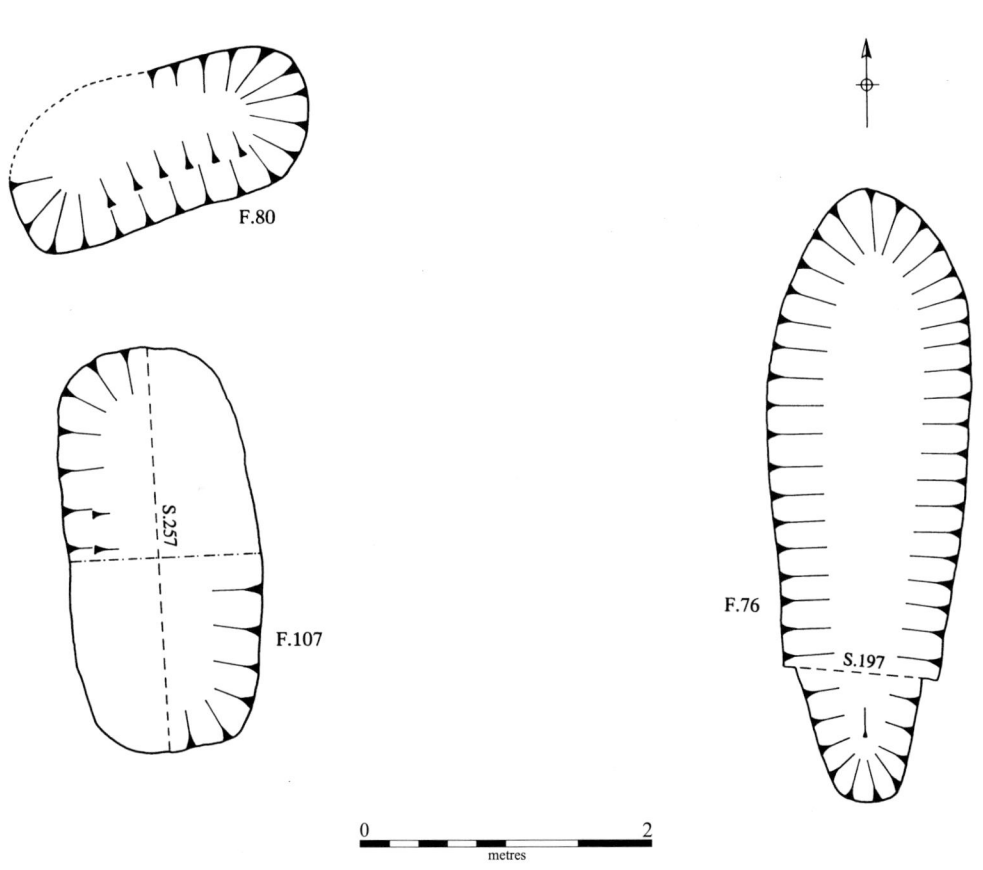

Figure 27 The West Central Entrance troughs (F. 76, 80 and 107)

37

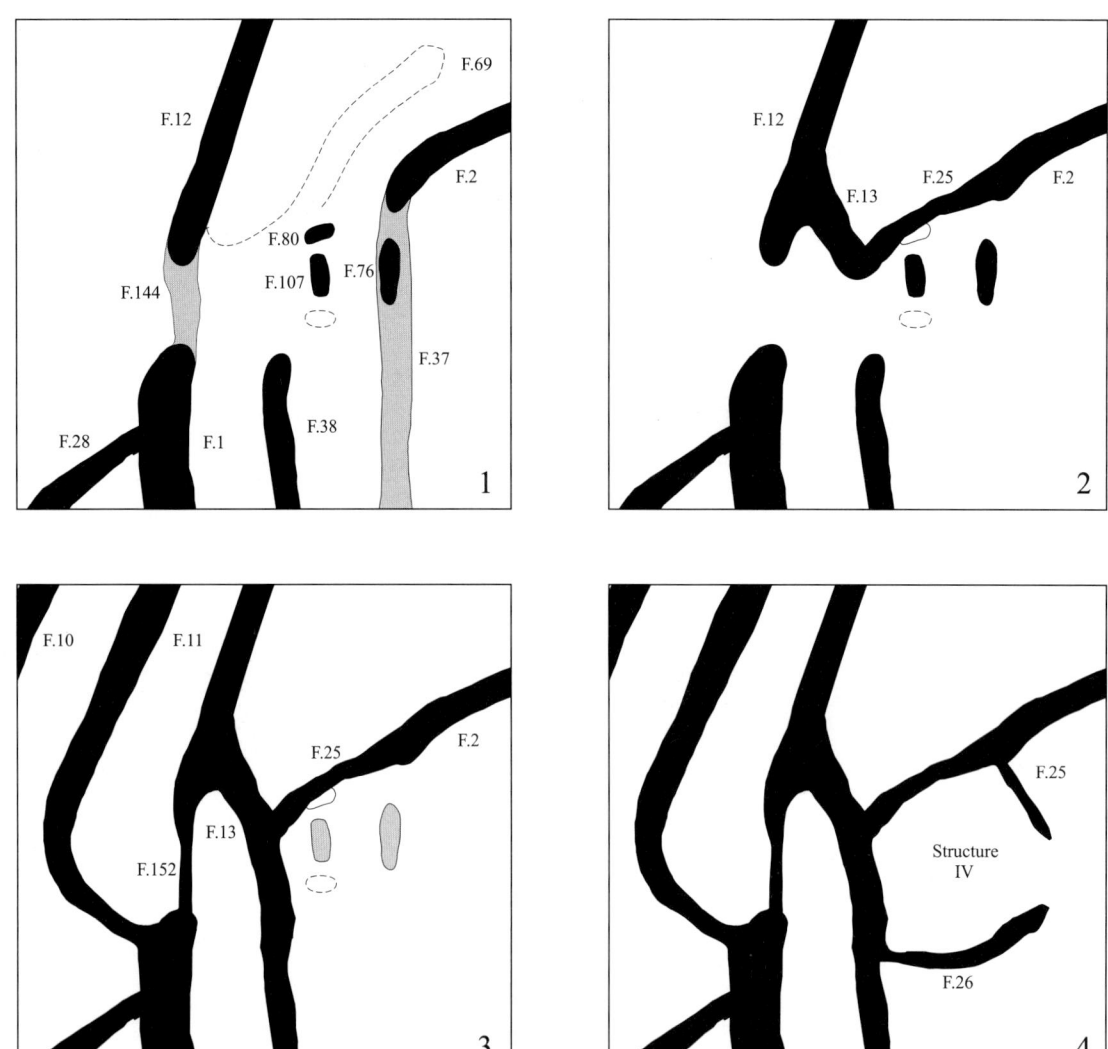

Figure 28 Development of West Central Entrance and Structure IV: (1) Phase 4 entrance, with F. 144 and F. 37 backfilled; (2) Phase 4, possible western extension of F. 2/25 and southern extension of F. 13 to encircle southern bank terminal (as defined by line of trough F. 69); (3) Phase 5, closure of West Central Entrance; (4) Phase 5, insertion of Structure IV.

becomes very difficult to account for the branching of ditch F. 12 at this point. Otherwise, why would the eastern F. 13 line cut across between the main circuits, and presumably through the major bank which they must have delineated (see below)?

Reconstructing the southern side of this entrance is relatively straightforward where it is marked by the changes in alignment and ditch profile: the original butt end of the inner F. 38 circuit would correspond directly with the large terminal of the outer circuit (F. 1), immediately south of and conjoining the backfilled length of ditch (F. 144). There would, however, be many more alternatives when trying to configure the entrance's north side; unfortunately, excavation within the area of the F. 12/13 junction was not sufficiently intense to provide resolution. While it may be the case that the F. 12 terminal, as re-cut after the backfilling of the F. 144 ditch, lay centrally at the junction of the F. 12/13 'Y' (or even turned in slightly along the line of F. 13), here it is presumed that it fell within the F. 12 arm alone, leaving an entrance interruption of *c.* 6.50m across the backfilled length of F. 144. No corresponding alteration need necessarily have occurred within the northern length of the inner circuit (F. 2): its line could simply have been left open beyond its junction with F. 37 following the backfilling of the latter, with the F. 69 trough marking the southern terminal of the bank behind the F. 12 ditch line. If so, access could theoretically have been gained to the Watergate *via* the gap between the end of F. 2 and F. 69 by traversed the 'corridor' between the F. 1 and F. 2 circuits. However, as indicated in Fig. 28, this bank's terminal may have later been enclosed with the arm of F. 13 extending to its junction with the northern length of the Structure IV circuit (F. 25), connecting it with the end of the F. 2 circuit in the east.

Two trough-like pits were found in this area. The eastern of these, F. 76, had been cut into the backfill of ditch F. 37 and was centrally aligned upon it. Of 'cigar-like' shape, it had rounded ends and was 4.20m long (0.30–0.60m wide), with a flattish base 0.60m deep. Its banded fills — alternating horizons of re-deposited clay natural with dark occupation-type deposits — may, at least in part, represent subsided floor surfaces (probably from Structure IV; see below). F. 107, located parallel 3.50m to the west, was of slightly more ovoid plan (1.40 x 2.80m; 0.45m deep) but lacked F. 76's mixed fill sequence, containing instead uniform light-mid brownish grey silty clay (see *Pits and troughs*, below, for discussion of the finds recovered from these features). In their form/scale and parallel setting, these two features are reminiscent of the blocking trenches associated with the north-eastern Watergate. This, and their location along the entrance axis, suggests that they also related to some kind of structure. (Given F. 76's re-cutting of ditch F. 37, it would otherwise be difficult to account for their purpose and stratigraphic situation.) Again, since no post-holes were apparent within their fills it must be assumed that any timber superstructure was supported by banks generated by their spoil (?set before F. 76/107).

It is assumed that F. 80 immediately to the north, of comparable size to F. 107, also relates to this gate-blocking structure. Whilst of similarly ovoid shape (1.00 x 2.20m), it was considerably deeper (0.70m). However, it is difficult to be certain of its true plan-form as the north side had been truncated by a later ditch (F. 25): it may even have been 'pear-shaped'. Certainly, the eastern end seemed to slope down broadly to a much larger concave western base. Its fill sequence appeared to represent two horizons of backfilling, re-deposited natural clays being separated by a major lens of very dark grey fine silt — an 'occupation layer' with a high density of artefacts. Although the function of this feature was indeterminable, the excavator speculated that it could have been a large post-hole. As such, it may be comparable to F. 56 and F. 59 associated with the Landward Entrance, and have held a large timber upright. Regardless of its precise role, if considered part of the F. 76/107 setting it would render their layout asymmetrical. With their upper profiles backfilled with re-deposited clays, it proved difficult to distinguish these features. Moreover, if another feature comparable to F. 80 had been situated symmetrically on the southern side of F. 107 it would have been obscured by the line of the post-medieval ditch passing through this area (F. 4), and may therefore have gone unnoticed. Its hypothetical position (as it were) is indicated on Fig. 28: it can only be regretted that this area was not investigated in greater detail.

Buildings and structures

Six round eaves-gully defined structures (Structures I–VI) were found within the interior of the Ringwork's innermost circuit. The two smallest had negligible finds densities: having no obvious residential function, they will be referred to as *ancillary structures*. While the easternmost (VI) probably did no more than encircle a haystack, the other, located beside the inner circuit near the Landward entranceway, could have controlled access into the Ringwork (II). The four remaining buildings *may* have consisted of two pairs. In both instances, the pennannular eaves-gully of the two main buildings (I and IV) opened onto a relatively minor structure immediately to the east which could have had an ancillary function. Such modular pairing of buildings is not uncommon on later prehistoric settlements (see Evans and Hodder forthcoming for overview). Yet other combinations are certainly possible, as will be explored below. Given their finds densities and form it seems probable that the two 'medial' category structures (Structures III and V) — those seemingly positioned in front of the main buildings — did see some degree of residence and will therefore be termed *minor buildings*. This is only a convenient term of reference, however, and should not rule out the possibility of their independent existence from Structures I and IV. As to phasing, it is only the latter two buildings that have any inferred stratigraphic relationship. These do not seem to have been directly contemporary, their succession being established through their relationship to backfilled ditch F. 37. The southern (Structure I) evidently pre-dated the northern (Structure IV), and the earlier building appears to have become the site of a midden whilst its later counterpart still stood.

Any discussion of the structural evidence has to confront the fact that almost no post-holes survived. A degree of ground-surface truncation — eradicating banks, floor surfaces and wall-lines — had certainly occurred. Yet it is difficult to see this as accounting for more than 0.10–0.15m, not the *c.* 0.30m depth or more of major post-holes. This could suggest that the buildings' load-bearing supports were largely carried on the ground surface, with posts possibly set on pads. This issue is, of course, essentially irresolvable. The gullies unquestionably represent buildings and it must simply be accepted that, for whatever reason, the structures' uprights left no trace.

From their scale, and the great quantities of finds within their surround ditches, there can be little doubt that the two western structures (I and IV) represented substantial buildings. In contrast to the smaller ditch-defined structures (III and V), these both have eastern entrance interruptions in their circuit — the most common orientation of Iron Age houses in the region. Another attribute the two western structures share in contrast to the others is irregularity of plan. The ditch-surround of Structure IV is of polygonal form, and only circular on its southern side, while Structure I was distinctly ovoid. Considerable ambiguity surrounds the status of the 'C'-shaped Structures II and III. If fully projected, the diameter of the south-westernmost (II) would continue into the circuit of the inner Ringwork ditch and the 'C', at least in this instance, would therefore seem complete in itself. The full plan of the larger 'half-circle' (Structure III) may well have 'risen' over an upstanding bank, however, and have subsequently been lost to plough damage. (Note that in the following descriptions diameter measurements are taken from the mid-points of gullies.)

Major buildings

Structure I
(F. 6, 61, 63, 67, 68, 85-92, 141 and 142: Plate IX; Fig. 29)
Although regular in its form, the eaves-gully defining this structure was of ovoid plan and elongated on its north-south axis (F. 6: 11 x 12.00m). Generally 1.00–1.25m wide and 0.35–0.55m deep, its profile varied from a rounded 'V' with splaying sides (locally with a flat base 0.10–0.15m across) to a broad concave form. Along its western perimeter, where it bordered ditch F. 37, its exterior edge splayed more broadly and the swathe between the two was reduced by 0.15–0.25m from (machined) ground level. Ditch F. 6 was continuous, apart from a 1.80m wide entranceway interruption on the east side defined by sub-circular terminals. However, a much more minor gully whose line extended the arc of the main gully (F. 67), 0.30–0.60m wide with a concave profile 0.15–0.20m deep, crossed this entranceway gap. The sub-circular butt of F. 67 continued just beyond the northern terminal of F. 6 (overlapping by 0.30m), but lay 0.40m west of it. Whilst in plan F. 67 would appear to block the F. 6 entrance, this would only be the case if they were contemporary. Instead, F. 67 seemed to pre-date the main F. 6 circle and a line of stake-holes extending west for 2.40m from its terminal would not seem to relate to the main building (F. 85–92, 141 and 142). The existence of this earlier gully might explain the ovoid shape of the larger F. 6 'circle' (*i.e.* as an expansion upon an original 'C'-shaped structure: Structures III and V below). Alternatively, and more likely, it was simply elongated on its north-south axis intentionally to avoid connection/overlap with the evidently contemporary western ditch F. 37.

There was, nevertheless, some re-cutting of the main eaves-gully. F. 63 and F. 68 were lengths of minor gullies, 0.35–0.60m wide and 0.10–0.25m deep, which seemed to truncate the interior edge of F. 6. Whereas these essentially respected the building's 'circle', F. 61 (*c.* 0.50–1.00m wide and 0.35–0.45m deep) re-cut and ran obliquely across the line of F. 6 (straight, 3.70m long); large quantities of bone waste were found within its eastern butt end. From post-excavation analysis, it is clear that this feature conjoined with a re-cut of the backfilled F. 37 ditch line (F. 148). This feature, 1.00–1.30m wide and 0.65–0.80m deep with a broad flat-based 'V' to 'U'-shaped profile, was consistently distinguished in section over a distance of 3.00m. By plan-configuration, it must have terminated only *c.* 0.50m to the south. While its northern extent is unknown, it was not visible in section beyond this point and is reconstructed as forming an 'L'-shape with F. 61. This probably relates to the 'demise' of Structure I and the establishment of a new western entrance across the Ringwork circuit (backfilling of the southern length of F. 38). While the F. 63 and F. 68 lengths may have connected with F. 61, one possibility is that they later acted to drain the area of the structure's interior after the building's demolition, when presumably its surfaces served as a yard.

Structure IV
(F. 13/25/26/111: Plate X; Fig. 29)
Measuring 11.00–12.00m in 'diameter', with a 4.10m-wide entrance interruption on its eastern side, this was set in the extreme north-western corner of the Ringwork. Of quasi-polygonal plan, it truncated both the inner Ringwork circuit (F. 2) and the backfilled ditch F. 37; its diameter locally incorporated the outwork Ditch F. 38/13. No contemporary interior features were recovered.

The north-eastern circuit (F. 25) terminated in a sub-square butt. It was 0.60–0.80m wide and *c.* 0.40m deep, with a 'U'-shaped profile. An

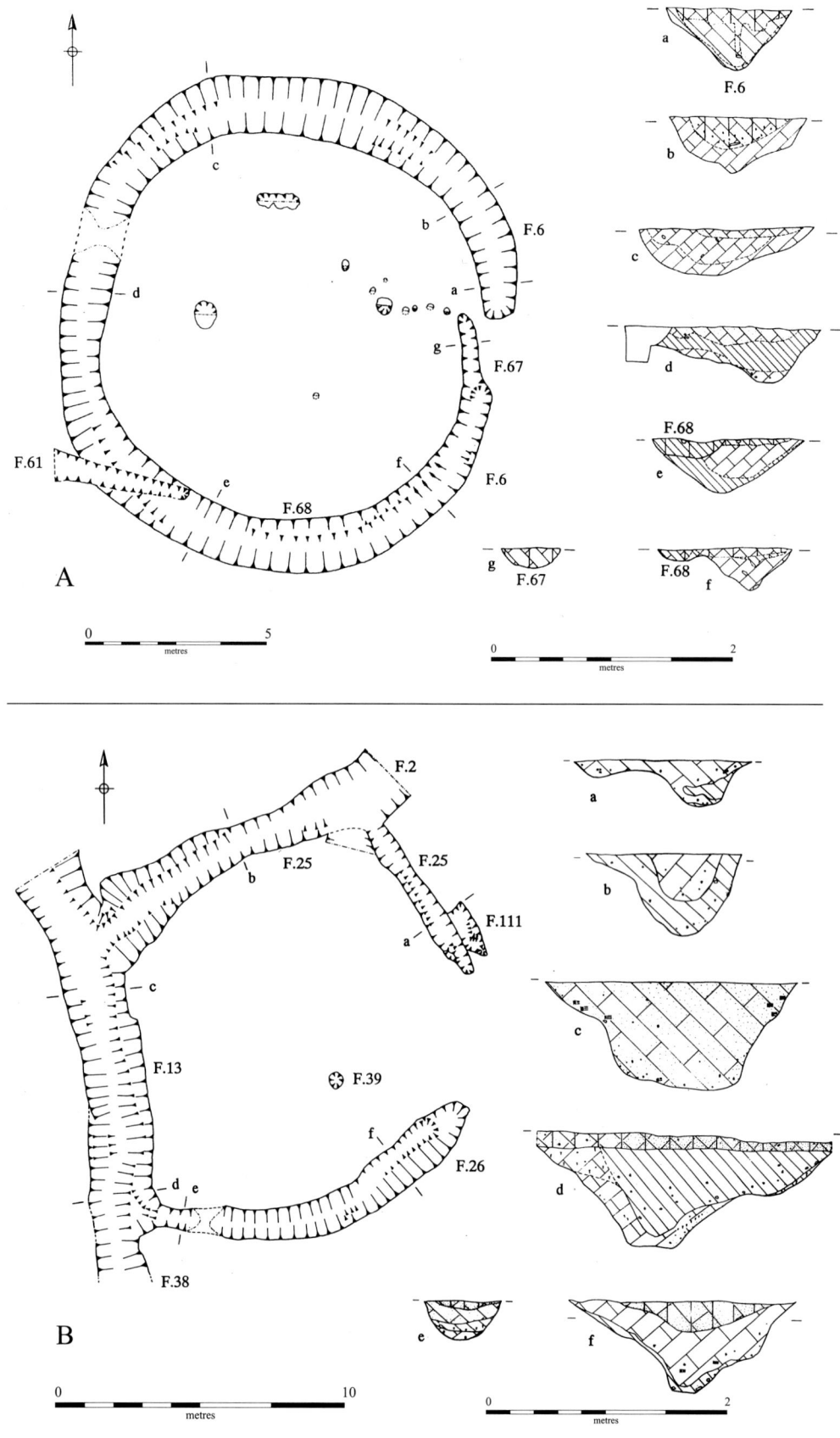

Figure 29 Main buildings: **A** Structure I; **B** Structure IV

Plate IX Structure I, looking west across the eaves-gully's entrance (photo by C. Price)

Plate X Looking west through the entrance terminals of Structure IV (photo by C. Price)

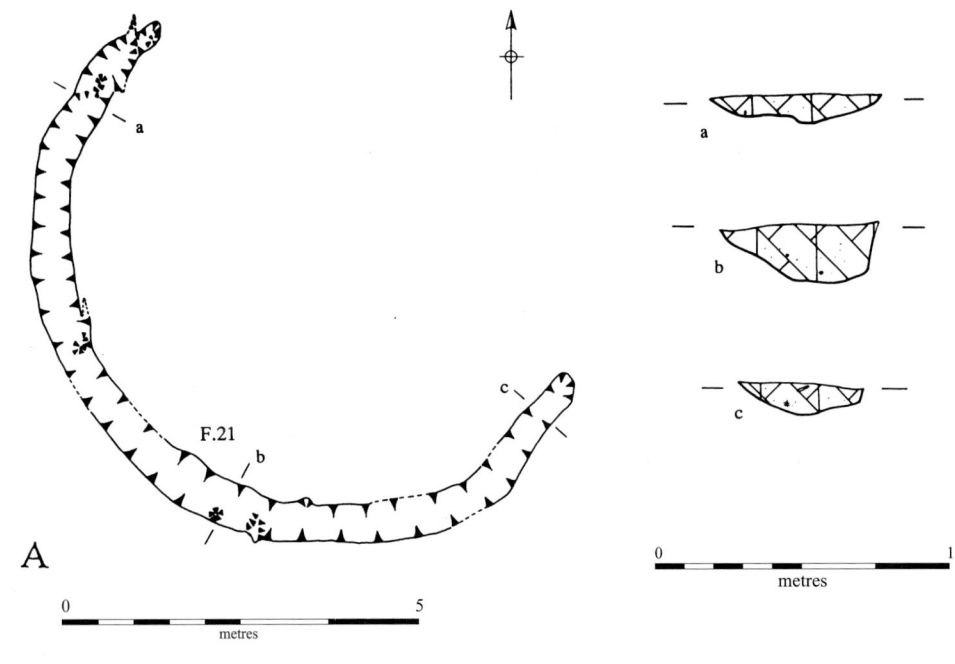
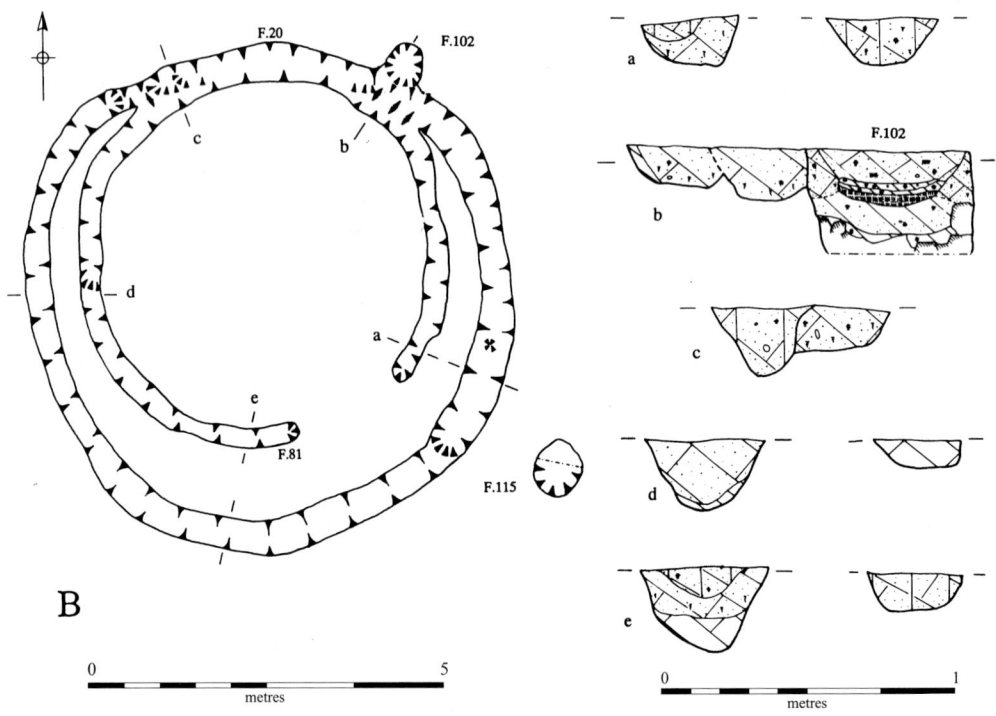

Figure 30 Minor buildings: **A** Structure III; **B** Structure V

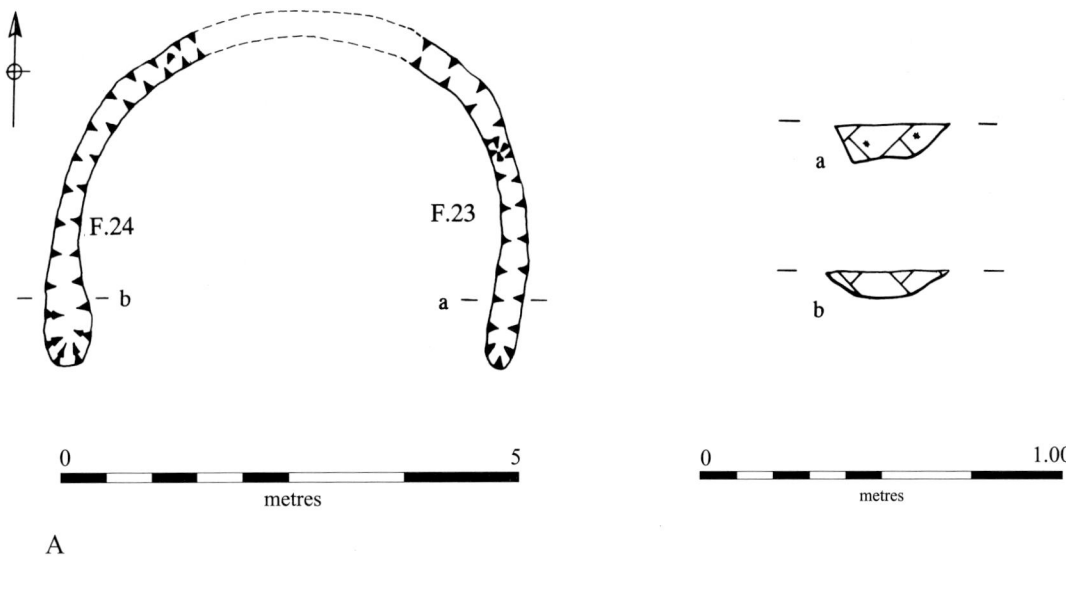

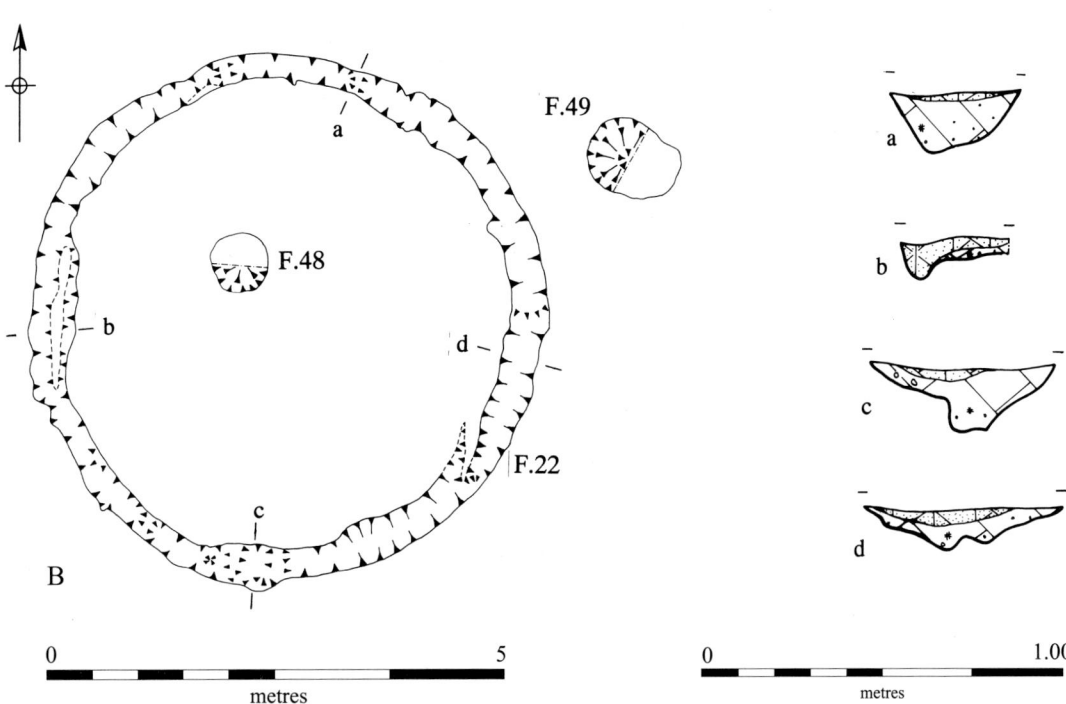

Figure 31 Ancillary buildings: **A** Structure II; **B** Structure VI

irregular trough, conjoining the eastern exterior side of the terminal, may have been a related feature (F. 111; 0.70 x 1.80m and 0.15m deep).

The northern edge of the north-western circuit (F. 2/25) continued uninterrupted from the junction of ditches F. 2/37 (apart from a slight southward deflection). This would seem, in essence, to be the western continuation of the inner Ringwork circuit — a length of ditch incorporated into the circuit of this structure, but not specifically dug for it. In the main 1.10–1.20m wide and *c.* 0.70m deep, with a 'U'-shaped profile, certainly this was much more substantial than the discrete eastern arm represented by F. 25.

With regard to the west side (F. 13/38), over a distance of *c.* 8.00m a length of the inner Outworks ditch corresponded with the line of this structure (2.10–2.30m wide and 0.90–1.10m deep). The ditching of the south side (F. 26) is the one length of the structure's perimeter that actually curves. Reflecting entrance-associated re-cutting, it was deepest and widest at the north-eastern end (1.60m across and 0.55m deep) and reduced to *c.* 0.65m width and 0.30–0.35m depth adjacent to the western end where it continued into the F. 13/38 Outworks ditch.

The irregular plan of this structure reflects its secondary status to, and its accommodation within, the Ringwork's 'corner'. Large quantities of finds and an array of 'special' objects were recovered from its ditches, including both La Tène-style decorated and Roman/Romano-British pottery, and fragments of human skull.

Minor buildings

Structure III
(F. 21: Fig. 30)
With a projected diameter of 7.50m, this 'C'-shaped gully was open to the north-east. Its shallow concave profile was 0.40–0.60m wide and 0.07–0.15m deep.

Structure V
(F. 20/81/102: Fig. 30)
This was a double ring-gully whose northern edges intercut. The inner ring (F. 81), with a 1.50m wide interruption on its south-eastern side, had a diameter of 5.00m and was 0.20–0.35m wide and 0.10–0.30m deep. The outer ring was actually slightly ovoid and elongated on its north-south axis (6.30 x 6.50m: F. 20), and was 0.30–0.55m wide and 0.23–0.35m deep. Both of these appear to have been open gullies rather than wall-trenches. While in the field it was thought that the outer gully re-cut the inner, with hindsight this relationship should probably be reversed. The building's sequence seems complicated: a phase-extended development could be proposed for the larger outer circuit (F. 20) since butt ends were apparent within its south-eastern and north-western arcs. Without corresponding terminals indicative of entrances, this could suggest that it was originally of 'C'-shaped plan open to the south-west (*i.e.* similar to/mirroring Structure III). This arc would then have only later been extended (and the circle closed) around that side where its layout was much more irregularly angular.

A substantial ovoid pit (0.60 x 1.20m in plan) 'conjoined' the north-eastern arc of F. 20, probably cutting it. This cut, F. 102, had vertical sides and a flat base 0.70m deep. Possibly a large post-hole, its base was packed with burnt cobbles and loomweight fragments.

Ancillary structures

Structure II
(F. 23/24: Fig. 31)
This 'C'-shaped gully, with a projected diameter of *c.* 4.80m, was open to the south. Its two gully segments (its arc petered out along northern side) were 0.24–0.35m wide and 0.02–0.10m deep; widening to *c.* 0.50m, these terminated in definite butt ends to the south.

Structure VI
(F. 22/48: Fig. 31)
This uninterrupted 'ring-ditch', 5.25m in diameter, had largely vertical sides (with spade-marks locally visible) and a flat undulating base (0.25–0.45m wide; *c.* 0.13m deep: F. 22). Situated off-centre within its interior was a steep-sided cut feature (0.60m diameter; 0.25m deep), possibly a post-hole (F. 48).

Pits and 'troughs'
(Table 1; Figs 32 and 33)
Almost all the pits proved to be small. The vast majority were of sub-circular/ovoid form, 0.50–0.70m across and only 0.10–0.30m deep. A few larger examples were up to 0.90–1.20m across and of *c.* 0.40m depth (Figs 32 and 33). Noteworthy is the complete lack of any large 'pit-wells'. Demonstrated as a 'type-artefact' of later Bronze Age/earlier Iron Age settlement (Evans 1999; Edmonds *et al.* 1999), their absence suggests that water was obtained from the deeper pooling points along the Ringwork's main circuit, possibly supplemented by run-off from building roofs.

There was no obvious evidence of placed or 'special' deposition within the site's pits. Lacking, for example, rare animal/bird species or human remains, they do not seem to have been venues for intentional 'placement' of objects. Producing only 12 and 8 sherds of pottery and 10 and 3 pieces of bone respectively, the pair of 'pits' *c.* 0.20m deep to the rear of Structure III may, for example, represent no more than hollows produced by scraping fowl. Even the pits in the diagonal setting extending north-west from Structure V were undistinguished apart from by their relatively high finds densities (8/23 sherds, 18/46 bones and 2/8 pieces of clay each; F. 35, only surviving as a scoop *c.* 5cm deep, produced only two pieces of pottery and bone). This, however, is generally true of the pits within the Ringwork as a whole. Those exterior to or between the F. 1/F. 2 circuit had very low artefact densities (5 or less pieces of pot or bone), with bone quantities being particularly low. The only exceptions to this were F. 83, cut by the western outwork ditch (nine sherds), and F. 104: 0.65–0.70m in diameter and only 0.10m deep, the latter feature yielded 129 sherds of pottery and has, in fact, the highest density of this material of any feature on site. Producing only 55 bones, it had a high pot-to-bone ratio (1/2.34) and the assemblage may reflect some degree of 'selection'. This becomes more marked given that it produced only one sherd of pottery, whereas the adjacent corner segment of the 'early' F. 64 ditch had a relatively high concentration of bone (36 pieces). Similarly, pit F. 104 may also relate to a nearby spread of burnt material (*376*), which produced both burnt clay and stone but no pottery or bone. While F. 104 may reflect Ringwork-entrance related activity, the quantities of material within it could equally point to settlement beyond to the enclosure system.

	Size(m)	*Depth (cm)*	*Number Pottery*	*Number Bone*	*Number Bt. Clay*
F. 32	1.40x3.50	40	81	158	18
F. 33/108	1.35x2.80	75	35	104	11
F. 65	1.50x5.50	35	21	6	13
F. 76	0.60x4.20	60	99	163	15
F. 80	1.00x2.20	70	44	69	14
F. 107	1.20x2.80	45	42	59	10

Table 1 'Trough-like' features: dimensions and finds density

Reflecting their ambiguous status, the one group of features that are themselves outstanding within the Figure 32 pit plot are the large 'troughs' (Table 1), which also produced considerable quantities of finds. It is questionable whether F. 65, located east of Structure III at the end of the F. 118 fence-line, should be included with these as it is relatively ditch-like and had been irregularly re-cut. The other features in this category (which all fall within the area of Structures I/IV), while superficially similar, display variability. Whereas F. 76, 32 and 33 are irregular, shallow and rather grave-like (F. 107 produced a human tooth), F. 80, 107 and 108 — the latter re-cut by F. 33 — are much more regular and, having affinities with the Watergate blocking pits (F. 29 and 30), could even have been structural. The dimensions of the latter, at least, might lead to suggestions of tanning. There is no obvious evidence of this, however, and it seems too easy an explanation for their form, clustering and 'unusual' character.

Pre-/early Ringwork enclosure
Having outlined the main components of the Ringwork and its interior, it is now appropriate to consider the site's more fragmentary elements. A number of features survive only as truncated 'shelves' along the upper sides of the later ditches, making them difficult to define and trace. Generally much more minor than those of the ensuing layout, most were backfilled and all lacked the peat fills of the later ditches. While many are clearly ancestral to, and in part determine, the Ringwork's final layout, for others their 'pre-' or 'early' Ringwork attribution is less certain.

The north-western dyke system
(F. 15, 73, 82, 93, 96 and 146: Figs 17, 34–36)
A pair of intercutting ditches ran NNE–SSW across the site's north-western margin. The easternmost, F. 15, extended 14.00m south from the limits of excavation, where it would have shortly terminated had its end not been truncated by F. 1 (it could not have continued for more than 16.50m). With a concave profile, 0.95m wide and 0.45m deep (as recorded in the edge-of-excavation section), it did not extend as far north as Trench VIII. However a very similar ditch in Trench VI, F. 140 (0.90m wide and 0.20m deep, with a flat base 0.50m across), appeared to represent a continuation of its line after interruption. A comparable feature, F. 93 (c. 1.20 wide and 0.30m deep), ran parallel, and just truncated the western side of ditch F. 15. Again, while it had been severely truncated by later features both its sub-circular terminals survived, and it was c. 10m long.

A series of more substantial intercutting ditches ran parallel with these 2.40m further to the west. The latest re-cut line was F. 82, which terminated in a sub-square butt at exactly the same point in the south as ditch F. 93. With a 'U'-shaped profile, F. 82 was 0.65–0.90m deep; it survived to 1.05m width (full estimated width 1.40m). Along its western side it cut ditch F. 73. Generally 2.20–2.50m wide and c. 1.00m deep, this had an angular splaying 'V'-shaped profile. (In the south it terminated in a sub-circular butt 0.65m deep and 1.40m across.) Following the alignment of this re-cut feature configuration (before the southernmost 3.80m of F. 82, which turned westwards), ditch F. 73 could be traced discretely over c. 4.50m. It was found to truncate a much larger feature, F. 146, whose southern end terminated in a sub-square butt. In section, just beyond that point, it was seen to have a 2.95m-wide, broadly 'U'-shaped profile with a flattish base 0.90–1.20m deep. In the segment immediately to the north, although having similar edges, the profile of this feature group was markedly different: c. 3.00m wide, it was there 1.50m deep with a splaying 'V'-shaped profile. No distinct re-cutting was apparent (e.g. no trace of F. 82), leading to the question of what had caused its greater depth at that point. Did it all represent ditch F. 73, or had that feature re-cut over the top of F. 146 which was there locally deeper? In longitudinal section north beyond this segment, the F. 73/146 ditch line was only 0.55–0.95m deep. Admittedly, this exposure fell short of the centre of the ditch (which was deeper westwards); given the configuration of its edges it must have terminated there and collectively have been 10.00–10.50m long. Although much more robust, its 'ends' (and alignment) exactly matched that of F. 93 to the east. However, the area where F. 73/146 ended in the north — and the junction of the later Ringwork ditches F. 10 and F. 14 — proved extraordinarily complicated. Although stepped in and staggered by some 0.50m on its western side, the northward ditch (F. 14) followed the line of F. 73/146, and their eastern edges directly coincided. Due to its peat infill (which was missing from the backfilled deposits of F. 73/146), there can be no doubt that F. 14 was a later Ringwork-contemporary boundary. Nevertheless, an earlier version — one broadly contemporary with F. 73/146 — must have continued northward on this alignment, one later re-cut by F. 14.

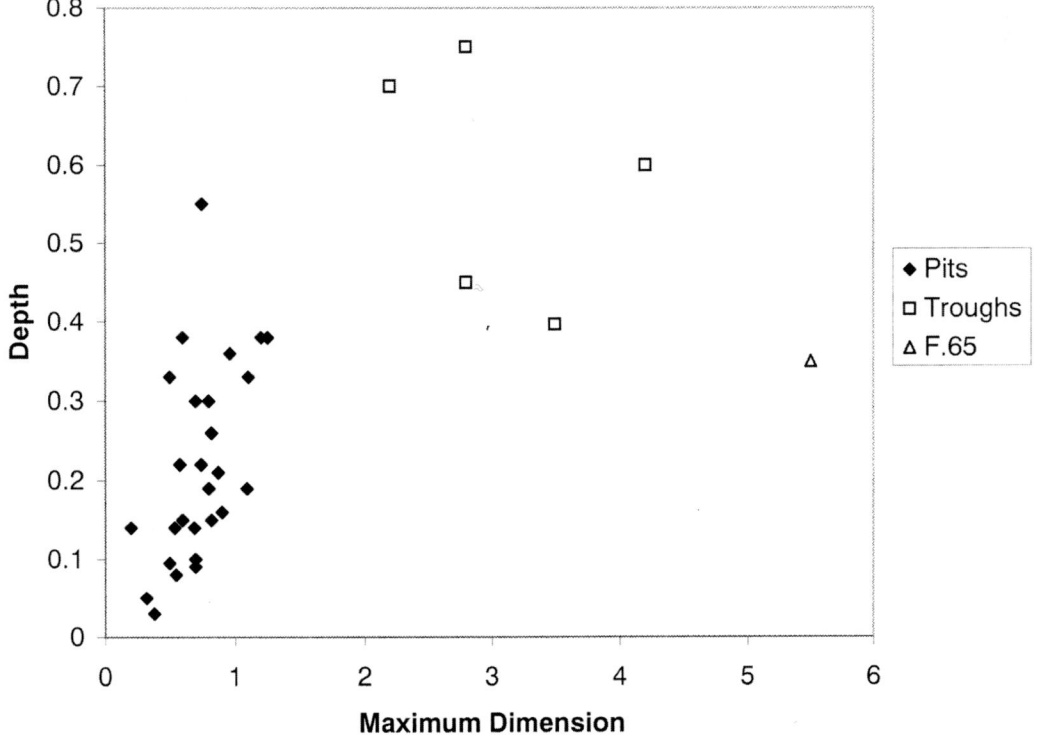

Figure 32 Plotting of pit/trough dimensions

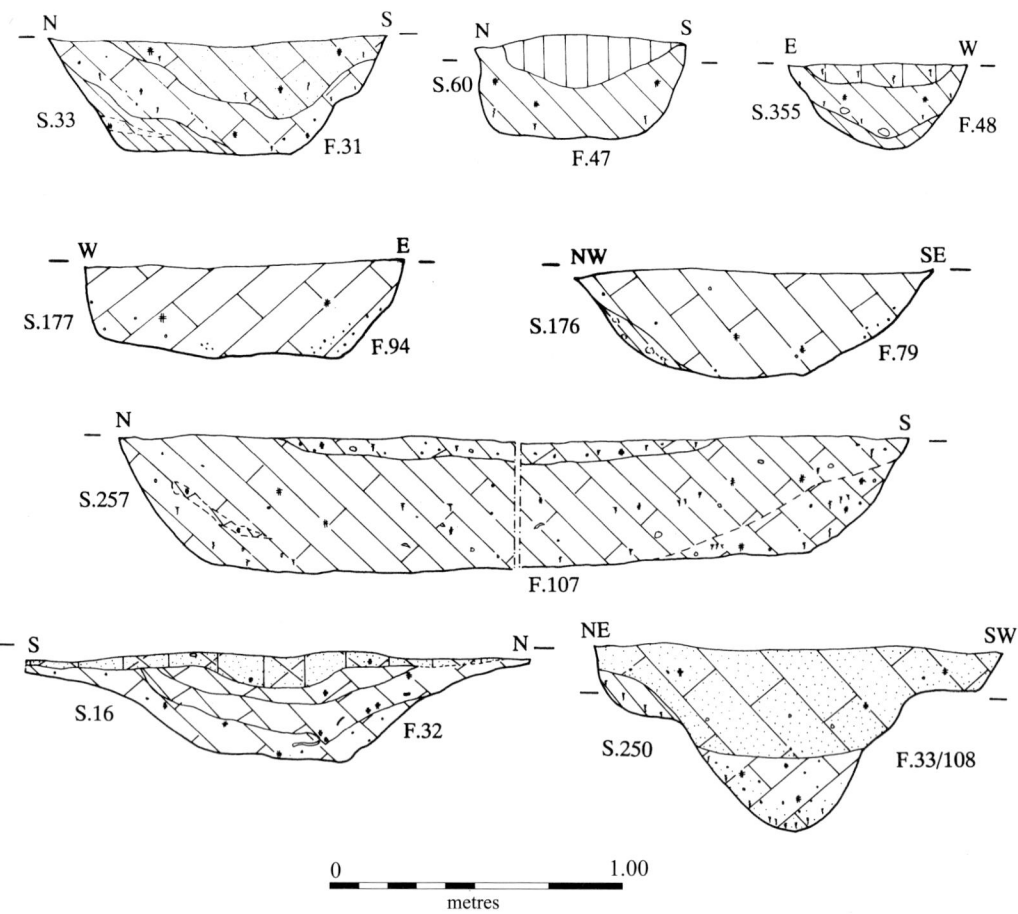

Figure 33 Pit/trough sections (F. 31–3, 47, 48, 79, 94, 107 and 108)

Although severely truncated along its eastern side (by Ringwork ditch F. 10), the full 7.75m length of an obviously 'early' NNE–SSW oriented ditch was identified along the western edge of excavation (F. 96). With sub-circular butt ends, this was c. 1.00–1.10m wide and 0.45m deep with a 'U'-shaped profile.

The rectilinear system
(F. 27, 37, 52, 57 and 127: Figs 17, 37–39)
A north-to-south oriented ditch, F. 37, ran straight between the two western ends of the main inner Ringwork circuit (F. 2). In the north its relationship to the Ringwork ditch had been lost through later re-cutting. In the south, however, it was clear that F. 37 had itself been cut by western extension of F. 2 and this is consistent with the fact that it had clearly been backfilled along its length. F. 37 was typically 2.10m wide and 1.10m deep, with an angular 'V'-shaped profile. While generally its profile was quite regular its upper eastern edge splayed broadly adjacent to Structure I, giving an overall width there of c. 2.70–3.00m. Over its southernmost 3.00–4.00m its alignment turned sharply westwards to run parallel with F. 46; adjacent to its southern terminal, F. 37 deepened to 1.25m.

In the south-eastern sector of the Ringwork's interior, lying just beyond F. 2 and truncated by it, was a series of rectilinear ditches. F. 27 was 'U'-profiled (c. 1.60m wide and 0.75m deep) and discretely visible over a distance of c. 11.50m, terminated in a circular butt end. It was continuously excavated in a series of metre segments over a distance of 8.00m west of this point. Beyond that, it was clearly seen to be truncated by the inner Ringwork circuit; in another segment still further west, its probable west end survived in the base of the later ditch. It would therefore seem that this east-to-west ditch was at least 14.00m long. With a gap of 1.20m, a ditch returned northward from the eastern butt end of F. 27. This feature, F. 52, was visible over a length of 8.00m, and was also truncated by the inner Ringwork circuit in the north. Again, however, its terminal appeared to be held 'within' the base of that feature, suggesting a total length of c. 10.00m. With a 'U'-shaped profile 1.20–1.50m across, this ditch was 0.50–0.60m deep.

West of the exposed butt of ditch F. 27, a straight ditch 3.80m long ran northwards to end in a sub-circular butt (F. 57). Its southern terminal was sub-square and fell only 0.10m short of the southern east-west ditch. F. 57 was different from the latter two ditches described inasmuch as it had a 'V'-shaped profile that sloped down to a flat base 0.15m wide. Otherwise, it was 1.00–1.05m across and c. 0.55m deep. Its regularity and its profile both suggested that it might have been 'structural' (i.e. building-related). Despite these differences in character, given their spatial inter-relationship F. 57 was probably contemporary with F. 27 in the south. Similarly, apart from having a comparable profile/size, the manner in which the southern end of F. 52 kinked towards F. 27 to form a 'gapped' corner indicates direct contemporaneity. Even more suggestive of their inter-relationship is the fact that all the ditches shared the same basic fill sequence: charcoal-flecked dark grey-brown clay primary deposits being sealed by backfill (grey-brown clays with substantial lenses of marl), the latter evidently upcast from the construction of the Ringwork.

The south-western end of a concave-profiled, 'cigar-shaped' length of ditch 3.65m long (0.60–0.73m wide and c. 0.25m deep) ran north-west from this corner (F. 127). Whilst considerably smaller than F. 27 and F. 52, it was very regular and 'real'; a small number of finds were recovered from its homogenous fills (mid-dark brown-grey silty clay: marl inclusions probably attest to backfilling). Perhaps rather than being directly associated with these ditches, this may have been some kind of entrance-blocking trench. (The clay sub-soil was quite mixed in the immediate area. Other would-be features investigated there ultimately proved to be of geological origin, and a swathe was further reduced to determine the status of these 'potentials'.)

Previously described in the context of the early configuration of the Ringwork's Landward Entrance above, F. 46 — there parallel with the terminal of ditch F. 37 — must also relate to this rectilinear system and broadly correlate with F. 27 to the east.

Outer circuit precursors
(F. 64, 84, 95, 100, 106, 145, and 147: Figs 17, 19, 23, 25 and 40)
The area immediately exterior to the south-western Ringwork entrance had evidently been reduced by c. 0.15–0.20m and sealed by the same peat as in the upper ditch profiles. This area was machined-stripped twice

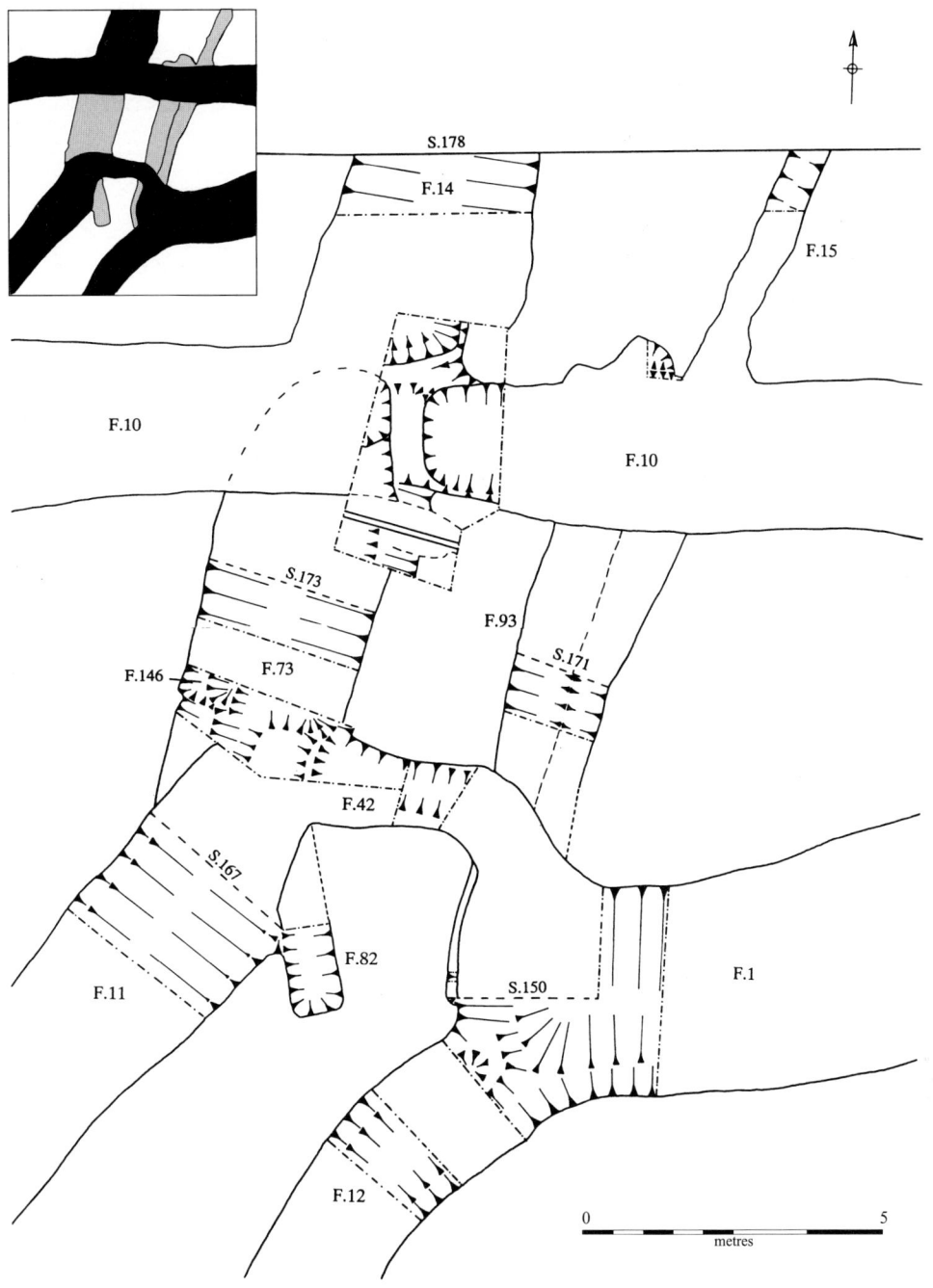

Figure 34 The north-west double-ditch system and the Outworks' junction with the Main Circuit terminal

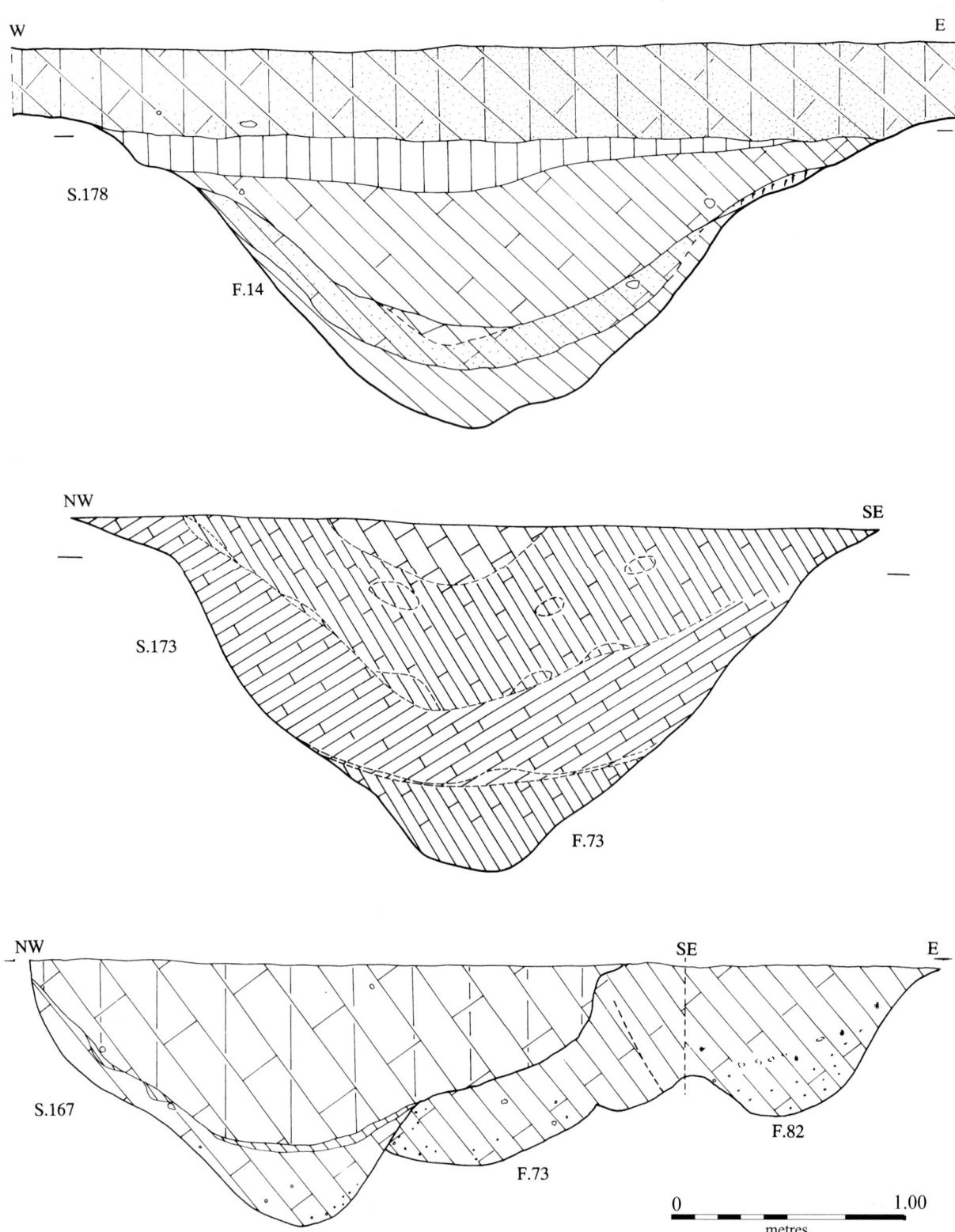

Figure 35 Sections: ditches in north-western quarter (area of Fig. 34; F. 11, 14, 73 and 82)

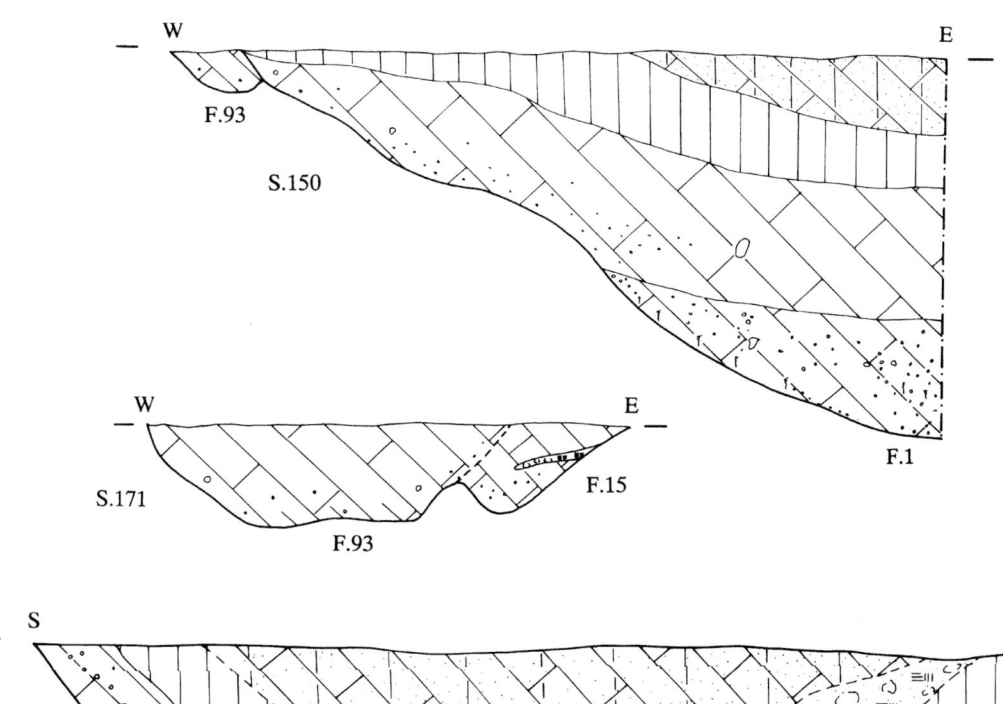
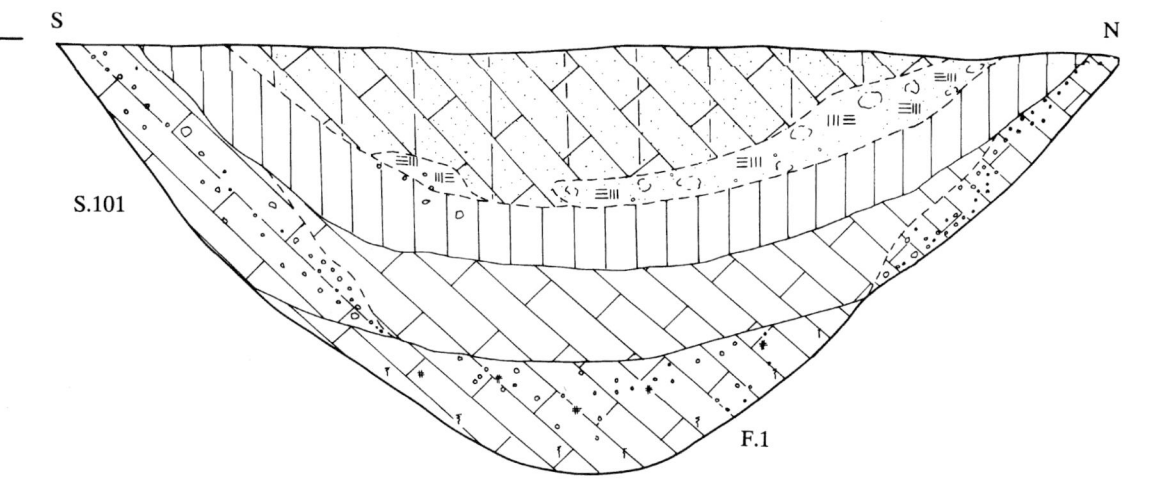
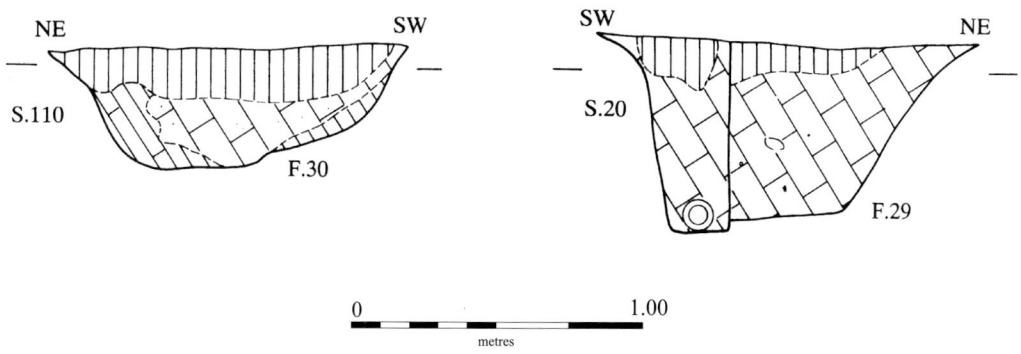

Figure 36 Sections: North Circuit features (F. 1, 15, 29, 30 and 93)

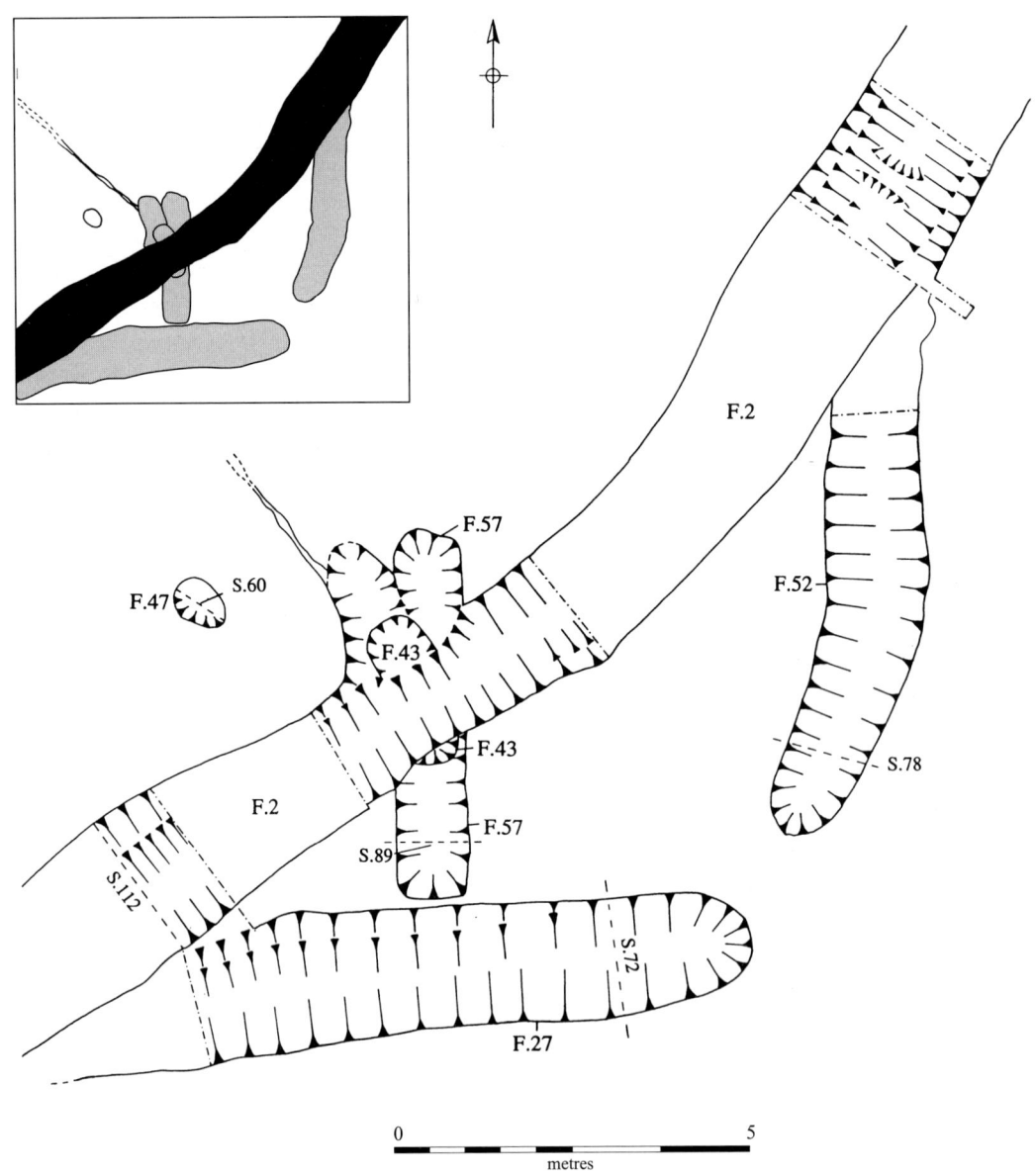

Figure 37 The South-East Rectilinear System

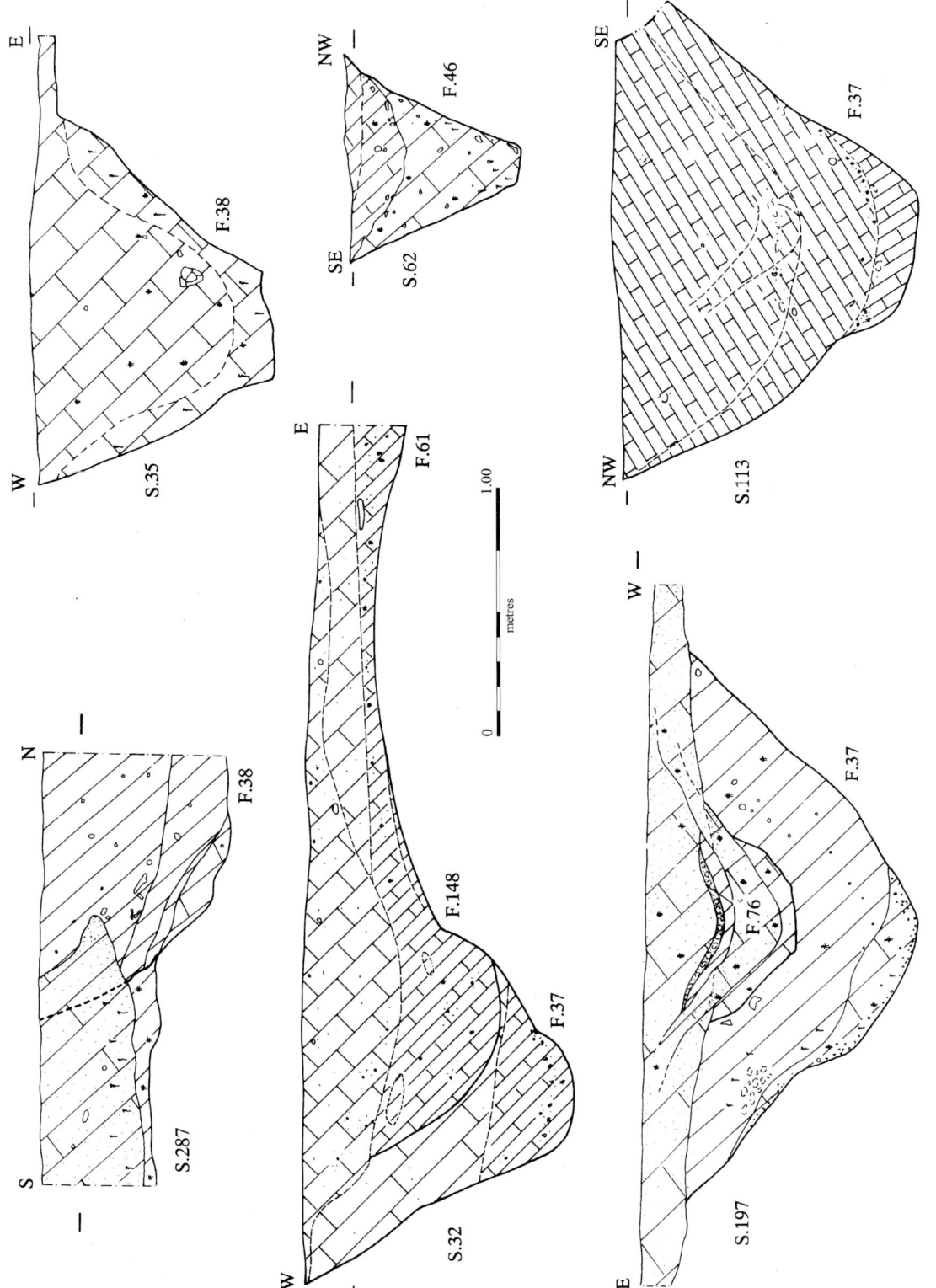

Figure 38 Sections: Inner Western Circuits (F. 37, 38, 46, 76 and 148)

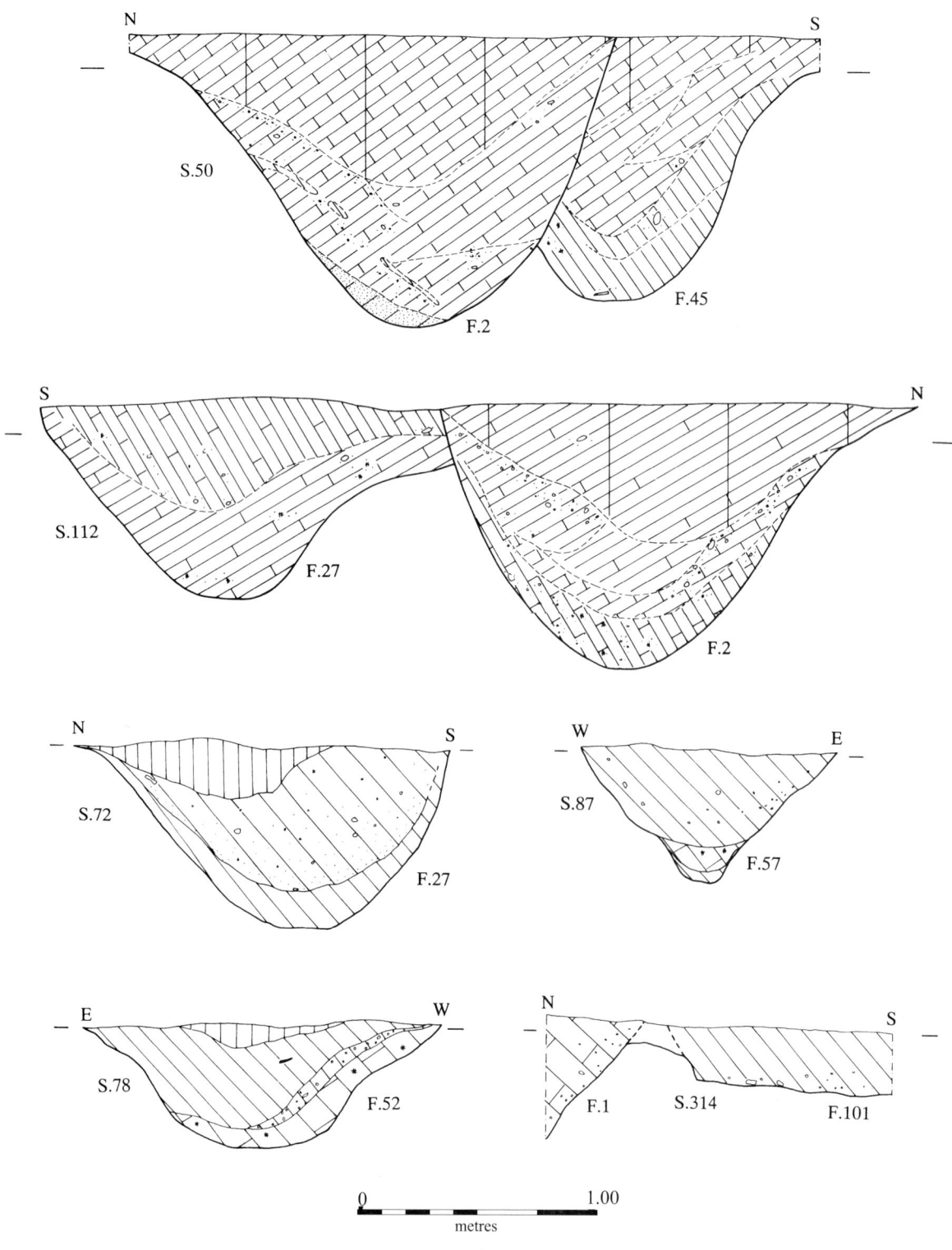

Figure 39 Sections: Southern Interior Circuit (F. 2, 27, 45, 52, 57 and 101)

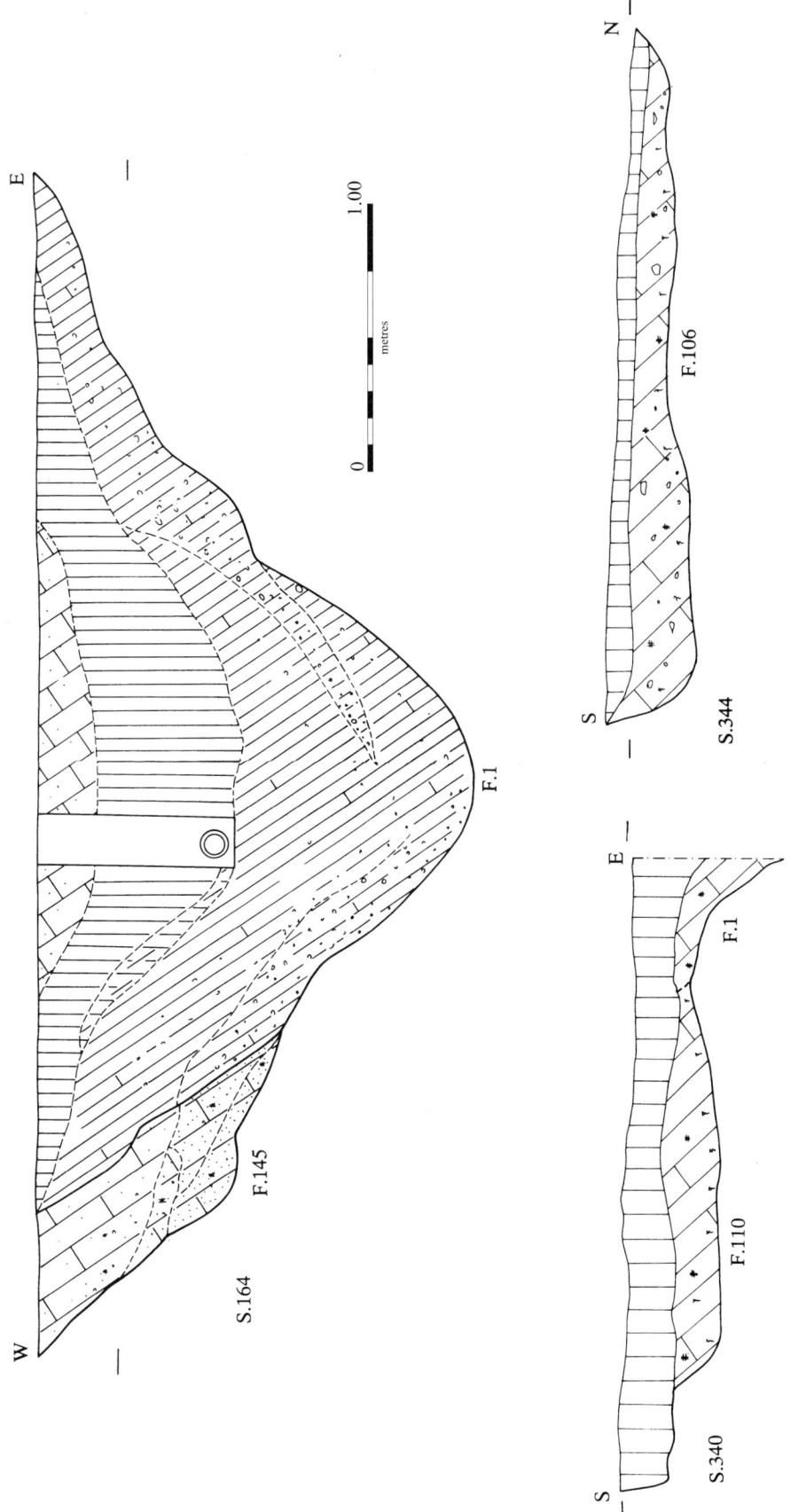

Figure 40 Sections: Southern Exterior Circuit (F. 1, 106, 110 and 145)

because of problems of feature-definition and machine access, and the additional reduction penetrated the clay sub-soil by as much as 0.20–0.25m. Consequently, the tops of features were also truncated, apart from within the area of a single baulk left across the middle of this zone. This issue pertains particularly to F. 64, a rather unusual 'U'-plan ditch configuration which was 1.80m across and 0.85m deep with a 'U'-shaped profile (as untruncated in the baulk: otherwise 1.10–1.25m wide and 0.60-0.70m deep). This had been backfilled with re-deposited clay natural; the overlying peats did not subside into its profile. A definite sub-circular northern terminal was identified along the southern edge of the main Ringwork ditch. From there F. 64 extended southwards and returned 'tightly' to the west, where it ran straight for a distance before curving north-westwards; there it was cut again by the line of the Ringwork.

A distinct 'shelf' (F. 84) was present within the northern edge of the main Ringwork circuit immediately opposite the north-eastern terminal of F. 64. This only survived over an area of 0.80 x 1.40m, where it was $c.$ 0.95m deep. Its western edge was straight (north-to-south), suggesting a terminal end. Although possibly once holding a timber element (and thus Ringwork gate-related), the fact that its northern edge continued eastwards before it was truncated by F. 1 indicates that it was probably a linear feature — in other words, a ditch. In section, $c.$ 1.50m east of this point another 'version' of this ditch (re-cutting) was observed in the northern edge of the Ringwork circuit. This feature (F. 145) was 0.90m deep and survived to a width of 1.05m (its base and south side truncated), ending in a western sub-circular terminal 0.50m beyond the section. Symmetrically situated in relation to the F. 64 ditch configuration, the western terminal of at least one 'early' east-to-west ditch was certainly present at this point.

Running slightly oblique to the line of the main Ringwork circuit, an earlier east-to-west ditch was traced for 21m along its southern edge (F. 100). This probably represents the eastern continuation of F. 145 (?and F. 84). Where untruncated, at its eastern end, it was $c.$ 2.60m wide; it was generally 0.20–0.37m deep with a flattish undulating base. There was definite evidence of re-cutting inasmuch as a deeper sub-circular western terminal was identified, beyond which another (?secondary) sub-square butt end lay $c.$ 3.50m further east (F. 106). These were filled, in the main, with light to dark grey-brown clay loam, the upper quarter to a third of their profiles being filled/sealed by the same peats that bedded into F. 1.

An extremely truncated earlier ditch also seems to have survived along the north-western interior edge of the main Ringwork ditch, within the south-western arc of its circuit (F. 95). Its profile varied from an angular 'V' (flat base 0.15m across) to a concave 'U', 0.90–0.95m deep. This survived to a width of 1.20m and is estimated to have originally been $c.$ 1.80m across: at no point did its full profile survive. Whilst the northern length of this feature had been truncated, to the south-west its sub-circular terminus was excavated. This ditch had largely been backfilled with re-deposited clay natural, and there were only limited traces of primary silting. A distinct shelf, surviving along the western side of F. 1 adjacent to its main western terminal, probably represents the continuation of F. 95 (F. 147). Not excavated discretely, this was 0.50m deep (with slight machine truncation, and probably 0.70m deep prior to this) and 0.50–0.90m wide ($c.$ 1.50m estimated full width).

'Diagonal' features
(F. 43, 65, 101, 109, 118 and 130: Figs 17, 37, 39 and 47)

Feature F. 43, re-cutting the north-western side of F. 57, appeared to represent the northern sub-circular butt end of a concave-profiled ditch/trough 0.30m deep and 0.95m wide. Further to the south it broadened to $c.$ 1.40m width, and its base held a steep-sided linear trough $c.$ 0.35m deeper than to the north (0.90m wide). Whilst certainty is impossible, the latter would appear to have been 2.20m long. South of the line of F. 2 (which truncated F. 43) there was a distinct drop in the base of F. 57 down to the same depth. If this lower stepped trough was one single feature/re-cut, its north-to-south axis would have had to turn sharply north-westwards. F. 43 was filled with grey-green clay. Though it is difficult to be confident of the phasing relations of these re-cuts, its relationship with the inner Ringwork ditch was unambiguous. F. 2 definitely truncated the full depth of F. 43; moreover, it terminated at the same northern point as F. 57. All this suggests an 'early' date.

A 0.10–0.20m wide trough, essentially straight (F. 118), ran from the north-western end of F. 43. This proved to be steep-sided with a flat base and was 0.05–0.07m deep. Its alignment did not correspond with those of any of the modern/post-medieval features; cut by a land drain and linking two unequivocal Iron Age features, it was certainly 'real' and may well have held a fence-line. In the north-west this trough conjoined F. 65 (above, *Pits and troughs*). Altogether 5.50m long (north-south) and 0.90–1.50m wide, this feature configuration included a number of re-cuts, most seemingly linear. Its 'bulk' form was 1.20–1.50m across and $c.$ 0.15m deep, with a flat concave base and $c.$ 4.50m long. Within it a deeper trough (0.35m depth in total) 2.70m long and $c.$ 0.70m wide was identified. Another linear feature, 0.12–0.25m deep with a concave profile (0.80m wide; 5.50m long), could also be recognised within it. While it is difficult to know how to interpret these intercutting troughs they did seem vaguely similar to F. 43/57 in the south-east.

Exterior to the Ringwork, the south-eastern corner of the site was also found to have been reduced by 0.20–0.30m and this was sealed by peats that were 'dirty' with occupation refuse (layer *495*). This horizon was subsequently stripped away (causing truncation of the tops of features by $c.$ 0.20–0.25m). There, roughly continuing the alignment of F. 118, a minor ditch F. 101 ran north-west from the corner of the edge of excavation to the main Ringwork circuit. With a concave profile, 1.20m wide and 0.45m deep in the edge-of-excavation (0.55m wide and 0.20–0.25m deep in plan exposure), it is hard to be certain of its exact stratigraphic relations. On the one hand, at its northern end it broadened into a 'reduction hollow' that had definitely been truncated by ditch F. 1. On the other hand, within this zone it had a deeper sub-circular butt end that terminated 0.25m short of the Ringwork ditch (*i.e.* possibly in relationship to it). A parallel ditch lay $c.$ 28m to the west (F. 109). Where test-excavated it had a 'U' shaped profile 0.45–0.50m wide and 0.20m deep (as strip-truncated), with an irregular flat base (*i.e.* matching F. 101). In the north, it terminated 0.30m short of the line of F. 100 (1.50m south of F. 1 — the main Ringwork circuit). While doubt must remain, this would suggest that these two obliquely-oriented ditches — which by their form/alignment must themselves have been directly contemporary — relate to an 'early' enclosure system and not to the Ringwork *per se*.

One other 'diagonally oriented' feature (F. 130: see Fig. 41, no. 7) was recorded. Falling within the interior of Structure I, this was a slight, 0.40–0.45m wide ditch oriented north-west to south-east and $c.$ 0.12m deep. Ending in a sub-circular terminal in the north, it was at least 4.20m long. It definitely pre-dated Structure I and, considering the pale character of its silty clay fills, may represent an 'early' ditch line, possibly of pre-Ringwork date.

Other 'features'
(F. 97–99: not illus.)

A slightly crescent-shaped east-to-west oriented trough was excavated west of the line of F. 1/95 in the south-west corner of the site (F. 99). This was 3:20m long and 0.64m wide; it had a flat-based 'U'-shaped profile and was 0.40m deep. Above a basal fill of dark brown/black charcoal-flecked clay loam, this feature appeared to have been backfilled with re-deposited (natural) clay; a few flecks of bone, burnt clay and flints were the only finds recovered.

A similar curvilinear feature lying roughly parallel to the north was also tested (F. 97). This was 5.25m long and 0.40m wide; it was 0.20–0.25m deep with a 'U'-shaped profile. A similar length of trough extended north-eastwards from its end (F. 98); 0.35m wide, this was truncated by the main Ringwork circuit and seemed much shallower (0.06m — though this was exaggerated by over-machining). These two features had 'clean' fills and a fragment of bone from F. 98 was the only find recovered. It is difficult to evaluate their status. Certainly pre-dating the main Ringwork, F. 97–99 were all probably of natural origin (either periglacial or tree-throw/-root derived).

III. Phasing dynamics and structuring principles

Because of the organic nature of the Ringwork's layout — its 'additive' character — it is difficult to know where to draw the line between major horizons of re-development, as opposed to accumulative small-scale changes. Nevertheless, its 'end' — the Outworks-elaborated Ringwork fort — was not necessarily pre-figured by its domestic-scale predecessor, and at some point in the course of the sequence a 'sea-change' occurred. In terms of its inter-relationship with the earlier enclosed settlement it is crucial that this (re-)defining 'moment' is distinguished, or at least explored.

With reference to the issues of presentation discussed in Chapter 1, phasing is both a 'first' and a 'last' thing — an *emergent* structure of *underlying* patterns. This raises the question of whether it should be stated at the outset of site reports and — however qualified — thereby become 'naturalised' from the start as the only ordering possible. Here a more discursive approach will be adopted, which

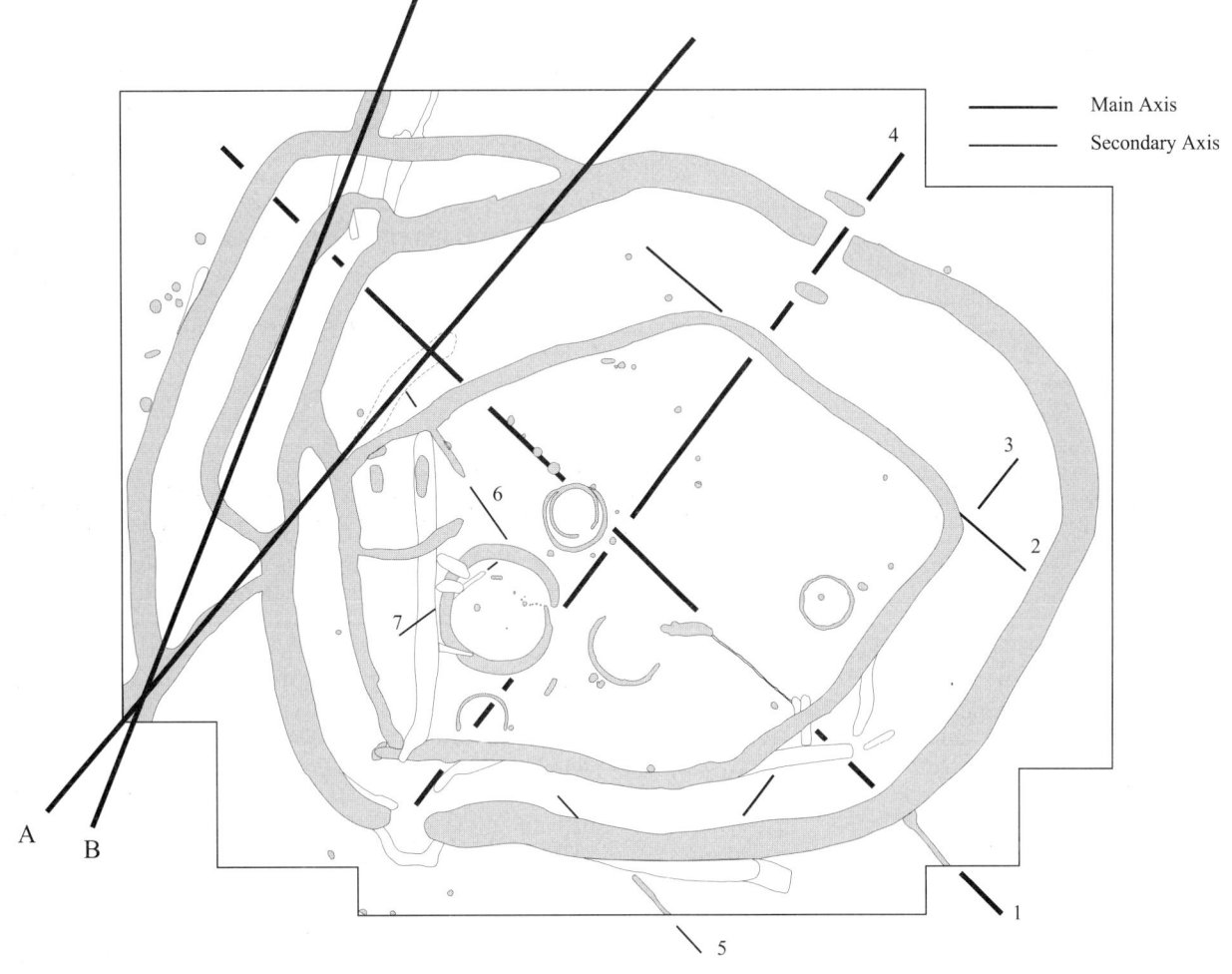

Figure 41 *Circles and Diagonals:* main spatial axes

allows phasing to 'unfold' through the presentation of different categories of data and levels of analysis. Only a basic framework will be offered at this stage, which focuses on the structural sequence of the Ringwork's development. Not surprisingly, uniform patterns of ditch and house re-cutting/-building are not apparent. There is, after all, no reason why the re-siting of a building need determine any re-working of its surrounding enclosure circuits. Only in Chapter 5, following the presentation of specialist and distributional studies, will the Ringwork's phasing be re-addressed, largely in terms of the possible interactions between its buildings. At this time, the outline presented below essentially charts the site's *constructional* sequence, and emphasises the initiation rather than the closure of significant features. Obviously, the latter has greater ramifications for the integrity of artefact assemblages, and their analysis must occur at a broader level (see Chapter 4 for a discussion of 'depositional horizons').

The character of the site's clay-based feature fills — with peat filling the upper profiles of the Ringwork's major features — did not prove particularly revealing of the subtleties of re-cutting. Moreover, given the cumulative character of the Ringwork's layout, most of its main features were obviously maintained and left open. Therefore, determination of the site's phasing must largely rely on broad principles of spatial organisation, rather than detailed stratigraphic succession. Consequently, it is first necessary to discuss the structural principles (and contradictions) of its 'design', its long-term spatial linkages and, furthermore, the scale and arrangement of its bank systems. Here, from the outset, attention should be drawn to a gradient of structural re-working that is apparent within the larger dynamics of the Ringwork's alterations. Running, as it were, from its south-western Landward Entrance across the interior to the Watergate, while the latter remained relatively pristine and unaltered (single phase), the enclosed structures went through a major re-building (two phases); the western access underwent two substantial re-modelling episodes (three phases). These different phasing rhythms attest to the crucial role of the Ringwork's landward approaches — its interconnection with the outside world — and the distinction between 'front' and 'back' space.

Straddling the 'lie of the land' and the locale's groundslope, the arrangement of the enclosure's circuits would have been apparent visually when approaching the site. While presumably the sheer scale of its defences would have blocked detailed appreciation from the western (landward) side, this would not have been the case from the eastern Cove-side marshes. As has been similarly argued with reference to the off-slope topographic situation of causewayed enclosures (Evans 1989b), the Ringwork's spatial structure could have been 'read'. This, however, seems unlikely to have been determined by perceptual concerns or a need for 'display'. Rather, with its location chosen according to strategic determinants, the system as a whole faced westward and the eastern marshes must essentially have been considered as a part of what was enclosed (*i.e.* 'in system').

Circles and diagonals: spatial determinants
(Fig. 41)
While at first glance the configuration of the site seems relatively straightforward — a bi-vallate circular enclosure with elaborate outworks on its north-western side — underlying this is a rectilinear series of backfilled ditches that were both clearly ancestral to its layout and integral to its early phases (F. 27, 37, 52 and 57). Their east–west axis is sympathetic to the eastward 'pull' of the Ringwork's main circuits. Moreover, there are a series of diagonal alignments, apparently both pre-dating and co-existing with the Ringwork, whose occurrence is far more difficult to account for. On one hand, there is the north-east to south-west axis as defined by the Ringwork's two main entrances: the south-western Landward and the Watergate in the north-east (Fig. 41.4). A series of opposing north-west to south-east diagonals also bisects the interior of the enclosure. These include the line of the north-eastern length of Structure IV's eaves-gully (F. 25) (to the east of which runs the parallel arrangement of four pits F. 31 and F. 34–6) and, in the south-east sector, the alignment of F. 118. The latter, if projected beyond the outer circuit, continues the axis of ditch F. 101 (Fig. 41.1; with which F. 109 to the west is parallel; Fig. 41.5).

These diagonals seem to conflict with, and even to cross-cut, the basic circular configuration of the Ringwork, and raise the issue of how two such apparently opposing structural principles could co-exist. The explanation for this lies in the 'design' compromises of the enclosure — the accommodation of a 'circle' with the north-east to south-west axis of the larger Wardy Hill system. The alignment of the early ditches in the extreme north-west of the site (F. 14, 15, 73 and 93, and possibly F. 96 in the west) clearly determined the alignment of the Ringwork's western outworks (Fig. 41.B). In the south-west the larger up-slope axis is conjoined by ditch F. 28, which was apparently maintained throughout the lifetime of the enclosure *per se*. (If projected north-eastwards it would correlate roughly with the 'ghosted' line of F. 69, whose end corresponds with the 'four pits' and the F. 118/101 alignment: Fig. 41.A.) Here it may even be relevant that the straight north-eastern side of the Ringwork's circuit did itself lie parallel with the F. 101/118 axis. Therefore, what we are seeing is a spatial compromise between a 'circle' and the diagonal layout of the larger Wardy Hill system. The diagonal 'dyke' system preceded the construction of the Ringwork itself and was maintained during its period of use; it is not a matter of one alignment superseding another but of the two co-existing in compromise. This was, of course, largely determined by the fact that the elongated east-to-west axis of the Ringwork circle (its axis being established by the Phase 2 rectangular alignment) did not complement the alignment of the larger landscape-scale system, but instead took advantage of the relative flatness of this immediate area of the skirtland peninsula projecting north-eastwards from the hill-top.

Linkages and embankment
(Figs 42 and 43)
At crucial points the Ringwork's 'design' was clearly determined by the position of earlier features, and the conjoining of its elements to them. This, in part, contributed to its 'pulled' layout. Aside from the maintenance of the landward approach in the south-west there are two such key linkages, both in the north-west quarter of the site. The first is that the north-western terminal of its outer circuit came off the southern end of the north-western double-ditch system; secondly, the original northern end of the inner F. 2 circuit met the northern terminal of ditch F. 37.

Whilst being wary of recourse to 'invisible' factors, the determination of the Ringwork's form also clearly related to various upstanding components. This itself involves two 'horizons': on the one hand remnant bank and/or hedge systems (probably of later Bronze Age origin); on the other the locations of Ringwork-related banks. The specific layout and impact of the first of these will be discussed within the phasing summary below. What is important at this stage is the recognition of the lingering influence — often disproportionate to their immediate scale — that relatively minor ditch and bank systems can have upon subsequent landscape development.

There is little question of where the Ringwork's banks would have been situated given the regular (for the most part) *c.* 4–5.00m wide interval between its concentric ditch circuits (Fig. 42). The only area of real debate is the wide berm between the inner F. 2 and outer circuits on its eastern and northern sides. It is here that the evidence of the F. 69 trough north of Structure IV is relevant. After weighing the evidence, essentially this must represent a path worn around the interior side of the bank behind ditch F. 13 (and possibly also a slight catchment channel for collecting bank run-off). If so, it would have left a berm 5.50–6.50m wide on its eastern side (*i.e.* facing F. 13) and *c.* 8.00m across in the north towards F. 1. It is the curvature of the north-eastern end of F. 69 that permits us to determine the location of the F. 1 bank along the sector in question. Not surprisingly (given the effort involved in shifting spoil any distance from a quarried source) it would have been alongside the main ditch and not midway between the two circuits. This would imply, moreover, that the interior blocking trench of the north-eastern Watergate would have lain abreast the bank system.

Locating the line of the bank on this side would indicate, therefore, that there had been a *c.* 5.00m wide swathe between its southern edge and the inner circuit along the northern side of the Ringwork (Figs 42 and 43). That this seems essentially to have been 'empty' raises the question of what purpose this annex-like space could have been put. Whilst the corralling of stock would seem an obvious suggestion, there was no enhancement of phosphate levels throughout this area of the kind that would have been expected had animals regularly been kept there. Given its apparent paucity of usage (and that there is no evidence of backfilling of any of the intervening portion of F. 2 to incorporate this swathe into the main interior), this must be considered a 'design' discrepancy. As such, its existence might infer that the construction of the inner circuit pre-dated that of the outer, whose wider interval on this side was determined by the apparent need to link it with the line of the ditch/bank in the north-west (F. 42/93 *et al.*).

Presuming that the upcast clay sub-soils would quickly settle and compact, no 'quarried' displacement factor has been added when calculating the height of the Ringwork's banks (*i.e.* 'one-to-one' re-deposition has been assumed). The width of the bank system assumes that a *c.* 0.50m-wide berm lay between their edges and the source ditches. By this means the Outworks' banks may be suggested to have been approximately 3.50m wide, that between F. 10 and F. 11 *c.* 1.10m high, and that behind F. 11 only *c.* 0.75m high. For most of its length the bank associated with the main F. 1 perimeter would have been *c.* 4.00m wide and 1.60m high. However throughout the north and eastern sectors (with its much wider berm with the inner circuit) the line of the F. 69 trough suggests that the bank may have been *c.* 6.00m across. If so, on this side it would have only been *c.* 1.05m high. Of course, there would probably have been considerable variability in the banks' levels. Generally, because the ditch perimeters are longer than their internally concentric banks, more spoil would then be generated than from direct ditch-to-bank displacement (and also through entranceway interruption). It is presumed that most of this 'excess' would have gone into the western perimeter behind the line of F. 12: although this ditch was relatively minor (*e.g.* comparable to F. 11) in all likelihood an 'F. 1-scale' bank stood behind it. (Note that for the purposes of the above calculations, the loss of *c.* 0.10m from the top of the Ringwork's ditches through plough damage has been assumed and factored in terms of the quantity of spoil generated, and below in reckoning ditch-to-bank-top heights.)

It is crucial that we bear in mind not just the height of the banks but also how high they stood in relation to the base of their flanking ditches. If, moreover, they were capped by hedge lines *c.* 1.00m high then the line of F. 1 would represent a 4–4.50m high barrier: even F. 10, for example, would have presented a 2.20–2.50m high 'face'. Collectively these would have been a formidable defence and the main perimeter bank, given its scale, probably warrants the term 'rampart' (see Fig. 134).

The status and location of any bank associated with the inner circuits is unknown, especially F. 2's bank pre-dating the outer circuit (F. 38's spoil probably contributed to the main F. 1 upcast). Logically it should have lain within that ditch, yet the one-to-one correspondence in the distribution of both finds densities and phosphate levels between its interior and perimeter zones would not suggest any 'interruption' (*i.e.* an internal bank to stop 'things' going into the ditch; see Chapter 5 concerning these distributions). The situation of Structure II immediately beside the ditch would also indicate that no bank intervened. However, this was sited beside the Phase 5 western extension to that circuit (*i.e.* contemporary with F. 1), at which time its spoil probably went onto the main perimeter bank. The F. 2 bank, if 2.50m wide (the berm between F. 2 and Structure VI) would, on average, have only stood some 0.70m high. While this circuit, if capped by a hedge, would have been a substantial barrier — 2.70m high from ditch base to bank 'hedgework', and therefore comparable to that associated with F. 10 — it was certainly not on the scale of the main perimeter feature. One possibility is that, with the construction of the main circuit, the F. 2 bank was levelled and the spoil either spread or transported to the main perimeter.

Phasing outline
(Figs 44–6)

Phase 1
(Fig. 44)

This is essentially marked by the establishment of the F. 73/93 *et al.* double-ditch system in the north-west. Whilst possibly flanking a minor drove, these are more likely to have bounded a bank system given the broader context of the site's early usage and the character of the North Field circuit (whose layout it presumably also influenced). If so (and if was turf-constructed at least in part, if not largely) this could have extended south beyond the flanking ditches (possibly to the F. 28 boundary). Cut by the Phase 5 Outworks, ditch F. 96 — lying south-west of, and parallel with, the double-ditch system — is shown as broadly contemporary. However, it could have always been of a later date with its alignment simply determined by the axis of this putative bank system.

Based on the discussion of the lasting impact that the series of diagonal axes evidently had on the Ringwork's layout, it is proposed that this development occurred against a background of remnant bank and/or hedge field systems aligned on the main axis of the Wardy Hill-top system — essentially the line of F. 28 in the extreme south-west corner. It is not certain whether or not a precursor of that ditch then lay in this position, only that it must represent the primary landscape axis within the area. From the collective location/alignment of later features, the main north-west to south-east bank on this axis can be reconstructed with some degree of certainty. As marked by the line of F. 101 and F. 118 (and the 'four pits') on the east side and the north-eastern length of the F. 25 gully, the 'half circle' of Structure III in the west (whose remainder presumably rose up over its flanks) and the line of 'disruption' through Structure V, this would have to be some 4–5.00m wide (and at least 0.20–0.30m high for the western half of the Structure III gully not to penetrate into the sub-soil). At this size it would, in fact, have been comparable to the putative north-west bank (as defined by F. 73/93 *et al.*). Alternatively, it could be postulated that this corridor-like 'seam' may instead have been the result of a pair of more minor banks running parallel at this width. Without some sort of levelling-up, however, this would not account for the siting (and subsequent 'loss') of the north-eastern half of Structure III (see Barrett *et al.* 1991, 149–151, concerning the comparable influence of an earlier field system upon the layout of the South Lodge enclosure).

Aside from ditch F. 130, Fig. 44 should not be read as indicating that the diagonal features shown actually pre-date the F. 73/93 system (F. 101, 109 and 118), nor necessarily even Phase 2, but simply that they follow this remnant alignment.

Phase 2
(Fig. 44)

This period sees the first substantial occupation on the site, which would have been initiated by the creation of the rectilinear ditch system with its south-western entrance (F. 27, 37, 52, 57 and 127). Structure I — the first great roundhouse — was certainly integral to its layout. Possibly, in a 'satellite-like' manner, the smaller round Structures III and V were integral to it too. The hayrick (VI) also seems contemporary as it is framed by the projected alignment of

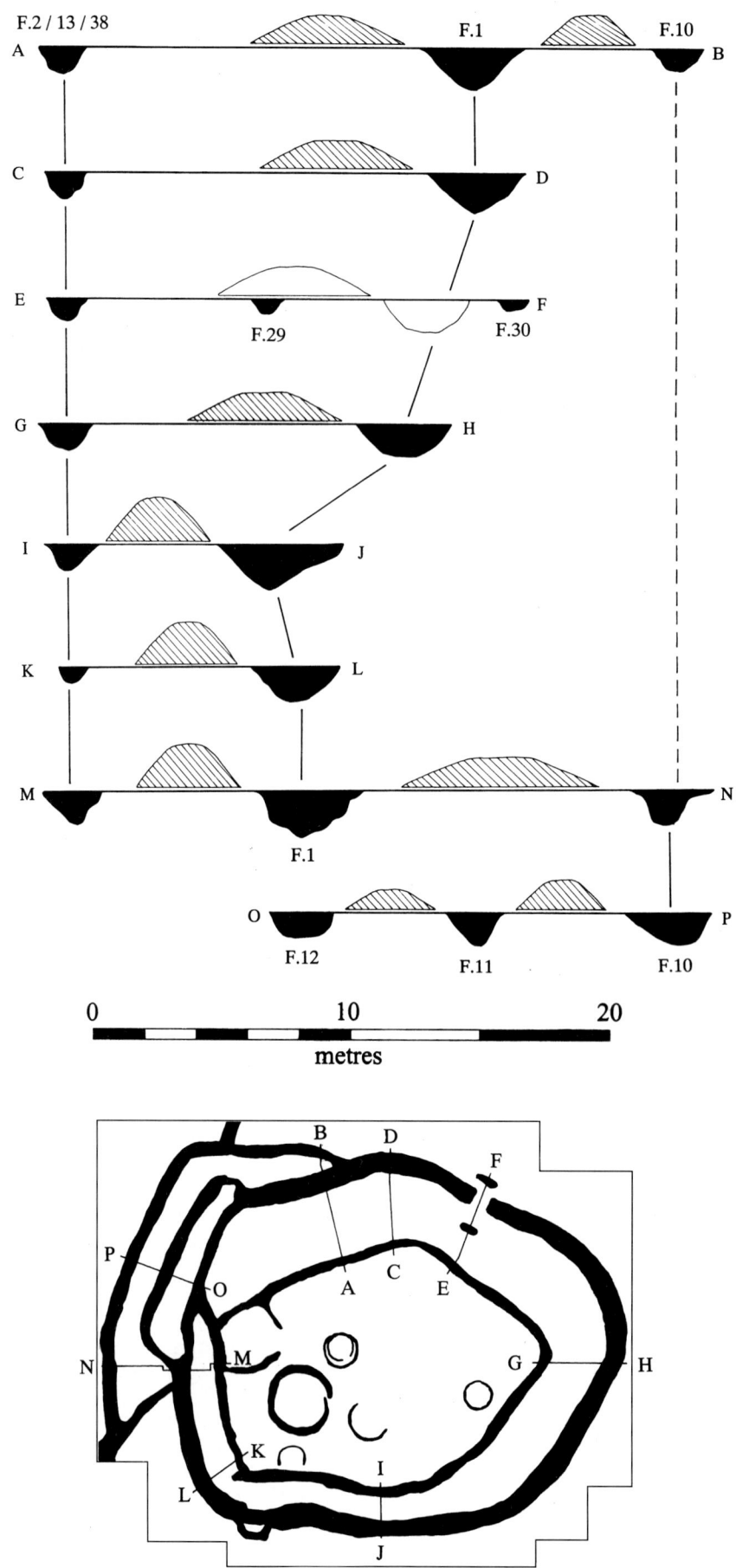

Figure 42 Ringwork banks: reconstructed transect sections

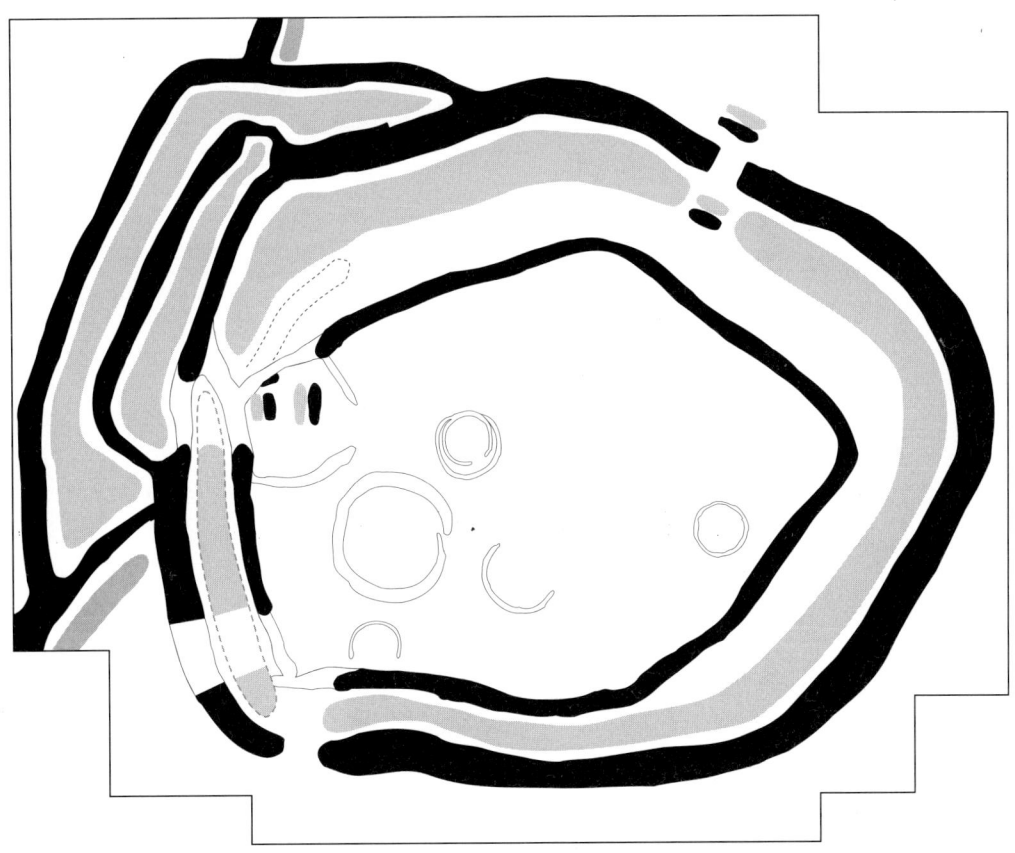

Figure 43 Ringwork banks: reconstruction plan

the eastern north-south boundaries of this ditch system (F. 52 and 57).

It is presumed that the antenna-like ditches that variously frame and radiate from this system's entrance were broadly contemporary. However, as these were all only truncated by the main Phase 4 perimeter there would be no stratigraphic reason not to assign them to Phase 3. Whereas a definite eastern end was found for the southern of these ditches (F. 100 *et al.*), there is far less certainty about the northern extent of the western ditch (F. 95). Whilst its end may have coincided with the main F. 1 terminal midway along that side, in all likelihood it continued as the backfilled F. 144 length of ditch F. 12; it may even have linked with the north-western double-ditch system. It is difficult to account for the layout of the F. 64 ditches; they seem to 'box' the approach to the system's south-western entrance. While a number of alternative options have been explored (was the feature a square barrow, for example?) it appears to do nothing more than frame the entrance, and presumably regulated access to it.

Ditch F. 109 to the south appeared to terminate in relationship with the east-to-west antennae ditch (F. 100 *et al.*) and is presumed, therefore, to be broadly contemporary. Together with F. 101, which ran parallel, these seem to represent elements of an enclosure-contemporary field system that had its origins in the remnant Phase 1 bank system, and was therefore probably of Later Bronze Age/Early Iron Age ancestry. The F. 118 'trough' shares the alignment of the eastern of these ditches. Apparently flanking the eastern side of the bank postulated along this line, it might represent a minor fence, or even a hedge. The F. 65 'pitted trough' configuration at its end is only loosely assigned to this phase on account of its parallel alignment with the rectilinear system. However both its function and affiliations, in all honesty, are indeterminable. There are also potential complications relating to the 'integrity' of the F. 27/46 ditch line, which are further discussed below (*Phasing alternatives and ambiguities*).

Phase 3
(Fig. 45)
This is marked by the establishment of the F. 2 circuit. The manner in which its north-western end 'springs' from the terminal of F. 37 indicates that this earlier north-to-south boundary must still have been operational, and served to close the western side of this circuit. Equally, it is presumed that the Phase 2 entranceway was still maintained. It must be emphasised that the phasing of the F. 2 circuit prior to the main outer perimeter (F. 1) is entirely inferential, and relates to the arguments outlined above regarding the site's spatial organisation: primarily, that the north-eastern perimeter of F. 2 follows more closely the site's main north-east to south-west diagonal axis, from which (almost in the manner of 'Chinese whispers') the corresponding portion of the outer circuit displays greater variability. Relevant, too, is the 'empty' annex-like swathe between F. 2 and F. 1 on the northern side; on the basis of phasing 'linkages', the displacement between the two circuits on that side would seem to relate in general terms to the secondary status of the outer of the two.

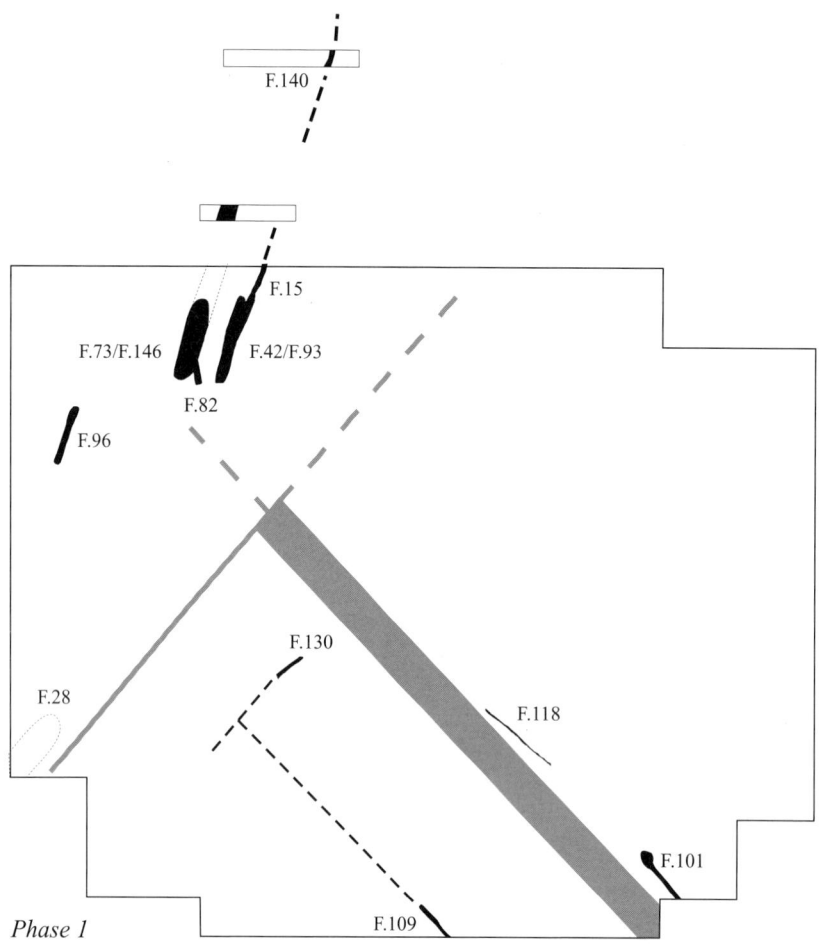
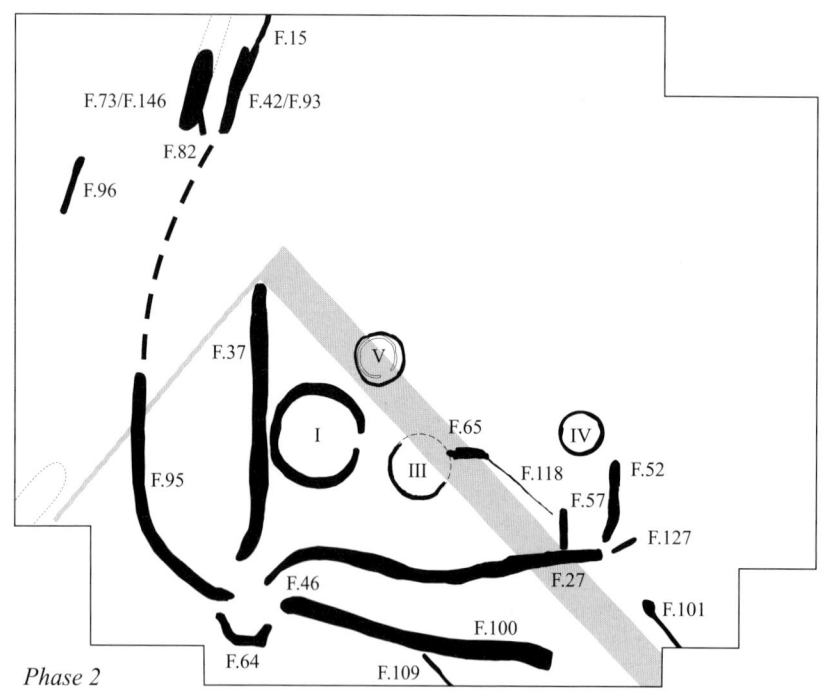

Figure 44 Phase plans (Phases 1 and 2)

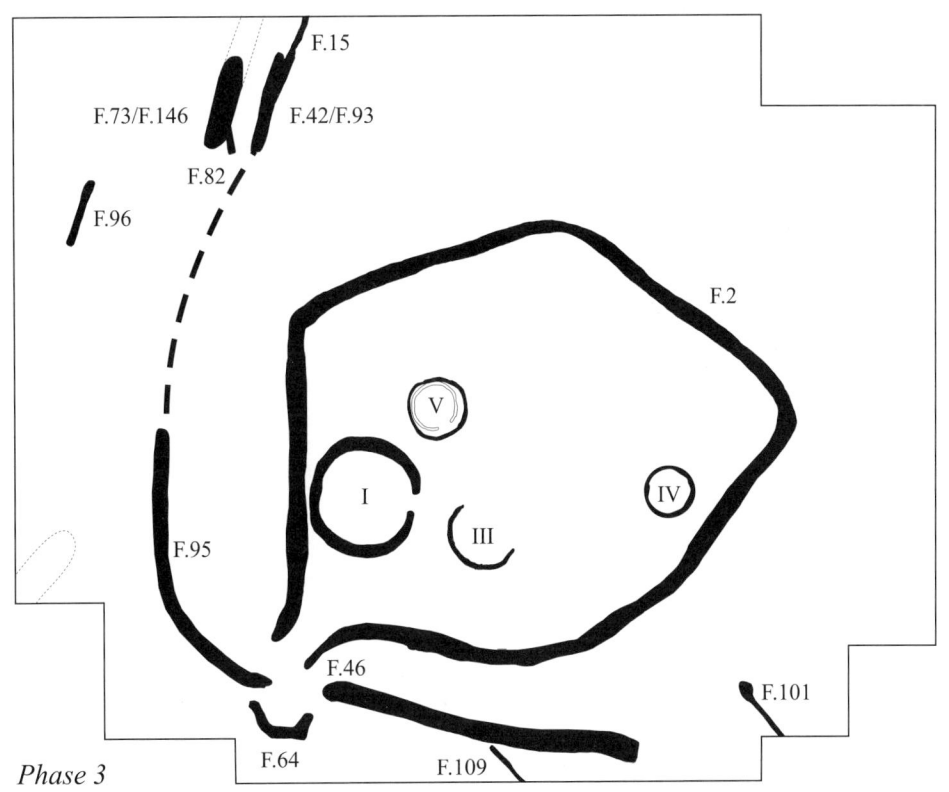

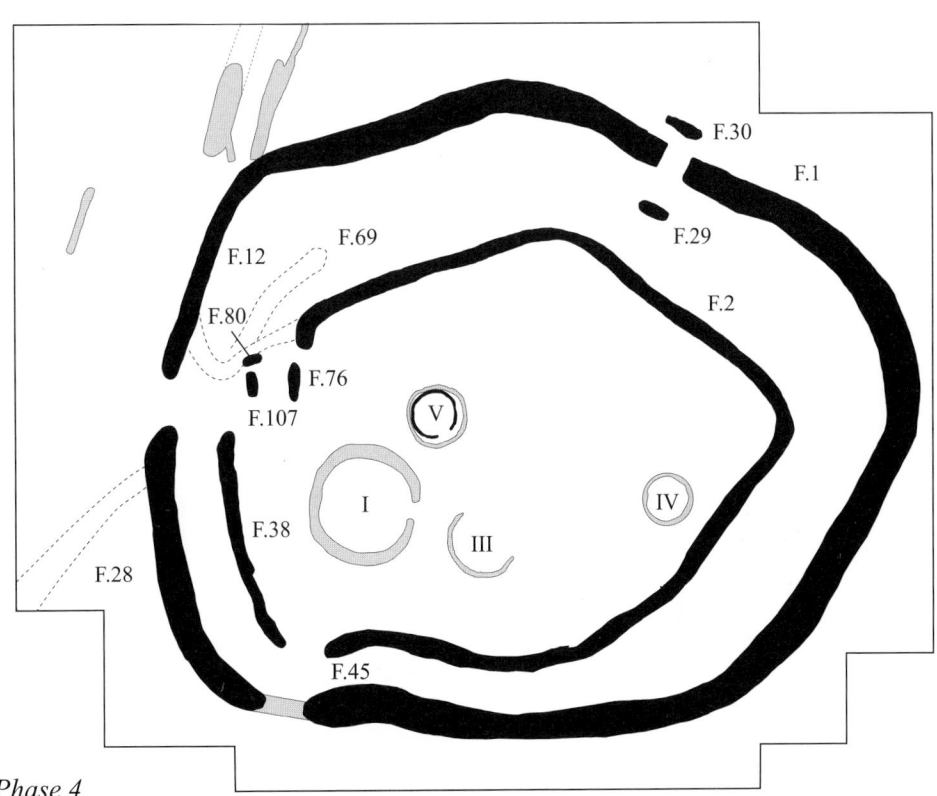

Figure 45 Phase plans (Phases 3 and 4)

Phase 4
(Fig. 45)
With the establishment of the outer circuit, there was a major expansion (and 'closure') of the enclosure system. To some extent, this episode forms the hub of the phasing scheme insofar as it marks a change from a 'domestic-type' compound to a 'fort' as such. Nevertheless, the Phase 3 layout determined key elements in this development. Once starting in the north-west from the southern end of the F. 73/93 ditch system, not only did the layout of the main perimeter roughly mirror the F. 2 circuit, but the location of the south-western landward access was maintained (though reconfigured) and, across its south-western sector, apparently it re-cut the line of the Phase 2 boundary (F. 95).

The establishment of the Ringwork's outer perimeter also saw the creation of the north-eastern Watergate. As discussed above, the extent to which the interior was accessible from this point is debatable. There is no direct evidence (*e.g.* from artefact or re-cut patterning) that the F. 2 circuit was bridged there. Perhaps entry from this axis was by traversing the western 'corridor' between the F. 1 bank and the inner circuit, with access to the latter being gained at the western end of F. 2. Another access way into the enclosure, the West Central Entrance, was also provided. Falling midway along the western perimeter, it indicates a degree of formal spatial organisation and emphasises the prominence of the east-to-west axis. As described above, it was also provided with a 'trough' or blocking-trench system (accompanied with large posts). However, this 'structure', unlike that associated with the Watergate, lay within the gap through the circuits. The Landward Entrance was evidently also re-worked at this time. There, the main factors to account for are the backfilling of the western Phase 2 ditch (F. 37) and its replacement by the inner circuit boundary along the south-western sector, F. 38. The establishment of the latter at this point was associated with the backfilling of the F. 64 system and the re-cutting of the F. 2/46 terminal as F. 45, and must indicate a bridged crossing of the outer perimeter (F. 151 causeway). With the addition of gateway posts (F. 56 and 59), this entrance — like the other two of this phase — was clearly also 'controlled'.

As indicated by the segmented 'long pit' impressions held in the F. 151 causeway, despite the fact that the outer perimeter extended across the line of the Phase 2 and 3 landward approach, a bridged entrance in this location seems to have been maintained during this phase. Perhaps this was an afterthought following over-enthusiastic perimeter digging (*i.e.* an organisational oversight). If so, having two entrances in the western half of the enclosure system would have made little sense if their approaches were not somehow separated. Therefore, it is presumed that the line of ditch F. 28, probably re-cutting the line of an earlier up-slope axis, was then established running north-east down to the F. 1 perimeter. Only from its existence would there have been a need for distinct western and south-western entrances: the latter being from inside the larger Wardy Hill-top system, the former from its outside. By the same logic, it could be argued that the north-eastern Watergate equally related to the establishment of the North Field circuit, curtailing access from the north-west.

This phase obviously saw major alternations to the enclosure system. Its overall layout suggests that it marks a re-orientation, with the east-to-west axis becoming

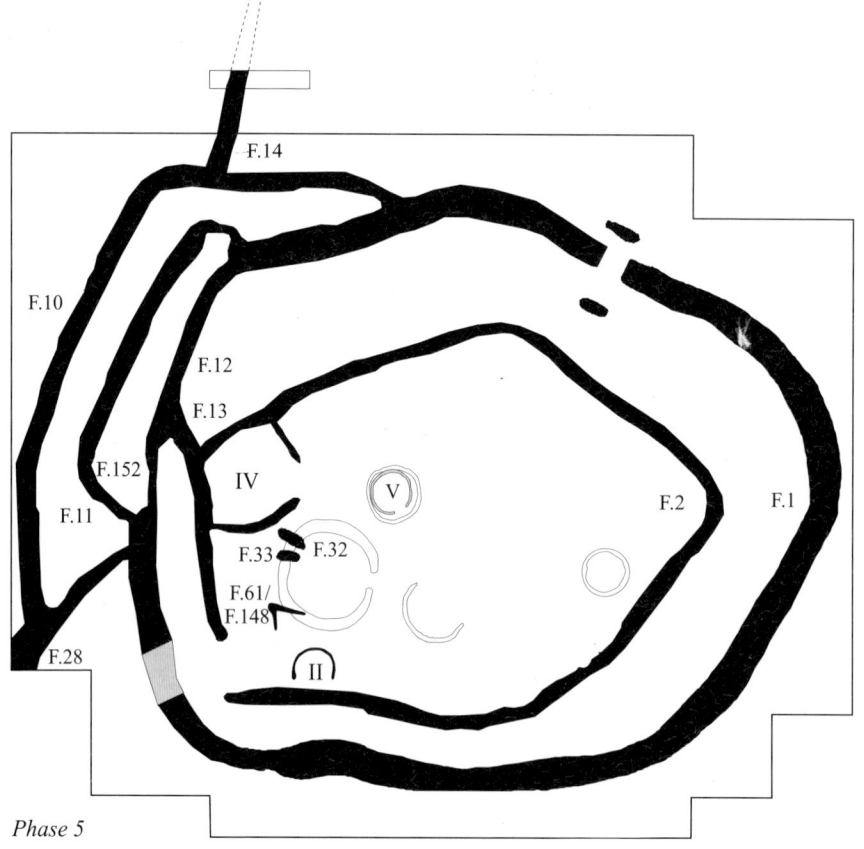

Figure 46 Phase plans (Phase 5)

paramount for the first time over the south-west to north-east one. Given all that this implies in terms of transformational change, a crucial issue then becomes which, if any, of the earlier buildings were still functioning within its interior. Strictly on the basis of stratigraphic succession, there would be nothing stopping direct continuity of Phase 3–4 occupation. The only grounds for doubting this relate instead to assumptions of the scale of these alterations *vis-à-vis* a continuity of domestic usage, and different rhythms of change as regards the elaboration of the Ringwork's perimeter and the duration of buildings. This issue will be further discussed below (Chapter 5).

Phase 5
(Fig. 46)
This sees the closure of the West Central Entrance: the southward extension of the F. 13 terminal to join the inner circuit on that side (F. 38), and the re-cutting of the backfilled F. 144 ditch linking the main western terminals of F. 1 and F. 12 (re-cut F. 152). These actions were clearly undertaken in anticipation of the addition of the western Outworks (F. 10 and 11), with the F. 14 boundary re-cutting the line of the north-western ditch system relating to the arc of the North Field circuit. The closure of the West Central Phase 4 entrance may well have also related to the western extension of F. 2 and, thereby, the cutting-off of the main Landward access in the south-west. It would then follow that the 'secondary' Western Crossing was established immediately to the north-west of this point. This was marked by the backfilling of the southern length of F. 38, with the corresponding portion of the outer circuit then presumably bridged.

Of the contemporary buildings, Structure II could only have been established with the western extension of F. 2, as it would otherwise have blocked the original south-western entrance. Similarly, it was only with the closure of the West Central Entrance that Structure IV could have been set within the north-western corner of the Ringwork's interior. However, the western circuit of that building (the southward extension of F. 13) was clearly not directly building-related. Its scale and alignment relate to the extension of the inner circuit on that side, and it was evidently not dug in the first instance as an eaves-gully. This therefore may indicate that the building had been inserted sometime later within this phase's development. Although located 'deep' within the site's defences behind the Outworks boundaries its position, set hard against the inner circuit, may well have compromised the Ringwork's defensive capability. If so this may, by extension, also imply the 'later' position of this building within this phase.

The two trough-like pits cutting across the north-western perimeter of its gully, certainly marking the demise of Structure I, are phased to this time (F. 32 and 33). While their function is unknown, they may have generally related to the 'L'-shaped ditch configuration cut into the southern 'junction' of that building's gully and the F. 37 ditch-line (F. 61 and 148). The latter's assignment to this horizon is based on the fact that its southern end seems to closely correspond with the 'secondary' terminal of the inner circuit (F. 38) and must relate to access through the newly-established western entrance across the main perimeter at this point.

Phasing alternatives and ambiguities
What has been presented can only be considered a basic 'growth model' for the site. For reasons outlined above, much ambiguity must remain concerning aspects of its development and alternative phasing scenarios are possible. Foremost amongst these would involve reconsidering whether or not the early 'antenna-like' ditch system, assigned to Phase 2, should actually be associated with the establishment of the inner Ringwork circuit proper (F. 2: Phase 3). There is neither a stratigraphic nor an inferential basis to determine their precise relationship.

Another possibility, presuming that the putative bank system flanked by the north-western double-ditches extended south beyond their line, is whether at one point the innermost line of the Outworks system — F. 11 in relationship to F. 1/12/144 — actually pre-dated the F. 10 bank line and bounded this earlier north-to-south bank. If so, this configuration could be a Phase 2 or even Phase 3 phenomenon; the separation of this outwork perimeter in the north (F. 42 to the north-western F. 1 terminal) would still relate to Phase 5. Although compelling in terms of the long-term impact of earthwork systems, this argument's downfall is that it implies the creation of the West Central Entrance during Phase 4. This would imply the localised levelling of this bank line, only to have it re-established with the further elaboration of the Outworks in Phase 5.

The subtleties of the southern Phase 2 ditch line (F. 27/46) and the complicated arrangement of ditches at its eastern end (F. 52 and 57; Fig. 44) are also not fully comprehended. Of the latter, while the irregularities in the line of the easternmost (F. 52) conform to the general layout of this phase's other ditches the marked straightness and situation of F. 57 is peculiar, and it seems to fulfil no obvious function. Particularly noteworthy is that its southern end does not conjoin with F. 27, but stops immediately short of it (its sub-square terminal obviously respecting the latter). To this should be added that this immediate area — at least as represented by densities within the subsequent F. 2 circuit at this point — not only saw significant artefact deposition but also much re-deposition of burnt material, and a high frequency of charred plant remains (Murphy, Chapter 3). The evidence collectively indicates that 'something' was clearly happening at this point. Though this may amount to no more than an (unduly) complicated entrance configuration (between the F. 52 and 57 terminals), this would not explain its layout satisfactorily. One real possibility is that F. 57 flanked the eastern end of a square/rectangular structure, whose southern eaves drained into the equally straight F. 27 ditch. If so, this was probably shed-like (*c.* 4–5.00 x 4–5.00m), and may have been used for storage. No beam slots or post-holes were found in association but neither, due to plough truncation, did they survive within the site's roundhouses. (The only other viable possibility is that F. 57 supported a free-standing timber partition, perhaps screening an area of outdoor working/processing. There was, however, no direct evidence that the feature itself held posts; nor would this interpretation account for the marked straightness of F. 27 to the south.)

This scenario would account for the straightness of the eastern F. 27 length of the southern ditch line. Yet beyond its western terminal it is, unfortunately, impossible to distinguish a distinct Phase 2 ditch line (extending west from F. 27) from the subsequent Phase 3 circuit (F. 2). It is actually possible that there was a gap between the end of F.

27 and the F. 46 ditch lengths, though no eastern terminal for the latter was identified. This interpretation, albeit speculative, could correlate with the fact that along its south-central side lenses of dirty trample were seen to bed down into reduced swathes bordering F. 2, and were apparently cut by it. (The inner circuit there also truncated two small pits, F. 55 and 126). Despite this evidence of 'early'/Phase 2 occupation activity, why the southern ditch might have been so interrupted is unknown. Nevertheless, the evidence does seem to confirm the independent status — however brief — of the straight eastern length of F. 27.

IV. Period III: historical usage
(Figs 47 and 48)

Artefacts recovered in the upper profile of the main Ringwork ditches confirm that the enclosure survived as a substantial earthwork until the first decades of the 20th century. Aside from a clutch of medieval coins in the top of ditch F. 11 (perhaps a dropped purse of the 13th–15th centuries) and a few sherds of that attribution, the vast majority of this material was of post-medieval date (18th–19th centuries). With some 590 sherds of this period recovered, its density suggests some dumping activity: perhaps it served as a village midden.

Features
Apart from claying trenches, and what resembled a sheep pen, the main features attributable to this phase are a series of north-to-south oriented ditches (Fig. 48). These divide the extant field into four equal-sized plots and must represent early post-medieval field boundaries. Two points of significance are as follows:

1. Their variable depths and disjunctions indicate that they were laid out in relationship to the Ringwork-as-earthwork (*i.e.* 'rising' over its ramparts).
2. They are not shown on 19th-century maps. This could suggest that they relate to an early arable phase of post-medieval agriculture involving drainage, with the land reverting to pasture in the 19th century only to go under the plough again during World War I (as reported by local people).

The three NNE–SSW oriented ditches ran parallel at a roughly regular interval across the site (30–34m apart: F. 3, 4 and 5). Filled with mid-dark brown humic loam, they consistently truncated Iron Age features; given their relationship to extant field boundaries, there can be no doubt of their post-medieval attribution. Generally they were 1.25–0.40m across and 0.30–0.60m deep with concave profiles; troughs and 'steps' in their bases suggested re-cutting. At points along their length the ditches were considerably larger (*e.g.* F. 5 measured 1.80 x 0.80m where it cut F. 1 in the south); elsewhere they were much more minor (*e.g.* F. 4, measuring 0.65m x 0.10m between F. 1 and 2 in the north). Generally they tended to 'shallow' and narrow between the main Ringwork circuits, where their fills were also mixed with clays (the northern end of the westernmost ditch, F. 4, stopped in relation to the F. 1 circuit). This must attest to some degree of bank/rampart earthwork survival.

In the eastern trench arm (IV), this 'grid' of north-to-south ditches continued in the form of F. 9 (0.90m wide and 0.40m deep), which ran north into Trench V. In Trench VI, a similar north-to-south ditch was also sectioned (F. 17: 1.10m wide and 0.45m deep). Roughly continuing northward along the interrupted line of ditch F. 4, this did not however extend as far south as Trench VIII. Otherwise, a series of narrower ditch-parallel troughs were investigated within the northern and eastern trenches (F. 8, 16, 17 and 18). Unlike the wide ditches, which had splaying tops, these peat-filled features were 0.55–0.60m wide with vertical sides and flat bases. 'Box-like', they appeared spade-dug. They do not seem to have been open features and the farmer's comment that these were claying trenches (intended to introduce alkaline clay into the acid peat) seems valid, though bush drainage remains another possibility. Two unexcavated ditches lying on the same orientation crossed the northern half of Trench VII (F. 138 and 139). Lying only 0.75m apart, and both *c.* 0.60m wide, it is not certain which was a ditch and which, if either, a claying trench.

Two lengths of an apparently 'C'-shaped half-circular gully *c.* 9.00m in diameter was exposed in the extreme south-east corner of the site exterior to the Ringwork's circuit (F. 50/51: Structure VII). These were 0.20–0.30m wide and *c.* 0.14m deep; they were filled with humic peaty loam, with only limited evidence of any basal silting. The two western terminals stopped just short of ditch F. 5 (by 0.40 and 0.90m) and the structure appeared contemporary with it. Therefore, through its plan relationships a 'late' date can only be postulated for it: perhaps it functioned as a sheepfold. Given, however, its plan similarity to the Ringwork's other 'half-circles', an earlier attribution (*e.g.* Roman) must also remain a possibility.

As detailed by Hall (below), a considerable quantity of 18th–19th century pottery was recovered. Whilst most derived from the fieldwalking, much was found in the uppermost peats of the main Iron Age features, again attesting to the Ringwork's earthwork survival. This quantity seems greater than what could be expected from a manuring spread alone and it is possible that, at least in early post-medieval times, the Ringwork was a frequented 'place' — one attracting dumping, and possibly animal penning. To this end, some of the reduced trample-zone transgression of the main circuit may date to animal action of this period (*e.g.* the swathe exterior to the south-eastern 'corner' of F. 1).

Pottery
by D. Hall
A total of 588 post-Roman sherds was recovered. There were only five medieval pieces, which must have been deposited with 'rubbish' spread there in the 18th–19th centuries. The 'stratified' contexts (*i.e.* upper profiles of earthwork features) had more 18th-century sherds than elsewhere, and finds from them included a single example of tin-glazed earthenware (Delft). This fabric was very rapidly superseded by white wares after 1740.

Largely of 19th-century date, most of the sherds were small and derive from household rubbish added to manure. 'White wares', including all types of cream ware, bone china, *etc.* (plain, blue and polychrome), comprise 48% of the collection. English stonewares form six percent and Staffordshire wares in a yellow fabric amounted to two percent. Most of the other sherds were various types of red earthenwares (43%). These ranged from coarse, glazed red earthenware bowls and large pancheons, glazed black with iron or white with a tin glaze, to fine red ware cups in Jackfield-type fabrics. Nearly all of the material recovered is likely to be of 18th- and 19th-century date.

Tobacco pipes
by D. Mackay
The assemblage consists of 34 pieces, 29 of which are plain stem fragments; of the rest, four are bowl fragments, and another is a stem with part of a spur remaining. The dating must necessarily be tentative, as stem fragments are notoriously hard to attribute unless a large number of similar date are recovered. The fieldwalking and test-pitting contexts account for the majority of pieces, 18 in total. From *013* came three bowl fragments of 18th-century type, but not enough of their form survives to narrow the date range. One stem is almost certainly of 17th-century date. The remainder of the stems are of general 18th- and 19th-century type.

Those from other contexts — largely the upper earthwork profiles of major Iron Age features — span a general 18th–19th century date range, with a fragment from a late 17th-century bowl and a late 18th–19th century decorated bowl fragment from the upper fills of F. 1. The latter is the only piece deserving further mention, its spur bearing the initials 'R.S.' and the bowl decorated with vertical fluting.

There are several candidates for its maker, the two most likely being Robert Sibley, manufacturing in Ely from *c.* 1830–60, and Risley Shelton, recorded in Cambridge in the 1830s.

This is a typical ploughsoil assemblage. Made up of small, often abraded, fragments of many types and periods of pipe, it is consistent with a build-up of material as a result of casual deposition, nightsoiling and rubbish tipping.

Metalwork
Most of the metalwork recovered from the site, including buttons, a clock escapement and various machine fittings, as described below in Chapter 4, is of 'late' attribution.

Artefact distributions
(Fig. 47)
The distribution of 'late' pottery within the ploughsoil was relatively uniform (range 0–22 sherds; 5 mean; 3.69 st. dev.: Fig. 47). Apart from two localised peaks within the northern interior of the former enclosure, higher-than-mean values were restricted to its western perimeter and to just beyond the south-eastern corner of the outer circuit. The latter corresponds to the reduced peaty loam-filled swathe immediately exterior to the main Ringwork ditch: it must reflect 'late' trample (probably by

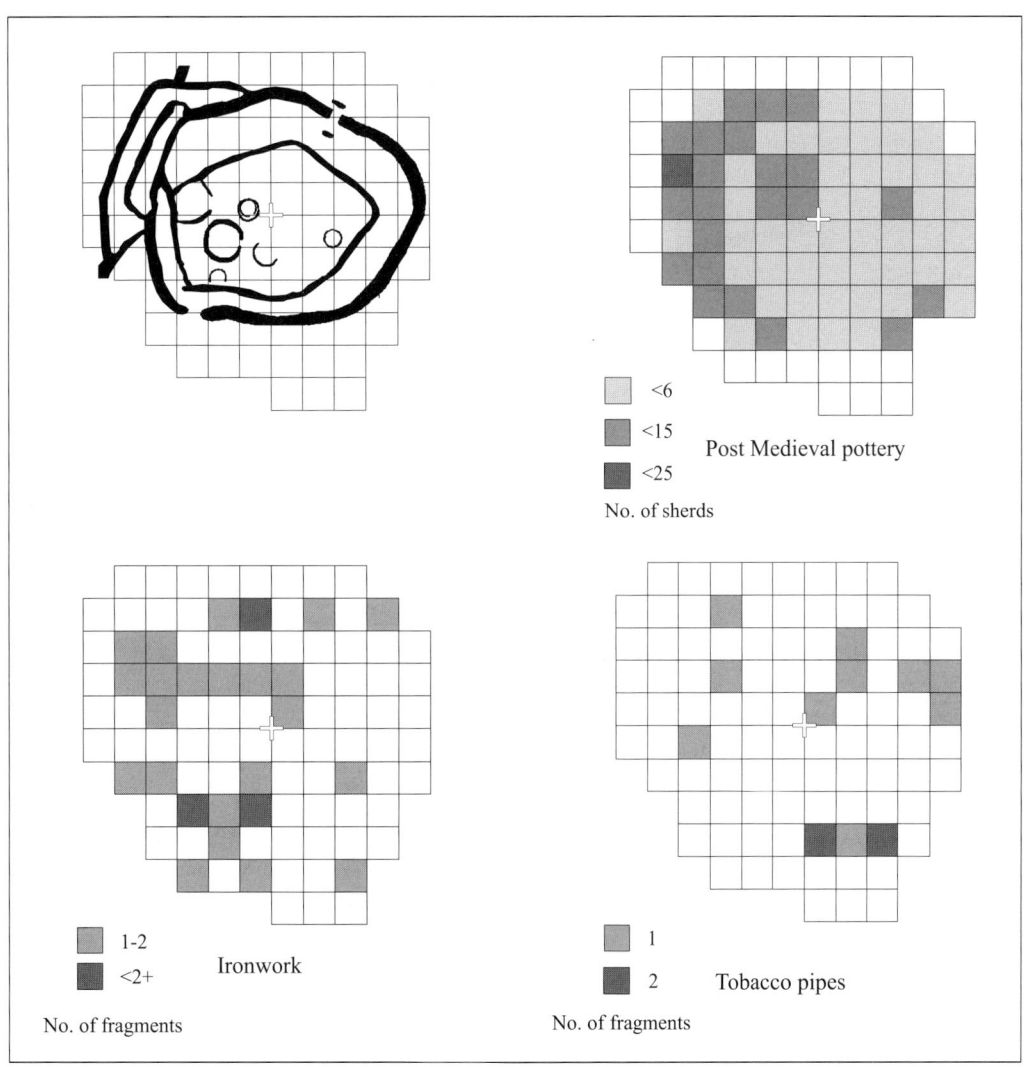

Figure 47 Post-medieval surface distributions

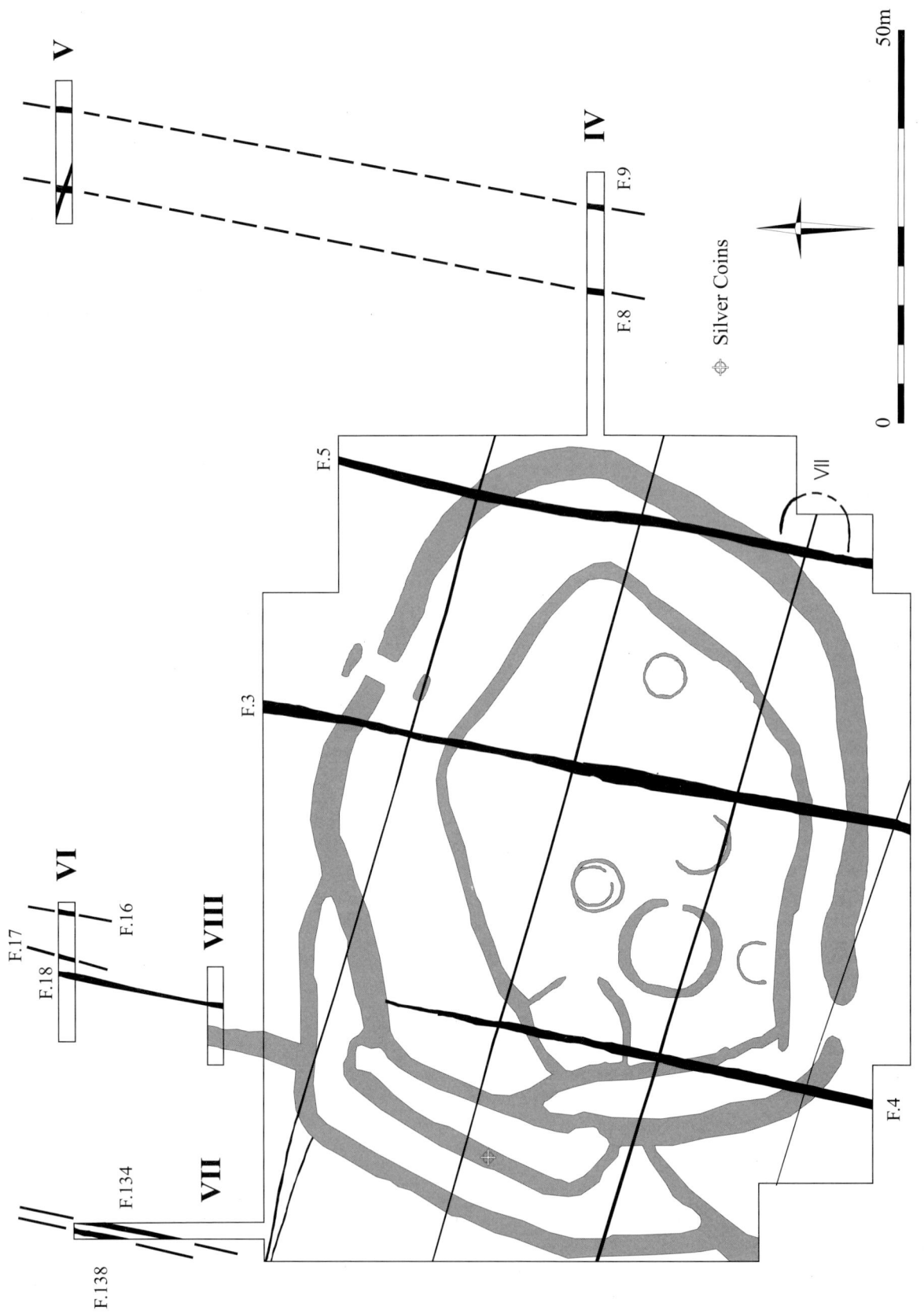

Figure 48 Historical usage (Period III)

stock), and possibly relate to the Structure VII animal pen. Generally, the distribution of this material — especially in the west, where it coincides closely with the line of the Iron Age enclosure system — must reflect the Ringwork's survival as an earthwork.

Occurring in densities of 0–4 pieces per 10m unit, with the majority of the material being nails, the distribution of the ploughsoil ironwork is similar and is most consistent across the western portion of the grid (Fig. 47). While the fact that none occur in the midden core area of the Iron Age distributions suggests the material is largely of 'late' date, the increased frequencies within the vicinity of the main south-western Ringwork entrance could indicate that a proportion of the nails derive from Iron Age (i.e. gate-related) structures. Beyond this western spread, the tendency for the iron to occur around the southern and northern sides of the grid across the eastern half of the collection area has affinities with the more marginal distribution of tobacco pipes. Though not concentrated in the area of the western 'late' pottery spread, equally these do not occur in the area of the Ringwork core distributions (Fig. 47). The only concentrations of any note are those in the south-eastern sector (corresponding to the reduced swathe exterior to the F. 1 circuit) and, more widely, in the north-east. This matches exactly the distribution of this material in the upper profiles of the F. 1 and F. 10 ditch circuits (12 pieces recovered in six segments). Otherwise, only one other piece was found in an excavated context (aside from the F. 8 claying trench): this was from the upper profile of F. 2 in the south-eastern sector, immediately adjacent to the occurrence of pipe in the outer circuit and fieldwalking grid.

Like that of the pottery, the distribution of the clay pipes certainly attests to the earthwork survival of the Ringwork's outer circuit. Probably reflective of manuring, the manner in which it varies from the distribution of the contemporary pottery (and to some degree the ironwork) suggests that another mechanism was responsible for the latter's more westerly main concentration: presumably including village-derived dumping.

Discussion: lost from history

The recovery of seemingly 'early' ditches dividing the field may relate to the fact that a substantial area of Coveney Fen (including the site) was enclosed prior to the 17th century (Hall 1996, 51–3, fig. 26). Known as 'The Dams', this reclamation extended over some 350ha. Hall notes that arable usage would probably have been impractical without pumps, but that the additional embankment (i.e. 'dams') would have extended the length of summer grazing. However, it is conceivable that the immediate location, lying relatively high on the skirtland of the Wardy Hill spur, was suitable for early arable usage.

The collective evidence suggests that the Ringwork probably survived in earthwork form until the time of its ploughing in World War I. Given this, it is remarkable that it was not then identified as a monument. While there are early maps that entitle the Wardy Hill spur as 'Warning Hill', and the fact that a World War II pill box was located on its crown, can be read as reflecting continuity of the locale's strategic function the site itself bears no name. This raises questions relating to landscape cognition and historical association: why was it not identified? Admittedly, it is unlikely to have ever been a monument to rival those of Hardy's Wessex. Nevertheless, its non-recognition may reflect the intensity and direction of local antiquarian interest (see Evans 1997b for further discussion of these themes). Within the specific context of the cultural landscape of the Isle of Ely, it may be more relevant that neither Wardy Hill nor Coveney (or the causeway linking the two) have any folkloric associations with the island's renowned Saxon figures or with Hereward's defence (as opposed, for example, to Belsar's Hill and the Aldreth causeway). This suggests that the attention of the region's antiquarians was governed both by expectations and 'lay' associations, with the final result that the site effectively became 'lost' from history until its excavation in 1992.

Local attitudes to the landscape's history
by N. James
(Table 2–5)

Inhabitants and 'outsiders' alike have long regarded the Fens as a distinctive countryside. The region is flat, open and damp, and the threat of floods is only kept in check by intensive and extensive engineering. The Fenland Survey Project helped to confirm that the peat or 'Black' Fens, in particular, are distinctive in their history too (see also Evans 1997b). To gather knowledge of Wardy Hill and assess contemporary attitudes to the landscape's development in general, we interviewed visitors to an open day at the excavation, advertised in the Isle of Ely in November 1991. We put a series of questions: about visitors' interest in archaeology; concerning their knowledge of fenland history and their opinions as to the future; about where they lived and whether or not they regarded themselves as fenlanders; and, for local people, whether they had known of the site before the dig.

The questionnaire was administered by students on the Cambridge University M.Phil. course in Archaeological Heritage Management. Explaining that they wished to ask some questions for an assignment, they succeeded in gaining sympathetic attention. Out of 556 visitors in all, 96 questionnaires were completed wholly or in part (families were interviewed collectively). In general, good data were collected on the second and third sets of questions but the students seem to have paid less attention to the first. One disadvantage of employing them to this end was that they did not have the knowledge to cross-examine visitors on 'suspect' answers. What, for example, does one make of the assertion that the Fens were under the sea until about 1870?

The questionnaire and results are included in the site archive. The tables accompanying the present summary distinguish the replies of those regarding themselves as 'fenlanders' from others ('No way', declared one local resident!). Answers as to when the Fens first became wetland were very diverse, but the 'Ice Age' figured prominently (Table 2). Another test was to ask about 'bog oaks': timbers commonly dragged up by farmers from beneath the peat topsoil. One of the best-known proofs that the landscape once looked quite different from today, they are often said all to lie in a particular direction, as if the trees succumbed to a common catastrophe. Concerning this, the replies were also diverse but flooding was a prominent theme, and again the Ice Age took some of the blame (Table 3).

We asked about the future too. Just as they know that the Fens used to be different, so too most visitors understood that the landscape is likely to change under the pressures of both development and climate change (Table 4). Many know that beneath the treasured peaty topsoil there lies clay, and local people seemed especially aware that the former is disappearing. Flooding also was regarded as a danger. Then we asked about preferences. Many respondents hoped that there would be more wetland but most wanted to preserve the present landscape (Table 5). This finding matches an opinion survey of about 70 visitors to an exhibition in 1989–90 on the history and future of the Fens (Fens Exhibition Project 1990).

The final question, for local residents only, was whether they had known about the site before the current dig. The landowner said that he had noticed crop-marks in the field. Two others also claimed to have seen marks, one back in the 1920s; another remarked that earthworks were once visible. Two others reported finds from the vicinity, one ascribing them to the Vikings and the other to the Bronze Age.

Visitors were clear about whether or not to identify themselves as 'fenlanders'. Yet, while one justified his chronology by adding 'That's what the old ones told me', it is probably on account of formal schooling that identity made no obvious difference to answers about history — although teachers should worry about the chronological estimates (Table 2)! On the other hand, it is not surprising that avowed locals were more conservative in their preferences for the future (Table 5).

In general, the responses showed awareness both of change in the Fens and of ecological processes in general, although, again, many remarks were very inaccurate. The concept of a 'dust bowl' was mentioned in anticipation of the future. Loss of the peat was as familiar an issue as the danger of floods, and there was reference to the role of engineering in maintaining the fields. In explanation of the landscape's early history, both the sea and glacial action were cited; in reference to bog oaks petrifaction, tropical storms and even plate tectonics were mentioned. The insistent reference to the Ice Age is thought-provoking.

Neither the Wardy Hill survey nor that the exhibition asked for respondents' ages but a couple of our students remarked that, while older people had hesitated to anticipate the future, younger visitors tended to favour provision for wetland habitats. A small but articulate proportion of the exhibition-goers, too, called for protection of habitat. Yet respondents to both surveys recognised the need for balance between local interests. These findings are interesting in view of plans announced by the National Trust, in 2000, for establishing much more wetland around the reserve at Wicken Fen.

	'fenlanders'	non-fenlanders
'long ago'/prehistory	3	1
Ice Age	5	3
end of/after Ice Age	6	5/6
c. 20–10 kya	1	2
7 kya–Roman	4	4
>1kya/Hereward's era	3	2
C12/3	2	
C17/8	1	2

Table 2 Visitor Survey: When did the fens become marsh? (kya–thousands of years ago; C–century)

'fenlander'	fell over	blown down	flood/?flood	flattened by glaciers	other
yes	3	2	6	1	3
no	2	2	3	3	2

Table 3 Visitor Survey: What caused 'bog oaks'?

'fenlander'	flooded	topsoil lower or gone	barren, clay, or built over	as today
yes	10	21	6	7
no	8	10	7	5

Table 4 Visitor Survey: How will the fens look a century from now?

'fenlander'	dry/unchanged	wet	mix, more wet
yes	28	11	6
no	17	10	5

Table 5 Visitor Survey: Would you prefer the fens to be dry or wet?

3. Environment Setting, Land-Use and Economic Practices

by A. Clarke, S. Davis, C. Evans, C. French, C. Gleed-Owen, P. Murphy, M. Robinson, D. Serjeantson, C. Stevens and P. Wiltshire

Although the Coveney marshes have not seen detailed palaeoenvironmental study, this chapter will progress from analyses relating to the site's landscape situation to its economic practices and evidence reflecting the intra-site distribution of these activities. Returning to the 'grand scale', it concludes with an attempt — by necessity 'broad brushed' — to model early land-use hypothetically within the area of Wardy Hill.

I. Soil micromorphological analysis
by C. French
(Fig. 49)

Located on slightly calcareous to near-neutral humic gley soils on grey clays of the Gault formation, the site's natural soils are fine textured, slowly permeable and poorly drained (Seale 1975). Three sample profiles from the excavations were analysed using the methodology of Murphy (1986) and Bullock *et al.* (1985) (Fig. 49 for location):

> *Profile 1 (251)*: possible remnant of buried soil beneath former rampart;
> *Profile 2 (072)*: hollow beneath the 'burnt flint mound' (Period I);
> *Profile 3 (206)*: upper fill of Iron Age eaves-drip gully (F. 6, Structure I; Period II).

Profile 1 (*251*)
This possible remnant of the *in situ* soil consists of one main (90%) and one subsidiary (10%) fabric in a partially homogenised matrix. The principal fabric is a sandy clay loam to loam which exhibits an angular to sub-angular, very fine (<5mm), moderately to strongly developed ped structure, with frequent very fine flecks of charcoal/organic matter intermixed with the fine groundmass. This fabric contains abundant non-laminated, dusty clay throughout the groundmass and occasional laminated dusty clay within it. The bulk of this clay illuviation probably occurs as within-ped slaking due to natural wetting and drying, rather than through soil disturbance. Indeed, the relative absence of illuvial clay in the inter-aggregate channels and intra-aggregate vughs indicates that it was well sealed by the Iron Age rampart from contemporary and later soil disturbance.

The minor, subsidiary fabric is an homogeneous silt loam with frequent amorphous organic matter and rounded sesquioxide nodules. This material is in discrete amorphous zones within, but not mixed with, the main fabric.

Structure: partially homogenised; angular to sub-angular, very fine (<5mm) blocky, moderately to strongly developed. *Porosity:* 10% inter-aggregate channels, irregular, horizontal and vertical, <0.5mm wide, <20um long, smooth to weakly serrated, walls partially accommodated; 5–10% intra-aggregate vughs, sub-rounded, smooth to weakly serrated, <2mm. *Organic components:* very few (<2%) large pieces of charcoal with cell structure partially degraded; frequent (15–20%) small, black flecks of charcoal/organic matter, rounded to sub-angular, no cell structure, well integrated with the groundmass. *Mineral components:* main Fabric 1: limit 100µm; coarse/fine ratio 25/75; coarse fraction 5% medium and 20% fine quartz, sub-rounded to sub-angular, 100–500µm; fine fraction 20% very fine quartz, 50–100µm, sub-angular to sub-rounded; 30% silt and 25% clay; speckled; light yellowish grey to yellow to amber to reddish brown (CPL), light yellowish-grey to orangey-brown (PPL), grey/light orange mottled (RL); >90% of total groundmass; subsidiary Fabric 2: limit 100µm; c/f ratio 10/90; coarse fraction 5% medium and 5% fine, sub-rounded to sub-angular, 100–250µm; fine fraction 20% very fine quartz, sub-rounded to sub-angular, 50–100µm; 70% silt and 10% clay; <10% of total groundmass, especially as amorphous zone infill in main groundmass. *Groundmass:* fine and related: porphyric, weakly to strongly reticulate striated; coarse: undifferentiated. *Pedofeatures: textural:* abundant (20%) non-laminated dusty clay throughout groundmass, yellow to amber (CPL), light yellow (PPL), moderately to strongly birefringent, mainly integral with groundmass and very rarely as linings of channels; occasional to many (5%) laminated dusty clay in groundmass, yellow to amber (CPL), moderately to strongly birefringent; *fabric:* few channel/vugh infills, partial/discontinuous, with groundmass of Fabric 1; *amorphous:* 50% of dusty clay impregnated with amorphous sesquioxides, orange (CPL); few zones (<5% of groundmass) of amorphous calcium carbonate; very rare (<1%) fragments of bone, <500µm.

This is an *in situ* soil which survives as a *c.* 8–10cm thick illuvial B horizon, with a natural shrink/swell clay component and a well-developed ped structure. The whole soil fabric is gleyed. There is the occasional infill/intrusive zone of organic, ungleyed A horizon material. It is probably representative of the former A horizon material immediately below the turf line.

The 'cleanliness' of the fabric, with little within-void illuviation of fines, suggests that the soil was subject to little disturbance until it was truncated and buried by the Iron Age rampart. This is corroborated by the well-developed ped structure, suggesting that this soil had not been ploughed. The distinct intermixing of the fabrics was probably caused by the associated activities of truncation (to generate material for the banks) and rampart construction itself.

Profile 2 (*072*)
The composition of this sample exhibited two fabrics, with the upper fabric grading downwards into a lower. The former was a loam to sandy clay loam with a moderately well developed, sub-angular, fine (<5mm) blocky ped structure, which petered out below a depth of about 2cm. It

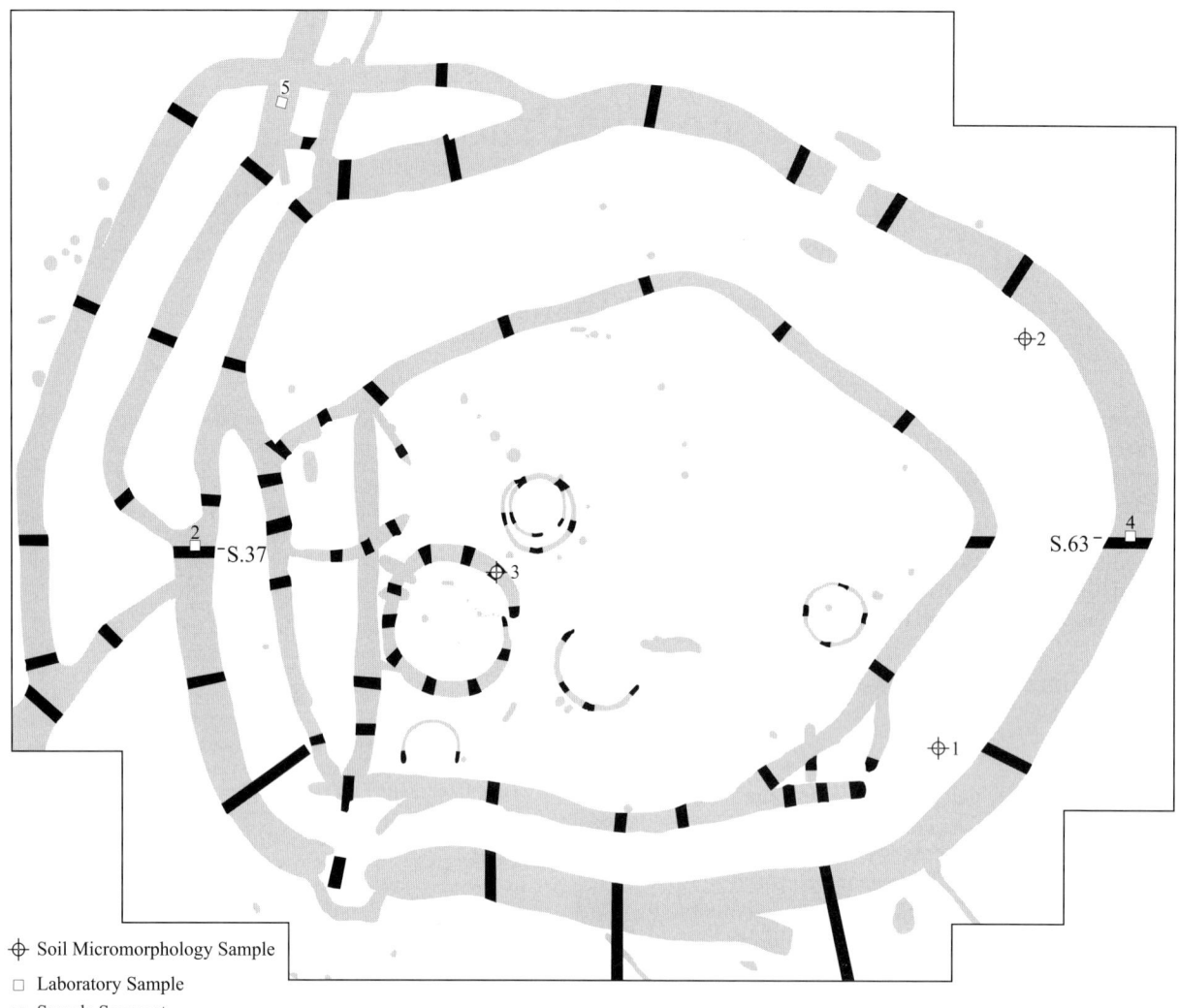

Figure 49 Location of environmental samples

- ⊕ Soil Micromorphology Sample
- ☐ Laboratory Sample
- ■ Sample Segment

was a dense fabric (<7% porosity) with little organic component, which was characterised by thin, horizontal concentrations of oriented laminated and non-laminated dusty clay with irregular zones of amorphous sesquioxide impregnation.

The lower fabric is similar, but with a much more open porosity (c. 30%), with all types of illuvial clay present throughout the groundmass and a few, irregular zones of amorphous sesquioxide impregnation.

Structure: upper 2cm exhibits a moderately developed, sub-angular, fine (<5um) ped structure which becomes poorly developed and a dense, homogeneous, well mixed fabric with depth. *Porosity*: main difference between fabrics; in upper/Fabric 1 5% vughs, sub-rounded, 100–500um; 2% channels, <300um wide, <8mm long, regular and vertical; in lower/Fabric 2 20% metavughs, irregular, up to 3mm; 5% channels, irregular, <1mm wide, <10mm long and <100μm wide and <10 mm long. *Organic components:* Fabric 1 very few (<2%) carbonised organic material, partially decomposed, <1mm; Fabric 2 very few(<2%) very fine flecks of organic material, <75μm, probably carbonised; <1% very occasional larger pieces of charcoal, 1–2mm. *Mineral components:* Fabric 1 limit 100um; c/f ratio 15/85; coarse fraction 10% medium and 5% fine quartz, 100–250μm, sub-rounded to sub-angular; fine fraction 35% very fine quartz, sub-rounded to sub-angular, 50–100um; 30% silt and 20% clay; moderately speckled; greyish white to golden brown (CPL), very light brown to brown (PPL), grey streaked with yellow (RL); Fabric 2 limit 100μm; c/f ratio 10/90; coarse fraction 5% medium and 5% fine quartz, sub-rounded to sub-angular, 100–250um; fine fraction 40% very fine quartz, 50–100μm, sub-angular to sub-rounded; 30% silt and 20% clay; light yellow to light greyish yellow (CPL), very light brown to golden brown (PPL), grey/orangey-brown (RL). *Groundmass:* Fabric 1: fine: weakly reticulate to striated; coarse: undfferentiated; related: porphyric; Fabric 2: fine: weakly reticulate to strongly striated; coarse: undifferentiated; related: porphyric. *Pedofeatures: textural:* in Fabric 1 abundant horizontal lenses or thin concentrations of oriented laminated and non-laminated dusty clay, <200um thick, yellow to gold (CPL); in Fabric 2 10% non-laminated dusty clay and 10% limpid clay throughout groundmass, moderate birefringence, yellow to amber (CPL); often both types exhibit laminations with limpid clay first and dusty clay second; *amorphous:* in Fabric 1 irregular zones of sesquioxide impregnation, <10% of groundmass; in Fabric 2 irregular zones of sesquioxide impregnation, up to 30% of groundmass.

This feature fill is probably a combination of freshly-eroded subsoil (Fabric 2) overlain by material derived from slow, natural infilling with 'B'-horizon-like material (Fabric 1, as for Profile 1), aided by the effects of rain-splash water-erosion and wetting/drying. The latter two soil formation processes give it its laminar appearance, and the whole groundmass is gleyed.

Profile 3 (*206*)
This spot sample was taken from the upper fill of the eaves-gully surrounding Structure I (F. 6). The infill material exhibits an apedal, heterogeneous, poorly mixed, clay loam fabric with abundant amorphous organic matter, frequent fine charcoal and iron-replaced pseudomorphs of plant tissue. The high organic matter content gives it a 'dirty' appearance. Very abundant non-laminated dusty clay, which has probably been derived by slaking from the adjacent subsoil, occurs throughout the groundmass. Some dusty clay coating the voids/channels is more indicative of recent disturbance, probably ploughing, as well as micro-laminated limpid clay occurring very rarely as fragments in the groundmass that are probably eroded remnants of the original subsoil. In addition, there are a few sub-rounded aggregates of silt within the groundmass, rare slivers of bone, neo-formed iron-phosphatic concretions, and amorphous zones of loam with soil faunal excrements and carbonised organic remains.

> Structure: In upper third homogeneous; in lower two-thirds apedal, poorly mixed and heterogeneous. *Porosity:* in upper two-thirds very dense; in lower two-thirds 5% channels, irregular to vertical, 50–500μm wide, up to 4cm lomg; 30%, vughs, sub-rounded, 100–400μm, smooth to weakly serrated, unoriented. *Organic components:* in upper third few (<5%) very fine flecks of charcoal; in lower two-thirds 5–10% charcoal with cell structure evident, sub-rounded to irregular, 200–400μm and 2–4mm; 25% amorphous organic matter, <75μm, some may be charred; amorphous zones of more organic fraction, up to 50% of groundmass; very few (<2%) iron pseudomorphs of plant tissue. *Mineral components:* in upper third 5% very fine quartz, 50–100um, sub-rounded to sub-angular; 50% silt and 45% clay; weak to moderate birefringence; light yellow to gold (CPL); in lower two-thirds limit 100um; c/f ratio 10/90; coarse fraction 5% medium and 5% fine quartz, 100–1250μm, sub-angular to sub-rounded; fine fraction 10% very fine quartz, 50–100um; 50% silt and 30% clay; moderately speckled; light yellow to golden brown (CPL), light yellowish-brown to brown (PPL), orangey-brown/grey mottled (RL). *Groundmass:* fine: striated to mosaic speckled to weakly reticulate striated; coarse: undifferentiated; related: porphyric. *Pedofeatures: textural:* bulk of fine fraction/ very abundant (25%) non-laminated dusty clay within groundmass, yellow (CPL), moderate to strong birefringence; <3% non-laminated clay, amber (CPL), moderate to strong birefringence; rare (<2%) micro-laminated limpid, dull/pale yellow (CPL), strong birefringence, as fragments in groundmass; *fabric:* few (2%) sub-rounded aggregates of silt within groundmass, 0.5-1.5mm; few (2%) amorphous zones of loam with strong, reddish black, sandy/silty clay loam with excrements and irregular fragments of carbonised organic material; *amorphous:* rare (<1%) bone fragments, <250μm; up to 20% imprenated with amorphous sesquioxides, reddish/orangey brown (PPL); few (5%), small (<250μm), sub-rounded sesquioxide nodules; few (2%) neo-formed iron-phosphatic concretions, amber (PPL), orangey-red/black (CPL), within groundmass; very rare (<1%) pottery fragments, 2 x 6mm, sub-angular.

This very organic feature fill contains redeposited natural soil and turf fabrics with a high artefactual component. Together these characteristics suggest redeposited settlement debris. The one component that is missing is any form of ash, which is unusual on a settlement site such as this. In addition, the neo-formed phosphates indicate the addition of urine; perhaps livestock were kept in this area of the site after the structure was abandoned and levelled.

II. Palynology
by P. Wiltshire
(Figs 50–53; Tables 6 and 7)

Two sequences of sediments were obtained from the outer enclosure ditch (F. 1) with the aim of demonstrating temporal changes and spatial differences in vegetation and landscape around the settlement. This was achieved by palynological analysis of sediments taken from two locations 80m apart. They were chosen by virtue of their topographical and hydrological differences, one section being on the extreme western and drier edge (Section 37: Figs 50–1), and the other on the wetter eastern side (Section 63: Figs 52–3).

Although palynomorph preservation and concentration were variable in these sequences, analysis was able to demonstrate both temporal and spatial variation in the plant communities that surrounded the Ringwork during the period of occupation. This work has demonstrated the virtue of multiple sampling at archaeological sites; even greater resolution would have been possible if additional sequences had been obtained from the enclosure ditch.

Methods

Sampling
Sub-samples consisted of approximately 2.0g were taken laterally within each core over 1cm depth of sediment. In Core 1 (Section 37) sub-samples were taken either contiguously or at 2.0cm intervals (Figs 50 and 51). In Core 2 (Section 63) sub-sampling was carried out at 2.0cm intervals from 2.0 to 10cm, and then at 4.0cm intervals from 10.0cm to 38.0cm. From 39.0cm to 50.0cm, sub-samples were contiguous.

Processing
Standard preparation procedures were used (Dimbleby 1985). Wet sediment was measured for 2.0cm^3 volume displacement (Bonny 1972). Tablets of *Lycopodium* spores (Stockmarr 1972) were added to allow estimates of palynomorph concentration (Benninghof 1962). Samples were lightly stained with 0.5% safranine and mounted in glycerol jelly.

Identification and nomenclature
Identification was aided by examination of modern reference material wherever necessary. Nomenclature follows that of Bennett *et al.* 1994, Moore *et al.* 1991 and Stace 1991. Cereal-type pollen refers to all grains of >40.0μm (Edwards 1989). No attempt was made to differentiate *Corylus avellana* (hazel) from *Myrica gale* (sweet gale), and both are included in *Corylus*-type.

Counting
Counting was carried out with a Zeiss phase contrast microscope at x400 and x1000 magnification as appropriate.

Pollen and plant spores
Palynomorph concentrations were variable throughout both sequences of sediments and it is likely that this was a function of sediment accretion rate and other taphonomic factors. Where palynomorphs were so sparse that counts of fewer than 100 were achieved, percentage data are shown on the pollen diagrams as open bars rather than blocks. Where counts are low pollen diagrams need to be interpreted with great care, but their inclusion is justified here simply to demonstrate the relative importance of the most common taxa.

Except for those sub-samples which are indicated on the pollen diagrams by open bars, counts in excess of 400 grains were achieved in every sub-sample. Palynomorphs that were too badly corroded for identification were also counted, being classified as 'unidentified'. This category included a small number of grains which eluded identification and remained as unknowns.

Microscopic charcoal
Errors are inherent in all quantitative methods of estimating the abundance of microscopic charcoal in pollen preparations. Chemical and physical processing of polleniferous sediments inevitably result in comminution of large fragments of charcoal into variable numbers of smaller particles. Another possible source of error is variation in the volume of sub-samples. Here, sub-sample volume was the same

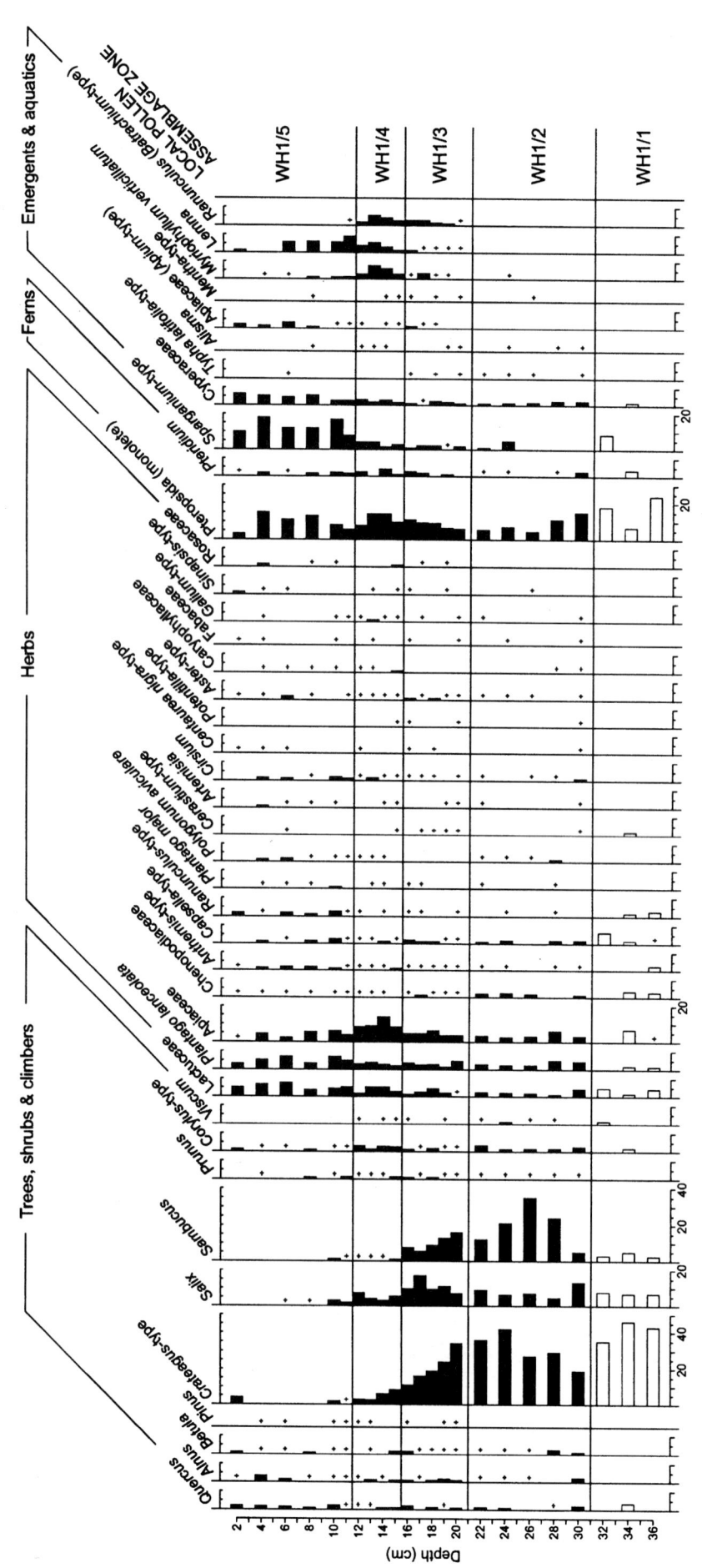

Figure 50 Pollen diagram (1/37)

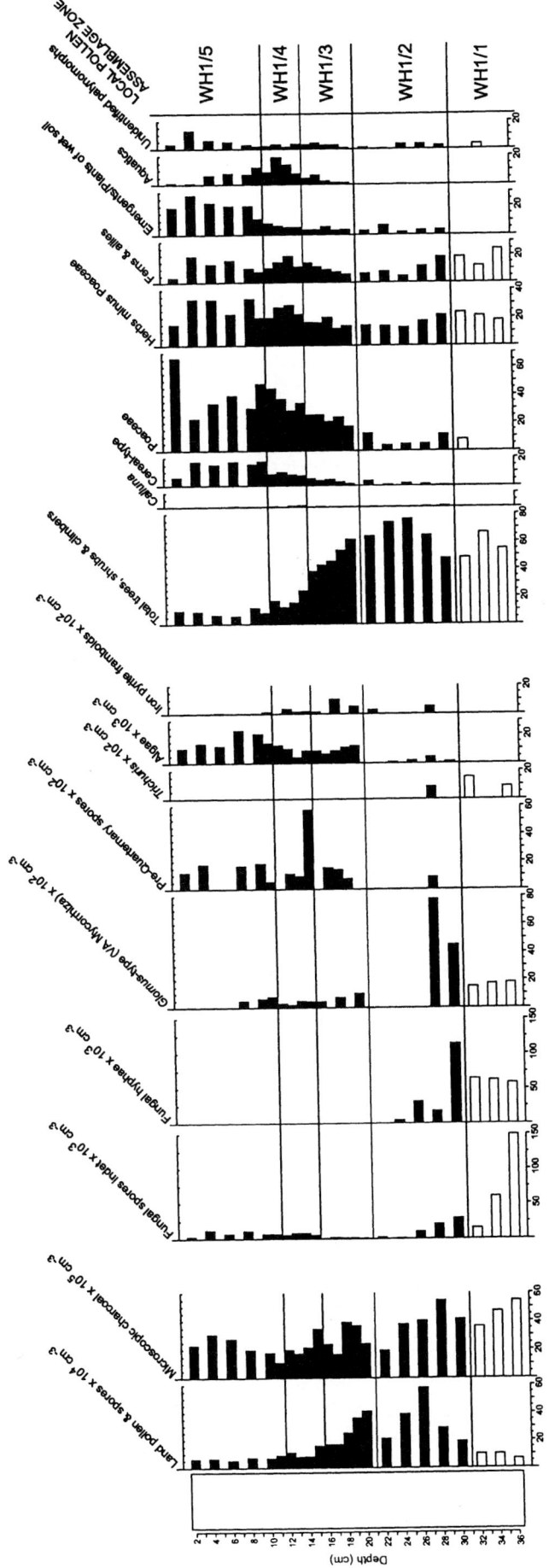

Figure 51 Summary pollen diagram (1/37)

throughout, and processing error was treated as a constant. All particles >5μm diameter were counted in relation to *Lycopodium* spores over fifteen traverses.

Iron pyrite framboids, and fungal and algal palynomorphs
These were counted in the same way as microscopic charcoal particles. Counts of fungal hyphae were achieved by tallying all individual pieces, irrespective of size, within the field of vision. If a hypha extended both margins of the field, it was scored as 1.

Expression and presentation of data
Pollen diagrams are simply aids to interpretation and the form of data expression must be appropriate for the specific data set. Diagrams were drawn with the computer programme Tilia and Tiliagraph (Grimm 1991). Land pollen and plant spore concentrations were expressed as numbers x 10cm, microscopic charcoal fragments as numbers x 10cm, and fungal and algal palynomorphs as numbers x 10cm. Pre-Quaternary spores, iron pyrite framboids, *Trichuris*, and *Glomus*-type were expressed as numbers x 10cm.

For the summary diagram, plant taxon groups and individual plant taxa were expressed as a percentage of total land pollen and plant spores (TLPS). Aquatic and emergent plants were expressed as a percentage of TLPS plus aquatics and emergents. All taxa achieving less than 1% of their appropriate sum are shown as '+' in the figures and tables. No attempt was made to calculate concentration values for plant taxa (Calcote 1998). Wherever pollen taxa were represented by less than 1.0% of the TLPS and occurred in fewer than five sub-samples they have been presented in tabular form in Tables 6 and 7.

Two pollen diagrams are presented for each feature: Figs 50 and 51 for Core 1 (Section 37), and Figs 52 and 53 for Core 2 (Section 63). Diagrams were divided into 'zones' for convenience of description, and were designated WH1/1 to WH1/5 (Core 1), and WH2/1 to WH2/3 (Core 2) accordingly. Zone boundaries were drawn subjectively based on changes in the palynomorph spectra.

Pollen Assemblage Zones

Core 1:37 (landward area of site)
(Figs 50 and 51; Table 6)

Zone WH1/1
Because palynomorph concentrations were low (not exceeding 10 x 10cm) and preservation was poor in this basal zone, counts of fewer than 100 were achieved. This means that percentage values must be viewed with caution; nevertheless, the main features of the local vegetation are discernible.

Fungal spores and hyphae were abundant, and *Glomus*-type also frequent. Trichurid eggs were also found at 32cm and 36cm. Iron pyrite framboids were found only in one level, and obligate aquatics were not found. However, pollen of emergents and plants of wet soil such as *Sparganium*-type, Cyperaceae and *Typha latifolia* were present. The only tree represented was *Quercus*, and then only at one level, but pollen of shrubs was abundant, particularly that of *Crataegus*-type, *Salix* and *Sambucus*. *Prunus*, *Corylus*-type and *Viscum* were also present. *Calluna* was found in one level, and herbs were represented by a relatively wide range of ruderal weeds and plants characteristic of grassland and pasture. Monolete Pteropsida (undifferentiated ferns) were relatively abundant and included *Pteridium* as well as *Thelypteris* and others.

Zone WH1/2
Palynomorph concentrations were markedly higher in this zone, reaching 58 x 10cm at 26cm. Iron pyrite framboids were found in two levels and algae were found in most samples. *Trichuris* and pre-Quaternary spores were present in one sample and algae were found in most. Fungal remains were high at the beginning of the zone but then declined progressively; *Glomus*-type was exceedingly high, reaching a peak in the level containing *Trichuris* and pre-Quaternary spores, but disappeared in samples above 28cm. *Sparganium*-type and *Typha latifolia* were well represented and Cyperaceae were found in every sample. Obligate aquatics such as *Alisma* (water plantain), *Mentha*-type (*e.g.* water mint), and *Myriophyllum verticillatum* (whorled water milfoil) were present. *Sphagnum* (*Sphagnum* moss) was also found throughout most of the zone. Monolete Pteropsida were well represented throughout the zone while *Ophioglossum* (adder's tongue fern) and *Selaginella* (club moss) were presented towards the end. *Pteridium* was present in most samples, and *Calluna* was found in the two basal samples in the zone.

Low numbers of *Quercus*, *Alnus* (alder), and *Betula* (birch) pollen grains were present in most samples but the dominant woody plants were *Crataegus*-type and *Sambucus*. *Crataegus*-type increased throughout the zone while *Sambucus* increased to a maximum at 26cm and then declined. *Salix* was present in every sample with values ranging between 4.5 and 13% TLPS. *Prunus* and *Corylus*-type were also represented in every sample, with *Viscum* appearing in all but the lowermost sample. Other woody plants include *Acer campestre* (field maple), *Hedera* (ivy) and *Rhamnus* (purging buckthorn). A wide range of herbs was present, and the assemblage contained taxa that might have been growing on local waste ground, along the ditch margins, in adjacent pastures and with crops. However, it is worth noting *Primula* (primrose), since this plant is typical of grassy banks and hedgerows. Microscopic charcoal remained high, though declining progressively towards the end of the zone. Cereal-type pollen reached percentages of between 0.6 and 3.4% TLPS.

Zone WH1/3
Palynomorph concentrations were high at the beginning of the zone (41 x10cm) but declined in a step-wise fashion to 17 x 10cm at the end. Iron pyrite framboids reached their highest concentration in the sequence, and algae increased both in frequency and abundance. Fungal remains were low and no hyphae were found, but *Glomus*-type was represented again and pre-Quaternary spores were frequent. Microscopic charcoal fluctuated, but did not reach the maximum levels of the previous zone. Pollen of Poaceae and cereal-type had increased percentages in every sample while other herbs reached similar levels as in the previous zone, although achieving higher frequency.

Emergents were represented in every sample, though only at previous levels, but obligate aquatics increased in both abundance and frequency. More floating aquatics such as *Lemna* (duckweed) and *Ranunculus* (*Batrachium*-type, *e.g.* water crowfoot) were present. Monolete Pteropsida were well represented. *Pteridium* was present in most levels, with *Calluna* appearing in just one level.

Low numbers of *Quercus* (oak), *Alnus* (alder) and *Betula* (birch) pollen grains were present in most samples, and *Pinus* (pine), *Tilia* (lime), *Ulmus* (elm) and *Fagus* (beech) were also present as single grains. But the dominant woody plants were *Crataegus*-type, *Sambucus*, and *Salix* (willow). *Crataegus*-type and *Sambucus* declined throughout the zone, but *Salix* increased and reached its highest percentages in the whole sequence. *Prunus* and *Corylus*-type were also represented in every sample, while *Viscum* and *Rhamnus* were also present. The herb pollen spectra were similar to those of the previous zone, although *Solanum dulcamara* (woody nightshade) and *Solanum nigrum*-type (*e.g.* black bindweed) were interesting additions to the assemblage. Cereal-type pollen was found in every sample and percentages ranged between 1.5 and 5.2% TLPS.

Zone WH1/4
The zone boundary between WH1/3 and WH1/4 was drawn where there was an even greater representation of obligate aquatic plants than in the previous zone (see Fig. 51 and Table 6 for aquatic taxa represented). There was also a marked increase in pre-Quaternary and fungal spores, accompanied by increased values for cereal-type, Poaceae, other dryland herbs and ferns, and a marked decline in the dominant shrubs. Iron pyrites framboids were present throughout the zone. There was a significant increase in the pollen of Apiaceae, and it is quite possible that the species included in this taxon were plants characteristic of high watertables such as *Oenanthe* spp. (water dropworts). *Sambucus* declined to values of <1% TLPS while there was a marked and sustained decrease in *Crataegus*-type and *Salix* values. The pollen of cereal-type, Poaceae and other herbs appear to have been enhanced by the changing environment but, of course, this could also be an artefact of percentage representation due to the decline in woody taxa.

Zone WH1/5
The boundary between WH1/4 and WH1/5 was defined by a decline in submerged aquatic plants, but a marked increase in emergent *Sparganium*-type (*e.g.* bur-reed), the floating aquatics *Lemna* (duckweed) and Nymphaea (water lily), algae and cereal-type. Pre-Quaternary spores, fungal spores and *Glomus*-type were present, indicating that soil was still eroding into the ditch; sporadic representation of iron pyrites framboids shows that the ditch sediments were waterlogged. The concentration of dry land palynomorphs was low (not exceeding 8.9 x 10cm), and this may be due to rapid accumulation of sediment rather than poor preservation. Some dry land herbs increased and, as before, these were ruderals and weeds of grassland and verges. Shrubs, even willow, declined to very low levels and mistletoe was not represented in this zone. There seems to have been a small increase in trees, particularly *Alnus* (alder) in the hinterland and *Pinus* (pine) was present throughout the zone. The top sample in the zone shows a dramatic increase in Poaceae (grasses) at the expense of many other taxa.

Local pollen assemblage zones	WH1/5				WH1/4				WH1/3					WH1/2					WH1/1		
Depth (cm)	4	6	8	10	11	12	13	14	15	16	17	18	19	20	22	24	26	28	30	32	34	36
Trees/Shrubs/Climbers																						
Acer campestre																			+			
Hedera		+																	+			
Rhamnus															+		+					
Tilia	+											+										
Ulmus												+										
Fagus										+												
Herbs																						
Aphanes						+																
Rumex acetosa-type	+	+							+										+			1.4
Rumex obtusifolius	+	+		+	+													+				
Sanguisorba minor			+									+							+			
Primula																+	+					
Silene vulgaris-type																+						
Geum												+	+	+								
Solanum dulcamara								+						+								
Solanum nigrum-type								+														
Epilobium							+				+											
Thalictrum							+															
Papaver	+																					
Urtica	+																					
Veronica-type	+																					
Ferns & allies																						
Thelypteris																					1.7	
Ophioglossum											+											
Selaginella									+						+							
Polypodium			+					+								+						
Osmunda					+																	
Emergents/Plants of wet soil																						
Sphagnum			+					+	+			+			+	+						
Filipendula	+		+					+	+													
Iris		+																				
Aquatics																						
Mentha-type																	+	+				
Potamogeton														+								
Nymphaea					+																	

Table 6 Pollen Assemblage Zones (Core 1/37)

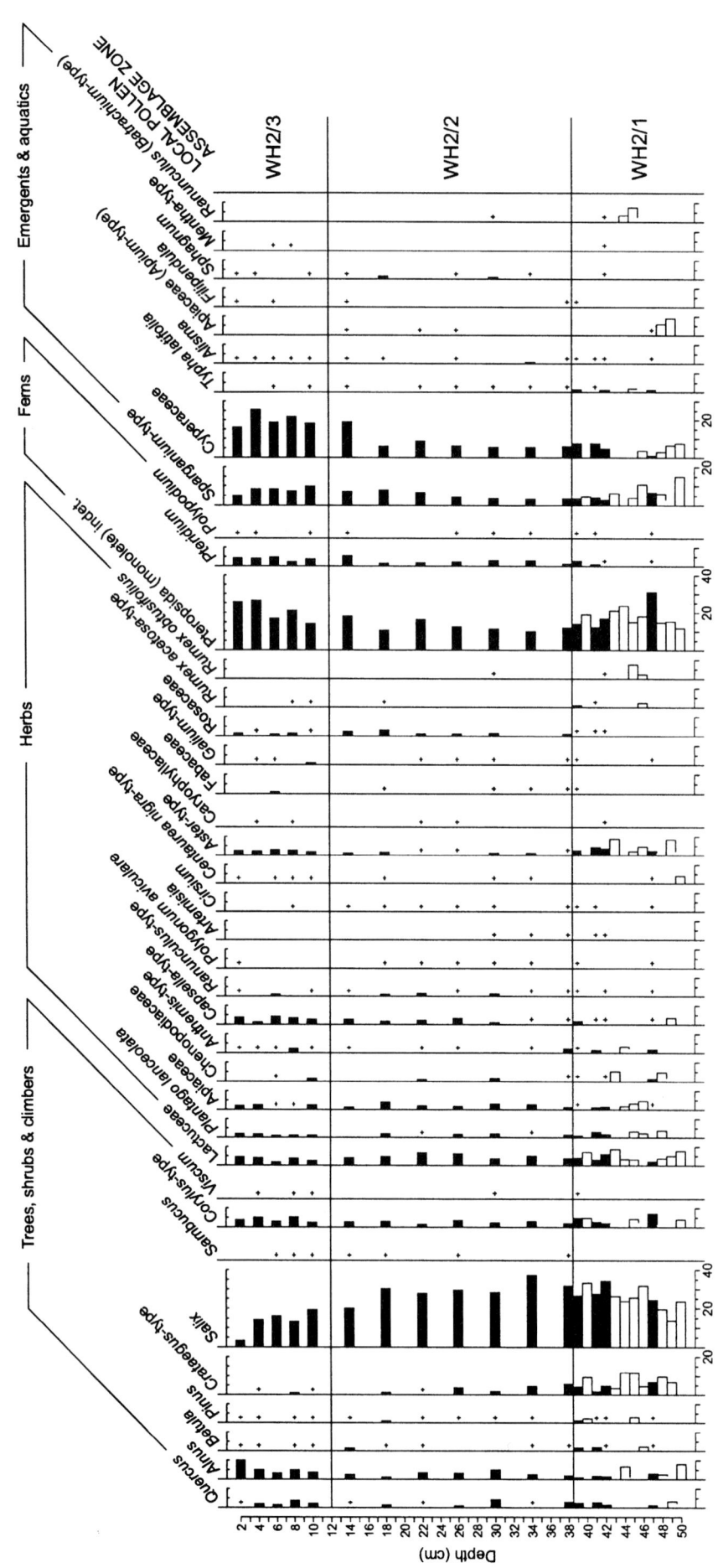

Figure 52 Pollen diagram (2/63)

Local pollen assemblage zones	WH2/3					WH2/2								WH2/1											
Depth (cm)	2	4	6	8	10	14	18	22	26	30	34	38	39	40	41	42	43	44	45	46	47	48	49	50
Trees/Shrubs/Climbers																								
Acer									+															
Carpinus			+																					
cf. Picea						+									+	+								
Fagus											+										+			
Fraxinus	+					+					+													
Hedera	+		+																					
Ligustrum							+		+				+											
Lonicera																				2.3				
Prunus																					+			
Rhamnus					+													3.4			+			
Tilia													+							2.3				
Ulmus	+																							
Viburnum opulus	1.1				+					+														
Herbs																								
Adonis	+																							
Arenaria-type	+				+							+												
Cerastium-type								+							+		1.8							
Epilobium-type				+																				
Geum										+														
Helianthemum						+				+					+									
Plantago major							+			+									1.1					
Plantago media									+															
Potentilla-type																					+	1.2		
Rhinanthus-type																			1.1					
Sanguisorba minor												+				+								
Solanum dulcamara								+								+								
Thalictrum		+	2.3									+				+			1.1					
Ferns & Allies																								
Equisetum													+					1.7						
Ophioglossum												+									+			
Aquatics																								
Lemna			+																					
Myriophyllum spicatum																				1.8	1.8			
Myriophyllum verticillatum																								10.0
Nuphar							+					+												
Potamogeton											+													

Table 7 Pollen Assemblage Zones (Core 2/63)

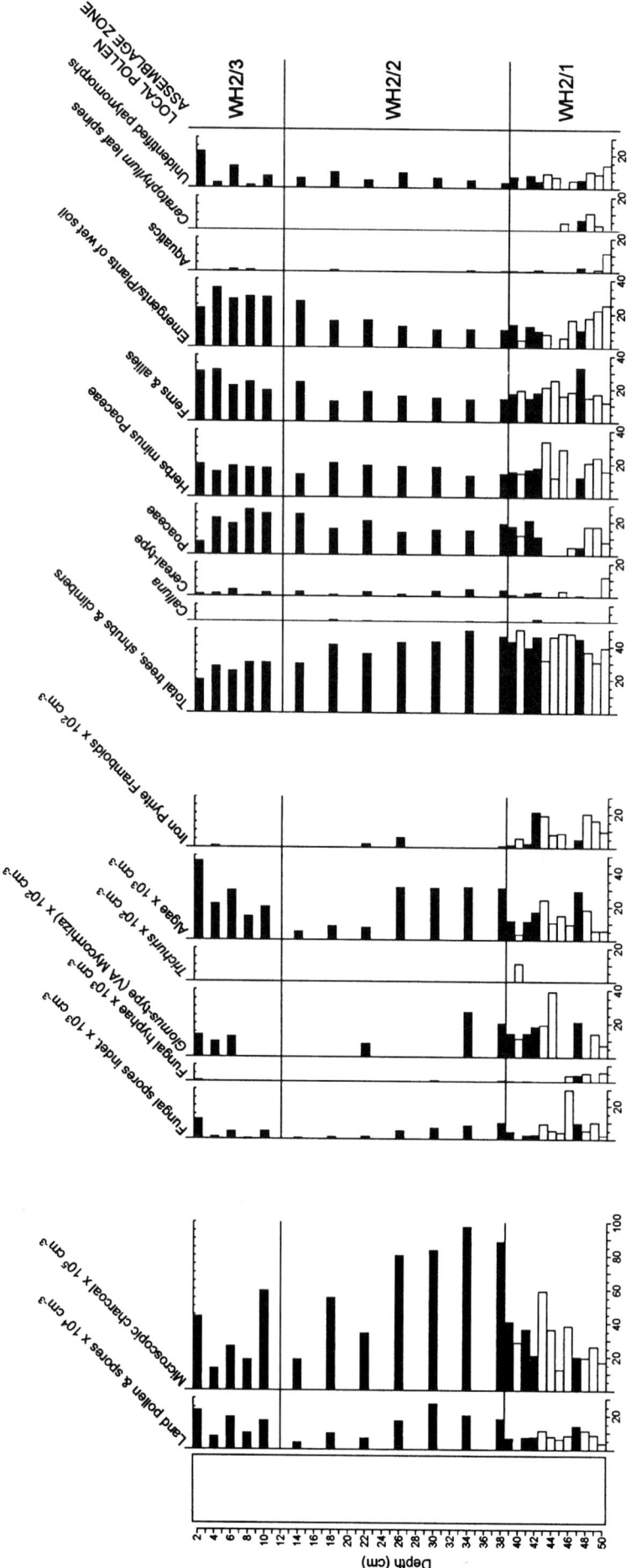

Figure 53 Summary pollen diagram (2/63)

Core 2:63 (fenward area of site)
(Figs 52 and 53; Table 7)

Zone WH2/1
Palynomorph concentrations varied very considerably in this zone (ranging between 4.6–14 x 10cm) and preservation was poor throughout the sequence. Counts of less than 100 grains were achieved in six levels so the percentage values must be viewed with caution. It is interesting, however, that the pollen curves are remarkably smooth in spite of the variable counts. Fungal spores, fungal hyphae, and *Glomus*-type were abundant and *Trichuris* eggs were found towards the top of the zone. Iron pyrite framboids were exceedingly abundant, reaching values of up to 20 x 10cm, though values fluctuated throughout the zone. A wide range of emergent plants, along with those usually forming tall herb communities in shallow swamps (*e.g. Filipendula*), were present. Obligate aquatics were also represented, but the most abundant herbaceous taxon was that of monolete Pteropsida (undifferentiated ferns).

The most abundant woody plant was *Salix* (willow) which reached the exceedingly high value of 14–34% TLPS. However, other shrubs were present such as *Prunus* (*e.g.* sloe), *Corylus*-type (*e.g.* hazel), *Rhamnus* (purging buckthorn) and *Sambucus* (elder). *Lonicera* (honeysuckle) was recorded in two levels, *Viscum* (mistletoe) was found in the uppermost sample of the zone, and *Solanum dulcamara* (woody nightshade) was present. The best represented tree was *Alnus* (alder) whose percentages ranged between 1.1 and 7.8% TLPS. However low percentages of *Quercus* (oak), *Betula* (birch), *Pinus* (pine) and *Tilia* (lime) were recorded. *Picea* (spruce) was also found. A wide range of herbs was found, but the most abundant were Poaceae (grasses), Lactuceae (dandelion-type plants) and *Aster*-type (*e.g.* fleabane and hemp agrimony). *Calluna* (heather) was found in several samples and occasional spores of *Pteridium* (bracken) were present. Other ferns (undifferentiated) were exceedingly abundant and *Ophioglossum* (adder's tongue fern) and *Equisetum* (horsetail) were found.

Zone WH2/2
Palynomorph concentration was higher in this zone and preservation was slightly better than in WH2/1. Iron pyrites framboids were found only in two samples (and then at much reduced values than the previous zone) but algae were much more abundant throughout the WH2/2. Microscopic charcoal levels were higher and fungal spores were consistently present. However, hyphae were less abundant and frequent and *Glomus*-type was present only in the two lowermost samples. Microscopic charcoal and algae were much reduced towards the end of the zone. Most taxa achieved similar values to those in the previous zone, although *Crataegus*-type was reduced, *Sambucus* appeared for the first time and *Quercus* was slightly better represented. Herbaceous taxa were less frequent than in the previous zone but *Pteridium* was slightly more abundant and *Calluna* was present. Cereal-type pollen, at a high of 4.4% TLPS, reached its highest value in the sequence.

Zone WH2/3
The zone line was drawn where there was a significant increase in emergent plants (particularly Cyperaceae) and aquatic taxa. It is interesting that *Nuphar* (yellow water lily) was recorded: this often covers large areas where there are open stretches of water within tall fen vegetation (personal observation). Ferns (including *Pteridium*) and Poaceae (grasses) also increased. Algae reached high levels in the upper part of the zone and *Glomus*-type and fungal spores were well represented. Iron pyrites framboids were also recorded in one level.

There was a noticeable increase in certain woody taxa such as *Alnus* (alder) and *Corylus*-type (*e.g.* hazel), while *Sambucus* (elder) had a higher frequency. *Viscum* was also present in the upper levels, and certain herbaceous taxa such as *Capsella*-type (*e.g.* shepherd's purse) and *Aster*-type (*e.g.* fleabane and hemp agrimony) increased. There was a marked decline in *Salix* throughout the zone, and *Crataegus*-type was recorded at low levels in only two samples. There was a slight increase in cereal-type pollen.

Interpretation

Core 1:37 (landward area of site)
(Figs 50 and 51; Table 6)

Zone WH1/1
The low concentration and corroded condition of palynomorphs suggests that the basal 4–5cm of sediment accumulated rapidly in the ditch. The high levels of fungal remains, including *Glomus*-type (Bagyaraj and Varma 1995), suggest that bioactive soil was eroding into the feature from adjacent areas and most of the pollen was probably carried with it. The presence of iron pyrite framboids (albeit in small numbers and in only one sample) indicates that standing water existed, at least periodically, in the floor of the ditch, but the absence of obligate aquatic plants probably means that it never persisted long enough for an aquatic community to develop.

The pollen of emergent taxa such as *Sparganium*-type (*e.g.* bur-reed), *Typha latifolia* (greater reedmace), and Cyperaceae (sedges) could have been blown from the adjacent fen, although sedges could also have been growing anywhere in the environs of the ditch. It is possible that ferns were growing within the ditch although, again, they could have been members of the fen community to the east of the site.

It is surprising that there was little evidence for Poaceae (grasses), although pollen of ruderal and grassland weeds was finding its way into the ditch. These taxa could have been derived from adjacent fields, from plants actually growing along the ditch edges, or even from debris strewn around the site. The only tree represented was *Quercus* (oak), and then only in one sample, but shrubs were well established by the time these sediments accumulated. The dominant shrub pollen taxon was *Crataegus*-type, and it is highly probable that most of this was *Crataegus* (hawthorn) itself. However, pollens of the Rosaceae (rose family), of which hawthorn is a member, are sometimes difficult to differentiate, and it is possible that *Rubus* (bramble) and *Rosa* (rose) were growing in association with the shrub. Indeed, seeds of *Rubus* and *Rosa* were found in the feature (Murphy, below). *Salix* (willow) and *Sambucus* (elder) were also well established, while *Prunus* (*e.g.* sloe) and *Corylus*-type (*e.g.* hazel) were present in the local community. It must be stressed that all these woody plants (except for *Corylus* and *Quercus*) are insect-pollinated and produce relatively small amounts of poorly-dispersed pollen. Generally, they are scarce in the pollen rain and their representation, certainly if high, strongly indicates either *in situ* growth or that they were very close to the feature.

Pteridium (bracken) and *Calluna* (heather) were found, and these suggest that dry, acidic soils were present in the catchment. However, their low representation indicates either that they were growing a considerable distance from the site or that they had been brought into the settlement for some domestic or industrial use. The high levels of microscopic charcoal suggests burning in the vicinity, and the presence of the eggs of the intestinal parasite *Trichuris* shows that dung was finding its way into the feature. Whether this was human or animal excrement is impossible to say. However, its presence does indicate eutrophication of the ditch sediment.

Zone WH1/2
The higher concentrations of pollen and spores in this zone might be a function of slower sediment accumulation rates so that each sample represents a longer period of time. However, the sediments themselves may also have been wetter and less aerated so that preservation was enhanced. There is certainly evidence for standing water in the ditch, but water could have occasionally flooded in from lower-lying sections, and the indicators of standing

water (iron pyrite framboids, algae, *Alisma*, *Mentha*-type and *Myriophyllum verticillatum*) might be secondarily derived. However, preservation was certainly better than in the previous zone and it equally likely that a rising watertable was resulting in episodes, or even prolonged periods, whne there was standing water in the ditch. *Sphagnum* moss, *Selaginella* (clubmoss) and ferns, including *Ophioglossum* (adder's tongue fern) might have been growing within the damp atmosphere of the ditch. Pollen from *Cyperaceae* (sedges) and other emergents could either have arrived in flood water, or have simply blown into the site from the adjacent fen.

Soil seems to have been eroding in the feature: fungal remains, and particularly *Glomus*-type (VA mycorrhiza), suggest that these soils were aerated and bioactive. Certainly, the influx of pre-Quaternary spores might indicate that either the ditch deposits were subjected to some strong erosive force, or that the feature was receiving weathered mineral material derived from elsewhere.

The very high levels of *Crataegus*-type (*e.g.* hawthorn) pollen in the previous zone must be viewed with caution because of the low pollen counts, but there is little doubt both *Crataegus*-type and *Sambucus* (elder) expanded and flowered prolifically at the site. *Sambucus* reached peak abundance in the middle of the zone, after which it declined a little, but it grows very quickly and probably succumbed to the increasing vigour of the slower-growing hawthorn (Grime *et al.* 1988). The range of shrubs which had matured close to the ditch included *Acer campestre* (field maple), *Hedera* (ivy), *Rhamnus* (purging buckthorn) and *Prunus* (*e.g.* sloe), while *Viscum* (mistletoe) was growing on one or more of them. *Salix* (willow) reached 4.5–13% TLPS: in view of its very restricted pollen dispersal, there is little doubt that it was growing in the ditch itself or even in the drier soil of the bank.

The shrubs were mature and might have been growing in a dense scrub close to this section of the ditch. It is interesting to note, however, that many of the plants were prickly and would have provided an effective barrier and fortification. It is tempting to speculate — especially since hedgerow plants like *Primula* were also found — that the ditch bank had been deliberately planted with thorny shrubs such as hawthorn and sloe, or that thorny plants, including *Rosa* (rose) and *Rubus* (bramble), had been encouraged by selective management. Hawthorn, sloe, and elder all make excellent hedging plants, the former two by virtue of their dense growth and prolific thorns, and the latter due to its resilience to coppicing, and lack of palatability and toxicity to mammals (Cooper and Johnson 1984). All these shrubs are intolerant of wet ground: this might provide additional evidence that they were growing on the ditch bank where the soil would have been raised above the watertable and high enough to avoid any flood water.

Many of the shrub species, particularly *Sambucus*, favour nutrient-rich soils, particularly those enriched with nitrogen and phosphate. The local soils might have been enriched by the organic pollution normally associated with human settlement, but the presence of intestinal parasitic worm eggs (*Trichuris*) also suggests eutrophication by animal dung.

The low levels of pollen of Poaceae (grasses) could indicate very heavy grazing at the site since grasses would fail to flower under such a regime. Many of the other herbaceous taxa, such as *Plantago lanceolata* (ribwort plantain) and *Centaurea nigra*-type (knapweed), could have been components of the local pastures but others, such as *Artemisia* (mugwort), Chenopodiaceae (*e.g.* fat hen and good King Henry) and *Polygonum aviculare* (knotweed) could have been growing on waste ground around the settlement. Any of them might have been growing on the ditch bank or adjacent verge (Dowdeswell 1987). Others, such as *Calluna* (heather) and *Pteridium* (bracken), could have been growing some distance away on drier, acidic soils, or have continued to be brought into the site for some domestic use.

The surrounding landscape seems to have supported very few trees. *Quercus* (oak), *Alnus* (alder), *Betula* (birch), *Tilia* (lime), *Ulmus* (elm) and *Fagus* (beech) were recorded, but all at low level or as single pollen grains. It is possible that richer and more extensive woodland was available in the catchment but, if this were the case, it was so severely managed that few trees managed to flower. On the other hand, the density of the local shrubs might have been acting as a screen, effectively preventing extra-local and more regionally-produced pollen from entering the site.

There is evidence for cereal cultivation and/or processing in this zone, with percentages of cereal-type pollen ranging between 0.6 and 3.4% TLPS. These are low levels if cereal cultivation or processing were carried out close by. The palynological evidence tentatively suggests that pastoral farming might have dominated during the period represented by this zone, although screening of extra-local pollen by shrubs cannot be discounted.

Sambucus reached its maximum representation in the middle of the zone while *Crataegus*-type reached its peak later, as *Sambucus* declined. *Salix* and *Corylus*-type increased slightly while other woody taxa achieved similar values to previously. However, at the end of the zone the overall trend for woody plants was downwards. The reduction in soil erosion indicators suggests there was a period of relative soil stability in the upper part of the zone and, apart from a slight increase in cereal-type and Poaceae (grasses), there was little change in the environment surrounding the pollen site.

Zone WH1/3

The boundary between WH1/2 and WH1/3 is drawn where there was a marked increase in frequency and abundance of algae, iron pyrite framboids, obligate aquatic and emergent plants, and *Salix*, indicating the presence of standing water for fairly long periods (if not permanently). There was also a reappearance of *Glomus*-type and pre-Quaternary spores, which suggests erosion and that bioactive soils were again being washed into the ditch. Towards the top of the zone, concentrations of pollen and spores declined, probably because of more rapid sediment accumulation rates rather than differential decomposition.

Most dryland plants were better represented, including trees, grasses and cereals, while the only taxa to show sustained declines were *Crataegus*-type and *Sambucus*. It is likely that the increase in aquatics and emergents and the indicators of soil erosion was real, but the reciprocal relationship between the dominant shrubs and other terrestrial taxa might be a statistical artefact. As *Crataegus*-type and *Sambucus* declined, so would the pollen percentages of other taxa increase. On the other hand, the decline of the dense shrubs would have allowed better dispersal of other pollen taxa into the site. The enhanced representation of dryland herb pollen might have been due to weeds growing on the bank being able to flower more prolifically as more light became available.

The strong evidence for increased wetness and soil instability in this zone suggests that the declines of *Crataegus*-type and *Sambucus* were real. Neither of these taxa can withstand wet conditions and the progressive nature of their demise, as shown by smooth pollen curves, suggests a gradual diminution of their vigour and performance in response to rising watertable. There is no evidence of any sudden onslaught on the vegetation and the changes seen in the pollen diagrams (Figs 50 and 51) were probably a consequence of natural changes in groundwater level rather than shifts in management.

Zone WH1/4
The persistence of iron pyrite framboids in the sediment, and the significant increase in aquatic and wetland plants and soil erosion indicators, suggests that the ditch became even wetter than before. It seems to have been receiving more eroded soil, possibly from water flowing up from the fen, or even from water sweeping over the floor of the settlement itself. The changes in the immediate local vegetation are reflected in the marked increase of most herbaceous taxa (both of wet and dry soils), the influx of soil erosion indicators and the demise of shrubs. The decline in *Crataegus*-type (*e.g.* hawthorn) and *Salix* (willow) was significant but appears to have happened rather gradually; *Sambucus* (elder), on the other hand, was affected quickly. This might be explained by hawthorn growing relatively high up on the bank and thus protected to some extent, while elder and willow were growing lower down and been subjected to prolonged waterlogging. Willow would tolerate the sodden conditions much more readily than elder. It is interesting that *Viscum* (mistletoe) was present in most samples, so some shrubs (probably hawthorn) were still vigorous enough to support this parasite.

The significant rise in abundance of floating aquatic plants suggests that they were able to establish in this part of the ditch, and the increase in *Sparganium*-type (*e.g.* bur-reed) hints that fen vegetation was beginning to colonise further into the settlement. The marked rise in Apiaceae might also indicate that aquatic members of this family, such as *Oenanthe* spp. (water dropworts) or *Conium maculatum* (hemlock), were choking the ditch.

The extra-local and regional vegetation seems to have been relatively unaffected in the pollen record, and this might emphasise the relatively local nature of the rise in groundwater levels. Furthermore, in spite of the obvious changes in the settlement, people were still active nearby. Microscopic charcoal levels were similar to those in the previous zone and cereals were still being grown and/or processed nearby. The increase in the representation of both cereals and grasses might indicate simply that more extra-local pollen was able to enter the ditch as the shrubs declined: certainly fen and swamp grasses such as *Phragmites* (reed) might have been blowing in from adjacent areas. However, the changes might also be tentatively interpreted as a small shift in agricultural practice. Domestic animals would have been moved from permanently sodden pastures, and consequently local grasses would have been able to flower more prolifically. For some reason, there might also have been greater pressure to produce cereals. Cereal-type pollen reached values of 7.4–9.6% TLPS in this zone, and such high percentages are indicative of cereal fields or cereal processing in the immediate vicinity.

Zone WH1/5
The pollen concentrations and the presence of soil erosion indicators suggest that the sediment in this zone accumulated rather rapidly. The ditch was still wet, but the water level could have been considerably lower than before by virtue of silting-up. Obligate aquatics which are generally found in deeper water, such as *Myriophyllum verticillatum* (whorled water milfoil) and *Batrachium*-type (*e.g.* water crowfoot), were much reduced, while *Lemna* (duckweed), which can exist on the surface of very shallow water, actually increased. The expansion of *Sparganium*-type (*e.g.* bur-reed) and *Cyperaceae* (sedges), and the abundance of Poaceae, might suggest that fen vegetation was spreading into the ditch and shading out the smaller aquatics.

The virtual extinction of the shrubs that had once dominated the site might have resulted in more extra-local and regional pollen entering the ditch. The regional vegetation is thus better represented in this zone than earlier in the sequence. The landscape was very open, with very few trees in the immediate locality. The environs of the settlement were dominated by grasses, herbs and fen vegetation although some *Crataegus*-type, *Salix*, *Sambucus* and *Prunus* were still present, possibly as occasional, stunted individuals.

Microscopic charcoal levels show that people were still active in the environs of the site, and cereal-type pollen was very high (reaching up to values of 17% TLPS). *Pteridium* (bracken) and *Calluna* (heather) were still represented and might still have been brought into the site.

The lowered levels of most taxa, and the massive expansion of grasses, in the uppermost level is difficult to explain, but it might either suggest an abandonment of the immediate area for grazing so that local grasses were able to flower, or that tall grasses had colonised the ditch. It is also possible that *Phragmites* reed had spread into this area of the feature, or even that it had been used for dumping hay or thatch material.

Core 2:63 (fenward area of site)
(Figs 52 and 53; Table 7)

Zone WH2/1
The high values for *Glomus*-type and other fungal remains, iron pyrite framboids, algae, *Ceratophyllum* (hornwort) spines and emergent and aquatic plants indicate that the ditch not only contained standing water during the period represented by this zone but was also receiving eroding soil, possible from the bank of the ditch or even from the settlement. The low palynomorph concentrations might point to a relatively rapid accumulation of these basal sediments. The *Trichuris* eggs might have been derived from human or animal excrement but they do indicate a degree of eutrophication of the ditch and might, in part, account for the relatively high values for algae (Round 1981).

Salix (with values up to 34% TLPS) dominated the site and the ditch had been constructed within, or immediately adjacent to, dense stands of the shrub. When the overwhelming representation of willow and the high values of ferns, emergent plants and obligate aquatics, and the presence of taxa such as *Equisetum* (horsetail) and *Sphagnum* moss, are all considered it seems reasonable to suppose that the areas to the east, thought to be open fen or reed swamp, probably supported dense willow carr. The relatively abundant Lactuceae and *Aster*-type may have been plants such as *Senecio aquaticus* (marsh ragwort) and *Pulicaria* (fleabane)/*Eupatorium* (hemp agrimony) respectively. All these can grow prolifically in carr, swamp and wet ditches. The relatively low value for Poaceae (grasses) provides additional evidence for the adjacent fen being willow carr rather than reed swamp, since much higher values for Poaceae might have been expected if *Phragmites* (reed) had been the dominant plant in the wet areas.

Although the ditch and its environs contained waterlogged soil it is obvious that there were drier areas in the immediate vicinity. These may have been provided by the ditch bank, or by the settlement slightly to the west. Many of the herbs recorded in this zone were ruderals characteristic of bare, drier soils or moist verges and would not have tolerated permanent sodden soil. Furthermore, *Crataegus*-type was relatively abundant, reaching values of up to nearly 10% TLPS. Like many other shrubs, including willow, this insect-pollinated plant is very poorly represented in the pollen rain. It must have been growing nearby to be represented by these values. *Prunus* (*e.g.* sloe), *Rhamnus* (purging buckthorn) and *Lonicera* (honeysuckle) were also growing close by and none of these can tolerate waterlogging. *Viscum* (mistletoe) was present so its host must have been growing close by. These plants are unlikely to have been components of the willow carr, or any other kind of fen vegetation, and it is likely that either they were growing as scrub in the settlement, or they had been planted on (or had colonised) the bank. They might even have been growing on the inner ditch bank rather than the outer, and this could account for their lower representation.

Trees were relatively well represented in this zone, including *Quercus*, *Alnus*, *Betula*, *Pinus* and *Fagus* (beech). *Alnus* and *Betula* are the only ones to tolerate waterlogging, and it is likely that most were growing on higher ground further away from the settlement. The presence of *Picea* (spruce) is particularly intriguing since it was thought to have become extinct in Britain in the last Ice Age. However, there is now convincing evidence that it was planted in several parts of East Anglia from the 1st to 4th centuries AD and in early medieval times (Wiltshire and Murphy in prep.); its pollen has been found in Hampshire at an early Romano-British site (Wiltshire 2000).

High levels of microscopic charcoal in the sediment showed that burning was occurring near this section of the ditch, while the consistent representation of cereal-type pollen indicates that crop-processing was being carried out in the vicinity. It is feasible that the cereal pollen could have been derived from cornfields, but the nearest ground suitable for cereal cultivation was a few hundred metres to the west. Cereal pollen is thought to travel very small distances from a growing crop, and the most likely explanation for its presence in the ditch is that pollen was derived from winnowing or threshing within the settlement. *Pteridium* and *Calluna* were also found at very low levels: either they were growing in dry, acidic soils further away from the site, or they were being brought into the settlement for some domestic use.

Zone WH2/2
The higher palynomorph concentrations, reduction in the indicators of soil erosion, and the virtual disappearance of framboids (except for two levels) might indicate more stable conditions, and perhaps shallower, more aerated water in the ditch (Wiltshire *et al.* 1994). Obligate aquatic plants, and many of the herbs which had been relatively abundant in WH2/1, declined; *Crataegus*-type was very much reduced, almost to extinction at the end of the zone. The curves for microscopic charcoal and algae mirrored each other, being high in the first part of the zone and falling off suddenly in the two upper levels. It is likely that the algae were responding to rapid fluxes in eutrophication of the wet soil by burnt material (Round 1981). The increase in cereal pollen may have been due to more cereals being processed or simply the reduction of *Crataegus*-type and other herbs may have allowed more pollen to enter the sediment. It is possible that the *Sambucus* (elder) pollen was derived from elsewhere in the settlement, since this shrub is exceedingly intolerant of wet soil; it was probably growing on drier soils in the vicinity since its pollen does not travel far from source (Wiltshire 1999).

The decline in obligate aquatic plants might have been due to the water becoming too shallow, or perhaps they were shaded out by overhanging willow. It is probable that there were changes in conditions within the ditch since plants which may have been growing on its wet sides such as certain Lactuceae, *Aster*-type and ferns all declined. However, so did plants such as *Plantago lanceolata* (ribwort plantain) and Chenopodiaceae (goosefoot family), which are normally components of drier areas. Yet it is possible that herbs growing on banks and small areas of raised ground were simply shaded by dense willow stands.

Zone WH2/3
There is little doubt that conditions at the site became considerably wetter in this zone and soil instability seems to have increased. Obligate aquatics and emergents/plants of wet soil, particularly Cyperaceae, increased. Ferns were also more abundantly represented and these may have been species such as *Thelypteris palustris* (marsh fern), which normally grow in fens and wet places. However, the water may have been shallow and reasonably well-oxygenated since iron pyrite framboids were found in only one level.

Nearly all taxa were better represented in this zone, including *Viscum* (mistletoe), Poaceae (grasses), *Pteridium* (bracken), most herbs, other shrubs and trees. Woody taxa such as *Hedera* (ivy), *Acer campestre* (field maple) and *Viburnum opulus* (guelder rose), and trees such as *Ulmus* (elm), *Carpinus* (hornbeam) and *Fraxinus* (ash) were represented in the sequence for the first time. Herbs such as *Thalictrum* (meadow rue) and *Ophioglossum* (adder's tongue fern), plants characteristic of wet meadows, were also present. The increased species richness and abundance in this zone was probably due to the progressive decline of *Salix* (willow), which dropped to a very low level in the uppermost sample.

Discussion

This study has illuminated the conditions prevailing both within the ditches and in the wider landscape, but it must be remembered that the local, extra-local and more regional pictures obtained of the landscape around Wardy Hill have varied according the density of the local vegetation at each of the two pollen sample sites over time. Both areas of the settlement were influenced by different pedological and hydrological conditions. It is not surprising, therefore, that the local vegetation should have varied between them.

As is the nature of ditches, both sampling sites had damp conditions, with the fenward site (Section 63) being wetter than the landward (Section 37). In both locations the initial infilling was probably quite rapid, and bioactive soil and weathering materials were being washed into the features. Later, each enjoyed a period of relative stability until rising water levels resulted in inwash and changes in the local communities.

The landscape around Wardy Hill was extremely open during the whole period represented by the ditch sediments. Although trees were present in the catchment, either they were a considerable distance away or were so sparse, or they were so heavily managed that little pollen was produced. Careful examination of the two pollen diagrams (Figs 50–53) shows that most of the trees in the record were probably growing on higher ground to the east, where the village of Coveney is today. Higher percentages and greater numbers of tree taxa were recorded from the sample site next to the original wet ground (Section 63), and it is surprising that the regional component has such a biased representation in these two sequences.

The area around Section 37 had been dominated by *Crataegus*-type (*e.g.* hawthorn and other thorny plants such as rose and bramble) for a considerable period before the sediments started accumulating. This is evidenced by the very high representation of this taxon even in the depauperate basal sediments. *Viscum* (mistletoe), which was probably using hawthorn as a host, was also present. This suggests that local shrubs were mature enough both to produce flowers and to be able to support the parasite. *Viscum* is most often found growing on trees where the relative humidity of the air is high. However, its host range is exceedingly wide and it has even been found growing on small hawthorn shrubs high on the North Downs in Surrey (personal observation). It is likely, therefore, that *Viscum* formed part of the local plant community, and no claim can be made for any ritual significance behind its presence.

The very high representation of *Crataegus*-type and *Sambucus* (elder), and the presence of other thorny taxa such as *Prunus* (*e.g.* sloe), suggest that these taxa had been encouraged, or even planted to form hedges on the enclosure banks. The value of thorny plants as barriers and fortifications is obvious, while the aversion that domestic animals have for elder also makes it a useful plant for defining boundaries. Section 37 had a rich herbaceous flora and these herbs could have been growing anywhere in the vicinity. Some taxa are characteristic of waste ground, others are typically found in pasture, while others might have survived well on the ditch bank or verge. Many herbs have a wide ecological tolerance range and it is unwise to infer too much from their presence.

Hedges come into existence in a variety of ways, including deliberate planting, creation of assarts from existing woodland and natural colonisation of pre-existing boundaries such as fences (Cameron and Pannett 1980). If there was indeed a hedge at Wardy Hill, and it had been deliberately planted, then there must have been a source of suitable seedlings and cuttings from scrub or woodland edges within manageable distance of the site. If, on the other hand, the hedge had arisen by natural colonisation and subsequent management, then its species composition (Fig. 51; Table 6) would indicate that it had been in existence for a considerable period. It has been suggested that, broadly, it is possible to attribute 100 years of a hedgerow's existence for every woody taxon present (Hooper 1971). The situation is certainly more complex than this, but wherever species richness of woody plants is high, and poor colonisers such as *Acer campestre* (field maple) and *Corylus avellana* (hazel) are present, then it is implied that either the hedge is old, or it has been selectively planted with a mixture of species. There are a number of ecological indicators for dating hedges: for example, it is generally agreed that a hedge is probably more than 400 years old if field maple is present (Dowdeswell 1987). Hedges, if cut periodically, can exist for hundreds of years with species richness increasing over time (*ibid.*). It is possible that hedges had existed around the Ringwork for very much longer than is suggested by the sediment profile, since active management might have involved periodic ditch clearance and the resultant loss of the earlier record. This enclosure ditch was not a primary Iron Age feature, and any 'hedgerow pollen' could have been derived from older established hedges in the settlement.

Eventually Section 37 became very wet; it is probable that the ditch flooded and that even the bank soils became sodden. This had an adverse effect on the shrub community and both elder and hawthorn declined, the former more abruptly than the latter. This may be due to their respective positions relative to the ditch and bank. Gradually aquatic and wetland plants colonised the site and, eventually, the shrub community seems to have disappeared altogether. With the removal of this effective screen to extra-local and regional pollen rain, a picture of the wider landscape was obtained. It revealed an open terrain dominated by herb-rich grassland and wetland. However, cereal production and/or processing was important, and the large amounts of cereal pollen might have been derived from Wardy Hill itself or from adjacent drier ground.

Section 63, which bordered the wetter areas of the locality, supported as expected a diverse assemblage of aquatic and emergent plants. However, it was dominated by *Salix* (willow). Like most of the shrubs already discussed, willow is insect-pollinated and even a few pollen grains indicate its local presence. With very high values (up to 34% TLPS) over a seemingly long period, the site probably supported a considerable population of the shrub. When the values for other wetland indicators are considered, it must be concluded that the area immediately to the east of the site was probably dominated by willow carr. However, there seems to have been some attempt at hedging and creating a boundary on this eastern side of the settlement because *Crataegus*-type and a range of other insect-pollinated woody shrubs and mistletoe were present locally, but they all eventually declined to virtual extinction at the site. As at Section 37, conditions eventually became very wet and more typical open fen vegetation expanded as even willow declined. With the reduction of willow, plants growing extra-locally and regionally were better expressed. Although the landscape was very open, it would seem that a wide range of trees and shrubs was growing in the catchment. Cereal-type pollen was never abundant in the sediments of Section 63, and it is probable that on this side of the settlement it was derived from cereal processing or the dumping of waste.

Both sample sites demonstrate a similar history, although their specific characteristics were very different. If the large concentrations of *Crataegus*-type and *Sambucus* pollen do represent hedges around the site, then they may have been less well-maintained at Section 63 than at Section 37, or perhaps they were never deemed to be as important. Perhaps the existence of dense willow carr and very wet, swampy ground was considered a good defence to the east of the site, while the more accessible landward margin would have needed greater fortification.

III. Plant macrofossils and molluscs
by P. Murphy
(Plate IX; Figs 54–59; Tables 8–21)

Although the clay soil at the site was composed of poorly drained organic (but now de-watered) sediments, formed in wet conditions, were present only in the base of the outer Ringwork ditch. Uncharred plant macrofossils from these deposits are discussed below. The majority of contexts sampled contained only charred plant macrofossils, sometimes associated with a few durable seeds, such as *Sambucus nigra* (elder) and *Lemna* sp (duckweed), which survive well in de-watered fills.

Ninety-four bulk samples were collected from features of all phases. The heavy clay matrix of the samples posed problems of disaggregation, so that conventional processing in a flotation tank was found to be ineffective. Pre-treatment, involving thorough air-drying followed by soaking in hot water, was found to be necessary to disaggregate the samples. For practical reasons, this necessitated a reduction in sample size to about 7 litres. Plant material was then separated from the disaggregated sediment by manual flotation/washover, collecting the flots in a 0.5mm mesh. The dried flots (or sub-samples of them) were sorted under a binocular microscope at low power. Charred plant macrofossils were identified by comparison with modern reference material. All samples included some intrusive modern plant material, principally fibrous roots and weed seeds, but also some modern bread wheat chaff and straw.

The results are tabulated in Tables 8–15; nomenclature follows Stace (1991).

Period	I	II.1		
Feature no.		73	83	99
Fill no.		345	406	562
Feature type	Burnt flint mound	Ditch	Pit	Gully
Sample no.	90	91	92	93
Cereal grains				
Cereal indet. (ca)				
Triticum sp (ca)				
Triticum aestivum s.l. (ca)				
Hordeum sp (ca)				
Hordeum vulgare L (ca)				
Avena sp (ca)				
Cereal chaff				
Triticum sp (gb)				
Triticum sp (spb)				
Triticum sp (ri)				
Triticum dicoccum Schubl (gb)				
Triticum dicoccum Schubl (spf)				
Triticum spelta L (gb)				
Triticum spelta L (spb/spf)				
Triticum aestivum s.l. (rn)				
Hordeum sp (rn)				
Cereal awns				
Triticum sp (a. fr)				
Hordeum sp (a. fr)				
Avena sp (a. fr)			x	
Culm fragments				
Cereal/large grass (cn)				
Cereal/large grass (culm frags)				
Other crops				
Linum cf *usitatissimum* (s.fr)				
Fabaceae indet. (large cotyledon frag)				
Herbs (weeds/grassland spp)				
cf *Agrostemma githago* L (fragment)				
Anagallis-type				
Anthemis cotula L				
Apiaceae indet.				
Atriplex sp				
Brassica sp				
Bromus mollis/secalinus				
Caryophyllaceae indet.				
Cerastium sp				
Chenopodiaceae indet.				
Chenopodium album L				
Chenopodium ficifolium Smith				
Euphrasia/Odontites sp				
Fallopia convolvulus (L) A. Love				
Galium aparine L				
Galium sp				

Period	I	II.1		
Feature no.		73	83	99
Fill no.		345	406	562
Feature type	Burnt flint mound	Ditch	Pit	Gully
Sample no.	90	91	92	93
Hyoscyamus niger L				
Lamiaceae indet.				
Leontodon sp				
Malva sylvestris L				
Medicago/Lotus/Trifolium-type				
Montia fontana subsp *minor* Hayw				
Persicaria lapathifolia (L) Gray				
Persicaria maculosa Gray				
Persicaria sp				
Plantago lanceolata L				
Poaceae indet. (large)				
Poaceae indet. (medium)				
Poaceae indet. (small)				
Polygonaceae indet.				
Polygonum aviculare L				
Ranunculus acris/repens/bulbosus				
Raphanus raphanistrum L				
Rumex acetosella L				
Rumex sp				
Stellaria graminea/palustris				
Stellaria media-type				
Tripleurospermum inodorum (L) Schultz-Bip				
Vicia/Lathyrus sp				
Wetland plants				
Cladium mariscus L			4	
Eleocharis sp				
Trees/shrubs				
Corylus avellana L				
Crataegus monogyna Jacq				
Prunus spinosa L				
Rosa sp				
Sambucus nigra L				
Charred fruit fragment cf Rosaceae				
Vegetative plant material				
Charcoal <2mm	xxx	xx	xxx	xxx
Charcoal >2mm	x			
Thorns				
Buds				
Stem/rhizome fragments	xx	x		
Unidentified seeds etc.			3	1
Sample volume (litres)	7	7	7	7
Flot volume (litres)	0.2	<0.1	0.1	0.1
% flot sorted	100	100	100	100

Table 8 Charred macrofossils, Period I and II.1 contexts (Note that for Tables 8–15 all taxa are represented by fruits or seeds unless otherwise indicated; Abbreviations: a – awn; ca – caryopsis; cn – culm node; fr – fragment; gb –glume base; s – seed; spb – spikelet base; spf – spikelet fork; rn – rachis node)

Feature no.	27	37	37	37	37	52	52	57	57	80	107
Fill no.	229	238	239	320	630	?227	230	272	285	414	550
Feature type	Ditch	Ditch				Ditch		Ditch			Pit
Sample no.	87	47	48	49	88	9	89	57	58	63	94
Cereal grains											
Cereal indet. (ca)		1				1				1	
Triticum sp (ca)						1					
Triticum aestivum s.l. (ca)											
Hordeum sp (ca)											
Hordeum vulgare L (ca)											
Avena sp (ca)											
Cereal chaff											
Triticum sp (gb)		1		2	1						1
Triticum sp (spb)									1		
Triticum sp (ri)											1
Triticum dicoccum Schubl (gb)		1			2						
Triticum dicoccum Schubl (spf)						2				1	
Triticum spelta L (gb)						1					
Triticum spelta L (spb/spf)											
Triticum aestivum s.l. (rn)											
Hordeum sp (rn)					1					1	
Cereal awns											
Triticum sp (a. fr)											
Hordeum sp (a. fr)											
Avena sp (a. fr)											
Culm fragments											
Cereal/large grass (cn)				1						1	
Cereal/large grass (culm frags)											
Other crops											
Linum cf usitatissimum (s.fr)											
Fabaceae indet. (large cotyledon frag)											
Herbs (weeds/grassland spp)											
cf Agrostemma githago L (fragment)											
Anagallis-type											
Anthemis cotula L				1							
Apiaceae indet.											
Atriplex sp											
Brassica sp											
Bromus mollis/secalinus		1				1					
Caryophyllaceae indet.											
Cerastium sp					2						
Chenopodiaceae indet.		1		1		4					
Chenopodium album L				2							
Chenopodium ficifolium Smith											
Euphrasia/Odontites sp											
Fallopia convolvulus (L) A. Love											
Galium aparine L											
Galium sp											
Hyoscyamus niger L											
Lamiaceae indet.											

Feature no.	27	37	37	37	37	52	52	57	57	80	107
Fill no.	229	238	239	320	630	?227	230	272	285	414	550
Feature type	Ditch	Ditch				Ditch		Ditch			Pit
Sample no.	87	47	48	49	88	9	89	57	58	63	94
Leontodon sp											
Malva sylvestris L											
Medicago/Lotus/Trifolium-type		3			1			1		2	
Montia fontana subsp *minor* Hayw											
Persicaria lapathifolia (L) Gray											
Persicaria maculosa Gray											
Persicaria sp											1
Plantago lanceolata L											
Poaceae indet. (large)							1				
Poaceae indet. (medium)	1			1							
Poaceae indet. (small)							1	1			
Polygonaceae indet.				1				1			
Polygonum aviculare L											
Ranunculus acris/repens/bulbosus											
Raphanus raphanistrum L											
Rumex acetosella L											
Rumex sp										1	
Stellaria graminea/palustris		1									
Stellaria media-type										2	
Tripleurospermum inodorum (L) Schultz-Bip											
Vicia/Lathyrus sp			1	1					1		
Wetland plants											
Carex spp											
Cladium mariscus L									1		
Eleocharis sp				1						3	
Trees/shrubs											
Corylus avellana L											
Crataegus monogyna Jacq											
Prunus spinosa L											
Rosa sp											
Sambucus nigra L											
Charred fruit fragment cf Rosaceae											
Vegetative plant material											
Charcoal <2mm	xx	xx	xx	xx	xx	xx	xx	xx	xx	xxx	xx
Charcoal >2mm						x				x	
Thorns											
Buds											
Stem/rhizome fragments	x					x					
Unidentified seeds etc.				1	1					2	2
Sample volume (litres)	7	7	6.5	6	7	6.5	7	6.5	6	7	7
Flot volume (litres)	<0.1	<0.1	<0.1	<0.1	<0.1	<0.1	<0.1	<0.1	<0.1	0.2	0.1
% flot sorted	100	100	100	100	100	100	100	100	100	100	100

Table 9 Charred macrofossils, Period II, Phase 2 contexts

Feature no.	6	6	6	6	6	6	6	6	6	6	6/67	61	61
Fill no.	202	206	209	213	221	225	236	398	420	425	218	268	325
Feature type	\multicolumn{11}{c}{Ring-gully}		Gully	
Sample no.	11	12	13	74	14	15	16	17	76	75	18	59	60
Cereal grains													
Cereal indet. (ca)	4	1		1		2	1	3	2	1	4	4	
Triticum sp (ca)											3	3	2
Triticum aestivum s.l. (ca)													
Hordeum sp (ca)						1						1	
Hordeum vulgare L (ca)													
Avena sp (ca)													
Cereal chaff													
Triticum sp (gb)	1	9	1			8	3				1	8	1
Triticum sp (spb)		1				1						1	
Triticum sp (ri)					2						1	1	
Triticum dicoccum Schubl (gb)	2	3		1		2				1	3	12	5
Triticum dicoccum Schubl (spf)		2				1						1	
Triticum spelta L (gb)		1				2						2	1
Triticum spelta L (spb/spf)													
Triticum aestivum s.l. (rn)						1							
Hordeum sp (rn)	1	1									1	1	
Cereal awns													
Triticum sp (a. fr)													
Hordeum sp (a. fr)													
Avena sp (a. fr)						x					x	x	
Culm fragments													
Cereal/large grass (cn)													
Cereal/large grass (culm frags)						x							x
Other crops													
Linum cf usitatissimum (s.fr)													
Fabaceae indet. (large cotyledon frag)													
Herbs (weeds/grassland spp)													
cf Agrostemma githago L (fragment)													
Anagallis-type													
Anthemis cotula L													
Apiaceae indet.													
Atriplex sp		2			1	1					1	2	1
Brassica sp													
Bromus mollis/secalinus		4			1	5				1	3	2	4
Caryophyllaceae indet.											1		
Cerastium sp						1							
Chenopodiaceae indet.	3	1			1	2			1		2	9	1
Chenopodium album L	2	2	1			1	1					6	1
Chenopodium ficifolium Smith	1				4							2	
Euphrasia/Odontites sp													
Fallopia convolvulus (L) A. Love													
Galium aparine L		1											
Galium sp					1								
Hyoscyamus niger L							1						
Lamiaceae indet.													
Leontodon sp													
Medicago/Lotus/Trifolium-type	11	3	1		1	4	1				3	1	3
Malva sylvestris L													

Feature no.	6	6	6	6	6	6	6	6	6	6	6/67	61	61
Fill no.	202	206	209	213	221	225	236	398	420	425	218	268	325
Feature type	\multicolumn{11}{c}{Ring-gully}		Gully	
Sample no.	11	12	13	74	14	15	16	17	76	75	18	59	60
Montia fontana subsp *minor* Hayw													
Persicaria lapathifolia (L) Gray													
Persicaria maculosa Gray													
Persicaria sp		1			1							2	1
Plantago lanceolata L													
Poaceae indet. (large)	1	1	1									1	
Poaceae indet. (medium)						1							
Poaceae indet. (small)		2	1		2	2	1			1	1	2	
Polygonaceae indet.													
Polygonum aviculare L				1		1						1	
Ranunculus acris/repens/bulbosus													
Raphanus raphanistrum L													
Rumex acetosella L													
Rumex sp		1			3						3	2	
Stellaria graminea/palustris													
Stellaria media-type			1		60	4		1				125	8
Tripleurospermum inodorum (L) Schultz-Bip												1	
Vicia/Lathyrus sp											1		1
Wetland plants													
Carex spp													
Cladium mariscus L													
Eleocharis sp	2	5			6	2				1	2	9	
Trees/shrubs													
Corylus avellana L													
Crataegus monogyna Jacq			1										
Prunus spinosa L													
Rosa sp													
Sambucus nigra L													
Charred fruit fragment *cf* Rosaceae													
Vegetative plant material													
Charcoal <2mm	xxx	xxx	xxx	xxx	xxx	xxx	xxx	xx	xx	xxx	xxx	xxx	xx
Charcoal >2mm	xx	xx	x	x	x	xx					xx		
Thorns	1												
Buds												1	
Stem/rhizome													
Unidentified seeds etc.	6	1	2		17	2		1		2	2	4	3
Sample volume (litres)	6.5	6	7	7	7	6.5	7	6.5	7	7	7	7	7
Flot volume (litres)	0.2	0.1	0.1	0.1	0.1	0.1	0.1	<0.1	<0.1	<0.1	0.2	0.1	<0.1
% flot sorted	100	100	100	100	100	100	100	100	100	100	100	100	100

Table 10 Charred macrofossils, Structure I

Feature no.	23	24	21	21	21	21	53	54
Fill no.	360	364	161	166	169	174	196	197
Feature type	Str. II		Str. III				Pit (Str. III)	
Sample no.	32	33	25	26	27	28	54	55
Cereal grains								
Cereal indet. (ca)			1			2	4	2
Triticum sp (ca)	2		2	3		2	1	
Triticum aestivum s.l. (ca)								
Hordeum sp (ca)					1			1
Hordeum vulgare L (ca)								
Avena sp (ca)				1		1		2
Cereal chaff								
Triticum sp (gb)	1	6	5	5	5	11	4	6
Triticum sp (spb)				1		1		1
Triticum sp (ri)					1			1
Triticum dicoccum Schubl (gb)	1	5	5	3	7	19	15	14
Triticum dicoccum Schubl (spf)	1		1			4	3	3
Triticum spelta L (gb)	8	2	1		2		2	1
Triticum spelta L (spb/spf)	1	1						
Triticum aestivum s.l. (rn)				1				
Hordeum sp (rn)								
Cereal awns								
Triticum sp (a. fr)								
Hordeum sp (a. fr)								
Avena sp (a. fr)			x			x	x	
Culm fragments								
Cereal/large grass (cn)	1							
Cereal/large grass (culm frags)		x						
Other crops								
Linum cf *usitatissimum* (s.fr)								
Fabaceae indet. (large cotyledon frag)								
Herbs (weeds/grassland spp)								
cf *Agrostemma githago* L (fragment)								
Anagallis-type								
Anthemis cotula L								
Apiaceae indet.								
Atriplex sp								
Brassica sp				1				
Bromus mollis/secalinus			1				1	1
Caryophyllaceae indet.								
Cerastium sp		1						
Chenopodiaceae indet.			2	2	1		1	
Euphrasia/Odontites sp								
Chenopodium album L			2		1		3	2
Fallopia convolvulus (L) A. Love						1		
Galium aparine L								
Galium sp								
Chenopodium ficifolium Smith		1		2		1		

Feature no.	23	24	21	21	21	21	53	54
Fill no.	360	364	161	166	169	174	196	197
Feature type	Str. II		Str. III				Pit (Str. III)	
Sample no.	32	33	25	26	27	28	54	55
Hyoscyamus niger L								
Lamiaceae indet.								
Leontodon sp								
Malva sylvestris L		1						
Medicago/Lotus/Trifolium-type			1		6		3	4
Montia fontana subsp *minor* Hayw								
Persicaria lapathifolia (L) Gray				1				
Persicaria maculosa Gray								
Persicaria sp			1	1			3	1
Plantago lanceolata L								
Poaceae indet. (large)							2	
Poaceae indet. (medium)						1		
Poaceae indet. (small)		1		2			2	3
Polygonaceae indet.								
Polygonum aviculare L								1
Ranunculus acris/repens/bulbosus								
Raphanus raphanistrum L								
Rumex acetosella L								
Rumex sp								1
Stellaria graminea/palustris								
Stellaria media-type							1	
Tripleurospermum inodorum (L) Schultz-Bip					1			
Vicia/Lathyrus sp			1		1			1
Wetland plants								
Carex spp				1				
Cladium mariscus L			1	1	1	2	1	2
Eleocharis sp		4			2		3	6
Trees/shrubs								
Corylus avellana L								
Crataegus monogyna Jacq						1		
Prunus spinosa L								
Rosa sp								
Sambucus nigra L								
Charred fruit fragment cf Rosaceae								
Vegetative plant material								
Charcoal <2mm	xx	xx	xxx	xxx	xxx	xxx	xxx	xx
Charcoal >2mm							x	
Thorns							1	
Buds								
Stem/rhizome							x	
Unidentified seeds etc.	1	1	1	3	1		5	2
Sample volume (litres)	6.5	7	7	7	7	7	6.5	7
Flot volume (litres)	<0.1	<0.1	0.1	0.1	0.1	0.1	0.1	0.2
% flot sorted	100	100	100	100	100	100	100	100

Table 11 Charred macrofossils, Structures II and III

Feature no.	20	20	20	20	81	81	81	81	81	81	102	102	102	102	22	22	22	48	49
Fill no.	432	436	440	444	446	449	453	454	458		508	509/10	511	512/3/4	128	137	141	177	179
Feature type					Str. V							Pits assoc. Str. V				Str. VI		Pits (Str. VI)	
Sample no.	21	22	23	24	64	65	66	67	68		69	70	71	72	29	30	31	52	53
Cereal grains																			
Cereal indet. (ca)	1	1	1	4	8		1	2	3		1			7					
Triticum sp (ca)				2	3				3				1	4					1
Triticum aestivum s.l. (ca)															1				
Hordeum sp (ca)		2	1	10	2				1		4								1
Hordeum vulgare L (ca)			1																
Avena sp (ca)				1		1													
Cereal chaff																			
Triticum sp (gb)		2	1	21	11				5		1			8		1	4		1
Triticum sp (spb)				4			2		2		1			2					
Triticum sp (ri)			1	7	1				1					1		1			
Triticum dicoccum Schubl (gb)		1	1	16	7		1	1			1			1		1	2		
Triticum dicoccum Schubl (spf)				4	1		2												
Triticum spelta L (gb)				10	2		1	1	2					1					
Triticum spelta L (spb/spf)			1						1										
Triticum aestivum s.l. (rn)					1														
Hordeum sp (rn)				6	1														
Cereal awns																			
Triticum sp (a. fr)																			
Hordeum sp (a. fr)																			
Avena sp (a. fr)				x							x								
Culm fragments																			
Cereal/large grass (cn)														1			1		
Cereal/large grass (culm frags)																			
Other crops																			
Linum cf usitatissimum (s.fr)	1																		
Fabaceae indet. (large cotyledon frag)											1								
Herbs (weeds/grassland spp)																			
cf Agrostemma githago L (fragment)							1												
Anagallis-type			1																
Anthemis cotula L																			

Feature no.	20	20	20	20	81	81	81	81	81	102	102	102	102	22	22	22	48	49
Fill no.	432	436	440	444	446	449	453	454	458	508	509/10	511	512/3/4	128	137	141	177	179
Feature type	Str: V									Pits assoc. Str: V				Str: VI			Pits (Str: VI)	
Sample no.	21	22	23	24	64	65	66	67	68	69	70	71	72	29	30	31	52	53
Apiaceae indet.																		
Atriplex sp	1			14					2	3					1			
Brassica sp			1															
Bromus mollis/secalinus				4		2	2		3									
Caryophyllaceae indet.										1								
Cerastium sp																		
Chenopodiaceae indet.		4		13	4			1			2	2	2					
Chenopodium album L	1		1	17	1				3	1			1					1
Chenopodium ficifolium Smith			1	5									1					
Euphrasia/Odontites sp													1					
Fallopia convolvulus (L) A. Love																		
Galium aparine L													1					
Galium sp																		
Hyoscyamus niger L																		
Lamiaceae indet															2			
Leontodon sp																		
Malva sylvestris L		1																
Medicago/Lotus/Trifolium-type		1		2	2				1				2					
Montia fontana subsp *minor* Hayw				1														
Persicaria lapathifolia (L) Gray									1									
Persicaria maculosa Gray								1										
Persicaria sp		1		1					2									
Plantago lanceolata L					1								1					
Poaceae indet. (large)					4				1					1				
Poaceae indet. (medium)													1					
Poaceae indet. (small)		1			2				2				1	1				
Polygonaceae indet.																		
Polygonum aviculare L												1						
Ranunculus acris/repens/bulbosus																		
Raphanus raphanistrum L										2								
Rumex acetosella L	1												1					

Feature no.	20	20	20	20	81	81	81	81	81	102	102	102	102	22	22	22	48	49
Fill no.	432	436	440	444	446	449	453	454	458	508	509/10	511	512/3/4	128	137	141	177	179
Feature type				*Str. V*							*Pits assoc. Str. V*				*Str. VI*		*Pits (Str. VI)*	
Sample no.	21	22	23	24	64	65	66	67	68	69	70	71	72	29	30	31	52	53
Rumex sp					2				2					1	1	1		
Stellaria graminea/palustris															1			
Stellaria media-type													1					
Tripleurospermum inodorum (L) Schultz-Bip				4														
Vicia/Lathyrus sp														1				
Wetland plants																		
Carex spp		1				1						1				1		
Cladium mariscus L			2	2														
Eleocharis sp	1			6					1	1		2	2			1		1
Trees/shrubs																		
Corylus avellana L										xxx	x		x					
Crataegus monogyna Jacq										x			1					
Prunus spinosa L										1			1					
Rosa sp																		
Sambucus nigra L													x					
Charred fruit fragment cf Rosaceae																		
Vegetative plant material																		
Charcoal <2mm	xx	xx	xxx	xxx	xxx	xx	xx	xxx	xxx	xxx	xxx	xxx	xxx	xx	xx	xx	xx	xxx
Charcoal >2mm		x		xx	x	x				x			x			x		xx
Thorns										1								
Buds													1					
Stem/rhizome fragments														x	x	x		
Unidentified seeds etc.	1	1	1	2	2		2			3	1	1	8	2			1	
Sample volume (litres)	7	7	7	7	7	6.5	7	6.5	7	7	2	7	8.5	6	6	6.5	6	6
Flot volume (litres)	<0.1	<0.1	0.1	0.1	0.2	<0.1	0.1	0.1	0.2	0.1	0.1	0.1	0.3	0.1	<0.1	<0.1	<0.1	0.1
% flot sorted	100	100	100	100	100	100	100	100	100	100	100	100	50	100	100	100	100	100

Table 12 Charred macrofossils, Structures V and VI

Feature no.	31	32	33	34	36	47	55	65	65
Fill no.	71	100	95	97	99	175	240	303	304
Feature type				Pits				Ditch/pit	
Sample no.	42	44	43	45	46	51	56	61	62
Cereal grains									
Cereal indet. (ca)	2	5	2		1		1	1	6
Triticum sp (ca)	5	2	2		3	1	1	1	5
Triticum aestivum s.l. (ca)							1		
Hordeum sp (ca)		2	3	1		3			1
Hordeum vulgare L (ca)								2	
Avena sp (ca)									
Cereal chaff									
Triticum sp (gb)	7	8	7			7		1	9
Triticum sp (spb)	3		3		1			1	2
Triticum sp (ri)	4			2				1	2
Triticum dicoccum Schubl (gb)	23	17	8	7		3			6
Triticum dicoccum Schubl (spf)	3	2	3	3	1			2	6
Triticum spelta L (gb)						4			5
Triticum spelta L (spb/spf)						1			
Triticum aestivum s.l. (rn)									
Hordeum sp (rn)	1	1		1		2		1	
Cereal awns									
Triticum sp (a. fr)									
Hordeum sp (a. fr)									
Avena sp (a. fr)	x		x	x		x		x	x
Culm fragments									
Cereal/large grass (cn)						1			
Cereal/large grass (culm frags)									
Other crops									
Linum cf *usitatissimum* (s.fr)									
Fabaceae indet. (large cotyledon frag)									
Herbs (weeds/grassland spp)									
cf *Agrostemma githago* L (fragment)									
Anagallis-type									
Anthemis cotula L									
Apiaceae indet.								1	
Atriplex sp	1	1	1		1	1		1	
Brassica sp									
Bromus mollis/secalinus	7	2	5					3	4
Caryophyllaceae indet.									
Cerastium sp									
Chenopodiaceae indet.	3	11	10	3		3		1	1

Feature no.	31	32	33	34	36	47	55	65	65
Fill no.	71	100	95	97	99	175	240	303	304
Feature type				Pits				Ditch/pit	
Sample no.	42	44	43	45	46	51	56	61	62
Chenopodium album L	10	6	9	2	1	1			1
Chenopodium ficifolium Smith	3	2	1						
Euphrasia/Odontites sp									
Fallopia convolvulus (L) A. Love	1	1	1			1		1	
Galium aparine L		1							
Galium sp			1						
Hyoscyamus niger L									
Lamiaceae indet.									
Leontodon sp									
Malva sylvestris L			1	1					
Medicago/Lotus/Trifolium-type	7	5	6	1	1	1		1	1
Montia fontana subsp *minor* Hayw					1				1
Persicaria lapathifolia (L) Gray		1							
Persicaria maculosa Gray									
Persicaria sp	1	2		1	2			1	
Plantago lanceolata L	1		1						
Poaceae indet. (large)		3	1						
Poaceae indet. (medium)								1	
Poaceae indet. (small)	2	3	3	1		1			
Polygonaceae indet.			1						
Polygonum aviculare L		1	4						
Ranunculus acris/repens/bulbosus			1	1					
Raphanus raphanistrum L									
Rumex acetosella L									
Rumex sp		1	5						
Stellaria graminea/palustris		1							
Stellaria media-type	42			1	1				
Tripleurospermum inodorum (L) Schultz-Bip									
Vicia/Lathyrus sp		1	2		2				
Wetland plants									
Carex spp	1	2							
Cladium mariscus L	1	8	4			1		1	
Eleocharis sp	14	6	22	1	2			2	1
Trees/shrubs									
Corylus avellana L									
Crataegus monogyna Jacq									
Prunus spinosa L						1			

Feature no.	31	32	33	34	36	47	55	65	65
Fill no.	71	100	95	97	99	175	240	303	304
Feature type				Pits				Ditch/pit	
Sample no.	42	44	43	45	46	51	56	61	62
Rosa sp				1					
Sambucus nigra L	1	1							
Charred fruit fragment cf Rosaceae									
Vegetative plant material									
Charcoal <2mm	xx	xxx	xx	xxx	xxx	xx	xx	xxx	xxx
Charcoal >2mm	x	x	x	xxx		xx		x	x
Thorns									
Buds	1								
Stem/rhizome fragments			x	x		x		x	
Unidentified seeds etc.	7	5	5	6	2	2			3
Sample volume (litres)	6.5	7	7	3	7	6	6.5	7	7
Flot volume (litres)	0.1	0.1	0.1	1	0.1	0.1	<0.1	0.1	0.1
% flot sorted	100	100	100	12.5	100	100	100	100	100

Table 13 Charred macrofossils from pits and other contexts

Feature no.	1	1	1	1	1	1	2	2	2	2	2	2	2	2	2	2	10	12	12
Fill no.	62	63	65	245	246	249	606	20	21	22	23	24B	26B	34	35	83	385	278	146	276
Feature type			Outer enclosure ditch							Inner enclosure ditch							Outwork ditches		
Sample no.	80	81	82	83	84	85	86	73	1	2	3	4	5	6	7	8	10	77	19	20
Cereal grains																				
Cereal indet. (ca)											1	1		1	4		3			1
Triticum sp (ca)								1		2	9		5		2		11			
Triticum aestivum s.l. (ca)																				
Hordeum sp (ca)										2							2			
Hordeum vulgare L (ca)																				
Avena sp (ca)															2					
Cereal chaff																				
Triticum sp (gb)								3		26	31		22	3	6		17			
Triticum sp (spb)										6	5		2	1	4					
Triticum sp (ri)										21	6		6	2	3		7			1
Triticum dicoccum Schubl (gb)										19	21		14	8	11		36			
Triticum dicoccum Schubl (spf)										1	3		1	2	6		2			
Triticum spelta L (gb)								4		6	16		7		3		12			
Triticum spelta L (spb/spf)																1				
Triticum aestivum s.l. (m)																				
Hordeum sp (m)						1				4					1					
Cereal awns																				
Triticum sp (a. fr)										x							x			
Hordeum sp (a. fr)										x										
Avena sp (a. fr)										x	x			x	x		x			
Culm fragments																				
Cereal/large grass (cn)						1					1									
Cereal/large grass (culm frags)												x	x		x					
Other crops																				
Linum cf Usitatissimum (s.fr)																				
Fabaceae indet. (large cotyledon frag)																				
Herbs (weeds/grassland spp)																				
cf Agrostemma githago L (fragment)																				
Anagallis-type																				
Anthemis cotula L																				
Apiaceae indet.																				

Feature no.	1	1	1	1	1	1	2	2	2	2	2	2	2	2	2	10	12	12
Fill no.	62	63	65	245	246	249	606	20	21	22	23	24B	26B	34	35	83	385	278	146	276
Feature type			Outer enclosure ditch						Inner enclosure ditch								Outwork ditches		
Sample no.	80	81	82	83	84	85	86	73	1	2	3	4	5	6	7	8	10	77	19	20
Atriplex sp										2	1				1		1			
Brassica sp																				
Bromus mollis/secalinus									2	21	20		7	3	4		22		1	
Caryophyllaceae indet.																				
Cerastium sp											1									
Chenopodiaceae indet.								1	3	14	3	1	2	1	8		18			
Chenopodium album L										1	1			1	2		2			
Chenopodium ficifolium Smith													1		2		3			
Euphrasia/Odontites sp														2						
Fallopia convolvulus (L) A. Love															1					
Galium aparine L															1					
Galium sp																				
Hyoscyamus niger L																				
Lamiaceae indet.																				
Leontodon sp																				
Malva sylvestris L								6	1	6	2		1	1	1		6			
Medicago/Lotus/Trifolium-type										1										
Montia fontana subsp *minor* Hayw											1						1			
Persicaria lapathifolia (L) Gray						1														
Persicaria maculosa Gray										2										
Persicaria sp											1									
Plantago lanceolata L										1	1		2	3				1		
Poaceae indet. (large)														1					1	
Poaceae indet. (medium)																				
Poaceae indet. (small)										147	3				1		3			
Polygonaceae indet.																	1			
Polygonum aviculare L													1							
Ranunculus acris/repens/bulbosus										2										
Raphanus raphanistrum L										1				1						
Rumex acetosella L																				
Rumex sp																				
Stellaria graminea/palustris																				

Feature no.	1	1	1	1	1	1	2	2	2	2	2	2	2	2	2	2	12	12
Fill no.	62	63	65	245	246	249	606	20	21	22	23	24B	26B	34	35	83	385	278	146	276
Feature type			Outer enclosure ditch							Inner enclosure ditch							Outwork ditches			
Sample no.	80	81	82	83	84	85	86	73	1	2	3	4	5	6	7	8	10	77	19	20
Stellaria media-type																	14			
Tripleurospermum inodorum (L) Schultz-Bip										18	1		3				2			
Vicia/Lathyrus sp																				
Wetland plants																				
Carex spp													1	2						
Cladium mariscus L										6	9		1	1	2					
Eleocharis sp								2	2	3			1	3			8			
Trees/shrubs																				
Corylus avellana L																				
Crataegus monogyna Jacq																				
Prunus spinosa L																				
Rosa sp																				
Sambucus nigra L										x										
Charred fruit fragment cf Rosaceae														1						
Vegetative plant material																				
Charcoal <2mm	x	xx	xx			xx		x	xx	xxx	xxx	x	xx	xxx	xx	xx	xxx	x	x	x
Charcoal >2mm	x	x	x			x	x	xxx			xx	x		xx			x			
Thorns																				
Buds												x								
Stem/rhizome										x								x		
Unidentified seeds etc.								4		7	3		3	2	7	7	9	1		7
Sample volume (litres)	7	7	7	7	7	7	7	7	7	7	7	7	7	6.5	7	7	7	7.8	6	7
Flot volume (litres)	0.1	0.2	0.2	1	1.5	0.2	0.5	0.1	<0.1	<0.1	0.1	0.3	0.1	0.1	0.1	0.1	0.1	<0.1	<0.1	0.1
% flot sorted	100	50	50	<10	<10	100	50	100	100	50	100	100	100	100	100	100	100	100	100	100

Table 14 Charred macrofossils, Outer and Inner Ringwork Circuits and Outworks

Feature no.	25	25	25	25	25/6	25/6	26	26	26	26	39
Fill no.	306	310	315	332	329	336	348	352	355	359	124
Feature type					*Structure IV*						Pit
Sample no.	34	35	36	37	79	78	38	39	40	41	50
Cereal grains											
Cereal indet. (ca)		1		1		2		1	1	6	
Triticum sp (ca)	2							1		3	
Triticum aestivum s.l. (ca)											
Hordeum sp (ca)										2	
Hordeum vulgare L (ca)											
Avena sp (ca)	1					1					
Cereal chaff											
Triticum sp (gb)	9	1			14	1			10	11	
Triticum sp (spb)	1				4				1	2	5
Triticum sp (ri)		1			4				2	6	
Triticum dicoccum Schubl (gb)	5	3			11	2	1	1	1	18	
Triticum dicoccum Schubl (spf)				1	7	1				3	
Triticum spelta L (gb)					5	1			1	3	2
Triticum spelta L (spb/spf)											
Triticum aestivum s.l. (rn)											
Hordeum sp (rn)									3	4	
Cereal awns											
Triticum sp (a. fr)											
Hordeum sp (a. fr)											
Avena sp (a. fr)								x	x	x	x
Culm fragments											
Cereal/large grass (cn)	2										
Cereal/large grass (culm frags)											
Other crops											
Linum cf. *usitatissimum* (s.fr)											
Fabaceae indet. (large cotyledon frag)											
Herbs (weeds/grassland spp)											
cf *Agrostemma githago* L (fragment)											
Anagallis-type											
Anthemis cotula L											
Apiaceae indet.											
Atriplex sp				1						1	1
Brassica sp											
Bromus mollis/secalinus		1			14				4		
Caryophyllaceae indet.									2		
Cerastium sp											
Chenopodiaceae indet.	3	1			1					4	1
Chenopodium album L		1	2							2	
Chenopodium ficifolium Smith					1					1	
Euphrasia/Odontites sp											
Fallopia convolvulus (L) A. Love											
Galium aparine L	2										
Galium sp											
Hyoscyamus niger L											
Lamiaceae indet.											
Leontodon sp											
Malva sylvestris L											
Medicago/Lotus/Trifolium-type			1						3		2
Montia fontana subsp *minor* Hayw											
Persicaria lapathifolia (L) Gray						1					

Feature no.	25	25	25	25	25/6	25/6	26	26	26	26	39
Fill no.	306	310	315	332	329	336	348	352	355	359	124
Feature type					Structure IV						Pit
Sample no.	34	35	36	37	79	78	38	39	40	41	50
Persicaria maculosa Gray											
Persicaria sp			1	1					1		
Plantago lanceolata L											
Poaceae indet. (large)	1										
Poaceae indet. (medium)											
Poaceae indet. (small)											
Polygonaceae indet.	1										
Polygonum aviculare L											
Ranunculus acris/repens/bulbosus										1	
Raphanus raphanistrum L											
Rumex acetosella L										1	
Rumex sp						2				1	
Stellaria graminea/palustris										1	
Stellaria media-type	1		1	1						1	1
Tripleurospermum inodorum (L) Schultz-Bip	1									2	
Vicia/Lathyrus sp					1						
Wetland plants											
Carex spp				1							
Cladium mariscus L			1	1					6	4	
Eleocharis sp	1		1	2	3			1	1	1	
Trees/shrubs											
Corylus avellana L				x							
Crataegus monogyna Jacq									1		
Prunus spinosa L											
Rosa sp											
Sambucus nigra L											
Charred fruit fragment cf Rosaceae											
Vegetative plant material											
Charcoal <2mm	xx	xx	xx	xxx	xx	xxx	xx	xxx	xxx	xxx	xx
Charcoal >2mm				x							xx
Thorns											
Buds											
Stem/rhizome										x	
Unidentified seeds etc.	3	2		1		6			6	11	3
Sample volume (litres)	6.5	6.5	7	7	7	7	7	6	7	7	6.5
Flot volume (litres)	<0.1	0.1	<0.1	0.2	0.2	0.1	<0.1	0.1	0.1	0.1	0.1
% flot sorted	100	100	100	100	100	100	100	100	100	100	100

Table 15 Charred macrofossils, Structure IV

Context Group	Period II.1 ditches and pits	Period II.1 Structures I, II, III, V, VI	Period II.1/2 ditches and pits	Period II.2 Ringwork ditches	Period II.2 Structure IV	Total frequencies
Cereal grains						
Cereal indet.	3	24	7	6	6	46
Triticum sp (wheat)	1	14	8	6	3	32
Triticum aestivum (bread wheat)		1	1			2
Hordeum sp (barley)		11	5	2	2	20
Hordeum vulgare L (six-row hulled barley)		1	1			2
Avena sp (wild/cultivated oats)		5		1	2	9
Cereal chaff						
Triticum sp (wheat glume bases)	4	26	6	7	6	49
Triticum sp (wheat spikelet bases)	1	11	5	5	5	27
Triticum sp (wheat rachis internodes)	1	11	4	7	4	27
Triticum dicoccum (emmer glume bases)	2	26	6	6	8	48
Triticum dicoccum (emmer spikelet forks)	2	11	7	6	4	30
Triticum spelta L (spelt glume bases)	1	16	2	6	5	30
Triticum spelta L (spelt spikelet forks)		3	1	1		5
Triticum aestivum (bread wheat rachis nodes)		4				4
Hordeum sp (barley rachis nodes)		6	5	2	2	15
Cereal awns						
Triticum sp (wheat)				2		2
Hordeum sp (barley)				1		1
Avena sp (wild/cultivated oats)		8	6	5	4	23
Culm fragments						
Cereal/large grass (nodes)	2	2	1	2		7
Cereal/large grass (fragments)		2		3		5
Other crops						
Linum cf *Usitatissimum* (?flax, seed fragment)		1				1
Fabaceae indet. (pulse cotyledon fragment)		1				1
Trees/shrubs						
Corylus avellana (hazel nutshell)		2			1	3
Crataegus monogyna (hawthorn fruitstone)		3			1	4
Prunus spinosa (sloe fruitstone)		1	1			2
Rosa sp (rose fruitstone)			1			1
Sambucus nigra (elder seed)			2			2
Charred fruit fragment (cf Rosaceae)		1		2		3
Total number of samples	**11**	**39**	**9**	**20**	**11**	**90**

Table 16 Summary of frequencies of charred cereal and other plant remains

Context and bulk sample number	Total grains	% grains	Total chaff	% chaff	Total herbaceous taxa	% herbaceous taxa	Principal herb taxon	Total count
Structure I, fill *221*, BS 14	0	0	2	2	98	98	*Stellaria media*-type	100
Structure I, fill *268*, BS 59	8	3.9	26	12.8	169	83.3	*Stellaria media*-type	203
Structure V, fill *444*, BS 24	17	11.9	68	47.5	58	40.6	Chenopodiaceae	143
Pit 31, fill *71*, BS 42	7	4.6	41	27.6	101	67.8	*Stellaria media*-type	149
Pit 33, fill *95*, BS 43	7	6.2	21	18.8	84	75	Chenopodiaceae	112
Pit 33, fill *100*, BS 44	9	9	28	28	63	63	Chenopodiaceae	100
Inner Enclosure Ditch, fill *22*, BS 2	4	1.3	83	26	232	72.7	Poaceae(small)	319
Inner Enclosure Ditch, fill *23*, BS 3	10	7.2	82	59.5	46	33.3	*Bromus*	138
Inner Enclosure Ditch, fill *385*, BS 10	16	8.9	74	41.1	90	50	none predominant	180

Table 17 Summary of assemblage composition

Structure number	I	II	III	IV	V	VI
Mean density of cereal grains (nos. per litre)	0.37	0.24	0.58	0.29	0.79	0.1
Mean density of cereal chaff (fragments/litre)	0.94	1.85	3.19	1.95	1.63	0.33
Mean density of 'weed seeds' (nos per litre)	4.58	0.93	2.41	1.68	2.25	0.56

Table 18 Plant assemblages from Structures I–IV

Section no.	37	37	37	37	63
Depth(cm)	*120–135*	*135–150*	*150–160*	*160–170*	*112–125*
Laboratory sample no.	LS 2	LS 2	LS 2	LS 2	LS 4
Trees and shrubs					
Crataegus monogyna Jacq.			31	25	
Crataegus-type (thorns)		1	3	3	
Quercus sp (leaf frags)			x	x	
Rosa sp					3
Rubus sect. Glandulosus Wimmer and Grab.	7	38	21	15	22
Rubus-type (thorns)		8	17	18	12
Sambucus nigra L. (see note below)	120	238	31	14	1
Solanum dulcamara L.	2	9	4	2	
Viscum album L. (Epidermis: leaf, stem, inflorescence) *		xxx			
Terrrestrial herbs					
Apiaceae indet.		1	5		2
Asteraceae indet.		1		3	
Atriplex sp		1			
Caryophyllaceae indet.	1				
Chenopodiaceae indet.		2		1	1
Cirsium/Carduus sp		8	10		4
Conium maculatum L.		1			
Dipsacus fullonum L.					2
Lamiaceae indet.		1			
Lapsana communis L.		3	3	1	
Mentha sp	1		1	1	5
Moehringia trinervia (L.) Clairv.			1	1	
Myosotis sp					1
Poaceae indet.		2			
Polygonaceae indet.		2			2
Potentilla anserina L.		1			
Rumex sp		4	1	2	
Sonchus asper (L.) Hill			4	1	
Sonchus sp		3		1	
Stachys sp	2				
Stellaria media-type		10	7	9	
Urtica dioica L.	10	108	22	6	4
Urtica urens L.					1
Plants of wet soils					
Bidens sp					5
Carex sp		1			1
Eleocharis sp					7
Eupatorium cannabinum L.					1
Filipendula ulmaria (L.) Maxim			1		
Juncus sp					x
Lycopus europaeus L.	1	6	3	2	20
Menyanthes trifoliata L.		1			
Aquatic/reedswamp plants					
Alisma plantago-aquatica L.					21
Alismataceae indet.	1	4			36
Apiaceae cf *O. aquatica*	22				
Characeae indet.					17
Cladium mariscus L.		5			
Lemna sp (see note below)	616	2	3	1	2
Oenanthe aquatica (L.) Poiret	5	1	2		1
Potamogeton sp			7	1	47
Ranunculus sceleratus L.	1				

Section no.	37	37	37	37	63
Depth(cm)	120–135	135–150	150–160	160–170	112–125
Laboratory sample no.	LS 2	LS 2	LS 2	LS 2	LS 4
Ranunculus subg. *Batrachium* (DC.) A. Gray	11	1	4	5	3
Sparganium sp					1
Typha sp			6		6
Zannichellia palustris L.					1
Heathland					
Pteridium aquilinum (L.) Kuhn (pinnules)				x	x
Other plant macrofossils					
Buds/budscales		x	x	x	x
Charcoal	x	x			x
Leaf fragments		x	xx	xx	
Mosses		x	x	x	
Twig fragments			x	x	x
Unidentified seeds etc.	5	6	11	8	20
Sample weight (kg)	1	1	3	3	3
% sorted	100	25	12.5	25	25

Table 19 Plant macrofossils from F. 1 sections
(N.B. Counts given for *Sambucus* and *Lemna* are estimated from sub-samples)

Section no.	63	37	37	37	37
Depth (cm)	112–125	160–170	150–160	135–150	120–135
Laboratory sample no.	LS 4	LS 2	LS 2	LS 2	LS 2
% Trees and shrubs	15.3	64.2	54.0	62.7	16.0
% Terrestrial herbs	8.8	21.7	27.3	31.6	1.7
% Plants of wet soils	13.7	1.7	2.0	1.7	0.2
% Aquatics and reedswamp plants	54.2	5.8	11.1	2.8	81.5
Total seeds	249	120	198	469	805

Table 20 Summary of plant macrofossils from F. 1

Section no.	37	37	37	37	37	37	63
Depth (cm)	100–110	110–120	120–135	135–150	150–160	160–170	112–125
Laboratory sample no.	LS 2	LS 2	LS 2	LS 2	LS 2	LS 2	LS 4
Freshwater molluscs							
Acroloxus lacustris (Linnaeus)	1						
Armiger crista (Linnaeus)	11	47	14				
Bathyomphalus contortus (Linnaeus)	7	4	1				
Bithynia sp.	12	39	7				
Bithynia sp. (opercula)	41	116	1		1		17
Bithynia tentaculata (Linnaeus)							
Gyraulus albus (Mueller)							
Hippeutis complanatus (Linnaeus)	1	2	2				
Lymnaea cf stagnalis (Linnaeus)							3
Lymnaea sp(p).	1	1					
Physa fontinalis (Linnaeus)	1						
Planorbarius corneus (Linnaeus)	7	9					4
Planorbidae indet.	7	18	4				
Planorbis planorbis (Linnaeus)	14	21	1				
Sphaeriacea indet.	5	3					
Valvata cristata Mueller	2	15				1	
Freshwater 'slum' molluscs							
Anisus leucostoma (Millet)	1	3	1				
Lymnaea truncatula (Mueller)	5	24	8				
Land/marsh molluscs							
Aegopinella sp.	1						
Cepaea/Arianta sp.					1		
Limacidae indet.		1					
Succinea sp.							1
Vallonia sp	2						
Zonitidae indet.		5					
Indeterminate (apices)	1	2	1				
Other taxa							
Ostracods						x	x
Fish bones (including stickleback)			x				
Amphibian bones					x	x	x
Vole cheek tooth						x	
Sample weight (kg)	**1**	**1**	**1**	**1**	**3**	**3**	**3**
% sorted	**100**	**100**	**100**	**25**	**12.5**	**25**	**25**

Table 21 Molluscs from F. 1

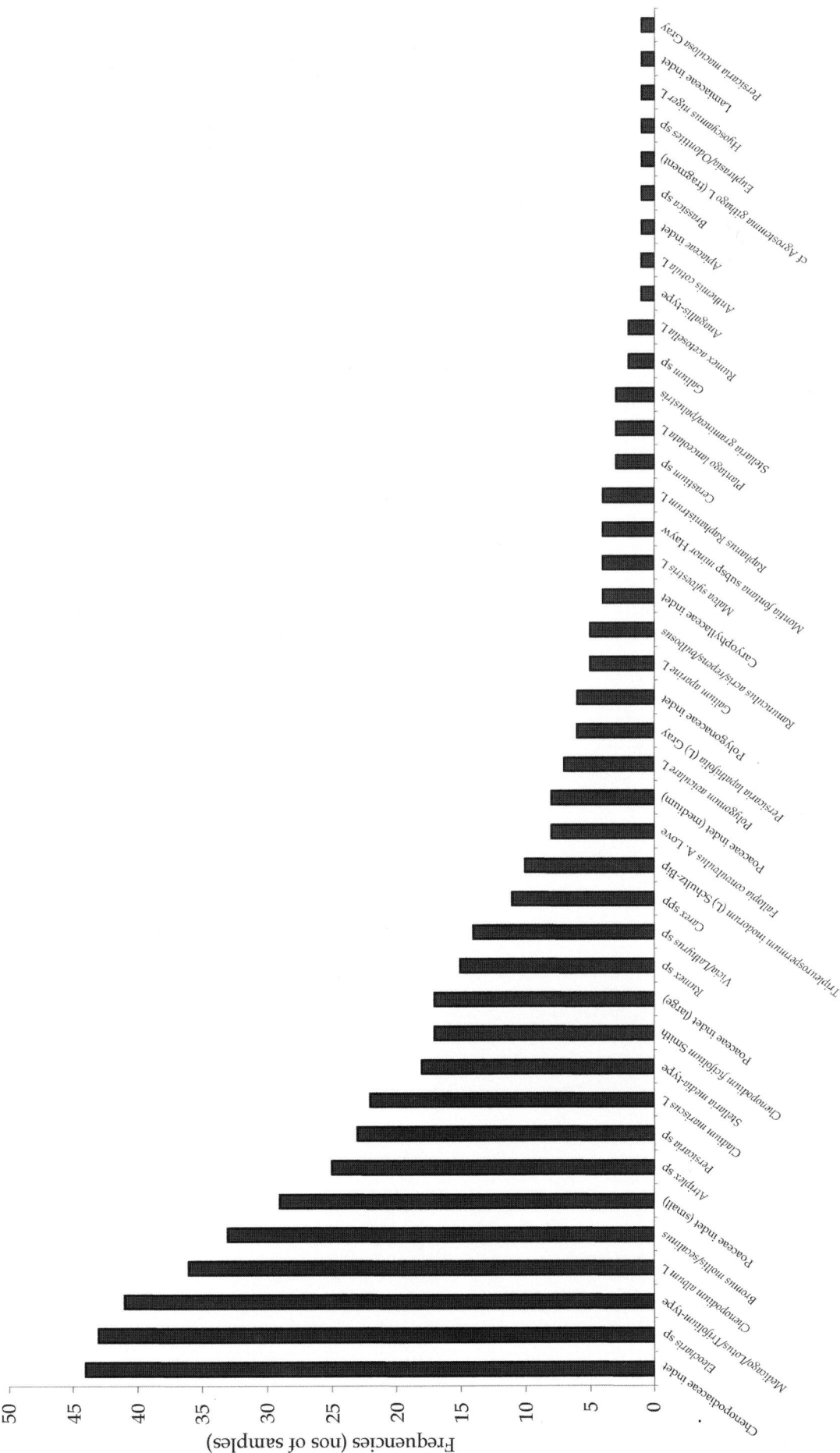

Figure 54 Frequency of herb taxa (Period II)

Pre-Ringwork features (Period I)
(Table 8)
A single bulk sample was taken from one of the 'hollows' associated with the burnt flint mound. Heat-shattered flint fragments were common, but the 7 litre bulk sample produced a relatively small flot (0.2 litres) composed of charcoal (mostly < 2mm) and charred fragments of indeterminate stems and rhizomes. No other macrofossils were noted, and no interpretation can be proposed.

Three samples were also processed from features relating to the north-eastern 'dyke system', thought to pre-date the Ringwork itself (Samples 91–3; F. 73, 83 and 99). The flot volumes obtained were again small (up to 0.1 litres) and consisted mainly of small charcoal fragments < 2mm. Apart from this, one sample included a scrap of *Avena* (oat) awn, with nutlets of *Cladium mariscus* (saw-sedge). Such very sparse assemblages are strictly uninterpretable: given the later activity at the site, the possibility of some intrusive material being present cannot be dismissed. However, there is certainly no evidence from these samples for any significant cereal processing.

The Ringwork occupation (Period II)
(Plate IX; Figs 54–59; Tables 9–21)

Cereals and other crops
(Fig. 55)
Frequencies of charred crop remains, and those of other economic plants in the ninety samples from contexts of Period II, are summarised in Table 16. The cereal crops represented were *Triticum dicoccum* (emmer), *Triticum spelta* (spelt), *Hordeum* sp (barley, including *H. vulgare*, six-row hulled barley) and *Triticum aestivum* (bread wheat), with *Avena* sp (wild or cultivated oat). Most of the wheat grains were not identified to species, though two samples included short *T. aestivum*-type grains. The barley grains were mostly badly deformed, though a few asymmetrical specimens from lateral spikelets of *H. vulgare* were present. A high proportion of the wheat chaff was very fragmentary or deformed. However, chaff fragments of emmer were well represented, followed by spelt and barley, with a very few rachis nodes of bread wheat. Awn fragments of *Avena* were frequent, with some of *Triticum* and *Hordeum*. Culm nodes and fragments of cereals and/or large grasses were moderately frequent, but never numerically abundant. Other probable crop remains comprised a seed fragment probably of *Linum usitatissimum* (flax) and a cotyledon fragment from a large pulse seed.

The wild flora
(Fig. 56)
Charred nutshell fragments of *Corylus avellana* (hazel), fruitstones of *Crataegus monogyna* (hawthorn), *Prunus spinosa* (sloe) and *Rosa* sp (rose), and seeds of *Sambucus nigra* (elder) occurred sporadically (Table 16), but the sparse charred macrofossils of edible wild plants do not suggest substantial reliance on wild fruit and nut collection.

Frequencies of charred macrofossils of herbaceous species are summarised in Fig. 54. The more frequent taxa (those present in >10% of samples) included common arable weeds: Chenopodiaceae, predominantly *Chenopodium album* (fat hen) and *Atriplex* sp (orache), with *C. ficifolium* (fig-leaved goosefoot), *Bromus mollis/secalinus* (brome grass), *Persicaria* spp (redshank, pale persicaria), *Stellaria media*-type (chickweed), *Rumex* spp (docks), *Vicia/Lathyrus* spp (vetches) and *Tripleurospermum inodorum* (scentless mayweed).

Small and large Poaceae (grasses) and *Medicago/Lotus/Trifolium*-type (small-seeded leguminous species including medicks, trefoils, clovers *etc.*),

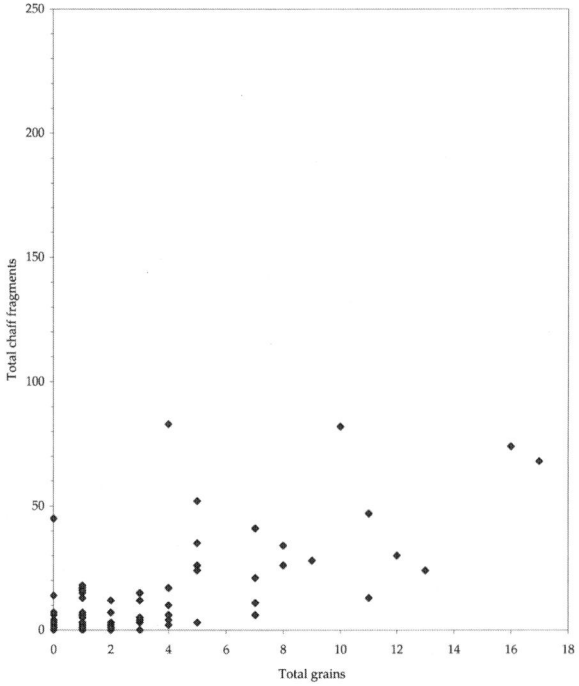

Figure 55 Total counts of grains and chaff fragments (Period II)

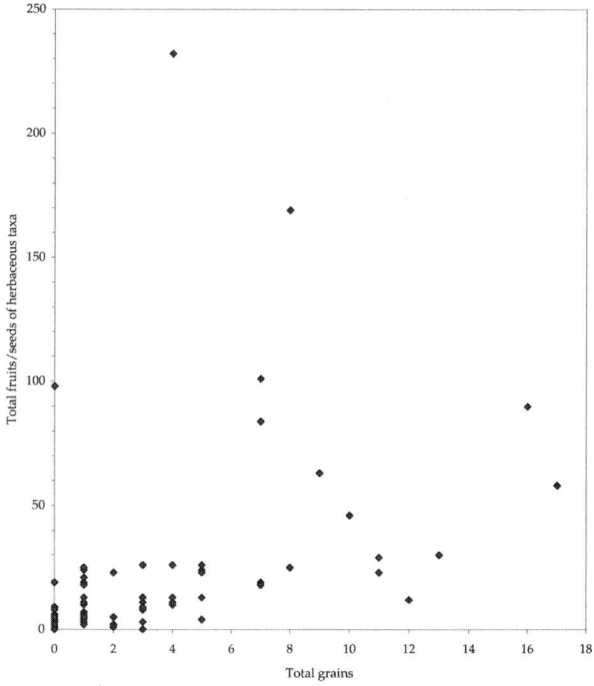

Figure 56 Total counts of grains and fruit/seeds (Period II)

were also common. Close identification of these taxa was not possible but they commonly occur in grassland, as do some other taxa represented at lower frequencies: *Ranunculus acris/repens/bulbosus* (buttercups) and *Plantago lanceolata* (ribwort plantain). Damp-ground species, particularly *Eleocharis* spp (spike-rush), but also *Persicaria* spp (redshank, pale persicaria) and *Carex* spp (sedges), were also frequent.

High frequencies of charred macrofossils of grassland and damp-ground plants in association with cereals are often taken as an indication that tillage was incomplete, so that grassland plants were able to persist in the arable fields (following Hillman 1981), and that cultivation extended onto poorly-drained land (as first suggested by M. Jones 1978). Following the latter interpretation, the abundance of *Eleocharis* and *Persicaria* could well indicate that the cereals from Wardy Hill had been grown on wet soils, and probably locally, as suggested by G. Jones for the cereal remains from Haddenham (G. Jones, forthcoming). However, caution must be exercised in such interpretation for it is likely that the taphonomy of charred assemblages from ditches, gullies and pits is complex. They could easily include charred material from more than one source including, for example, hay, litter and thatching materials, besides cereal crops and their contaminants.

One common species from Wardy Hill — *Cladium mariscus* (saw-sedge) — definitely could not have occurred as a crop weed. It grows in reedswamp and fen, usually in pure dense stands. It has traditionally been used for thatching and as kindling for fires, and these activities no doubt account for its abundance in the samples.

Some other weed species, occurring at lower frequencies (often only single specimens) are unlikely to have been growing in poorly-drained arable fields on clay soils. These include *Rumex acetosella* (sheep's sorrel) and *Raphanus raphanistrum* (wild radish), both of which are more typically found on well-drained sandy soils. There is therefore some very slight evidence to suggest that crops grown elsewhere may have been processed on site. If so, however, there is no reason to think that this was on any significant scale.

Crop-processing activities
(Figs 55 and 56)
Bearing in mind the above *caveats* regarding the taphonomic complexity of the samples, assemblage composition can be used to provide information on crop processing activities on-site. Figures 55 and 56 summarise total counts of grains, chaff fragments and fruits/seeds of herbaceous taxa from all contexts of Period II. It is plain that in many samples grains made up a relatively minor component (though obviously the smallest assemblages are not informative). Chaff fragments and, in some samples, fruits/seeds of herbaceous taxa were much more abundant. It is thought that crop-processing waste- or by-products are generally represented, rather than material derived from prime grain charred by such accidental processes as granary fires or poor temperature control during grain drying or malting. The samples probably relate to disposal by fire of waste products from the cleaning of small batches of cereals taken from bulk stores and/or from the use of such products as fuel. Cereal by-products used as fuel would have been partly generated by on-site crop cleaning, though van der Veen (in press) has suggested that such material was also an actively-traded resource in later prehistory. However, at Wardy Hill the composition of the weed flora gives no support for any large-scale importation of by-products grown elsewhere.

Assemblage composition for samples including more than 100 macrofossils is summarised in Table 17. In almost all these samples small weed seeds predominate (*Stellaria media*-type, Chenopodiaceae, small Poaceae), and crop-cleaning by sieving is probably represented. One sample (BS 3; F. 2 *23* consisted largely of chaff and of large caryopses of *Bromus mollis/secalinus*; this is more likely to be a winnowing residue.

Spatial patterning of charred macrofossil discard
(Figs 57 and 58)
The spatial distribution of charred plant macrofossils from the site (Period II) is presented in Fig. 57, in terms of numbers of charred macrofossils (grains, chaff fragments and fruits/seeds of herbaceous species only) per litre of soil processed. The first, and most obvious, point is that densities were very low outside the F. 2 ditch circuit. No sample from F. 1, the Outwork Ditches or associated features contained more than one macrofossil per litre, even in the vicinity of the entrances. The bank between F. 1 and F. 2 evidently prevented large-scale dispersal of charred material beyond F. 2 (except, presumably, by wind-blow), and there is no evidence for any significant crop-processing activities outside the defended circuit.

Three samples from the south-eastern part of F. 2 produced some of the highest densities of material from the site: *022* (91 macrofossils/litre), *023* (20/litre) and *385* (26/litre). It was suggested above that both sieving waste and coarser winnowing waste were represented. These contexts did not produce particularly high densities of artefacts, and fieldwalking before excavation showed that that this part of the site was not where the main middens were located. A plausible interpretation is that crop cleaning took place in this part of the enclosure, the waste products were burnt on bonfires, and the charred residues found their way into the adjacent fills of F. 2.

There are several points worth noting with regard to the fills of the eaves-gullies of Structures I–VI and contexts directly associated with them. Mean densities of charred grains, chaff fragments and 'weed seeds' for the structures are summarised in Table 18 and Fig. 58. The fills of ring-ditches associated with Structures II and VI included the lowest mean densities overall, and this correlates with the interpretation of these structures as 'ancillary'.

Apart from this, it is probably unwise to place too much emphasis on mean densities for the entire structures, for these can be biased by particularly rich samples. For example, one sample from the gully associated with Structure I (*268*, BS 59) contained 29 macrofossils/litre, the highest density of material in any context associated with the structures. This sample, composed predominantly of small weed seeds, has biased the mean density for the Structure I as a whole. It is would therefore be unreliable to attempt to differentiate types of activities taking place in each structure. However, interpretation in general terms can be offered. It seems reasonable to interpret the charred material from the gully fills as residues swept out from internal domestic hearths on which cereal-processing by-products had been burnt: either deliberately as fuel or

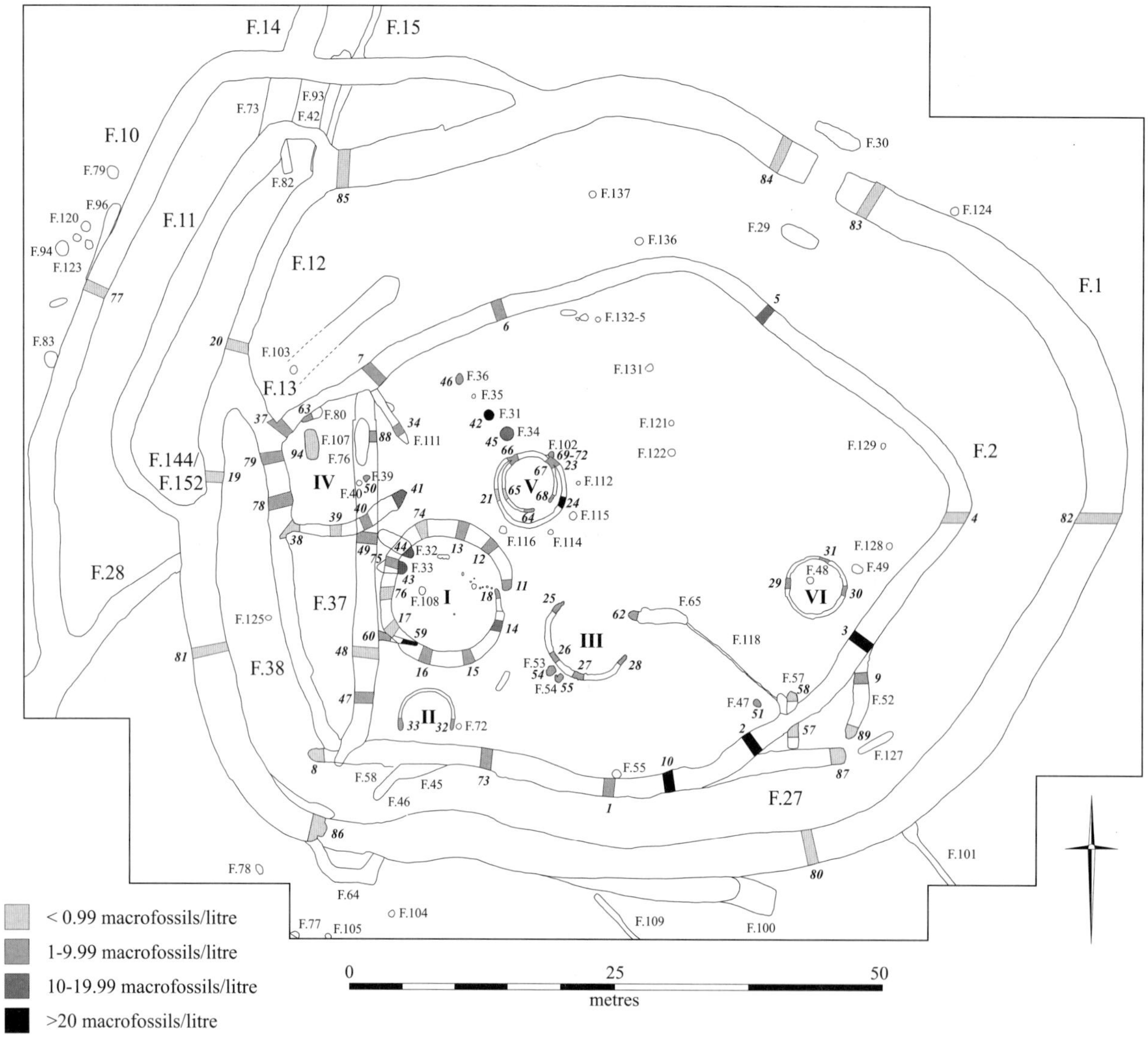

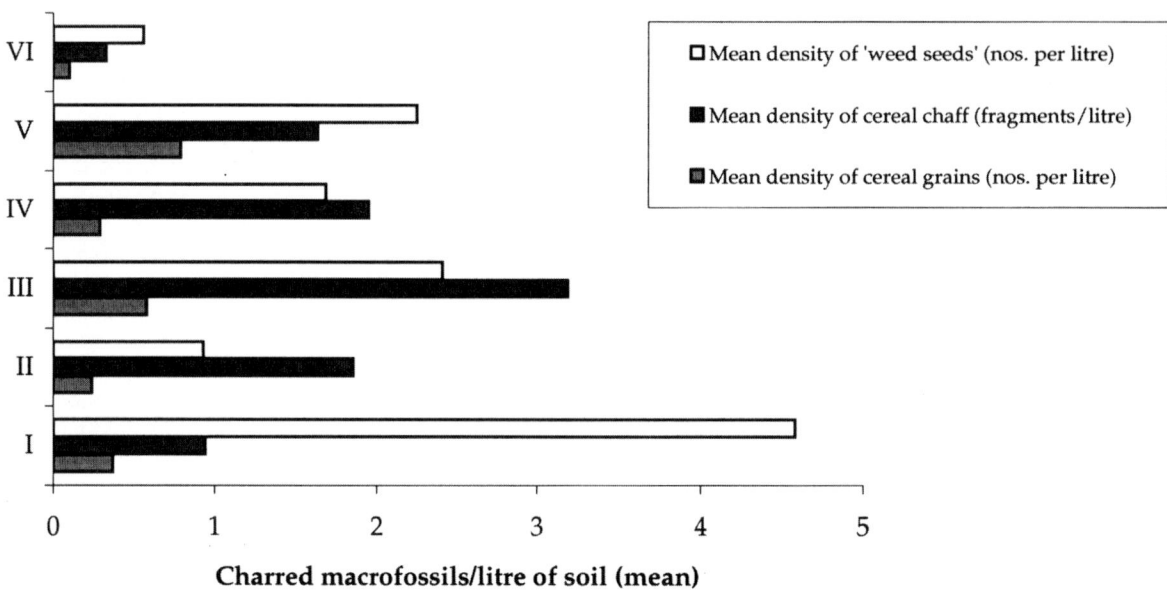

Figure 57 Overall density plot of macrofossils per litre

Figure 58 Densities of charred plant macrofossils (Structures I–VI)

incidentally as waste. Structures I and IV included relatively high densities on the southern side of their doorway entrances, just where such sweepings might be expected to accumulate. The low densities of charred material in fills associated with Structures II and VI may imply that they lacked internal hearths.

Uncharred plant macrofossils
The vast majority of bulk-sampled contexts were shallow and their fills, though wet or moist when excavated, had not provided permanently anoxic conditions. Consequently, though charred plant macrofossils were common, survival of uncharred plant material was minimal apart from a few durable propagules in some samples. These included seeds of Lemna (duckweed), which survive surprisingly well in de-watered fenland clays. However, organic deposits were present in the basal fills of the main circuit F. 1. Samples were taken at two locations. Section 37 was on the higher part of the site, whilst Section 63 was on low ground adjacent to the fen. The upper fills (not sampled) comprised topsoil, 20th-century bank-levelling deposits and dark clays ramified by modern roots.

In addition, some macrofossils were recorded from a monolith taken primarily for pollen assessment from the early ditch in the north-eastern sector, F. 73 (*345*, Laboratory Sample 5). There was insufficient material from this sample for analysis to be profitable.

The sediments

Section 37
At this point the ditch was cut through very stiff, impervious clay. The lower fills were as follows (depths from top of section):

100–120cm: extremely firm brown to greyish-brown clay; virtually stoneless; well-developed columnar peds; mollusc shells locally common; fibrous roots (*52*);

120–135cm: firm brown clay; virtually stoneless; some dark brown organic inclusions; large orange-brown mottles; fibrous roots (*52*);

135–170cm: slightly firm dark greyish-brown organic clay; some marl fragments; orange-brown mottles; visible leaf impressions; poorly preserved twigs and seeds; mollusc shells; becoming moist towards base, but essentially de-watered (*68*).

Laboratory Sample 2 (LS2) was a column sample taken for macrofossil analyses, vertically subdivided at 100–110, 110–120, 120–135, 135–150, 150–160 and 160–170cm.

Section 63
This part of the ditch was dug through clay and marl and was relatively free-draining, although at a lower elevation; all deposits were dry (de-watered).

70–80cm: very firm dark greyish-brown clay; virtually stoneless; well-developed columnar peds; fibrous roots abundant (*58*);

80–112cm: very firm greyish-brown clay; virtually stoneless; prominent orange-brown mottles; off-white marl inclusions; vertical off-white streaks of gypsum; degraded mollusc shell fragments (*58*);

112–125cm: very firm dark greyish-brown organic clay; virtually stoneless; some orange-brown mottles; off-white marl inclusions; white laminations; mollusc shells throughout, but particularly common at base; fibrous roots.

Laboratory Sample 4 (LS4) was a column sample taken for macrofossil assessment, vertically sub-divided at 70–80, 80–90, 90–100, 100–112 and 112–125cm.

Small sub-samples from both Sections were initially disaggregated and washed out over a 0.5mm mesh, and the retents assessed to establish where there was preservation of uncharred plant macrofossils. On the basis of assessment, samples from 120–170cm in LS2 (Section 37) and the sample at 112–125cm in LS4 (Section 63) were analysed. Samples were initially disaggregated by pre-soaking in a dilute NaOH solution, and macrofossils were then separated using the methods of Kenward *et al.* (1980). The sample weights processed, and the proportions of the organic fraction sorted, are given in Table 19. All identifications were verified by comparison with modern reference material.

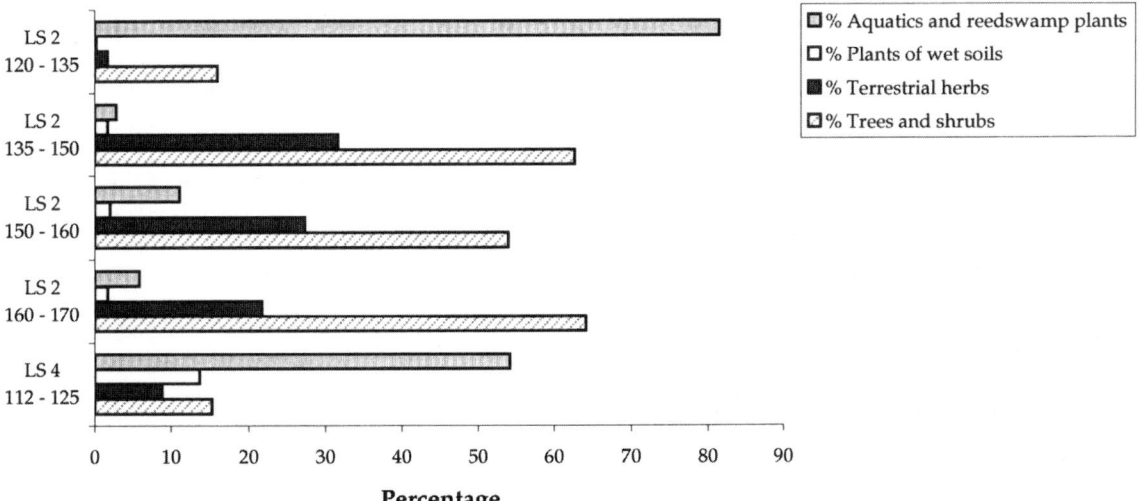

Figure 59 Plant macrofossil assemblages from F. 1

Discussion

The plant macrofossil assemblages from these five samples are listed in Table 19, and summarised in Table 20 and Fig. 59. Macrofossils derived from four main ecological groups of plants were recorded: aquatics/reedswamp species, plants of wet soils, terrestrial herbs and trees/shrubs. In addition a few pinnules of *Pteridium aquilinum* (bracken) were noted in the basal samples from both sections. Bracken is unlikely to have been growing locally or on-site, given the predominantly poorly-drained clay soils in the vicinity. It may have been intentionally imported for use as flooring material or animal bedding.

Aquatic and reedswamp plants were common in the basal fill of F. 1, Section 63 (112–125cm): accounting for 54.2% of all seeds from the feature. The predominant taxa were Alismataceae, including *Alisma plantago-aquatica* (water plantain), charophytes (stoneworts) and *Potamogeton* spp (pondweeds). This section was on the lower-lying 'fen' side of the enclosure, and plainly the ditch had held standing water in this area whilst the basal sediment accumulated. In the basal three samples from Section 37 (135–170cm), however, macrofossils from these plants were sparser (maximum 11%). Whilst conditions must plainly have been wet within the sediment (otherwise macrofossils would not have been preserved), these lower frequencies of aquatics and reedswamp plants suggest either that areas of standing water over the sediment surface were more restricted, or that the ditch was only intermittently flooded at this point. The assemblage from 120–135cm in Section 37 was quite different in character, being dominated by macrofossils of aquatic plants (81.5% of total macrofossils), and in particular by *Lemna* sp (duckweed). It was also at this level that significant numbers of freshwater mollusc shells first occurred (Murphy in prep.), and these increased in abundance in sediments above, though these were too de-watered for plant macrofossil preservation. Much wetter conditions are indicated, probably relating to a widespread, perhaps regional, rise in the watertable.

There was, again, a contrast between Sections 37 and 63 in terms of the percentages of macrofossils from trees and shrubs. Taxa identified from fruits, seeds and leaves included *Crataegus monogyna* (hawthorn), *Quercus* sp (oak), *Rosa* sp (rose), *Rubus* section *Glandulosus* (bramble), *Sambucus nigra* (elder) and *Solanum dulcamara* (woody nightshade), whilst *Crataegus*-type and *Rubus*-type thorns were also present. In the basal sample from Section 63, macrofossils of trees and shrubs comprised 15.3% of the total count, though this percentage has been depressed to some extent by the abundance of aquatics. In the base of Section 37, below 150cm, percentages of 64.2–54% were recorded. At 135–150cm the overall percentage for trees and shrubs was 62.7%, but by this level the main taxon was *Sambucus*, which was comparatively rare below. *Sambucus* was also common at 120–135cm, but its percentage representation was again depressed by the abundance of *Lemna* seeds in the sample. In two samples from Section 37, the woodland herb *Moehringia trinervia* (three-veined sandwort) was associated.

It is suggested that these macrofossils represent woody plants growing directly adjacent to the ditch, most likely on the internal bank. The unusual abundance of thorny species in the basal fills of these two sections, especially 37, is thought to indicate at least that growth of such plants locally was permitted by excluding grazing animals, and it is even possible that they were intentionally planted. Either way, a belt of thorny vegetation on the bank would have formed an effective barrier that would not have easily been penetrated. Whether this vegetation was a managed hedgerow or no more than an untidy zone of scrub is impossible to say, since there was virtually no preservation of woody stems from which growth forms could be inferred. Characteristic hedging features on roundwood — including right-angle bends in stems which may be generated by hedge-laying and management — have been noted in Iron Age contexts from Fisherwick, Staffordshire (Williams 1979) and St Ives, Cambridgeshire (Taylor 1996).

The increased abundance of *Sambucus* seeds above 150cm in Section 37 is not simply a consequence of the well-known durability of these seeds in aerated deposits: though represented in the lower fills, they were not common. A real local expansion of elder scrub may be inferred, perhaps relating to abandonment of the site whilst these upper fills accumulated.

One very unusual identification, of *Viscum album* (mistletoe: Plate XI), was made by Dr Mark Robinson, who comments:

> The paraffin flotation of a 1.0kg sample from Section 37, 135–150cm, to recover insect remains also resulted in a large quantity of plant epidermal tissue floating. It had the khaki, translucent appearance which is often characteristic of the remains of evergreen shrubs, and was eventually identified as *Viscum album*. The remains included epidermis of leaves, stems and inflorescences. The leaf fragments had a coarse cell pattern with scattered stomata that gave way on the rounded leaf margin to rows of cells and no stomata. Indistinct fragments of the venation adhered to the epidermis. The stem fragments had a more regular pattern of quadrate cells which gave a tuberculate surface. Stomata were present at intervals. The inflorescences comprised the characteristic united bracts with setaceous margins. The coarse pattern of equilateral cells gave a reticulate, tuberculate surface to the bracts.
>
> The concentration of mistletoe remains was such that the deposit might have contained an entire plant. It is possible that the mistletoe had been deliberately placed in the ditch.

Dr Robinson's suggestion that the mistletoe was intentionally placed is intriguing. However, it must be noted that samples from this ditch section included remains of rosaceous shrubs and oak, which can be parasitised by mistletoe. The plant may have been growing locally on scrub and trees, and have been incorporated into the ditch fill by entirely natural processes.

The rather low frequencies of plants characteristic of wet soils in Section 37 (only up to 2%), though 13.7% in Section 63, seem at first sight surprising at a fen-edge site. This probably relates to the nature of the 'seed' catchments in the two sections, and to the shading-out of some open fen species by scrub growth. In 37, the ditch seems to have been an isolated wet feature bounded by scrub in an otherwise *comparatively* well-drained area, so that habitats for open fen species were restricted. In 63, by contrast, the ditch was adjacent to the fen. The remaining group of terrestrial herbs comprises mainly weeds, with *Urtica dioica* (stinging nettle) predominating. These are uninformative.

Mollusca

Within the outer circuit, mollusc shells were present in the basal fill of Section 63 (LS 4: 112–125cm) and in most samples from Section 37 (LS 2: 100–170cm). Sediment descriptions for these two sections have been given in the

Plate XI Mistletoe (*Viscum album*; Section 37, 135–150cm): (1) leaf fragment (x15.5); (2) leaf tip (x13.5); 3) bracts of inflorescence (x15); 4) leaf tip, bracts and leaf base (x6).

report on uncharred plant macrofossils. A significant characteristic of the clayey sediments in these sections was the presence of gypsum, and probably of re-precipitated calcite, as white laminations and vertical streaks. In de-watered fenland clays, sulphur acids (HSO and HSO) produced by oxidation of pyrite commonly react with the calcium carbonate component of shell to produce gypsum (CaSO.2HO). It is therefore evident that some shell destruction has occurred, and this is particularly clear in the lower fills: some samples from Section 37 included no shells, and in the sample from Section 63 the main items surviving were the dense opercula of *Bithynia* sp, with a few shells of large *Lymnaea* spp and *Planorbarius corneus*. A few decalcified crushed periostraca were also noted.

Shells were extracted, together with plant macrofossils, from the samples using the methods of Kenward *et al.* 1980. Meshes of 0.5mm were used throughout.

Discussion

Mollusc shells from Sections 37 and 63 are listed in Table 21.

In Section 37 there was virtually no preservation below 135cm. Shelly clays at 100–135cm, however, included relatively abundant shells. The assemblages included a small component of terrestrial species, but there were too few shells to provide any information on dry-land habitats around the ditch. Freshwater slum taxa, characteristic of stagnant conditions and intermittent desiccation, were present: *Anisus leucostoma* and *Lymnaea truncatula*. These two snails, particularly *A. leucostoma*, are commonly reported from ditches and other wet archaeological features, and generally seem to represent the fauna resident in the feature (O'Connor 1988). However, the assemblages from this section were dominated by more typically freshwater species, including some snails such as *Planorbarius corneus*, which are not tolerant of poor, enclosed habitats, but are largely confined to large bodies of well-oxygenated water (Boycott 1936). Consequently, the assemblages are thought to have been emplaced as a result of widespread flooding from the fen, rather than representing a resident ditch fauna.

The sample from the base of Section 63 was plainly differentially preserved, consisting of large shells and durable elements, but *P. corneus* was again present. Flooding again seems to be indicated.

IV. Insects
by M. Robinson
(Fig. 60; Tables 22 and 23)

Organic sediments were discovered in the outer enclosure ditch (F. 1). Two sample columns were taken from the ditch for the analysis of plant and invertebrate remains, Section 37 and Section 63. Insect remains were found to be preserved in those parts of the columns from which useful assemblages of macroscopic plant remains were recovered, so those sample units were also analysed for insects.

The sample units had been disaggregated by soaking in dilute sodium hydroxide solution and had then been washed over onto a 0.25mm mesh to recover organic remains. Some insect remains had been picked out when sub-samples of these flots had been sorted for macroscopic plant remains, but the flots had not been fully sorted for insects. They were therefore subjected to paraffin flotation onto a 0.2mm mesh to recover further insect remains. The insects were identified with reference to the collections of the Oxford University Museum of Natural History. The results are given in Tables 22 and 23 as the minimum number of individuals represented by the fragments identified from each sample unit. The tables also give sample weights. Nomenclature for Coleoptera follows Kloet and Hincks (1977).

Preservation of remains was good in the bottom three sample units from Section 37 (135–170cm), and reasonable-sized insect assemblages were recovered from them. The coleopteran results from these samples have been displayed by species groups as percentages of the total terrestrial Coleoptera in each sample unit (Fig. 60) largely following Robinson (1991, 278–81). Preservation was less good in the top sample from Section 37 (120–135cm) and in Section 63.

Interpretation

Conditions in the ditch

Water beetles were well-represented in all the samples. They were all species of stagnant water, likely to have been living in standing water in the bottom of the ditch. *Helophorus* cf. *brevipalpis*, *Hydrobius fuscipes* and *Ochthebius minimus* were amongst the more numerous species. One beetle, *Noterus clavicornis*, is characteristic of calcareous conditions. Scirtid beetles, probably *Cyphon* sp., which have aquatic larvae, were also very numerous. Amphibious beetles, such as *Anacaena bipustulata* or *limbata*, probably lived in damp vegetation debris on the ditch sides, along with terrestrial species of waterside habitats such as *Lesteva longoelytrata*. Coleoptera which feed on marsh and aquatic plants were present in all the samples. The weevil *Tanysphyrus lemnae*, which feeds on *Lemna* spp. (duckweed), was probably associated with this small plant floating on water in the ditch. *Prasocuris phellandrii*, which feeds on aquatic Umbelliferae such as *Oenanthe aquatica* gp. (water dropwort), was identified from the top organic sample from Section 37 (120–135cm) and from Section 63. It is possible that this plant had colonised the ditch but the remains could also have been introduced through flooding, or the beetle could have flown in from the fen. Many of the samples also contained a few donaciine chrysomelid beetles which are dependent on tall reedswamp monocotyledons (reeds *etc.*). They were almost certainly from the fen, and are considered below.

Woodland, scrub and hedges

Around 2.5% of the terrestrial Coleoptera from the bottom three samples from Section 37 fall into Species Group 4 (wood- and tree-dependent taxa). Such a value suggests a landscape that was largely open but with a significant presence of woodland or scrub. Indeed, while many of the other Coleoptera can occur in woodland habitats there were only a very few, for example the arboreal caterpillar-feeder *Calosoma inquisitor*, which do not also occur in open habitats. The host-specific species of the tree and shrub- dependent Coleoptera included several examples of *Anthonomus* cf. *chevrolati*, which feeds on *Crataegus* spp. (hawthorn) and *Chalcoides* sp., which feeds on

Populus and *Salix* spp. (poplar and willow). The most numerous of the dead-wood-feeding Coleoptera was *Acalles turbatus*. This is particularly associated with dead twigs and small diameter branches of *Crataegus* sp. in hedges, which it bores into. One possible interpretation of the evidence would be that there was a hedge associated with the ditch of the Ringwork, rather than that there was a general scattering of hawthorn scrub over the area of the site. Other beetles characteristic of hedgerow included the cerambycid *Tetrops praeusta* and the *Rubus* spp. (blackberry, *etc.*) feeding weevil *Anthonomus* cf. *rubi*.

Grassland
Grassland was clearly a major aspect of the landscape around the Ringwork. Chafer and elaterid beetles with larvae that feed on the roots of grassland herbs (Species Group 11) ranged from 2.5 to 4.3% of the terrestrial Coleoptera from Section 37. The most numerous were *Phyllopertha horticola* and species of *Agriotes*. However, there were also several examples of *Agrypnus murinus*, which requires well-aerated, non-waterlogged soils. The more host-specific of the phytophagous Coleoptera that feed on grassland plants included *Mecinus pyraster*, which feeds on *Plantago lanceolata* and *P. media* (plantains), *Mantura chrysanthemi*, which in Britain appears to be associated with *Leucanthemum vulgare* (ox-eye daisy) and *Hypera punctata* on *Trifolium* spp. (clovers) and *Medicago* spp. (medicks). Beetles of the genera *Apion* and *Sitona* which tend to be favoured by hay meadow conditions (Species Group 3) were well represented, reaching 9.5% of the terrestrial Coleoptera. They included *Apion pisi*, which feeds on *Medicago* spp., and *A. craccae*, which feeds on *Vicia* spp. (vetches *etc.*). Such a high value for this group would be appropriate to the presence of hay meadow. However, these beetles would also have been able to flourish if a hedge left a strip of grassy vegetation protected from grazing along the edge of the ditch.

Scarabaeoid dung beetles which feed on the droppings of the larger herbivorous mammals on pasture (Species Group 2) were very abundant. They rose from 12% of the terrestrial Coleoptera in the bottom sample from the ditch at Section 37 (160–170cm) to over 29% in the sample from 135–150cm. The most numerous species were *Aphodius contaminatus* and *A.* cf. *sphacelatus*, which are still very common in Britain. However, there was an example of *Onthophagus nutans*, which is now extinct in Britain although it is known from other Iron Age sites (Allen and Robinson 1993, 138). Those beetles which occur more generally in decaying organic material (Species Group 7), such as *Megasternum obscurum* and *Anotylus sculpturatus* gp., could also have been living in animal droppings. These results suggest a strong concentration of domestic animals on the site. It is likely that the Ringwork or one of the associated enclosures was used to herd stock.

Arable and other disturbed or waste ground habitats
There was only a slight presence of insects that favour arable habitats. For example, there was only a single individual from Species Groups 6a and 6b (carabid beetles of disturbed or sparsely vegetated ground). However, the phytophagous insects included a small element that is associated with waste ground vegetation. The weevil *Apion malvae* feeds on Malvaceae, particularly *Malva*

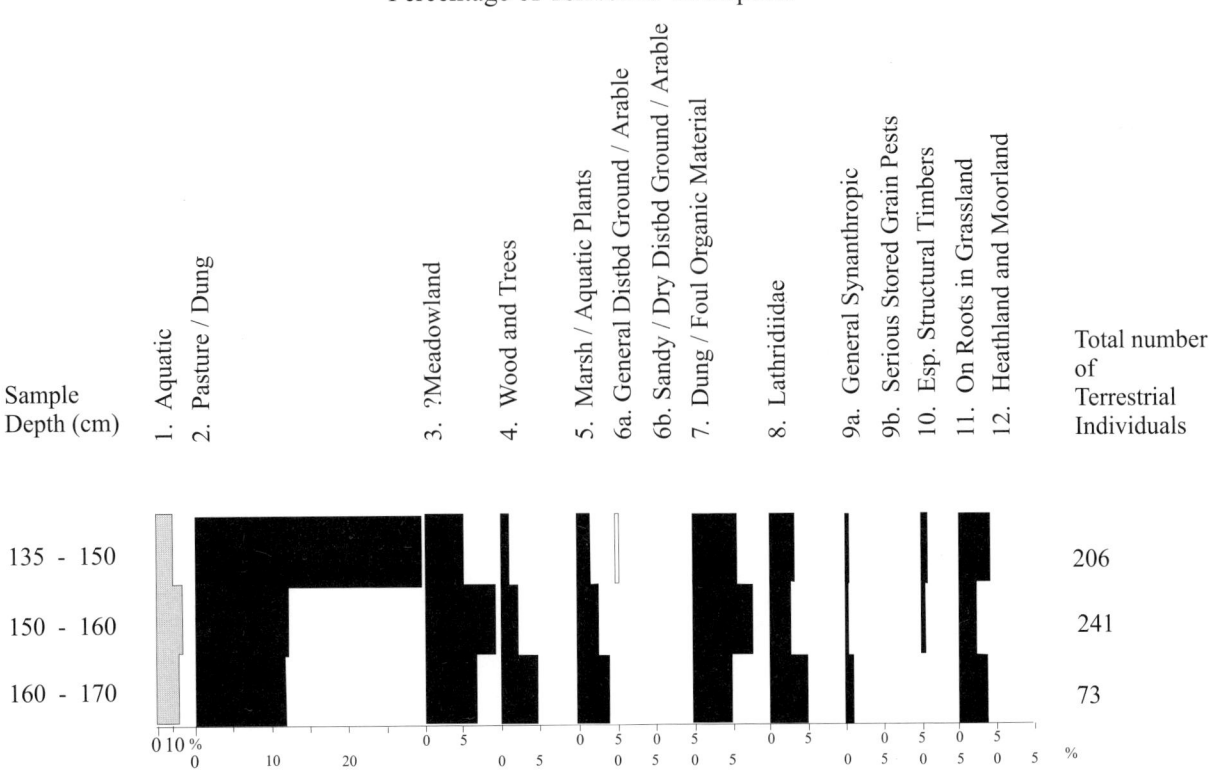

Species groups expressed as a percentage of the total terrestrial Coleoptera (ie aquatics excluded)
Not all the terrestrial Coleoptera have been classified into groups

Figure 60 Species groups of Coleoptera

	\multicolumn{5}{c	}{*Minimum Number of Individuals*}	*Species Group*
Section	37	37	37	37	63	
Depth (cm)	160–170	150–160	135–150	120–135	112–135	
Context	68	68	68	52	52	
Sample number LS	2	2	2	2	2	
Sample weight kg	3.0	3.0	1.0	1.0	3.0	
Carabus monilis F.	-	1	-	-	-	
Calosoma inquisitor (L.)	1	-	-	-	-	
Trechus obtusus Er. Or *quadristriatus* (Schr.)	1	11	1	-	-	
Bembidion properans Steph.	1	-	-	-	1	
B. assimile Gyll.	-	1	-	-	-	
B. biguttatum (F.)	-	2	1	-	-	
B. guttula (F.)	-	1	-	-	-	
Bembidion spp.	-	-	2	-	-	
Pterostichus melanarius (Ill.)	-	1	-	-	-	
P. minor (Gyll.)	-	1	-	-	-	
P. nigrita (Pk.)	-	3	-	-	-	
P. anthracinus (Pz.) or *nigrita* (Pk.)	-	-	1	-	-	
P. cupreus (L.) or *versicolor* (Strm.)	1	2	1	-	-	
Calathus fuscipes (Goez.)	1	-	1	-	-	
C. melanocephalus (L.)	-	2	1	1	-	
Agonum sp. (not *muelleri*)	-	1	-	-	-	
Amara spp.	-	1	1	-	-	
Harpalus rufipes (Deg.)	-	-	1	-	-	6a
H. ardosiacus Lut. or *sabulicola* (Pz.)	-	1	-	-	-	
H. affinis (Schr.)	-	1	-	-	-	
Acupalpus cf. *dorsalis* (F.)	-	1	-	-	-	
Chlaenius nigricornis (F.)	-	1	-	-	-	
Haliplus sp.	1	2	1	-	1	1
Noterus clavicornis (Deg.)	-	1	-	-	1	1
Hygrotus inaequalis (F.)	-	1	2	-	-	1
Hydroporus spp.	-	1	1	-	2	1
Agabus bipustulatus (L.)	1	1	1	-	2	1
Agabus sp. (not *bipustulatus*)	-	1	1	-	-	1
Colymbetes fuscus (L.)	1	1	1	-	-	1
Gyrinus sp.	-	-	-	-	1	1
Helophorus aquaticus (L.) or *grandis* Ill.	1	1	1	1	-	1
Helophorus sp. (*brevipalpis* size)	2	3	2	-	9	1
Coelostoma orbiculare (F.)	-	1	1	-	1	1
Sphaeridium bipustulatum F.	-	1	1	-	-	
Cercyon haemorrhoidalis (F.)	1	-	2	-	1	7
C. sternalis Shp.	-	1	-	-	-	7
C. ustulatus (Pres.)	1	2	-	-	1	7
Cercyon spp.	-	1	-	-	-	7
Megasternum obscurum (Marsh.)	-	8	5	1	1	7
Hydrobius fuscipes (L.)	1	4	1	-	1	1
A. bipustulata (Marsh.) or *limbata* (F.)	-	3	1	-	1	1
Helochares lividus (Forst.) or *obscurus* (Mull.)	-	-	-	-	1	1
Enochrus sp.	-	1	2	-	3	1
Cymbiodyta marginella (F.)	-	1	-	-	-	1
Chaetarthria seminulum (Hbst.)	-	1	-	-	-	1
Hister quadrimaculatus L.	-	-	2	-	-	
Paralister cf. *carbonarius* (Hoff.)	-	-	1	-	-	
Ochthebius minimus (F.)	-	1	-	-	-	1
O. cf. *minimus* (F.)	2	6	6	1	3	1

	Minimum Number of Individuals					Species Group
Section	*37*	*37*	*37*	*37*	*63*	
Depth (cm)	*160–170*	*150–160*	*135–150*	*120–135*	*112–135*	
Context	*68*	*68*	*68*	*52*	*52*	
Sample number LS	*2*	*2*	*2*	*2*	*2*	
Sample weight kg	*3.0*	*3.0*	*1.0*	*1.0*	*3.0*	
Hydraena testacea Curt.	2	4	1	-	1	1
Limnebius aluata (Bed.)	-	3	-	-	2	1
L. nitidus (Marsh.)	-	1	-	-	-	1
L. papposus Muls.	-	2	-	-	-	1
Ptiliidae indet. (not *Ptenidium*)	-	-	2	-	-	
Choleva or *Catops* sp.	-	1	-	-	-	
Acidota cruentata Man.	-	-	1	-	-	
Lesteva longoelytrata (Gz.)	2	4	2	-	-	
Omalium spp.	2	4	1	-	-	
Bledius sp.	1	-	-	-	-	
Carpelimus bilineatus Steph.	-	1	-	-	-	
Carpelimus sp. (not *bilineatus*)	-	-	2	-	-	
Platystethus arenarius (Fourc.)	-	-	1	-	-	7
P. cornutus gp.	-	1	1	-	-	
P. nodifrons (Man.)	-	2	1	-	-	
A. nitidulus (Grav.)	-	-	1	-	-	
A. rugosus (F.)	-	2	1	-	-	7
A. sculpturatus sp.	2	5	3	1	1	7
Stenus sp.	-	-	1	-	-	
Paederus sp.	-	1	-	-	-	
Lathrobium (not *multipunctum*)	1	1	1	-	-	
Xantholinus glabratus (Grav.)	-	1	-	-	-	
X. longiventris Heer	-	2	2	-	1	
X. linearis (Ol.) or *longiventris* Heer	-	1	-	1	1	
Philonthus spp.	1	3	2	1	-	
Staphylinus olens Müll.	1	1	1	-	-	
Tachyporus sp.	-	2	1	-	-	
Aleocharinae indet.	2	3	5	-	1	
Pselaphidae indet.	-	-	1	-	-	
Geotrupes sp.	1	1	1	1	-	2
Colobopterus erraticus (L.)	-	-	1	-	-	2
C. fossor (L.)	-	1	-	-	-	2
Aphodius ater (Deg.)	1	1	2	-	-	2
A. contaminatus (Hbst.)	1	8	19	-	2	2
A. depressus (Kug.)	-	-	-	-	1	2
A. cf. *fimetarius* (L.)	1	2	-	-	-	2
A. foetidus (Hbst.)	-	1	1	1	-	2
A. granarius (L.)	-	4	6	1	-	2
A. pusillus (Hbst.)	-	3	6	-	-	2
A. cf. *sphacelatus* (L.)	3	6	15	2	2	2
Aphodius sp.	-	-	2	1	-	2
Oxyomus sylvestris (Scop.)	1	2	1	-	-	
Onthophagus nutans (F.)	1	-	-	-	-	2
O. ovatus (L.)	-	3	7	-	-	2
O. vacca (L.)	-	-	1	-	-	2
Onthophagus spp. (not *ovatus*)	1	-	-	-	-	2
Phyllopertha horticola (L.)	1	1	2	1	-	11
Cetonia aurata (L.)	-	1	-	-	-	
cf. *Cyphon* sp.	5	22	14	6	-	

	\multicolumn{5}{c	}{*Minimum Number of Individuals*}	Species Group
Section	*37*	*37*	*37*	*37*	*63*	
Depth (cm)	*160–170*	*150–160*	*135–150*	*120–135*	*112–135*	
Context	*68*	*68*	*68*	*52*	*52*	
Sample number LS	*2*	*2*	*2*	*2*	*2*	
Sample weight kg	*3.0*	*3.0*	*1.0*	*1.0*	*3.0*	
Simplocaria maculosa Er. or *semistriata* (F.)	1	-	-	-	-	
Byrrhus sp.	-	1	1	-	-	
Dryops sp.	-	1	1	-	-	1
Agrypnus murinus (L.)	1	1	2	-	-	11
Athous hirtus (Hbst.)	-	1	2	-	-	11
A. obscurus (L.)	-	1	2	-	-	11
A. sputator (L.)	-	-	1	-	-	11
Agriotes spp.	1	3	-	1	-	11
Cantharis rustica Fall.	-	-	1	-	-	
Cantharis sp.	1	1	1	-	-	
Grynobius planus (F.)	1	-	1	-	-	4
Anobium punctatum (Deg.)	-	2	2	-	-	10
Ptinus fur (L.)	1	1	-	-	-	9a
Kateretes rufilabris (Lat.)	-	1	2	-	-	
Brachypterus sp.	-	3	4	1	-	
Brachypterus pulicarius (L.)	-	1	-	-	-	
Meligethes sp.	-	1	1	-	-	
Omosita colon (L.)	-	-	1	-	-	
Atomaria spp.	-	1	1	-	-	
Cryptophagidae indet. (not *Atomaria*)	-	1	1	-	-	
Phalacrus sp.	-	1	-	-	1	
Olibrus sp.	-	1	-	-	-	
Stilbus sp.	-	-	1	-	-	
Subcoccinella vigintiquattuorpunctata (L.)	-	-	1	-	-	
Stethorus punctillum Weise	-	4	1	-	-	
Adalia bipunctata (L.)	1	-	-	-	-	
Coccinella septempunctata L.	-	-	-	-	1	
Propylea quattuordecimpunctata (L.)	-	1	-	-	-	
Lathridius minutus gp.	-	2	4	-	-	8
Enicmus transversus (Ol.)	-	1	1	-	-	8
Corticariinae indet.	4	4	2	-	1	8
Typhaea stercorea (L.)	-	-	1	-	-	9a
Anaspis sp.	-	-	1	-	-	
Anthicus antherinus (L.)	-	1	-	-	-	
Tetrops praeusta (L.)	-	2	-	-	-	4
Bruchus or *Bruchidius* sp.	-	1	-	-	-	
Donacia clavipes (F.)	1	-	1	-	-	5
D. impressa Pk.	-	2	-	-	1	5
D. vulgaris Zsch.	1	-	-	-	1	5
Plateumaris affinis (Kz.)	1	-	-	-	-	5
P. braccata (Scop.)	-	2	-	-	1	5
Donacia or *Plateumaris* sp.	-	1	1	1	-	5
Chrysolina sp.	-	-	1	-	-	
Gastrophysa polygoni (L.)	-	-	1	-	-	
Prasocuris phellandrii (L.)	-	-	-	1	1	5
Phyllotreta atra (F.)	-	1	-	-	-	
P. nigripes (F.)	-	1	-	-	-	
P. cf. *nodicornis* (Marsh.)	-	1	-	-	-	
P. nemorum (L.) or *undulata* Kuts.	-	2	-	-	-	

	Minimum Number of Individuals					Species Group
Section	*37*	*37*	*37*	*37*	*63*	
Depth (cm)	*160–170*	*150–160*	*135–150*	*120–135*	*112–135*	
Context	*68*	*68*	*68*	*52*	*52*	
Sample number LS	*2*	*2*	*2*	*2*	*2*	
Sample weight kg	*3.0*	*3.0*	*1.0*	*1.0*	*3.0*	
P. vittula Redt.	2	4	1	-	1	
Aphthona striata (Goez.)	-	-	1	-	-	
Longitarsus spp.	5	4	5	-	1	
Altica sp.	-	-	1	-	-	
Crepidodera ferruginea (Scop.)	-	-	1	-	-	
Chalcoides sp.	2	1	-	-	-	4
Mantura chrysanthemi (Koch)	-	-	1	-	-	
Chaetocnema concinna (Marsh.)	1	6	3	-	2	
Psylliodes sp.	-	2	2	-	-	
Rhynchites aequatus (L.)	-	1	-	-	-	4
R. cf. *germanicus* Hbst.	-	-	1	-	-	
Apion malvae (F.)	1	-	1	-	-	
A. urticarium (Hbst.)	-	1	-	-	-	
A. pisi (F.)	-	1	-	-	-	3
A. craccae (L.)	-	1	-	-	-	3
Apion spp.	4	18	9	1	5	3
cf. *Phyllobius* sp.	-	-	1	-	-	
Barypeithes sp.	1	1	1	-	-	
Sitona hispidulus (F.)	-	-	1	-	-	3
Sitona spp.	1	3	1	-	-	3
Hypera punctata (F.)	1	-	-	-	-	
Tanysphyrus lemnae (Pk.)	-	2	1	-	1	5
Acalles turbatus Boh.	1	2	1	-	-	4
Notaris acridulus (L.)	-	-	1	-	2	5
Ceutorhynchus erysimi (F.)	-	3	-	-	-	
Ceuthorhynchinae indet.	-	4	1	1	-	
Anthonomus cf. *chevrolati* Desb.	-	2	1	-	-	4
A. cf. *rubi* (Hbst.)	1	1	1	-	-	
Tychius sp.	2	-	1	1	-	
Mecinus pyraster (Hbst.)	1	2	1	-	-	
Gymnetron labile (Hbst.)	-	-	-	-	1	
Hylastinus obscurus (Marsh.)	1	-	-	-	-	
Total	**84**	**282**	**229**	**27**	**62**	

Table 22 Coleoptera from F. 1

	\multicolumn{5}{c	}{*Minimum Number of Individuals*}
Section	*37*	*37*	*37*	*37*	*63*
Depth (cm)	*160–170*	*150–160*	*135–150*	*120–135*	*112–125*
Context	*68*	*68*	*68*	*52*	*58*
Sample number LS	*2*	*2*	*2*	*2*	*4*
Sample weight (kg)	*3.0*	*3.0*	*1.0*	*1.0*	*3.0*
Odonata indet. – adult	-	1	-	-	-
Forficula auricularia L.	2	6	1	-	-
Heterogaster urticae (F.)	-	-	1	-	-
Drymus sylvaticus (F.)	-	2	-	-	-
Dictyla convergens (H.–S.)	-	1	-	-	-
Anthocorinae indet.	1	1	1	-	-
Gerris sp.	1	-	-	-	-
Philaenus or Neophilaenus sp.	1	1	-	-	-
Megophthalmus sp.	-	1	-	-	-
Aphidoidea indet.	2	6	21	-	2
Trichoptera indet. – larva	1	1	1	-	-
Trichoptera indet. – larval case	-	-	-	1	5
Myrmica rubra (L.) or ruginodis Nyl. – worker	-	-	1	-	-
M. scabrinodis gp. – female	-	-	1	-	-
M. scabrinodis gp. – worker	-	2	2	-	1
Myrmica sp. – male	-	-	1	-	-
Lasius flavus gp. – worker	-	1	-	-	-
L. niger gp. – worker	-	-	6	-	1
Lasius sp. – male	-	-	-	-	1
Apis mellifera L. – worker	-	2	1	-	1
Hymenoptera indet. (not Formicidae)	2	12	8	-	2
Chironomidae indet. – larva	+	-	+	-	+
Dilophus febrilis (L.) or femoratus (Meig.)	3	13	3	-	4
Diptera indet. – puparia	-	12	1	-	2
Diptera indet. – adult	1	7	-	-	4

Table 23 Other insects from F. 1

sylvestris (common mallow), a plant that does not readily withstand grazing. The nitidulid beetle *Brachypterus* sp. and the heteropteran bug *Heterogaster urticae* feed on *Urtica dioica* (stinging nettle). It is likely that these plants were growing in neglected corners within the Ringwork or at the base of any hedges.

Fen
The hinterland of the site was peat fen, which was reflected by the insect fauna. There were several examples of the nitidulid beetle *Kateretes rufilabris*, which feeds on the pollen of *Juncus* spp. (rushes) and *Carex* spp. (sedges). All the samples also contained species of donaciine chrysomelid beetles, which feed on tall reedswamp and fen monocotyledonous plants. These included *Donacia clavipes* and *Plateumaris braccata*, which feed on *Phragmites australis* (common reed), and *Donacia impressa*, which feeds on *Schoenoplectus lacustris* (true bulrush). Two other species from the ditch, *Donacia vulgaris* and *Plateumaris affinis*, feed on a wider range of these plants, particularly *Carex* spp. (sedge).

Structures and settlement activities
There was a slight presence of synanthropic beetles. *Anobium punctatum* (woodworm beetle; Species Group 10) was identified from two of the samples and it is likely that it had emerged from structural timbers. Two other species from the ditch, *Ptinus fur* and *Typhaea stercorea*, are general synanthropic beetles (Species Group 9a) which are most usually found inside buildings or in old straw and hay, but they also have habitats unrelated to human activity. *P. fur*, for example, can live in nests. The Lathridiidae (Species Group 8), mould feeders which flourish in damp thatch and hay, were not unusually abundant, and the occurrence of beetles of foul organic material (Species Group 7) was no more than might be expected given the evidence for domestic animals from the scarabaeoid dung beetles of Species Group 2.

Remains of four workers of *Apis mellifera* (honey bee) were identified. They were found at both Section 37 and Section 63. These finds do not prove that the occupants kept bees: they could, for example, have been from a feral colony living in a nearby hollow tree. They do, however, confirm that the resources of the hive would have been

Feature/context	Description
F1 *011*	Completely desiccated twig fragments with bark. Unidentified.
F1 *062*	Clay blocks with black leaf fragments; reticulate venation but leaf margins not preserved. Also includes small degraded fragments of bark and decayed traces of wood. Unidentified.
F1 *065*	Two wood frags. Cell structure totally degraded. Unidentified.
F1 *067*	Sixteen twig frags, no bark, *c.* 4–15 mm diam very badly fissured and degraded. Unidentified.
	Five miscellaneous wood frags. Very badly fissured and degraded. Unidentified.
F.1 *068*	Fourteen fragments of twigs, 3–7mm diam. One with well-preserved *Crataegus-type* thorns. Cell structure of some moderately well-preserved. These retained for possible identification.
F1 *091*	Completely desiccated roundwood frag with bark. Unidentified.
F1 *245*	Straight roundwood stem, no bark, 500mm long; compressed, stem diams 30 x 20mm. *Fraxinus* sp. Other roundwood frags probably also of *Fraxinus*.
	Larger wood frags with some bark; compressed and fissured; cell structure badly degraded. Possibly *Fraxinus*.
	Four roundwood twig frags *c.* 10–20mm. Diameter; compressed and fissured; cell structure badly degraded. Unidentified.
	Roundwood stem, no bark, 210mm long; fissured and compressed, *c.* 20mm diam; rotted at one end, giving spurious impression of artificial point; *Fraxinus* sp.
F1 *246*	Five roundwood stem fragments with bark loosely attached, up to 170mm long; diams *c.* 25–30mm, fissured and compressed; cell structure totally degraded. Unidentified.
	Twig fragments *c.* 10mm diam. Similarly poorly preserved. Unidentified.
F1 *247*	Eighty-three twig and roundwood frags *c.* 4–30mm diam. Some with traces of bark. Most completely compressed, fissured and distorted. Three relatively well preserved stems with coherent cell structure retained for identification. These are stems with contorted growth, semi ring-porous with wide rays. ?*Prunus*.
F1 *249*	Two timber fragments, 120–30 x 15mm, 50 x 60 x 5mm. Larger piece probably *Fraxinus* but cell structure of both badly degraded.
F1 *396*	Two large timber fragments, no bark, 110 x 70 x 45mm and 180 x 120 x 50mm. Very badly fissured and distorted. Both *Quercus* sp.
	Two 10mm diam. twig fragments, no bark, fissured and distorted. Unidentified.
	Completely desiccated fragments of bark. Unidentified.
F1 *397*	Four thin (*c.* 5mm) radially split fragments of timber. Splitting due to natural fissuring during decay along rays. Cell structure totally degraded. Unidentified.
	Fragment of large roundwood, *c.* 40mm diam, fissured and degraded but probably *Fraxinus*.
	13 twig frags, *c.* 5–12mm diam. One with traces of *Prunus/ Crataegus-type* thorns. Fissured and degraded. Unidentified.
	23 miscellaneous wood fragments all very badly fissured and distorted. Unidentified.

Table 24 The wood assemblage

available to the settlement. Honey bee was also recorded at the Iron Age settlement of Mingies Ditch, Oxon (Allen and Robinson 1993, 139).

Differences between the sections and chronological change
Insufficient insects were recovered from Section 63 to detect any ecological differences between the insect assemblages from the two sections other than that there was a higher proportion of aquatic beetles from Section 63. Section 37, however, did offer some evidence of chronological change. The percentage of scarabaeoid dung beetles (Species Group 2) more than doubled ascending the profile, whereas the proportion of weevil favoured by hay meadow (Species Group 3) declined. Whether this reflected very local changes or a more general intensification of grazing is uncertain. There was no evidence from the insects for any increase in flooding over time.

Generally, the insect results have given a picture of the Wardy Hill Ringwork which is consistent with the other archaeological evidence. The settlement itself was not intensively occupied, and was possibly surrounded by a hedge. The landscape was relatively open and included much grassland against a background of fen. The herding of domestic animals appears to have been a major activity at the settlement and it is possible that beekeeping was practised. Such results would quite possibly be typical of Iron Age settlements on the fen-edge, and certainly fall within the range of results from Iron Age settlements in the upper Thames Valley (*e.g.* Allen and Robinson 1993).

V. Wood
by P. Murphy
(Table 24)

Wood was collected by hand during excavation, almost entirely from the enclosure ditch F. 1. Preservation was variable but predominantly very poor. Macroscopically the wood was semi-desiccated, with fissures splitting along the rays; bark, where it survived, was usually only loosely attached to the shrunken wood. Many stems were compressed by the overlying clay. Microscopically the cell structure of most wood samples was completely disrupted. Some had identifiable tissue surviving, though even in these samples the rays were irregularly sinuous and vessels deformed. In these circumstances there was no prospect of detecting any wood-working evidence, and identification was rarely possible. The material was all inspected and notes are given in Table 24. The identifications of *Fraxinus* (ash) and *Quercus* (oak) simply reflect the fact that only species with very distinctive structure could be identified amongst the poorly preserved wood. Much of the twiggy material is from irregularly-grown stems including *Prunus/Crataegus*-type thorns, which would be consistent with evidence from seeds and pollen for the proximity of sloe and hawthorn hedgerow/scrub.

VI. Animal bone
by S.J.M. Davis
(Figs 61–64; Tables 25–37, 72–82 (Appendix))

From the 17,228 pieces of bone recovered from the site, a total of 1412 identifiable bones, mandibles and isolated teeth were recorded (the ploughsoil material is not here considered: see below). Most of the animal remains were recovered by hand. Some smaller bones of large animals and bones of smaller animals and isolated teeth may well have been missed (*Sieved fraction*, below). Most bones (and their surface structures) are well preserved, though some have suffered from the action of carnivores prior to incorporation into the soil.

For a full description of the methods used, see Davis 1992. In brief, all mandibular teeth and a restricted suite of 'parts of the skeleton always recorded' (*i.e.* a predetermined set of articular ends/epiphyses and metaphyses of girdle, limb and foot bones) were recorded and used in counts (Table 25). In order to avoid multiple counting of very fragmented bones, at least 50% of any given part had to be present for it to be counted. Single metapodial condyles of caprines and cattle were counted as halves, as were each of the two central pig metapodials.

A mammal-bone epiphysis is described as either 'unfused' (when there are no spicules of bone connecting epiphysis to shaft so that the two separate easily) or 'fused' (when it cannot be detached from the metaphysis). Caprine teeth were assigned to the eruption and wear stages of Payne (1973 and 1987); pig and cattle teeth were assigned to the eruption and wear stages of Grant (1982).

Measurements taken on the humerus and cattle metapodials are illustrated in Davis (1992; figs 1 and 2) and on pig teeth follow Payne and Bull (1988). In general, other measurements taken are those recommended by von den Driesch (1976).

Species size and representation
(Figs 61–64; Tables 25–27; Appendix)

Sheep and goat
Caprine teeth and bones are generally difficult to determine to species. Some, such as the dP and dP, astragalus, metapodials and terminal phalanges (Payne 1969, 1985; Boessneck 1969) are relatively easy to identify as either sheep or goat. As Table 25 indicates, most of the caprine bones at Wardy Hill belonged to sheep. There was no evidence for the presence of goat. In the British Iron Age goats were only kept in very small numbers (Grant 1984a). For the purposes of further study (*e.g.* biometry and age at death), the sheep/goat teeth and bones are referred to herein as *sheep*.

The sheep at Wardy Hill, as well as sheep from several other Iron Age, Roman, medieval and post-medieval sites in England, are compared with a sample of 26 modern unimproved Shetland ewes using a log ratio diagram (Figs 61–63). Sheep stature and shape undoubtedly changed over time in England, though evidence for this is only beginning to emerge from zooarchaeological studies. As more assemblages are studied biometrically, it is becoming increasingly clear that sheep significantly increased in size during the early post-medieval era.

The medieval/post-medieval data from Launceston Castle (Albarella and Davis 1996) are shown in the figures to serve as a scale against which earlier changes may be compared. These figures show that the widths and depths of Wardy Hill sheep bones were similar to those from the other Iron Age sheep in Hampshire, as well as the small sample from Barrington in Cambridgeshire. These Iron Age sheep were clearly very gracile, with the majority of the measurements in the width and depth dimensions falling well to the left of the '0' line in these log-ratio plots. Since the standard sample comprised ewes only, and the archaeological sheep probably included some rams, these Iron Age sheep must have been very small indeed. Moreover, the lengths of a number of the bones lie well to the left (Fig. 62) and suggest that many of the Wardy Hill sheep were also of very short stature. Of the two Roman samples from Owslebury and Lanes (Carlisle) those from Owslebury are somewhat more robust (t + 3.1 p < 0.01), but the difference is slight. The medieval sheep from Launceston are slightly more robust than the Iron Age and Roman ones shown here.

Cattle
The cattle at Wardy Hill appear to have been fairly small, and similar to the ones found at Barrington (Table 28; Davis 1995).

Equids
Equid bones and teeth can also be difficult to identify to species (most ass and horse bones are sometimes easily confused). The Wardy Hill equid teeth undoubtedly belonged to horse: the enamel folds on the biting surfaces of the mandibular teeth had 'U'-shaped lingual folds, and the buccal folds partially penetrate between the flexids in the molars (Eisenmann 1981). Given the difficulties in distinguishing skeletal remains of horses and donkeys, the presence of the latter species cannot be ruled out.

There are four horse metatarsals (see Appendix). Their lateral lengths in millimetres are 218.6 (*605*), 219.7 (*603*), 231.7 (*355*) and 245.6 (*404*). Multiplying these measurements by Kiesewalter's factor (*i.e.* 5.33; von den Driesch and Boessneck 1974) indicates their withers heights ranged from 1.17–1.31m, or from 11 hands 2 inches to 13 hands. Since the pony/horse boundary lies at 14 hands 2 inches, the Wardy Hill metatarsals belonged to ponies rather than horses. According to Coy and Maltby (1987) Iron Age ponies ranged from 10–14 hands.

Pigs
The absence of any especially large specimens of Sus suggests that the small sample of pig bones and teeth belonged to the domestic pig rather than its large relative, the wild boar, which survived in England until the 17th century (Harting 1880, 102). In Fig. 64 the pig measurements are compared with the 'standard' values calculated

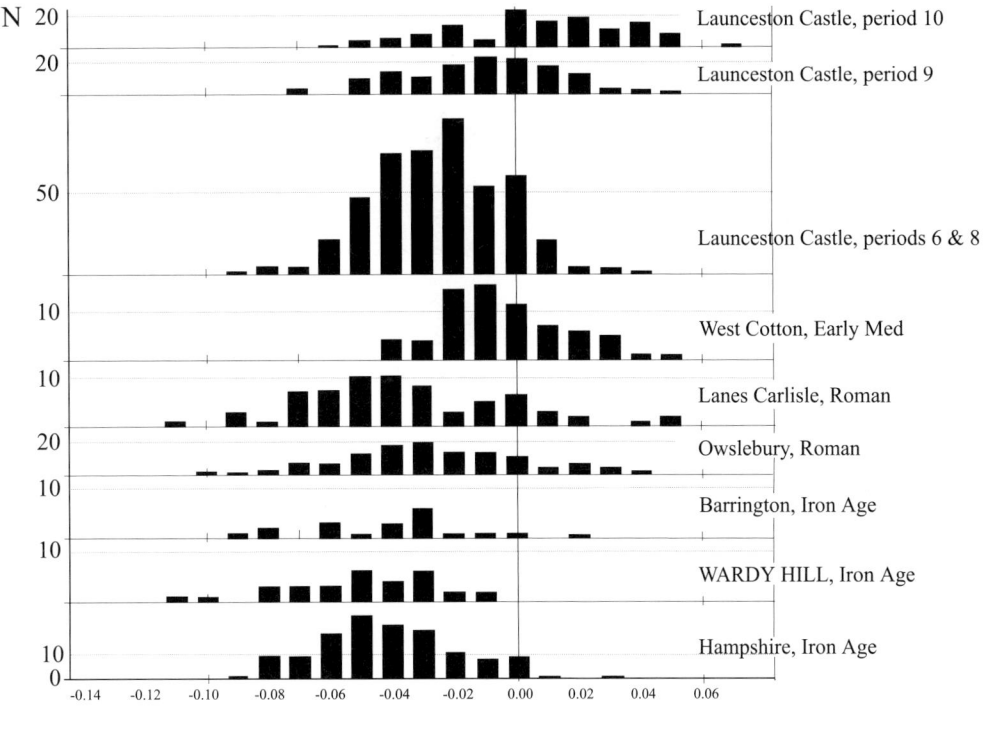

Measurements of the widths of the Wardy Hill sheep bones compared with the mean values of widths (the '0' line) of a sample of 26 modern Shetland ewes – Log ratio diagrams (from Davis 1996). The following measurements are pooled: [humerus BT + metacarpal Bd + tibia Bd + astragalus Bd + metatarsal Bd]. Values which are greater than the Shetland mean are positive and lie to the right of the zero line, values which are less are negative and lie to the left. Samples of sheep bones from other sites are included for comparison, as follows, from bottom to top: four Iron Age sites in Hampshire (Balksbury, Micheldever Wood, Owslebury and Rope Lake Hall; from the Animal Bones Measurement Project of the University of Southampton – ABMAP); Wardy Hill, Cambridgeshire (this report); Barrington, Cambridgeshire (Davis 1995); Owslebury, Hampshire (Maltby 1987); Lanes, Carlisle (Connell and Davis in prep.); West Cotton, Northamptonshire (Albarella and Davis 1994); Launceston Castle, Cornwall (Periods 6 and 8 are medieval, periods 9 and 10 are post-medieval; in Albarella and Davis 1996). Data from Owslebury were kindly supplied by Mark Maltby, and from ABMAP by Kate Clark.

Figure 61 Sheep size in England: log ratio of mean widths

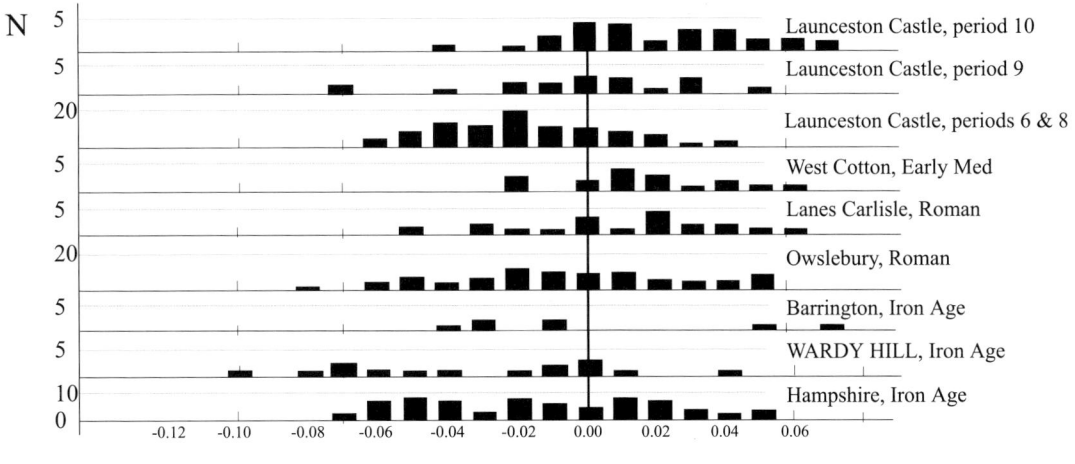

Measurements of the lengths of the Wardy Hill sheep bones compared with the mean values of lengths (the '0' line) of a sample of 26 modern Shetland ewes – Log ratio diagrams (from Davis 1996). The following measurements are pooled: [metacarpal GL + tibia GL + calcaneum GL + astragalus GL + metatarsal GL]. Values which are greater than the Shetland mean are positive and lie to the right of the zero line; values which are less are negative and lie to the left. Samples of sheep bones from other sites are included for comparison, as follows, from bottom to top: four Iron Age sites in Hampshire (Balksbury, Micheldever Wood, Owslebury and Rope Lake Hall; ABMAP); Wardy Hill, Cambridgeshire (this report); Barrington, Cambridgeshire (Davis 1995); Owslebury, Hampshire (Maltby, 1987); Lanes, Carlisle (Connell and Davis in prep.); West Cotton, Northamptonshire (Albarella and Davis 1994); Launceston Castle, Cornwall (Periods 6 and 8 are medieval, periods 9 and 10 are post-medieval; in Albarella and Davis 1996). Data from Owslebury were kindly supplied by Mark Maltby, and from ABMAP by Kate Clark.

Figure 62 Sheep size in England: log ratio of mean lengths

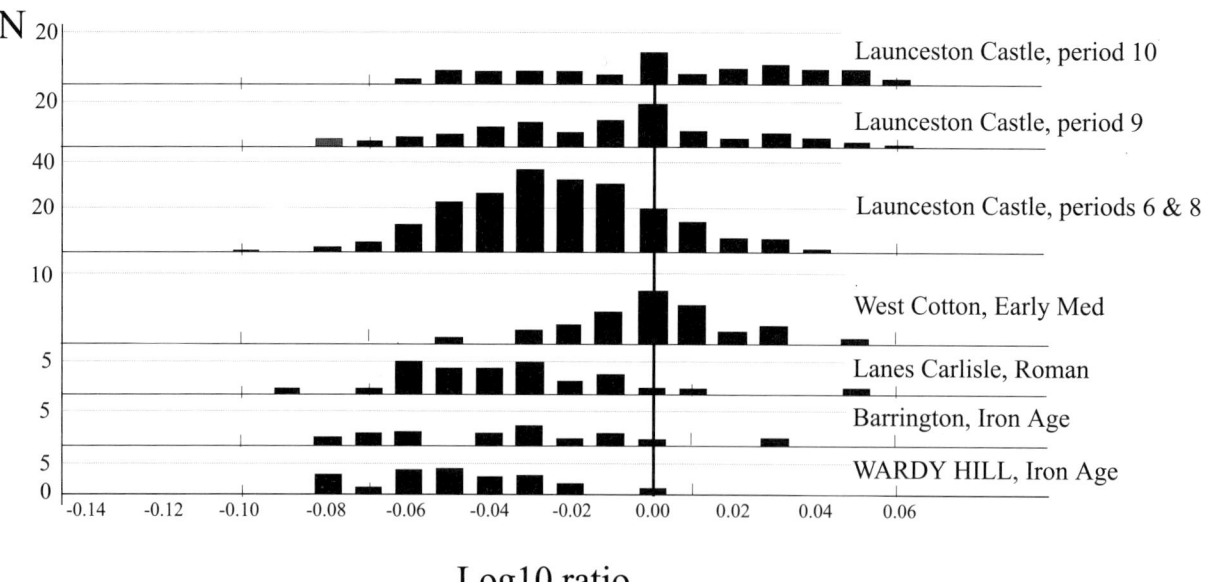

Measurements of the depths of the Wardy Hill sheep bones compared with the mean values of depths (the '0' line) of a sample of 26 modern Shetland ewes – Log ratio diagrams (from Davis 1996). The following measurements are pooled: [humerus HTC metacarpal DEM + astragalus Dd]. Values which are greater than the Shetland mean are positive and lie to the right of the zero line, values which are less are negative and lie to the left. Samples of sheep bones from other sites are included for comparison, as follows, from bottom to top: Wardy Hill, Cambridgeshire (this report); Barrington, Cambridgeshire (Davis 1995); Lanes, Carlisle (Connell and Davis in prep.); West Cotton, Northamptonshire (Albarella and Davis 1994); Launceston Castle, Cornwall (Periods 6 and 8 are medieval, periods 9 and 10 are post-medieval; in Albarella and Davis 1996).

Figure 63 Sheep size in England: log ratio of mean depths

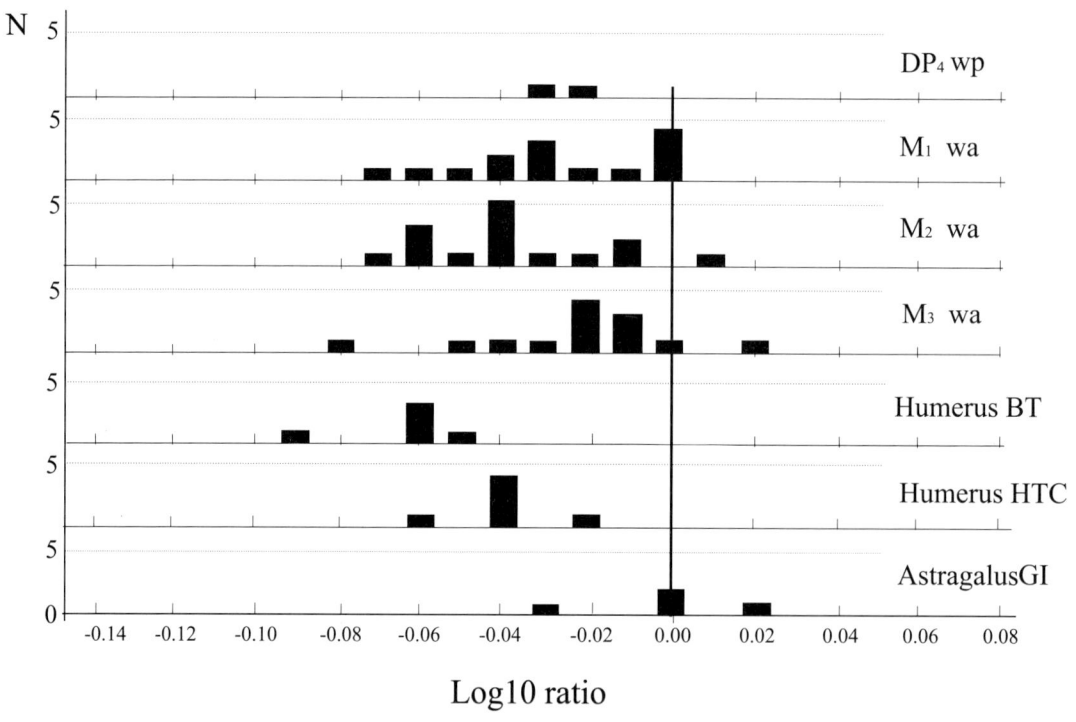

Measurements of the Wardy Hill pig teeth, humeri and astragali compared with the mean values (the '0' line) of a sample of Neolithic pig teeth from Durrington Walls (Albarella and Payne forthcoming) – Log ratio diagrams. Values which are greater than the Durrington Walls 'standard' are positive and lie to the right of the zero line, values which are less are negative and lie to the left.

Figure 64 Wardy Hill pig bone measurements compared with Durrington Walls

		Cattle	Sh/Goat	Pig	Horse	Dog	Hare	Others
Teeth (mandibular)	I	22	15	24	[14]			Water Vole 3
	dI	3	2	2				
	C			19 (13m+6f)	[3]	[6]		Cat 1
	dC							
	P1							
	P2	4		4	3	2		
	P3	11	30	12		3		Cat 1. Fox 1. Otter 1
	P4	13	49	19	2	4		Cat 1. Otter 1
	dP2	10	16					
	dP3	16	41 (37=Sh)	1	2			
	dP4	22	64 (64=Sh)	3	3			
	M1	19	79	17		5		Cat 1. Otter 2. Water Vole 2
	M2	16	62	17		4		Fox 1. Water Vole 2
	M3	33	85	16	1	1		
	M1/2	29	98	6	1			
Scapula (glenoid)	U		5	1				?Red Deer 1
	F	8	9	4	2	1		
	?	4	4	3	1			
Distal humerus	UM	1	1					
	UE							
	F	10	17 (11=Sh)	9	4	3		Badger 2
Distal radius	UM	2	7	1	1			
	UE	1		2				
	F	4	4			1		
Distal metacarpal	UM		7	0.5				
	UE							
	F	6	4 (4=Sh)					Fox 1
C2		1	1					
Ischium (acetabulum)		16	15	3	3			
Distal femur	UM	2	3	1				
	UE	1	3				1	
	F	2	2		1	1		Fox 1
Distal tibia	UM	1	8	3				
	UE		1	1				
	F	15	13	4	4	1	1	
Calcaneum	U	4	4					
	F	1	5					
	?	17	3	2	1			
Astragalus		11	9 (3=Sh)	4	2	1		
Distal metatarsal	UM	2	4					Otter 1
	UE	1						
	F	6	5 (5=Sh)	0.5	4			
Phalanx 1 proximal	UM	6	11	1				
	UE	1						
	F	29	18	1	6	5		
Phalanx 3		17	1 (1=Sh)	3	1			
Distal metapodial	UM	1.5	0.5					
	UE	1	2					
	F	1.5	0.5		1	7		
Other bones								2 Red Deer antler frags
Totals		371	708	183	52	42	2	
	%	27	51	13	4	3	present	

Table 25 Numbers of mammal teeth and bones

Some sheep/goat bones could be identified to species and their numbers are given in brackets; where this was possible all were sheep (=Sh). UM = unfused metaphysis, UE = unfused epiphysis, F = fused end, m = male, f = female. The antler fragments are red deer. * The count of horse incisors and horse and dog canines include both upper and lower teeth, their totals are therefore halved to compute the total bone counts.

	n	%	N Molars	% Molars
Cattle	371	27	97	20
Sheep/Goat	708	50	324	64
Pig	183	13	56	12
Red Deer	0			
Horse	2	4	2	
Hare	2			
Dog	42	3	10	2
Fox	4		1	
Cat	4		1	
Otter	5		2	
Badger	2			
Water Vole	7		4	1
Galliform	5			
Raven	3			
Corvid	2			
Duck	12	1		
Goose	2			
Swan	1			
?Crane	1			
Woodcock	1			
?Thrush	1			
Buzzard	1			
Amphibia	2			
Pike	1			
Total	**1412**		**496**	

Table 26 Animal bones and teeth
The right hand column considers the numbers of molar teeth only. In view of the probable poor preservation of many of the bones — especially of sheep — these numbers may well provide a truer estimate of the original frequencies of mammals at Wardy Hill.

from the Neolithic sample of pigs from Durrington Walls (Albarella and Payne forthcoming). This method allows different measurements to be compared. Thus most of the Wardy Hill pig measurements are to the left of the '0' Durrington 'standard' line. It seems likely then that after the Neolithic period the size of the English pig decreased.

Dog
There is nothing particularly remarkable about the dog bones and teeth. Most of their measurements indicate dogs of medium size (see Appendix). By way of comparison, most fall in between the AML reference collection Collie (18 inches at the shoulder) and the AML reference collection Labrador (23 inches at the shoulder). Small lap dogs did not apparently appear in Britain until Roman times and were, as indeed they are today, a luxury (Harcourt 1974).

Otter
Otter-hunting was once a popular amusement in England 'pursued with much pomp and circumstance' (Bell 1837, 132). Bailey *et al.* (1981) found an otter mandible in an Iron Age context at Meare Village West.

Galliform
The bones of chicken (known from the late Iron Age in Britain: Bate 1934), guinea fowl and pheasant (both of which were known to the Romans) are difficult to distinguish although some parts, such as the tarso-metatarsus and the femur, can help in this respect. Unfortunately, no diagnostic galliform bones were found. The chicken is descended from the red jungle fowl of south and south-east Asia. It was introduced westwards and had become common in the Mediterranean by the 6th century BC (Crawford 1984). Chicken is known from the Hallstatt and La Tène periods in central Europe and was perhaps introduced into Britain during the centuries before the Roman invasion. Julius Caesar wrote that chickens were kept by the ancient Britons for amusement (*Gallic War* V, 12).

Pike
Apart from a pike mandible, nine pike vertebrae were found in *328* and *329*. They measure approx. 18 x 16mm in diameter, and therefore derive from quite large fish probably over a metre long (Locker *pers. comm.*). This 'exceedingly common' fresh-water fish was, according to

	Wardy Hill	Cat's Water	Haddenham	Barrington	Danebury	Market Deeping	Baldock	Meare Village
Sheep/Goat	50	39	63	47	58	37	49	61
Cattle	27	45	18	25	21	41	28	24
Pig	13	7	4	14	11	7	18	13
Red Deer	+	+		?+	1	+		
Horse	4	7		5	4	13	5	1
Dog	3	2		3	4	2	1	2
N	**1412**	**5782**	**840**	**670**	**46,358**	**320**	**[80]**	**1876**

Table 27 Percentages of the main animals species at Wardy Hill compared to those from some other Iron Age assemblages in England
Comparative assemblages: Cat's Water Fengate (Biddick 1984), Haddenham (Evans and Serjeantson 1988), Barrington (Davis 1995 and 1998), Danebury (Grant 1991), Outgang Road, Market Deeping (Albarella 1997), Baldock (Chaplin and McCormick 1986), and Meare village, Somerset Levels (Bailey *et al.* 1981). 'N' is the total count of identifiable bones from which these percentages have been calculated. An exception is Baldock, where the minimum numbers of individual animals were used and N is the total MNI.

Yarrell (1836), highly esteemed in medieval times. He quotes a Rev. Sheppard who noticed 'an annual migration of Pikes which takes place in spring in the Cam into which river they come in great shoals, doubtless from the fens in the neighbourhood of Ely, where they are bred' (1836, 384). Yarrell also describes how pike were caught in the Norfolk Broads using liggers or cylindrical floats, made of wood, cork or rushes 8–15 feet long from which hooked bait was suspended.

Other taxa

The remains of hare, fox, badger and birds, as well as the pike and otter, though scarce, all testify to some hunting, fowling and fishing by the inhabitants of Wardy Hill. There were probably more fish, bird and small animal bones, which were not recovered (*Sieved fraction*, below). There are two fragments of deer antler (probably red deer): one is sawn, suggesting the use of this material for tool production. The absence of other deer bones is worth noting, but in view of the total size of the assemblage may not be of any great significance. According to Grant (1984a) wild animals are very rare on most Iron Age sites in Britain.

Frequencies of taxa

To take the site as a whole, of the 1412 recorded bones and teeth 50% belonged to sheep, 26% to cattle and 13% to pig. Scrutiny of the counts of teeth and bone in Table 25 indicates that the 'minimum numbers' of the different species can be estimated as follows: sheep 60 (first + second molars divided by 4); cattle 17 (third molars divided by 2); pig 10 (first + second molars divided by 4); horse 3 (deciduous + permanent fourth pre-molars divided by 2). Undoubtedly hand collection has meant that many of the smaller bones and teeth, especially of the smaller taxa, were lost during excavation. A closer look at Table 25 shows that both sheep and pigs were probably considerably more common than cattle than is indicated by the total bone counts. There are approximately three times as many sheep molars (324) as cattle molars (97). These tend to be well preserved, are less likely to be destroyed by dogs, and are easier to see during excavation. They may, therefore, provide a better estimate of the ratio of sheep to cattle at Wardy Hill (*i.e.* 3 to 1). While the molars suggest three times as many sheep as cattle, the bones suggest a very much lower sheep/cattle ratio (18 sheep and 11 cattle humeri; 15 sheep and 16 cattle ischia; and only 12 sheep but 22 cattle calcanea). Similarly, the pig/cattle ratio was perhaps 1:2, with 56 pig molars and 97 cattle molars. In summary, the ratio of sheep/cattle/pig was then probably 6:2:1. Given the small size of sheep teeth, sheep were probably even more common than this 'molar ratio' suggests. Notwithstanding recovery (as well as preservation) bias, and given the greater size of cattle (a cow in the Iron Age probably equalled six sheep in terms of dietary yield), the inhabitants of Wardy Hill probably had two beef meals for every one of lamb/mutton and pork.

How does Wardy Hill compare in terms of the relative numbers of cattle and sheep with other contemporary fen-edge sites, and with other Iron Age sites in England in general? At Cats Water, Peterborough, cattle comprise 45% and sheep only 39% (Biddick 1984). At Outgang Road, Market Deeping, cattle comprise 42% and sheep only 38% (Albarella 1997). But at another fen-edge settlement — Enclosure V, Upper Delphs, Haddenham — sheep far outnumber cattle (Evans and Serjeantson 1988). In general terms Wardy Hill, with its high sheep/cattle ratio, is typical of contemporary sites across the country (Table 27). The abundance of sheep compared to cattle appears characteristic of 1st millennium BC sites in England, especially of the second half of this period. This general increase in the numbers of sheep throughout the 1st millennium is linked to the spread of downland arable farming, with even higher frequencies of sheep occurring on sites located on higher ground such as chalk downland (Grant 1984a, Cunliffe 1991). At Danebury, for example, sheep numbers were as high as 70% (Grant 1984b). Robinson and Wilson (1987) noted that the percentages of sheep remains on twelve Iron Age sites in the Midlands ranged between 25% and 63%, while on fifteen Romano-British sites these percentages dropped to between 12% and 45% with pig and cattle becoming more frequent (see also King 1978). Thus, with its predominance of sheep over cattle and pig the Wardy Hill fauna is typical of most, but not all, Iron Age sites in southern Britain. However, given the problems of recovery and preservation, variations of the sheep/cattle ratios must be regarded cautiously. Another point of interest is the rather low percentage of pig. Grant (in press) suggests that in the Iron Age there is a correlation between relatively high proportions of pig remains and high-status occupation, although she cautions that the 'high' percentages are rather lower than those of Roman and medieval periods. Those with little pig are low-status or ordinary rural sites; the Celts prized pork above all other flesh, and regarded it as the food of the gods (Ross 1967, 313).

Skeleton parts present, carnivore activity and butchery

There are insufficient bones to investigate possible body-part preferences in any detail, though there is little evidence from the counts of postcranial bones in Table 25 for any especial preference for particular parts of the skeleton. All parts of the skeleton of cattle, sheep and pig are represented, if rather unequally. Variations between the different parts probably reflect differential preservation (Brain 1967) and recovery (Payne 1975).

The numbers of teeth compared to bones in Table 25 reveals a very striking disparity. Take the sheep for example. From the teeth alone 60 animals (*i.e.* numbers of [M + M + M] 4) are represented, while there are at most only eleven individuals (from the numbers of tibiae) indicated by the limb-bones. This exceptionally high ratio of teeth to bones is probably due in part to the poorer rate of preservation of bone as well as to the action of dogs, which tend to avoid teeth. It appears characteristic of many rural sites where the rate of deposition may have been lower than in towns, and where dogs were perhaps more common (Albarella and Davis 1994). Indeed some bones at Wardy Hill had been gnawed (21 or 13% of cattle, 6 or 14% of pig, 3 or 10% of horse and only 6 or 4% of sheep). Several bones, all small sheep bones, show the typical pattern of partial digestion described by Payne and Munson 1985: two astragali (*055* and *352*), two calcanea (*316* and *328*), a distal metapodial condyle (*401*) and a complete proximal phalanx (*031*). These, and the gnawed bones, probably reflect carnivore activity. This generally poor rate of preservation makes it difficult to draw firm conclusions regarding the age-at-death patterns of the more common animals (below). (In contrast, the low ratio

	Barrington			Wardy Hill		
	n	*mean*	*sd*	*n*	*mean*	*sd*
M3 length	5	36.3	1.8	22	35.2	1.6
M3 width	10	16.1	0.8	25	15.5	1.0
Tibia Bd	9	56.3	5.0	10	54.3	3.4
Astragalus Gl 1	5	61.4	2.4	9	57.4	2.9
Astragalus Bd	7	38.6	2.5	9	36.2	2.7
Metatarsal Bd	3	50.4	3.1	4	51.6	4.3

Table 28 Cattle measurements: Wardy Hill compared to Barrington

	Butchered	Gnawed	Total number of bones
Cattle	5	21	182
Horse	?1	3	30
Pig	3	6	44
Sheep	3	12	170*
Dog	0	0	20

* 6 of which are semi-digested

Table 29 Wardy Hill: numbers of butchered and gnawed bones

	Main Building		Inner Ringwork Circuit		Outer Ringwork Circuit	
	Bones	*Mandibles*	*Bones*	*Mandibles*	*Bones*	*Mandibles*
Cattle	41	18	34		43	46
Sheep	45	58	50	84	20	31
Pig	11	23	8	16	6	
Horse	3		8		16	
Dog			1		15	23
N=	188	65	87	25	86	13

Table 31 Distribution of animal bones (Bones) and mandibles with two or more teeth (Mandibles) in different parts of Wardy Hill
The figures are percentages, and N represents the total counts for each column. Note that sample sizes are small especially for the mandibles so interpretation must be treated with caution.

	Main Buildings		Inner Ringwork Circuit		Outer Ringwork Circuit	
	Cattle	*Sheep*	*Cattle*	*Sheep*	*Cattle*	*Sheep*
Limb Bones	31	57	14	22	23	14
Phalanges 1+3	29	11	5	16	8	1

Table 32 Distribution of numbers of main limb-bones (scapula, humerus, radius, metapodials, pelvis, femur and tibia) and phalanges (proximal and terminal) of cattle and sheep in different parts of Wardy Hill
Note that sample sizes are small, so interpretation must be treated with caution.

Sheep/Goat

	0	1	2	3	4	5	6	7	8	9	10	11	12	13	14	15	16	17	18	19	20	21	22	23	24	Unassigned
dP4							2	1	5	10		1	25	11	37	1	1	2	3	3						3
P4					1		5	6	3	32	2	2	12	1	1	1							1	1		
M1			1	3	1	2	9	17	7	37		2			3	8										2
M1/2			4		4	6	3	3	1	41	1	1	2		1	1										2
M2	2		3			2	4	2	6	8	9	1	1													2
M3	5	1	4	1	6	5						27														2

Cattle

	a	b	b/c	c	c/d	d	e	f	g	h	j	k	l	m	n	Unassigned
dP4	1	1		1				9	4		6	4				
P4						1	1	6	2	1					1	
M1	1							3	2		6	4	2			
M1/2	3	5		1			1	5	3		3	4	2	1		
M2	2	1						2	5	1	1	1	3			
M3	3	5		2		1	1	1	8	1	2	4	1	3		

Pig

	a	b	c	d	e	f	g	h	j	k	l	m	n	Unassigned
dP4			1						1					
P4		3	8	5	1		1			1				
M1		1		4	2	4	1	1	3				1	
M1/2			1	2	2									
M2	2		5	5	2		2						1	

Table 30 Dental wear stages of the sheep/goat (after Payne 1987), cattle (after Grant 1982) and pigs (after Grant 1982) at Wardy Hill

of horse teeth to horse bone is worth noting, but difficult to explain.)

A few bones (two cattle, three sheep and two pig) had cut marks and a few had crop marks (three cattle and one pig bone: Table 29), but these numbers are too small to allow meaningful comparisons between taxa. It is a little surprising that so few animal bones appear to show signs of butchery.

Age distribution
(Table 30)
Given the extremely poor preservation of the faunal assemblage at Wardy Hill, age-at-death data have to be treated with great caution. One standard technique used by zooarchaeologists is to assign complete or nearly-complete mandibles to eruption and wear stages (for caprines, for example, using the criteria of Payne 1973). This works well for sites where the majority of teeth are still in their mandibles. However, for assemblages of very fragmented bones — and Wardy Hill certainly falls in this category — many of the younger (more fragile) mandibles will have broken up. Hence, a bias favouring adult ageable mandibles results.

Table 30 shows that over 60% of the sheep/goat mandibles at Wardy Hill are in age classes 'F' (3–4 years) and 'G' (4–6 years). Closer inspection of Tables 25 and 30, however, indicates a somewhat different picture. Note firstly the high proportion of dPs. This last milk pre-molar tooth is not shed in sheep/goat until the end of the second year, when it is replaced by P. The ratio dP:P is 64:49. I would not interpret this as a predominance of one- and two-year old animals: P is a much smaller tooth than dP and therefore much less likely to be recovered, especially in an assemblage such as that from Wardy Hill consisting mostly of isolated teeth. Perhaps it is safer to consider the dP:M ratio. The third molar, of similar size to dP, erupts at about the same time as the dP–P replacement. The dP:M ratio of 64:80 indicates that perhaps around 44% of the sheep were being slaughtered by the time they reached the age of 24 months, and the scarcity of dPs in very young wear stages suggests many of these were slaughtered at over 6 months of age (see Deniz and Payne 1982). Since many of the Ms are in Stage 9, which lasts until animals are at the end of their third year, the overall pattern is one of culling in the first three years of life, suggesting an emphasis on meat-production. This does not of course mean that sheep were not milked nor shorn of their fleeces too, merely that the emphasis was on meat. A similar conclusion can be drawn from the cattle teeth data, with a dP:M ratio of 22:33 again indicating a probable emphasis on meat.

This emphasis on mutton and beef is similar to the finding at Outgang Road, where Albarella (1997) interpreted the dental data as indicating sheep were probably kept for their meat as well as wool and milk, and the cattle were probably more highly valued for their traction power and milk. At Barrington, too, the majority of the sheep were culled quite young, suggesting an emphasis on meat (Davis 1995); Albarella (1997) suggests that meat may have been the main product of sheep husbandry during the English Iron Age. However, according to Grant (1984a) there was considerable variation in sheep husbandry practices in the Iron Age. Wool may have become increasingly important, as evidenced by the findings of loomweights, spindle whorls and weaving combs (Ryder 1983).

Robinson and Wilson (1987) also suggest that the provision of meat from relatively young animals was a major aim of sheep husbandry, though there may well have been considerable demand for secondary products. In Roman times, evidence suggests that sheep were slaughtered at later ages, implying greater emphasis on milk and wool (Robinson and Wilson 1987).

As is generally the case for pig, an animal bred mainly for its meat and fat, most of the pigs at Wardy Hill were culled when young. The dental eruption and wear data for pigs indicate that the majority were probably slaughtered in their second and third years. Note that there are relatively few dPs in comparison to Ps (the dP is shed and P4 erupts during the pig's second year: Bull and Payne 1982), and most of the Ms are in early wear stages. Unfortunately there are insufficient pig bones to corroborate the dental evidence.

Small numbers of bones/teeth of foetal or newborn sheep, pigs, cattle and horses indicate that these animals were probably bred at Wardy Hill, rather than being imported from elsewhere. This suggests, rather unsurprisingly, that the people of Wardy Hill were themselves husbanders of livestock.

These culling patterns for the Wardy Hill sheep and cattle may corroborate the archaeological interpretation of the site. If indeed it served as a 'local centre' (Evans 1992, 1997) then the animal bones may represent the leftovers of meals served to visiting guests. In other words, rather than being a small farming settlement existing at subsistence level, the farmers of Wardy Hill were having to supply meat meals to their visitors. Yet a word of caution is required here. If Wardy Hill was a high-status settlement then its inhabitants, in addition to locally reared livestock, may have purchased prime meat animals from surrounding settlements whose economy might well have been based upon milk and/or wool. One way to test this would be to study the animal bones from surrounding settlements to see whether those sheep were slaughtered at a later stage of their lives.

Other anomalies and pathology
In artiodactyls the lower third molar tooth is characterised by having three pillars. The third pillar, or hypoconulid, is somewhat smaller than the others and occasionally fails to develop. The cause of this failure is not understood and it may be an inherited trait. Of the 31 cattle Ms at the site whose completeness could be assessed, two have missing hypoconulids. However, due to a high degree of fragmentation at Wardy Hill most teeth are isolated. Hence one or two Ms with missing hypoconulids (*i.e.* with only two pillars, and therefore resembling Ms or Ms) may have been identified as MS. Of twelve Ms in mandibles containing at least one other tooth (*i.e.* cases where identity of the tooth as M is certain) one has a missing hypoconulid. Given this, perhaps it is more prudent to suggest that the frequency of cattle Ms at Wardy Hill with missing hypoconulids is 1/12.

An equid distal femur from *120* has an eburnated articular surface. A distal cattle metatarsal from *307* has rather bad eburnation on its articular surface and the medial condyle had expanded medially, giving the whole distal part of the bone an asymmetric appearance. These conditions may develop in old individuals and could be associated with old work animals and animals which have suffered excessive strain.

The environment
The presence of otter, water vole, geese, ducks, swan and amphibia indicate the presence of water at or near the site: this is hardly surprising given its fen-edge location. At other fen-edge Iron Age settlements such as Haddenham (Evans and Serjeantson 1988) and Outgang Road (Albarella 1997) these taxa were also found, though, unlike at these two other sites, beaver is strikingly absent from the Wardy Hill assemblage.

Intra-site variability
With so few bones, comparisons between different dwellings have little statistical significance (below). However, the following three main feature types — the main buildings, the inner Ringwork circuit and the outer Ringwork circuit contain — between them yielded approximately 80% of the animal remains from Wardy Hill. An attempt has been made to examine to what extent these three feature types differ zoo-archaeologically. The species frequencies (Table 31) reveal that there are rather more bones of large animals (cattle and horse) and dogs than small food-animals (sheep and pig) in the outer Ringwork than in the inner circuit or the main buildings. Indeed almost all the dog bones derive from the outer Ringwork circuit. One possible explanation for this discrepancy between the inner and outer precincts is simply that large bones, being more obtrusive, and bones of animals which were not consumed (dog and ?horse), tended to be preferentially jettisoned to the periphery of the site. Wilson (1992) discusses the deposition of animals bones on Iron Age sites and considered that it is not surprising that bones of horse and dog were treated differently from those of the main foods animals. At the Iron Age site at Mingies Ditch, Wilson (1992) writes: 'horse and dog bones appeared less commonly associated with domestic activity areas (hearths and houses) and occurred peripherally ... a pattern suggesting waste disposal of coarse debris including articulated bones of dog'.

Besides species frequencies, the ratio of limb-bones to proximal + terminal phalanges has also been considered (phalanges are small: Table 32). If indeed large bones were preferentially jettisoned away from the site's centre then we might expect the limb-bone/phalanges ratio to be higher in the outer Ringwork circuit than in more central areas of the site. For the cattle bones this does appear to be the case, since there are more limb-bones than phalanges in the outer Ringwork circuit than in the main buildings, although the inner Ringwork circuit resembles the outer one! The result for the sheep bones is unclear, however, and they do not show any interpretable pattern.

Summary and conclusions
Most of the faunal remains from Wardy Hill were from animals eaten in antiquity. Teeth are hugely over-represented compared to bones, probably reflecting considerable attrition by dogs and weathering prior to their incorporation into archaeological deposits. The probable ratio of sheep/cattle/pigs, on the basis of the numbers of their molar teeth, was 6:2:1. Taking into consideration the greater weight of cattle compared to sheep, the frequencies of the species at Wardy Hill indicate that most of the meat consumed at Wardy Hill was probably beef, followed by lamb/mutton and some pork. The relatively high percentage of sheep (as indicated by the dental remains) seems to concur with many, though not all, Iron Age sites in England.

The sheep (there was no evidence for goat) were similar in size, and probably also conformation, to Roman and medieval sheep. They were small compared to modern unimproved Shetland sheep. The rather higher proportion of lamb as opposed to adult sheep teeth suggests that the sheep were kept with an emphasis upon meat production. No doubt their milk and wool were exploited too.

There were also remains of medium-size dogs. The presence of aquatic animals such as otter, swan, duck and pike is hardly surprising in view of the site's location at the edge of the fen.

VII. Surface bone, sieved fraction and herpetofauna
by C. Evans with A. Clarke, C.P. Gleed-Owen and D. Serjeantson
(Plate XII; Tables 33 and 34)

In total 1591 animal and fish bone were recovered from the flotation residues, with small bone recovered in 75 of the 94 6–7 litre samples that were processed (pieces 5mm or greater counted). From these, the following animals and birds were identified by S. Davis: *Apodemus* sp (wood mouse: 3); *Arvicola terrestris* (water vole: 6); *Microtus agrestis* (vole: 1); *Sorex araneus* (shrew: 2); sheep/goat (7); pig (3); cat or fox (1); and duck (1). The low rate of identification of the material reflects its small size and high degree of fragmentation: with a total weight of 508g, the pieces would have a mean weight of only 0.32g (more than six times less than the mean weight of the ploughsoil bone).

Identified by D. Serjeantson, remains of small fish were present in eleven samples from six features (Table 33). Most are from two samples from F. 1, while the remainder are sparsely scattered over the site. They are in good condition, if fragmented, with the exception of one that is encrusted. The only species positively identified is pike, *Esox lucius*; one vertebra is certainly not from pike and may be from perch, *Perca fluviatilis*. Pike remains were also identified among the hand-collected material: with the exception of a single cyprinid bone, this was the only fish species found at the nearby site of HAD V (Serjeantson *et al.* 1994).

The identified elements from the sieved samples are a caudal fin and precaudal and caudal vertebrae. The unidentified fragments are vertebrae, fin rays and head bone fragments. All the fish present, both identified and unidentified, are small (*i.e.* below approximately 200mm in length) or tiny (below approximately 80mm). Three vertebrae from ditch F. 1 (*246*) are probably from the same fish, a small pike.

There are three possible origins for these fish. They may have been caught and eaten by the occupants of the Ringwork, an interpretation more likely for the small pike than for the tiny fish. They may be fish which became incorporated in the features and died there (*i.e.* flood introduced), as presumably did amphibians which were also found at the site. This would fit with the rather sparse scatter of bones over the site. A third possibility is that they are the prey of a fish-eating predator such as heron, which also preys on amphibians. This last is the least likely

Feature	Sample No	Element	Size	Species	Notes
F1	246	Caudal vertebra	small	*Esox lucius*	probably same fish
F1	246	Caudal vertebra	small	*Esox lucius*	probably same fish
F1	246	Caudal vertebra	small	*Esox lucius*	probably same fish
F1	246	scale		*Esox lucius*	
F1	246	Caudal vertebra	tiny	unidentified	possibly *Perca fluviatilis*
F1	246	Skull fragment	small	unidentified	
F1	246	fragments	small	unidentified	
F1	249	vertebra	small	unidentified	encrusted
F2	23	Caudal vertebra frag.	small	unidentified	broken
F2	385	Vertebra fragment	tiny	unidentified	
F2	24B	Vertebra frag.	tiny	unidentified	broken
F6	206	Precaudal vertebra	small	*Esox lucius?*	
F6	206	Caudal vertebra	small	unidentified	
F21	166	vertebra	tiny	unidentified	
F21	166	Vertebra fragment	tiny	unidentified	
F21	169	Caudal fin	small	*Esox lucius*	
F25	306	Fin ray		unidentified	
F25	310	Precaudal vertebra	small	*Esox lucius?*	
F102	503	Fin ray		unidentified	

Table 33 Fish remains from flotation samples

explanation, since bones from such deposits would be expected to occur in concentrations.

Herpetofauna remains were forthcoming from 41 of the sample residues (Plate XII). Identified by C. Gleed-Owen, the assemblage comprised *Trituras cristatus* (crested newt), *Triturus* sp., *Bufo bufo* (common toad), *Bufo* sp., *Rana temporaria* (common frog), *Rana* sp., *Anura* indet., *Anguis fragilis* (slow-worm), *Natrix natrix* (grass snake) and *Ophidia* indet. The occurrence of crested newt implies the presence of mature ponds with rich aquatic vegetation. All the amphibians require fish-free ponds for successful breeding, and during their terrestrial life are generally found in an open herbaceous environment, or possibly open woodland. Common toad tolerates drier situations than the other species and prefers (though not exclusively) deeper, less well-vegetated ponds. Grass snakes tend to hunt for fish and amphibians in ponds and streams, and together with slow-worm are associated with rich herbaceous vegetation (Arnold and Burton 1978); the slow-worm requires unploughed land as it lives in leaf litter and subsoil. While this is the first indication of a slow-worm on an Iron Age site, all the other species have been recorded on other sites of the period in Eastern England (Gleed-Owen 1998, 1999).

Because sampling was not undertaken on a volumetric basis (non-proportional to overall feature/context capacity), it is not possible to use the residue bone as a direct check on hand-excavated retrieval from the same contexts (2708 pieces/16,265g; mean weight 6.00g). What it does inform us, however, is about site formation processes, and that there was much bone incorporated into its occupation matrices. Herpetofauna aside, that so much of it is unidentifiable indicates that this derives from the reduction of larger pieces through trample and redeposition rather than the incorporation of 'small species'.

During the course of final post-excavation analysis, in an attempt to further elucidate the character of the Ringwork's surface spreads the animal bones from both the four central test-pits and the midden zone as represented in the fieldwalking collections (sixteen units with densities greater than six bones) were examined by A. Clarke of the CAU. Amounting to only 1125 bones, this group is a minute sample of the 79,500 that have been estimated to have been incorporated in the topsoil across the enclosure's interior. The material from these contexts was, moreover, small (2.06 and 2.03g mean weight) and accordingly only a small fraction could be identified to species (9.2% and 8.8% respectively).

Cattle bone is predominant (Table 34), and this remains true even if we add to these figures the 108 bones only generally attributable to cow- and sheep-size animals (cow 53.3%; sheep/goat 41.9%). It warrants mention that the percentage for pig is somewhat enhanced by the occurrence of three such bones in test-pit 1 sited above the Structure I eaves-gully (from which the single bird and dog bones were also recovered); the frequency of pig from the surface collection alone is 6.2%.

VIII. Discussion

Situating and denying 'the Wet'
(Fig. 65; Tables 34–37)

All the environmental evidence, including the herpetofauna remains, would attest to the wet conditions across the site as a whole, and especially its eastern sector, and that the Ringwork's outer ditch circuit held standing water. Moreover, the frequency of dung beetles and the palynological evidence of excreta would indicate this was quite a noxious divide: a marked barrier, both physical and cognitively (wet/dry; clean/dirty).

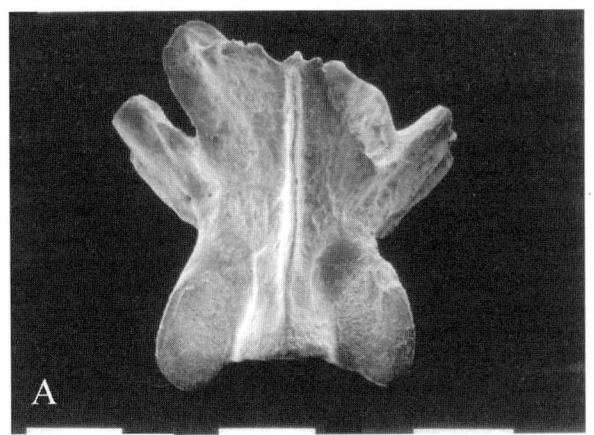
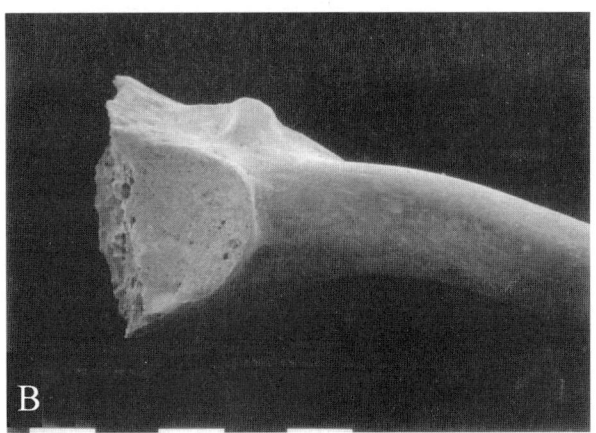
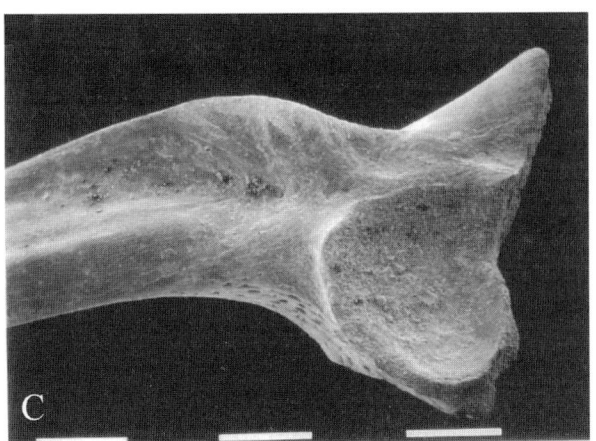
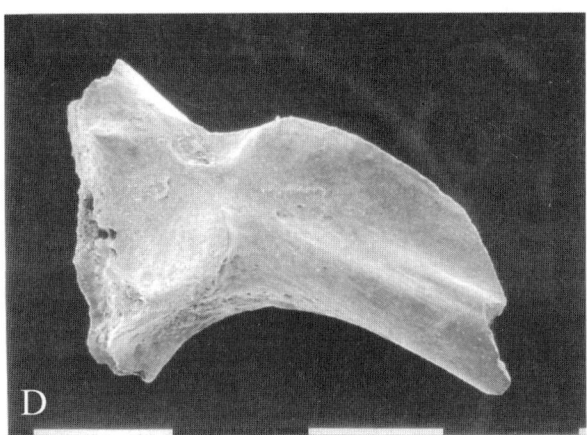
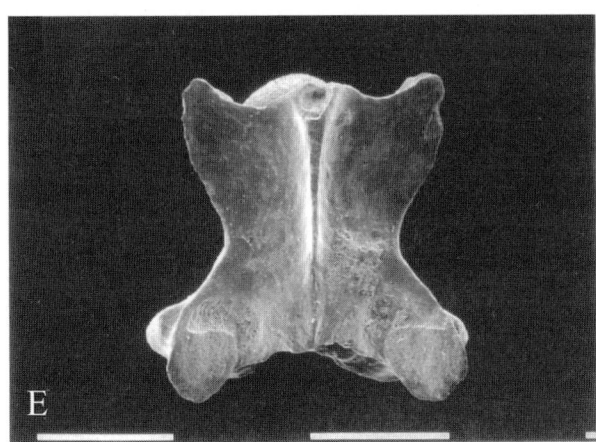
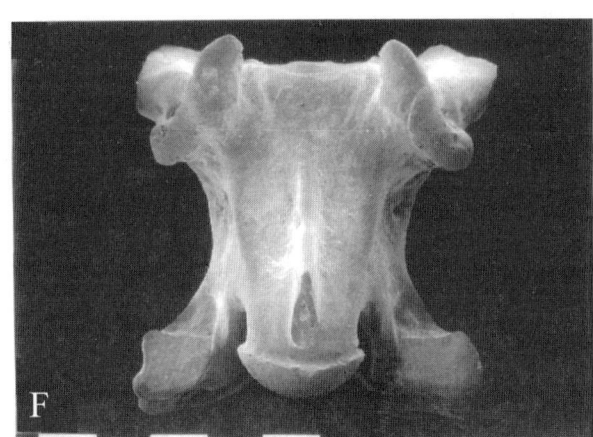

Plate XII Herpetofanual remains
(a) trunk vertebra (dorsal view) of *T. cristatus* (F. 52 227); (b) right ilium (lateral view) of *B. bufo* (F. 2 083); (c) left ilium (lateral view) of *Rana* cf. *temporaria* (F. 2 035); (d) right ilium (lateral view) of juvenile *Rana* cf. *temporaria* (F. 2 083); (e) trunk vertebra (dorsal view) of *A. fragilis* (F. 37 630); (f) trunk vertebra (ventral view) of *N. natrix* (F. 52 227)

	Cow	Sheep/Goat	Pig	Deer	Dog	Bird
Number	50	42	7	1	1	1
Percent	49	41.2	6.9	0.9	0.9	0.9

Table 34 'Midden core' animal bones

	300 yr span	100 yr span
Sheep	1.4 per year	4.2 per year
Cattle	0.4	1.2
Pig	0.23	0.7
Horse	0.07	0.2

Table 35 Estimates of annual kill-off rates

| | Structures ||||| Site Total ||
	St. I	St. II	St. III	St. IV	St. V	No.	%
Main Domesticates							
Cattle	64 (53.33%)		1 (7.14%)	51 (26.42%)	1 (20%)	371	26.27
Sheep/Goat	32 (26.67%)		6 (42.86%)	96 (49.74%)	2 (40%)	708	50.15
Pig	22 (18.33%)	1 (100%)	7 (50%)	40 (20.73%)	2 (40%)	183	12.96
Horse	2 (1.67%)					52	3.68
Total no.	120	1	14	193	5	1314	
Total %	96	100	61	94	100		93.06
Other							
Dog			6				
Red Deer	1						
Badger	1						
Water vole	1						
Amphibian				1			
Fowl				2			
Duck	2		2	6			
Heron				1			
Goose				1			
Swan				1			
Woodcock				1			
Total % Others	4	-	39	6	-		6.94
Grand Total	**125**	**1**	**23**	**205**	**5**	**1412**	

Table 36 Number of identifiable bones and teeth by Structure (excluding flot residue); bracketed numbers indicate percentages of main domesticates

	Cattle	Sheep/Goat	Pig	Horse	Other
Wardy Hill (2.–3.00m OD)	26	50	13	4	7
Hurst Lane (2.–4.00m OD)	45	41	9	3	2
Watson's Lane (6.00m OD)	25	60	11	2	2
West Fen (6.50m OD)	35	57	8	*	*

Table 37 Faunal remains from the Ely sites (percentage by NISP)

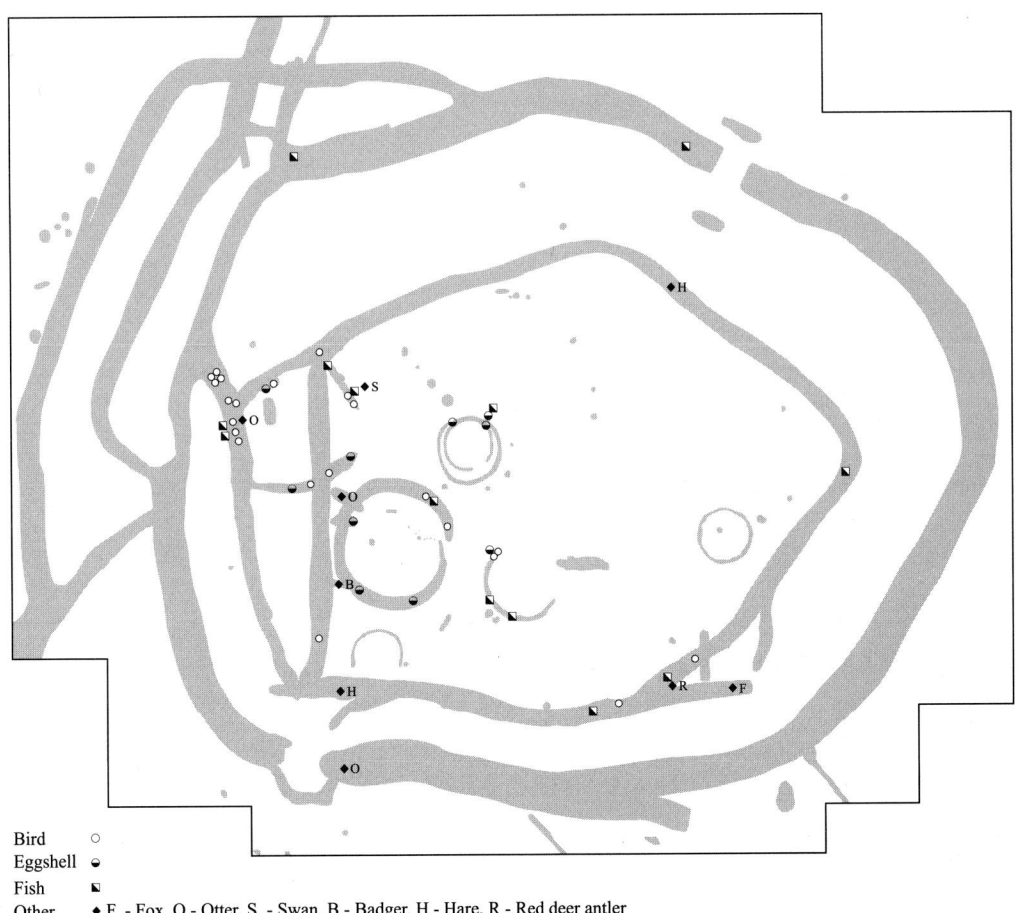

Figure 65 Bone distribution plots

135

Although only located some 80m apart, the evidence of the two main column samples attests to the 'betwixt' situation of the Ringwork, with the 'fenward' column (Section 63) consistently reflecting a much wetter reedswamp environment than the upslope location (Section 37). The locational propensity for Iron Age settlement in the region between the dry and wet (at least seasonally) — that straddles the 2–3.00m OD contour — has been discussed in the context of the enclosures at the Upper Delphs, Haddenham (Evans and Hodder forthcoming), and is also part of a more widespread phenomenon (*e.g.* Cunliffe 1991). It would appear to relate to maximising the arable potential of better drained up-terrace slopes, and allowing ready access to seasonal marshland resources (primarily pasture and thatch). Equally crucial is that these situations — at the edge of the wet — would ensure within-site sources of water supply (Evans 1997a).

Generally the environmental remains indicate open grassland, with localised stands of woodland in the vicinity (especially the fenward Section 63 with its representation of willow carr). Beyond this, the picture of changing land-use within the site catchment is complicated. Whereas the uncharred plant macrofossils and molluscs show evidence of increased wetness, the same is not true of the insect remains. These, as denoted by the increase in dung beetle, suggest a greater intensification in grazing (Robinson, above). Similarly, whilst in the landward column the pollen shows a marked increase in arable within the upper half of the column, the palynological evidence generally attests to increasingly wet conditions. In this regard, the evidence could generally be interpreted as reflecting a greater intensification of agriculture — both immediate pasturage and off-site arable — despite the fact that the Ringwork itself was subject to higher water levels.

That cultivation was undertaken at some distance from the Ringwork, probably upon Wardy Hill itself, would receive support from the evidence of the pollen columns, since evidence of arable was much more apparent in the landward sample location (Section 37). Equally, amongst the insects the low, almost negligible, representation of species favouring arable environments as opposed to the frequency of those attesting to animals — variously hay meadow habitats and dung beetles — would attest to immediate grazing. In this regard, the larger Wardy Hill dyke defences (with marsh on the east) may equally have enclosed pasture and stock. Given this scenario, the defences could have been approached through fields and, if so, crops would have been vulnerable to razing. While obviously relating to environmental factors (wet *vs.* dry land) this, however, may have also involved perceptions of value, and an evaluation of status that favoured stock.

As Murphy notes, the presence of a few weed types within the charred plant remains could provide evidence for the importation of cereal crops. This must be tentative, however, and it is conceivable that they derive from crops grown on nearby pockets of lighter gravel subsoils. Yet these all lie low within the immediate landscape and, despite their 'lightness', would probably have been saturated at that time. Otherwise, the only other evidence for the importation of plants would be the occurrence of bracken macrofossils within the column samples, which may have been brought in for flooring or animal bedding. Amongst the charred weed assemblage the frequency of sawsedge, which grows in reedswamp and fen, suggests its usage and not merely accidental incorporation within harvested crops. This was presumably used for thatch and as fire kindling.

The identification of the remains of four honey bees (Robinson, above) need not mean that hives were kept, but only that honey was available locally as a resource.

That the occurrence of *Prunus/Crategus*-type thorns within the wood assemblage and the uncharred plant macrofossils might attest to hawthorn hedging, as discussed by Murphy, would seem confirmed by Wiltshire's palynological analysis. In the case of the latter, that it even maintained its presence when wetter conditions otherwise occurred suggests that it was growing nearby in an elevated situation. Collectively, therefore, the evidence demonstrates that the Ringwork was hedged: these hedges, probably planted atop its banks, may have contributed to its defences. In terms of the pollen alone two points warrant emphasis. First is the evidence of mature hedges in the basal profiles, as this might attest to hedges pre-existing to the establishment of the Ringwork proper and may possibly correlate to the lingering presence (extensive alignment) of the F. 73 *et al.* dyke system. Second is the frequency of mistletoe. Probably a parasite hosted by the hedge, it belies arguments for any kind of special deposition (*viz.* Druidic associations) as might be advocated from the identification of its tissues amid the insect samples. Hedge trimming, rather than intentional placement, probably explains its occurrence in this context.

Now recovered from a number of later prehistoric sites, the wider evidence of hedging from the region has recently been discussed, along with its implications for the lasting influence of minor and/or otherwise 'invisible' boundaries (Evans 1999; Pollard 1996). What is unique in the case of Wardy Hill is the evidence that it may have contributed to a defensive superstructure. Again, this is important on two accounts. On the one hand, the addition of a timber element to banks — whether grown or cut (*i.e.* a stockade) — could have made 'moderate-scale' enclosures (as represented by their below-ground traces) into much more formidable defences. On the other hand, the employment of what is essentially an agricultural means of allotment/division is, in this instance, consistent with the 'baseline' affinities of the Ringwork: elaborating the 'domestic' into something else.

The distribution of charred remains would confirm the 'boundedness' of the site's occupation, and that no crop-processing occurred beyond the line of the F. 2 circuit. Similarly, the density of plant remains corresponds closely with the artefact densities. With Structures I and IV having the highest densities, the low frequencies in Structures II and VI indicate that they were without hearths and were of ancillary/non-residential function; Structures III and V would have been of medial status. Interestingly enough, in samples from the south-east sector of F. 2 — well away from the main houses — both sieving and coarser winnowing waste seem to be represented in the charred assemblages. This would correspond with the evidence of the eastern pollen column (WH2/2) that this was an area of cereal processing.

Dominated by sheep (50%), generally the representation of domesticated taxa from the site is in keeping with other sites of the period in the region. The frequency of pig warrants attention, however. Often held to be a marker of status, at *c.* 13% its overall site value is relatively low. However, its deposition seems to have been house-centred and rises in frequency to 18% and 21% in Structures I and IV respectively, more than a third higher than for the site as a whole. (In Structure III it was 50%, though the building assemblage is much too small to be statistically meaningful.) Taking the main house figures, the percentage of pig would, therefore, lie at the lower end of high status sites which demonstrates, if nothing else, the problem of employing site-wide species 'means' alone. Equally noteworthy, and possibly telling of a relative and strictly local measure of status, is that out of all the recent Ely sites the percentage of pig is highest at the Ringwork (Table 37).

Generally, Wardy Hill shows very little indication of the exploitation of wild produce. Thatching (and perhaps flooring material) aside, essentially it drew upon the domesticated landscape and Murphy notes that the representation of edible wild plants (fruit and nuts) is very sparse. Most telling — and certainly in marked contrast to HAD V, where fenland produce (especially beaver and birds) were being taken in considerable numbers (Serjeantson in Evans and Hodder forthcoming; Evans and Serjeantson 1988) — is the faunal assemblage. The isolated occurrence of otter, badger, fox, hare and birds other than galliforms (*e.g.* swan) suggests only opportunistic taking, and that wild species did not contribute significantly to the site's subsistence. Equally, the limited occurrence of red deer antler without accompanying bone suggests only a pattern of 'pick-up', and not a hunting strategy as such. Such a paucity of wild species is, surprisingly enough, typical of fenland sites of the period. This is all the more noteworthy since most of these communities, living in what were certainly then wet landscapes, seem to have ignored a range of available marshland produce.

Also common on fenland prehistoric sites is the occasional representation of pike: a big fish. Based on the (non-) recovery of fishbone at Haddenham and the later Bronze Age settlement at Runnymede Bridge (both sites where substantial sieving programmes were conducted) Serjeantson has argued that, probably as a reflection of taste, fish did not contribute significantly to the later prehistoric diet (Serjeantson *et al.* 1994). However, in the case of Wardy Hill — where extensive bulk-artefact sampling was not feasible and finds-retrieval control had to rely instead upon the finer mesh flotation residues from an intense environmental programme — the consistent occurrence of fishbone (and eggshell) from the four main roundhouses (I, III–IV) could suggest a more regular exploitation of marshland resources. Their numbers are so low that birds and fish are unlikely to have been a major component of the diet, yet they are sufficient to indicate something 'more' than just sporadic activity.

Based on the estimated total site population of more than 114,000 animal bones (Chapter 5), the frequency of domestic taxa recovered would suggest that Davis' species figures (by teeth) should be multiplied by at least seven-fold: 420 sheep, 119 cattle, 70 pigs and 21 horses. Such one-to-one calculation must carry *caveats* concerning animal part representation relating to differential surface and sealed context preservation, and we must be wary of naive interpretation (ethnographic and historical record-informed excavation suggest bone survival of less than 2%: *e.g.* Guilday 1977, Serjeantson, *pers. comm.*). Nevertheless, it does provide a relative measure of possible consumption kill-rates:

From this, a long chronology (at least *vis-a-vis* the duration of intense occupation) would have to be considered unviable given the representation of stock. Even the rates for the shorter span are terribly low in reference to normative patterns of stock maintenance (see Pryor in Evans and Hodder forthcoming; for sheep and pig they are, nevertheless, marginally higher than the Danebury figures, despite that enclosure's much greater size: see Grant 1991). Of course, this is not a matter of 'hard' economics or maximal herd management (*cf.* Pryor 1996), and one might expect, for example, that each year a certain number of sheep may have been sent out in gift exchange. Nevertheless, some mechanism of 'loss' would still have to be evoked. Either a substantial portion of the bone must have somehow been taken off-site (*e.g.* midden manuring and/or scavenging) or most body-part/species identification has been eroded through trample reduction and/or human and animal on-site consumption practices.

In terms of the distribution of animal bone, aside from sheep and cattle which were recovered throughout (Fig. 65) there is an obvious association between pig remains and the main roundhouses. Horse, on the other hand, seems more restricted to the margins of the Ringwork, with there being a marked concentration in the area of the 'landward' entrance. Nevertheless, two pieces of the latter were found in the southern terminal of Structure I. Equally, apart from a tooth and two bones within the southern terminal arm of Structure IV, four other pieces were recovered in association with that building; the latter, however, was found in its north-western sector at its junction with the main Ringwork circuit (F. 13).

Aside from five bones and a tooth from Structure III, the distribution of canine remains was also marginal. They occurred sporadically around the northern circuit of F. 2 and in the eastern terminal of the landward entrance (F. 1). Eleven bones of dog (plus four teeth) recovered from excavated segments at the junction of ditches F. 10/28 probably indicate the deposition of a complete carcass.

Of the 23 bird bones plotted, all but three were associated with the main round structures. Two each were recovered from the northern terminals of Structures I and III; aside from occurring in both terminals of Structure IV, there was a distinct concentration throughout the north-western sector of that the building (nine pieces adjacent to the F. 13/Ringwork junction). Otherwise, of the wild species, fox occurred in the eastern end of the primary Ringwork ditch F. 27, and a single otter bone was recovered from the eastern F. 1 terminal of the landward entrance. (Single otter teeth were present along the 'backside' of Structure IV, and nearby in the contemporary pit F. 32.) Single bones of both badger and hare occurred within the south-western extension of the inner circuit adjacent to its terminal (the length blocking the F. 1 landward entrance). Another bone of hare was recovered from the F. 2 circuit opposite the Watergate. The other occurrence of badger was in the F. 61 trough. Antler was found in the south-eastern sector of F. 2.

Little can be said concerning the distribution of the 'wild' material. Leaving aside the bird bone (which definitely concentrated within Structure IV, including swan), and the occurrences of fox and antler in the south-eastern sector, it was only found adjacent to or in the enclosure's main entrances, and features cutting/post-dating Structure I (F. 32 and 61). The otter tooth in Structure IV was the only such find directly associated with a building.

Avian eggshell was recovered from samples from all four of the main round houses (Structures I, III–V), and otherwise only occurred in pits F. 33 and 80. Similarly, albeit in low numbers, samples from the same four buildings also produced fishbones (at least pit F. 102 in the case of Structure V). Apart from this, fish were present in samples from along the south-eastern sector of the inner Ringwork circuit, and in two instances along the northern side of the main ditch F. 1. Of the latter, both Murphy and Serjeantson note that they are relatively common in the sample from the western terminal of the Watergate. As such, remains did not occur in the adjacent length of the inner circuit, this could suggest specific deposition relating to processing immediately outside the Ringwork (*i.e.* bringing in the 'catch'). Alternatively, given that fishbone also occurs in another sample along this fenward length of the main circuit, it is conceivable that the fish were introduced into it during a flood episode.

Regarding the distribution of bone within the structures (Table 36), only Structures I and IV produced sufficient numbers to allow a comparison of the frequencies of taxa. While there is little difference in the percentages of pig, the frequencies of cattle and sheep vary. Thus in Structure I the cattle are 53% and sheep 27% while in Structure IV the percentages are reversed, with cattle 26% and sheep 50%. The remains from Structure IV are actually the most representative of any building of the site's excavated assemblage as a whole, and what is particularly striking is the high frequency of cattle within Structure I. This must reflect specific depositional practices. It could well be the case that this building, upon becoming the site of a midden (with material dumped into its upper ditch profile), received more bone from larger animals (horse and cattle) which otherwise would have been relegated to the site's margins. The analysis of the surface context bones would equally support this interpretation: within that horizon cow also occurred at a frequency of *c.* 50% (sheep *c.* 41%; the low percentage of pig bone — *c.* 6% — could also add weight to the observation that its deposition was building-related).

As indicated in Table 37 the differences in species representation across the site — particularly between Structures I and IV — occur only within the range of variability observed between the other recent Ely assemblages. The Ringwork's assemblage, in some respects, has its closest affinities with that from Watson's Lane, Little Thetford. Regarding the absolute height of these sites there seems no obvious pattern in terms of species representation and their immediate landscape situation, except perhaps that the more elevated sites — Watson's Lane and West Fen (1995) — have the highest frequencies of sheep. Yet this would be at odds, for example, with the results from the HAD V enclosure, lying at *c.* 2.50m OD, a more low-lying site with 68% sheep (Evans and Serjeantson 1988; Serjeantson in Evans and Hodder forthcoming). Based on the Ringwork's analysis and its degree of intra-site variability, what undermines any temptation towards simple land-use modelling for these sites is that the Watson's Lane and West Fen (1996) excavations only involved small portions of much more extensive settlements, and the results may not be representative of their total assemblages. The fact that, for example, the latter excavations were more house-focused (with little site periphery representation) could, based on the Ringwork's distributions, have led to a lower frequency of horse.

Despite the fact that the Wardy Hill assemblage has the highest frequency of 'others', the 'wild' species still seem to have been incidental takes and the community appears to have practised an essentially dryland economy while living on the edge of a marsh. This itself may reflect the relative 'weight' of its western landward defences, and that the eastward wetland was evidently envisaged as a barrier. Although, as discussed, this effective denial of marsh is common on sites of the period in the region (*e.g.* Cats Water, Fengate or the Colne Fen compounds), in this specific instance it may also tell of the Ringwork's *raison d'être*. It was not primarily sited to exploit maximally the area's mixed environs, but for defence and the control of landscape access.

Agricultural processing: an overview
by C. Stevens
(Figs 66–67; Tables 38 and 39)

Wardy Hill is one of a number of excavated sites within Ely — Hurst Lane and West Fen Road (1995 and, in 1999, the Cornwell sub-site) — and the surrounding region (Watson's Lane, Little Thetford) that have produced good Iron Age and Roman archaeobotanical data sets (Chapter 1 for background; site summaries in Chapter 5). It has been argued elsewhere (Stevens 1996, in press) that the majority of charred assemblages relate to the taking of crops from storage on a regular 'day-by-day' basis for processing into flour, dough, bread and gruel *etc.* for immediate consumption. The wastes from these events are then discarded onto the hearth, from whence they become incorporated into archaeological features. That such domestic processes may be repeated countless times a year, over the lifespan of a settlement, explains the high frequency of remains from post-storage processing, as opposed to the pre-storage processing of crops after harvest in late summer. These processing events produce assemblages that reflect the stage at which the crop was stored. Charred assemblages then have the potential to reveal these day-to-day processes: those carried out shortly after the crops were harvested in late summer, and the state in which the crop was stored (*i.e.* as clean, semi-cleaned grain, sheaves or partially threshed ear). To this end, the data from the five sites were compared to see how storage and processing activities might have varied between them.

The crops grown
Similar crops — emmer, spelt and barley, and weeds — to those at Wardy Hill dominated the other assemblages. As with Wardy Hill, while free-threshing type grains were occasionally recovered at few sites were they well represented. The exceptions were two Roman samples from the 1999 West Fen Road Cornwell site, where a number of free-threshing type wheat grains were found.

Harvesting practice
The way in which crops were harvested, by uprooting, plucking, sickle or scythe, may be determined by the weed assemblage (Hillman 1981; 1984). The presence of low-growing species (under 30cm high) may be taken as indicative of harvesting by cutting close to the ground. Such species seeds were present in samples from Wardy Hill: for example *Prunella vulgaris* (self-heal), *Rumex*

Site	Hurst Lane	Wardy Hill	West Fen Rd (Cornwell)	West Fen Iron Age	Cornwell Roman	West Fen Rd (1995)	Watsons Lane	Watsons Lane IA	Watsons Lane RB
All samples	21	66	6	3	3	10	41	29	12
Total litres	182	841	196	53	35	100	608	428	180
Big weeds	271	291	99	40	59	794	400	293	107
Small weeds	841	989	81	56	25	268	333	190	143
Intermediate	97	116	16	8	8	8	74	18	56
Unclassified	21	20	5	4	1	3	28	17	11
Grain (total)	186	227	172	30	142	360	474	369	105
Free-threshing wheat grain	1	2	81	7	74	0	3	1	2
Barley grain	21	42	30	4	26	27	13	11	2
(Actual) est. Hulled wheat	(97) 161	(0) 162	(8) 13	(7) 11	(1) 2.1	(216) 325	(147) 441	(131) 350	(16) 91
Glumes (inc. Spikelet forks)	572	1034	450	390	60	1832	1797	1119	678.00
% Big weed seeds to small	22.42	20.85	50.51	38.46	64.13	74.21	49.57	58.48	34.97
% Weed seeds to grain	86.86	86.18	53.89	78.26	39.57	74.88	63.79	58.40	75.12
% Seeds to glumes	68.26	57.80	30.88	21.69	60.78	36.94	31.72	31.64	31.86
Log. Est. grain/glumes	−0.55	−0.80	−1.54	−1.55	−1.46	−0.75	−0.61	−0.50	−0.87

Table 38 Ely environs: Actual counts for weed seeds, cereal grains and chaff. Percentages for all samples and the Log of estimated hulled wheat grains divided by glumes (1 spikelet fork=2 glumes)

Site	Hurst Lane	Wardy Hill	West Fen Rd (Cornwell)	West Fen Rd Iron Age	Cornwell Roman	West Fen Rd (1995)	Watsons Lane	Watsons Lane IA	Watsons Lane RB
No. samples used	15	28	6	3	3	9	26	17	9
Mean – % weed to grain	89.83	82.43	60.25	43.51	76.98	75.33	63.63	58.26	73.78
Median – % weed to grain	89.66	84.75	57.92	39.82	79.55	76.29	63.56	55.88	75.00
Mean – % large (classified)	24.34	29.52	55.38	69.92	40.83	66.15	48.40	54.60	36.68
Median – % large (classified)	22.73	24.24	48.20	77.27	47.83	75.00	48.53	52.63	37.50
No. samples used	9	28	4	1	3	9	26	17	9
Mean – Log grain/glumes	−0.81	−0.80	−1.55	−1.78	−1.47	−0.77	−0.56	−0.33	−0.98
Median – Log grain/glumes	−0.57	−0.81	−1.62	−1.78	−1.47	−0.74	−0.56	−0.43	−0.91
Mean – % seeds to glumes	64.18	56.48	33.45	40.00	31.27	39.90	38.40	41.55	32.46
Median – % seeds to glumes	62.50	55.10	27.78	40.00	15.56	37.74	39.78	44.68	38.89

Table 39 Ely environs: Mean and median percentages for each analysis and the number of samples used. The first shows the percentage of all weed seeds to all cereal grain and the percentage of all classified large weed seeds (>2.5mm) from a total of all weed seeds whose size could be determined. The second shows the log of estimated hulled wheat grains divided by glumes as above and the percentage of all weed seeds agains glumes (1 spikelet fork = 2 glume bases).

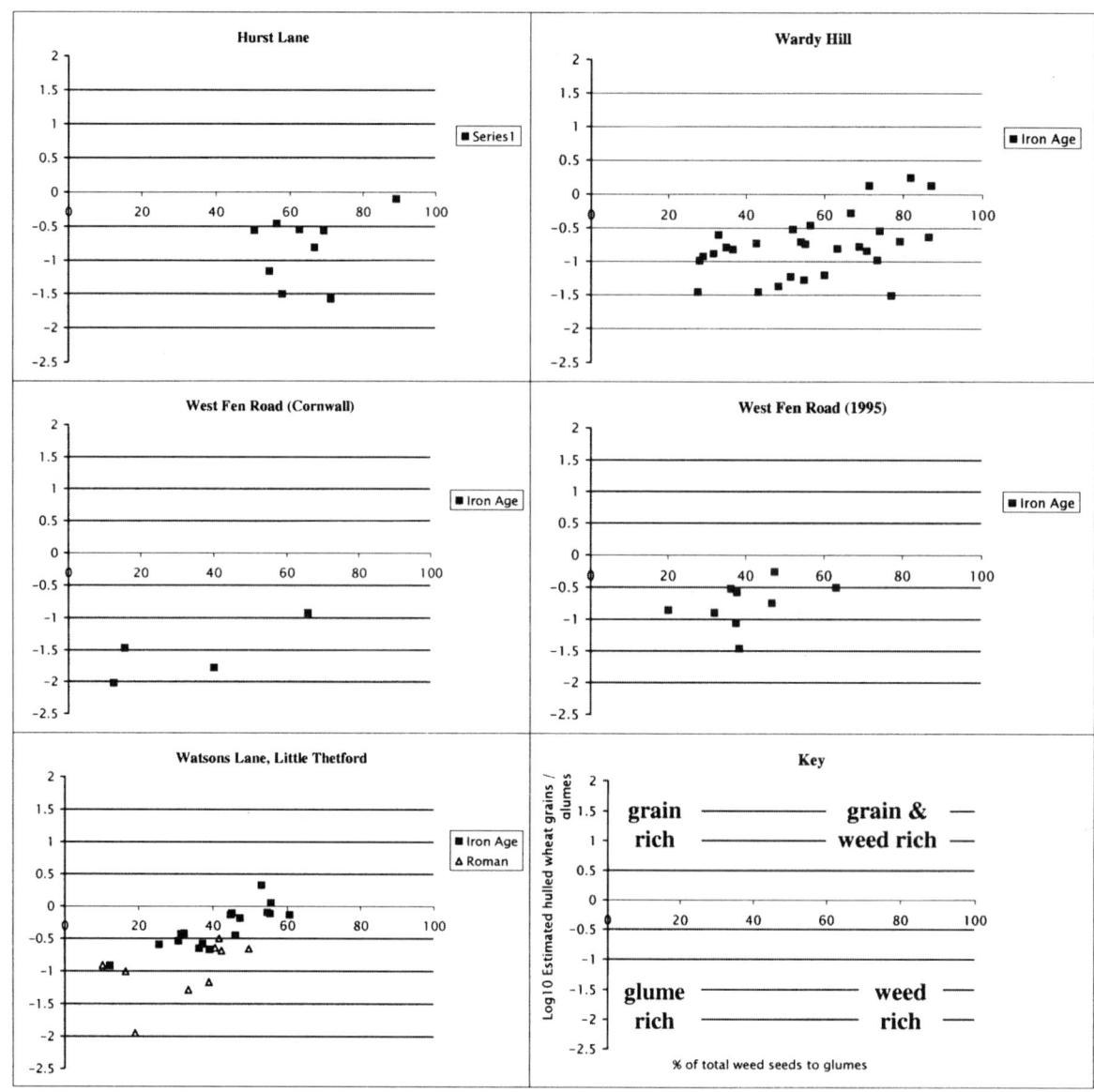

Figure 66 Ely Environs: The ratio of estimated grains of hulled wheats divided by glume bases (1 spikelet fork=2 glumes) plotted against the percentage of weed seeds to glumes

acetosella (sheeps sorrel) and *Anagallis arvensis* (scarlet pimpernel). Seeds of *Trifolium* spp (clover species), which grow under 30cm, were common from the other sites.

Harvesting by scythe is generally believed to have been a Roman innovation and, rather than for cutting cereals, was more probably used for harvesting hay (Rees 1979). The evidence from the Ely sites then suggests that harvesting was conducted with sickles, close to the ground.

Scheduling of processing activities
After harvest, farmers would have been faced with the decision whether to store the crop unprocessed as sheaves, as partially threshed whole ears, partly processed as semi-cleaned grain, or fully processed as cleaned grain. Such decisions will have revolved around the number of people on hand for such operations, pressure of time and (possibly) the availability of large barns. Successful storage requires that grain be stored in a dry condition. As such, the crop must be harvested and processed when either a large number of predictably dry days are available, or the presence of a barn facilitates further processing. For prehistoric British farmers who may have not had access to barns, and with few predictable dry days, processing prior to storage may have been problematic. To process crops to a clean state would have been reliant on the ability to organise large amounts of labour. The organisation of both harvesting and processing events can be seen from historical accounts of many traditional European societies to have been embedded within social structures through ritual and tradition (*e.g.* Frazer 1890). The evidence for the

processing of the crop may then reveal something of how peoples organised and scheduled such activities.

Storage practice
Charred remains have the potential to reveal past storage practices, and it is probable that hulled wheats, emmer and spelt would have been stored in the glumes (Hillman 1981). The pounding and separation of the glumes is highly time-consuming, and would probably have been carried out as and when clean grain was required. In addition, storage within the glumes would have greatly limited problems related to insect predation as well as fungal attack.

The first analysis tests the hypothesis that the assemblages relate to post-storage processing practices. The ratio of estimated hulled wheat grains was divided by the number of glumes (*cf.* van der Veen 1992, 83). The estimated number of hulled wheat grains was calculated in a similar fashion to van der Veen. However, for samples where no grains were identified to wheat or barley it was assumed all were of hulled wheats. A similar approach was taken where wheat grains were not identified to hulled or free-threshing varieties.

'Daily-processing' waste
The figure used for plotting the samples (Fig. 66) and presented in Table 38 is the estimated number of hulled wheat grains divided by the total number of glumes (each spikelet fork counts as two glumes). For this analyses only samples with at least fifteen glumes, and grain or weed seeds, were used. Where glumes outnumber grains a negative figure is returned; where grains outnumber glumes a positive figure results. Where grains equal glumes a figure of zero is returned. As seen from the plots most samples were glume- rather than grain-rich (Fig. 66). Charring experiments show that glumes are more readily destroyed than grain (Boardman and Jones 1990), and it is probable that many samples were more glume-rich prior to charring and deposition. This suggests samples came from the charring of waste from 'daily-processing': the waste from the separation of glumes after storage.

The Y-axis shows the ratio of weed seeds to glumes. Weed seeds will be more prolific where crops were stored in a less processed state so that the number removed after storage will be that much greater. Alternatively, samples representative of the processing of barley and free-threshing wheats will produce weed seeds, but not readily-preserved glumes.

The plots show mixed results. A general trend is seen with the number of glumes increasing as the number of weed seeds and grains decrease. This may reflect preservation conditions, with poorer conditions destroying glumes more readily than grains or weed seeds. Wardy Hill and Hurst Lane demonstrate a higher proportion of weed seeds than glumes, though glumes were more prolific than grain. Neither site had higher proportions of barley and free-threshing cereals than hulled wheats (Table 38).

Analysing storage practices
The second analysis tests the hypothesis that the Wardy Hill and Hurst Lane settlements may have been storing crops in a less processed state (Fig. 67; Table 39). Processing separates both chaff and weed seeds from grain. As we move through each stage the purity of the crop increases, and the ratio of grain to weeds increases also. Grain-sized weeds (*c.* 2.5–4.5mm) tend to stay with the crop, while those that are small, light and/or remain in the seed-head are removed more readily. These grain-sized seeds are the last weed seeds to be removed, often by hand as the final stage before the clean grain is ground (Hillman 1981).

These observations give two more ratios to examine. The first is that of weed seeds to grain. The initial analysis demonstrates that the assemblages represent glume waste from at least the later pounding stages. Both grain and weeds will be lost at each processing stage. However, the ratio of grain to weed seeds within both crop and the waste will increase through the processing sequence. Crops stored as semi-clean or fully-cleaned grain will be grain-rich. Grain is lost during pounding, but many of the weeds will have been removed after harvesting prior to storage. The second ratio uses the fact that large weed seeds are removed at the sequence end, with smaller seeds separated in the earlier stages. The ratio of large to small weed seeds therefore increases through the processing sequence (*cf.* Jones 1984; 1987).

Samples were plotted using the ratio of weeds to grain against the ratio of large (average width/length of 2.5mm or greater) to small weed seeds (Fig. 67). Only samples with fifteen or more weed seeds were used in the analysis. The circles show the predictive distributions for samples coming from crops stored in an unclean condition (top right), and as semi-clean grain or spikelets (bottom right).

The plots show the samples from Wardy Hill and Hurst Lane falling within the expected distribution for samples coming from crops stored in a less-processed state, as unthreshed or partially-threshed ears. They are dominated by small weed seeds. The samples from Little Thetford show a clear division, with small weed seeds dominating later Roman samples while larger seeds are more common in those of Iron Age date. The samples from West Fen Road (Cornwell) show the reverse scenario, with later Roman samples dominated by grain and large weed seeds. The samples from West Fen Road (1995) were mainly dominated by large seeds of *Avena* spp (oats) and *Bromus* spp (brome grass). As such, they did not entirely conform to the expected distribution for waste from storage of unclean or fully processed crops; one sample fell within the expected range for storage of uncleaned grain. The reasons for this distribution are unclear. The few floret bases found were of the wild type rather than the cultivated variety. However, the possibility that the majority of seeds of oats represent the cultivated, rather than the wild variety, cannot be entirely dismissed. If seeds of oats were removed from the analysis, then the samples would be dominated by small, not large, seeds. Another possibility is that cultivation practises, such as winter sowing, may lead to a predominance of weeds of oats in the field at the expense of smaller seeded species, such as *Chenopodium* spp. Lastly, it may be that improved or more scrupulous separation techniques led to less grain wastage, and so to dominance by seeds of oats. However, the distribution from the first analysis (Fig. 66) did not reveal the high ratios of glumes that might be expected under such a scenario.

Scheduling processing practises
Small weed seeds dominated both the samples from Wardy Hill and the Iron Age and Roman samples from

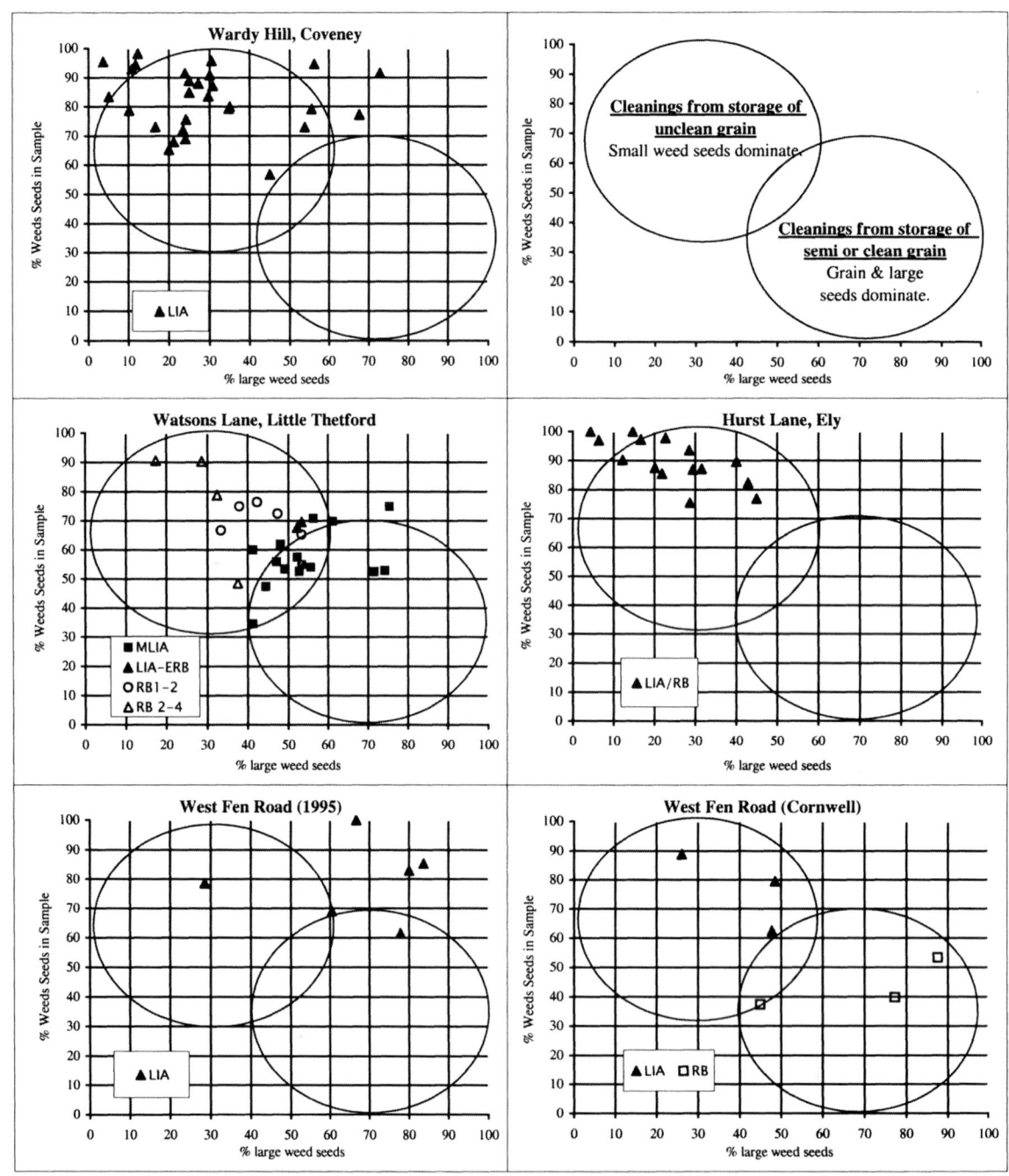

Figure 67 Ely Environs: The percentage of all weed seeds to cereal grains plotted against the percentage of large weed seeds (>2.5mm) from a total of all classified weed seeds

Hurst Lane. At both sites it would appear that crops were stored relatively unprocessed, implying that activities revolving around harvest were probably organised on a small, household, level. The site at Watson's Lane would appear to have been similar during the Roman period. There is some indication that in the Iron Age crops were stored in a more fully processed state. It is uncertain whether charred assemblages represent single or multiple events spread out over a week, a month, a year, or many years. The nature of the site — with many feature re-cuts, and Roman occupation overlying the Iron Age settlement — was such that some mixing of earlier and later charred material had certainly occurred. It is possible that some blurring resulted, with possible reworking of later material into earlier deposits. A transition from larger-scale organisation on a multiple household level to the organisation of processing by households may have occurred. Such a change would imply a scenario in which

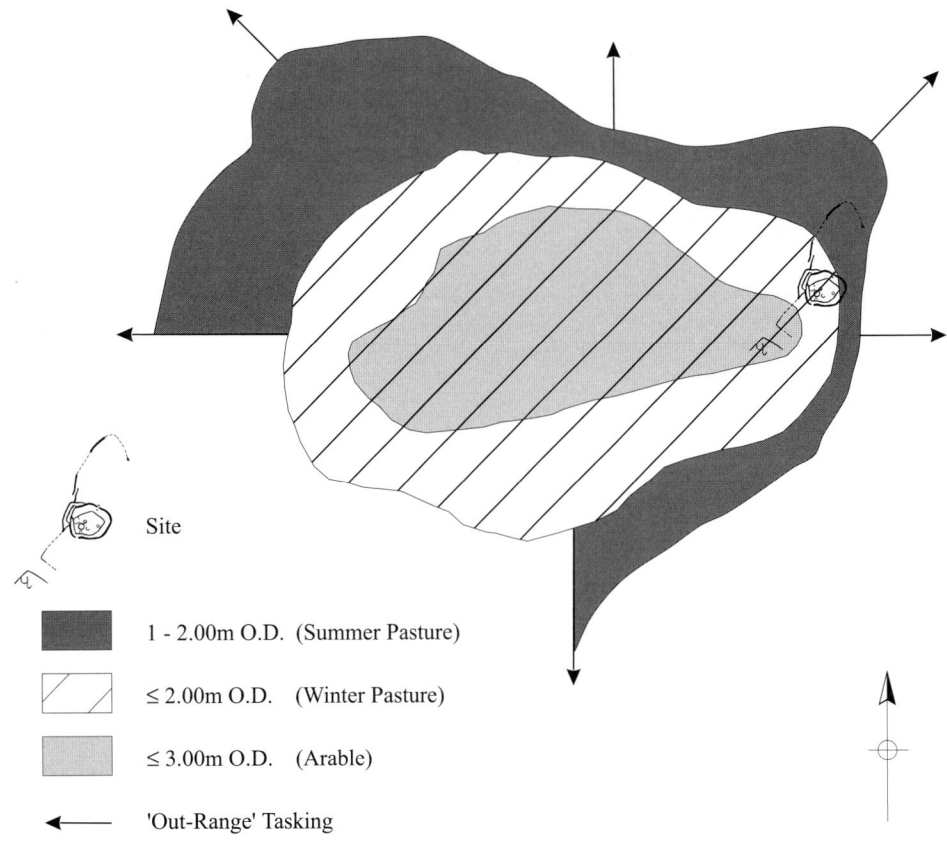

Figure 68 Land-use model

processing activities, rather than being concentrated after harvest, were spread throughout the year. For the West Fen Road sites, the 1999 Cornwell site excavations revealed a change from crops stored in a relatively uncleaned state to those stored as semi-clean grain. This sees a change in the organisation of agriculture to one in which crops are stored in a more processed state, involving barns and/or larger numbers of co-operating people. It is possible that the 1995 site represents a similar pattern to that seen in the Roman period. The high number of oat seeds may indicate that something that was once a tolerated impurity in the crop was now more carefully extracted than previously.

Carrying capacities and land-use modelling
(Figs 68 and 69)
When estimating the carrying capacity of the immediate Wardy Hill landscape, typical of fenland situations, the main constraints are set by the availability of elevated dry land for arable and winter pasture. For crop production, Wardy Hill itself (excluding the area of the site at its eastern end) would offer some 25ha at an elevation above 3.00m OD (Fig. 68). In the context of the Haddenham Iron Age research, Stevens (in Evans and Hodder forthcoming) reviewed the period's production techniques and field/cereal capacities. Using a cereal return figure of 15cwt per acre, he calculated that fifteen people would require fields over an area of *c.* 1.9ha, with 25 people needing some 3.2ha. From this, the hilltop would potentially have had the capacity to support a population of *c.* 200 persons.

In terms of winter pasturage for stock, in the forthcoming Haddenham report Pryor calculates that sheep could be grazed at a rate of 9.3 head per hectare. Within the Wardy Hill environs it is estimated that there would be upwards of *c.* 65ha of land available above *c.* 2.00m OD (again, excluding the site), presumed to be the maximum range of seasonal flooding. Given this, potentially there would have been land to support some 605 stock. As outlined by Pryor, if a household was to be regularly kept in meat — consuming *c.* 25 lambs a year (one every fortnight) — then a breeding population of 600 ewes theoretically could support some 24 family groups. (In terms of arable capacity the hilltop could support up to 33 six-member families.) Such 'ballpark' estimates are underlain by assumptions concerning the maximisation of production that are unlikely to have been applicable in prehistory. They take no account, moreover, of the coverage of woodland lots equally necessary to sustain early settlement (Darrah in Evans and Hodder forthcoming). The point is, however, that even if we halve these figures the Wardy Hill environs could have readily supplied the resources needs of upwards of 12–15 family groups.

Of course, when attempting to model the Wardy Hill 'territory' the range of out-field pasture would have to be added to the above. If winter grazing is potentially calculated at a level of 65ha, then 50ha for summertime usage could be considered reasonable since grass would then be growing (F. Pryor, *pers. comm.*). If it is presumed that this was largely provided for by fen-edge meadows, and that this would be feasible to a depth/height of c. 1.00m OD,

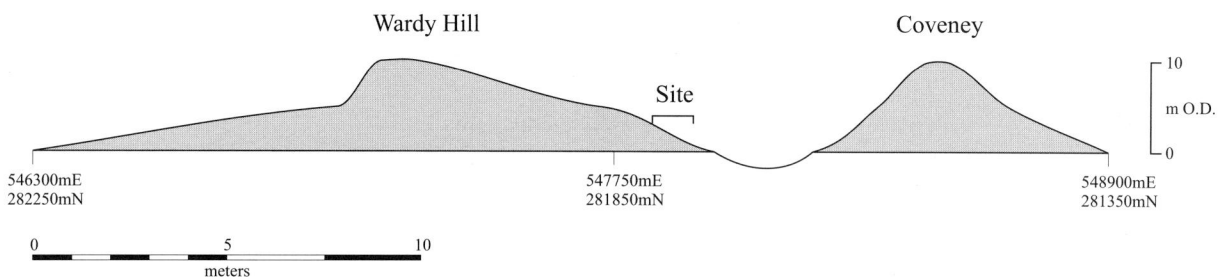

Figure 69 Schematic elevation of Wardy Hill and Coveney Islands

then this area could be accommodated within a *c.* 300–350m radius along the northern and eastern sides of the site (Fig. 68). Being so 'sided' (*i.e.* fenward), this alters the otherwise concentric hilltop land-use model thus far presented. Combining these hypothetical land-use zones would give the Ringwork a potential agricultural range of *c.* 175ha. This approximates the 200ha territories that Cunliffe postulated for the 'Woodbury-type' farmsteads within Danebury's environs, to each of which he tentatively assigns some 40–80 individuals (1984, vol. 2, 552). However, this would be significantly less than the 0.5m and 1.5m in-/out-field radii respectively that Clarke proposed for the Glastonbury 'lake village' (*c.* 450ha), which he estimated as supporting a population of 60–120 (1972). Extrapolating from these figures, Clarke's model would give a per hectare/'head' ratio of 0.13–0.26 (13–26 per 100ha). Based on these figures, as defined here, the Wardy Hill environs would support a residential population of *c.* 21–43: the equivalent of two to three times the average population of 'typical' domestic compounds of the period. Cunliffe's estimates of residential densities for the extended families within his Woodbury-type enclosures are substantially greater (0.20–0.40 per ha). From this basis, Wardy Hill could have supported 35–70 persons. In their re-appraisal of Glastonbury, Coles and Minnitt presented a detailed critique of Clarke's model and their analysis of the settlement suggested a higher population: 125 and 200 respectively for its Middle and Late Phases (1995, 200–6). Applying these to Clarke's 'home-range' radii produces land-use carrying figures much more similar to Cunliffe's — 0.27–0.44 per ha — with its Wardy Hill equivalent being 47 to 77 persons.

Given this land-use modelling, and presuming that the adjacent fringes of the Coveney marshes would offer sufficient immediate summer pasture for regular subsistence supply of the site's inhabitants, there is no reason to evoke mechanisms of long-distance pastoral transhumance on the part of the Wardy Hill community (see Evans 1987, Evans and Hodder forthcoming, for further general discussion). There may well have been off-site overnighting by shepherd 'boys', but this need not have involved sustained displacement by sub-sets of its residential groups. 'Outland' movement would only be required if there was competition for local summer pasture by more distant communities, and/or the site's inhabitants specialised in stock rearing at a level required for 'export' production. Yet — and while this remains a truism — no site is an 'island', and it must be envisaged that there would have been much 'going out' beyond this home range for social visitation, trade and specific landscape 'tasking' (*i.e.* resource procurement).

From the above discussion, the occurrence of skirtland ringing fenland islands is obviously a critical factor in the determination of their settlement potential: did the islands' edges drop sharply to below wet marsh levels, or were their flanks more gradually sloping? The latter situation would have provided, in effect, an 'escape' mechanism, since arable land and settlement could be concentrated on the high ground with summer pasturage around their off-crown flanks. Otherwise the restricted area of these dry rises would also have to accommodate pasture, thereby reducing their potential arable (and settlement) component. In this context Wardy Hill and Coveney itself offer interesting contrasts (Fig. 69). While extending over 4.1ha, the latter has very marked edges with little skirtland, as opposed to Wardy Hill's wide berm; to date, no significant archaeology has been found upon Coveney island (Hall 1996).

4. Material Culture

by C. Evans, K. Gdaniec, J.D. Hill, G. Lucas, K. Robbins and D.F. Williams, with A. Dickens and L. Horne

This chapter is concerned with the material environment of the Ringwork's inhabitants. The site's general artefact frequencies and depositional dynamics will be addressed in Chapter 5, although specific 'type' distributions will be considered here in the final section. In terms of these intra-site analyses, the differential sampling fraction between the Ringwork's buildings (100% excavation) and its inner and outer circuits (25% and 10–14% respectively) must be born in mind when considering finds representation.

I. Iron Age and Early Roman pottery
by J.D. Hill with L. Horne (and with contributions by G. Lucas and D.F. Williams)
(Figs 70–88; Tables 40–50)

The assemblage consists of 5311 sherds, weighing 60,988g and with a mean sherd weight of 11.48g (Table 40). This figure does not include the pottery collected from fieldwalking prior to excavation. The assemblage is one of the largest excavated from a later Iron Age/Roman transitional site in northern East Anglia or the East Midlands (Table 41). Relatively few sites of this date have larger assemblages, and even that from Cats Water, Fengate is only twice as large as Wardy Hill (11,600 sherds: Pryor 1984).

The material consists of sherds from both handmade and wheelmade vessels recovered from over 70 features. While most features produced only limited quantities of often small and abraded material (less than 10 sherds), several of these groups (*e.g.* those from F. 46 and 64) comprised unusually large and fresh sherds. Only twelve features produced groups weighing more than 1000g each, and three contributed 48% of the total assemblage (Table 42). These were gullies surrounding the large circular buildings (Structure 1 — F. 6; IV — F. 25/26) and the inner circuit of the Ringwork itself (F. 2). Both of the main buildings' gullies produced substantial portions of individual vessels. Compared to most Pre-Roman Iron Age assemblages from northern East Anglia, there are a relatively large number of complete or near-complete reconstructable vessel profiles, most coming from the gullies surrounding the two large structures (I and IV).

The material is generally well preserved and sherd recovery from the hand-dug features was good, despite the difficult weather conditions at the time of the excavation and the heavy clay feature fills (*Sieved fraction*, below). These factors did affect the retrieval of detailed information that may have been of value in distinguishing specific contexts and features, however. At the same time, the heavy clay on which the site was located clung persistently to many sherds, even after washing. The difficulties in washing many of the sherds may account for the low occurrence of carbonised food residues and other evidence for use, including wear *etc.* Many sherds in softer fabrics show signs of wear from the cleaning process, and the burnished or wiped surfaces of some may have been removed.

The collection was recorded using the system recommended by the Prehistoric Ceramics Research Group's *Study of Later Prehistoric Pottery: General Policies and Guidelines for Analysis and Publication* (1997). Pottery from each context was divided by external surface finish and technology, before being ascribed to a fabric group after macroscopic examination; sherds were weighed to the nearest whole gram and external surface treatment (burnishing, scoring *etc.*) recorded. Every diagnostic sherd (rim, base, shoulder or decorated body sherd *etc.*) was examined and assigned a form type as appropriate, with further detailed variables recorded as suggested in PCRG 1997. Each fabric was described following the system laid out in that publication, and consideration has been given to comparing the fabrics from this and other later Iron Age sites from the region. A standard rim and base form typology has been developed to allow direct comparison with other later Iron Age assemblages, such as those from HAD V (Hill and Braddock forthcoming) and Little Thetford (Hill and Braddock 1998). Close attention has been paid to recording the following variables to address the questions asked of this assemblage as outlined above: fabric, vessel form and size, surface treatment, sherd size and condition, and the presence of carbonised residues. Copies of the archive on which this pottery report is based are held at the CAU and the British Museum. The archive consists of a primary spreadsheet, stored electronically and in paper copies, containing all the data entries recorded during the analysis.

Phasing and dating
The bulk of the pottery dates to the later Pre-Roman Iron Age and the first four or five decades after the Roman Conquest. Establishing tighter dating is inhibited by both the complex nature of the site and the difficulties in precisely dating both hand- and wheelmade pottery in this and other parts of Eastern England. The details of the complex and difficult structural phasing of the site have been outlined previously in Chapter 2 of this report. It is important to stress here that this structural sequence cannot be used to produce simple, distinct groups of pottery that correspond to this phasing. In particular, many earlier-phase features may contain significant quantities of pottery from later phases. This is because:

1. The upper fills of these features may have accumulated some time after their initial infilling;
2. Later re-cutting of parts of the Ringwork ditches *etc.* might have led to their 'contamination' by later pottery.

In perfect excavation conditions, it might be possible to distinguish and separate later accumulating or intrusive pottery. However, this has not always been possible on this site. As such, simple totals of pottery from particular

		Wardy Hill	Haddenham V	Watson's Lane
	No.	*5311*	*15015*	*1212*
	Wt. (g)	*60988*	*174055*	*13662*
Mean sherd wt.		11.4	11.6	11.3
Rims (wt.)		19.60%	14.9%	15.00%
Bases (wt.)		17.90%	9.30%	14.21%
Surface treatment				
Scoring		1.78%	25.90%	4.13%
Burnishing		10.48%	8.20%	17.22%
Technology				
Handmade		76.50%	99.90%	95.32%
Wheelmade		23.50%	<0.10%	4.68%

Table 40 Characteristics of pottery assemblage

Site	*County*	*Wt. (g)*
Little Waltham	Essex	500,000
Haddenham V	Cambridgeshire	174,055
Weekley	Northamptonshire	142,670
Wardy Hill	**Cambridgeshire**	**60,988**
Greenhouse Farm	Cambridgeshire	52,271
Enderby	Leicestershire	35,180
Fison Way, Thetford	Norfolk	34,750
Birchanger	Essex	20,820
Gamston	Nottinghamshire	19,300
Werrington	Cambridgeshire	19,160
Watsons Lane	Cambridgeshire	13,660
Wavedon Gate	Buckinghamshire	9702
Tort Hill (East and West)	Cambridgeshire	9352
Haddenham IV	Cambridgeshire	7696
Silfield	Norfolk	6831
Wotton Hill (Phase 2)	Northamptonshire	3610
Marions Close	Cambridgeshire	1438

Table 41 Comparative pottery assemblage sizes

Feature		Sherd no.	Wt. (g)	MSW (g)	% total sherd no.	% total wt.
F27	Earlier Inner Ringwork ditch South-East Entrance	59	1275	21.61	1.11	2.08
F76	Pit inside Structure IV	93	1283	13.8	1.75	2.1
F61	Structure I eaves-gully	114	2424	21.26	2.14	3.96
F26	Structure IV eaves-gully	233	2534	10.88	4.37	4.14
F13	Outer Ringwork ditch/Structure IV	246	2647	10.76	4.62	4.33
F37	Earlier Inner Ringwork ditch	276	2739	9.92	5.18	4.48
F1	Outer Ringwork ditch	247	3391	13.73	4.64	5.54
F2	Inner Ringwork ditch	809	7525	9.30	15.18	12.30
F6	Structure I eaves-gully	711	9009	12.67	13.34	14.72
F25	Structure IV eaves-gully	1050	12,876	12.26	19.70	21.04
Total		**3838**	**45,703**	**136.19**	**72.03**	**74.69**

Table 42 Ten main features producing pottery

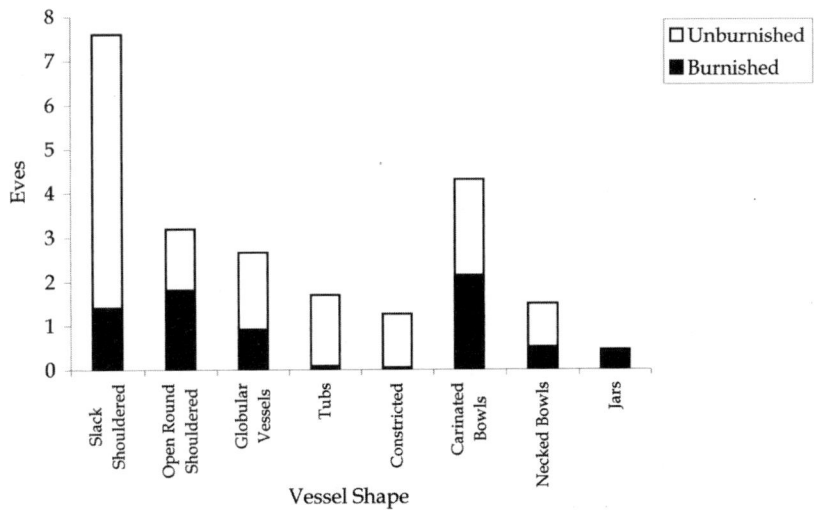

Figure 70 Numbers of different vessel types

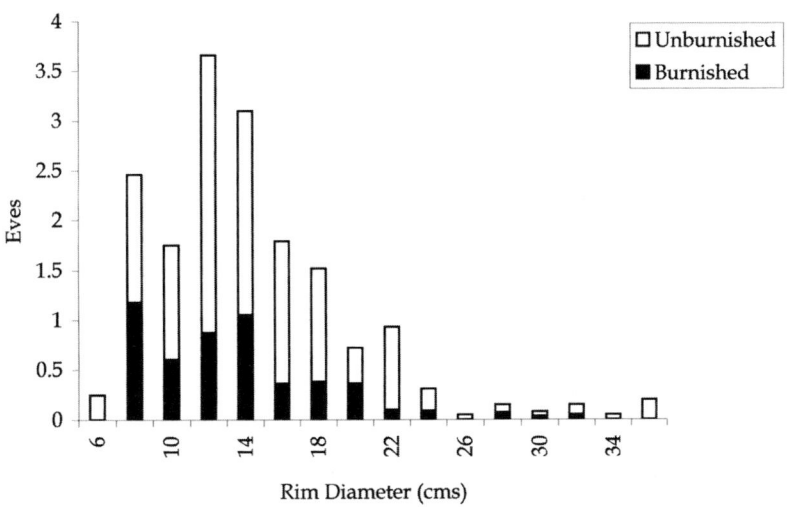

Figure 71 Size of handmade pots

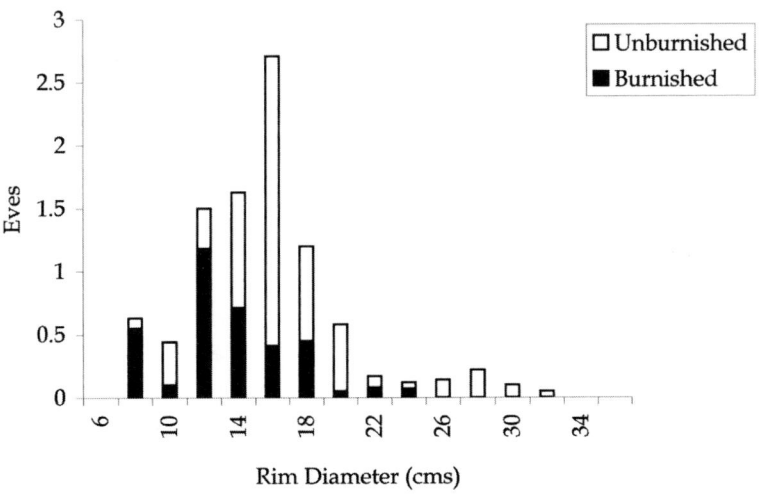

Figure 72 Size of wheelmade pots

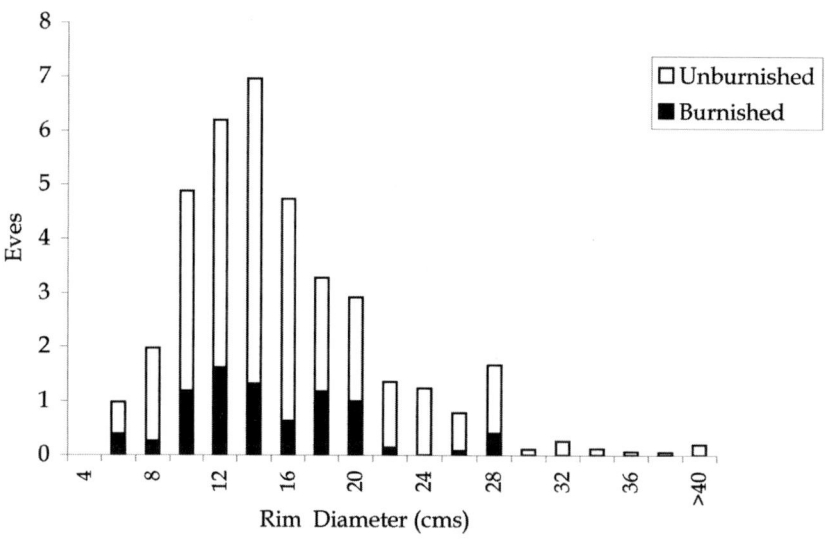

Figure 73 Haddenham V pot sizes

features may contain pottery from different periods of the site's use. These problems are not unique to Wardy Hill, but are of great importance here because of the desire for close dating to relate the changing nature and function of pottery assemblages with important developments occurring locally and regionally in the 1st centuries BC and AD.

Equally, it is worth reiterating that no pottery assemblage is ever the product of a simple constant ceramic 'fall-out' throughout a site's occupation. Rather, it represents a palimpsest of material entering archaeological deposits through a range of processes, with the larger deposits presenting a picture of 'punctuated' deposition — often marked by very short events of deposition separated by long periods when relatively little of the pottery used on the site may have entered subsoil features. The long use-lives of particular vessels, curation of broken sherds, and feature backfilling using midden material that may have accumulated over long periods all cloud the issue of close dating of features and deposits at the site.

Overall, the pottery can be divided into three or four main chronological groups: Late Bronze Age material, handmade later Iron Age vessels, 'Belgic'/'Aylesford-Swarling' wheelmade vessels (hereafter ASW) and clearly early Roman pottery: the latter includes parts of at least two Samian vessels. Table 43 shows the overall quantities of different pottery fabrics in terms of the overall phasing of features. Because of the issues just discussed, these figures should not be taken to indicate that wheelmade pottery was actually in use in either Phase 1 or even 2, nor that burnt flint-tempered pottery was still being made during this period.

To some extent the site's phasing nomenclature as employed in this section relates more to 'depositional horizons' rather than to the elucidated structural sequence, which is based essentially upon immediate construction events rather than longer-term processes of feature infilling. While Phase 1 directly correlates with the described ditch system, Phase 2 in effect becomes a 'shorthand' for the construction, use and filling of the features associated with that structural horizon. This involves the rectilinear ditch system and, primarily, Structure I, but also Structures III and V. Yet, as outlined in Chapter 2, its buildings certainly continued in use throughout Phase 3, if not later. The primary distinction in terms of the later 'depositional horizon' — that is, Phases 3–5 — is: first, the establishment of the F. 2 circuit (Phase 3); then the main perimeter (F. 1; Phase 4); and eventually the Phase 5 outworks (and Structure IV). A product of organic expansion, these circuits were all evidently still open at the time of the enclosure's abandonment. It is the long-term maintenance of these boundaries, and the differentials between the intervals of their construction and the building succession, that gives rise to the discrepancy between structural and assemblage-based phasing.

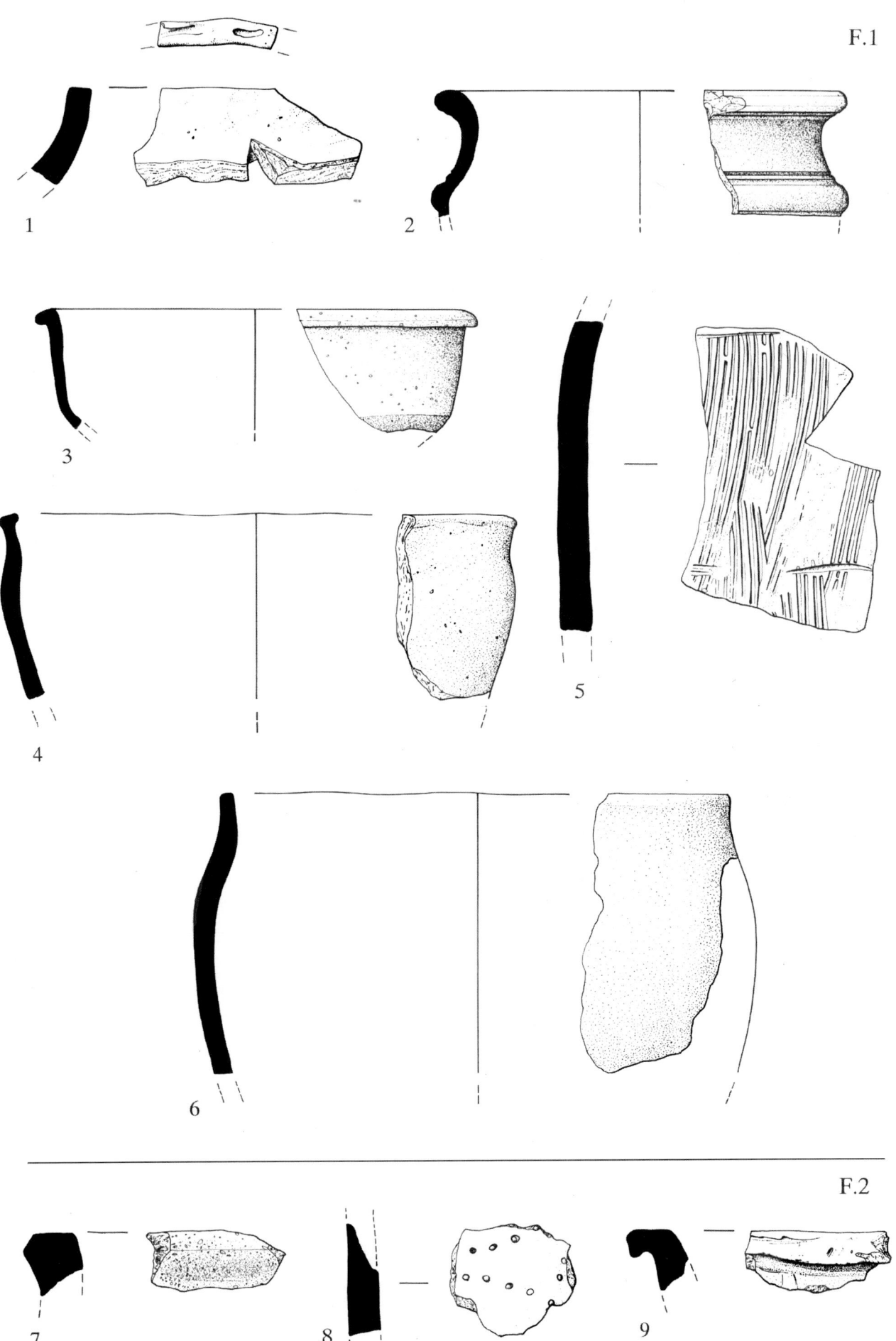

Figure 74 Pottery: Outer Ringwork ditch, F.1 (1–6); Inner Ringwork ditch, F. 2 (7–9). Scale 1:2

149

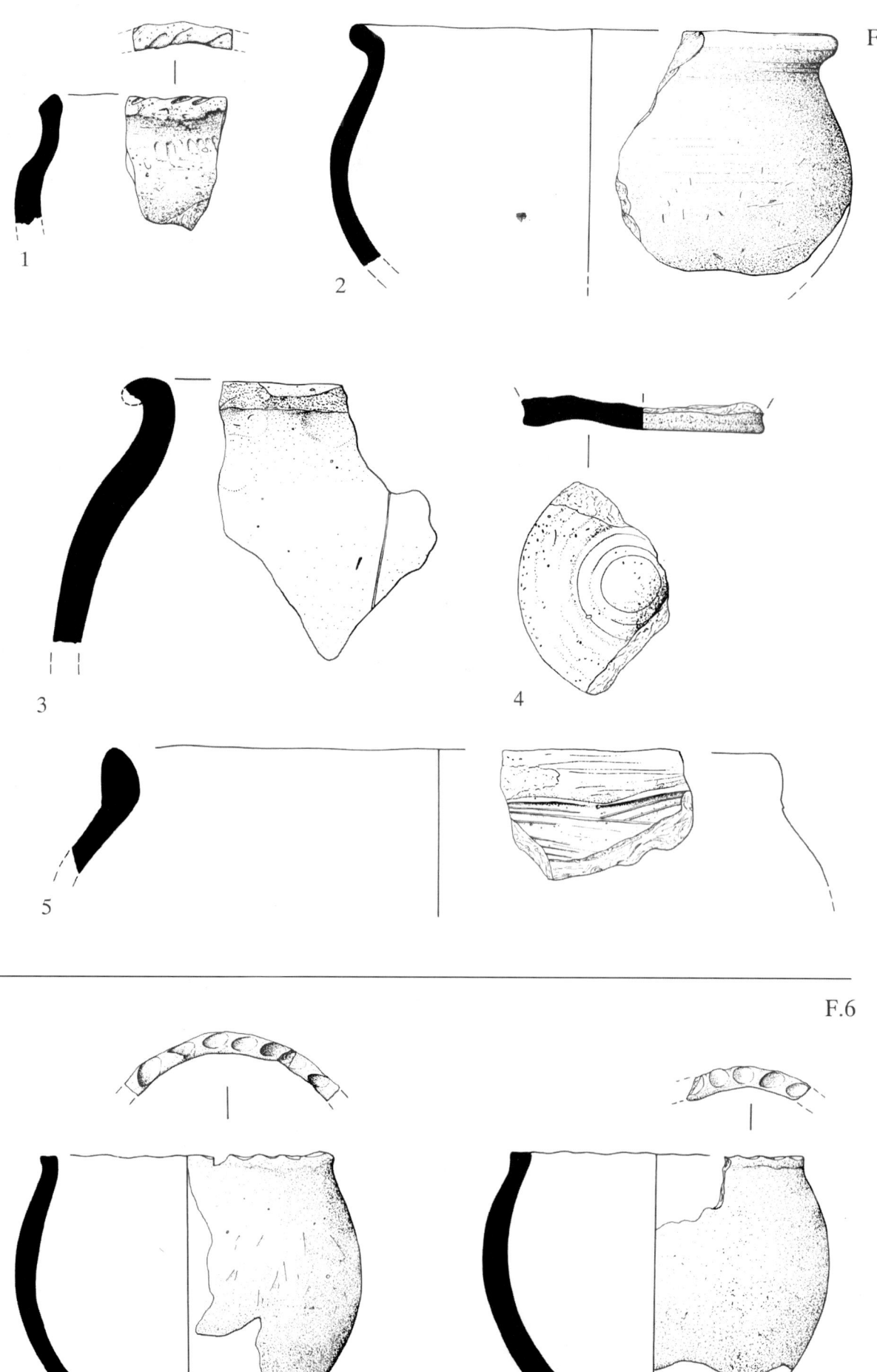

Figure 75 Pottery: Inner Ringwork ditch, F.2 (1–5); Structure I, eaves-gully F. 6 (6 and 7). Scale 1:2

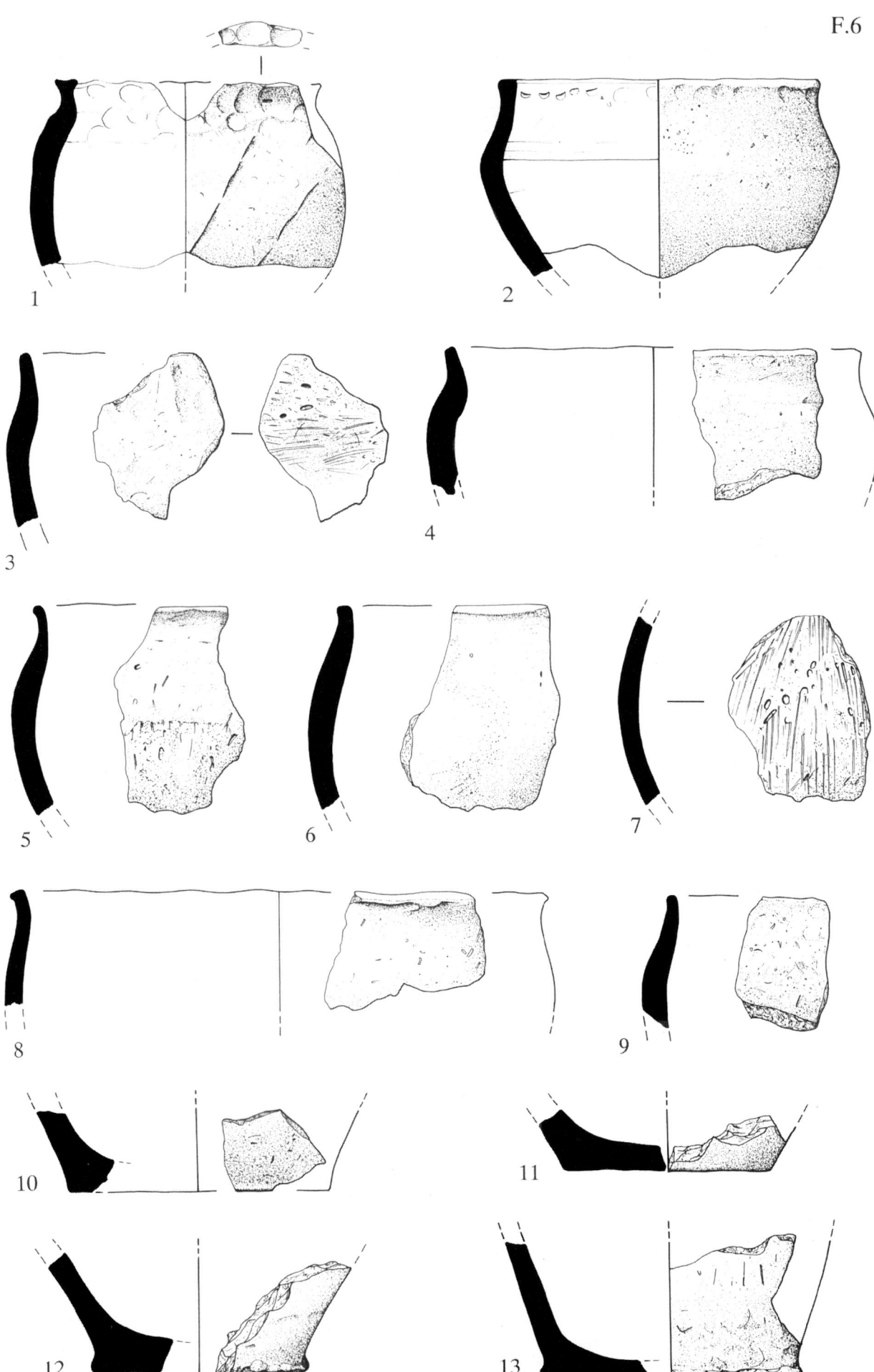

Figure 76 Pottery: Structure I, eaves-gully F. 6. Scale 1:2

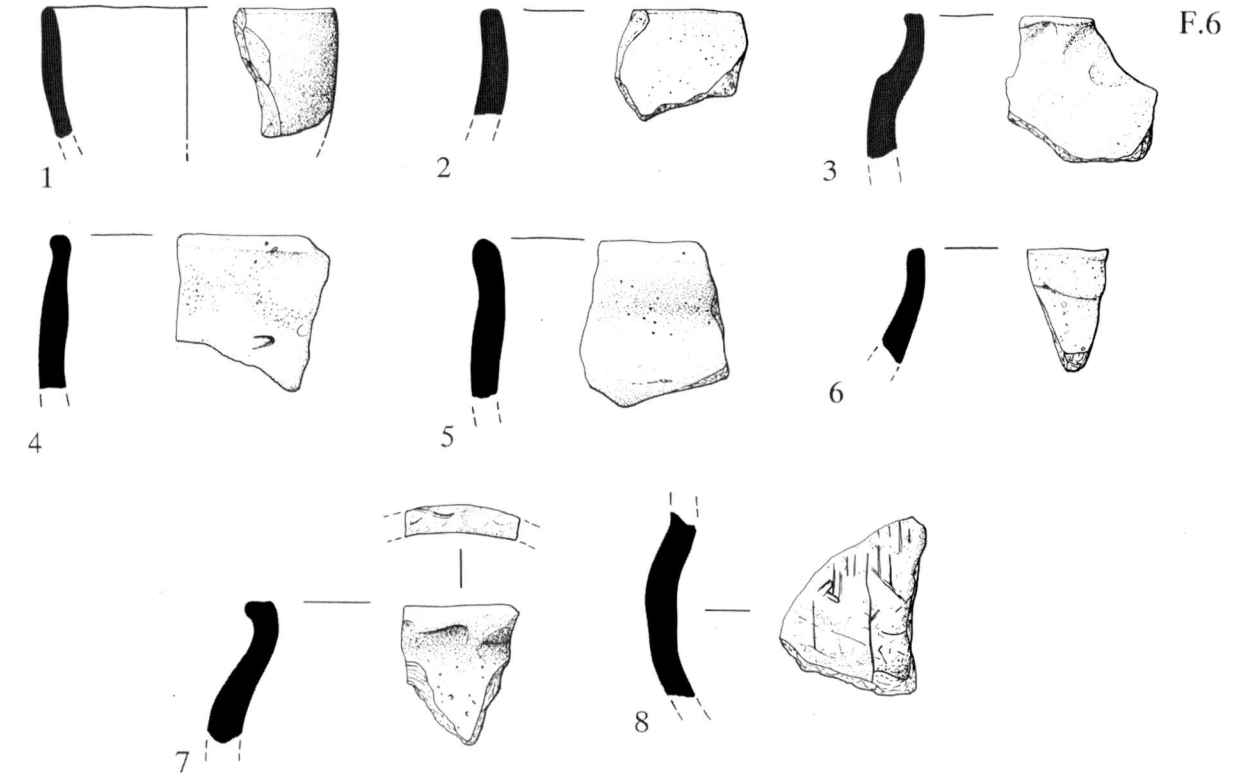
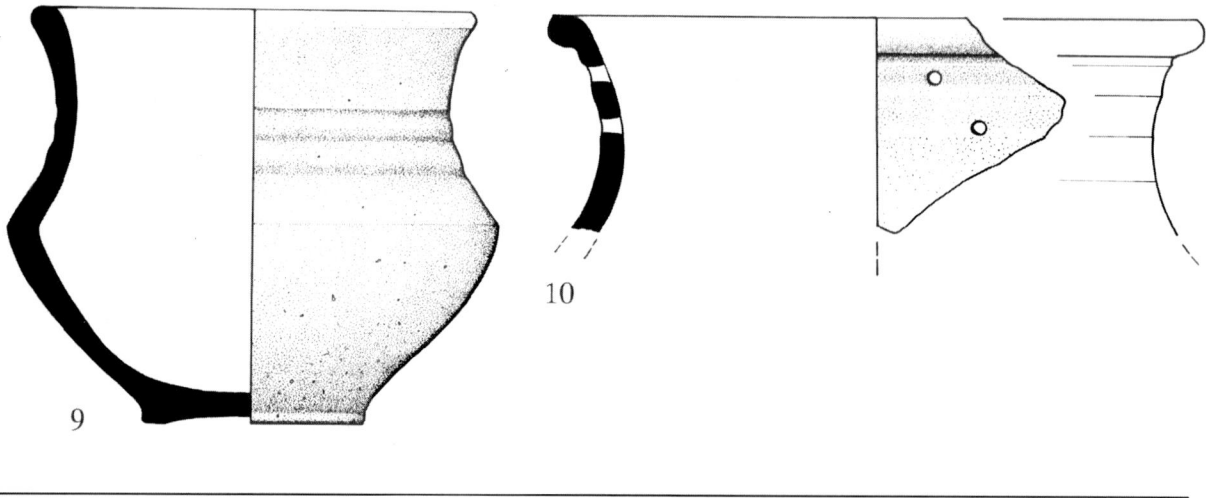

Figure 77 Pottery: Structure I, eaves-gully F. 6 (1–8); Outworks Ditch F. 11 (9 and 10); Outworks Ditch F. 12 (11). Scale 1:2

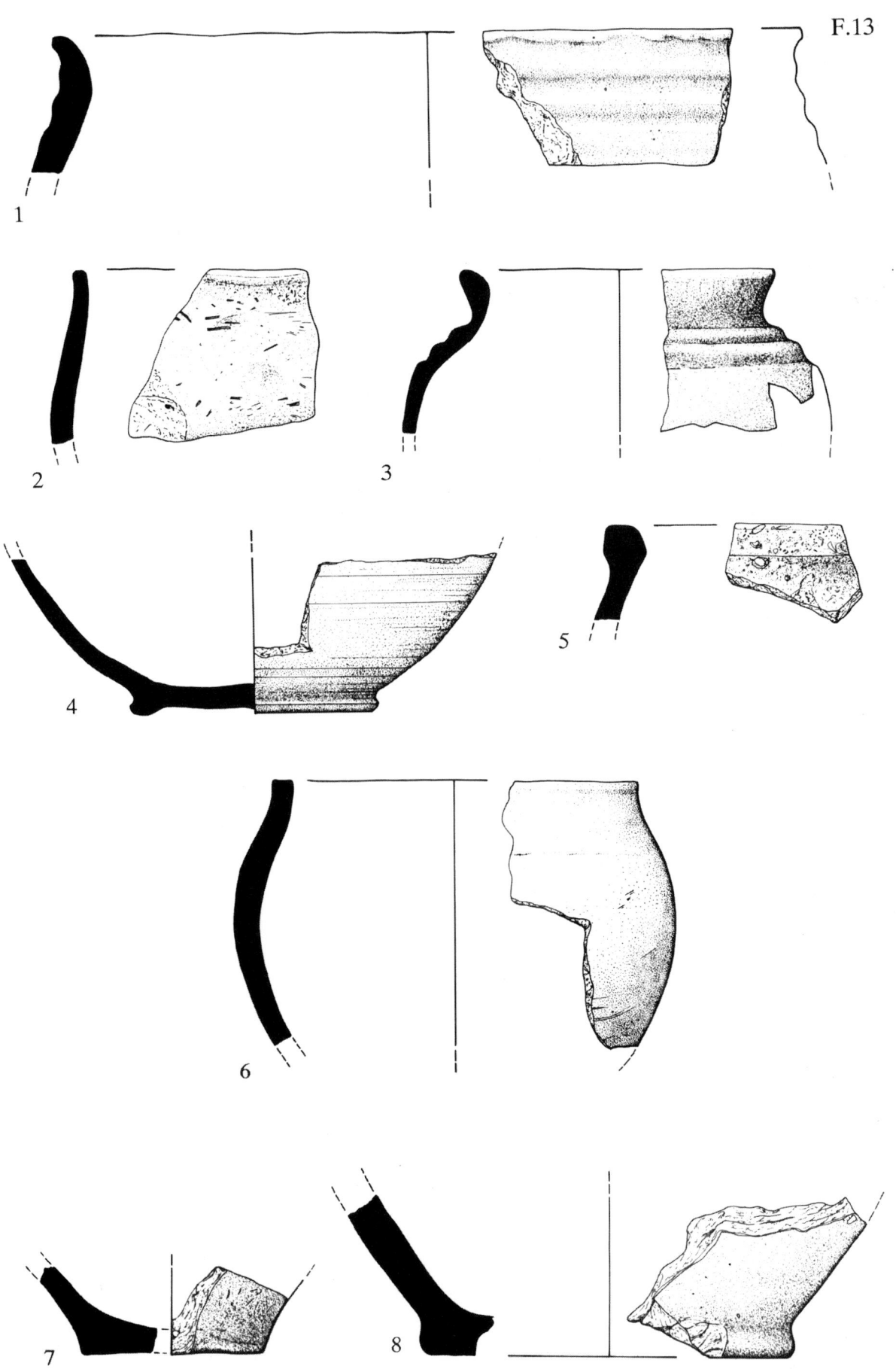

Figure 78 Pottery: F. 13, ditch blocking West Central Entrance; west circuit Structure IV. Scale 1:2

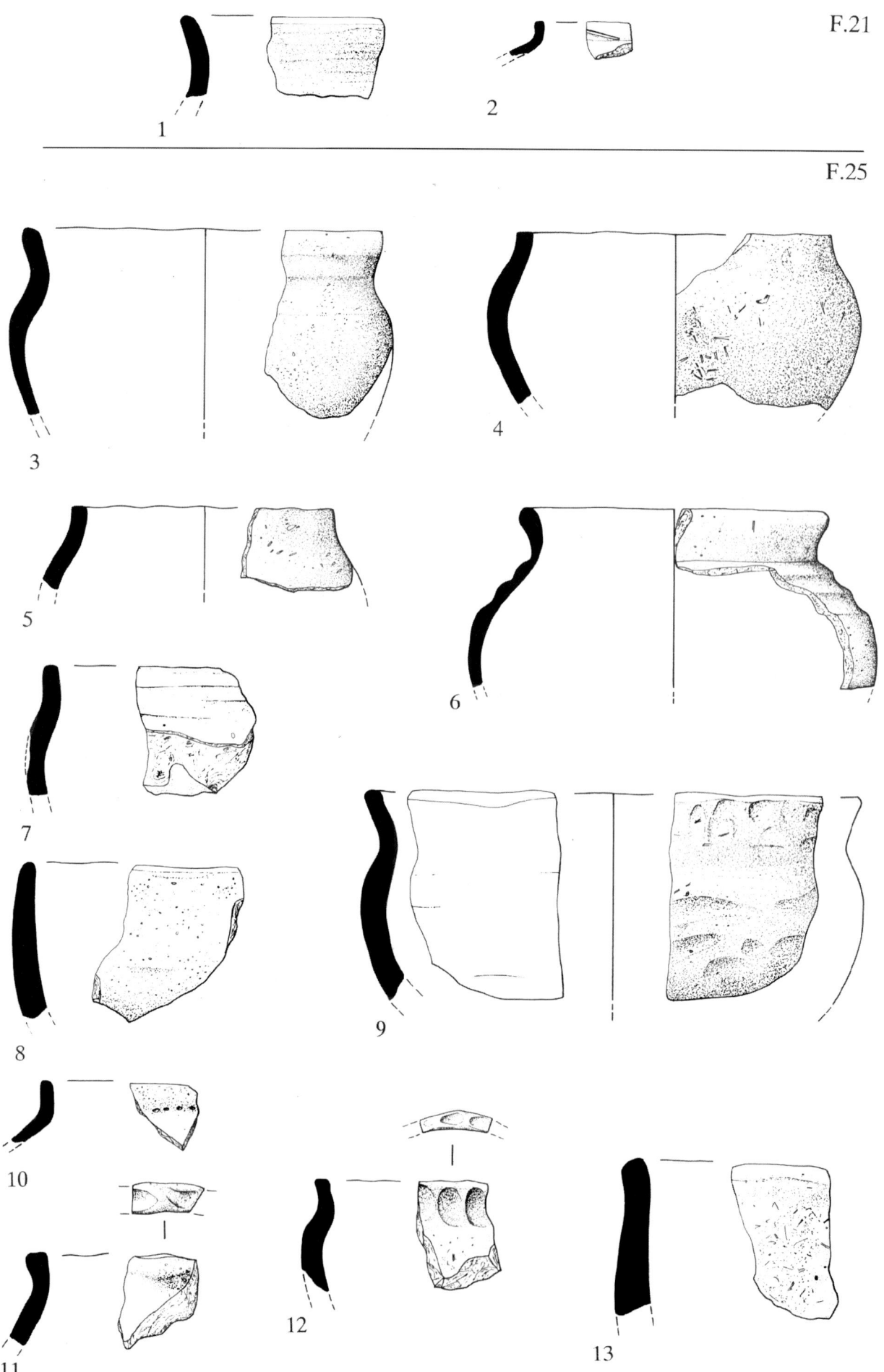

Figure 79 Pottery: Structure III, eaves-gully F. 21 (1 and 2); Structure IV, eaves-gully F. 25, ditch blocking West Central Entrance; west circuit Structure IV. Scale 1:2

F.25

Figure 80 Pottery: Structure IV, eaves-gully F. 25. Scale 1:2

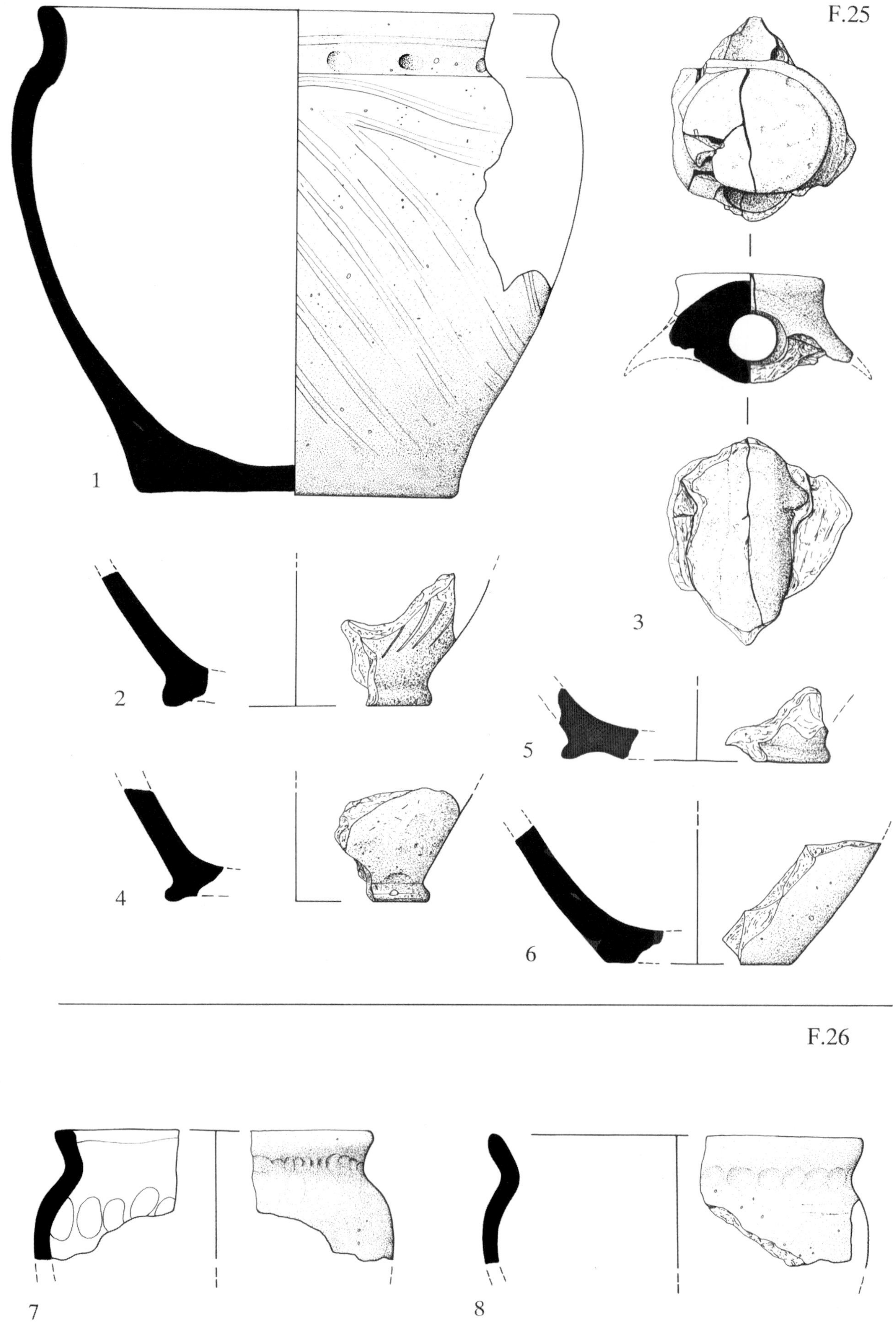

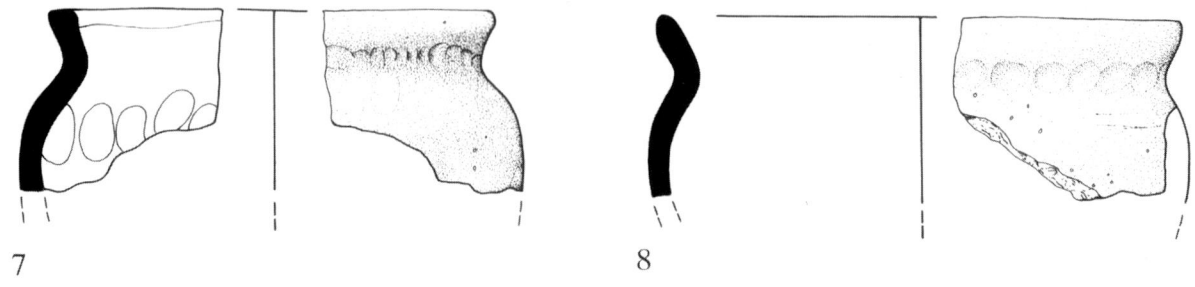

Figure 81 Pottery: Structure IV, eaves-gully F. 25 (1–6) and F. 26 (7 and 8). Scale 1:2

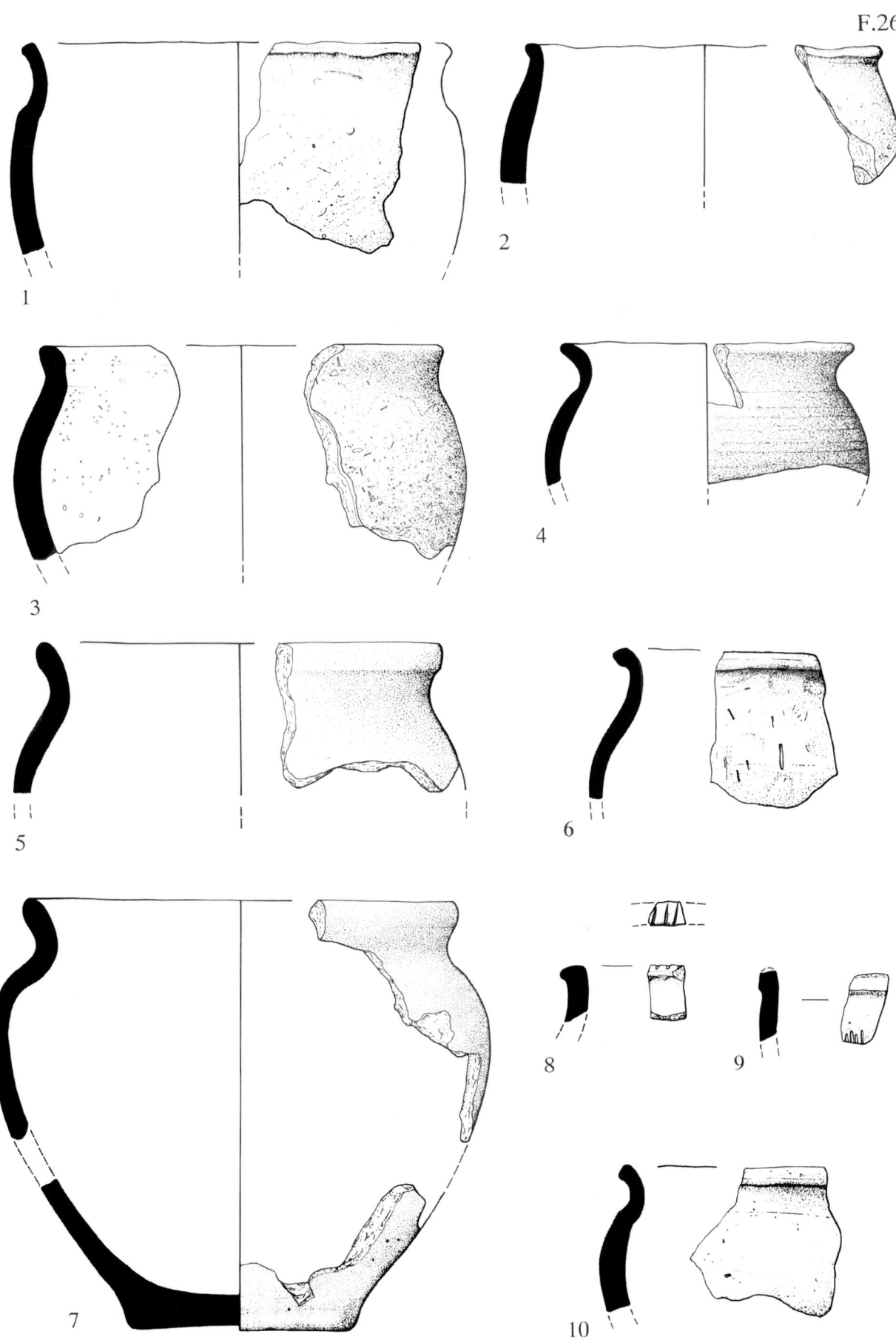

Figure 82 Pottery: Structure IV, eaves-gully F. 26. Scale 1:2

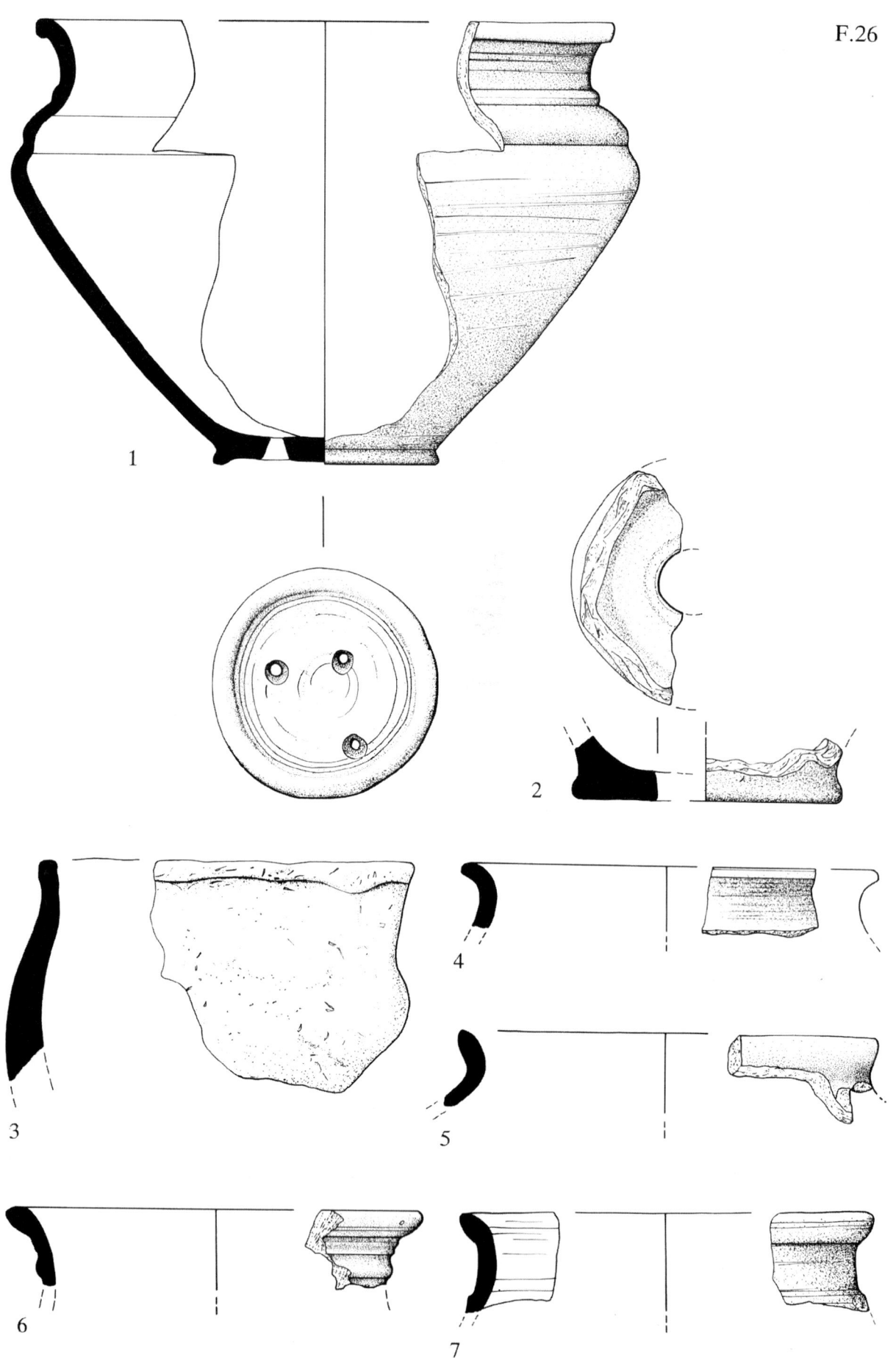

Figure 83 Pottery: Structure IV, eaves-gully F. 25 ('2' from F. 21). Scale 1:2

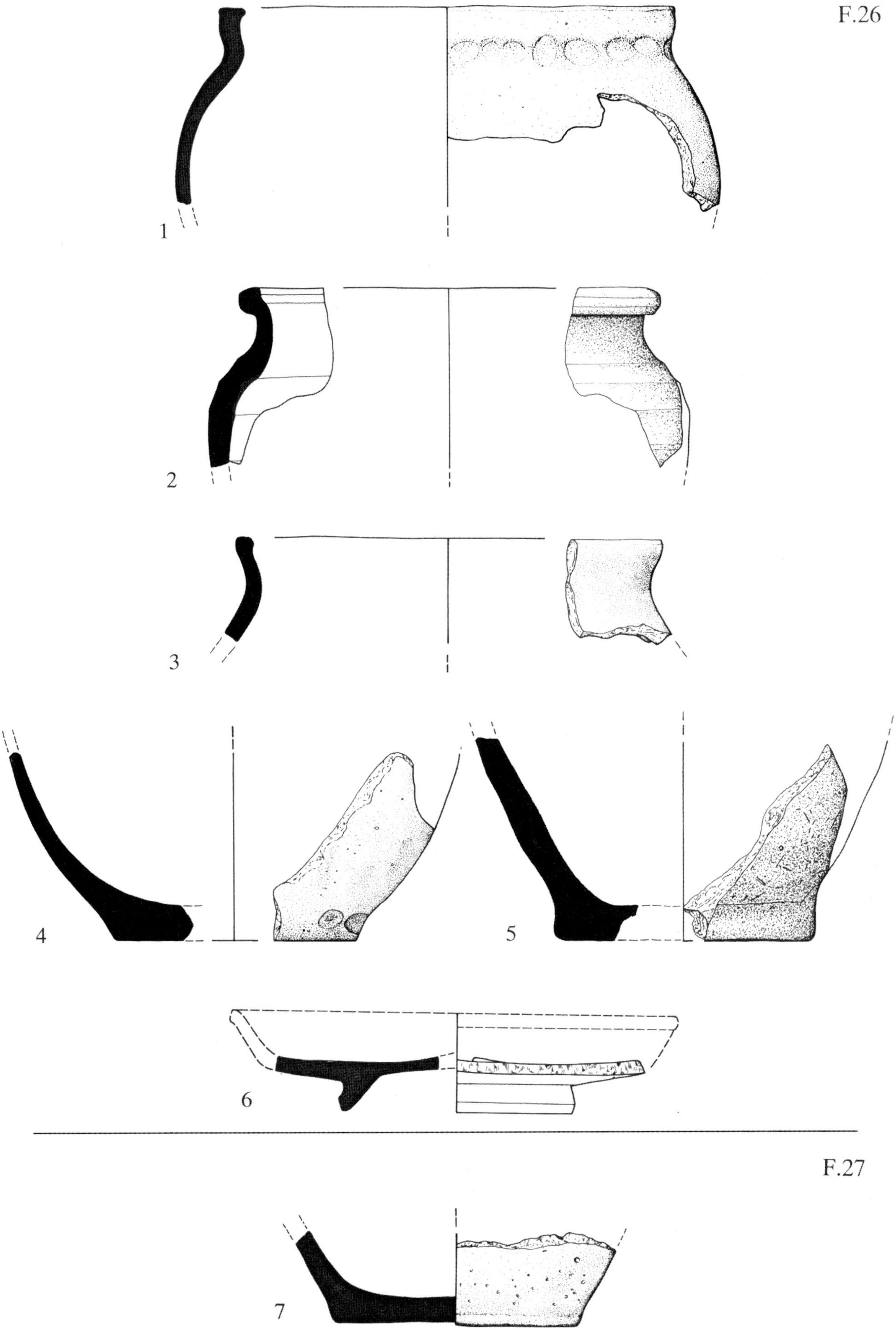

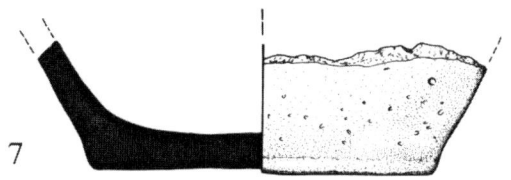

Figure 84 Pottery: Structure IV, eaves-gully F. 25 (1–6); Phase 2, 'Inner' Southern Ditch F. 27 (7). Scale 1:2

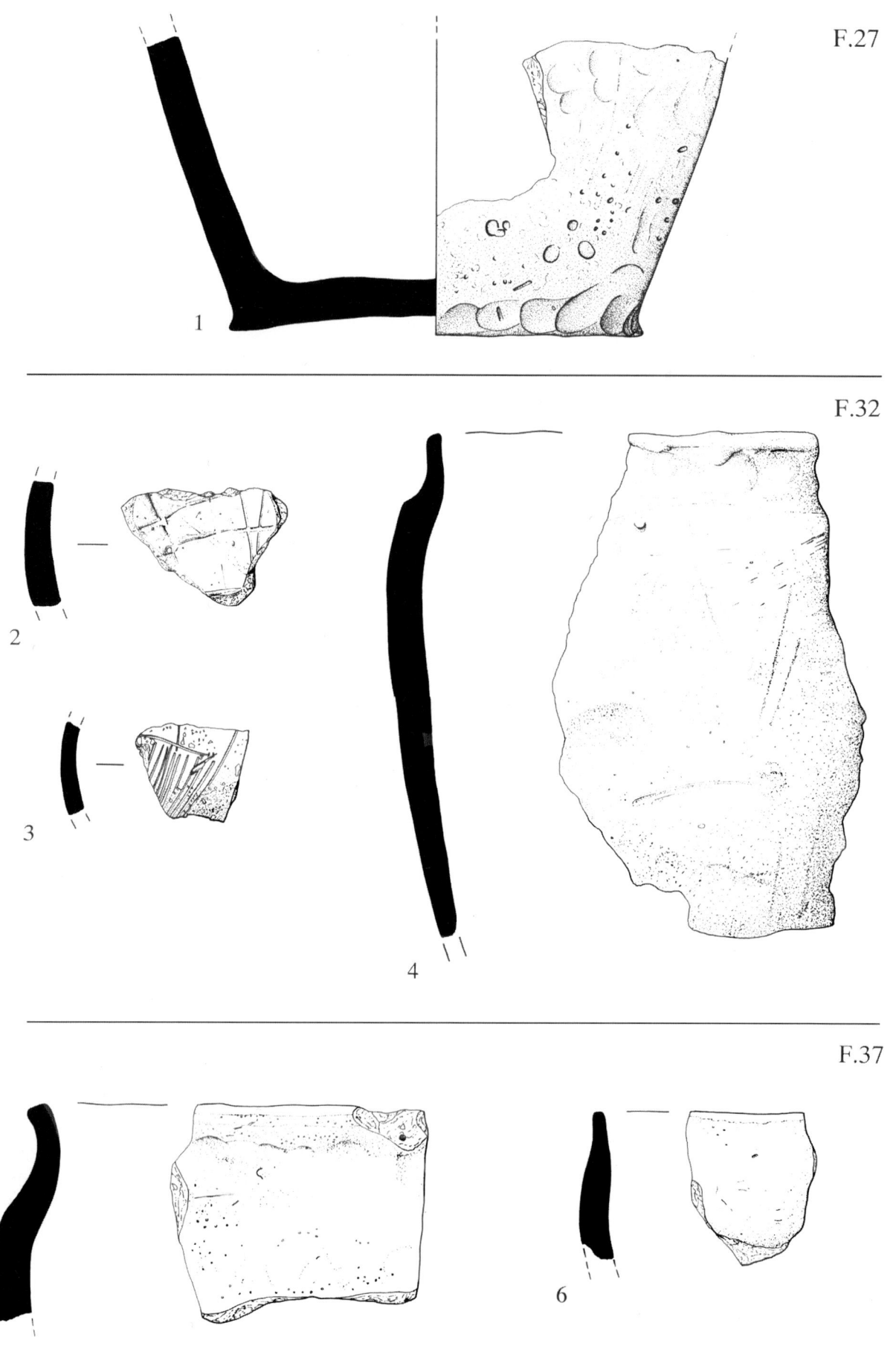

Figure 85 Pottery: Phase 2, 'Inner' Southern Ditch F. 27 (1); pit cutting Structure I, F. 32 (2–4); Phase 2, 'Inner' Western Ditch F. 37 (5–6). Scale 1:2

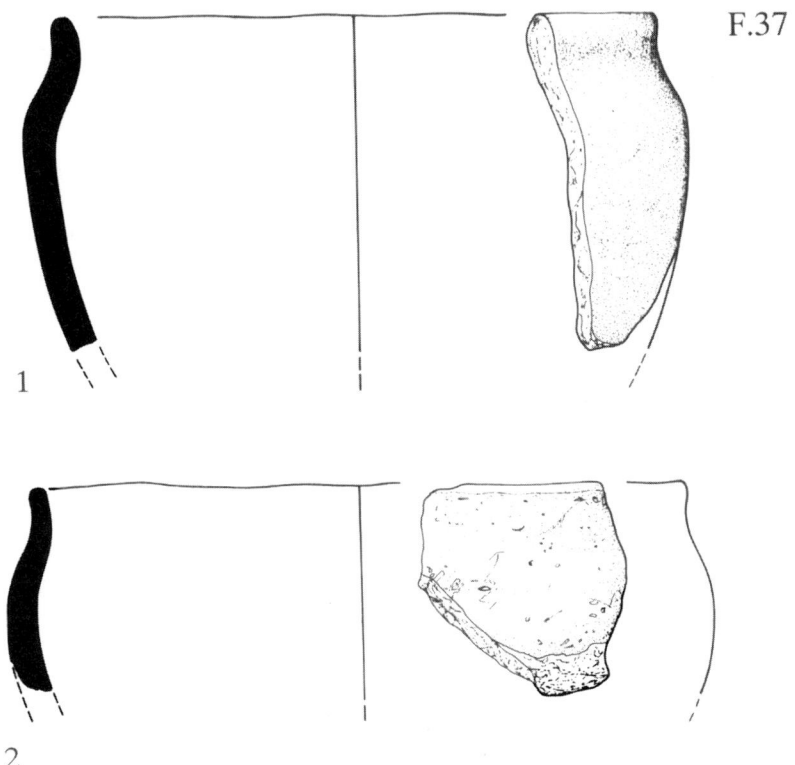

Figure 86 Pottery: Phase 2, 'Inner' Western Ditch F. 37. Scale 1:2

Period I (pre-Iron Age)
There is a quantity of Late Bronze Age and, possibly, Early Iron Age pottery in the assemblage (3.4%). Characterised by added burnt (*i.e.* calcined) flint temper, this material occurs residually in a number of later features (Fig. 87). There is only one well-preserved diagnostic sherd (Fig. 75.1), but the rarity of any other fingernail/impressed body decoration points to a Late Bronze Age (Plain phase PDR) date for this material (*c.* 1200–800 BC).

Period II (Iron Age)
(Figs 70–88; Tables 40–50)

Phase 1
There is no evidence to suggest that any wheelmade pottery was used on the site when either Phase 1 or 2 began. The little pottery in primary and secondary contexts for Phase 1 features is handmade later Iron Age Plain Ware. Traditionally called Middle Iron Age (or before that Iron Age 'B') pottery, this ceramic tradition had emerged by the start of the 3rd century BC but clearly continued up to and after the Roman Conquest in some parts of the region. It is marked by a narrow range of forms: some were burnished and others were not, but there was little or no scoring on unburnished vessels. It is usually made from sandy fabrics. This assignment covers a range of local traditions across East Anglia and the southern East Midlands that share much in common, but with many local features (*e.g.* Percival 1999, Sealey 1997, Cunliffe 1991), some of them yet to be defined.

Unfortunately, there is insufficient diagnostic pottery from Phase 1 features to enable a closer dating than *c.* 300 BC–AD 1 to be made.

Phase 2
A 2nd- or 3rd-century BC date is likely for the start of Phase 2. The main circular building, ancillary buildings and related pits *etc.* contain no wheelmade pottery in primary or secondary deposits. The largest assemblages of pottery from the buildings date their end-use and not their 'beginnings', as the material was recovered from eaves-gullies that would have been regularly maintained. Although not all cleaning-out of these ditches need have been that deep, it is likely the 'fresh' pottery in these features was discarded or placed in the gullies late in the use of the buildings. These deposits contain a range of handmade later Iron Age bowl/jars, typical of those found on many Cambridgeshire sites but with local peculiarities. Chronological change in the forms of later Iron Age plain ware vessels has been difficult to identify. Although recent excavations at Hurst Lane provide a chronological sequence for plain ware later Iron Age pottery possibly spanning the 4th century BC to the late 1st century AD, the range of typical vessel forms at Wardy Hill does not compare with the earlier 4th–3rd century material from the latter site. (This is a moot point with regard to the site's absolute dating: *Chronology and sequence*, below.) At West Stow, Suffolk, there is also evidence for an increasing proportion of burnished rounded bowls with everted or sinuous profiles in the later phases (1st century AD: Forms F and G, West 1990). There is evidence from

some Cambridgeshire sites for a similar change, with these becoming more common in the early 1st century AD or slightly earlier. There are very few of these rims in the eaves-gully of Structure I (Phase 2), where burnished forms were either Type A (usually with rounded bodies) or Type L vessels (see below for a description of this typology). Type F, and especially Type G, vessels are most common in the Ringwork ditches and in the gully of Structure IV (Phase 5), however. The pottery from Phase 2 can be compared with the material from the settlement at Watson's Lane, Little Thetford. This latter assemblage contains similar plain ware vessels in sandy fabrics. The latest building (dating probably to 1st century BC) at this site, F. 3, produced only one 'S'-profile Type G vessel in the lowest fills of the gully (Hill and Braddock 1998). This gully and others produced rim sherds of handmade cordoned neckless bowls similar to that found in F. 13, *680* (Fig. 78.1), which were suggested to date to the 1st century BC at Little Thetford on the basis of parallels to similar wheelmade vessels in southern East Anglia.

There was no pottery from the interior features of Structure I. The eaves-gully of Structure I contained a large assemblage of pottery (11,616g). Only 244g of wheelmade pottery come from the gully (2.3%), of which 93g is represented by a large body sherd and small rim sherd of undiagnostic form in Fabric G2 from F. 61, *325*, the linear gully re-cutting the house circle. The rest of the wheelmade pottery probably also post-dates the demolition of the structure. Where it was possible to distinguish primary and secondary fills in the eaves-gully (*233–235, 237, 252*) no wheelmade pottery was present in the lower fills. This might suggest that the other wheelmade pottery, all in sandy fabrics typical of Phases 3–5, came from the midden that covered the front area of the former building at this time.

Structure III contained only two sherds of wheelmade pottery (2.67% out of 821g of pottery), again made from Fabric G2 (F. 21, *169*, 7g: *164*, 15g). Later sandy wheelmade sherds and Roman grey ware sherds were recovered from the two pits by this gully (F. 53 and 54), which probably are either intrusive or indicate that these features date to Phase 5. A tiny fragment of Samian weighing 1g came from the gully (F. 21, *172*). It is probably intrusive.

Again, the eaves-gully of Structure V contains a very small amount of wheelmade pottery (135g out of 1053g: 12.8%). Of this, 34g represent eleven tiny sherds of sandy fabric pottery, which are probably intrusive or had accumulated in the upper hollow of the gully in Phases 3–5. However, two sherds of Fabric G2 weighing 101g that came from F. 20 *443* are probably contemporary with the main assemblage. They represent 9.6% of the total pottery from this eaves-gully.

No wheelmade pottery was recovered in primary contexts from the main settlement features at the contemporary site of Watson's Lane, Little Thetford, nor at HAD V. The relatively high proportion of vegetable-tempered pottery would also point to a date early in the later Iron Age for Phase 2 through parallels to other sites (*i.e.* 3rd–2nd century BC). The ceramic evidence is consistent with the radiocarbon evidence suggesting that Phase 2 deposits date to the period when handmade Middle Iron Age forms were current without any wheelmade pottery. A 3rd–2nd century BC date could be proposed for the pottery deposited in the lower fills of these features. The presence of grog-tempered sherds in their upper fills suggests later activity, perhaps in the 1st century BC or the early 1st century AD.

The Ringwork
Tying the dating of the Ringwork to the buildings it enclosed is difficult. Again, pottery recovered from different ditches that form part of the Ringwork does not necessarily date their original excavation. If these features were also regularly maintained and cleaned out, pottery from their main fills date the time when this process stopped, or at least when their fills were not dug out to their original depth. These difficulties are complicated by later remodelling, blocking and re-cutting of parts of the Ringwork. The inner and outer Ringwork ditches contain large quantities of wheelmade, sandy pottery that post-dates the horizon seen in the eaves-gullies with just grog-tempered wheelmade pottery. However, there are parts of the Ringwork that appear to have 'collected' their pottery assemblages earlier than this, confirming suggestions that the Ringwork was originally constructed to enclose an existing settlement.

Here the original south-east corner of the enclosure is particularly important, as it was later cut off and back-filled. The ditches at this point contained medium and large sherds of handmade pottery (F. 27 and 52), the majority being in the western (F. 27) arm (*228* and *049; 215, 216* and *217*). There are only small numbers of tiny (<5g) sherds of wheelmade pottery in these features, which are probably intrusive. No grog-tempered wheelmade pottery is represented. The sections through the adjacent portion of the inner F. 2 circuit contain small amounts of pottery, but the few wheelmade sherds in *149* are larger than the handmade sherds from the same and neighbouring sections (*148–151*).

The north-east entrance has very little pottery from its excavated sections. Most are small sherds of handmade pottery, and it lacked any of the similar-sized wheelmade sherds which occur in many other features in the western and southern parts of the site. However, there is a large part of a single handmade vessel in a distinct fabric, Q25, from the north-western terminal of the outer Ringwork ditch (F. 1 *397*).

Finally, the blocking of the south-west entrance clearly dates to a time when wheelmade sandy fabrics (Phase 5) were commonplace (Fig. 87). The western original inner ditch, F. 37, mostly produced just handmade pottery — with the exception of segment *293*. Within the lower/primary silts of its terminal was found a small assemblage similar to that in the house gullies, with 42g of grog-tempered pottery (Fabric G2) out of 233g of pottery in total (*059* and *060*). The latter includes a small part of a necked bowl in Fabric G2; the other pottery is all handmade. However, the upper fills of these sections through the terminal contained 264g of pottery that includes sherds (151g) of wheelmade pottery, including those from later sandy/Early Roman grey ware vessels. The only pottery from F. 46 — the eastern terminal — was 51g of Fabric Q12, a later mid-1st century/early Roman sandy grey ware fabric. Sections across the main inner ditch F. 2 that mark the blocking of this entrance contained wheelmade sandy fabrics, including more of this early grey ware type fabric, in the primary and lower fills.

The evidence from both the inner and outer Ringwork ditches suggests a complex history of infilling, cleaning

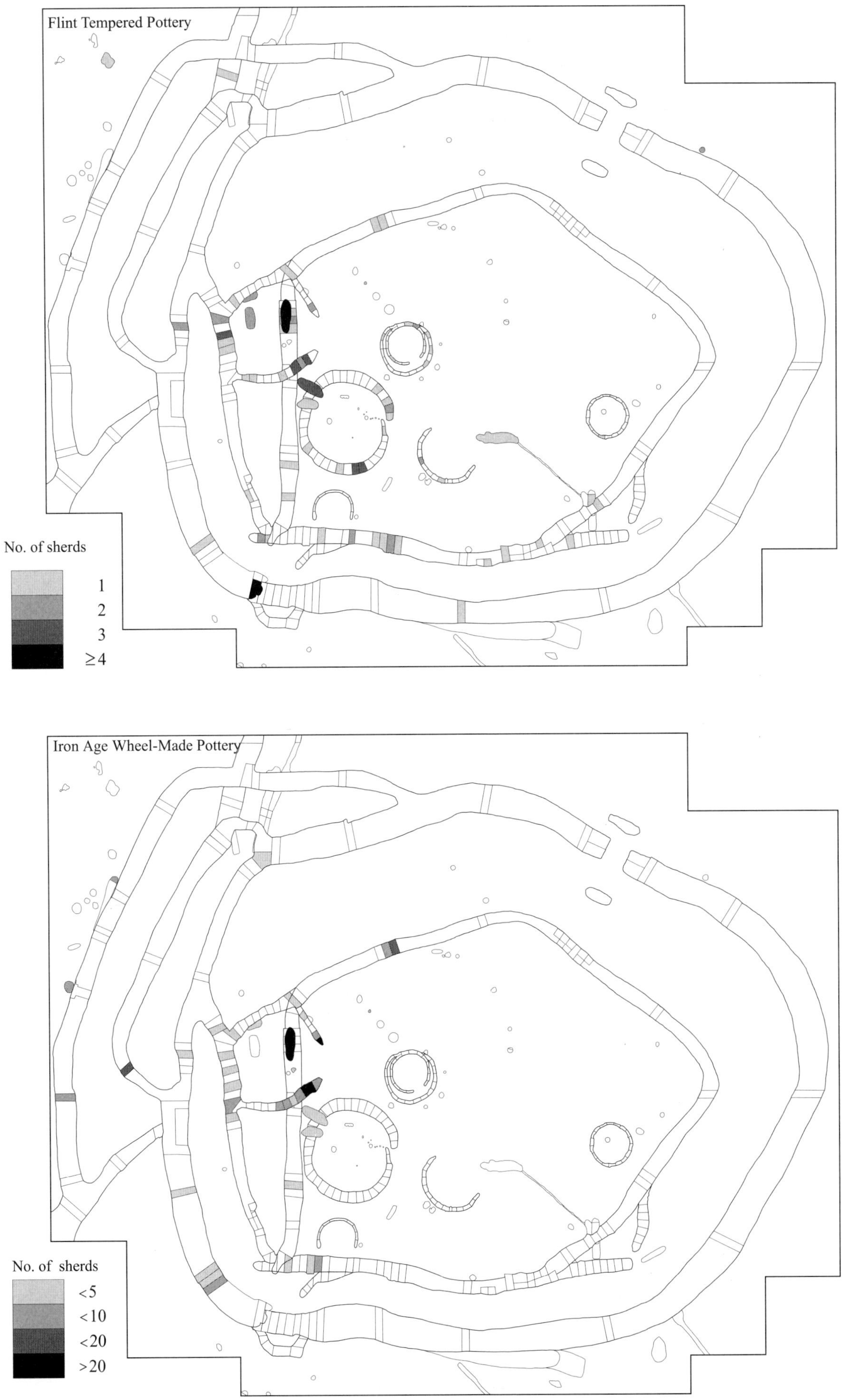

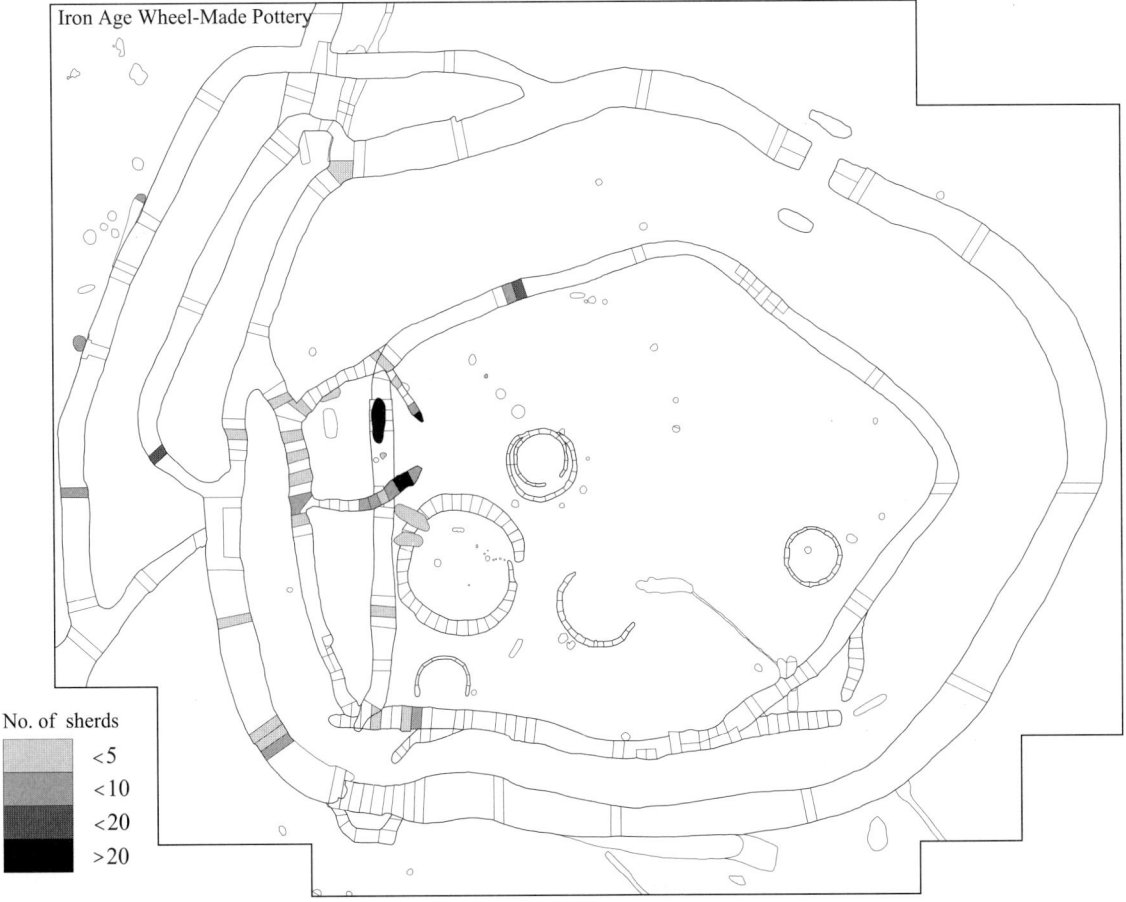

Figure 87 Distribution of flint-tempered (top) and wheelmade Iron Age wares

and re-cutting. In the east of the enclosure, the primary silts of the inner ditch, F. 2, contain only handmade pottery, and in some sections contain no pottery in the upper fills. This picture is also true for the northeast entrance. The last pottery deposited in the base of the terminals of the south-western entrance included pieces of handmade ware that are probably of mid to late 1st century BC date, along with grog-tempered vessels. The remodelling and blocking of this entrance probably dates to Phase 5.

Phases 3–5
(with G. Lucas)
The main differences between the pottery assemblages of Phases 2 and 3–5 are the higher proportions of wheelmade pottery, now in a range of sandy fabrics. Many have oxidised external surfaces, but one fabric appears to be an early version of a Roman Grey Ware (Fabric Q12). The forms are mostly typical of later ASW/mid-1st century AD wheelmade pottery, but include forms that are clearly Early Roman in date (F. 1, Fig. 74.1; F.12, Fig. 77.11; F. 13, Fig. 78.4; F. 25, Fig. 81.1; F. 26, Figs 83.1 and 83.6 and Fig. 84.2). This is found alongside later Iron Age handmade pottery in Structure IV and large parts of the western Ringwork (Figs 87 and 88). ASW forms such as carinated bowls and necked bowls were current from the 3rd decade BC in Hertfordshire and Essex (F. 11, Figs 77.9 and 77.10; F. 13, Figs 78.1 and 78.3; F. 25, Fig. 79.6). However, it remains unclear when these became common in many other parts of Eastern England. In southern Cambridgeshire it is this later ASW pottery that is made from sandy fabrics, in contrast to the use of grog temper elsewhere (Thompson's Area 7; 1982). Vessels of this type and fabric appear to have been common in the pre-Conquest features in Alexander's Cambridge excavations (Alexander and Pullinger 2000) and are known from other south Cambridgeshire sites. They may have been current from the start of the 1st century AD, but work in the Nene Valley demonstrates they are only common there from the 20s and 30s AD. A similar situation probably holds true for the fens.

These ASW forms continued to be made for several decades after the Roman conquest in many parts of south-east and eastern England, although the introduction

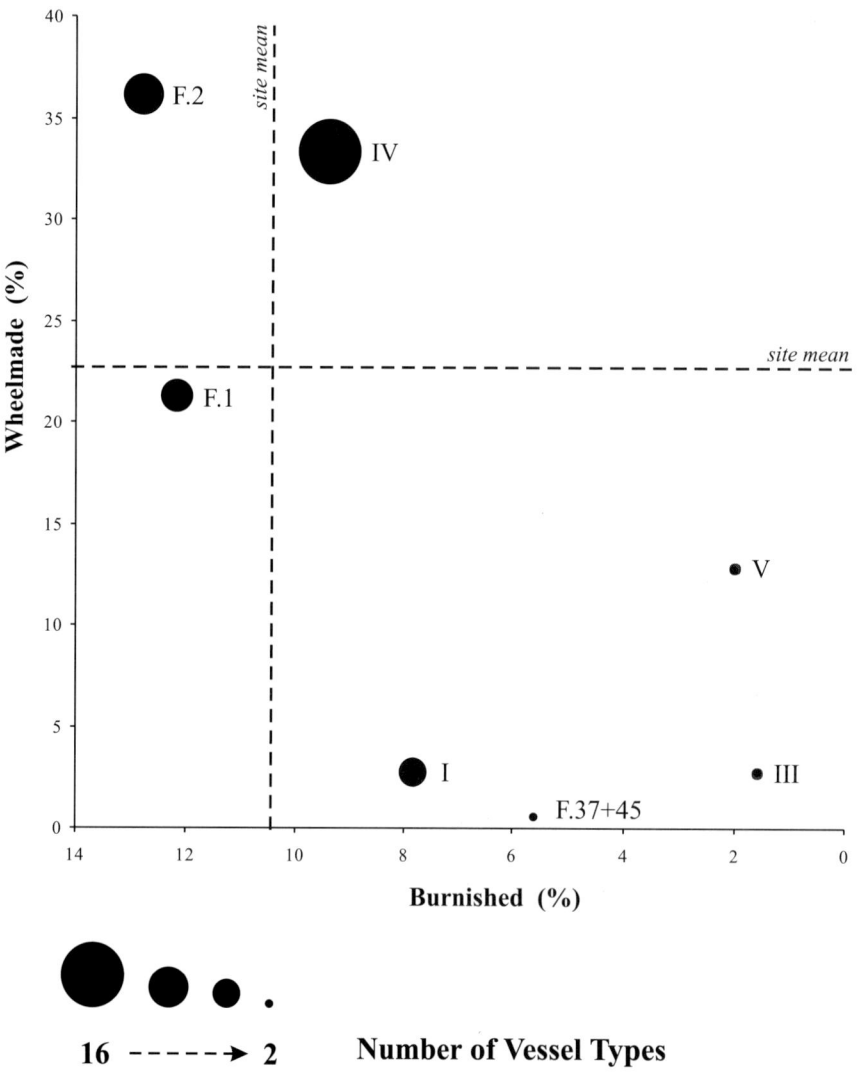

Figure 88 Plot showing relative frequency of wheelmade and burnished Iron Age pottery within main Ringwork features and structures

	Fabric	II	II?	II or III	II or III.1	III.1	III.1?	III.2	III	Unphased	Total	% Total
Handmade												
Burnt Flint	F1	25		1		1062	7	306	521	45	1983	3.3
	F2				13	542		77		8	640	1.0
Sand	Q1			70		2217	88	1806	71	65	4317	7.1
	Q2	11	1	96	104	3911	125	8533	261	1234	14,258	23.4
	Q3			17	21	1116	42	1245	10	310	2761	4.5
	Q6	11		37		756	23	1263	619	187	2705	4.4
	Q8			30	50	2139		2391	35	183	4828	7.9
	Q18							1823			1823	3.0
	Q16					15		283		50	348	0.6
	Q30				38	169		323		7	537	0.9
Sand and Shell	Q4			20	11	654	45	978	230	81	2019	3.3
	Q15					615	32	630		19	1296	2.1
	Q25					23		240			263	0.4
	Q28							230			230	0.4
Shell	S1	6	488			419	85	1154	35	56	2243	3.7
	S2					120	350	787		192	1449	2.4
	S4	14		3		155		26		3	201	0.3
	S5	10				151	59	262	39	5	526	0.9
Vegetable	V1	13		4	292	2634	72	837	284	96	4232	6.9
Total Handmade		90	489	278	529	16,698	928	23,194	2105	2541	46,659	76.5
Wheelmade												
Grog	G1					106		225			331	0.5
	G2					182	104	928	19	116	1349	2.2
	G4							481			481	0.8
	G6							26	114		140	0.2
Grog and Sand	G7							55	4	9	68	0.1
	Q23					11		58	11		80	0.1
	Q24					4		44			48	0.1
Sand	Q10		74					1117		49	1240	2.0
	Q12		768			145		3228	247	67	4455	7.3
	Q13							605	93	54	752	1.2
	Q14			2		101	25	2380	163	143	2814	4.6
	Q19							442	37		479	0.8
	Q31					66		478	28	32	604	1.0
	Q40			5	16	80	9	461	206	40	817	1.3
Shell	S7							320	163	15	498	0.8
	Samian					2		66			68	0.1
	RB Grey Ware					36		27		42	105	0.2
Total Wheelmade		0	842	7	16	733	138	10,941	1085	567	14,329	23.5
Overall Total		**90**	**831**	**285**	**545**	**17,434**	**1066**	**35,118**	**2704**	**2827**	**60,988**	**100.0**

Table 43 Weight of different pottery fabrics from phased features

of kiln firing (as recorded at Cherry Hinton, Greenhouse Farm, Fen Ditton and Swavesey) represents a significant change. They gradually evolve into well-known local Roman coarse ware forms from the mid Flavian period onwards. It is suggested below that Fabric Q12 is a 'proto-grey ware', but it is not known if this was first produced before 43 AD. Wheel-turned pottery did not completely replace handmade pottery on many sites in the fens or on the fen-edge for several decades at least (*e.g.* Pryor 1984, Mackreth 1988, West 1990). The persistence of 'Middle Iron Age' handmade pottery alongside ASW and Flavian wheelmade forms is a feature of many parts of Eastern England (Willis 1997a). This is the case here, where approximately two-thirds of the pottery from Phases 3–5 was still handmade. Distinguishing wheel- from handmade vessels has proved difficult for many body sherds, where careful surface finishing has obscured the manufacturing process. It is possible that some wheelmade and handmade forms were made by hand and finished on a turntable.

As such, the Wardy Hill settlement complex may have received increasing numbers of wheelmade sandy vessels from the 20s and 30s AD. However, many of the deposits of material in the Ringwork and Structure IV took place later than this, in the decades after the Roman Conquest. One sherd, from F. 2 *028* (cat. 930) is in a fine, sandy grog-tempered fabric (?Essex) and is the 'stunted pedestal' base of a jar in the Late Iron Age tradition (*cf.* Thomson Type A6). Such a vessel is not likely to date much beyond the post-Conquest period, and is probably pre-Flavian or even earlier. However, jars from F. 13 *347*, F. 12 *410* and F. 26 *256* and *354* are all probably post-Conquest. More unambiguous post-Conquest forms include large parts of vessels from parts of the western outer Ringwork, such as the fine bowl from F. 12 *410* (Fabric Q12, Fig. 77.11) and jar from F. 13/38 *347* (Fabric Q10, Fig. 78.4). These forms are Flavian in date, as is the bowl from F. 53 which is in a proper Roman Grey Ware, unlike the sandy 'proto-grey ware' Fabric Q12. Pottery of a similar Flavian date was recovered from F. 25, part of Structure IV (*e.g.* jars from *354* FS160 in Q10 and FS55 in Q12: FS=Feature Sherd). Some of these forms have mid, not early, Flavian parallels. Finally, a bowl from F. 1 is of 2nd-century date (*053*; Fig. 74.3).

The final evidence of such a late date for the end of the occupation is the Samian base, also from *354* in F. 25. This is half of a base of a South Gaulish Drag. 18 platter (Fig. 83.6). Lacking the increasing bowl characteristics of a Drag 18/31, this form was current in the mid–late 1st century AD. The platter was originally stamped, but the sherd had broken around the stamp. The Samian and other vessels from *354* suggest the gullies around Structure IV were backfilled in the mid-Flavian period (70s or 80s AD). If Q12 is a post-Conquest fabric it will date much of the reworking of the western part of the Ringwork, including the blocking of the south-west entrance, to the 40s AD or later. A further sherd of Central Gaulish Samian came from Structure III (F. 21 *172*).

From the fieldwalking (*013*), there were five Roman sherds: three of wheel-thrown sandy coarsewares (two body sherds from one jar and a beaded rim from another), one Nene Valley beaker or cup in dark brown colour-coat, and finally a possible Central Gaulish Samian sherd.

Fabric types
(Tables 43–46)
Fabric categories presented in later prehistoric pottery reports give the impression of being solid, tightly-defined 'real' entities. But the pottery from this site acutely spotlights the problems in our definitions of fabrics. Because it straddles the Iron Age–Roman transition, this site contains both later prehistoric types of fabrics (broadly-defined basic clay recipes used across many sites) and early Roman fabrics (far more consistent products which can often be identified as specific products from particular locations).

A total of 37 different fabric types belonging to eleven broad groupings have been identified on the basis of the characteristics of the clay, type and nature of inclusions, preparation and firing (Tables 43–46 provide a breakdown of the characteristics of each fabric). This is a comparatively large number of fabrics for the size of the assemblage in this part of Eastern England. However, the variety of fabric types present reflects the possible status of this site as a local centre, and suggests that small amounts of pottery from a much wider range of non-local sources were being used in comparison with other contemporary settlements.

Each fabric is identified by a unique letter and number combination as recommended by the PCRG (1997), based on the dominant inclusions visible to the naked eye (*e.g.* S1 = shelly Fabric 1). Samples of each fabric were described using a binocular microscope (x20 power), and also labelled according to the broad system developed by David Knight and Carol Allen that allows the dominant inclusions by modal size and abundance to be represented as a shorthand convention (PCRG 1997, 27–8). This labelling system allows fabrics to be more easily compared between sites. The coding provides a four-letter description of the principle inclusion type, its frequency and modal size. The first two letters describe the inclusion (*e.g.* QU = quartz; SH = shell; BF = burnt flint; GR = grog *etc.*). The third letter identifies the frequency, or density, of the inclusion (*e.g.* R= rare [<3%]; S = sparse [3–9%]; M = moderate [10–19%]; C = common [20–29%] *etc.*), while the final letter describes the modal size of the inclusion (*e.g.* F = fine [<0.25mm]; M = medium [0.25–1mm]; C = coarse [1–3mm]; V = very coarse [3–9mm]; E = extremely coarse [>9mm]). It should be noted that many different fabrics identified here share the same four-letter description. The fabrics can be divided into four main groups:

1. Handmade burnt flint tempered fabrics: Late Bronze Age;
2. Other handmade fabrics: later Iron Age/Early Roman;
3. Wheelmade 'Iron Age' fabrics: later Iron Age/Early Roman;
4. Wheelmade Romanised fabrics: Early Roman.

Handmade burnt-flint-tempered fabrics
F1 and F2, accounting for 4.3% of the total assemblage, are coarse and fine burnt flint tempered fabrics. Both are typical Late Bronze Age fabrics for the region. No diagnostic forms were recovered and the assemblage essentially consists of small sherds (5–10g) that were residual in later features.

Handmade fabrics associated with later Iron Age forms
Pottery in these fabrics accounted for 72.5% of the total assemblage.

Sandy fabrics
The majority of the pottery (71.8% of all handmade sherds without burnt flint tempering) is made from sandy fabrics, with the single largest group belonging to Fabric Q2 (32.2% of all handmade sherds without burnt flint tempering). Most sandy fabrics were probably made locally from alluvial fenland clays (see below). Local potters were not exploiting the readily-available geological clays (Kimmeridge and Ampthill) on and around the Wardy Hill settlement complex. In reality, many of the separate fabrics identified here might represent a basic continuity. Q1, Q2, Q3 and Q6 differ slightly in terms of the density and size of the rounded sand grains they contain, probably reflecting slight differences between local clay sources or even within the same clay beds. However, there are differences in the range of vessel types made in each.

Every type of handmade vessel present at the site was, at some time, made from Q2 except for non-local shapes Z1 and Z2. But, for example, twice as many of the small number of Type C vessels were made from Q1 than from Q2, even though overall five times as many vessels (measured by Eves) were made from Q2 than Q1. The more common constricted vessel form, B, was also often made from Fabric Q1: 30% of all rims by Eves of this form are in Q1, 36% in Q2. Q2 and Q3 were also commonly used to make Type L globular vessels (56% of all Type L vessels by Eves are in Q2, 23% in Q3). These three fabrics also differ in terms of their preparation. The laminated structure of Q3 might suggest less care in preparing the clay than for the other fabrics, while Q2 consistently contains small quantities of burnt-out plant material. All these sandy fabrics have medium/fine sand grains. Q2 was used to make vessels of all sizes up to 36cm in rim diameter. However, no vessel made from Fabric Q1 or Q3 was larger than 24cm in rim diameter. There are no 'coarse' sandy fabrics, and all these probably local fabrics were used to make burnished and unburnished vessels of all sizes. The largest vessels in these sandy fabrics were, however, often made from Fabric Q8. Associated with the thickest body sherds, this has greater densities of medium sand than found in Q2, along with rarer coarser sand grains. The origins of this clay are unclear. It could be a different clay with no added temper, or it might represent the same sources used for Q2 but with extra sand added to provide strength for making the larger vessels. Few rims in Q8 are large enough to distinguish the shapes of the vessels they came from, a general problem with the larger vessels in this and other assemblages. The limited evidence suggests Q8 vessels were either of large Type F or of Type T form.

Three sandy fabrics are clearly mineralogically different to the others in this group, and are probably not 'local'. Q30 is marked by a dense, black fabric with very fine sand grains and moderate quantities of small flint pebbles/gravel (1.2% of all handmade sherds without burnt flint tempering). This coarse fabric was used for several different forms, and occurs in low quantities throughout Phases 1–5. At least five different vessels were made from this very coarse fabric, including Type G, L and N vessels of a small to medium size (12–16cm rim diameter). Q16 (0.8% of all handmade sherds without burnt flint tempering) is a distinct oxidised fabric with plant/seed voids on and close to the surfaces – suggesting it was wiped or 'dusted' with grass or straw – and, distinctively, contains some glauconitic pellets that do not occur in other handmade sandy fabrics. At least four different vessels were made from this fabric, which occurs throughout the life of the settlement. Finally, Q18 is the distinctive fabric of the stamped and roulette decorated jar from F. 25 *305/307* (Fig. 80). It contains red/rose transparent quartz grains, unlike the white and often opaque sand grains in the common sandy fabrics, set in a dark blue grey matrix. It does also, however, include disaggregated pellets of glauconite.

The small decorated sherd from F. 2 *281* (Fig. 74.8), was originally assigned to Fabric Q2. However, petrological examination shows that it is made from a geologically different sandy clay, which includes some glauconite, and iron oxide coated sand grains. Nevertheless, it was made to a similar recipe to Fabric Q2.

Sandy fabrics were often burnished (17.6%), but were less commonly scored than other fabrics. Most of these are fine to medium/coarse; there are few coarse, very or extremely coarse sandy fabrics, and the one fabric of this group that is noticeably coarse — Q30 — is possibly not locally produced.

Sand and shell fabrics
These represent 8.6% of all handmade sherds without burnt flint tempering. Four fabrics are distinctive in having sand and shell inclusions. The shell varies in nature from fabric to fabric. Q4 and Q15 are similar, except that Q4 contains more frequent natural clay pellets. Both contain sparse densities of thin white shell fragments (recent or Quaternary sub-fossil fresh water shell?). At this site, vessels ranging in size from 12–28cm were made in these fabrics. Although only 9% of all handmade rims (by Eves) were made from Q15, 15% of the constricted-mouthed Type B vessels are in this fabric. Q25 and Q28 both share the dark, often bluish, grey matrix that typifies geological clays in the region (Kimmeridge, Oxford, Ampthill *etc.*) containing few large sand grains. Both contain small quantities of thick fossil shell. Only small to medium-sized vessels were made from this fabric (rim diameters of 8–16cm); very few vessels made of these fabrics were burnished, although all are medium/fine in terms of coarseness.

Shell fabrics
These represent 10% of all handmade sherds without burnt flint tempering. They contain no sand and had only shell inclusions. Although comparable to the common shelly fabrics at HAD V, they need not come from the same source. S2 is a very coarse fabric, often with scored external surfaces; S1, a typical medium-fine fabric, is the only shelly fabric with burnished surfaces at Wardy Hill. The finer shell fabrics on this site were used to make small to medium-sized vessels (8–18cm rim diameter), but the coarser shelly Fabric S2 was used for some large and very large vessels (rim diameters of 12, 22, 30 and 40cm), and was clearly used for some large vessels primarily of storage type. It appears to have been more common in Phases 3–5 than in Phase 2.

Plant-tempered fabrics

These account for 9.6% of all handmade sherds without burnt flint tempering. Plant-tempered pottery is now recognized as an important component in all later Iron Age handmade assemblages in the region. It occurs in relatively large quantities on a number of 3rd–1st century BC sites in the region, including West Stow (55% of the Phase 1 assemblage), Marions Close, Cambridge (16%), Hinchingbrooke Park (24%) and Barley (Cra'aster 1961 — based on author's re-examination of the pottery). However, less than 1% of the pottery at HAD V was vegetable-tempered. At Wardy Hill, this fabric only occurs in Phases 1 and 2, and is made from a silty clay with little visible sand to which cut plant temper has been added. Vessels made from this fabric were not burnished. Apart from one Type A slack-shouldered, upright-rimmed vessel, this fabric was only used to make tub-like straight-sided vessels (Type T) at this site — probably a vessel type used for storage and cooking. However, those vessels with measurable rims fall into a narrow size range of small vessels (8–16cm). Of the seven rims in the assemblage displaying direct evidence for cooking in the form of carbonised food residues, one is a Type T-shaped vessel in this fabric.

Wheelmade 'Iron Age' fabrics ('Aylesford-Swarling')

Overall, 22.5% of all the pottery was wheelmade in a range of ASW fabrics, although these were clearly still being made after the Roman Conquest. The bulk of this pottery was clearly not made on the site or close to it, and the majority was probably not made on the Isle of Ely. This pottery can be sub-divided into four main groups in terms of their main inclusions: pure grog, grog and sand, sand, and shell. They occur in two or three main colour groups: those with dark brown or black exterior surfaces (G1, G2, Q10 and Q13); those with dark grey surfaces (Q12); and those with oxidised red/orange/brown surfaces (G4, Q14, 19 and 31). In general terms, unoxidised surfaces occur on the smaller wheelmade vessels (8–18cm), which are also those most likely to be burnished and carinated forms. Oxidised exteriors occur most commonly on the larger wheelmade vessels (14–22cm rim diameters).

Grog-tempered fabrics

These three fabrics only make up 3.7% of the total assemblage, of which the bulk is accounted for by one, G2. A 'classic' Late Iron Age wheelmade grog-tempered fabric (9.9% of all wheelmade pottery), this has a dark grey, well-prepared, extremely dense, fine silty matrix with sparse fine crushed grog as an added temper. This is the only wheelmade fabric to occur in Phase 2. This fabric was used to make smaller vessels in the 8–16cm rim-diameter range, with a marked concentration at the small end of this range. The coarser grog fabrics (G1 and G4) were used to make larger vessels with rim diameters between 16 and 24cm. Most vessels made of G2 are carinated forms, but with some Type S and one of the Type H vessels. The only large rim in G1 is a large carinated form; that made of G4 is a large necked bowl (Type S). Both G1 and G2 have unoxidised dark brown exterior surfaces, but G4 has oxidised red/orange exteriors.

Grog- and sand-tempered fabrics

As discussed above, most wheelmade pottery in southern Cambridgeshire by c. AD 20–30 was made from sandy fabrics, rather than using the grog tempering favoured in other parts of south-east England. Almost all of the wheelmade pottery from Phases 3–5 falls into this category. However, close examination suggests that while many of these fabrics have only sand inclusions there was also a tradition of adding grog to sandy fabrics. These four fabrics make up 10.6% of all the wheelmade pottery. All four differ in terms of matrix or type of sand grains. Q10, like all but one of the wheelmade fabrics examined petrologically, contains glauconitic pellets, but in a micaceous clay. Q23 contains distinctively angular fine sand grains, while those in Q24 are distinctly dull, rounded and rectangular shaped in a reddish, iron-rich matrix. Q23 and Q10 are unoxidised fabrics with black or dark brown surfaces, while Q24 and Q31 are oxidised.

Sand-tempered fabrics

These six fabrics form the bulk of the wheelmade pottery. However, just two of them make up 50% of all the wheelmade pottery at Wardy Hill (Q12 and Q14). Q14, Q19 and Q40 are all oxidised red/orange/brown fabrics; Q12 and Q13 are unoxidised, with grey or grey brown surfaces. Q12 is a dense sandy fabric with coarse glauconitic pellets whose matrix is usually grey, and its surfaces are often grey or grey brown. In appearance, it could be considered a prototype for later grey wares in the area. Q12 was used to make vessels ranging in rim diameter from 10 to 22cm, and some from 28 to 30cm; most, however, were small (14–16cm). All the sandy wheelmade fabrics examined by thin section have been found to contain glauconite, which was not present in the main handmade fabric, Q2. This suggests that not all were made locally, or even on the Isle of Ely (see below).

Shell-tempered fabrics

There is a small quantity of wheelmade, unoxidised shelly pottery with dark grey to black exterior surfaces (S7; 3% of all wheelmade pottery). Only found in Phases 3–5, some vessels made in this fabric were rilled. Unlike the other handmade shelly fabrics it has a distinctly calcareous-rich clay matrix, as well as shell inclusions. This suggests a different source(s). Vessels in this fabric were all small (10–16cm rim diameter).

Fabric	Grand Total (g)	Percentage of Assemblage
G2 Wheelmade	1349	2.2
G4 Wheelmade	481	0.8
Q19 Wheelmade	479	0.8
S7 Wheelmade	498	0.8
Q19 Wheelmade	479	0.8
S5 Handmade	526	0.9
Q31	604	1.0

Table 44 Fabrics selected for petrological analysis

Roman fabrics

In Phases 3–5 there is a very small quantity of obviously 'Roman' pottery. This consists of 32g of true Roman grey wares from four separate contexts and three finds of Samian. The latter are two tiny sherds of Central Gaulish Samian and part of the South Gaulish Drag. 18 platter discussed above. Together the Roman pottery accounts for less than 0.2% of the entire assemblage. In addition, one Nene Valley sherd was recovered from fieldwalking.

Petrology
(Table 44)

Rather than simply sampling one sherd from every fabric identified during the recording of the assemblage, a targeted strategy was adopted following an extensive programme of petrological analysis carried out for the pottery from HAD V. A range of samples was selected to address four key questions:

1. What was the origin of the common sandy fabrics that form the bulk of the assemblage (Q2 and its variants Q1 and Q8)?
2. Do the shelly fabrics at this site differ mineralogically from each other and from the HAD V samples?
3. Are the clearly wheelmade 'Aylesford-Swarling' and early Roman vessels in sandy fabrics also local products, made in the same clays as used to produce Q2, or were they not made on the Isle of Ely?
4. Finally, what are the origins of the jar decorated with La Tène-style stamped and rouletted decoration from F. 25 *307/308*, and the one sherd from another decorated vessel from F. 2 *281*? Were they local products, or made off the Island?

Analysis
by D.F. Williams

Situated north-west of Ely, Wardy Hill roughly lies on the boundary between formations of Kimmeridge Clay, Alluvium and Peat Fen deposits (Geological Survey 1" Map of England, Sheet No. 173). There are scattered outcrops of Boulder Clays a mile or two to the south of the site, and slightly further south around Ely are deposits of Lower Greensand. Fourteen representative sherds of Iron Age pottery were thin-sectioned and examined under the petrological microscope (Table 44). Detailed descriptions of each of the sample fabric sherds are presented below in the catalogue. These have been arranged into broad fabric groupings based on the predominant non-plastic inclusions present. From these a number of general points can be made:

1. Firstly, it is clear from the examination of this small group of samples that there is a wide variety of fabrics present, pointing to a number of different production centres. While some of these sources may well have been located close to the site, others were almost certainly not. Secondly, there appears to be a clear fabric distinction between earlier handmade sherds and later 'Belgic' wheelmade ones. It appears, for example, that the sherds containing glauconite belong exclusively to the later wheelmade fabrics, and that glauconite is absent from the early handmade wares. At the same time, shell is lacking in the later wheelmade fabrics; when it is present in the group as a whole, it is found only in the earlier handmade fabrics. (It seems to be absent in the organic Fabric V1.)

2. Two of the earlier sherds, S3 and S3 (between them accounting for 4.4% of the assemblage), had been made from a calcareous-rich clay. Both include fossils of bryozoa, an aquatic invertebrate animal that is particularly found in Jurassic formations. With the Kimmeridge Clay being so close to the site, there seems to be no reason to suspect anything other than a local source. This may also be true for S5, which contains frequent small platelets of (undistinguished) fossil shell (0.8% of the assemblage).

Q2, the most common fabric of the earlier handmade wares — indeed within the site assemblage as a whole — is a reasonably sandy fabric (22.6% of the assemblage). However, the actual sherd of this particular fabric examined also contains isolated plates of fossiliferous shell and a piece of oolitic/shelly limestone. (It may be that in this respect the sherd is perhaps 'unrepresentative' of what is basically a large group of sandy fabric sherds.) The latter inclusion points to a Jurassic origin, though the comparatively small calcareous content in the fabric suggests that the clay itself was clearly different to that used for S7, S3 and S5. The source, therefore, was probably a non-Jurassic clay, though of a variable nature. In local terms one of the Fenland clays may have possibly been used, though on this basis it is difficult to be certain.

3. The later wheelmade sample sherds form an interesting assemblage. In terms of fabric, they can be divided into two groups: one dominated by inclusions of glauconite, and the other by grog (previously fired pottery deliberately broken and introduced into the clay as temper by the potter). Two of the wheelmade sherds, Q12 and Q19, contain roughly equal amounts of glauconite and quartz in what are noticeably sandy fabrics, where the frequent fairly large glauconite pellets are easily seen in the hand-specimen. The nearest glauconite-rich sand source would seem to be the area of Lower Greensand around the Isle of Ely, which consists of glauconitic sands and sandstones, or possibly the Cambridge Greensands of the region (Chatwin 1961; Worssam and Taylor 1969). The La Tène decorated vessel, Q2*, contained only slightly less glauconite than the above two sherds, with slightly less again for Q20.

The remainder of the wheelmade fabrics, G2, G4, Q10 and Q31, all contained small pieces of grog, a common feature of much 'Belgic' pottery of the region (Thompson 1982). It is interesting to note that all four of these fabrics also include a number of small glauconite pellets in the clay matrix, which again probably suggests a non-local source. In the case of Q31, some of the grog was also seen to contain glauconite pellets.

4. In general terms, many of the fabrics present at Wardy Hill are mirrored at the Iron Age site at HAD V to the south. A number of the large group of fossil shell fabrics from that site were also found to contain small pieces of bryozoa, although since this fossil is fairly widespread it is probably not particularly significant. Many of the sandy fabrics at Haddenham contained glauconite and, as at Wardy Hill, the quantity present varied between the sherds. Both sites also produced

organic (?tempered) pottery. However, none of the pottery from Haddenham examined included grog-tempering.

Thin-sectioned sherds

Quartz sand
1. Fabric Q2. Handmade (FS 111 <1589> F.13 *320*). This is a predominantly sandy fabric with a moderately frequent scatter of poorly-sorted quartz grains. However, in addition to the quartz grains there are isolated platelets of fossiliferous shell, a fragment of oolitic/shelly limestone, a few fairly well-rounded pieces of flint and some opaque iron oxide. There is also a scatter of elongate voids where organic material has burnt out. The small number of voids suggests that these are in all probability naturally occurring organic material present in the clay, such as tree roots, plants *etc.*

Fossil shell/limestone
2. Fabric S7. Wheelmade (FS 137 <1445> F. 25 *306*). This is a calcareous-rich, moderately vesicular fabric. Scattered throughout the clay matrix are small plates of fossiliferous shell, including bryozoa, and small pieces of cryptocrystalline limestone. Also present are sparse poorly-sorted grains of quartz and a few clay pellets.
3. Fabric S1. Handmade (<2150> F. 37 *239*). This is also a calcareous-rich fabric. It contains frequent small pieces of fossil shell, including bryozoa, and some small fragments of shelly limestone, with sparry calcite cement. Also present are moderately sparse grains of quartz and a few phytolith fragments (silica skeletons of plants).
4. Fabric S5. Handmade (FS 8 <1746> F.6 upper *223*). This has a fairly fine-textured clay matrix, which contains moderately frequent small platelets of shell or thin curved voids surrounded by reaction rims where the shell has dissolved. Also present are a few grains of quartz, some small pieces of flint and opaque iron oxide.

Organic
5. Fabric V1. Handmade (<1746> F.6 *233*). The fabric is dominated by elongate organic voids, some of which still contain carbonised plant remains. Also present are moderately frequent, slightly poorly-sorted quartz grains, a few small pieces of flint, and some flecks of mica and opaque iron oxide. The frequency of the voids suggests that the organic material (?mainly grasses) may have been deliberately introduced into the clay as temper.

Glauconite/quartz
6. Fabric Q19. Wheelmade (<2686> F. 11 *649*). In the hand-specimen this sherd has a very distinctive-looking sandy fabric. Under a binocular microscope (x20) it can clearly be seen to contain frequent grains of quartz and soft, light red to dark brown coloured, oxidised pellets of glauconite, in roughly equal amounts. This identification is confirmed in thin section. The sherd has a fairly clean clay matrix, within which are set frequent pellets of glauconite and grains of well sorted quartz. The glauconite and quartz are disaggregated and randomly dispersed throughout the clay matrix. Also present are some small pieces of flint.
7. Fabric Q12. Wheelmade (FS 175 <169> F. 25 *334*). In composition, the fabric of this sherd is somewhat similar to 6. However, it is a reduced fabric, in contrast to the oxidised fabric of that sherd; it also contains noticeable elongate organic voids, which are scattered throughout the clay matrix and can also be seen on the surfaces of the sherd.
8. Fabric Q2*. La Tène decorated vessel (FS 473 <2187> F. 2 *281*). This is another glauconite–quartz fabric, although the glauconite is not quite as frequent as in sherds 6 and 7. In the hand-specimen it is more difficult to distinguish the glauconite pellets from the quartz grains, as both have a dark (?iron) staining.
9. Fabric Q18. La Tène decorated vessel (FS 247 <1664> F. 25 *307/308*). A slightly micaceous isotropic clay matrix containing frequent moderately well-sorted monocrystalline grains of quartz and some disaggregated dark brown oxidised pellets of glauconite. Also present are a scatter of elongate organic voids, some quite large and occasionally containing charcoal, and two small fragments of fine-grained micaceous limestone.
10. Fabric Q20. Wheelmade (FS 248 <2315> F. 12 *410*). This sherd has a groundmass of frequent silt-sized quartz grains and a scatter of larger, poorly-sorted, grains, some of which are polycrystalline in texture. The clear size grade division between these two sets of quartz grains raises the possibility that the larger grains may have been deliberately added as temper. In addition to the quartz, there are a number of small, light reddish-brown pellets of glauconite scattered throughout the clay matrix (these can readily be seen in the hand-specimen). Also present is a small piece of well-rounded siltstone.

Grog-tempered
11. Fabric G2. Wheelmade (FS 110 <1589> F. 13 *327*). In thin section this can be seen to contain small inclusions of grog, set in a slightly micaceous clay matrix. The fabric also contains a groundmass of silt-sized quartz grains, with a moderately sparse scatter of slightly larger grains, the odd piece of flint, a few small pellets of glauconite and sparse elongate voids.
12. Fabric G4. Wheelmade (FS 56 <1673> F. 26 *354*). There are similarities in fabric between this oxidised sherd and the reduced fabric of No. [11]. Both share the same range and size grade of non-plastic inclusions, set within a somewhat micaceous clay matrix. However, the inclusions in this sherd are slightly more frequent than in the previous one, making for a more sandy fabric.
13. Fabric Q10. Wheelmade (FS 182 <1678> F. 26 *355*). This is a somewhat similar fabric to 11. In this sherd carbonised plant remains can still be seen in a number of the organic voids.
14. Fabric Q31. Wheelmade (FS 167 <1765> *356*). Small pieces of grog can be seen set in a slightly micaceous clay matrix. Also present are moderately frequent well-sorted angular-shaped quartz grains, some small pellets of glauconite and a few small pieces of flint. It is interesting to note that one or two of the fragments of grog also contain glauconite, suggesting a certain continuity of production.

Production and exchange

There has been little detailed research into the production and exchange of Iron Age pottery in Eastern England, except to examine very distinctive fabrics of decorated vessels. When summarizing the evidence for exchange across Britain, Morris (1994) suggested the available evidence pointed to predominantly local production in eastern England. Work at this site and at HAD V has looked at the range and possible sources of different fabrics in greater detail than for most other sites in the region. Both confirm that the bulk of pottery used on later Iron Age sites was made locally, perhaps within their immediate vicinity. However, both assemblages point to a complex picture of exchange of pottery, possibly over long distances, alongside the predominant use of locally-made vessels.

Wardy Hill, like HAD V, is located in a diverse geological and physical environment. The definition of 'local production' used by Morris employs a distance of 7km to define local sources of clay. Ethnographic studies show that it is unusual for potters to travel more than this distance to collect clay (Arnold 1985). For potters living inside the Wardy Hill enclosure, or in the associated settlement complex outside it, travelling this far by land would allow them to exploit a wide range of very different clay sources. Water transport could have made access to more distant sources feasible. The settlement itself is located on Ampthill and Kimmeridge clays; both are rich in fossil shell with dark grey geological clays and some bands of lighter calcareous clays. The Kimmeridge clay contains fewer calcareous horizons. Both were used as sources of clay in different parts of the region in the Iron Age. These clays make up the underlying geology of most of the north part of the Isle of Ely and the islands to the north and west. Within 6–7km to the south of the site the spine of the southern part of the Isle of Ely is Lower Greensand, a source of glauconitic, sandy-derived clays. There are extensive deposits of Boulder Clay on Ely, while the surrounding fenlands contain a range of alluvial-derived clays, often now covered by later peat.

Evidence from HAD V suggested that very local sources of clay, lying no more than 2km from the site, were used there. This was on the basis that the most commonly occurring fabrics were those made locally, and that — to judge from ethnographic evidence — potters probably used only one or two clay sources at any one time. A similar model can be proposed for Wardy Hill. Whether pots were made by every household in the settlement complex, or by just a few potters, is not clear. However, the bulk of the handmade pottery is made from sandy, apparently alluvial, clays (Q1–3, Q6, and Q8). A source within the fenlands is probable, the clays being washed down from river valleys to the west. Potters chose not to use the fossil shell-rich, dark grey and sometimes calcareous geological clay sources immediately around the settlement. However, these local, alluvial clay source vessels only made up 65% of all the handmade pottery. Other handmade pottery used very different clays. Given the rich range of different clay sources within a day's travel of the settlement, all the other fabrics could have been made on the settlement. However, ethnographic evidence points to a pattern of the use of a small number of clay sources over long periods of time in many situations with household production. As at HAD V, it is suggested here that local potters only used a small number of clay sources. If so, some or most of the other handmade fabrics present on the site were not made by potters living at the Wardy Hill settlement complex. If the plant-tempered pottery was also locally made — it is commonly found on many sites — it might suggest that as much as 80% of pottery used in Phase 2 was made on the Wardy Hill settlement, or at other settlements close by. Although this fabric did not use a sandy natural clay to which temper was then added, it might or might not have been made locally. Other pots made from distinctive and different fabrics arrived at the settlement through a range of possible exchanges — some over short distances, others possibly longer. None of these non-local pots need have been acquired through markets; gift exchange of either the pots themselves or their contents might be envisaged. The non-local material includes the shelly wares. While a high proportion of the finer shelly fabric (S1) was burnished, the vessels made from the very coarse Fabric S2 were often scored. Only one fabric, Q16, contains any glauconite. This mineral is common in the wheelmade fabrics, and a southern Ely or Cam Valley source is possible.

The fine, dense grog-tempered fabric found alongside the handmade pottery in Phases 3 and 4 is very distinctive. It was probably not made locally, and sources in southern Cambridgeshire, Hertfordshire or Essex are likely. However, given that this type of pottery was probably made by a few specialist potters in southern Cambridgeshire alongside the continued widespread production of handmade pottery at this time, there is no reason to suppose a similar situation did not apply on the Isle of Ely.

The main difference between Phases 2 and 3–5 is the increased proportion of non-local pottery, which became predominantly wheelmade while the locally-produced pottery remained handmade. There is no evidence that any of the wheelmade pottery was made locally. All the sandy and sand-with-grog fabrics examined by thin sectioning contain varying proportions of glauconitic pellets. There are differences between the individual fabrics, suggesting that the minor fabrics of this type such as Q23 and Q24 come from sources other than those exploited for the wheelmade pottery. Most of the wheelmade glaucontic pottery is almost certainly derived ultimately from the Lower Greensand. This outcrops both on the south of the Isle of Ely and also to the south in the valley of the Cam, providing two distinct possible sources for this pottery. However, to date there are no known mid–late 1st century AD pottery kilns on the Isle of Ely. They clearly were quickly adopted in the Cam Valley (*e.g.* Cherry Hinton; Greenhouse Farm, Fen Ditton). This suggests that much of the wheelmade pottery could have been made in the lower Cam Valley, with river transport being a relatively easy means of importation.

The majority of the handmade pottery continued to be made in the same local sandy fabrics as before. The non-local handmade fabrics present in Phase 2 still occurred, although with the addition of two new fabrics (Q28 and Q18). There is even more of the very coarse shell fabric (S2) than previously. There is almost no plant-tempered pottery in the later features, suggesting the use of this tempering had ceased by the mid–late 1st century BC — unless its absence reflects changes in the function and status of the site.

Forms, surface treatment and decoration
(Tables 45–50)

A typology has been developed based on a study of vessels illustrated in published reports from sites throughout Eastern England. This typology does not use the basic overall form of the vessel, as in that developed for Danebury which is now widely used in southern-central England (Brown 1991; Woodward 1997). Complete or even partial vessel profiles are rare from Iron Age sites throughout eastern England, and Wardy Hill is no exception. Instead, a typology has been devised that describes base and rim/shoulder forms separately. From the complete or partial profiles illustrated in pottery reports across the region, there appears to be a relationship between rim and shoulder form with the overall shape of the vessel in many, but not all, examples. This allows basic vessel forms to be reconstructed from just the shoulder and rim where these survive. This approach has limitations. Relying as it does on just the rim and shoulder it cannot easily distinguish between bowls and jars for some vessel types (especially Type A slack-shouldered vessels). Most, but not all, burnished Type A vessels are bowls or bowl-like, with unburnished vessels tending to be more jar-like. In the future, this system can be used alongside the specific description of partial profiles using the Brown (1991) system employed in Wessex.

The rim/shoulder and base typologies used for this and all the other assemblages discussed are listed below. For rims and shoulders the classification system is alphanumerical, where the first letter describes the shoulder/neck/rim profile and the following number denotes the actual shape of the rim itself. For example, A1 is a rim from an open vessel with a slacked shoulder and simple, distinct upright or near-upright neck (A) and a flat-topped rim end (1). The appropriate number on its own indicates where the rim is too small, or does not have enough of the shoulder surviving to allow an identification of the original upper vessel profile, only the shape of the rim. For example, 8 is a 'T'-profiled rim from a vessel of unknown shape. In addition, the diameter and the proportion of the original complete rim surviving have been measured where possible for every rim sherd. For bases a simple numeric system has been employed. Each base sherd has been ascribed to one of ten basic forms, and the

	Fabric	Eves	%Eves	% Handmade Eves	Burnished	Rilled	Combed	\multicolumn{5}{c}{Rim-top treatment}
								A	B	C	D	E
Handmade												
Burnt flint	F1	0.67	2.4	3.7						0.10		0.10
	F2	0	0.0									
Sand	Q1	1.35	4.8	7.5	0.28						0.10	0.10
	Q2	6.92	24.8	38.5	1.80				0.13	0.14	0.50	0.87
	Q3	1.15	4.1	6.4	0.28			0.25	0.05			0.30
	Q6	1.17	4.2	6.5	0.03							
	Q8	0.30	1.1	1.7								
	Q18	0.20	0.7	1.1								
	Q16	0.35	1.3	1.9					0.10			0.10
	Q25		0.0									
	Q28		0.0									
	Q30	0.49	1.8	2.7								
Sand and shell	Q4	0.64	2.3	3.6	0.24							
	Q15	1.63	5.8	9.0	0.10		0.075			0.22		0.22
Shell	S1	2.01	7.2	11.1	1.05							
	S2	0.23	0.8	1.3								
	S4		0.0									
	S5	0.45	1.6	2.5								
Vegetable	V1	0.34	1.2	1.9								
Total Handmade		17.90	64.2	100.0	3.78		0.075	0.25	0.28	0.46	0.60	1.69
Wheelmade				% Wheelmade Eves								
Grog	G1	0.55	2.0	5.6	0.05							
	G2	1.75	6.3	17.7	1.24							
	G4	0.15	0.5	1.5								
	G6		0.0									
Grog and sand	G7		0.0									
	Q23	0.10	0.4	1.0								
	Q24		0.0									
Sand	Q10	1.92	6.9	19.4	1.11	0.22						
	Q12	2.22	8.0	22.5								
	Q13	0.05	0.2	0.5								
	Q14	0.94	3.4	9.5	0.12		0.12 Diagonal					
	Q19	0.35	1.3	3.5								
	Q31	0.84	3.0	8.5								
	Q40	0.05	0.2	0.5								
Shell	S7	0.55	2.0	5.6	0.45							
Samian		Base only										
RB Grey Ware		0.41	1.5	4.1								
Total Wheelmade		9.88	35.4	100.0	2.97	0.22	0					
Grand Total		**27.85**	**100.0**	—	**6.75**	**0.22**	**0.075**	**0.25**	**0.28**	**0.46**	**0.60**	**1.69**

Table 45 Fabric, surface treatment and rim decoration by Eves

	Fabric	Total (g)	Burnished	Combed	Rilled	Scored	Wiped
Handmade							
Burnt Flint	F1	1983	6				
	F2	640				8	
Sand	Q1	4317	508			269	
	Q2	14,258	2004			23	127
	Q3	2761	236			27	201
	Q6	2705	6	34		96	
	Q8	4828				46	148
	Q18	1823					
	Q16	348					
	Q30	537					
Sand and shell	Q4	2019				50	
	Q15	1296	88			11	10
	Q25	263					
	Q28	230					
Shell	S1	2243	669			19	
	S2	1449				216	
	S4	201					
	S5	526		15			
Vegetable	V1	4232				51	
Total Handmade		**46,659**	**3517**	**49**	**0**	**816**	**486**

Table 46 Fabric and surface treatment

Vessel shape	Total (Eves)	% All forms	Burnished (Eves)	% Burnished	Rilled (Eves)	Combed (Eves)	Rim-top decoration	% Rim-top decoration
A	6.16	26.2	1.24	20.1			0.99	16.1
B	1.11	4.7	0.05	4.5			0.30	27.0
C	0.15	0.6						
D	1.44	6.1	0.16	11.1			0.10	6.9
F	1.07	4.6	0.20	18.7				
G	2.12	9.0	1.61	75.9			0.05	2.4
H	0.45	1.9	0.45	100.0				
K	0.30	1.3						
L	2.20	9.3	0.61	27.7			0.40	18.2
M	0.15	0.6	0.15	100.0				
N	0.32	1.4	0.15	46.9				
Q	2.53	10.8	1.31	51.8				
R	1.77	7.5	0.83	46.9				
S	1.50	6.4	0.51	34.0	0.3			
T	1.40	6.0	0.08	5.7			0.14	10.0
V	0.12	0.5						
Z1	0.20	0.9	0.20	100.0				
Z2	0.20	0.9						
Z3	0.08	0.3				0.08		
RB	0.22	0.9	0.15	68.2				
Total	**23.49**	**100.0**	**7.7**	**32.8**	**0.3**	**0.08**	**1.98**	**8.4**

Table 47 Vessel form characteristics

diameter and proportion of the original complete rim/base surviving measured where possible.

Three vessels falling outside the existing typology used for this and other sites have been catalogued as Z1–3. Z1 is a handmade jar with stamped and roulette decoration made in Fabric Q18. Found in contexts *307/308* in F. 25, the eaves-gully of Structure IV (Fig. 80), it is clearly a special item. The second vessel, Z2, is an 'S'-profiled rim and shoulder from a tall 'barrel'-shaped, thick-walled storage vessel. Handmade in Fabric Q15, this vessel comes from context *618* in F. 2, the inner Ringwork ditch (Fig. 75.3). Z3 is an upright-rimmed storage vessel of a type that can be paralleled on a number of Late Iron Age/Early Roman sites outside the region. From F. 2 *616*, this sherd is handmade from Fabric Q15 and has combing on its shoulder (Fig. 75.5).

Eves measurements (Estimated Vessel Equivalents), and not the number of sherds, are used in this report to analyse the quantities and size ranges of different types of rims and bases. Work on this assemblage, and that from HAD V, shows that Eves can be used to quantify later prehistoric pottery assemblages, despite their small size compared to pottery from later periods and problems with the irregularity of handmade rims. An Eve is calculated from the percentage of the circuit of the rim or base of a vessel represented by a particular sherd. These percentages are added together for each phase, rim form, surface treatment, *etc.* and divided by 100 (PCRG 1997, 36; Orton 1989; Orton *et al.* 1993, 168–73). The resulting figure provides a statistically accurate method of comparing the quantities of pottery with different attributes, as it is based on the percentage of the original mouth or base surviving.

Rim and shoulder form typology
A. Simple, but distinct upright (or near-upright) rim with neck, the rim rising from a slack-shouldered to ovoid body. Essentially an open vessel form. This is the typical rim form for many later Iron Age vessels in Cambridgeshire, and includes vessels that might be called jars (*i.e.* are slightly taller than they are wide) and bowls. Where burnished or smoothed, these vessels often have more ovoid bodies. These vessels blend into Type L vessels (*e.g.* Figs 75.6 and 75.7; Figs 76.1–76.3).
B. Simple but distinct upright (or near-upright) form with neck and rim rising from a very pronounced dog-legged shoulder, so that the diameter of the vessel's mouth is distinctly smaller than the vessel's maximum girth. A constricted vessel form, its neck and rim form is essentially the same as Type A: the distinguishing feature is the constricted vessel mouth (*e.g.* Fig. 74.1; Fig. 79.10).
C. Upright rim with no or little manifestation of a neck on shouldered or rounded bodied vessel, where the diameter of the vessel's mouth is distinctly smaller than the vessel's maximum girth. A constricted vessel form (Fig. 81.7).
D. Simple but distinct outwardly-flared straight neck and rim rising from a slack-shouldered body. An open vessel form, this is closely related to Type A but differs principally in the outward angle of the straight neck and rim away from the vertical (Fig. 79.9).
E. Simple, very distinct short neck and rim rising vertically (or near-vertically) from a very pronounced high, rounded shoulder. Type E is closely related to Type A, differing principally in the presence of the very distinctive high shoulder giving a marked dog-legged shoulder and rim profile. The neck is usually short in comparison to the total height of the body.
F. Round-bodied vessel with distinct rounded shoulder and neck leading to an everted rim. An open vessel form, Type F is closely related to Type G. They differ principally in the degree to which the vessel's profile is markedly a flowing 'S'-shaped profile. Type F is less markedly 'S'-profiled (Fig. 82.1).
G. Pronounced round-bodied open vessel with a relatively high round shoulder, and distinct rounded concave neck with an everted rim. This form has a distinct flowing 'S'-shaped profile to the whole body. An open vessel form, Type G is closely related to Type F. They differ principally in the degree to which the vessel's profile is a markedly flowing 'S'-shape; Type G is more markedly 'S'-profiled, with a high shoulder (Figs 82.4 and 82.7).
H. High-shouldered round-bodied vessel with a distinct angular profiled neck and a straight, outward-flaring rim (Fig. 78.3).
J. Open, high-shouldered vessel with straight walls and a distinct angular-profiled shoulder and neck leading to a straight outward-flaring rim. Type J is related to Type H. It differs principally in that it has straight-sided walls and a marked angular profile, while Type H has rounded walls and shoulders.
K. Ovoid or rounded, slack-shouldered vessels with no necks. The rim is essentially where the vessel wall ends and is not treated as a distinct entity. An open vessel form, it is sometimes similar to Type A, but lacks any neck; includes both tall tub and more open bowl vessel profiles (Fig. 79.8).
L. Globular to ovoid vessels, with a slight change in wall profile creating a distinct rim separate from the wall of the vessel. An open vessel form, Type L is similar to Type K though it differs in the degree to which a distinct, separate rim zone is distinguishable. While Type L is similar to Type C (a constricted vessel form), it is an open vessel form (Fig. 79.4).
M. Round, globular 'fish bowl'-shaped vessels with no neck. The rim may essentially lie where the wall ends, or be marked as a separate entity by beading *etc.*
N. Round, 'fish bowl'-shaped vessels with a neck and short, everted rim. Type N is very similar to M, differing only in that there is a noticeable neck and everted rim.
P. 'Flower pots' and other tub-shaped open vessels that may have straight or slightly concave sides finishing with no distinct neck.
Q. Carinated open bowl; often wheelmade. This form includes carinated cups, bowls and *tazzae*, and also 'S'-profiled cups and bowls (Figs 77.9 and 77.10); may be more closely defined using Thompson's 1982 typology).
R. Cordoned-necked open vessels. Straight or slightly curved, long-necked vessels marked by bands of cordons. Usually a bowl form, but may also occur as jars. This form is usually wheelmade (may be more closely defined using Thompson's 1982 typology).
S. Wheelmade round-bodied, necked vessels, usually with an 'S'-shaped profile; includes cordoned-necked bowls (may be more closely defined using Thompson's 1982 typology).
T. Tall straight-sided 'beakers' with relatively narrow but open mouths and no necks.
U. Shallow dishes with curved sides and no neck.

Rim end typology
1. Simple flattened direct rim (basic flat end)
2. Simple rounded direct rim (basic rounded rim end)
3. Simple tapered direct rim (basic tapered rim end)
4. Flat or slightly curved top with a distinct exterior thickening or lip
5. Flat or slightly curved top with a distinct interior thickening or lip
6. Flat or slightly curved top with a thick flattened exterior lip and a square/rectangular profile
7. Flat or slightly curved top with a thick flattened interior lip and a square/rectangular profile
8. 'T'-profile rim with a flat or slightly curved top
9. Round beaded rim end
10. Tapered beaded rim end
11. Distinct expanded rim with flat top and side at right-angles to it

Base form typology
1. Simple flat base with the vessel wall rising from the bottom of the base
2. Stepped base with the vessel wall rising from the top of the base
3. Pinched-out, protruding simple flat base where the clay has been pulled down and outwards around the bottom of the base
4. Pedestalled base
5. Omphalos or very short foot ring not protruding outwards from under the bottom of the vessel
6. Pinched-out, protruding stepped base where the clay has been pulled down and outwards around the bottom of the base
7. Foot-ringed base
8. Wheel-turned beaded flat base
11. Handmade beaded flat base

Of the rim sherds, 23.49 Eves were sufficiently large for specific rim and shoulder form designation. Another 3.86 Eves of rim sherds could only be assigned to a specific rim-end shape. Table 47 provides a breakdown of vessel forms in terms of overall numbers, surface treatment and decoration. Table 48 summarises the different

Vessel shape	6	8	10	12	14	16	18	20	22	24	26	28	30	32	34	36+	Total (Eves)	% All Forms
A		0.35	0.80	1.76	0.72	1.64	0.35	0.05	0.05	0.09		0.15	0.1		0.05	0.05	6.16	26.20
B				0.20	0.23	0.32	0.08	0.05	0.08	0.10						0.05	1.11	4.70
C					0.05		0.10										0.15	0.60
D		0.13	0.10	0.18	0.32	0.37	0.20	0.10	0.04							p	1.44	6.10
F			0.20	0.25		0.15		0.08	0.25		0.14						1.07	4.60
G			0.05	0.10	1.44	0.07	0.05	0.18		0.05		0.13		0.05			2.12	9.00
H				0.45													0.45	1.90
K	0.25							0.05									0.30	1.30
L		0.50	0.20	0.80	0.05	0.15	0.30	0.05	0.12				0.03				2.20	9.30
M			0.15														0.15	0.60
N						0.12		0.05	0.15								0.32	1.40
Q		0.08		0.68	1.03	0.19	0.45	0.05	0.05								2.53	10.80
R		0.55	0.19	0.11	0.37	0.15	0.25	0.05	0.10								1.77	7.50
S				0.28	0.08	0.36	0.33	0.38		0.07							1.50	6.40
T		0.08	0.20	0.3	0.10	0.39	0.09	0.03	0.11					0.10			1.40	6.00
V				0				0.12									0.12	0.50
Z1							0.20										0.20	0.90
Z2						0.20											0.20	0.90
Z3												0.08					0.08	0.30
RB							0.22										0.22	0.90
Total	0.25	1.69	1.89	5.11	4.39	4.11	2.62	1.24	0.95	0.31	0.14	0.36	0.13	0.15	0.05	0.1	23.49	100.00

Table 48 Rim diameter by Eves

sizes of the various types of vessel, while Table 49 summarises the overall distribution of the sizes of burnished/unburnished, handmade/wheelmade vessels, *etc*. Rim diameter in most Iron Age vessels is directly proportionally to the original size and volume of a vessel (Woodward 1997). This allows the distribution of rim diameters of different types of vessel to provide a direct measure of the actual size range of vessels used by the site's inhabitants/users; Fig. 70 shows the proportions of different-shaped vessels.

Handmade pottery
The site's handmade pottery is typical of later Iron Age assemblages in the region. There are 17.12 Eves, which are composed of essentially open forms in slack, ovoid, globular and ellipsoid shapes. Very few vessels were in constricted forms (Forms B and C). Approximately a quarter to a third of these vessels were burnished, and were probably used mainly as serving forms. Burnished vessels occur in slack-shouldered, ovoid and globular forms (Forms A, F, G, L, M and N: 5.14 Eves in total). These never have decorated rims, but a tiny number could have borne incised or stamp/rouletted decoration. Burnishing is a time-consuming activity, in many ethnographically-observed cases taking as much, or more, time than forming the vessel. Evidence at HAD V and other sites suggests handmade burnished vessels were primarily, but not exclusively, used as serving forms. Although unburnished vessels need not all be for storage or cooking, many probably were. Only unburnished vessels have rim-top decoration; the majority have plain rims (2.07 Eves = 17.2% of unburnished handmade rims). Scoring is only present on unburnished vessels.

The twelve handmade rim/shoulder forms present in this assemblage can be grouped into six main shapes of vessel: *open slack-shouldered* vessels, *open round-shouldered* vessels, *globular* vessels, *high-shouldered* vessels, *tubs*, and *constricted* vessels. Each group has a characteristic shared basic form and other shared features, such as the occurrence of burnishing, scoring or rim top decoration *etc*. The form and other characteristic features are related to the vessels' intended use in the range of food storage, preparing, cooking and serving activities. The proportions of burnishing, scoring and rim-top decoration for each vessel group are presented in Table 49.

Slack-shouldered open vessels (Types A and D) with ovoid or ellipsoid bodies comprise the majority of the measurable handmade rims (approximately 50%). The typical vessel form in south and central Cambridgeshire later Iron Age assemblages is the slack-shouldered open vessel with a short upright rim (Type A), which alone comprises 42% of the rim assemblage here. This vessel type comes in a range of sizes and shapes. It can be burnished or unburnished (20% of Type A and 11% of Type D rims are burnished). Burnished vessels might be squatter and more globular and bowl-like, but not always (and hence not strictly slack-shouldered: see above). Type A vessels occur in all sizes with rim diameters from 8–34cm (Table 48). Most are in the size range of 10–18cm, with two distinct peaks in the distribution at 12cm and 16–18 cm. Type A rims occur in 14 different fabrics, including all the handmade fabrics with the exception of Q8, Q18 and Q30. The exception of Q8 is interesting, as this fabric appears to have been particularly associated with very large storage vessels. Type D vessels have an everted or out-turned rim. Less common, these vessels show a unimodal size distribution peaking at 14–16cm (range 8–22cm). There is often no sharp distinction between forms: some Type D's are similar to Type B vessels and also have fingertip decoration around the bottom of the rim, and even inside the body (FS 163 and 218: F. 25 *353* and F. 25 *357*).

Constricted-necked vessels with upright rims (Types B and C) are related to the slack-shouldered vessels, but have smaller rims compared to their maximum girth. There are relatively few of these at Wardy Hill; only 8% of handmade vessels, compared with 22.5% at HAD V. Ranging in size from 8–22cm in rim diameter, they occur in only a few fabrics, with the finer sandy Fabric Q1 being over represented. At least one vessel was made in a possible non-local fabric, Q15. These vessels were rarely burnished (only 4.5% of 'B's were burnished) but were those most commonly bearing ornamented rims (27% of B rims were decorated, as opposed to 16% of A rims). Some also have finger impressions under the outside of the rim (*e.g.* FS6 F. 6 *223*).

Round-shouldered open vessels with distinct necks and everted rims (Types F and G) comprise 20% of the handmade assemblage. They are relatively rare in Phase 2, becoming more common in Phases 3–5. These more sinuous vessel forms gradually replace slack-shouldered open jars at West Stow over the course of the last centuries of the later Iron Age (West 1989, Phases 2 and 3). Along with the globular neckless bowls, they may represent fine or table wares (see below), and may have replaced the globular vessels in Phases 3–5. Many were burnished (29% of Fs and 75% of Gs — this latter figure is distorted by the presence of 100% of the rim of one G vessel made from Fabric S1 in Phases 3–5). They rarely or never have rim-top decoration, and may have been mainly serving forms. However, some large Type F forms were unburnished and made from Fabric Q8 (associated with large storage vessels) and the very coarse Fabric S2. These types have a wide size range with rim diameters between 8 and 30cm, and two concentrations in size at 12cm and 20–22cm. The contrast in Type F and G forms is marked in terms of fabric. Type F forms include large storage types and most are in local sandy fabrics. However, G vessels are mostly non-local (less than 21% of Type G rims are local sandy products). This form was also made on the wheel in Fabrics Q10 and S7. Neither vessel type is represented in the plant-tempered fabric.

Globular, neckless vessels (Types L, N and M) are an important component of the assemblage (18% of all handmade pottery). Like the round-shouldered/necked Type G vessels, many of these may have been table wares (see below). A few Type L vessels were unburnished and had rim-top decoration; there are two vessels of this type, both small (rim diameters of 8cm). Most other vessels in this group were burnished (Table 47) or had smooth surfaces. Thin-walled globular vessels in the region tend to have been the main form to have had incised, impressed or rouletted La Tène style decoration. At this site Type L vessels, with a distinct flattened rim top, are the most common type, with only four Type N and M vessels represented by rims. Rim diameters for Type L vessels range from 8–22cm and 28–30cm, with a peak at 12cm (Table 48). Most Type L vessels are made in local sandy fabrics, with a normal distribution of a small number of rims in other fabrics. Of the three Type N vessels one is made of

Q2, one in Q30, and another possibly in Q31 (*i.e.* possibly wheelmade).

Straight-sided or barrelled tubs (Types K and T) are a common component in many assemblages, but they occur in varying proportions. Less than 10% of the handmade pottery here falls into these shapes, with only two Type K vessels represented. One of the Type K vessels is a very small simple bowl, the smallest vessel in the assemblage. Coming from F. 6 *202*, this is comparable to a number of small 'cups' and bowls on other sites (Fig. 77.1). The size of these tubs is small (8–22cm) compared to sites such as HAD V, and it might be that large tub-like vessels are a feature of Scored Ware assemblages. Both Type K vessels were made in local sandy Fabrics Q2 and Q1, but Type T vessels occur in a range of fabrics and are one of the only two recognisable vessel shapes made in plant-tempered Fabric V1 on the site.

Other vessels: there is a single vessel (Type Z1) that falls outside of the typology of northern East Anglian vessels (Fig. 80; Plate XIII). This is the tall jar with stamped and roulette decoration that was found in the gully surrounding Structure IV (F. 25 *307/308*), where it sits alongside clearly mid–late 1st century vessels. There is no direct parallel for this vessel. There are two main foci for similarly-decorated pottery in eastern England: south Essex and Lincolnshire. In both areas these types of vessel date to the 1st century BC or earlier (Elsdon 1975). In both areas, the interlocking arch motifs with circular stamp impressions similar to this vessel are common (Elsdon 1975). This pattern is dominant in Essex, while it occurs alongside other designs in Lincolnshire. On this vessel the main lines are tooled, but the outsides are followed round with a roulette leaving one or two lines of small dots. Flask-like vessels, often with omphalos bases, occur in both areas (see pictures in Elsdon 1975; 1997). However, taller constricted jars like this are unknown, the closest parallel being a tall jar from Canewdow, Essex (Elsdon 1975, fig. 13).

Wheelmade pottery

There are 9.91 Eves of wheelmade rims in the assemblage. The forms are typical of the 1st century AD ASW vessels and early Roman coarse wares found on other sites in Cambridgeshire and the East Midlands. The pottery can be essentially divided into two main groups: carinated vessels (shapes R and Q) and necked bowls (shape S). In addition, there are a small number of other forms present, including wheelmade Type G bowls and Type T tubs. There are two wheelmade Type G vessels. One is a small rim sherd from a small bowl in Fabric S7 from the primary fill of the blocking of the southwest entrance, F. 2 *32*. The other, feature sherd 106, is the complete profile of a vessel from Structure IV (F. 25 *305*) that is more jar-like in its proportions than a common Type G vessel. About 25% of the original vessel is present. It is made in Fabric Q14 and has diagonal combed decoration across the surface. Although in a wheelmade fabric, this vessel does not appear to have been wheelmade. There are also two Type H vessels which correspond to Thompson's Type B2-1 (1982). Both survive as large portions from two burnished vessels from the gully of Structure IV: FS116 F. 25 *332* in Fabric S7 and FS110 F. 13 *327* in Fabric G2. This form is common in 'Aylesford-Swarling' assemblages in southern East Anglia, where it may be handmade and is predominantly a 1st century BC type.

Types R and Q are carinated vessels. Classic *tazza*-type carinated vessels fall into class Q (*e.g.* Figs 77.9 and 77.10). Other carinated vessels, sometimes with less clear shapes, but also many of those with a curved carinated neck arising from a rounded convex lower body (*i.e.* an 'S'-profile), are classed as Type R (Figs 77.11 and 83.1). These vary in size, with rims diameters between 8 and 22cm, but there is a distinct peak at 12–14cm (Table 48). Very high proportions have surviving burnished surfaces (Tables 47 and 49). Type Q forms are made in a wider range of fabrics than Type R and there are more Type Q vessels made in Fabric Q10 than Q12, while the opposite is true for Type R forms. As such, 48% of all Type R vessels were made from just grog-tempered fabrics (G1 and mostly G2), 12% were made in Q10 and 28% in Q12. These are all dark, unoxidised fabrics. Of Type Q vessels, 21% were made from G2, 27% from Q10, but only 7% from Q12. Twenty percent were made from Q14, 10% from Q19 and 9% from Q30 (*i.e.* 39% of these forms are in oxidised fabrics).

Approximately a quarter of the wheelmade vessels fall into Type S. Most are Thompson D1-1, typical necked bowls (1982), with a very small number of rilled cooking vessels. Two, possibly three, are jar forms, including a faceted early Roman jar from F. 26 *356* (Fig. 83). All of the non-rilled vessels have smoothed surfaces, and 34% have highly burnished surfaces. These vessels have a tight size distribution of between 12 and 20cm. They are most commonly made from Fabric Q10 (49%), but very rarely from Q12 (6%) — the common fabric from which Type R vessels are made. Ten percent of these vessels were in G4, 11% in G1 and 17% in Q31.

At least one wheelmade vessel in the assemblage had been broken and repaired in antiquity. Feature sherd 245 from F. 11 *649* has small holes for an organic binding to repair the broken rim of this carinated vessel (Fig. 77.10). Such repair holes are absent on handmade later Iron Age vessels in this and other assemblages known to the author. It provides an insight into how (some) wheelmade vessels might have been highly valued and kept for long periods in this community (*cf.* Senior 1995). Another large carinated vessel was re-used after part of the wall/rim had been broken, by being trimmed down to the point where the wall meets the base and having three holes drilled into the base to turn it into a strainer or steamer. This came from Structure IV, F. 26 *354*, and was in Fabric G4.

The Drag. 18 Samian platter from Structure IV, F. 25 *353* (Fig. 84.6; Plate XIII) also seems to have been modified or 'repaired' at some stage. It came from the same part section through the gully as the steamer/strainer. The upright wall of this platter appears to have been trimmed off, possibly after it had become chipped or broken. Only 50% of the complete trimmed vessel is present in the gully: it had broken around the potter's stamp, leaving the stamp on the missing half. Willis has recently reviewed the roles and status of Samian on 1st century AD sites and has shown that they are rare on rural sites (<2–1% of total assemblages). Here the small numbers on the contemporary fenland site of Werrington are very comparable (Mackreth 1988). Willis has demonstrated that Samian on rural sites of this date was often curated, kept and not broken for long time periods, but often occurs in termination deposits which contrasts to its low use. On all types of sites in Early Roman Britain, Willis has suggested that

Samian vessels were often used in deposits that marked structural changes and 'endings' (Willis 1997b, 1998).

In contrast to many well-known pre-/post-Conquest ASW and Early Roman assemblages, the narrow range of forms on this and other northern East Anglian sites is significant (Hill forthcoming). Missing are specialised drinking or serving forms such as Beakers, Cups, Flagons and Platters (except the one Samian plate). Equally, there are few rilled cooking jars or channel-rimmed jars. This wider range of vessels is a feature of many sites in southern East Anglia from the early–mid 1st century BC onwards and accompanies (indeed possibly causes) the adoption of the potters' wheel (Hill forthcoming). These changes reflect and make possible a wide range of socially important changes in food preparation, and in the appearance and format of meals and drinking. This picture of a functionally diverse pottery assemblage is also a characteristic of classic Roman assemblages (Evans 1993). A limited range of wheelmade forms in mid-1st century AD assemblages is found on many sites in and around the fens (see data summarised in Hill forthcoming). Woodward (in Hancocks *et al.* 1998, 40), has very usefully tabulated the range of wheelmade forms on key sites on the north-west fen-edge and Nene Valley, and this shows a similar pattern to that seen at this site. The commonest forms by far are carinated bowls (sometimes called 'cups') that fall into Thompson's 1982 Types E1-1 and E1-2, along with round-shouldered, necked bowls (Thompson's Types D1-1 and D2-1). There are also smaller numbers of jars such as Thompson's Types B1-1, B2-1 and B3-1. Exact numbers and proportions of these vessels vary from site to site. Tort Hill West has more jar forms (B1s, B2s and B3s) than either carinated or necked bowls (Hancocks *et al.* 1998). However, the quantified forms from Cats Water, Fengate, closely fit the proportions of wheelmade vessels witnessed in this assemblage, with carinated forms outnumbering necked bowls by two to one (*i.e.* Types Q and R here versus Type S).

Bases

There are 27.8 Eves of measurable base sherds in the assemblage. These range in size from 6 to 22cm diameter, most commonly being 8–10cm across (11.4 and 8.8 base Eves respectively). This suggests that the frequently-broken smaller vessels, with rim diameters between 12 to 14cm, sat on bases between 8 and 10cm wide. Very few bases were larger than 10cm in diameter (17.8% of all bases). Most were either of the simple variety where the vessel wall rises straight from the bottom of the base (Type 1: 40.8%), or have a marked stepped profile, where the vessel wall starts from the top of the base and gives a distinctive dog-legged profile to the lower part of the pot (Type 2: 28.4%). Stepped bases and those with pinched-down clay to give a concave profile at the bottom of the vessel (Type 3) were most frequently used on unburnished pots.

Wheelmade bases account for 36.9% of all bases, with most being of the simple Type 1 form (5.01 out of 11.3 Eves). Omphalosed bases are rare (1 Eve = 1 vessel), although foot-ring bases are more common (3.2 eves out of 10.3 Eves of wheelmade bases), and there are a small number of bead bases (0.75 Eves).

Surface treatment

Burnishing

Overall, 10.48% of all sherds in the assemblage are burnished, although the percentage for rims is considerably higher (32.3). This discrepancy could be due to greater care taken to clean and record burnishing on rim sherds. It could also be produced, however, by the fact that far more of the large vessels were unburnished; larger vessels produce far more sherds. This can be compared with HAD V where, overall, 8.2% of sherds larger than 4g and 11.1% of all measurable rims were burnished, and with Little Thetford, where 17% of all sherds were burnished.

There is a clear pattern observable, with a higher proportion of wheel-turned sherds and rims being burnished than handmade sherds and rims (7.5% compared to 20.07% of all sherds by weight, and 42.7% compared to 61.1% of all rims).

Most handmade burnished vessels were small: 37.3% of all handmade burnished rims have rim diameters of 12–14cm, but there are low numbers of larger and very large vessels with diameters up to 32cm (Table 49). By comparison, while there is a similar high proportion of unburnished handmade vessels with a rim diameter range of 12–14cm, there are significantly greater proportions of unburnished handmade vessels in the 16–22cm size range. Wheelmade burnished vessels show a similar size pattern to the unburnished vessels, with a distinct rim diameter peak of 12–14cm. However, there are no wheelmade burnished vessels larger than 24cm in rim diameter. Unburnished wheelmade vessels are larger on average than burnished ones.

Scoring

There are a very small number of sherds with scored body surfaces, and a few of these show the intensive scoring typical of East Midlands Scored Ware vessels. The low level of scoring at Wardy Hill is what might be expected in a Plain Ware assemblage, one of whose defining features is that unburnished cooking/storage vessels are not scored before firing. This was the case in contemporary Scored Ware assemblages in other parts of the region (Elsdon 1992), some as close as Haddenham and Earith (see Hill and Braddock forthcoming for a discussion of Scored Ware in Cambridgeshire). At Wardy Hill only 1.7% of the handmade pottery is scored and no surviving rims/shoulders have scoring. This can be compared with the Scored Ware assemblage at HAD V where 25.9% of all sherds larger than 4g in weight are scored, with 11.1% of all rims scored. However, the Wardy Hill figures are very similar to the contemporary Plain Ware assemblage from Little Thetford, where only 4% of all sherds were scored. Scoring is present on a small number of sherds in a wide range of fabrics, local and non-local, sandy and shelly. Only one shows any strong tendency to be scored: the very coarse shelly Fabric S2, of which 14.9% of sherds are treated in this manner. This fabric is similar to the coarse shelly fabric that is often scored found on East Midland Scored Ware sites at the mouth of the Ouse into the fens (*e.g.* Earith, HAD V) or further to the north-west.

There are a small number of vessels with combed, rilled or finger-impressed surface decoration.

							Diameter (cm)									
	6	8	10	12	14	16	18	20	22	24	26	28	30	32	34	>36	Total
Handmade rims																	
Burnished		1.18	0.60	0.87	1.05	0.36	0.38	0.36	0.10	0.09		0.07	0.03	0.05			5.14
Unburnished	0.25	1.28	1.15	2.79	2.05	1.43	1.14	0.36	0.83	0.22	0.05	0.08	0.05	0.10	0.05	0.20	12.03
			0.34	0.24	0.34	0.20	0.25	0.50	0.11	0.29		0.47	0.38	0.33			
Total	0.25	2.46	1.75	3.66	3.10	1.79	1.52	0.72	0.93	0.31	0.05	0.15	0.08	0.15	0.05	0.20	17.17
Wheelmade rims																	
Burnished		0.55	0.10	1.18	0.71	0.41	0.45	0.05	0.08	0.07							3.60
Diagonal combing								0.12									0.12
Rilled				0.12			0.18										0.30
Unburnished		0.08	0.34	0.32	0.92	2.30	0.75	0.53	0.09	0.05	0.14	0.22	0.10	0.05			5.89
Total		0.63	0.44	1.62	1.63	2.71	1.38	0.70	0.17	0.12	0.14	0.22	0.10	0.05			9.91
Total rims	**0.25**	**3.09**	**2.19**	**5.28**	**4.73**	**4.50**	**2.90**	**1.42**	**1.10**	**0.43**	**0.19**	**0.37**	**0.18**	**0.20**	**0.05**	**0.20**	**27.08**
Handmade ornamented rims		0.70	0.10	0.44	0.10	0.38	0.22	0.05	0.08								2.07
% Handmade unburnished rims with ornamentation	0%	55%	9%	16%	5%	27%	19%	14%	10%	0%	0%	0%	0%	0%	0%	0%	17%

Table 49 Rim diameter by vessel type

179

Body decoration

Three vessels bear clear decorative designs. There is a small sherd from F. 32 *290* with an irregular incised possibly diagonal design (Fig. 85.3), and parts of two vessels bear La Tène-style decoration. A single decorated sherd in Fabric Q2* (FS473) was recovered from F. 2 *281*, a length of the inner Ringwork ditch east of the blocked south-west entrance. This context produced a small assemblage of fourteen handmade sherds weighing 228g. The decorated sherd has part of a pattern of incised dots made by a sharp tool (Fig. 74.8). Although apparently in the common local sandy Fabric Q2, closer examination shows this is made from a geologically distinct clay matrix, even if the basic recipe is similar to Q2. This is probably from a non-locally made vessel or, if local, one made from a distinctly different clay source. There is also the large part of the stamp-and-roulette decorated jar from F. 25 that has already been discussed above (Fig. 80).

These parts of just two La Tène decorated vessels contribute to a recurring pattern that can be recognized on many later Iron Age assemblages across the region. Most assemblages, such as Wendons Ambo (Hodder 1978) and Birchanger (Medlycott 1994), have no such decorated pottery. Those sites that do only have it in tiny amounts, and there may be evidence for it having been deposited in a distinctive manner. Usually, only one or a few sherds from one or two vessels are present. This is the situation at Greenhouse Farm, Fen Ditton (Hill and Braddock 1999), Little Thetford, HAD V (Hill and Braddock 1998 and forthcoming), Lakenheath (Gell 1949), West Stow (West 1990) and Fengate (Pryor 1984). Complete decorated vessels are unknown and substantial parts of them, such as the jar in Fabric Q18 here, are rare. A complete profile of a decorated bowl was excavated at New Addenbrookes, Cambridge (Cra'aster 1961).

Where it is possible to reconstruct the original form of the decorated vessels used in the region, most appear to have come from globular, burnished bowls (Type L, N and M vessels). The jar from this site is atypical. The decoration is usually either incised lines, or rouletting with circular stamps. The Addenbrookes vessel has only an incised curvilinear design. Where studied in detail, their fabrics are usually atypical for the site, but decorated vessels studied so far do not share a common fabric that might suggest a single location for their specialist production. At Greenhouse Farm, the decorated sherds are in an unusual vegetable-tempered fabric unlike the more common vegetable tempered fabrics from the site. At HAD V a tiny sherd from a probably La Tène decorated vessel was in a sandy fabric, suggesting it was not made on the site as three-quarters of all the pottery there was made from shelly fabrics. At Wardy Hill, both vessels are in distinct and unique fabrics. Both, however, have glauconite inclusions, which implies that they may have been produced from the same southern Ely or Cam Valley sources as the rest of the wheelmade wares.

Decorated vessels might also have been marked out for distinct treatment when broken; they did not enter pits and ditches in the same ways as other vessels. Their deposition commonly involves a small number of sherds, and only rarely large portions of freshly broken vessels. This appears to be the case at Greenhouse Farm, where a small part of a burnished globular bowl was the only pottery placed in the small pit it was found in (Hill and Braddock 1999). At Little Thetford, the two decorated sherds come from similar positions around the circuits of different house gullies (Hill and Braddock 1998). The large sherds from the jar at Wardy Hill were placed near the terminal of a house gully during its deliberate backfilling (Structure IV). Unfortunately, nothing is known about the depositional context of the large portion of the decorated vessel from New Addenbrookes.

La Tène decorated pottery is a characteristic feature of three areas of Eastern England: Northamptonshire, Lincolnshire and south-east Essex (Elsdon 1975; 1997). In Northamptonshire decorated globular burnished bowls are present, usually in very small quantities, on a number of later Iron Age sites. The only recorded exceptions to this are the hillfort at Hunsbury and the settlement at Wakerley. This common Northamptonshire pattern of frequency, use and deposition closely matches that described here. Petrographic analysis confirms that decorated vessels found in that county came from a range of different sources, including south-western/Glastonbury style vessels made from distinctive fabrics that are only found in Cornwall (Williams 1986–7). The decorated pottery from later Iron Age Lincolnshire occurs in distinctive forms and styles of decoration that differentiate it from that of Northamptonshire. This pottery also appears to have been more plentiful, although this may be a factor of the very large assemblages of pottery found at Dragonby (May 1995) and Old Sleaford (Elsdon 1997). The pottery from southern Essex is less well understood, coming as it does largely from stray finds and old excavations.

Across East Anglia and the East Midlands, it would appear that small quantities of decorated pottery were in use and circulation. These distinctive vessels may have had quite specific uses and have been highly valued. They may have been made locally or at a considerable distance from the site they were eventually deposited on. If local products, they are rarely made from common fabrics used to produce similar vessels on the same site. This may imply that these vessels were made by only a limited number of specialist potters, and that they could have passed through many hands before ending up on the site where they were deposited. There is also some evidence to suggest that the whole vessels, or broken parts of them, were kept for some length of time. At Wakerley a sherd from a decorated vessel was deposited along with wheelmade pottery (Gwilt 1997). The large jar from Structure IV at Wardy Hill was possibly several generations old before it entered the ground. Traditionally, these vessels are dated to the 2nd and 1st centuries BC and are not a feature of ASW assemblages. They tend to be burnished globular bowls, a form which appears to have been essentially for consuming food or drink. These unusual versions of such vessels might be assumed not to have been used on a day-to-day basis, but might have been used on special occasions. The decoration on these vessels would stand out in the essentially plain assemblages of pottery they were used alongside. The associations between the La Tène style of ornamentation found on these pots and on metalwork is probably not coincidental. Given that La Tène ornamentation is largely restricted to weaponry, torcs and horse furniture in the region, this may suggest an association between male activities and ideologies and this style of ornamentation. That this distinctive, 'exotic' pottery was often then marked out for special treatment once broken should not come as a surprise.

Shape	RTA	RTB	RTC	RTD	Total
A	0.35	0.28	0.21	0.15	0.99
B		0.08	0.12	0.10	0.30
D			0.05	0.06	0.11
G				0.05	0.05
L		0.05		0.35	0.40
T		0.10		0.04	0.14
Total	**0.35**	**0.51**	**0.38**	**0.75**	**1.99**

Table 50 Rim ornamentation by vessel type

Rim-top ornamentation

Rim-top ornamentation or treatments are a characteristic feature of some unburnished handmade vessels in both Plain and Scored Ware traditions. This 'restricted' decoration is the most common way in which vessels may have been 'decorated'. In total, 17% of all unburnished handmade rims have decorated rim tops, compared to 28.2% of the total number of rims at HAD V. This treatment occurs usually on flat-top rims of Type A, B, D, L and T vessels (Table 47). Only four basic types of rim-top treatment were current at Wardy Hill:

RT A. Fingernail or other lines perpendicular across the rim
RT B. Fingernail or other lines, diagonally from left to right looking from the inside of the pot
RT C. Deep fingernail impressions, in a narrow ellipsoid shape created by the end of the finger as well as the nail
RT D. Dots or small fingertip impressions.

Of these treatments, D was the most common, followed by C (Table 50). Certain treatments were more common on some fabrics rather than others. Most vessels with rim-top decoration in Q2 have treatment Type D; Q3 vessels only have treatment A or B, if any treatment is present. This suggests that there were real cognitive distinctions made between these two similar local fabrics. Only vessels with rim diameters between 8cm and 22cm have rim decoration. The vessels most commonly ornamented in this way have constricted mouths (Type B), a pattern repeated at HAD V. Only Type A slack-shouldered, upright-rimmed vessels have fingernail impressions or other perpendicular lines across the rim; deep fingernail impressions, in a narrow ellipsoid shape created by the end of the finger as well as the nail, are only found on Type A, B and D vessels.

The evidence for rim-top ornamentation becomes most significant when the size range of vessels treated this way is compared to that of the burnished handmade vessels. Both appear more frequently on the same smaller-sized vessels (Table 49). As burnished rims virtually never have rim-top ornamentation, it would seem that within the smaller range of vessels there are two distinct vessel types that are not principally defined by either form or fabric.

Use
(Table 51)

Residues
Direct evidence of vessel use is rare in this assemblage, with only limited evidence for carbonised food residues and no recorded lime-scale. This is probably because of the difficulties in washing off the sticky clay that coated most sherds. For example, 16% of all sherds at Little Thetford have evidence for residues or limescale (Hill and Braddock 1998). Here only 0.8 Eves of rims (3.4%) and 1064g (1.7%) of all sherds have any use evidence, all in the form of carbonised food residues: all appear to be burnt carbohydrate-rich porridge, stews, *etc*. Of the total number of sherds with residues, most come from unburnished vessels (662g), but a significant proportion are burnished sherds (402g). However, of these burnished sherds, 307g are from wheelmade vessels.

Because of the small number of rims with residues, it is difficult to review which different sizes of vessels were used for cooking, as was possible at HAD V. However, of the seven rims with food residues on them, all had rim diameters of only 8–12cm (Table 51). Six were handmade and occur in both Phase 2 and Phases 3–5. As at Haddenham, cooking — of these foodstuffs at least — took place in handmade unburnished vessels, some often with decorated rims (4.9% of all handmade unburnished rims have food residues). Although only 7.1% of all rims in the assemblage have rim-top decoration, 15.1% of the rims with residues have rim treatments. Vessel shapes A, D, L and T were all used for cooking in this way, and vessels in fabrics Q2, Q3, S2 and V1 have residues.

At least one wheelmade vessel was used for cooking foods that created carbonised residues: this was a burnished necked jar (F. 1 *412*, shape S9, Fabric Q10). Yet handmade vessels were also used at the same time. It is evident that the 'burnished:unburnished'/'serving: cooking'distinction for handmade vessels does not apply to the way in which wheelmade vessels were used on this site. Wheelmade vessels were used for food preparation here, but these tended to be rounded bowls.

The evidence of carbonised residues from Wardy Hill demonstrates an apparent break from the perceived logic of appropriate fabric types for cooking. Carbonised residues appear equally on coarse and fine fabrics (532g each). There are 776g of hand- and wheelmade sandy sherds with residues (1.8%), and 288g of shelly fabrics with residues (5.8%). As such, there appears to have been no preference for cooking vessels to have been manufactured in only the supposedly more suitable shell or grog fabrics rather than the sandy wares. The higher percentage of the small number of non-locally made (?) shelly fabric vessels with residues is interesting. None of the sherds with carbonised residues has received any surface alteration such as scoring, which has been argued improves the thermal properties of cooking vessels.

Another relevant point that emerges from the evidence of the carbonised residues relates to the size of the vessels on which they occur. If the limited number of rims with residues is representative, cooking that produced residues was more prominently associated with the smaller vessels. This pattern does not conform to the evidence from HAD V, where residues were found on rims up to 28cm in diameter. If we are to assume that the diameter of, for example, a 12cm pot has the same measurement in height — this would be in keeping with the overall nature of these types of later Iron Age vessels — then the calculated volume would be approximately 1356cc.

Perforated bases
Only two vessels in this assemblage had perforated bases. From Structure IV, F. 26 *354*, there is a complete lower

Feature	Context	Fabric	Sherd No.	Wt (g)	Surface	Sherd type	Shape	Dia (cm)	Eve	Rim Top Decoration
F. 61	268	Q2	1	13		Rim	1	8	0.05	RTC
F.6/67	218	Q1	1	29		Rim	D3	?	<0.05	
F. 20	445	V1	1	49		Rim	T1	10	0.15	
F. 76	379	Q3	2	99		Rim	A1	12	0.25	RTA
F. 1 upper	560	S2	3	33		Rim	A1	12	0.05	
F. 1	412	Q10	1	54	Burnished wheelmade	Rim	S9	12	0.20	
	495 'spread'	Q2	1	26		Rim	L2	12	0.10	

Table 51 Rims with residues

part of a relatively flat-bottomed *tazza*-type vessel (Type R) made in Fabric G4 (Fig. 83.1). This appears to have been carefully trimmed around where the carinated vessel wall joins the base, suggesting that it had been broken and then re-used. Three holes have been drilled into its base to turn the re-used vessel into a steamer or strainer. There is a clear ring of abrasion with a diameter of 14cm on the bottom of this base, suggesting the strainer/steamer had sat on top of another vessel with a mouth of that size, against which it had frequently rubbed and turned.

The other perforated base is very different. Part of a globular vessel in Fabric Q2 was found in the eaves-gully of Structure III (F. 21 *172*; Fig. 83.2). This was perforated with a single large hole (16mm) made after firing in the centre. The very different style of perforation on this base would seem less suited to a function as a sieve or steamer. Might this represent the deliberate 'killing' of a vessel, as suggested for burnished, globular vessels at Wakerley, Northamptonshire (Gwilt 1997)?

Size and function
Ann Woodward has emphasized the importance of studies of vessel size in understanding different aspects of Iron Age societies (1995, 1996; Woodward and Blinkhorn 1997). The identification of possibly specific size-ranges of Iron Age vessels can shed light on the standardisation, and hence scale and mode, of pottery production. Size groupings, and how these differ between regions and different contexts of use (domestic and mortuary *etc*.), also provide a tool to investigate the primary functions of vessels. This approach has been used to consider the assemblage from HAD V in detail (Hill and Braddock forthcoming). As almost all British Iron Age pots are simple cylinders in basic form there is, as such, a direct relationship between the diameter of a vessel's rim and the volume it could hold. This allows rim diameter to be used as a measure of vessel size, even though most eastern English assemblages lack partial or complete vessel profiles from which to measure volume directly. This approach provides one way to move from vessel typologies and sherd numbers to an understanding of the ways in which people were using pots in daily and special activities.

The results presented above show clearly that the most important distinction made when producing and using pots was between burnished vessels and those with plain or scored surfaces. Burnishing the exterior of vessels is a time-consuming activity that produces a polished, smooth surface. In terms of a production step index (Feinman *et al*. 1981), this represents a distinctly larger labour input in manufacture. A range of vessel forms was burnished, and for several vessel shapes it was the size and not the shape of the vessel that determined if it was burnished. The most common burnished handmade vessels were the globular and round-shouldered rimmed bowls, along with smaller slack-shouldered jars (Table 47). Not every globular bowl or round-shouldered rimmed bowl was so treated but none have scored surfaces, and those not burnished have smoothed surfaces.

As Figure 71 shows, most handmade burnished vessels have rim diameters between 8 and 14cm. The majority of burnished vessels are 14cm and less in diameter (68% of burnished vessels) and 93% of all burnished rims are smaller than 20cm. The sizes of unburnished vessels show a distinctly right-skewed distribution. The majority of vessels in the assemblage are between 8 and 16cm in diameter; the maximum diameter recorded at Wardy Hill is 40cm.

Work on breakage rates also shows that distribution graphs of vessel size seriously distort the proportions of different sized vessels in the original 'living' assemblages. This is because frequently-handled vessels and/or those used in daily cooking are more likely to break than are special, infrequently-used vessels and rarely-handled large storage vessels (Hill 1995, 129–31). Therefore, small and medium-sized vessels used frequently to prepare, cook and serve food are likely to have been broken at Wardy Hill relatively far more often than the larger, infrequently-used cooking, serving and storage vessels.

In a cross-cultural study by Mills (1989), serving and cooking vessels had mean life spans of 1.5 (range of means from five studies; 0.23–2.7 years) and 2.14 (range of means from eleven studies; 0.4–2.6 years) years respectively. Storage vessels, however, had average spans of 5.4 years (range of means from eight studies; 1.2–12.5 years; see also Nelson 1991 and Shott 1996). As such, when imagining what vessels a household may have owned at any one time at Wardy Hill, the peak of smaller and medium sized vessels needs to be lowered. The large number of these vessels in the assemblage over-represents their original numbers on the settlement at any one time because they were more likely to have been broken.

Analyses of rim size distributions are becoming more common for Iron Age assemblages (Woodward 1995, 1996; Woodward and Blinkhorn 1997; Woodward in

Hancocks *et al.* 1998; Hill and Braddock forthcoming). This assemblage can be directly compared with the larger HAD V assemblage that is contemporary with Phase 2 and was located only approximately 10km from Wardy Hill. However, HAD V was a community that made and used a Scored Ware assemblage in shelly fabrics, while Wardy Hill produced a Plain Ware assemblage in sandy fabrics. In general, the distributions of vessel sizes are similar for both sites. While there are differences, these might be a product of chance depositional factors. However, the discrepancies may indicate significant distinctions in the numbers and sizes of vessels on these sites. The main difference between the sites is visible in the overall shape of the size distribution graphs. At Wardy Hill, the graph shows two distinctive peaks at 8cm and 12–14cm, with a gradual decline in numbers from 16–24cm and then a persistent small number of very large vessels. This differs from the pattern at HAD V where the graph shows a single peak between 10–16cm, with a small peak at 28cm.

These variations reflect specific differences in the sizes of burnished and unburnished vessels at both sites. In contrast to Wardy Hill, at HAD V there are distinct peaks in the size of burnished vessels, with three major groups with rim diameters of 10–14cm (Small), 18–20cm (Medium) and 28cm (Large: Fig. 73). There is also a higher proportion of burnished vessels with large rim diameters and larger vessels (diameters >20cm; 20% compared to 7%). This pattern mirrors similar concentrations in the sizes of unburnished vessels with evidence for cooking. This triple peak distribution is not visible at Wardy Hill. Instead there is a double peak of vessels with rim diameters sized between 8cm and 12–14cm; there is then a plateau with a number of vessels with rims between 16 to 20cm, followed by a tail of low numbers of larger vessels. There appear to be higher proportions of small, unburnished vessels (rim diameters 8–12cm) compared with HAD V, with again a distinct peak of unburnished vessels at 28cm. Although rim numbers are small, analysis of the assemblage of handmade later Iron Age pottery from Tort Hill West, south of Peterborough (Hancocks *et al.* 1998, fig. 47) shows a similar size distribution to HAD V.

The one other contemporary assemblage of Plain Ware pottery on the Isle of Ely that has been studied in detail — Watson's Lane, Little Thetford — has only 40 measurable rims. This is too small a number to make reliable statements about the distribution of different sized vessels. However, the broad features of its size distribution are familiar to that from Wardy Hill. There is a distinct concentration of burnished and unburnished vessels with rims between 10–16cm (small-sized vessels), and far fewer fit between this small sample of rim sizes from Little Thetford and the triple peaks witnessed at HAD V. Analysis of the large assemblage of later Iron Age pottery recently excavated from West Fen Road will help to establish if the differences between HAD V and Wardy Hill represent a real difference between East Midland Scored Ware assemblages and Plain Ware assemblages in general.

The wheelmade pottery used in Phases 3–5 shows a distinctive distribution that contrasts with the handmade material. As at Tort Hill and Fengate, Cats Water (Hancocks *et al.* 1998, fig. 47), most of these mid-1st century AD vessels had rims between 12cm and 20cm, the largest number having rims of 16cm diameter. However, at Wardy Hill the evidence shows that burnished wheelmade vessels, which tend to be carinated forms, fall in the smaller end of this size distribution: unburnished wheelmade vessels, often necked bowls, are larger (Table 48). The smaller vessels have dark, unoxidised exterior surfaces, while the larger vessels tend to have oxidised surfaces.

To conclude, in this and other later Iron Age assemblages there is a clear distinction between burnished vessels and unburnished vessels, which might have rim-top ornamentation. From other sites, as well as this one, it would appear that burnished vessels were primarily used for serving food and drink, while unburnished vessels were used to store, prepare and cook food. The serving vessels that were most frequently broken at Wardy Hill were relatively small (*i.e.* <15cm rim diameter), perhaps not being able to hold more than 1–1.25 litres of food or drink. There were larger burnished vessels, and a few of extremely large size, but these were relatively rare. This either suggests that there were very few of these very large vessels and/or that they were rarely moved/used and thereby only infrequently broken. There is no need to envisage a strict separation of burnished serving and unburnished vessels for cooking *etc*. Unburnished vessels were probably twice as common as burnished vessel in all sizes. Few of these larger than 20cm rim diameter vessels had rim-top ornamentation. This size range of ornamented unburnished vessels parallels closely the size of most burnished vessels. The large and very large vessels (>20cm) were probably used for storage and food preparation but could, if needed, be used for cooking large quantities of food.

Wheelmade vessels were used alongside handmade vessels, possibly in increasing numbers in the mid–later 1st century AD. Many of these were burnished, although only a limited range were acquired through exchange. Interestingly, there are few of the rilled or smaller combed vessels that typify the common ASW/Early Roman cooking forms, or of the channel-rimmed jars common in parts of the East Midlands. How many of the wheelmade vessels were primarily used as serving forms is not clear, and some were probably used for cooking alongside handmade forms. It would be difficult to argue, based on the one wheelmade rim with residues, that only the larger necked bowls were used for cooking, with the carinated forms used for serving. However, the fact that more of the carinated forms were both highly burnished and share the same rim size-range of the handmade burnished vessels suggests they were primarily used to serve, and not to prepare, food. They also share a similar colour to the handmade burnished vessels — dark colours being associated with these primarily serving forms. However, many of the larger wheelmade vessels were strikingly different in colour, being orange, light brown or even red, and would have been noticeably different at 'table'. There are no specialist drinking forms at the site such as cups or beakers, nor the flagons to pour their contents from. Equally there are no platters, except the one (possibly two) Samian vessels. The Samian platter is an oddity in the context of this assemblage, and not just because of its striking colour (Plate XIII). Clearly old before entering the ground, and having been 'repaired'/modified, this vessel has no parallels in the assemblage and was probably not used in the manner it was intended for. Equally, the La Tène decorated jar seems 'alien' in its shape and look.

The small range of essentially open wheelmade forms fits with evidence from a number of other northern East Anglian sites (Hill forthcoming, Woodward in Hancocks *et al.* 1998). On the sites where wheelmade vessels were introduced in the mid-1st century BC onwards, they occur in a limited range of essentially open forms, mirroring the limited range of open forms already made that had been used for several centuries. Although these wheelmade vessels would have been visually very distinct from the handmade forms used alongside them, they appear in the main to have been used according to pre-existing forms of food preparation, cooking and table manners, rather than accompanying changing food practices as seen further south (Hill forthcoming).

Sieved fraction
Ranging from 1–16 pieces per sample (4.4 mean), 191 pieces of pottery (161g) were recovered from the flotation residues. Their minute size — 0.85g mean — is emphasised by comparison with the 787 sherds (7958g) recovered by hand from the same contexts (mean sherd weight 10.11g). As discussed above in relation to the small bone sample these figures, being a non-volumetric sampling fraction, are not directly comparable. They do tell, nevertheless, of the 'smallness' of what escaped hand-recovery. As a measure of artefact reduction, and therefore the intensity of occupation, it is relevant that no pottery was recovered from the samples from either Structures II (two samples) or VI (three); nor from the outer circuit, F. 1 (seven) or the outwork ditches (F. 10 and 12, three samples). They occur otherwise in all of the structures, and in six out of ten samples from the inner Ringwork circuit (F. 2). This evidence attests to the location of a sphere of intense usage/trample, and also that house floor sweepings were not basketed out beyond a certain radius — the F. 2 ditch circuit.

II. Metals
(with A. Dickens)

In total ninety pieces of metal were recovered from the fieldwalking and excavation. Of these by far the majority were iron (80/89%), the rest consisting of five copper alloy pieces, two lead fragments and three silver coins. The material will be dealt with in three groups based on means of recovery: fieldwalking, preliminary machining and detailed hand-excavation. Only the last of these will be considered in any detail.

Fieldwalking
Of the forty-five pieces of metal recovered, all barring two lead fragments were of iron. Of the iron, 29 were nails (64%; Figs 89.4–89.7), all of which were square-sectioned; where heads survive there are examples of both square-round and folded 'T'-shape. Their distribution has been previously discussed within Chapter 2.

Apart from these objects, various clamps and probable machinery fittings (*e.g.* tractor parts) were recovered, all seemingly of post-medieval attribution.

Machining
This material is only treated separately because of the necessarily generalised nature of its recovery. Sixteen objects were recovered during machining, of which all but two were iron nails. The two remaining pieces were unidentifiable fragments. Thirteen of the pieces came from the upper levels of F.1, two from F.10 and one from F.91.

Excavation
Forty-five pieces, plus the three coins, were recovered during the main phase of hand excavation.

Iron
Apart from an extraordinary rivet-decorated piece (*Other finds*, below) only five pieces of any note were recovered from excavated contexts:

F.6	*208* <1788>: rectangular object 4 x 1.5cm; 4mm thick. One end broken, the other ending in a straight edge; possibly a chisel.
F.25	*333* <1650>: fragment, no object form discernible (3.1 x 1.6cm; 2mm thick). Red surface colour probably natural oxide weathering products or the result of burning.
F. 25	*316* <1629>: object, 6.8 x 1.1cm (max). Two different sections visible, one end circular (7mm dia.); opposite, sub-rectangular and flattened (1.2cm x 4mm). Two rivets/lined rivet-hole visible in X-ray at latter end suggests its attachment as a tang; this could indicate that the piece was some kind of hafted punch.
F.107	*550* <2240>: sheet fragment and ?rivet, broken, some delamination in one surviving corner.
F.13/38	*336* <2239>: sub-rectangular object/sheet 3.5 x 3cm+; 3mm thick with two surviving edges with rounded corner. In two fragments, tapering feature of decay, unlikely to be a blade.

Otherwise, only very small and degraded pieces were recovered from F. 13 (*336* <2429>), from F. 26 (*357* <1739>) and as a surface find (*574* <2354>). Nails were recovered from F.1, 2, 13, 25 and 29 (12 in total: a square-sectioned piece from F. 21 covered in concretion may also have been a nail); the implications of their distribution are discussed below.

Copper alloy
Aside from a post-medieval button (F.10; *016* <946>) and a clock escapement (Fig. 89.3; *016* <2469>), the following material was recovered:

F.4	*086* <944>: complete finger ring formed from strip in a spiral. Diameter 2.1cm internal, 2.6cm external; Late Iron Age/Early Roman (Fig. 89.1; *cf.* Farwell and Molleson 1993, 94, nos 23 and 25).
F.13	*330* <1599>: possible stud, rounded, c. 8mm in dia.
F.26	*359*, <2597>: ring fragment, 1.3cm dia x 2mm. Thin curved strip, one edge damaged (Fig. 89.2).

Silver
Three silver coins, evidently the contents of a dropped purse, were found together in the top of ditch F. 11:

<2700>	Edward I half penny
<2701>	Poss. Henry VI
<2702>	Edward III half groat

This modest assemblage can only be considered unremarkable and offers little insight into the Ringwork's usage. Given its context, noteworthy is the absence of broaches, Roman coins and evidence of bladed implements (*e.g.* billhooks, knifes, *etc.*). With the exception of the Late Iron Age/Early Roman spiral finger ring, and the three medieval coins, none of the objects recovered can be firmly dated, and few of them other than the nails may even be identified.

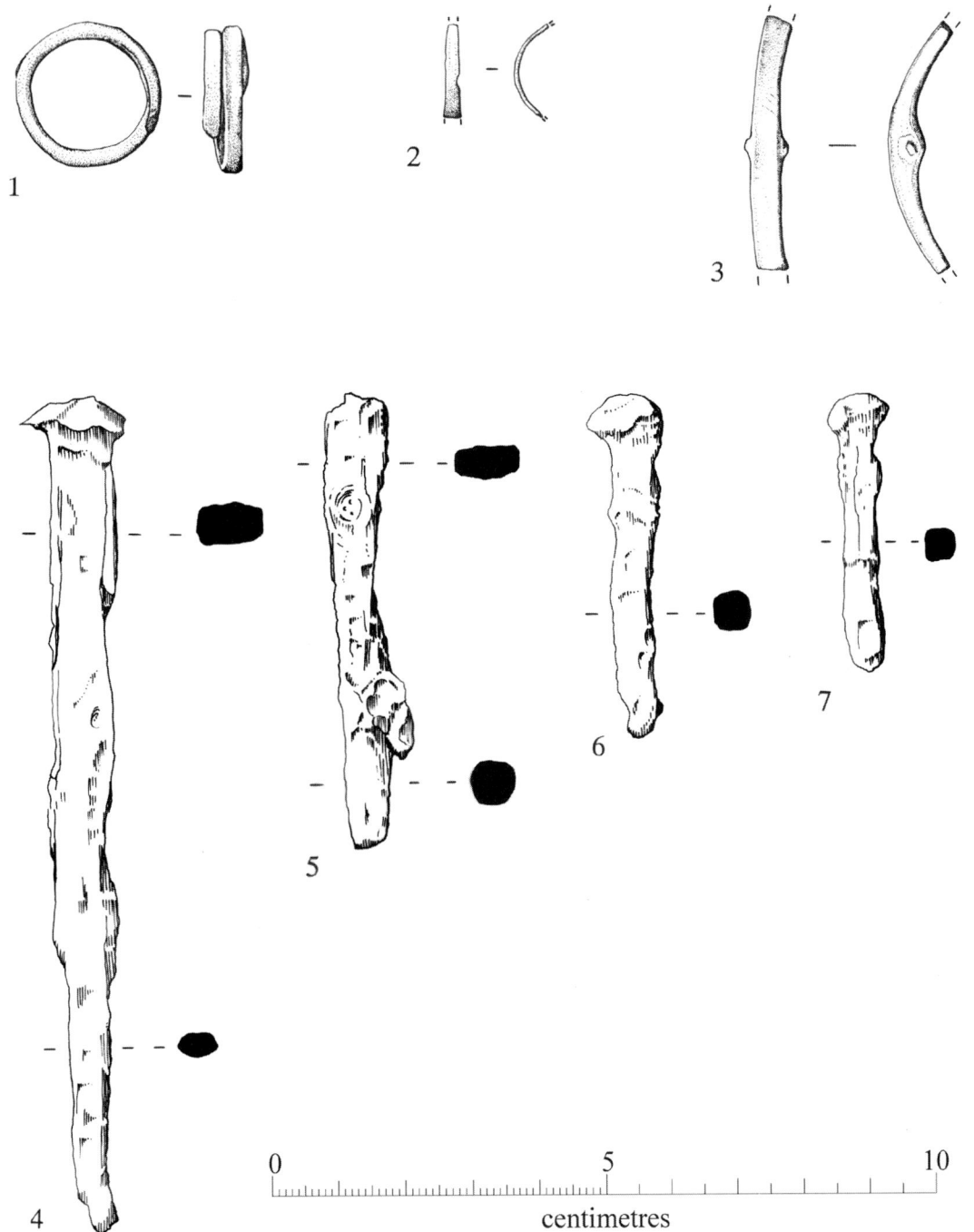

Figure 89 Metalwork: (1) spiral ring (<944> *086*); (2) ring fragment (<2597> *359*); (3) clock escapement (<2469> *016*); (4)–(7) iron nails (<836> *010*; <1629> *316*; <1421> *090*; <1108> *088*). Scale 1:1.

III. Metalworking debris
by K. Robbins
(Fig. 90; Tables 52 and 53)

In total 145 fragments of metalworking debris were recovered from the site. Apart from a handful of outliers, the vast majority of this material comes from the vicinity of the two large roundhouses (Structures I and IV) and specifically their eaves-gullies (respectively F. 6/61 and F. 25/26). Its occurrence in F. 13, 12 and 38 is from ditches adjacent to the northern building (IV), in which most of the metalworking debris was found. While no furnaces or hearths survived, localised very high 'rogue' readings in the magnetic susceptibility survey in the area of Structure IV could suggests their 'ghosted' location.

Analytical methods and definition of terms
The metalworking debris consisted of materials such as earth, clay and stone that contain silicates of one sort or another. These materials will melt (or fuse) if heated to sufficiently high temperatures, but such extremes were not generally obtained in antiquity even when a good draught

was provided for the fire. However, even somewhat lower temperatures, around 1000 °C, affect silicate materials. The ash in the fire, which is rich in alkalis, reacts with silicates (it is said to *flux* them) producing glassy (vitreous) materials which are usually called slags. These alkaline slags are often known as fuel ash slags and are not in themselves evidence for any specific industrial process; they simply indicate a fire at a high temperature. Association with diagnostic material such as metal-rich slags or crucibles can indicate the process of which they are by-products (Bayley 1985).

Energy-dispersive X-ray fluorescence (EDXRF) was employed to identify any traces of metal on the surfaces of the fragments, with the ultimate aim of determining the nature of the metal that was melted in the crucibles. The proportions of the non-ferrous metals present in the fragments depends not only on their original concentrations in the metal melt but also on their chemical nature. Elements like silver which are relatively unreactive do not survive as well as lead, and particularly zinc. The concentrations of lead and zinc are enhanced as they can act as glass-forming elements and the EDXRF was used as a qualitative analytical method and not a quantitative one.

The metalworking debris was identified, on the basis of its fabric and morphology, as comprising crucible fragments, metalworking slag, hearth lining, fuel ash slag, baked clay, vitrified stone and possibly Niedermendig lava. When dealing with samples of a small size, fragment identification is difficult: any pieces where identification is uncertain are prefixed with a question mark in the table. The very nature of the fragments prevents them from being fitting into well-defined categories. For example, materials intermediate between metalworking slag and fuel ash slag are found; these are described here as 'mixed' slag. For this reason the various properties used to identify different types of material must be defined.

A number of small fragments of clay proved difficult to identify and were therefore classified as baked clay, their grey colouration indicating that they had been subjected to heat; they may have been fragments of crucible or hearth lining. The samples initially labelled by the excavators as 'slag/bloomery' appear in fact to have been a mixture of ferrous slag, fuel ash slag and baked clay, which is porous and brittle. A fragment from each sample bag was analysed by EDXRF.

Crucible fragments
The initial factor considered was the shape of the sample — does it have two original parallel surfaces characteristic of a curved body sherd or rim? The majority of the crucible fragments had vitrification on their interior and outside surfaces. The thickness of the fragments, together with their fabric in cross-section, was also characteristic; all the crucible samples had a fine-grained structure with a high amount of quartz (Fig. 90). Six of the crucible fragments had visible metal droplets on their surfaces.

Metalworking slag and fuel ash
The metalworking slag was heavier and denser than the fuel ash slag due to its iron content. The fuel ash slag was less dense and lighter, with voids caused by trapped gasses and burnt material. The metalworking slag was generally a darker grey than the fuel ash slag, which had a lighter grey/brown colour.

Hearth lining
The external surface that was subjected to heat was usually vitrified. The cross-section displays a colour gradation from the ordinary fired clay, ranging from orange in colour (furthest from the fire) to a light grey, and on to a dark grey and often vitreous surface. All the hearth lining fragments are fine-grained with a high amount of quartz. Only one original surface survives.

Results
All the samples, with the exception of a small number of fragments, show vitrification to some degree, which indicates exposure to fire at high temperature. The fabric of the samples was mainly fine-grained, with a large number of quartz inclusions. Where this is not the case, the fragments were identified as metalworking slag or as fuel ash slag or vitrified stone. The crucible, hearth lining and baked clay fragments all have the same fine-grained fabric with quartz inclusions. The site is situated on a spur of Ampthill Clay, which may have been exploited as a raw

	Sample			Fragment identification				
Context	Feature	Number of fragments	Crucible	Metalworking slag	Fuel ash slag	Hearth lining	Other	Fine-grained quartz
35	2	2					Baked Clay	*
161	21	1			?1			
141	22	2					Vit. Stone	
218	6/67	2			2			
238	37	1	1					
306	25	2			1		Baked clay	*
332	25	4		1	3			
352	26	1					Vit. Stone	
359	26	1		1				
414	80	4					Baked clay	*
446	81	1		1				

Table 52 Metalworking debris from flotation residues

Sample Context	Feature	Number of fragments	Crucible	Metalworking slag	Fuel ash slag	Hearth lining	Other	Fine grained *quartz	Morphology	Visible metal droplets	Fragment analysed	Identified by XRF
117	38	13	1	1	4	7		*	1 rim		Crucible	(T) Cu
89	1	1				1		*				
203	6	1				?1		*				
205	6	1				?1		*				
207	6	1	1					*	1 body sherd		Crucible	Cu, Sn, Pb
211	6	1				1		*				
212	6	2					Baked clay	*				
225	6	2					Baked clay	*				
234	6	5	1	1		1	B.C+N.Lava	*	1 rim	1 *	Crucible	(H) Sn, (t) Pb + Cu
Low 235	6	1	1					*	1 rim		Crucible	Cu, Sn
Upper 235	6	2	13			1		*	1 body sherd		Crucible	Cu, Sn, Pb
268	61	3						*	2 rims + 1 b.s	1 *	Crucible	Cu, Sn, (t) Pb
269	61	2			2			*				
271	1	1					Baked clay	*				
316	25	4	3			1		*	3 body sherds	1 *	Crucible	(H) Sn, Cu, Pb
329	13	2				2		*			H. Lining	(T) Cu
332	25	2	1				Baked clay	*	1 body sherd			
333	25	7	5			?2		*	2 rims + 3 b.s	1 *	Crucible	(H) Sn, Cu, Pb
334	25	5	2			3		*	1 rim + 2 b.s		Crucible	Cu, Sn
335	25	5				3	Baked clay	*			Baked clay	(T) Cu
336	13	2					Baked clay	*				
347	13/38	1	?1			?1		*				
500	80	4		2	2			*			F. A slag	Cu, Sn
550	107	10		1	7		Baked clay	*				
550	107	4		2		?1	Baked clay	*				
554	12	1		1				*				
565	37	2				2		*				
566	76	3	1		1		Baked clay	*	1 body sherd		Crucible	(T) Cu
576	37	5		1	2	2		*				
596	122	3					Vit. Stone		1 rim?			
630	37	1	?1					*				
680	13	17	9	1	4		Baked clay	*	4 rims + 5 b.s	2 *	Crucible	(H) Sn, Cu, Pb
688	106	1			1							

Table 53 Metalworking debris: XRF analysis

187

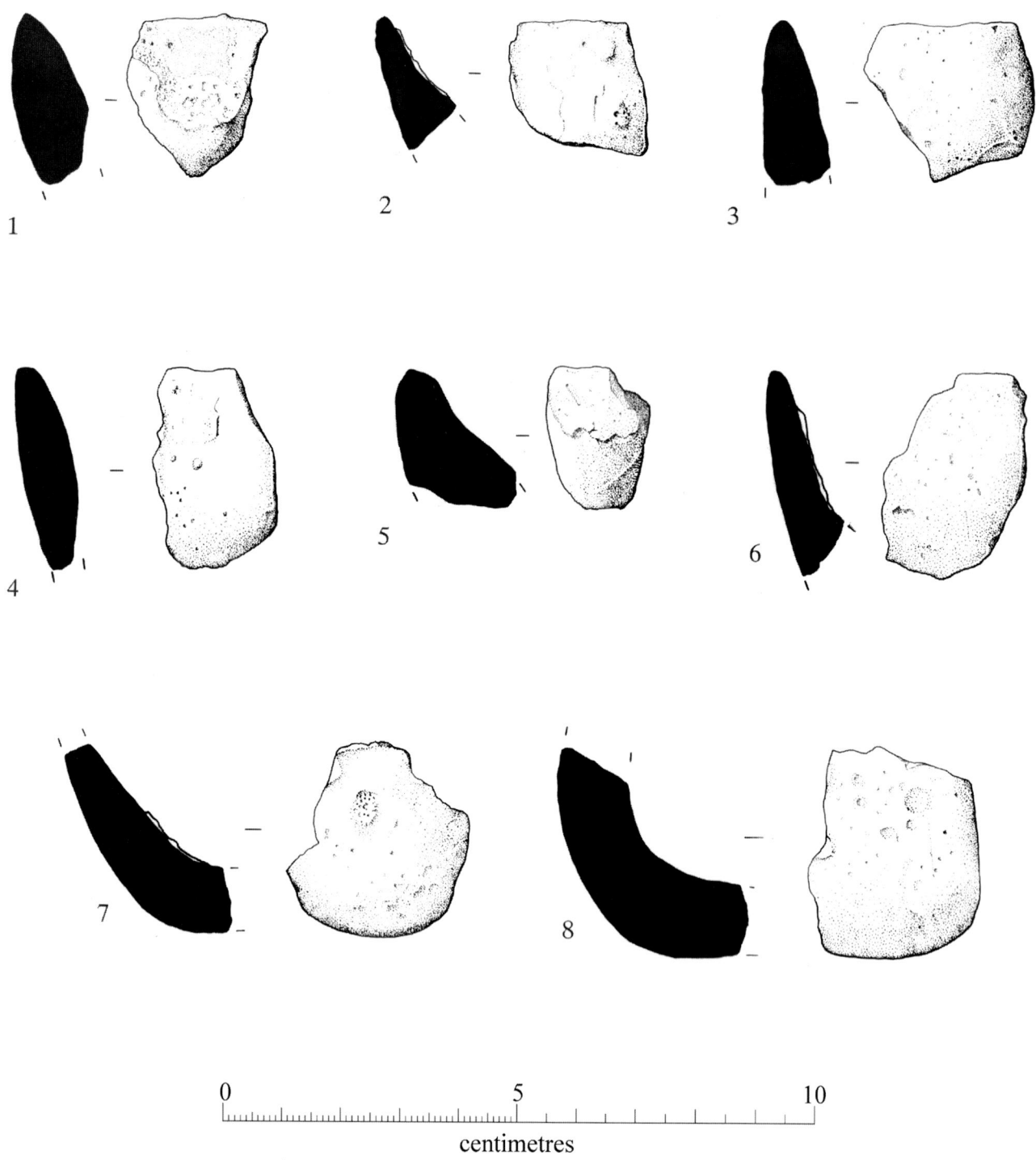

Figure 90 Crucible fragments: (1) <1697> *334*; (2) <1799> *234*; (3) <1307> *117*; (4)–(6) <2563> *680*; (7) <1627> *316*; (8) <1697> *334*. Scale 1:1.

material. The flotation debris contained metalworking slag and fuel ash slag.

EDXRF analysis was undertaken on at least one sample from each context and feature. Apart from single samples of hearth lining, baked clay and fuel ash slag, only the crucible fragments had non-ferrous metals present on their surfaces. The EDXRF identified copper and tin together with a relatively small amount of lead, indicating that bronzeworking had taken place. The lead was probably an impurity. Analysis of the metalworking slag and 'mixed' slag identified iron only on the surface of the fragments.

One sample is a piece of vesicular lava, probably from Niedermendig in the Middle Rhine. It was exploited as a grindstone or millstone as the fabric of the lava naturally provides a new cutting surface when the old surface is ground away, due to its vesicular structure.

Interpretation and conclusions

The highlighted features — the eaves-gullies (F. 6/61 and 25/26) of the two roundhouses (respectively Structures I and IV), the ditches (F. 13, 12 and 38) adjacent to the northern building (IV) and the earlier backfilled features within this area (F. 37/76, 80, 107) — all exhibit a similar range of fragment types. The related features in the area all contain fragments of crucible, metalworking slag, fuel ash slag, hearth lining and 'mixed' slag. This appears to support the idea that the debris found in association with Structure IV is largely redeposited, since it also occurs within earlier features within this area.

Examination of the iron-rich slag suggests it was probably not a smelting (iron-production) slag. The slag was more likely to have been produced by blacksmithing, when metallic iron was formed into objects. The other material examined, the fuel ash slag and hearth lining, may have been associated with metalworking. A single fragment of hearth lining has detectable levels of copper on the surface; one fragment of fuel ash slag was determined to have copper and tin on its surface, which indicates they were from hearths used in non-ferrous metalworking.

The analysis of the crucible fragments indicates that bronzeworking took place at Coveney. Evidence for non-ferrous metalworking in the Iron Age has been produced from dozens of sites. The finds are very varied and indicate three distinct types of metalworking, but very few sites produce evidence for more than one of these three. The first is casting debris, where metal was melted in crucibles and cast into objects using investment moulds. The second type comprises evidence for wrought industries, where crucibles are rare but tools and scrap metal are more common. Metal may have been melted but was only cast into ingots or blanks, smithed to give sheet metal, rods and wires which then were cut and worked further to produce objects. The final type of metalworking was restricted to the Late Iron Age and involved the use of coin pellet moulds to produce blanks for striking coins (Bayley 1992). Northover has noted the association of different types of metalworking with different types of sites (1984); casting debris appears to be found mainly on undefended lowland sites, while much of the best evidence for wrought metalworking comes from hillforts.

Non-ferrous metalworking sites of the Iron Age most often produce crucibles (nearly half of the sites doing so are hillforts: Bayley 1992) but often these are represented by only a single sherd, as for example at Breedon-on-the-Hill (Wacher 1964; Cunliffe 1974). Two distinct shapes are seen where the form can be reconstructed; the size and number of the Coveney fragments however prevent positive identification, other than to say that they appear consistent with the normal indicators of either investment casting where no moulds have survived, or of bar ingots or blanks. Moulds are not essential for this: a temporary groove in the ground would serve and leave no trace to be found.

The 30 small fragments of crucible recorded at Coveney do not appear unusual or unique when considered with other sites on the edge of the fens. Such sites as Sleaford, Lincs. (Jones *et al.* 1976; Robbins forthcoming) produced several thousand fragments of coin pellet moulds together with crucible fragments (see also Mortimer 1991 for finds from Snettisham, Norfolk). The site of Fison Way, Thetford (Wilthew, Bayley and Linton 1991) included finds of coin pellet moulds, crucible fragments and investment moulds, indicators of two different types of metalworking.

The metalworking evidence from Wardy Hill should be put in perspective. The ironworking on the site produced a total weight of the 'mixed' type slag of only 350g, the weight of the metalworking slag and fuel ash slag was even less, and the crucible fragments were restricted to around 30 small fragments. If metalworking was occurring on only a moderate scale over a number of years, one would expect a much greater amount of slag. This material would appear to represent metalworking on a small scale, perhaps only over a short period of time. What we are seeing could be a small metalworking operation serving the production/repair needs of a small population.

IV. Worked stone
by G. Lucas
(Fig. 91; Tables 54 and 55)

A large assemblage of stone was recovered from the site, much of it seemingly non-local, but only a small proportion appeared to be worked. Many of the fragments were small and some ambiguity surrounds their attribution: therefore, generally only the clearest cases of working are recorded here. All the sourcing of the raw material was done by S. Laurie of the Sidgwick Museum (University of Cambridge); almost all of it was probably derived locally from glacial erratics.

The worked stone identified falls into five categories: quernstones and rubbers, whetstones/grindstones, spindle whorls and beads, and others.

Quernstones and rubbers

Two conclusive examples of saddle querns were identified, both displaying fairly flat bases, angled sides and a 'dished' upper surface: <1789> *208*, F. 6 (444g; Fig. 91.3) and <1756> *346*, F. 13 (942g; Fig. 91.4). <1789> was a fine-grained, igneous rock (possibly basalt) with laths of plagioclase feldspars; probably an erratic, its original source is either Oslo or the Scottish borders. <1756> is a fine-grained sandstone (?Upper Carboniferous), probably also an erratic. Two other fragments were irregularly shaped but may have come from a large (?rotary) quern: a fragment from fieldwalking on the north side of the enclosures above F. 1 (*i.e.* non-building associated; *013* <587>) and another larger piece from F. 2 (*031* <2539>; Fig. 91.6). The former is lavastone (basalt or andesite) from Oslo, probably an erratic; the latter is porphyrite (feldspars), also an erratic from Oslo or the Scottish Borders. Finally, what may have been a small, almost 'mini', rotary quern came from F. 1 (*084* <1264>).

As well as these items, one half of an oval quartzite cobble (?Upper Carboniferous; erratic) had clearly been used as a rubber as it has a very smooth, worn face on one side; this came from F. 6 (*237* <1870>; Fig. 91.1). This piece raises issues about the identification of others, since it is clearly a naturally water-worn cobble which has been utilised as a rubber. Many of the fragments recovered were also of this nature but had much more ambiguous evidence for use-wear, as opposed to natural abrasion: it is only in cases where differential smoothing can be observed around the surface of fragments that a more confident identification is possible.

Cat.no.	Context	Feature	Count	Weight (g)	Type	Petrology
1028	027	F. 2	1	751	block	Micaceous sandstone
1187	057	F. 1	1	323	block	Ortho-quartzite
1230	095	F. 33	1	199	dressed slate	Quartzite
1120	211	F. 6	1	78	?	White micaceous sandstone
1626	330	F. 13	1	145	dressed block	Quartzite
1934	425	F. 6	1	179	?	White ortho-quartzite
2318	517	F. 102	7	2625	blocks	-

Table 54 Grind-/whetstones

Cat. no.	Context	Feature	Petrology
1637	332	F. 25	Ortho-quartzite
1712	202	F. 6	Grey quartzite sandstone
1863	235	F. 6	Very fine grey sandstone/siltstone
1180	207	F. 6	Chalk, with chert cement

Table 55 'Other' stone

Whetstones/grindstones
The caution expressed with regard to identifying fragments of quern and rubber certainly applies in the case of whetstones/grindstones, which formed the largest category of worked stone. These have been identified on the basis of having one worn surface, usually very flat and definitely very smooth in contrast to the other faces of the stone, which are variously rougher to the touch depending on the raw material used. Most of the fragments came from large grindstone blocks rather than small, hand-held whetstones (Figs 91.2 and 91. 5).

All the raw materials are probably erratics: the orthoquartzites and sandstones probably from Northern England (?Upper carboniferous) and the quartzites from the Midlands (Permian-Triassic).

Spindle whorls
Two complete spindle whorls from chalk were recovered from the site, one a fairly rough, 'chunky' example (<943> *013*, 46g, Fig. 92.1) and another from F. 2, more finely made (in fragments) with incised decoration in the form of radial lines (<948> *032*, 20g, Fig. 92.2).

Beads
Two fragments of tiny disc beads, probably in jet, were recovered through flotation (<2595> *239*, F. 37; <2596> *310*, F. 25).

Others
Four other pieces of stone were examined: none of them could unambiguously have been said to be worked, but they are included here nonetheless. <1637> was a small disc-shaped pebble that may have been used as a gaming piece, while the others were more substantial blocks. The chalk may derive from the Cambridge/Newmarket area and the sandstone/siltstone may also be fairly local; the others are sourced as above.

Discussion
Clearly crop-processing was going on at Coveney (Murphy, Chapter 3) and the querns are undoubtedly associated with this, although the use of saddle querns against the more equivocal presence of rotary querns is interesting in a Late Iron Age context. One might expect rotary querns to outnumber saddle querns by the 1st century AD/LPRIA, as is the case at Winnall Down (Jecock 1985, 77–80), yet social/regional differences may account for this, although it must be cautioned that the numbers involved are very small. Nonetheless, both examples came from the roundhouse structures which have been dated to the LPRIA. The worked stone from Coveney is perhaps most interesting, however, in terms of the number of whetstones/grindstones recovered: these far outnumber any other items, especially querns. The use of these for sharpening metalwork (and possibly also for polishing other tools?) is significant; although little was actually found in the way of metal tools/weaponry from the site, the evidence of the metalworking debris is unambiguous. Moreover, most of the fragments appear to come from large blocks, rather than small hand-held pieces, suggesting the sharpening of larger items of metalwork. As with the querns, the whetstones/grindstones mostly came from, or are associated with, the roundhouse structures.

V. Fired clay
by K. Gdaniec and G. Lucas
(Figs 92 and 93; Tables 56 and 57)

A total of 19.2kg (1761 fragments) of fired clay was recovered, the greater part of it coming from features F. 6, F. 37

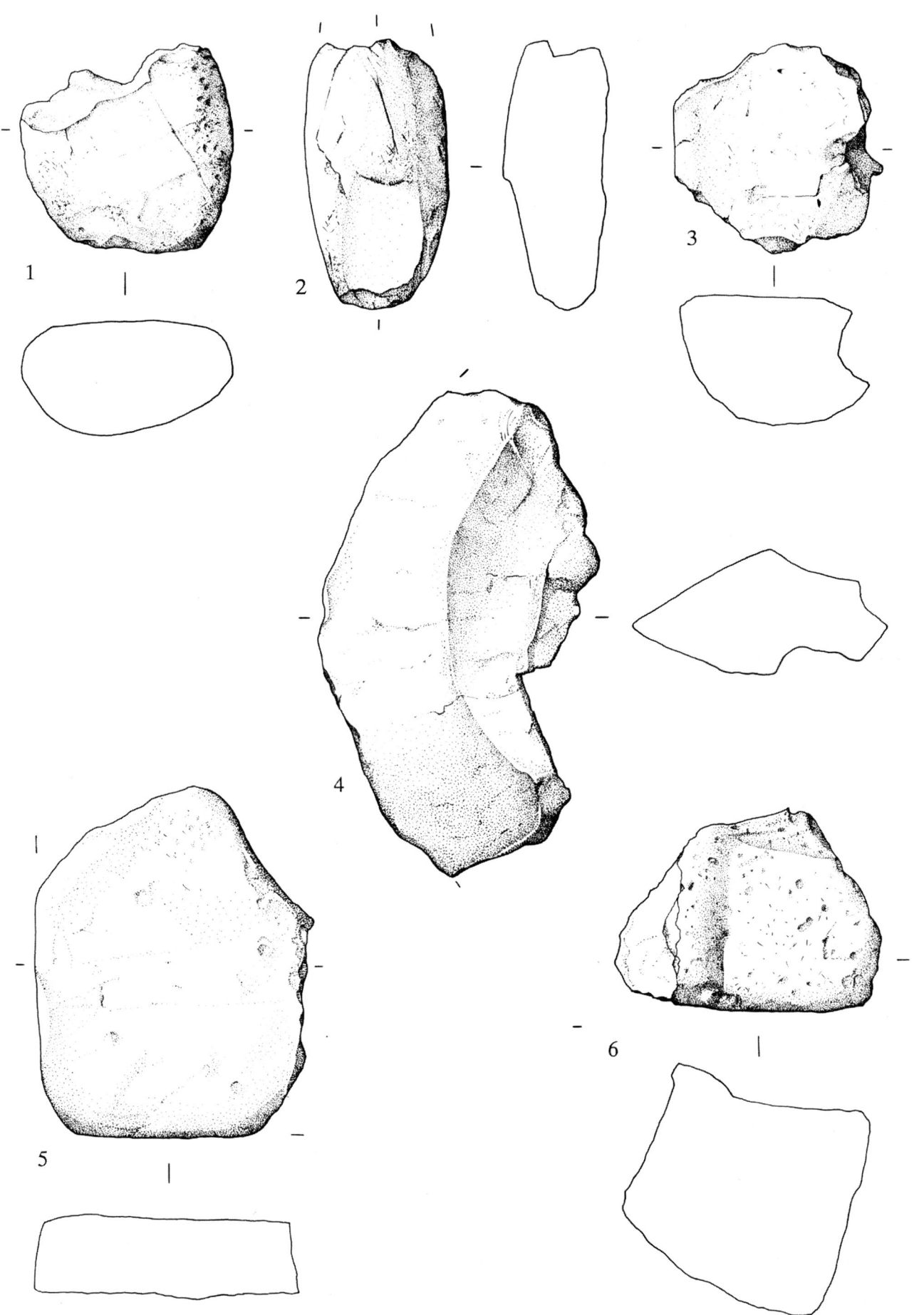

Figure 91 Worked stone: (1) rubber (<1870> *237*, F. 6); (2) grindstone (<1187> *057*, F. 91); (3) quern (<1789> *208*, F. 6); (4) quern (<1756> *346*, F. 13); (5) grindstone (<1028> *027*, F. 2); (6) quern (<2539> *031*, F. 2). Scale 1:2.

Form	Fabric					Total
	A	B	C	D	E	
Loomweight		6008 (175)	4034 (36)	1090 (1)		11,132 (212)
Spindle whorl				24 (1)		24 (1)
Oven	2885 (49)					2885 (49)
Undiagnostic	4881 (1462)				97 (37)	4978 (1499)
Total	**7766 (1511)**	**6008 (175)**	**4034 (36)**	**1114 (2)**	**97 (37)**	**19,019 (1761)**

Table 56 Fired clay fabrics

Specimen	Fabric	Weight (g)	Feature	Perforation (mm)	Thickness (mm)	Base (mm)	Sides (mm)
1184	B	1653	F.6	10	65	160	160
1200	B	1661	F.6	10	65	160	150
705	C	1720	F.102	-	60	160	150
1705	C	1239	F.102	-	60	160	150
1191	D	1090	F.6	10	65	160	160

Table 57 Summary data on complete loomweights

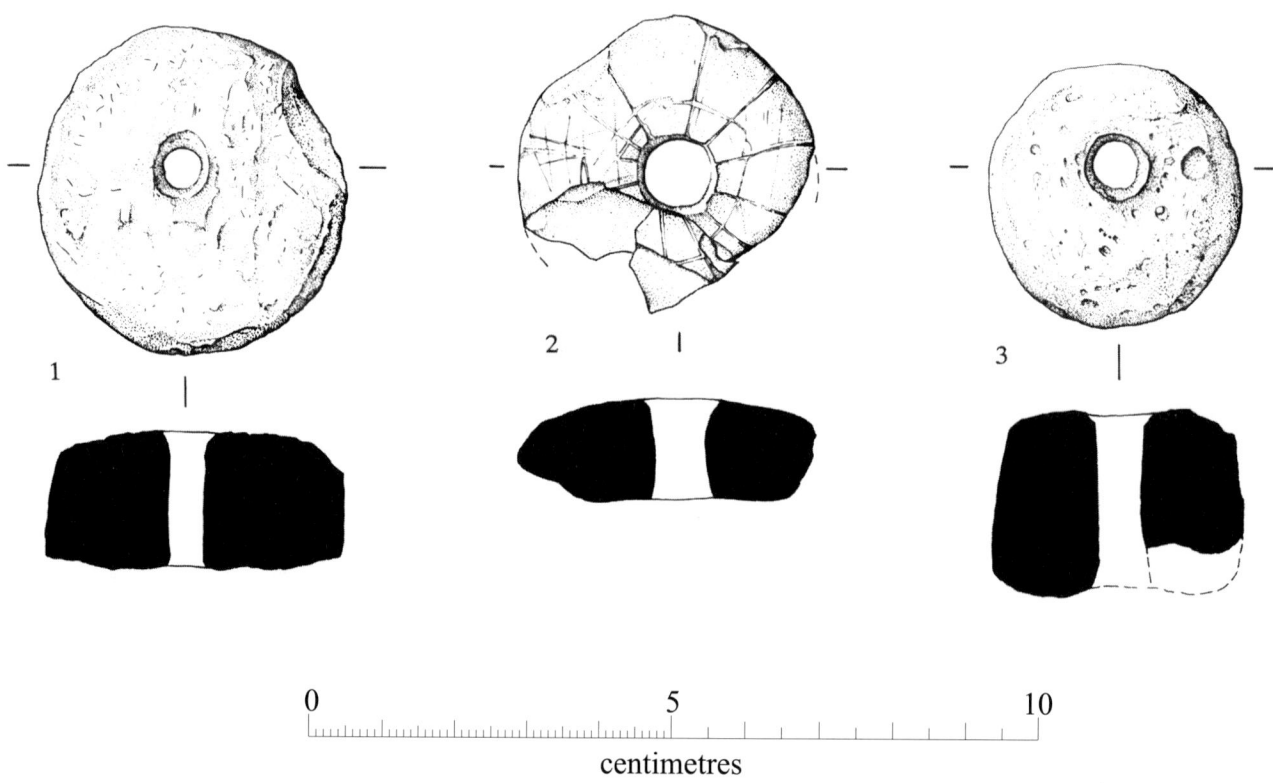

Figure 92 Spindle whorls: (1) chalk (<943>, unstrat.); (2) chalk (<948> *032*, F.2); (3) fired clay (<2699> *680*, F. 13). Scale 1:1.

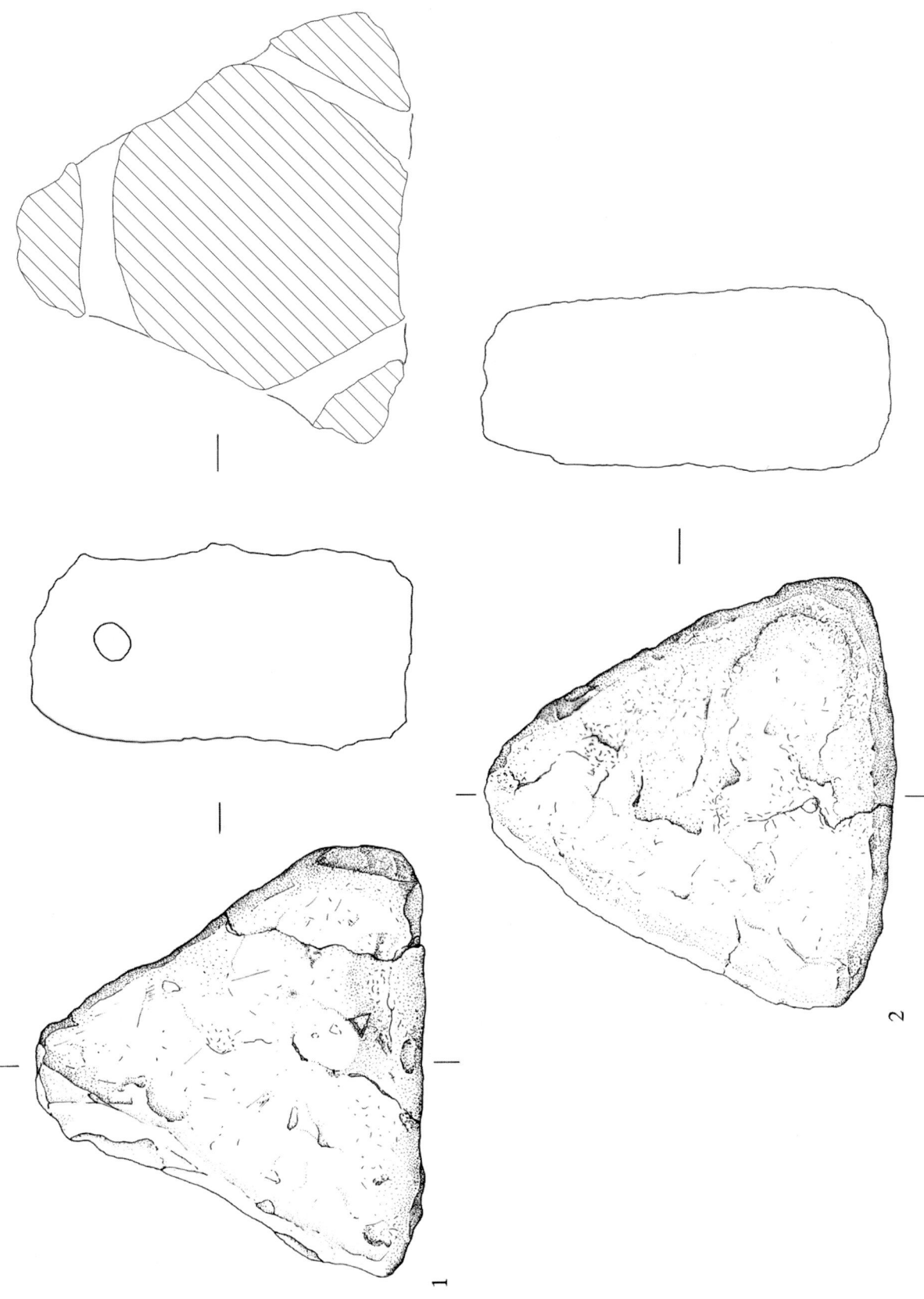

Figure 93 Loomweights: (1) <1184> *210*, F. 6; (2) <1705> *507*, F. 102. Scale 1:2.

and F. 102, all associated with Structures I and V. By weight, the majority of the assemblage comprises loomweights, although, by fragment count most are small, undiagnostic pieces. In order to facilitate analysis and make formal identifications, the assemblage was divided by fabric groupings on the assumption that these would correspond with known forms, of which three were recorded: loomweights, spindle whorls and clay ovens. Five fabrics were identified:

> *Fabric A.* Soft to slightly hard, orange-red with moderate to frequent vegetable temper and occasional coarse chalk, shell and grog fragments. Some fragments are very poorly fired and crumbly in texture.
> *Fabric B.* Slightly hard, buff-pink to reddish pink, usually with dark grey core and smoothed surfaces; occasional coarse shell, chalk and grog inclusions.
> *Fabric C.* Soft to slightly hard, pale orange red with occasional chalk and shell. Poorly fired and slightly sandy texture.
> *Fabric D.* Slightly hard, grey to pink-orange with frequent medium-sized chalk and shell. This is possibly a more shell-rich version of Fabric B.
> *Fabric E.* Soft, buff-grey, with very open texture and abundant vegetable tempering. This may be a variant of Fabric A.

Table 56 shows how these fabrics correlate with the forms (first number is weight; second, in brackets, fragment count).

Quite clearly, the diagnostic forms correspond to the fabric divisions. Moreover, it appears that most of the undiagnostic fragments can be attributed to clay ovens, as they are in the same fabric (A). The few fragments in Fabric E may derive from the same source, especially as these two fabrics resemble each other in the inclusion of vegetable temper, although other sources might be suggested such as daub. More generally, it is perhaps safe to say that Fabrics A and E, characterised by high vegetable temper and a softer and more open textured matrix, are structural (oven or daub) while Fabrics B, C and D, characterised by a harder, closer texture are artefactual (loomweight or spindle whorl). There are, however, significant differences in the artefactual fabrics and these were shown to correspond to differences in form. (Note that no briquetage was identified: see Morris 1996 and Lane and Morris 2001, 398–402 for discussion.)

Loomweights

Five complete examples were identified, along with fragments of several others (Table 57). While all were the triangular kind, two different types were identified, perforated and unperforated (Fig. 93.4). All the perforated types were in Fabrics B and D, while the unperforated one was in Fabric C. This distinction also seemed to manifest itself in the shape, in that perforated types tended to be equilateral in form while the unperforated ones had a slightly larger base (isoceles) and were also thinner.

The different shapes may or may not relate to the presence of perforation but, given that the methods of suspension will have been different, shape may have been a related factor. Moreover, the two kinds of loomweight also correspond with two depositional contexts, perforated types being associated with Structures I (F. 6) and IV (F. 37, 107) and unperforated ones with Structure V (F. 102), which may signify differences in traditions of loom construction.

The table is also useful in estimating the total numbers of loomweights, since by averaging the weights by fabric the combined weight of the fragments can be used to yield an estimated number of individuals. Fragments in Fabric B amount to 2694g, which suggests no more than two further loomweights in this fabric beyond the two whole ones, while 1075g of fragments in Fabric C suggest only one more. This would bring the total population of deposited loomweights for the site to eight. On this topic, it is also interesting to note that two different weights seem to occur with the two types; for the perforated types; this difference is also reinforced by a difference in fabric (B is heavier, D lighter).

Spindle whorl

The spindle whorl is in Fabric D, suggesting an association with the perforated loomweights, although its depositional association is with Structure IV (<2699> *680*, F. 13; Fig. 92.3). This was complete except for a chip and was conical in section, with flat faces and sloping sides (24g; 34mm diameter, 21mm thick, perforation 6mm diameter).

Oven fragments

Very few fragments of oven were diagnostic, many being spalls from the oven walls. However, some substantial shaped pieces came from F. 37 *386* and *369*, identifiable as supports which were either free-standing or (more probably) integral with the walls. Other larger pieces came from F. 61 *325* and F. 6 *203*. Overall, two-thirds of oven fragments (including undiagnostic pieces) are associated with the structures, the remainder mostly occurring in ditches and other features around the site. Of those associated with the structures, the majority occur with Structures I (2249g) and IV (2450g). They are found to a lesser extent with III and V (111 and 307g respectively), and rarely with II (1g) and VI (7g).

VI. Worked bone

Unfortunately this material was misplaced and, therefore, detailed description cannot be provided. The assemblage included portions of two pins (*035* <2468>; *026* <947>) and a weaving comb fragment (*026* <847>), all from F.2. Also found was what seemed to be a spindle whorl from Structure IV (F. 26 *357* <1265>); a bone handle was reported from F.1 (*267* <1662>) and a rectangular shaped piece from ditch F. 38 (*117* <945>). Otherwise, perforated drilled pieces were recovered from Structure IV and F. 57 (respectively, F. 25 *332* <2594>; *285* <2064>), and as surface finds (*014* <735>; *368* <958>). A possible toggle with two drilled perforations was found within Structure I (F. 6 *234* <1855>).

VII. Other finds
(Plate XIII; Fig. 94)

Decorated stave

Perhaps the most remarkable single find from the excavation was a metal-decorated, slightly curved wooden fragment (7.9 x 5.2 x 0.6cm: Plate XIII; Fig. 94) recovered from the south-eastern sector main ditch circuit (F. 1 *061* <848>). The top and bottom have been broken perpendicular to the wood grain; the vertical edges (parallel with the grain) are clean fractures. The wood is very degraded and the concave interior face shows no obvious evidence of working, though this is probably attributable to surface deterioration. Although possibly distorted through

Plate XIII
(Top) '*Ceramic Appearances*': indicative of the range of pottery types associated with Structure IV and their variability of finish and colour: right, the La Tène-style decorated jar (F. 25, *307* <1664>; see Fig. 80); upper left, wheelmade, necked bowl (F. 26, *359* <1685>); lower left, the Samian dish (F. 26, *354* <1673>; see Fig. 84.6), with the recovered piece set within a near-complete example of the same vessel-type recently excavated from Earith, Cambs.
(Bottom) The decorated stave (F. 1, *061* <848>). Note the smoothness of the band in which the rivets are set, obviously reflecting the original finish of the entire vessel (and attesting to its 'strap' protection). Both photos by G. Owen, University of Cambridge Museum of Archaeology and Anthropology.

compression, from its curvature it is estimated that the piece would have had an exterior diameter of c. 15cm.

Set within a smoothly-worked central band (2.8cm wide) across the width of the piece were seven square-headed fittings (7–8mm square). Although covered in what seems to be iron-derived corrosion, as is clear from Plate XIII, these are in fact copper alloy and the sharp edges of those in the right-hand setting indicated that they had been attached as fittings (*i.e.* not applied hot as any manner of adhesive). They are arranged in four-square/-cross chequerboard patterns, leaving their central squares empty. The fittings do not pierce the thickness of the wood and are attached to its exterior surface. X-ray images show bright lines around their edges. These are probably the result of the folded metal edges which, staple-like, attach the fittings to the wood. That the square-head settings obviously run as a pattern along the length of the smoothly worked zone suggests their inter-relationship, and clearly 'something' protected the surface of the wood in this strip. Given that there are no traces of corroded metal within it, it can only be presumed that this container was bound with a strap of leather attached by the decoratively set square-headed fittings. Judging from this, and the size of the wood fragment, it would be logical if this had been stave-built. However, M. Taylor, who examined it, does not think that the piece is oak but suggests that it could be alder. If so, the staves would have to be carved individually as alder does not split thin and cleanly like oak. Moreover the grain runs vertically, as would be expected if the piece was carved. (In stave-built vessels the grain runs across the body pieces to prevent splitting and make them waterproof.) In this piece the grain is radial and, therefore, it may derive from a two-piece carved vessel (*i.e.* a carved cylindrical body with inserted base) that may simply have split to resemble a stave (M. Taylor, *pers. comm.*; see Taylor in Evans and Hodder forthcoming concerning two-pieced carved vessels, which occur from the mid-1st millennium BC).

Although certainly not beautifully worked, this is a unique object within the archaeological record. It is, in fact, conceivable that its decorative design was once more complicated, with small inlay panels set in the centre of each of the four-square settings (?bone, antler or even red arsenic: see below). While the slight 'lipping' of the fittings in relationship to their 'void' central squares could be enlisted to support this, there is otherwise no direct evidence of this.

Judging from its projected diameter the piece could have been either from a small bucket or a large tankard (Evans 1989, 191–4, table 1). In terms of organic containers, general parallels could be drawn with the small Great Chesterford bucket (Stead 1971) or, further afield, the Glastonbury vessels (Earwood 1988); the Stuntney Fen bucket is considerably larger (Clark and Godwin 1940). The Wardy Hill piece is interesting on two counts. On the one hand, that its level of technological sophistication is not particularly great suggests its probable local manufacture and that it was not an imported item. Yet, on the other hand, if it is from a tankard then this object resonates within the context of findings of vessels of this type (Corcoran 1952). Usually represented by their

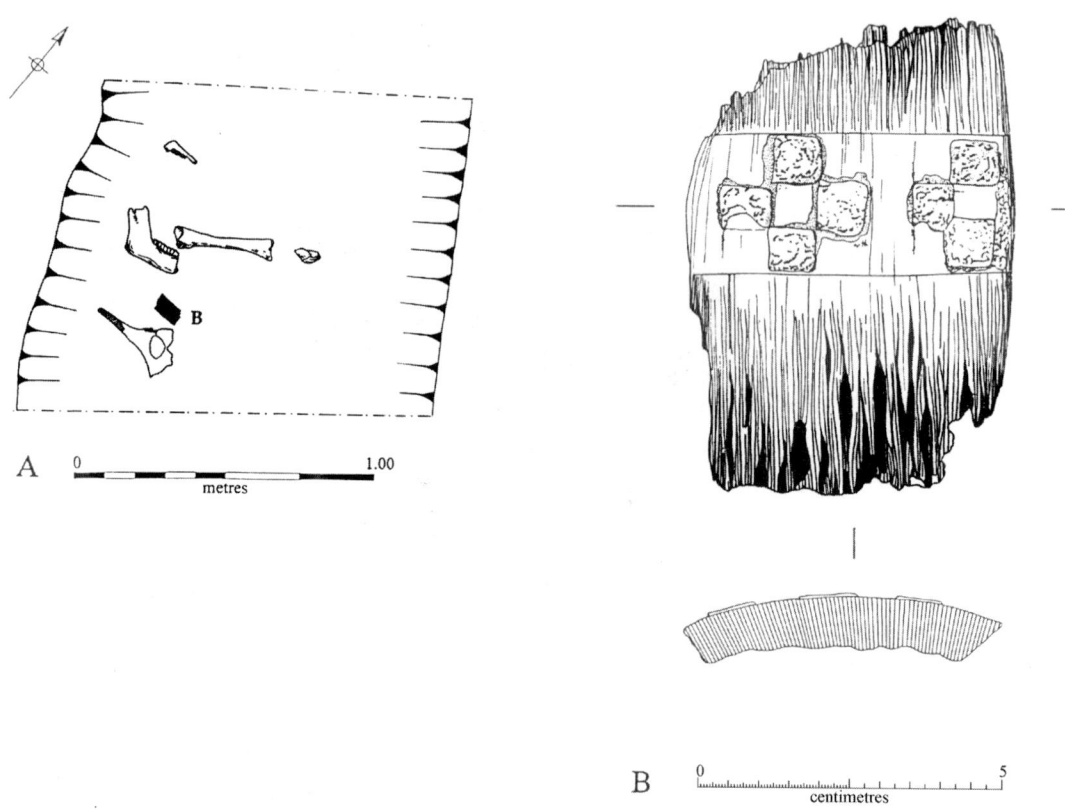

Figure 94 The decorated stave (B), and its location within the base of the F. 1 circuit (A)

metal fittings alone, these generally accompany only wealthier burials. Their occurrence, like that of more formal later Iron Age drinking sets, tells of the importance of drinking (alcohol). Maybe this piece represents a crude version of a high-status good — which in many respects seems to typify the inhabitants of the Ringwork.

Given the greater decay of the wood otherwise observed in the site's main circuit (Murphy, Chapter 3), the survival of this piece is probably attributable to its metal fittings. It recovery adds to the growing number of organic containers known from the region in recent years: an Early Iron Age bowl/scoop from Lingwood Farm, Cottenham (Evans 1999) and a carved later Bronze Age bowl (in imitation of ceramic form) from Eye Quarry, Peterborough (McFadyen 2000). Nevertheless, that they still only occur in a remarkably low ratio in relation to ceramics belies earlier arguments for the overwhelming dominance of organic containers in relationship to pottery (*e.g.* Clark and Godwin 1940; *c.f.* Evans 1989).

A red mineral
A cluster of small salmon pink/red translucent crystalline fragments with orange-yellow powder on their surfaces, recovered from Structure IV (F. 25 *307*), was submitted to the Ancient Monuments Laboratory for identification. Reported upon by M. Canti and J. Dillon, these were subject to transmitted polarised light microscopy and EDXRF and found to be an arsenical mineral, probably Realgar (arsenic monosulphide AsS). It is not possible to determine conclusively whether or not this derives from a natural geological source or was a corrosion product from a manufactured object. However, the latter is thought unlikely given the quantity of arsenic present, and the fact that arsenical copper is unknown from Iron Age Britain (P. Craddock, *pers. comm.*).

This unusual mineral could not have developed within fenland soil conditions and has probably been imported to the site, with Cornwall being the nearest British source. While amongst arsenic's more recent uses is as an opacifier in glass and for tanning, given its context its employment as a colour pigment (*i.e.* as 'red arsenic') is perhaps more likely. If so, it may even have been imported as an exotic material; it is very rare even in south-west British deposits, especially in grades that could be used as pigment (P. Craddock, *pers. comm.*).

VIII. Discussion
(Figs 95–97)

Situating activities
As attested to by the quantity of materials — particularly of 'small finds' — recovered from the house floors which survived at the HAD V enclosure (Evans and Hodder forthcoming), the loss of *in situ* surfaces at Wardy Hill severely limits any observation concerning distribution patterning and 'complete' representation of the site's assemblages (estimating scales of production and status *etc.*). Nevertheless, accepting these *caveats*, certain basic distribution trends can be distinguished.

Metalwork
Given that we cannot be certain of the status of the nine nails with regard to possible later introduction into the tops of features, they warrant little discussion. They only occur singularly in two of the structures (III and IV) and the only concentration of any note is near the Watergate (four in total; Fig. 24). Otherwise, of the ironwork found in context, aside from single fragments in pits F. 104 and 115, and in the Structure I gully, the remaining five pieces are all associated with Structure IV. Similarly, of the few pieces of copper alloy recovered, apart from the tankard stave from the main ditch at the point of its probable terminal bridging in the south-east, the stud and the two finger rings all come from the Structure IV ditches. Whereas the one ring fragment was recovered from the southern terminal (<2597>) and was probably deposited there (perhaps in sweepings), the complete spiral ring actually comes from the F. 4 post-medieval ditch at the point where it cut the north length of the gully (*i.e.* not from a ditch butt). An area from which human bone was recovered (see Fig. 116), this ring conceivably derives from an exhumed inhumation.

Overall, little can be said of the distribution of the metalwork given its scarcity, aside from the fact that it displays a marked concentration within Structure IV.

Metalworking debris
Aside from single occurrences of fragments of slag in ditches F.12/144 and F. 37, and, again singularly, in Structures III and V, all the crucible and slag pieces were found in association with Structures I and IV (Fig. 95). (Hearth lining fragments show a similar distribution, confined entirely to the latter two main structures apart from a single outlier in the eastern terminal of the Watergate.) The most marked concentration is in and around the F. 107 pit/trough within Structure IV and along that building's north-western circuit (the latter corresponding with an area of high magnetic susceptibility values).

Querns and loomweights etc.
Querns and grindstones have a more widespread distribution and occur in both of the Ringwork's two main circuits (F. 1 and 2; Fig. 96). However, apart from in pit F. 102 associated with Structure V, they only occur with Structures I and IV. Loomweights, also recovered in numbers within the packing of pit F. 102 (and a singular occurrence within F. 1), were otherwise only recovered from Structures I and IV. However, the distributional contexts of the latter two were quite different. While in Structure I they were spread around much of its eaves-gully's circuit (F. 6), in the case of IV none were recovered from its surrounding ditch, and instead only from pit F. 107 and the upper profile of ditch F. 37. However, one might not wish to make too much of this distinction as two of the site's four spindle whorls came from the Structure IV ditch. (The third spindle whorl came from the F. 2 extension across the south-eastern landward terminal; the one weaving comb recovered was from F. 2 adjacent the Watergate entrance.)

With only four spindle whorls and eight loomweights, the site's inventory is not particularly distinguished and this impression is reinforced by the paucity of metalwork recovered. What we are seeing seems very much to represent household-scale production. There is, for example, no evidence for 'special' grain-storage facilities or processing, or for particularly intense wool production. Certainly the distributions suggest that the *house*hold *per se* was the unit and focus of production. Admittedly this is biased by the manner in which the surviving eaves-gullies dominate the assemblages' representation, and that so much has been lost through the ploughing out of surfaces

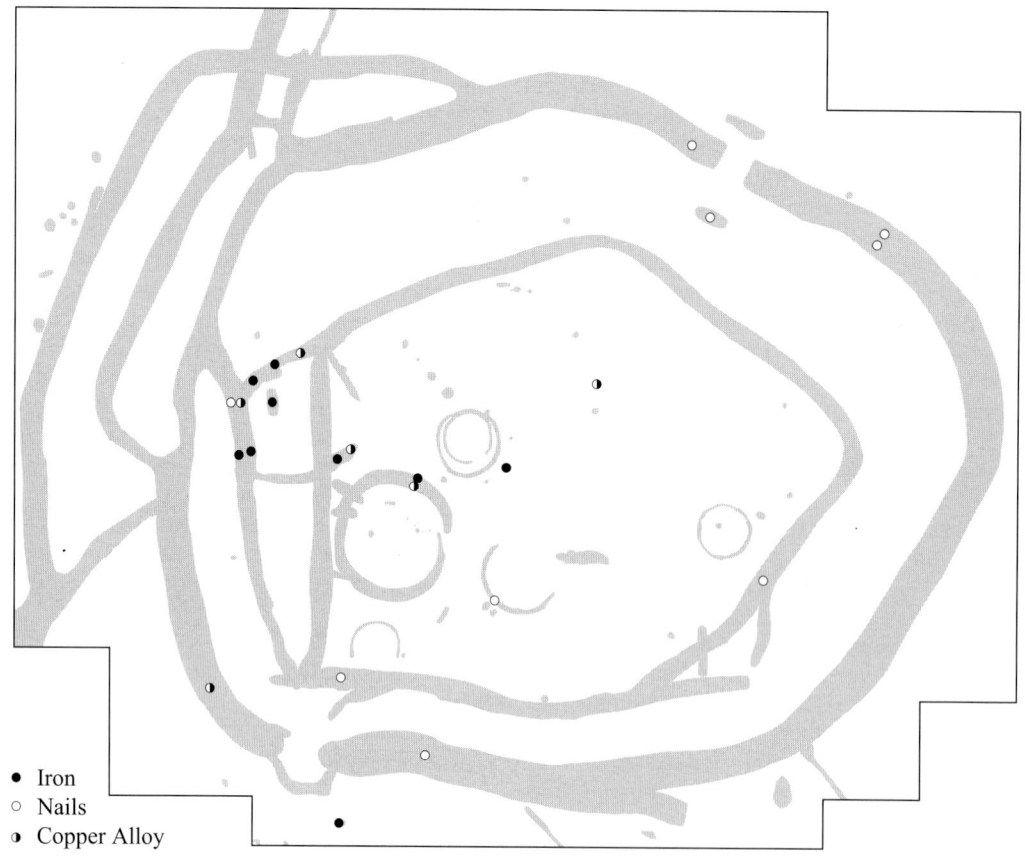

- Iron
- Nails
- Copper Alloy

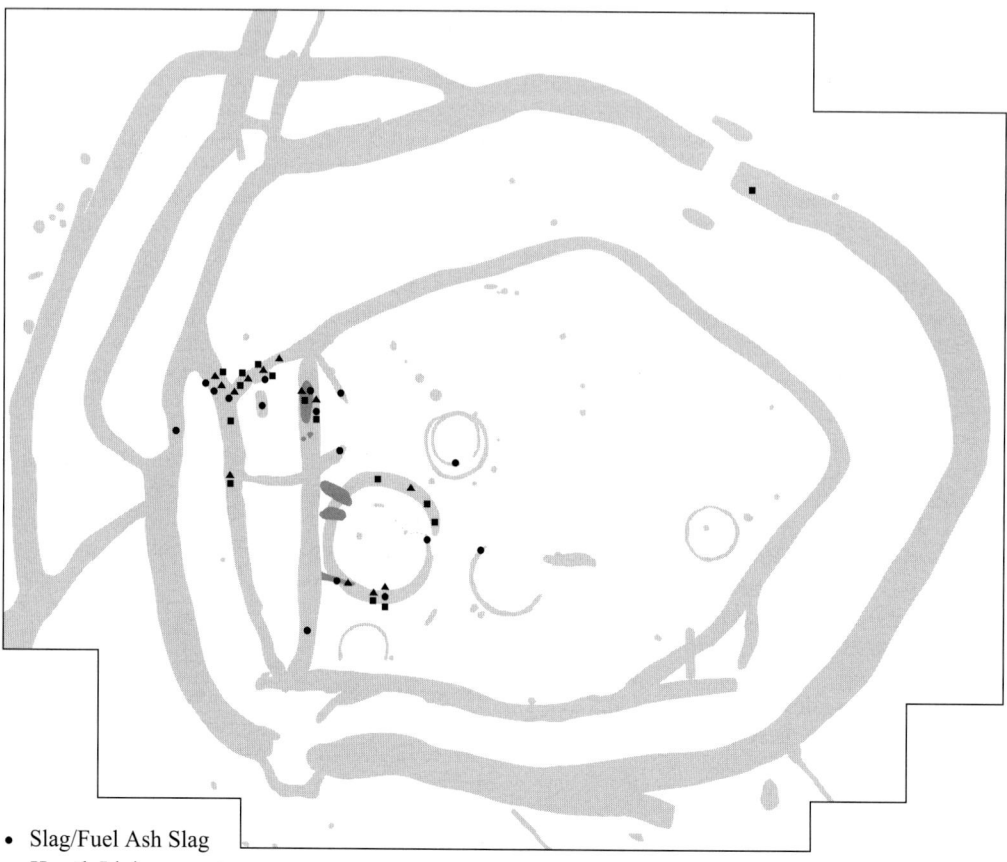

- Slag/Fuel Ash Slag
- Hearth Lining
- Crucible Fragments

Figure 95 Distributions: top, metalwork; below, metalworking debris

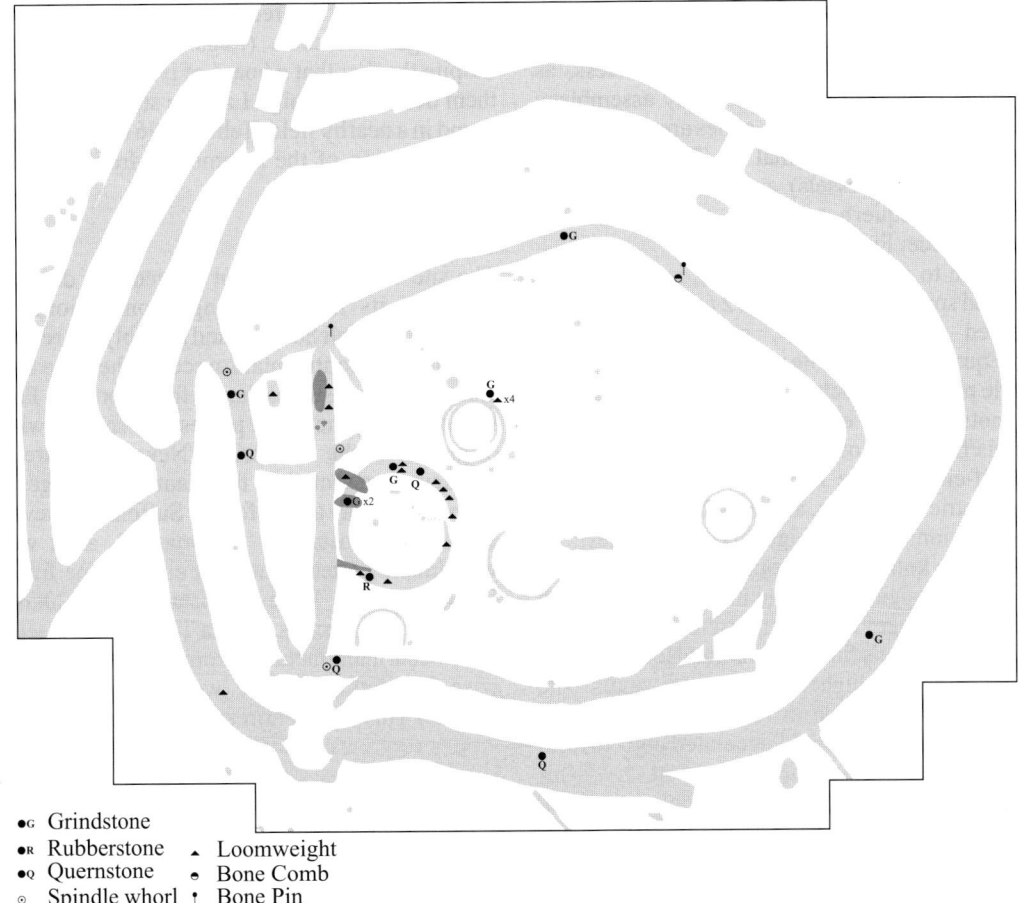

Figure 96 Distributions: worked stone, loomweights, spindle whorls and worked bone

and building-exterior middens. Nevertheless, when compared to recovery within the Ringwork's circuits — especially F. 2 bounding the interior ground — the evidence suggests that most production occurred within the houses themselves. Applying to both metalworking, weaving and food preparation, it is only the possible evidence of grain processing in the south-eastern corner and the greater dispersion of worked bone artefacts (possibly relating to sewing and wool-carding) that suggest outdoor activities.

As remarked upon above by Robbins, in recent years evidence of metalworking (especially of iron) has become increasingly commonplace on settlements of the period: locally, for instance, at the HAD V enclosure on the Upper Delphs (Evans and Hodder forthcoming). However it is not, for example, evident at the series of later Iron Age compounds excavated at Colne Fen, Earith (Regan and Evans 2000). While clearly metalworking did not involve centralised regionally-based production — an issue that still requires much more detail study — within the range of local settlement systems it may still have been a restricted activity.

Decorative styles

While only three pieces out of the site's substantial finds assemblage (aside from the medieval coins and various wiped/combed surface treatments to pottery) received surface decoration — the metal-decorated wooden fragment and the La Tène style pottery — when compared to most sites of this period within the region this represents a

Figure 97 Decorative styles: (A) incised spindle whorl; (B) wooden stave rivet pattern; (C) La Tène-style pottery motifs. Scale 1:1.

ne' cold morning (photos by Kasia Gdaniec)

5. Articulating Settlement Structure and Re-Addressing Sequence

Having outlined the site's structural sequence in Chapter 2, at this point the Ringwork's general artefactual and 'chemical' (*i.e.* magnetic susceptibility and phosphate) distributions will be considered. This discussion will be at a basic level of density/value patterning, the details of specific 'type' distributions having already discussed in Chapters 3 and 4 above. Instead, here the focus will be upon the inter-relationship between buildings and their artefactual and chemical densities compared to the Ringwork's circuits, and how these analyses act to bridge the site sequence and specialist studies. Moreover, in an effort to tease out 'the invisible', much attention will be given to ploughsoil densities, and particularly to the possibility that midden-type deposits had once extended across much of the interior of the inner enclosure. Having major implications concerning the interpretation of the site as a whole, these are important matters in trying to articulate the Ringwork's 'daily' operational structures and depositional practices. However, equally crucial are a suite of terminal phase patterns which seem to cross-cut the western Ringwork circuits and reflect a significant re-working of the immediate enclosure system. These analyses clearly demonstrate the importance of statistical ploughsoil sampling. As will become apparent, whilst they complement the excavated distributions, there are also instances where the surface spreads are independent of in-depth patterns, thereby offering distinct insights into the site's broader usage. Having addressed these issues, the Ringwork's building and constructional sequence will be re-addressed and summarised and its absolute chronology outlined. Finally, for comparative purposes, there will be thematic discussion of key results from other more recent 'Cove' excavations.

I. Ploughsoil distributions
(Figs 98–101, 108–11; Table 58)

In this section, the results of the surface distributions will be followed by discussion of the test-pitting results. This will essentially be confined to the phases of the Ringwork's usage *per se*, with the earlier lithics and subsequent post-medieval distributions having been previously discussed in Chapter 2.

Iron Age pottery
Across the fieldwalking grid the density of later prehistoric pottery varied from 0 to 36 sherds per 10m unit, with a site-wide mean of 6.9 pieces (9 st. dev.; Fig. 98). There is a distinct enclosure-centre 'high' (pulling south-westwards) composed of values consistently greater than fifteen pieces per unit, with densities of more than 25 sherds occurring throughout its 300m core.

Only one sherd of Later Bronze Age date was recovered and, when compared to the excavated assemblage, flint-tempered wares seem under-represented within the surface collection. Conversely, sixteen wheelmade sherds were recovered (Figs 99 and 111). While this seems an over-representation of the larger assemblage, accounting for only 5.5% of the total fieldwalking pottery, this is actually markedly less than its proportion of the overall assemblage. The 'impression' of its greater frequency is because so much of the wheelmade pottery recovered from excavated contexts was focused upon a single structure (IV), and was not generally spread widely through features (*Transgressing circuits*, below). Only occurring at a frequency of 1–2 pieces per 10m unit, the surface distribution of wheelmade wares is without any marked concentrations. Spread throughout the central/south-western quarter of the Ringwork, it is noteworthy that they do not extend throughout the northern portion of the core area of overall high Iron Age pottery density, and instead are distributed around its western and southern sides.

The mean size and weight values of the surface pottery were 1.95cm (long axes) and 7.30g respectively. When compared to Table 60, while the ploughsoil material is smaller than from the Ringwork's main roundhouses and ditch circuits, it is larger than that within the non-residential ancillary structures (II and VI). This suggests that the surface material derives from ploughed-out occupation deposits. While later arable activity has no doubt reduced its size, it was not manuring-derived in the first instance.

Roman pottery
Only twelve sherds of Romano-British pottery were recovered (Figs 98 and 111). Given these numbers there is obviously little if any sense in their distributional patterning, aside from the fact that the only two occurrences of more than one piece per 10m unit were on the western margin of the Iron Age pottery 'core' zone — immediately in front of Structure IV. Little can be said of the character of such a small assemblage. Noteworthy, however, is that the one piece of Samian recovered in the surface collection was from above the area of Structure III, whose eaves-gully produced another piece.

Bone
While densities ranged from 0–43 fragments per 10m unit (6.9 mean; 10 st. dev.), it is conceivable that at least some of the bone recovered from the fieldwalking derives from the later historical usage of the site (*i.e.* post-medieval; Fig. 98). However, its distribution so closely matches that of the Iron Age pottery — with a marked 1400m enclosure-central high with values between 16 and 25 pieces (and a comparable 300m core with still higher densities) — that it must reflect comparable depositional practices.

Phosphate
Reflective of the presence of organic waste, the distribution of phosphates directly complements those of the bone and Iron Age pottery, which are also high immediately

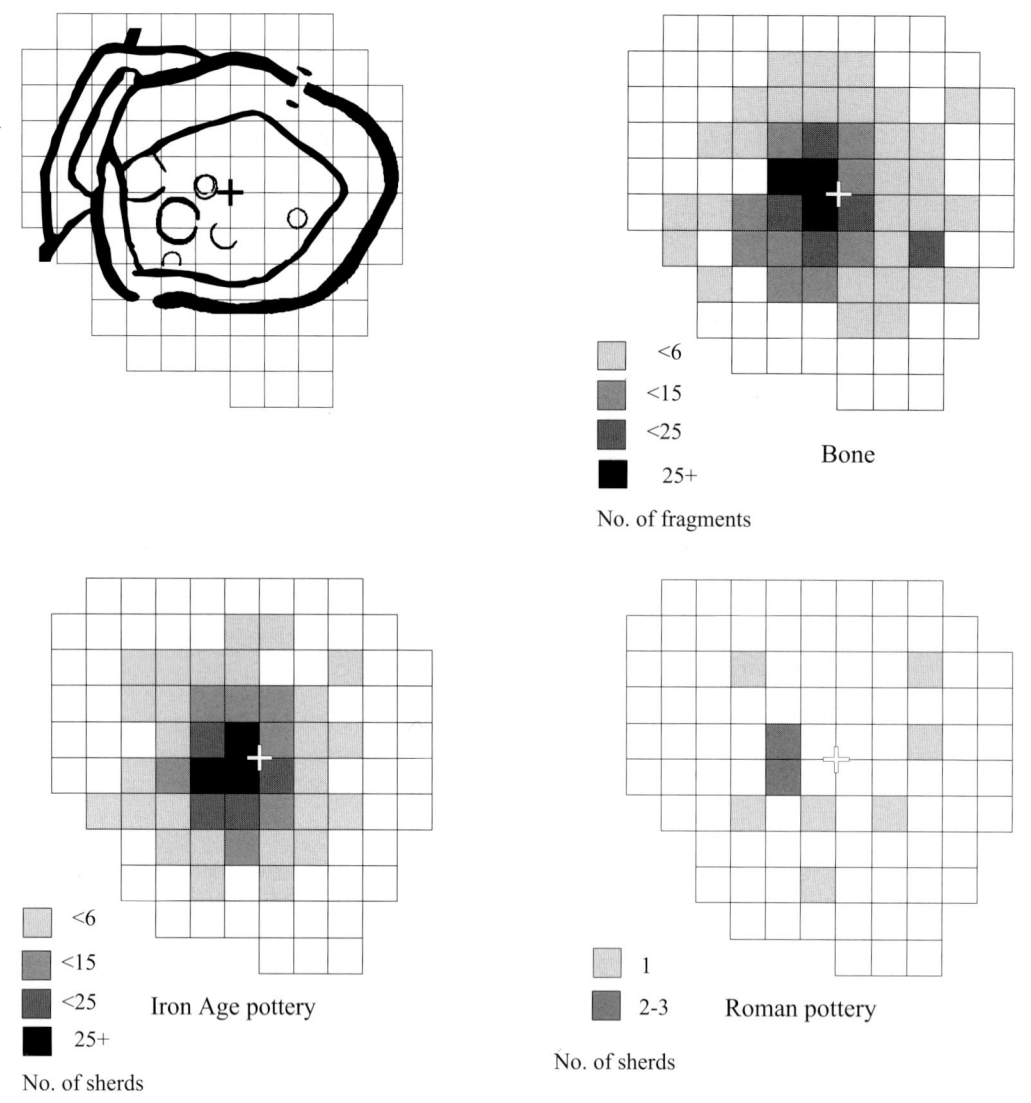

Figure 98 Ringwork-related surface finds densities

Spit	TP 4			TP 1		
	Pottery	*Bone*	*Bt. Clay*	*Pottery*	*Bone*	*Bt. Clay*
1 (uppermost)	16 (34.8)	130 (33.1)	15 (30)	1 (11.1)	7 (21.9)	9 (64.3)
2	18 (39.1)	121 (30.8)	22 (44)	5 (55.5)	18 (56.2)	1 (7.1)
3 (basal)	12 (26.1)	142 (36.1)	13 (26)	3 (33.3)	7 (21.9)	4 (28.6)
Total	**46**	**393**	**50**	**9**	**32**	**14**

Table 58 Test-pit finds densities, by spit (NB: only later prehistoric pottery has been included, and not post-medieval material; bracketed numbers indicate percentage of category total)

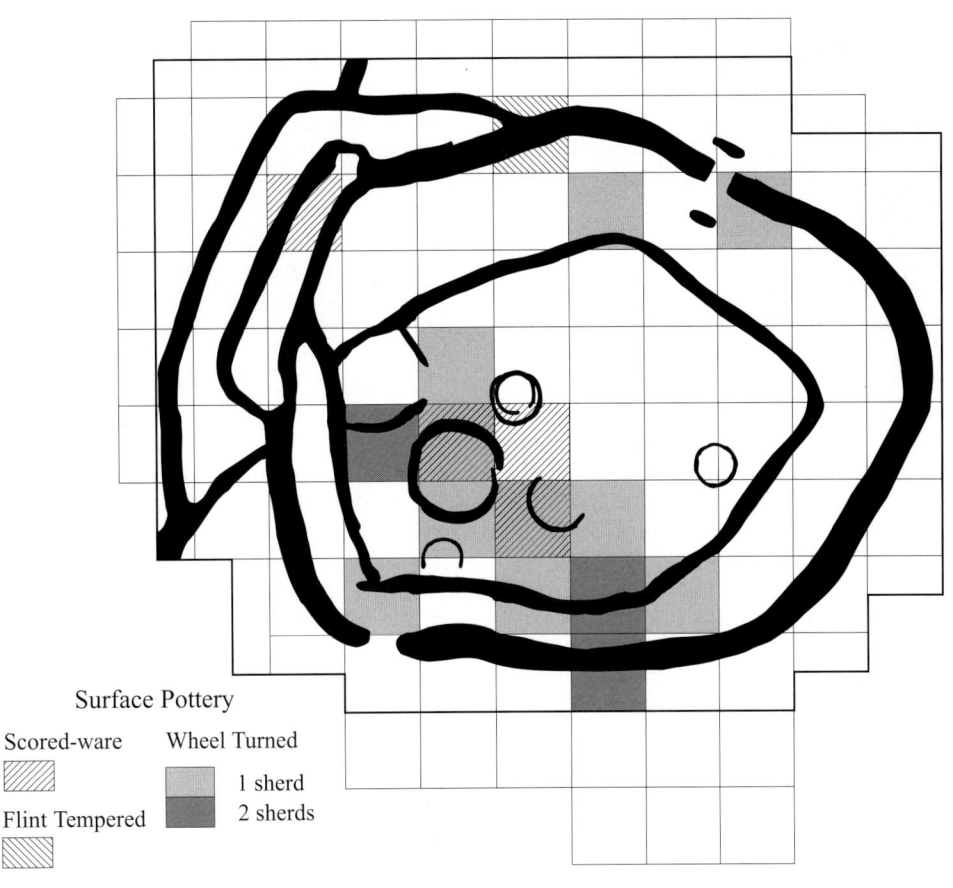

Figure 99 Iron Age pottery surface distributions (by type)

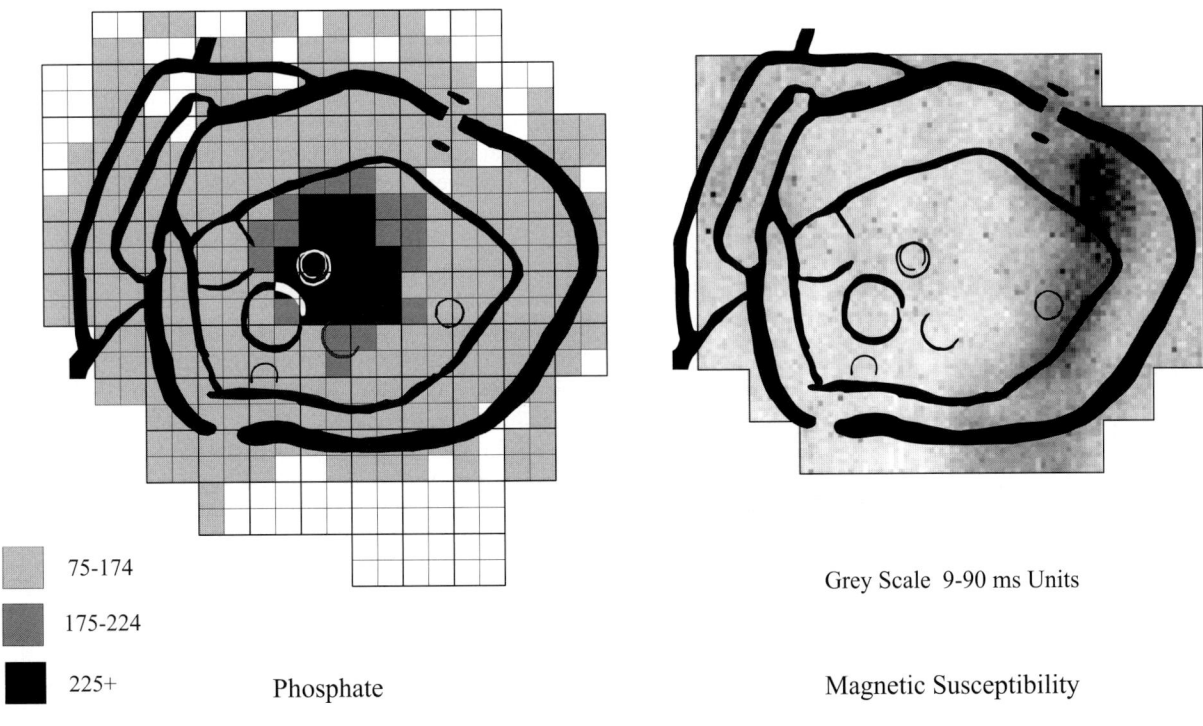

Figure 100 Surface survey results: phosphate and magnetic susceptibility

before the two main roundhouses (Fig. 100). Particularly relevant is the fact that no 'tails' run from this area outwards to any of the Ringwork's main entrances, as would be anticipated had this pattern primarily related to the penning of animals. (French, though, identified what are probably residues of animal urine in the soil sample from Structure I: Chapter 3, above.)

Magnetic susceptibility
Complementing the phosphate work, previous to the site's stripping A. Challands undertook a magnetic susceptibility survey throughout the area of the enclosure on a metre grid, using a Randall meter (200mm dia. field coil; Fig. 100). With a range of 9 to 90 ms units, the patterning clearly indicates that the highest values fall consistently across the eastern third of the sampling gird, where they are dominated by the 'signature' of the Period I burnt flint mound (and its ploughed-out tail to the south). Moderately high values continue north beyond the line of the main Ringwork circuit and extend throughout the area of the north-western outworks, leaving its central interior as a low value 'hole'. This is quite the opposite pattern to that of the phosphate results. It suggests that this technique was not particularly sensitive at this level and, aside from the specific eastern 'high', that the patterning was influenced by later agricultural practice. This being said, sporadic higher values register in the vicinity of the three northern roundhouses (I, IV and V). While that in front of Structure I may have some validity as being indicative of 'early' activity, as can be seen in Figure 100, the one extending between Structures I and III (from where it continues north along the western side of V) clearly related to a larger linear 'pull' which, again, was probably determined by agriculture. Enhanced imaging of this central portion of the grid, filtering out the influence of the eastern 'high', showed no clearer patterning.

Upon stripping of the topsoil, two areas were selected for further magnetic susceptibility survey at reduced depth. One, a 30 x 55m swathe through the enclosure's centre, will be discussed in detail below. The other was a 10m square in the core area of the burnt flint spread. While in the latter the southern side of the enclosure circuit registered strongly (due evidently to the quantity of burnt flint within its matrix), the values from the postulated area of the mound proper were unexceptional. This would indicate that the lithics had not been fired *in situ* but rather had been collected and heaped at this point.

Discussion
The marked site-central 'highs' in the distributions of bone and Iron Age pottery reflect the core of the settlement and the location of the main Iron Age houses (Structures I–III and V). Although in both instances these high zones effectively erupt against the general background densities across the area of the Ringwork, within them the densities 'build' regularly to (or fall off from) their respective 300m core values. As will become apparent below, what seems anomalous is that while this core zone coincides with the high artefact densities of Structure I neither they, nor even the minimum delineation of these high zones (the 6+ sherds and bones per 10m unit contour), extend to the area of Structure IV — the later great house that had even higher densities than I. Most telling of the character of these densities is the fact that in the cases of both pottery and bone the highest core values focus upon Structure V — a building of ambiguous status which had low artefact densities. Whilst these enclosure-central high-value swathes must reflect, in part, the general intensity of Iron Age occupation, more specifically the location of their highest cores would suggest the presence of contemporary middens. These probably occurred across the area of Structures I and V — before (east) and immediately south-east of Structure IV, argued to be the last main house on the site. While the latter building was evidently 'closed' with material backfilled into its eaves-gully, it did not become the site of a surface midden.

Of course, it could be argued that these various distributions only reflect differential plough damage. However, this would be countered by the fact that some of the spreads are mutually exclusive (*e.g.* burnt flint *vs.* Iron Age pottery) and, as will be shown below, that the enclosure-central 'highs' directly reflect the pattern of deposition within the Ringwork's inner circuit (*i.e.* largely mirroring in-depth depositional patterns). Even more telling is that they complement the results of the test-pitting, whose densities beyond this core zone are so low that site-wide patterning — other than the 'eruption' of the enclosure-central values — cannot really be distinguished.

II. Test-pit densities
(Fig. 101; Table 58)

When discussing the test-pit densities, two points warrant emphasis. Firstly, that it proved unfeasible to break the clayey ploughsoil down into anything less than 'fist-sized' lumps. Therefore, even in the case of the sieved squares, these figures must offer a relative and not an absolute measure of finds density. (In compensation, the spoil from one — 790/200 — was kept and dried. Approximately half of it was broken down so that it could pass in its entirety through a 5mm mesh. This resulted in substantially higher values than were recorded anywhere apart from the four-square core — 6 pot/11 bone — and indicates that total artefact numbers from the topsoil as a whole have been seriously underestimated. Secondly, the non-'four-core' test-pits were actually dug out by mini-digger, with their spoil barrow-sorted. Because of their machine-excavation, these were generally 10–20% larger than the sieved squares that were entirely hand-excavated.)

Two of the four central sieved test-pits were spit-excavated (three *c.* 10cm deep horizons each). While the application of this technique was insufficiently widespread to be statistically meaningful, it does provide insights into the vertical distribution of artefactual material within the ploughsoil (Table 58).

Attesting to the thoroughness of plough-action mixing, the frequency of the material appears to be relatively uniform by depth and does not concentrate at any particular level (although, aside from burnt clay, in TP 4, the values are greatest in the middle spit). Equally relevant — in relation to the very high values recovered from TP 1 within the south-westernmost test station, attributable to it being above (and even slightly dug into) the southern terminal of the Structure I eaves-gully — is that even here there was no significant vertical distinction. If these high values are attributable to the eaves-gully then its distributional trace is still apparent even in the uppermost spit.

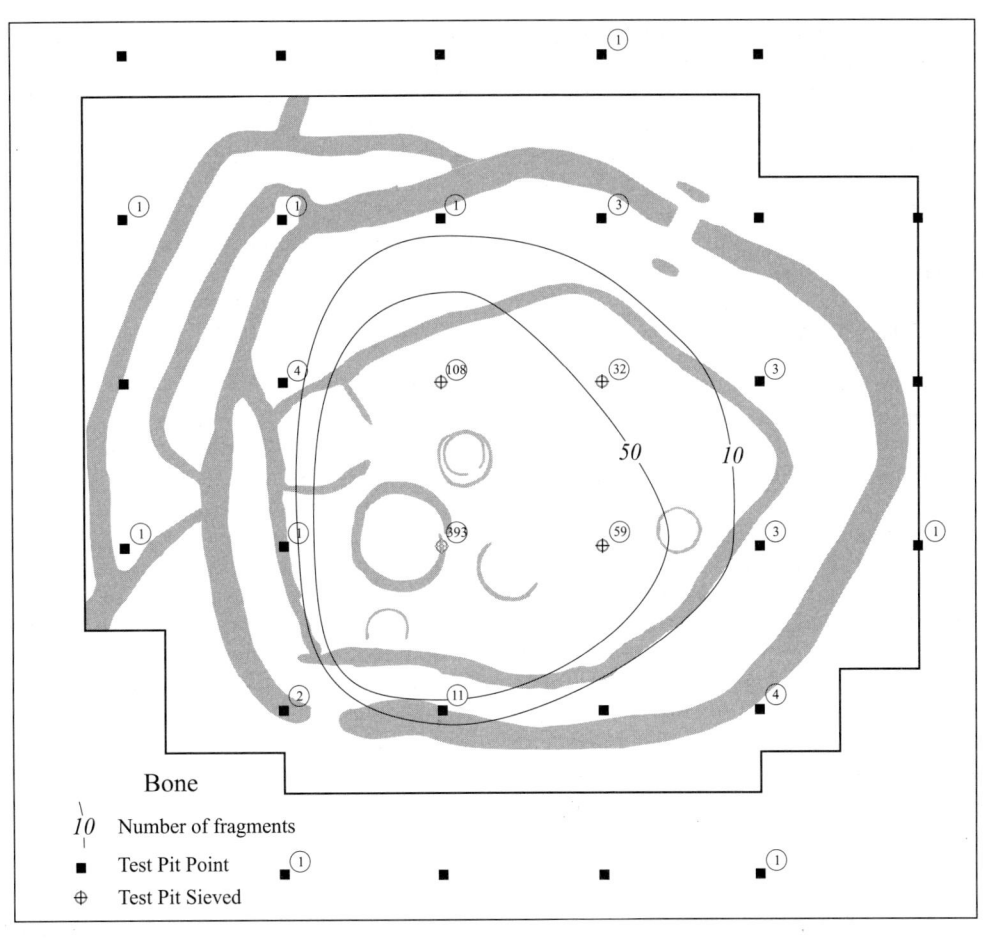

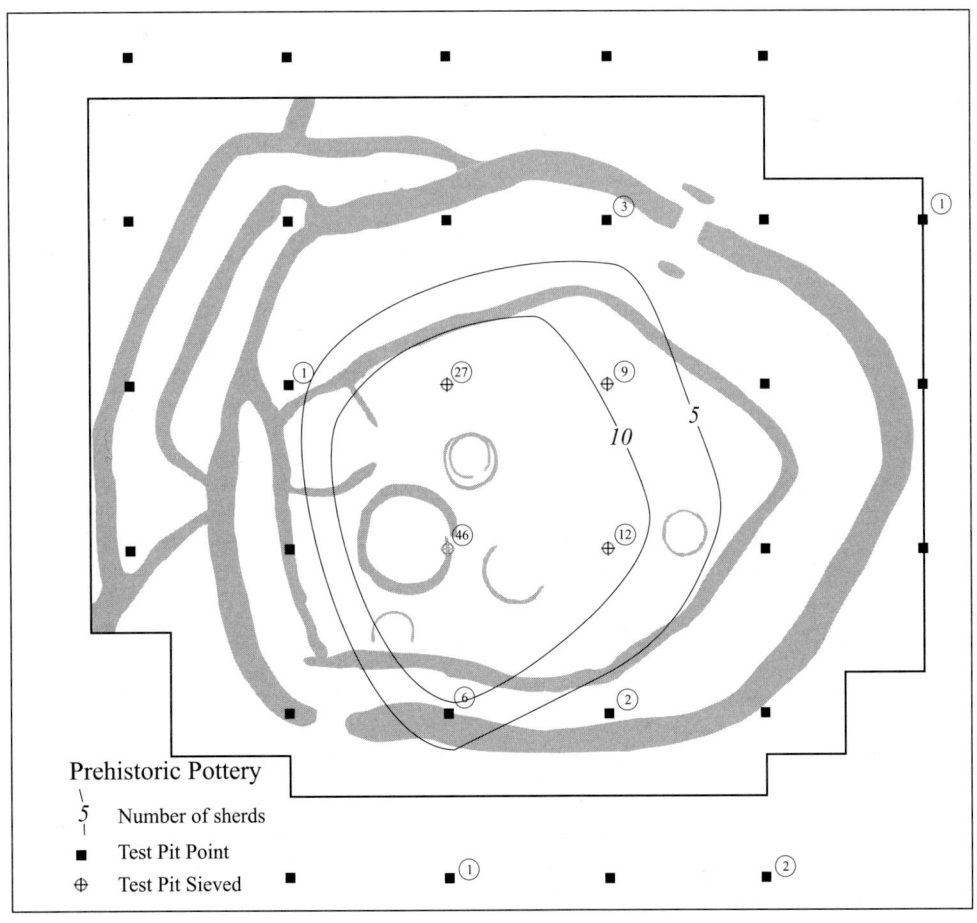

Figure 101 Test-pit finds densities

This indicates that there must have been very little lateral displacement of finds through ploughing within the site's heavy clay soils.

Bone, occurring in 20 out of 31 test-pits, was more consistently widespread than pottery (eleven test-pit occurrences; Fig. 101). This must relate in part to cognitive factors involved in the retrieval of small artefacts, it being more difficult to distinguish minute black pieces of pottery than lightly-hued bone against the ploughsoil background. Nevertheless, the test-pit densities do help to offset the reduced quality of the fieldwalking grid around its margins. Evidently the Ringwork's circuits were not an absolute barrier in terms of deposition. This is especially true along the southern side where the consistent occurrence of finds (albeit at low values) suggests Ringwork–exterior access, and possibly even settlement activity outside.

There is a massive discrepancy between the densities from the 'four-core' sieved test-pits and those across the remainder of the site. Whereas those sieved produced an average of 148 pieces of bone each (range 32–393), the twelve non-sieved/-core pits within the area of the Ringwork proper had an average of only 2.5 pieces (0–11 range). The same also holds true for the pottery: 23.5 sherds sieved average (9–46 range) *vs.* 1 (0–6 range; Fig. 101). Given the manner in which the pottery and bone frequencies 'sky-rocket' in the four central test-pits, with hindsight it was obviously a mistake to have sieved only these, as it becomes impossible to determine to what extent this technique of recovery is responsible for the higher frequencies. Support for the suggestion that these much higher central values reflect a real trend in the site's distributions, and not just differential recovery, comes from the surface distributions (Iron Age pottery, bone and phosphate). That their 'highs' directly correspond both shows that the four central test-pit values are not just a product of more controlled recovery and that the high surface densities there do not only reflect differential plough damage.

III. Feature patterning
(Figs 102–7; Tables 59–64)

Figure 102 shows the distribution of *excavated* pottery and bone according to standard deviation by individual features (by metre segment, with the value of longitudinal half-sectioned segments doubled). The problem with such plotting is that it is scaled relative to individual features, and therefore each of these — be it a minor eaves-gully or major Ringwork ditch — will be shown having their own 'highs' and 'lows'. Therefore, the unshaded 'low' value lengths of a main building gully may still have greater numbers than the highest (blackened) values of relatively minor and less finds-dense features.

These shortcomings aside, the plots portray important distributional trends: primarily how low the densities are across the north-western outworks (over the northern middle of their lengths) and in both Ringwork circuits in the eastern half of the enclosure. In terms of the latter, particularly relevant is that while somewhat increased pottery values occur within the terminals of the north-eastern Watergate in F. 1, this has no apparent co-relationship in the adjacent length of the inner circuit (F. 2). This suggests that F. 2 did not have a bridged crossing at this point, and either that the two did not operate together (inasmuch as the cutting of the F. 2 circuit made the F. 1 Watergate redundant) or that access across the inner circuit was staggered in this sector (*i.e.* F. 2 was circumvented further to the west along its northern perimeter). The plots indicate that the main areas of high density generally correspond with the location of the four main buildings across the western third of the Ringwork interior, and that the high values within the main outer circuit are generally confined to the area of its successive entrances on the landward side in the south-west. This indicates that deposition was largely from the Ringwork interior outwards — reflecting lines of access — and that finds do not seem to have been deposited in a manner reflecting uncurtailed access to the Ringwork's outer perimeter. The one distribution pattern that seems at odds with this logic is marked by the 'aligned highs' in the southern end of the Outworks ditches (west from Structure IV along the projected line of F. 2). This anomaly warrants more detailed discussion below.

What the plots also show, apart from the now-commonplace pattern of high artefact deposition within and approaching building eaves-gully terminals (see below), is that the area of highest ploughsoil surface distributions of pottery and bone stops just short of Structure IV (Fig. 98). This seems extraordinary, since that building's eaves-gully had the highest overall densities from the site. Again requiring further consideration, this issue will be returned to later in the chapter.

In order to interrogate the site's distributions in greater detail, and particularly to discuss building densities in relation to adjacent lengths of the inner Ringwork ditches and the ploughsoil data, we must deal in absolute finds numbers. Accordingly, these are shown in Figure 103 with the F. 2 circuit axially 'unwound'. It is in enabling this kind of analysis that the site's radially concentric sampling gird comes into its own, as it allows for direct registration between circuits and the enclosed buildings. Aside from an occurrence of higher-than-mean pottery values in the south-eastern corner of F. 2, this demonstrates a close match between bone and pottery 'highs' around this circuit. Equally, it shows how close the correspondence is between the contour plotting of the high 'surface' test-pit values and F. 2's deposition. This adds further credence to the suggestion that the inner circuit densities essentially reflect surface spreads, and probably the existence of middens within the area of the four main buildings (Structures I, III–V).

Buildings and eaves-gullies
Building-associated artefacts were almost entirely restricted to their eaves-gullies. Although the potential factoring for the respective scale of their gully-surrounds will be dealt with below, at this point the data is considered 'raw' (Table 59). As is clear from Figure 104, the structures break into three distinct pairings in terms of their finds numbers, with I and IV having by far and away the greatest numbers (both in excess of 4500 finds) and with II and VI having negligible densities of less than 25 pieces in total. Between these extremes Structure III and V have a medial status, each having between 250 and 550 finds.

Figure 105 indicates the distribution of material around the circuits of the structures' gullies by metre segments. From this plotting, the fact that Structure III shows little evidence of artefact density increase at the two ends of its eaves-gully could indicate that these were not in

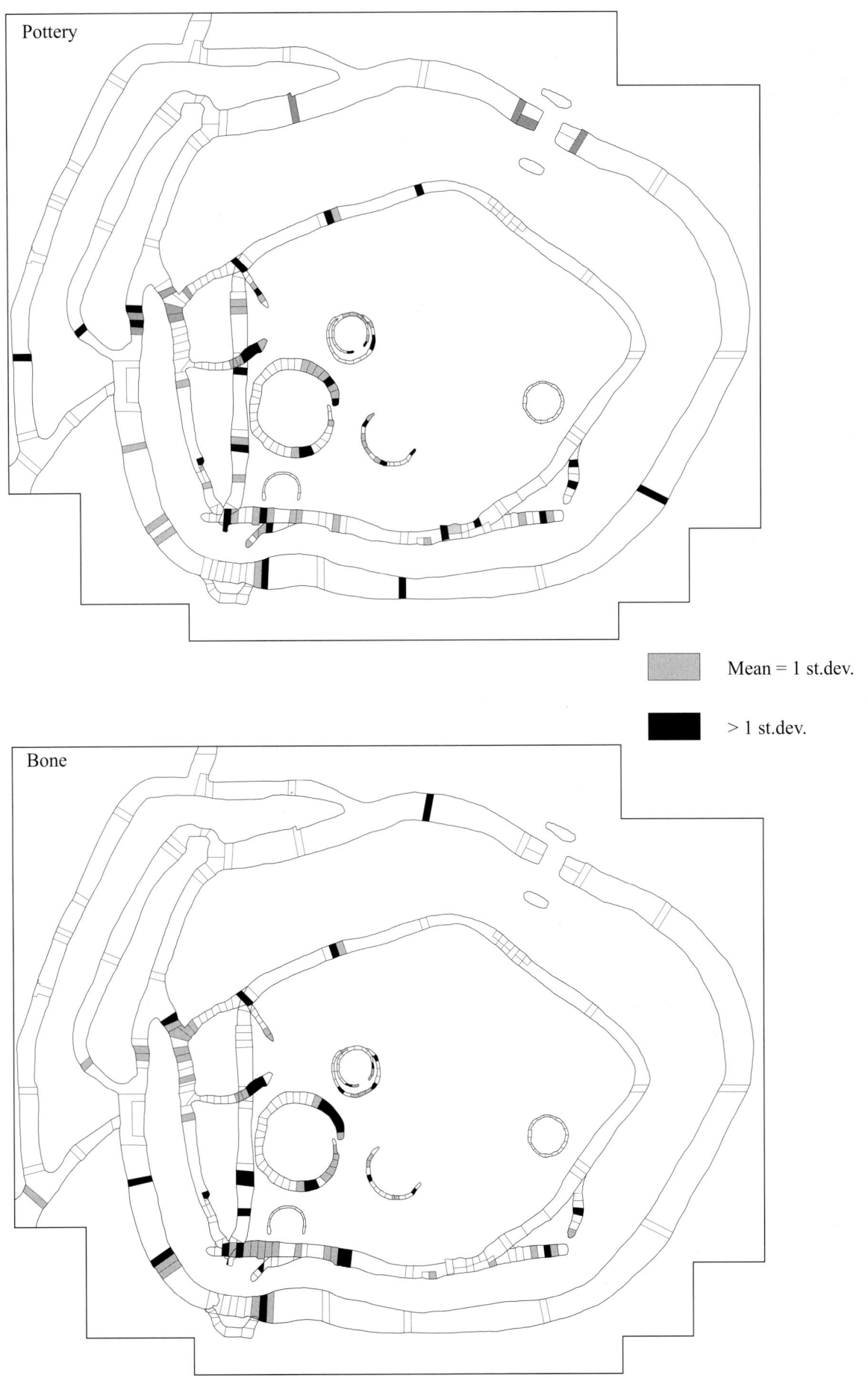

Figure 102 Excavated finds densities (pottery and bone by standard deviation)

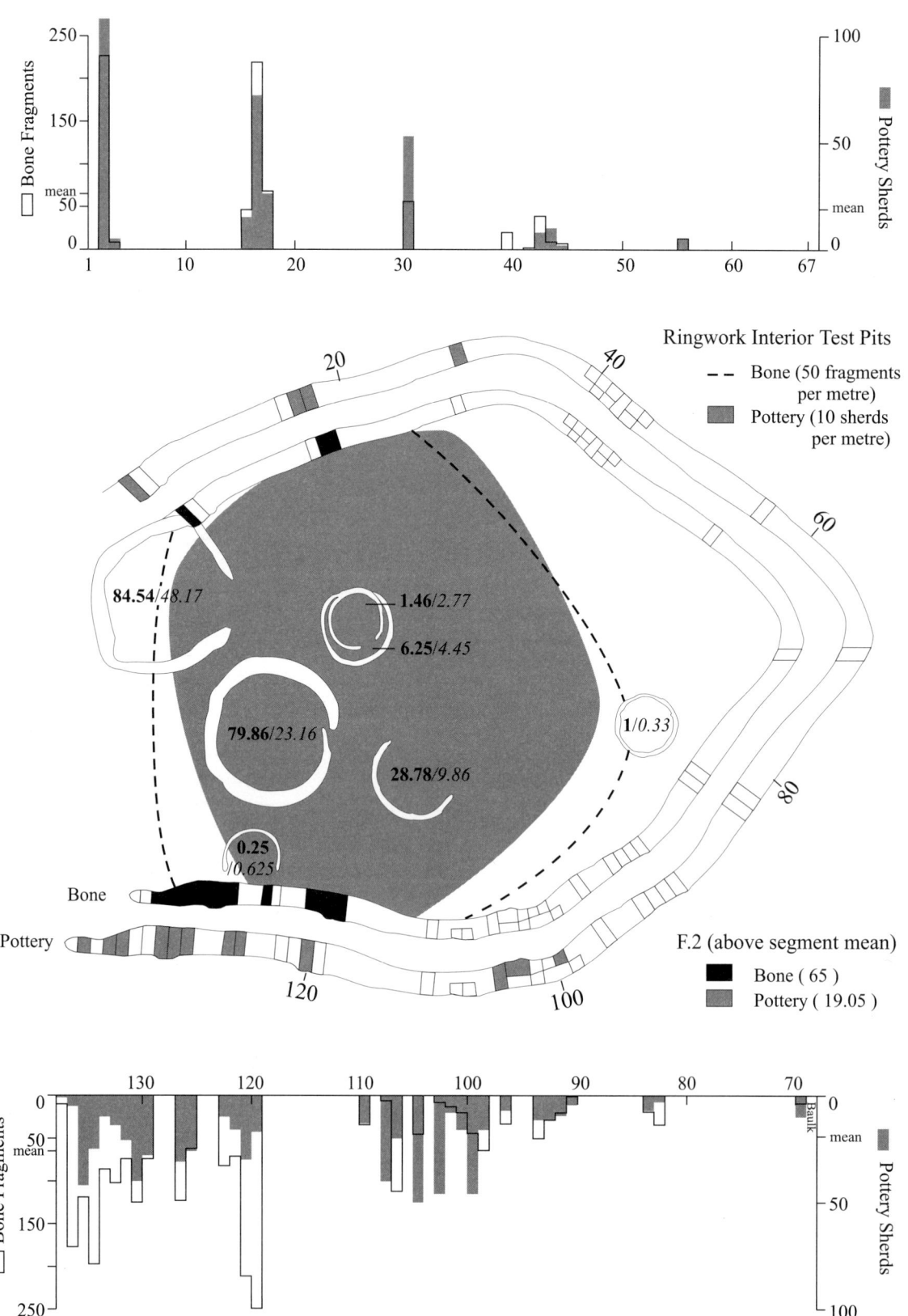

Figure 103 Comparative plotting of inner circuit and test-pit finds densities

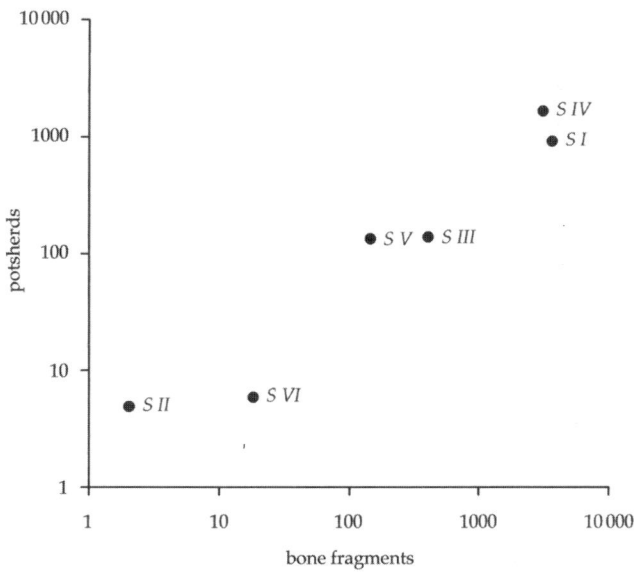

Figure 104 Frequency of pottery and bone by Structure

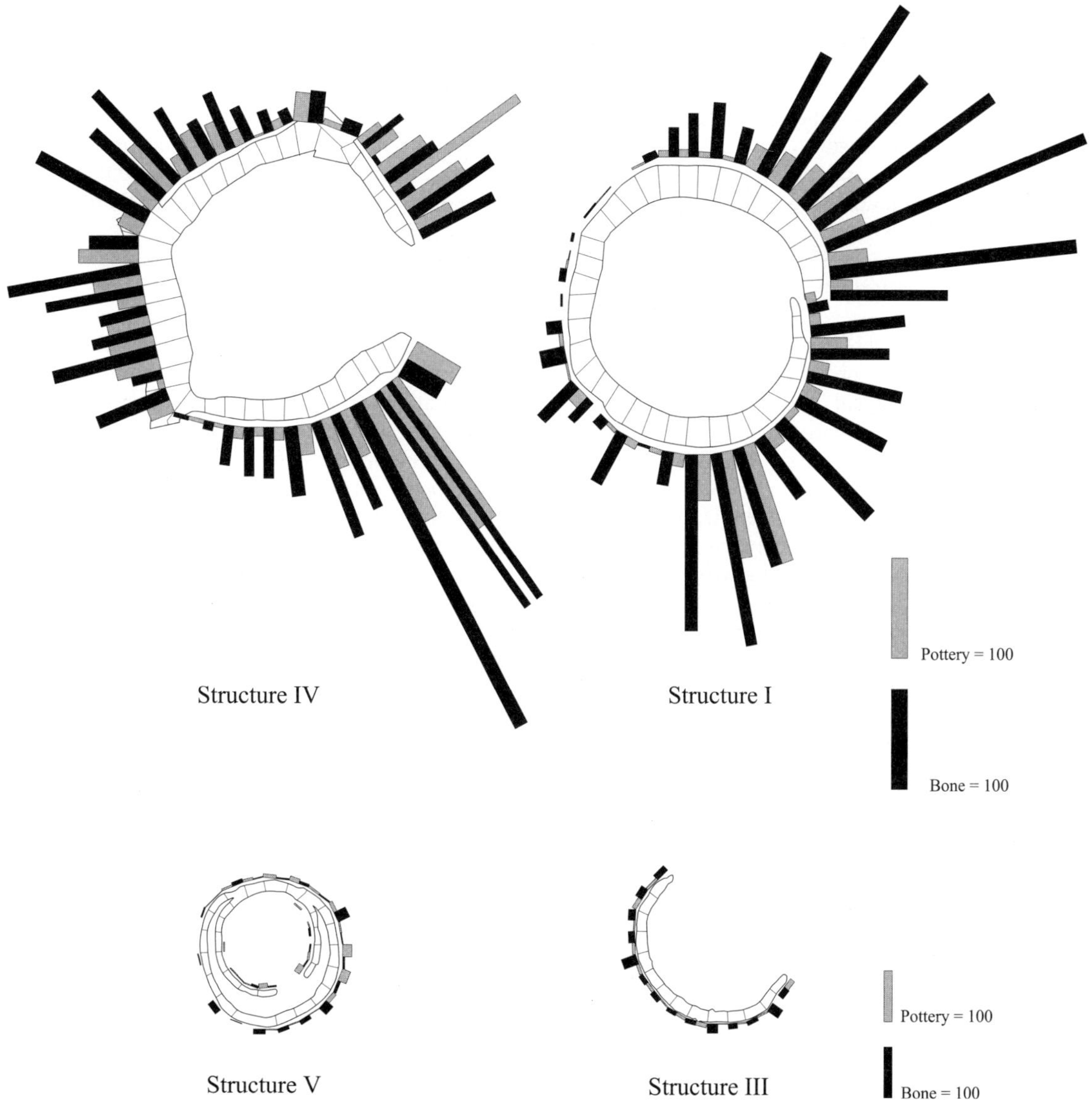

Structure IV   Structure I

Pottery = 100

Bone = 100

Structure V   Structure III

Pottery = 100

Bone = 100

Figure 105 Main Structure finds densities plotted by metre segment

	Pot	Bone	Metal	Metalwork debris	Worked stone	Flint	Burnt Flint	Burnt Clay	Stone
Structure I	931	3662	1	20	8	88	105	332	160
Structure IV	1689	3016	9	47	4	38	30	366	72
Structure III	138	403	1	1	0	9	19	20	7
Structure V	132	144	0	1	7	5	16	123	50
Structure II	5	2	0	0	0	0	0	2	0
Structure VI	6	18	0	2	0	1	3	4	2

Table 59 Number of artefacts recovered by Structure

fact its terminals, and that the circuit has in part been ploughed away. A slight, albeit subtle, rise in pottery numbers at the terminals of the inner circuit of Structure V does, however, show a pattern indicative of access-related deposition. Otherwise for that structure, whereas bone is generally higher throughout the south-eastern arc of the outer ring, pottery values are increased on the eastern and northern sectors, being greatest in the mid-east.

Of the two main buildings, deposition around the circuit of Structure I is generally high throughout the eastern half of its gully, with a marked rise along its southern arc where pottery values are greatest (bone is highest along the north-eastern arm). Generally this pattern would seem to reflect two factors: firstly, front/terminal deposition during its lifetime as a building (the situation of ditch F. 37 behind it would have made the western gully almost inaccessible); secondly, dumped deposition across its eastern and southern sides when it was dismantled.

Whereas Structure I's patterning seems straightforward, this is not the case for Structure IV. While again showing eaves-gully terminal 'highs' reflecting ease of access and toss, it is more difficult to explain the relatively high consistent values around its western and north-western sectors. Here, one of two potentially inter-related processes can be envisaged. Upon abandonment of the Ringwork the building may have simply been 'closed', with midden material being backfilled around its circuit (in which case the greater scale of the western perimeter may have been relevant). Alternatively, and more likely, much of this material may relate to the preceding Phase 4 access at this point — the West Central Entrance — and reflect both general discard and deposition within what had been its terminals.

The Ringwork catchment: feature densities and depositional processes

Comparing the recorded artefact densities demonstrates that the Ringwork's circuits saw structured deposition. In a ripple-like manner, densities decrease with distance from the main houses, with Structures I and IV having the greatest values (Table 60; Fig. 106). While densities within the inner circuit F. 2 are generally comparable to those of Structure I, they are still c. 20% less than in the eaves-gully of that building. Reflecting the patterning of the ploughsoil collection, the most significant decrease occurs beyond the line of F. 2, densities within the outer and outworks circuits being c. 45–60% less than those of Structure I.

The sense of 'catchment' within the Ringwork's circuits can be more readily appreciated if densities are compared between only the radial sample units. In Table 61, unlike in Table 60, entranceway-adjacent values are omitted in order to focus on general distribution patterns — the penetration of circuits — and the respective arcs of the north-western outworks are presented individually. Aside from expressing the regular fall-off of finds values from the Ringwork's core, it is also clear how little deposition occurred in the westernmost sector (F. 10) when compared to the main F. 1 circuit. This may reflect some degree of exterior access to the latter, and that the western axes marked the 'outside' of the larger Wardy Hill enclosure system.

As indicated in Table 60, densities within the primary inner circuit on the western axis (F. 37) are directly comparable to that of its later maintained, eastward extent, F. 2. Given that the line of F. 37 was backfilled and superseded, from a basic reading of these figures it could be argued that deposition within F. 2 occurred under similar circumstances and, therefore, only 'early' in its usage (i.e. solely contemporary with F. 37). However, a number of factors must be taken into account concerning the depositional dynamics of the inner Ringwork circuit. Particularly, these include the immediate proximity of Structure I to ditch F. 37, and the fact that the depositional foci around its perimeter would have shifted in relation to the change in residence between Structures I and IV. Otherwise the Phase 2 ditches had much lower artefact densities. Only along the main southern line, F. 27/45, could they be considered in any way substantive, although even here the mean segment density of pottery and bone was, respectively, some 50% and 60% less than that of F. 2.

Mean sherd weight generally varies in inverse relation to artefact density across the Ringwork's circuits. While falling at 9.30g for the inner circuit (F. 2; 9.92g for F. 37), it is lower than in the main building eaves-gullies (generally 11–12.5g), presumably reflecting its greater reworking and subsequent fragmentation away from the buildings. In both the main circuit and outwork ditches it was higher still (13.73g and 17.76g, the latter being an average of individual circuit mean sherd weights ranging from 4.20–38.35g). What this indicates, quite simply, is that while more minor quantities of material were deposited in the outer circuits, their transportation to the Ringwork perimeter was probably by more direct means — placing

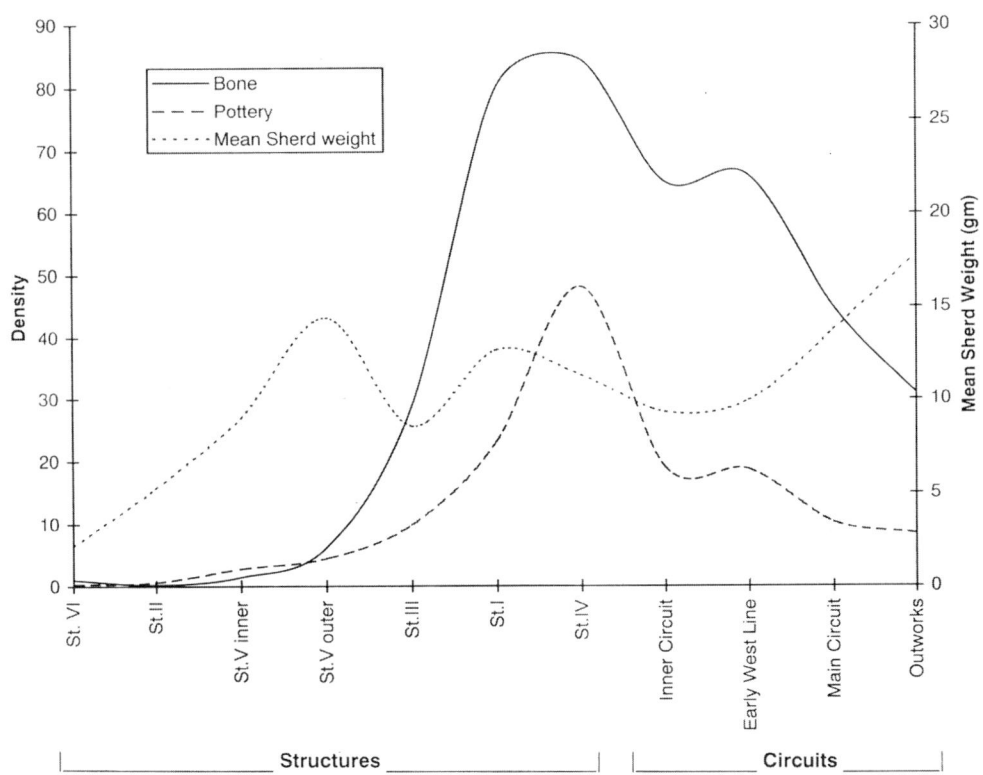

Figure 106 Mean segment finds densities (and mean sherd weights) from main Ditch Circuits and Structures

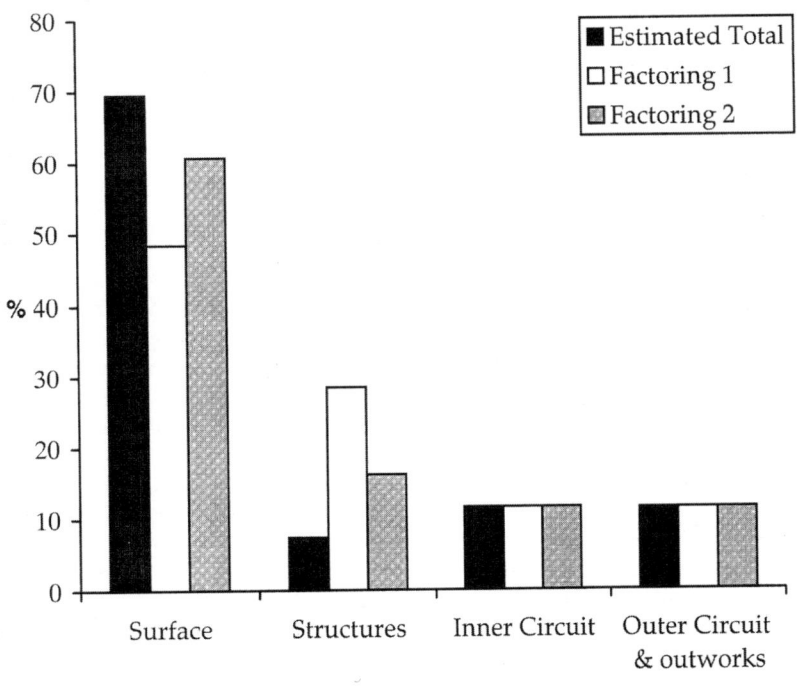

Figure 107 Total finds estimates by Ringwork component

	Structures							Circuits				Test pits
	Str. VI	Str. II	Str. V		Str. III	Str. I	Str. IV	Inner (F. 2)	Early West line (F. 37)	Main (F.1)	Outworks (F. 10–12, 28, 38; excl. Str. IV)	1–4
			Inner	Outer								
Bone no.												
Range	0–5	0–1	0–5	0–25	18–62	0–292	5–363	1–249	12–203	1–326	0–340	33–393
Mean	1.00	0.25	1.46	6.25	28.78	79.86	84.54	65.00	66.08	44.96	30.96	148.2
St. Dev.	1.61	0.46	1.85	6.54	13.19	82.19	77.41	65.36	74.05	67.56	67.65	166.3
Mean bone weight (g)*	1.50	(13.**)	3.21	6.28	5.87	7.71	6.01	6.18	6.31	12.58	7.36	2.06
Pottery no.												
Range	0–4	0–4	0–12	0–18	0–21	0–124	2–172	1–100	1–51	0–25	0–41	9–46
Mean	0.33	0.625	2.77	4.45	9.86	23.16	48.17	19.05	18.75	10.3	8.46	23.5
St. dev.	0.97	1.41	3.72	5.32	6.01	33.09	46.68	20.21	16.05	7.19	11.35	16.94
Mean sherd weight (g)*	2.17	5.25	9.00	14.40	8.55	12.67	11.3	9.30	9.92	13.73	17.76	4.32
Ratio pottery/bone (by no.)	1/3	2.5/1	1.9/1	1/1.4	1/2.9	1/3.4	1/1.7	1/3.4	1/3.5	1/4.4	1/3.7	1/6.3

Table 60 Main Circuit pottery and bone densities (per 1.00m segment: *NB.* mean sherd and bone weight calculated by feature not segment); ** the bracketed mean bone weight for Structure II must be considered unrepresentative as the population in this instance only consists of two pieces.

	Outworks			Structures		Main circuits	
	F. 10	F. 11	F.12/13	Str. IV	Str. I	F. 2	F. 1
Bone no.							
Range	1–6	10–51	3–172	5–363	0–292	18–219	3–111
Mean	3	27	67	85	80	55	24
Pottery no.							
Range	0–25	0–21	1–38	2–172	0–124	5–72	0–22
Mean	7	7	14	48	23	1	9

Table 61 Mean pottery and bone densities from main Structures (I and IV), and non-building (Structure IV west side) and non-entrance related metre segments from designated sample units from main ditches

or tossing the better parts of vessels by hand — than the more complex processes of re-deposition occurring within the Ringwork's interior.

Although the mean sherd weights of the main buildings (Structures I and IV) are comparable, that of Structure III at 8.55g is low; perhaps the relatively minor scale of its eaves-gully offered less protection for deposited material. However, the same cannot be true for Structure V, the profile of whose gullies was comparable to those of III but whose mean sherd weight was the highest for any building (14.40g for F. 20 alone, with F. 81 being lower).

Similar depositional propensities, although not quite so regular, are apparent in the bone weights, with the outer circuit having the highest overall mean (12.58g; Davis, in Chapter 3, also comments upon the occurrence of larger bone within the outer perimeter). With the Outworks having somewhat surprising low weights, the next highest value is that in the Structure I gully (771g). However, in this case, the values for Structure IV are also relatively low, with the means for both the outer gully of Structure V and the F. 2 circuit being slightly higher (6.01 *vs.* 6.28 and 6.18g respectively). Nevertheless, while both the mean sherd and bone weights for Structures I, IV and V (outer gully only) can be considered generally comparable, IV is consistently the lowest. If we read greater mean artefact weight as reflective of 'more primary' acts of deposition, then this may indicate that both the outer gully of Structure V and much of the circuit of Structure I became overlain by later midden deposits, whose larger component items — possibly generated in part by the Structure IV occupation — became caught in the upper profiles of their eaves-gullies. Either Structure III was not subject to this dynamic or the infilling of its gully, for whatever reason, did not permit the trapping of these midden deposits.

	Structures							Inner Circuit	Test Pits
	Str. VI	Str. II	Str. V Inner	Str. V Outer	Str. III	Str. I	Str. IV	(F. 2)	1–4
Capacity (m)	0.035	0.02	0.03	0.07	0.06	0.32	0.58	1.02	0.30
Bone no.									
Mean	1	0.25	1.46	6.25	28.78	79.86	84.54	65	148
Factored									(54.81)
Mean	28.65	16.03	44.51	95.13	504.91	249.56	146.26	63.73	493.30 (180.87)
Pottery no.									
Mean	0.33	0.625	2.77	4.45	9.86	23.16	48.17	19.05	23.5
Factored									(15.66)
Mean	9.46	40.06	84.45	67.73	172.98	72.38	83.34	18.68	78.34 (51.68)

Table 62 Metre segment artefact densities factored to give estimates of finds capacity per cubic metre
The bracketed numbers in the Test Pit column indicate a second stage of factoring to compensate for possible plough reduction. This would first involve reducing the pottery density by a third to account for their lower mean sherd weight when compared to that of Structures I, III–V and F. 2 (10.87g av. mean). Giving a sherd density of 15.66 per metre (51.68 per m), using the same reduction factor the bone density would then be 98.8 pieces per metre (326.04 m). It still, however, remains unaccountably high and occurs at a ratio to 6.3/1 to the pottery. If taking the more representative 1/3.5 pottery-to-bone ratio (see Table 60), then from a figure of 15.66 sherds a corresponding bone density of 54.81 pieces per metre could be estimated (180.87m). From these more conservative figures the mid-Ringwork interior midden would have an estimated population of more than 8221.5 sherds and 28,775.25 bones (not including midden-marginal values). In other words, the numbers are still substantial. This second factor reduction of the test pit figures means the ground surface pottery densities would no longer be comparable to any of the main structures, and its value would instead fall between Structures II and V (the bone density falling between Structures V and VI: *i.e.* not comparable to the main buildings).

Relative frequencies: modelling abandonment

As indicated in Table 60 the ratio of pottery to bone generally varied from 1/3–4.4 (by number). However, Structures IV and V and the 'early' southern line (F. 27 and 45) have considerably higher relative pottery densities. In the case of the latter, it is difficult to establish much sense of any mean ratio for the 'early'-phase features. Certainly when compared to the western axis (F. 37) and Structure I (though this is probably distorted by midden processes), it would seem to indicate a higher pottery fraction.

Of the later high pottery/bone ratios, the highest relate to Structure V. Although this might indicate a direct depositional relationship with Structure IV, its densities are so low that little can be said of their cause (*e.g.* this could alternatively suggest a non-residential function). In the instance of the final 'great' house, Structure IV, this figure is attributable to a high density of pottery, as its mean bone density is roughly comparable to its 'sister building' Structure I (respectively 84 and 80 pieces per metre segment); the mean density of pottery — 48 *vs.* 23 pieces — is more than 50% greater. How do we account for this?

At this juncture the 'terminal' status of this building becomes relevant, and its abandonment procedures must be conceptualised. While leaving the site and 'closing' this building is unlikely to have involved some extraordinary slaughtering of stock *en masse*, it may have entailed sorting its contents to decide what warranted transportation. Discarded items may well have included a range both of common vessels and of those broken pieces that it was always intended to repair (see *e.g.* Hayden and Cannon 1983). The latter may have included damaged 'special' vessels — either stored up in the rafters of the building or discretely tucked away around its perimeter — which had a sherd broken from their rim or whose base had fallen out.

The La Tène-style decorated vessel found in the northern arm of this building's eaves-gully terminal or the Samian base could well have fallen within this category. Only upon the decision to leave the site were intentions of repair finally left unrealised, and the vessels discarded. Aside from the obvious cases of a few specific vessels this proposal is not, however, borne out by the mean sherd weights from the two main buildings, as these are roughly comparable. Intentional vessel discard could still have occurred on abandonment, but only if these were otherwise smashed (with some deliberation) upon their deposition within the gully.

The alternative explanation for the pottery density associated with Structure IV is that, at least at some time during its occupation, its usage differed from of Structure I. Either its residents had a greater number of vessels, or perhaps on occasion it hosted larger group gatherings (*i.e.* people with vessels). The latter argument could be countered by the fact that rates of meat consumption for these two buildings, if used for a roughly comparable span, would seem to have been comparable on the basis of bone representation from their eaves-gullies. However, if the later occupation contributed most of the material within the enclosure's interior middens (including finds dumped in the upper profile of the earlier eaves-gullies) then any 'equivalence' based on bone number is irrelevant: the midden-reflective test-pit densities have the highest representation of bone-to-pottery on the site. This issue has major implications for the interpretation of the site sequence, and will be returned to below.

Reduction dynamics and cubic capacity

In Table 60 no account or compensation was made for the respective scale of features. This seems valid as only portions of the main house gullies could remotely be considered 'full of finds'. Otherwise, their densities would not directly relate to feature capacity — twenty sherds deposited within the inner circuit would equate with the same number in the outer. (This logic, of course, only pertains to direct artefact deposition, whether of primary, secondary or tertiary status. If finds entered a feature through midden dumping — *i.e.* mixed within a soil matrix — then feature-scale would be a more critical factor as artefact densities would relate to fill volume.) It is only in the case of Structure III that feature proportions seem to be a major issue. Although only *c.* 540 finds were recovered from it, potentially this equates to densities comparable to Structures I and IV as its eaves-gully is only approximately a third to a quarter the size of that of the 'great' buildings. If, in addition, its only partial enclosure of the building and its smaller diameter is factored for then it would have an adjusted finds total of *c.* 5050. (Structure V's 'full-circle' gully was of comparable dimensions to that of III, and therefore its densities are truly significantly less.)

Although cubic capacity may therefore not be relevant at the general level of basic inter-feature comparison it must, however, be considered if their densities are to be compared with the ploughsoil finds. The mean values of pottery and bone from the four central test-pits are potentially representative of densities within the midden deposits thought to have extended throughout the central swathe of the Ringwork interior. While the high figure for its bone density, when taken 'raw' (in Table 60), is almost twice that of the two main buildings (I and IV), the mean 23.5 sherd density per metre is comparable to that of both F. 2 and the Structure I ditch (being less than half that for Structure IV). It is, however, inappropriate to compare densities directly between a metre unit of ploughsoil (0.30m) and metre-long ditch segments of diverse depths and profiles. Therefore, in compensation, these figures have been factored in Table 62 as an expression of cubic metre density. From this the ploughsoil/midden densities, at 78 sherds per cubic metre, are no longer directly comparable to that of the F. 2 circuit, but compare instead to the 68–84m mean range of Structures I, IV and V. After factoring the ploughsoil bone density it still has 'rogue' status, being 2–11 times greater than that of those three structures. (It is nevertheless comparable to the factored figure for Structure III — 505 bones per m. Despite having a gully of very minor proportions, this building's cubic metre densities are extraordinarily high; at 173 sherds per m it appears more than twice as rich as that of any other structure.)

If extending over some 525m (the area of the 224+ phosphate core), then the average figures of 148 bones and 23 sherds per metre throughout the midden's core would give a total estimated population of 77,700 bones and 12,337 pieces of pottery. Similar figures are forthcoming if the test-pit contour densities (as shown in Fig. 101) are calculated instead: 79,500 bones and 15,912 sherds. While obviously still no more than a rough estimate, these however are more conservative as they apply to the entire interior of the F. 2 circuit and not the area of the midden core alone.

It could be argued that these figures are still much too high, and do not account for fragmentation wrought by plough damage and the over-representation of the test-pit densities by sieving (Table 62). Yet how much splintering and breakage would occur to bone as a result of later agricultural practice? Larger pieces of pottery would, of course, have fragmented upon impact with the plough, but smaller sherds and most bones would simply move and not break. Also relevant is the sheer quantity of small bone present on the site. This is evident in the bulk samples frequencies (mean bone weight 0.32g) and, for example, the fact that the mean weight of bone within Structure VI is less than that within the test-pits (1.50g *vs.* 2.06g; Table 60). This attests to the fact that the processes of occupation themselves resulted in the reduction of bone down to smaller sizes than those seen in the test-pits. The sieving programme undertaken across preserved floor surfaces at the HAD V enclosure demonstrated that great quantities of small artefacts had been trampled into their matrices (Evans and Hodder forthcoming). Such surface material has clearly been incorporated in the ploughsoil population at Wardy Hill. Therefore, to 'conveniently' factor away much of this background occupation matrix by statistically lowering the test-pit values is probably erroneous.

Modelling artefact populations

While recognising the elusive character of 'totalities' (Evans and Hodder forthcoming), because of the strict sampling procedures adopted in the site's excavation, and the delineated character of its occupation, it is possible to estimate the Ringwork's total artefact populations (Table 63).

By extrapolating from the test-pit densities and the percentage of each ditch circuit excavated, the Ringwork alone would have had a total artefact population in excess of 140,000 pieces of pottery and bone. This figure can only represent an estimate. On one hand, the F. 1 and F. 2 densities are probably somewhat over-estimated as almost all of their respective entrance-adjacent segments were dug, and this must skew their total artefact estimates upwards. Yet, on the other hand, the enclosure's discrete features (*i.e.* pits) and (aside from F. 37) the Phase 2 ditches have not been included. While it is assumed that these various factors together balance each other, the total population can only be considered approximate. This is, nevertheless, a useful measure of the intensity of the Ringwork's occupation. Certainly, given that the surface densities only include the test-pit estimates within the perimeter of the F. 2 circuit, when combined with the figures of the houses/structures and the inner circuit they indicate what proportion of the site's finds were confined within the area of the inner circuit (84%). Yet it is estimated that the Ringwork's main circuit must once have held upwards of 10,000 bones and 2300 sherds. This is a not-inconsiderable figure, and suggests sustained access to the area from 'outside'.

From the estimated total number of finds, while the building eaves-gullies would have produced only 6.5% of the total bone assemblage they accounted for nearly twice that percentage of the site's pottery — 12.5%. On the whole, however, the eaves-gullies/structures would have only represented 7.4% of the total population, as opposed to 69.5% being assigned to general surface finds. Yet by this means house floor deposits are subsumed within the latter figure, and factoring is therefore required to estimate the missing floor spreads. To facilitate this, in the first instance, for the main buildings (I, III, IV, V) the midden-core test-pit densities have been used — 148 bones and 23 sherds per metre — in relation to their floor area alone. For Structures II and VI the overall F. 2 interior

	Recovered		Estimated Total	
	Pottery	*Bone*	*Pottery*	*Bone*
Surface Finds				
Test Pits	110	631		
Fieldwalking	289	311		
Surface Total	399	942	15,912	79,500
Structures				
I (100%)	931	3662		
II (100%)	5	2		
III (100%)	138	403		
IV (100%)	1689	3016		
V (100%)	132	144		
VI (100%)	6	18		
Structures Total	2901	7245	2901	7245
Circuits				
Inner				
F. 2 (25%)	871	2464	3484	9856
F. 37 (28%)	282	879	1007	3139
F. 38 (17%)	99	348	582	2047
Outer				
F.1 (14%)	327	1408	2336	10,057
Outworks				
F. 10 (12%)	34	70	283	583
F. 11 (10%)	22	86	220	860
F. 12 (21%)	102	208	486	990
Circuits Total	1737	5463	8398	27,532

Table 63 Artefact population estimates; percentages of individual ditch circuits excavated shown in brackets. Note that there has been no factoring for plough-induced feature truncation (*i.e.* the north-eastern sector of Structure III) since finds displaced from them have, like those from 'lost' floor and other surfaces, contributed to the ploughsoil numbers.

density mean of 38.5 bones and 7.7 pot per metre has been applied (Table 64: factoring 1). These adjusted figures significantly alter the total artefact representation of the buildings — up to 28.5% — and accordingly reduce the generic surface proportion to 48.4%. A shortcoming of such factoring exercises with regard to the estimation of overall building totals is their extrapolation from mean surface densities. Working from site-wide averages, the higher frequency of pottery within (for example) the eaves-gully of Structure IV becomes 'smoothed' by such generalised surface calculations.

Because topsoil distributions are rarely interrogated in such detail, it is difficult to establish a basis for comparing total building finds numbers. Regionally, only the HAD V compound on the Upper Delphs provides an appropriate dataset (Evans and Hodder forthcoming). There, due to alluvial covering in the wake of abandonment, all floor surfaces were preserved. Superficially at least, its building artefact densities are remarkably close to the Ringwork's. Its great roundhouse (Building 4), which essentially matches the size of Structures I and IV, remarkably enough produced *c.* 15,500 artefacts in total — almost exactly mirroring the numbers of pot and bone (alone) postulated for the two main Wardy Hill buildings. Similarly its two 'lesser' round buildings, 6 and 7, respectively generated *c.* 2070 and 4630 finds. This is obviously comparable to the 3893 and 2995 totals proposed for Structures III and V respectively. (The one comparable non-residential ancillary structure at HAD V — Building 5, a 'half-circle' animal pen — produced only 116 finds, substantially less than Structures II and VI at Wardy Hill.)

Yet while the main building totals at Haddenham seem roughly comparable to those at Wardy Hill, there are marked differences between the ratio of their eaves-gully to surface finds. Based on the application of the midden density (factoring 1), 70–90% of the respective building totals at Wardy Hill would be floor-generated whereas at Haddenham this ratio is much lower (37–49% floor-derivation). It is difficult to know how to view these alongside each other. In each of the respective classes of buildings at Haddenham the surrounding eaves-gullies are substantially larger than their Wardy Hill counterparts, and it could be the case that a higher proportion of the surface material ended up in their surrounding ditches. Alternatively, the midden-based estimation of the Wardy Hill floor densities may simply be too high. If applying a figure of 45% gully-to-floor totals then the buildings at Wardy Hill would generate *c.* 11% of the Ringwork's total finds, with the generic surface deposits representing *c.* 66% of the site total (Fig. 107). Yet, apart from the cases of Structures II and VI (generating totals of 10 and 35 finds respectively), these figures seem too low: 6660 and 6822

Category	Estimated Total (Unfactored) No.	%	Surface Adjusted Total (Factoring 1) No.	%	Surface Adjusted Total (Factoring 2) No.	%
Surface	95,412	69.5	66,431	48.4	88,360	60.7
Structures						
I	4593		15,468		9298	
II	7		297		10	
III	541		3893		1993	
IV	4705		15,580		9410	
V	276		2995		1452	
VI	24		894		35	
Total	10,146	7.4	39,127	28.5	22,198	16.2
Inner Circuit F.2 and 38	15,969	11.6	15,969	11.6	15,969	11.6
Outer Circuits F. 1 and Outworks	15,815	11.5	15,815	11.5	15,815	11.5

Table 64 Breakdown of the site's estimated 'total' pottery and bone assemblage by Ringwork component, showing different factoring procedures to account for 'missing' floor proportion: (1) midden-density calculation; (2) according to 74 finds per metre figure (*c.f.* Table 62; excludes F. 37).

finds respectively for Structures I and IV, whose buildings must, after all, have been broadly comparable to Building 4 at HAD V with its 15,506 artefacts. Moreover, this approach seems inappropriately 'mechanical', as there is no necessary reason to suppose any direct relationship between floor and eaves-gully densities.

In another attempt at factoring, the house-floor densities from the main round buildings at Haddenham have simply been averaged. Producing a mean of 74 finds per square metre, in Table 64 (factoring 2) this has then been applied to the main Wardy Hill buildings (Structures I, III–V), with Structures II and VI retaining their low eaves-gully-to-'floor' ratio (these structures are unlikely to have had floors as such). This generates a much more 'reasonable' suite of figures suggesting that the buildings held *c*. 16% of the site's pottery and bone population, with general surface finds accounting for *c*. 61% (Fig. 107). Whilst admittedly involving a substantial element of subjective appraisal, these 'second' factoring figures are considered the most representative.

It should be noted that in none of the above analyses has any adjustment been made for the probable loss of most of the ditch circuit of Structure III. Theoretically, this should result in a ring of higher ploughsoil densities encircling the projected diameter of its 'half' gully (and would affect the estimation of its floor-area finds). Based on calculation of the potential scale of its loss, this could add as many as 4500 finds to the building totals — taking its final overall site representation to 19.4%, and accordingly reducing the generic ploughsoil value to 57.4%. Of course, if eaves-gully 'loss' figures in this range are at all accurate, they would be sufficient to pull the ploughsoil representation of the midden spread further south beyond its true extent.

IV. Chemical signatures
(Figs 108–10; Table 65)

As has been mentioned, upon machine-stripping but prior to excavation a 1350m swathe across the central portion of the enclosure was subject to intense magnetic susceptibility survey by A. Challands (5310 readings on a 0.5m interval; Fig. 108). With a range of 3–53ms units at this depth, unlike in the topsoil survey, at least some of the buildings clearly register. While only the eastern terminals of the eaves-gully of Structure IV and the eastern arc of V show, the complete excavated circuits of Structure I and III are apparent (the former registering much more strongly along its eastern and southern sectors). With its very slight gully, Structure II produced no obvious trace.

While isolated 'highs' occur within the buildings' interior, there are no indications of (for example) hearth locations from the plots. (The higher-value cluster in the eastern centre of Structure IV probably relates to subsidence along the backfilled ditch F. 37, whose line otherwise is only visible south of that building.) Of the other Ringwork ditches aside from F. 37, the western arc of the main circuit shows very clearly, especially at its northern terminal. While the line of F. 38 is only very weak, the fact that it cannot be distinguished at all over its southernmost *c*. 4.00m within the plot could confirm that this length had been backfilled on the establishment of a new western entranceway across the line of F. 1. The complex ditch junction in the northwest corner of the plot (Fig. 108.E) — where Structure IV conjoins with the outwork ditches — clearly registers as an area of intense activity. While correlating with the south-eastern end of the moderate high-value swathe extending throughout the north-western outworks visible is the topsoil survey, this also corresponds to an area of high artefact density and suggests that 'something' was clearly happening there. The fact that the narrow portion of ditch F. 12 (F. 152 re-cut north of the F. 1 terminal) does not really register at all could equally confirm that it also had been backfilled in connection with 'late' access at this point — the West Central Entrance.

The plots certainly indicate that there are no area-wide, building-specific magnetic susceptibility 'signatures'. No circle, for example, is apparent to complement or complete the southern half-gully of Structure III, and essentially only the gullies register. Given

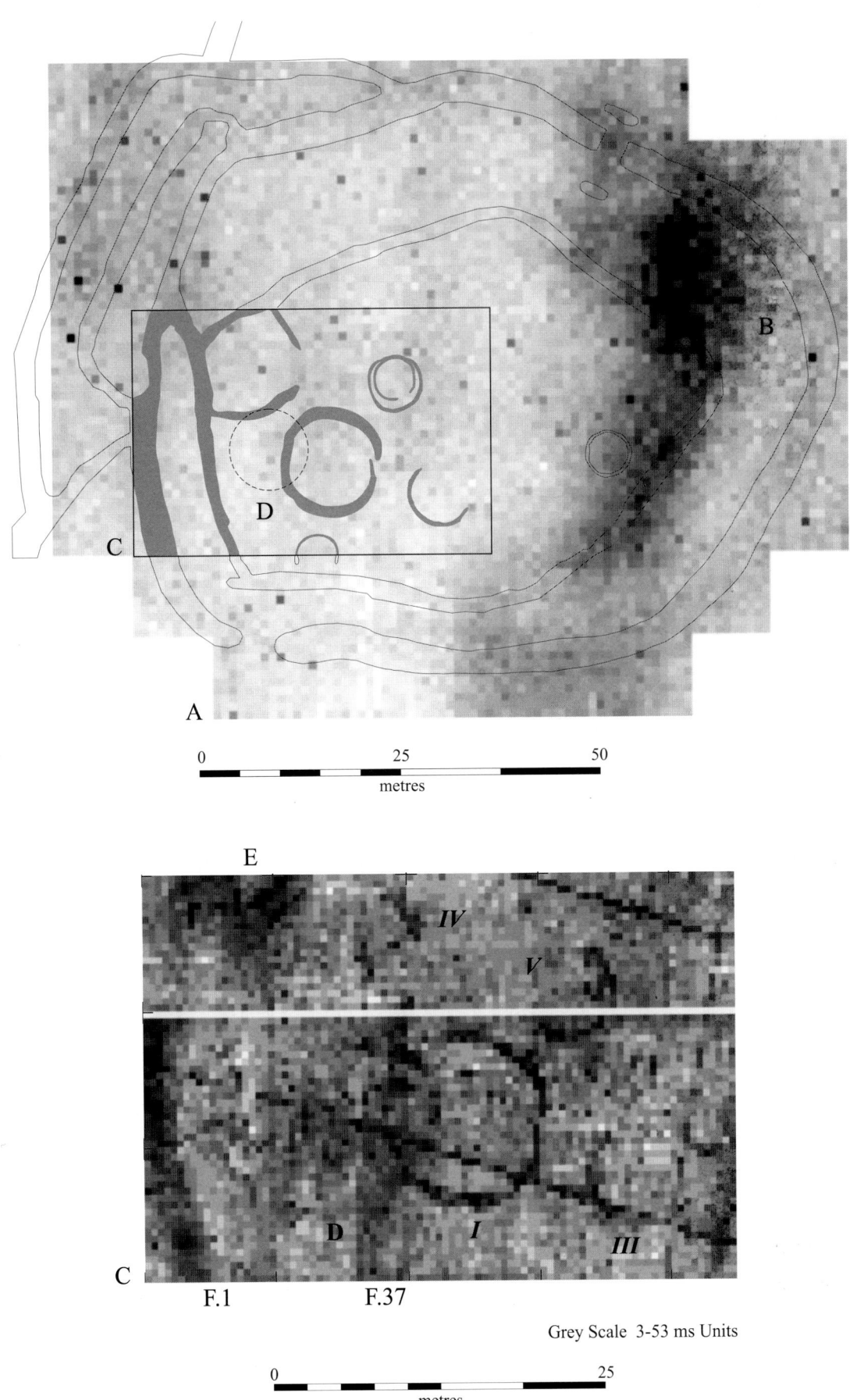

Figure 108 Magnetic susceptibility survey results: surface survey (top); bottom (Area 'C') shows detailed plot of stripped surface

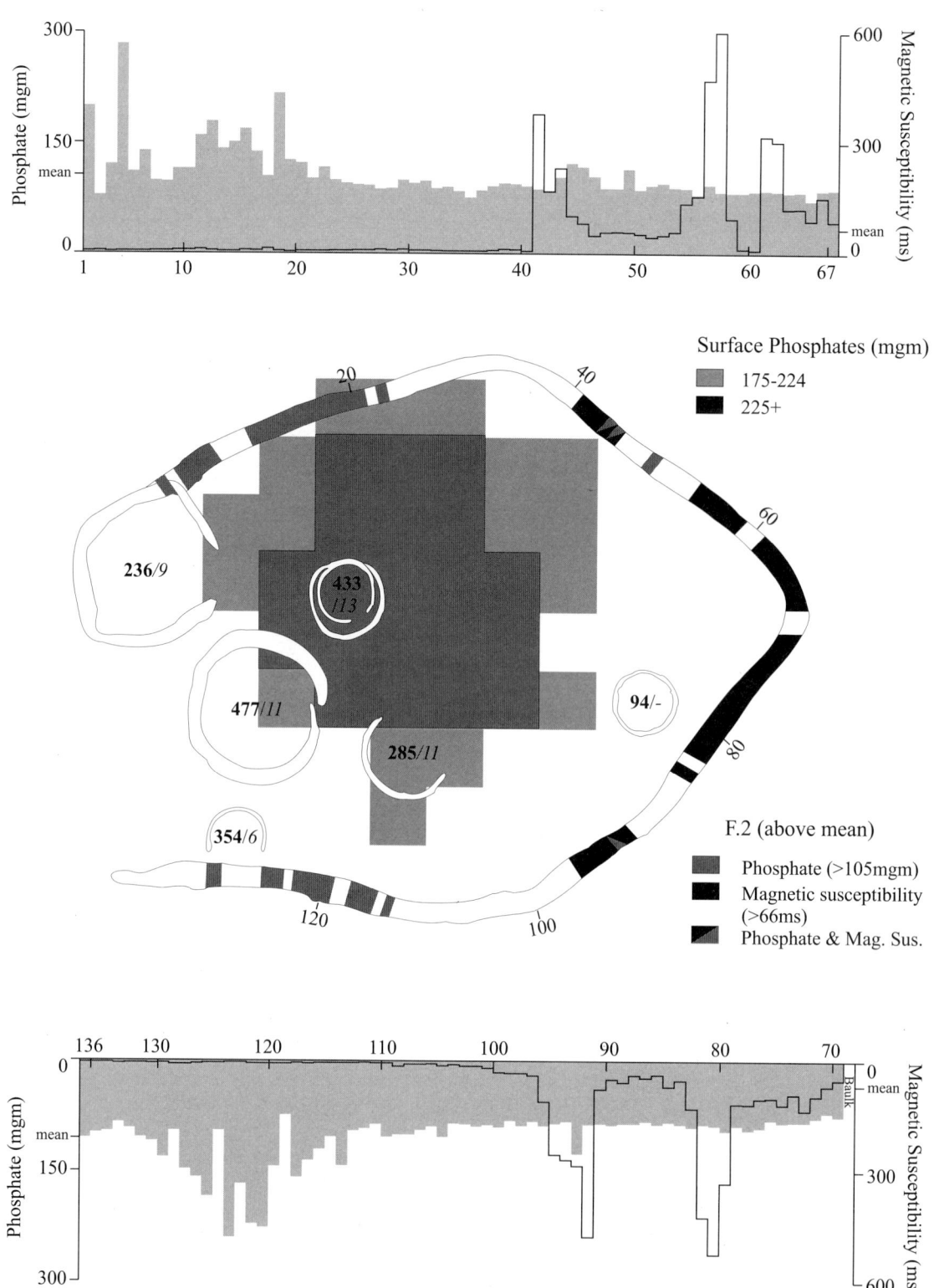

Figure 109 'Chained' phosphate and magnetic susceptibility values around Inner Circuit compared to surface results

this, the fact that a *c.* 10.00m diameter high-value circle appears to overlap the western side of Structure I is something of an anomaly, and could even suggest the location of a 'missed' structure (Fig. 108D).

'Chained' phosphate readings were taken from the enclosure's buildings, with samples collected on a metre interval around their eaves-gullies; the same collection policy was also applied to the Ringwork's inner circuit F. 2 (Table 65). Taking the mean values of their respective lengths, the structures rank in descending order as follows: I, V, II, III, IV, VI. Their values seem to relate directly to the high core (ploughsoil) readings that are thought to attest to the location of middens (Fig. 109). Structures I and V, falling within the core area proper, have

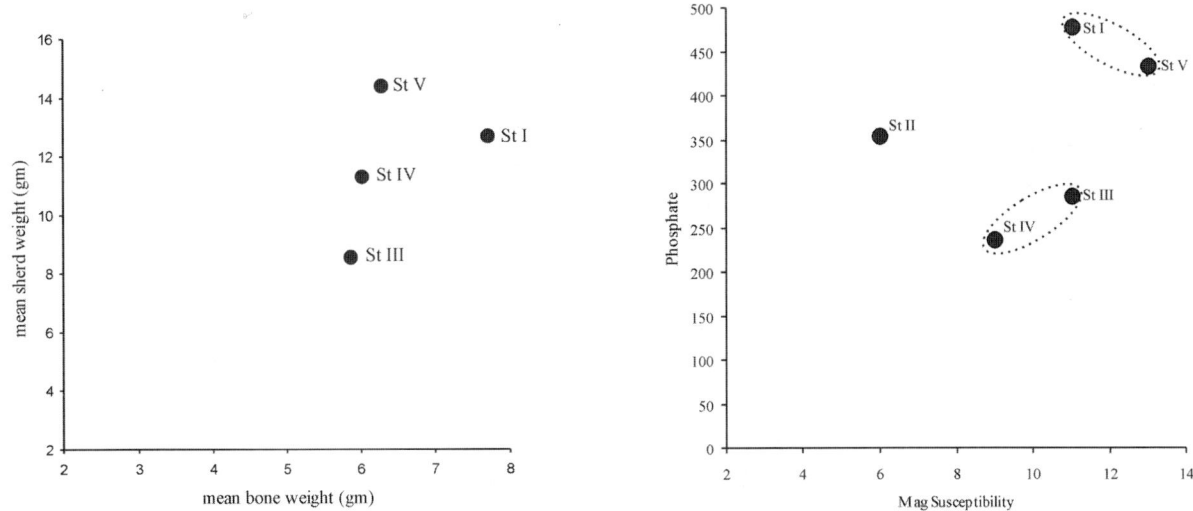

Figure 110 Plotting of Structures by (left) mean bone/sherd weight and (right) phosphate/magnetic susceptibility values ('chained' survey)

	Str. I F. 6	Str. II F. 23/24	Str. III F. 21	Str. IV F. 25/26	Str. V F. 20	Str. VI F. 22	Inner Circuit F. 2
Phosphate							
Range	272–700	321–75	206–372	72–527	258–574	81–113	71–284
Mean	*477*	*354*	*285*	*236*	*433*	*94*	*106*
St. Dev.	92	20	61	115	88	9	36
Count	35	7	16	33	20	18	136
Magnetic susceptibility							
Range	4–30	4–8	5–35	4–48	5–50	-	5–601
Mean	*11*	*6*	*11*	*9*	*13*	-	*67*
St. Dev.	5	1	6	5	10	-	113
Count	202	16	45	215	51	-	134

Table 65 Mean phosphate and magnetic susceptibility values from Structures and Inner Circuit

comparable mean values greater than 400, whereas Structures III and IV, situated on its margins, fall between 200–300. However, the interim status of Structure II is noteworthy. With a mean of 354, this seems unaccountably high given its slight character and low artefact density. Thought to have had a non-residential function, it lies immediately adjacent to the Ringwork's south-western entrances (well beyond the area of high ploughsoil phosphate levels) and may have related to the control of access. Obviously not deriving from midden deposits, the high phosphate levels associated with this structure could relate either to the movement of animals into the enclosure at this point (*e.g.* 'path' access) or to the actual penning of animals. Although perhaps far-fetched given its location, screened human defecation would offer another possibility (*e.g.* a toilet).

With a mean of 106, the F. 2 metre-'chained' readings are generally substantially lower than the mean building values. Nevertheless, their patterning shows a close co-relationship with the enclosure's occupation *per se*, as almost all of the consistently higher-than-mean readings fall within the western third of the ditch's arms adjacent to the buildings. When coupled with the evidence of accompanying artefact densities around the inner circuit (Fig. 103), the F. 2 phosphate plots are obviously sensitive to the settlement structures/foci it enclosed. Their seemingly direct relationship would confirm that no upcast bank lay within that ditch, allowing a one-to-one interaction between deposition within it and interior activities. For example, Structure VI in the east of the enclosure (the probable haystack, having the lowest phosphate levels of any structure) has no corresponding peak in the neighbouring length of F. 2. In fact, the only potentially significant 'high' throughout the east half of its circuit is that immediately aligned with the Watergate entrance. This also showed a corresponding increase in the magnetic susceptibility values, and could therefore suggest specific entrance-related enhancement. However, with a mean of 67ms unit — markedly higher than the 6–13 values from the structures — all the higher-than-mean readings in the case of the magnetic susceptibility 'chain' come from the eastern third of the enclosure. Clearly not relating to the enclosure's buildings, it becomes difficult to evaluate whether any of these relate to the Ringwork's occupation as such, or if they only reflect other patterns of usage. On the one hand, these eastern 'highs' must reflect the pull of material from the burnt flint mound into the ditches. However, *in situ* scorching was apparent in the upper fills of the F. 2 circuit in this area. Apparently 'structureless' — inasmuch as burnt elements could not be distinguished, only the orange scorching of the fills' clays — this must attest to later agricultural burning (*i.e.* 'root/pit' fires) and not to catastrophic damage to the Ringwork's defences. Given this, the only localised 'highs' within F. 2 that might otherwise be relevant are the cluster at the western end of the southern circuit. Corresponding with where Murphy has recognised some of the highest densities of plant macrofossils as occurring (and with the recovery of fishbone in this sector), this could suggest either the location of an early building relating to ditches F. 52 and 57 and/or the deposition of burnt household refuse and possibly waste from crop-processing.

There is only limited variability in the means of the main structures' magnetic susceptibility values if their eaves-gullies are compared alone, which rank in descending order: V, I/III, IV and II (VI being excluded from the stripped surface survey). Aside from the fact that Structure II has such a low register relative to its phosphate mean, in general the patterning is not unlike that for the phosphate inasmuch as it still seems essentially to reflect proximity to the building cluster core. While it may be relevant that Structure V appears to have seen more burning than I (and more than a third more than IV), other factors may have contributed. For example, the shallowness of Structure V's gully implies that primary activity (*e.g.* dumping of smouldering materials) may have been registered more directly than for the more robustly-ditched buildings. Equally, the greater proximity of its building's threshold to the gully could have resulted in a more direct reflection of depositional activity (*e.g.* hearth dumps and sweepings).

In Figure 110 the mean values are plotted for the structures' chained magnetic susceptibility and phosphate readings. In contrast to Figure 104 they suggest a different basis for 'pairing', or at least for inter-relationship, with I/V and III/IV having the greatest affinity. (While the plot of II confirms its high phosphate level, comparison cannot be made with Structure VI as it lay outside the area of the detailed magnetic susceptibility survey.) What is most interesting in terms of this pattern are the 'diagonal axes' of these apparent relations. Dealing with remnant chemical traces, however, this may not so much reflect building affinities as the structuring of later activities, particularly the location of the postulated midden. Largely generated by the terminal Structure IV occupation, while deposited in front of that building, it may not have extended as far south as Structure III. (A similar argument has been previously proposed for its southern 'distortion', based on the potential surface over-representation of that building due to the ploughing-out of its eaves-gully.) It warrants mention that, although certainly not a matter of 'pairing' as opposed to an *ordering*, the mean sherd and bone weight of these four structures could also be enlisted to support this interpretation. In both categories, Structures V (outer gully) and I variously have the greatest values, followed by Structures IV and III in descending order.

V. Transgressing circuits
(Fig. 111)

Artefactual paths
So far this discussion of the site's various distributions has largely been confined to articulation of the 'known': how the Ringwork's circuits structured depositional practices. There is, however, one type of distribution that clearly cross-cuts its circuits: the wheelmade ceramics extending across the line of the western outworks (Fig. 111). Directly corresponding with the axis of higher-than-mean pottery features values, discussed above, this is specifically because their distribution transgresses the concentric boundary system that it warrants inclusion at this point.

Generally the distribution of the wheelmade wares is restricted to the western third of the site, and across its central south-east portion none occur within the primary Ringwork phase features (the one sherd in F. 37 probably derives from the F. 148 re-cut). Focusing upon Structure IV, they occur within pits F. 32 and F. 33 cutting Structure I (see *Building types and inter-relationships*, below, concerning their lower frequencies in Structures I, III and V). Equally, whereas within the south-western terminal of the inner F. 2 circuit no wheelmade sherds were present within the area of the primary Landward Entrance, they occur north-west of this point in the F. 1 circuit — in the area of secondary western access.

The aligned occurrence of this material along the south-west to north-east axis of Structure IV, particularly their presence in the outworks west of that building (in F. 10–12), could suggest one of two interpretations. First, that this marks the approach to the Phase 4 West Central Entrance and, as a result, that material caught up in surface spreads there has later weathered into the outwork ditches along this axis. The second would see this as attesting to a terminal route of *transgression* across the line of the enclosure's defensive outworks, and perhaps that the site's defensive perimeter had become redundant (*i.e.* was regularly progressed through). The very fact that Structure IV was set 'hard' against the inner circuit, and presumably immediately beside the inner rampart, could also support a decline or change within the site's defensive status. (That wheelmade sherds however also occur in F. 83 and 96 — respectively a pit and ditch cut by the outermost of the outworks' circuits — could indicate that the establishment of that ditch line was a late event. Alternatively, the latter stratigraphic relationships may just relate to prolonged maintenance of that ditch, and what this distribution shows could be no more than a north-western focus to Late Iron Age settlement activities.)

Comparison of the distribution of wheelmade wares between excavated contexts and surface collection indicate that, while they overlap in the vicinity of the four main structures, the fieldwalking material extends further throughout the central-southern portion of the Ringwork's interior. Possibly reflecting the focus of 'late' patterns of movement and surface deposition, it is equally important to note where it did *not* occur: across the outworks axis and in the central core of the postulated midden zone beside Structure V. In relation to the latter, as will be discussed below, this could be interpreted as indicating that these dense surface deposits had started to accumulate prior to the Ringwork's terminal usage.

The distribution of the few early Roman wares recovered is similarly concentrated within the area of Structure IV. Here, however, they occur only in the building's southern circuit (and the southern end of its western side); a sherd also occurs within the area of the northern terminal of the Phase 4 West Central Entrance. Otherwise, apart from two isolated occurrences in F. 1 (and the 'rogue' Samian in Structure III), the only other piece is from the western portion of the inner circuit, by its blocking of the Landward Entrance. In short, there is a close correspondence between the wheelmade Iron Age wares and where the early Roman ceramics occur. This does not, however, explain the latter's distribution along only the southern side of Structure IV, and not the remainder of its circuit. Although greater complication must be suspected, from this it could be argued that its deposition occurred in opposition to the La Tène decorated vessel in the north-eastern length of this building's gully: certainly it was discrete from it. The latter, of course, must have been curated if it entered the ground at approximately the same time as the Early Roman pottery.

By comparison with the excavated contexts, the distribution of the Roman pottery found in the fieldwalking collections is dispersed with the only consistent 'spread' being in front of Structure IV, from where it extends south to Structures I and III and into the area of the secondary western entrance.

Occupation dynamics
These extended analyses are justified by the basic insights that finds distributions provide into the site's occupation dynamics. Whilst by necessity providing open-ended results, far too often the information locked in such datasets is left uninterrogated. Without it we are left with only a sequence-based logic of building succession, which seems an inadequate response to the complicated (and broader) matrices of occupation and visitation. If for no other reason than that it leaves so much data unmobilised, the processes and practices of daily life — cross-cut by the 'exceptional' — simply cannot be fully accounted for through a 'building block' approach.

Estimating the site's total artefact population provides a useful gauge in relation to other sites. Unfortunately, too few sites have been excavated in such a manner as to provide direct comparisons. Again, however, the extraordinary preservation of the HAD V enclosure does offer some reference potential here. With some 45,000 finds recovered, it can be estimated that its total population may have been in the region of 60,000 pieces. While admittedly with a much smaller compound area (c. 40% smaller than the Ringwork's interior), with seven buildings (although only one 'great' house) in three phases the intensity of its occupation is comparable. Given that Wardy Hill evidently saw some 2.3 times more finds (total estimate), this could be enlisted to suggest that it included something other than just domestic occupation *per se* — the finds' densities seem too great just for daily living. (Even if we were to add a second 'great' house occupation to the estimated HAD V total, or an extra c. 20,000 items, it would still be substantially less than the estimated Ringwork total by some 40,000 finds — a typical compound's total finds of the period.) After trying to estimate the ratio of the site's house finds to generic surface finds, the key issue is accounting for the some 80,000 (c. 61%) pieces finally assigned to the latter category. While only an issue because of the current excavation's ploughsoil sampling programme, in many respects the site's interpretation turns upon it.

As modelled from the surface phosphate levels (and generally corroborated with the core test-pit finds densities) the area of the postulated Ringwork-interior midden sealed, or at least overlapped in part, Structures I and V. It is, therefore, only reasonable to assume that it was broadly contemporary with the terminal Structure IV occupation (Phase 4–5). Yet this need not imply that it did not originate earlier in the sequence. Some buildings may have been dismantled before others and their 'footprints' given over to refuse disposal. Equally, smaller refuse heaps could have built up alongside still-functioning structures whose 'piles' were later incorporated into what seems to have been a 'communal' midden in front of Structure IV. Regardless of its precise relationship with regard to buildings, what is important is the very existence of this otherwise 'lost' feature. From its putative scale, what warrants emphasis is its location in the core of the occupation area. As at the contemporary HAD V enclosure (Evans and Hodder forthcoming; Evans 1997a) and the Later Bronze Age occupation at Runnymede Bridge (Needham and Sorensen 1988; Needham and Spence 1997) this indicates a high tolerance of refuse alongside settlement activities, and shows that it was not necessarily destined to be carted off for agricultural purposes (*cf.* Crowther's midden models in Pryor and French 1985 and Crowther 1983). Given this, 'midden' may be too mechanical or weighted a term to apply to these deposits and 'spread' more appropriate, implying as it does a cumulative matrix of occupation and dumping. Nevertheless, that its phosphate values do not continue into the central floor area of either of the two main buildings suggests that it reflects more than just ploughed-out floor surfaces and that, despite *caveats*, it does seem to have extended across the front of Structure IV. Ultimately, a vast quantity of material (relative to its eaves-gully/house signatures) seems bound up in these deposits, and the crucial issue is determining what practices account for its accumulation. Evidently largely generated by the final phases of the Ringwork's usage, is it just a matter of intense occupation or does it attest to extra-residential group gathering?

VI. Building types and inter-relationships
(Figs 112–15)
When compared to other settlements of the period in the region the layout of the Wardy Hill compound seems relatively 'pristine': there is no overlapping of its buildings and it lacks the organic intensity of such sites as Little Thetford, Hurst Lane or Fengate, Cats Water (Pryor 1984). It should therefore provide ideal circumstances to investigate the inter-relationship between main buildings and potentially ancillary structures — the 'modular compounding' of household space (see Clarke 1972, Parker Pearson and Richards 1994 and Evans and Hodder forthcoming for further discussion). Yet, due to plough damage, the site's round buildings were poorly preserved and offer few structural details. When compared, for example, to those in the HAD V compound they lack any floor surfaces, and even accompanying post-holes. As a result, since they are represented only by their eaves-gullies this is not an appropriate site to problematise

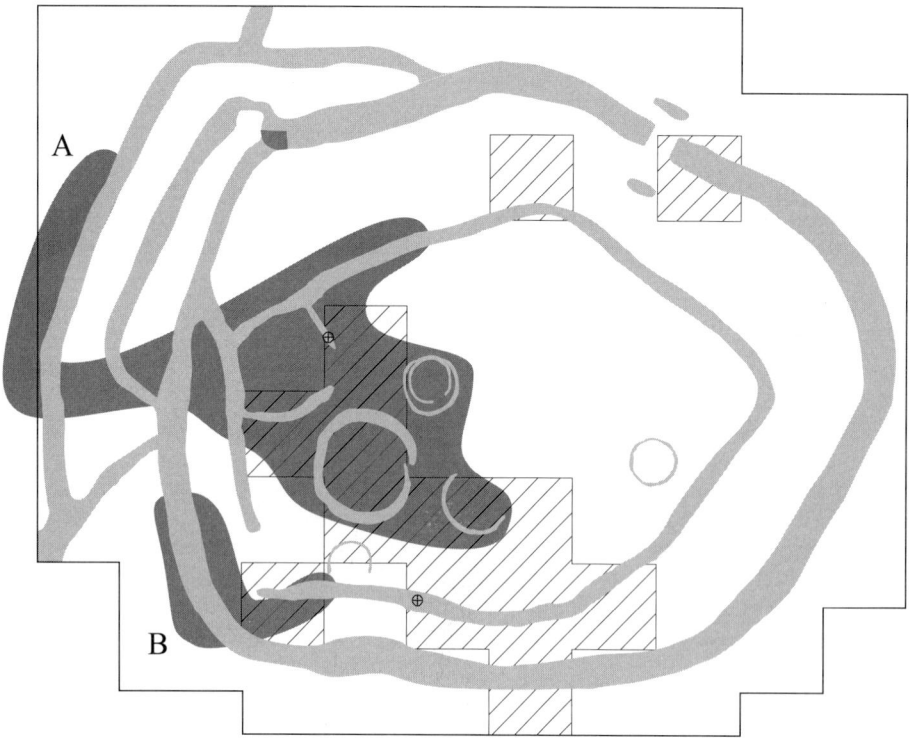

⊕ La Tene decorated Vessel

Distributions of wheel-made pottery (as excavated)

Fieldwalking distributions of wheel-made pottery

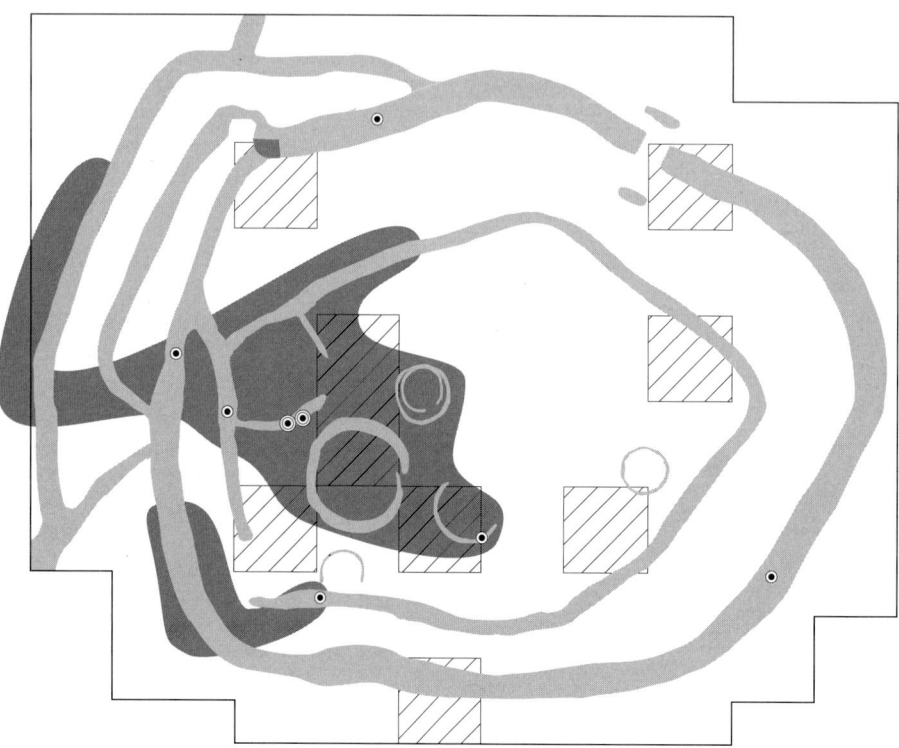

⊙ Roman Pottery

Fieldwalking distributions of Roman pottery

Figure 111 Distribution of wheelmade Iron Age wares (top) and Roman pottery (bottom) compared with ploughsoil distributions

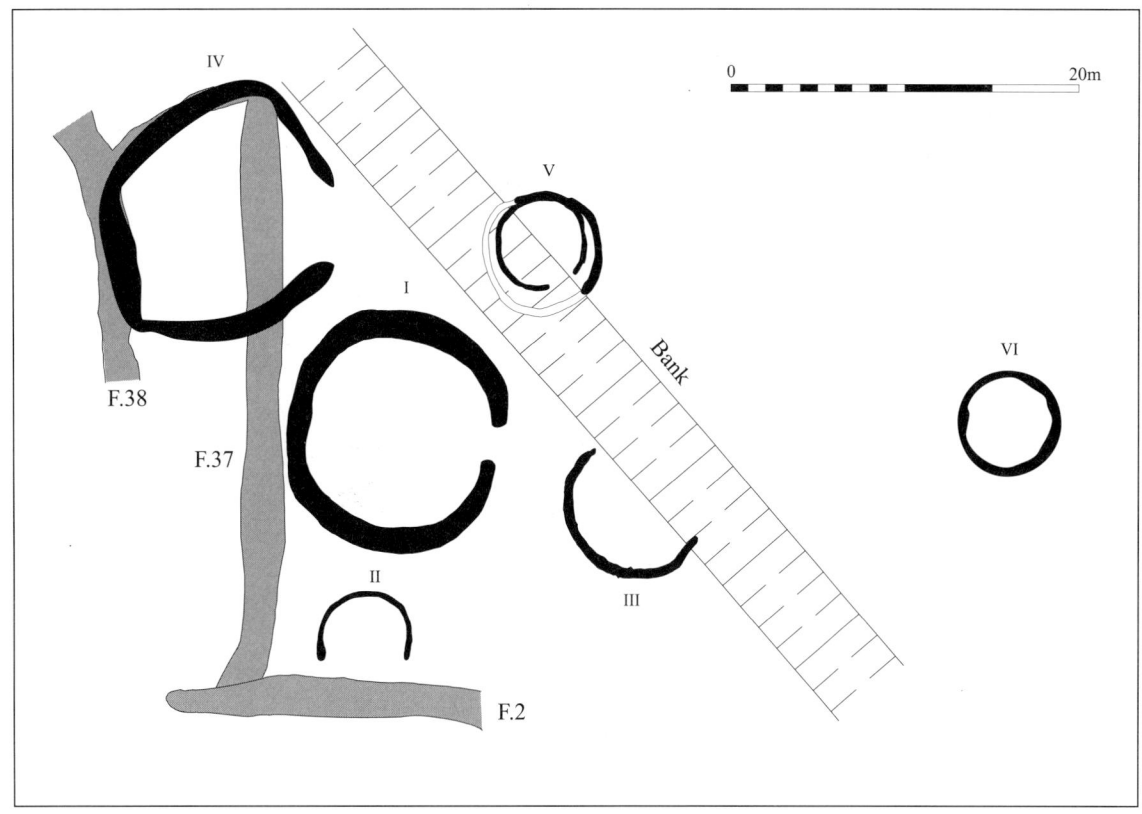

Figure 112 Ringwork interior: constraints upon building location

the character of the Iron Age roundhouse. Rather it/they must be treated as an assumed or normative entity – a 'building block' of Iron Age settlement.

The planforms of the site's building gullies show great variability. Two (Structures II and III) were half-circular in plan. Given its ditch-side situation the smaller of these, Structure II located adjacent to the Landward Entrance, could never have described a complete circle. For reasons already outlined, it cannot have been any kind of house. This does not seem to have been the case for Structure III, and its 'C'-shape is attributable to the fact that the remainder of its circuit must have continued up over the diagonal-aligned Period I bank (Fig. 112).

This putative bank-line also seems to have influenced the layout of the other three structures in this portion of the Ringwork, I, IV and V. The construction sequence of the latter is the most complex of any on the site. Possibly reflective of its central location within the Ringwork, certainly this contrasts with the fact that it had the lowest number of finds and artefact density of any of the four buildings *per se*. As shown in Figure 113, it evidently started as a 'half-circle' open to the south-west. Its original form mirrored Structure III and, like it, the remainder of its gully (and floors) must have continued upon the flanks of the earlier Structure I bank. That its outer circle was only later completed over the south-western sector (without significant difference in depth to the remainder) indicates that the bank must subsequently have been levelled at this point and a flat ground surface established. Only some time thereafter was the small pennannular gully inserted into its interior (see also Pryor 1983 concerning 'missing'/inferred building layouts).

The angular quasi-polygon plan of Structure IV is largely attributable to its 'secondary' status: its insertion within the north-western corner of the Ringwork's interior and the incorporation of existing ditch lines (F. 13 in the west and, possibly, the northern length of F. 25). As a result, only its southern side is strictly circular and the straightness of the north-eastern length of its gully must be because it there flanked the western edge of the Period I bank. Similarly, the marked ovoid form of Structure I, while largely determined by the avoidance of its gully with the western F. 37 ditch line, also appears to relate to this early bank as its arc in the north-east seems to flatten along this diagonal axis. Yet, despite these irregularities, circles of *c.* 11.00m diameter can be imposed on the plans of both the gullies of Structures I and IV. Based on normative principles of roundhouse reconstruction (*e.g.* an eaves overhang of *c.* 1.00m), the buildings defined by them would have been some 9.00m in diameter (Fig. 113). Though in the range of the largest roundhouses known in the region, they are not the biggest. Of, for example, the 25 Iron Age roundhouse gullies at the Hurst Lane settlement, three were of approximately the same scale (10.70–11.00m diameter); seven were larger, with the largest being 15.20m across. This is of comparable scale to Structure 3 at Little Thetford (dia. *c.* 15.40m; Figs 127 and 128) where four of the other seven Iron Age round buildings present had gullies comparable to Structures I and IV at Wardy Hill. Therefore, if building size alone is taken as the measure of household status then those at Wardy Hill would not fall into the first rank. However, plotting of the eaves-gully diameters (from centre points) shows that the majority fall between 7.00m and 11.00m

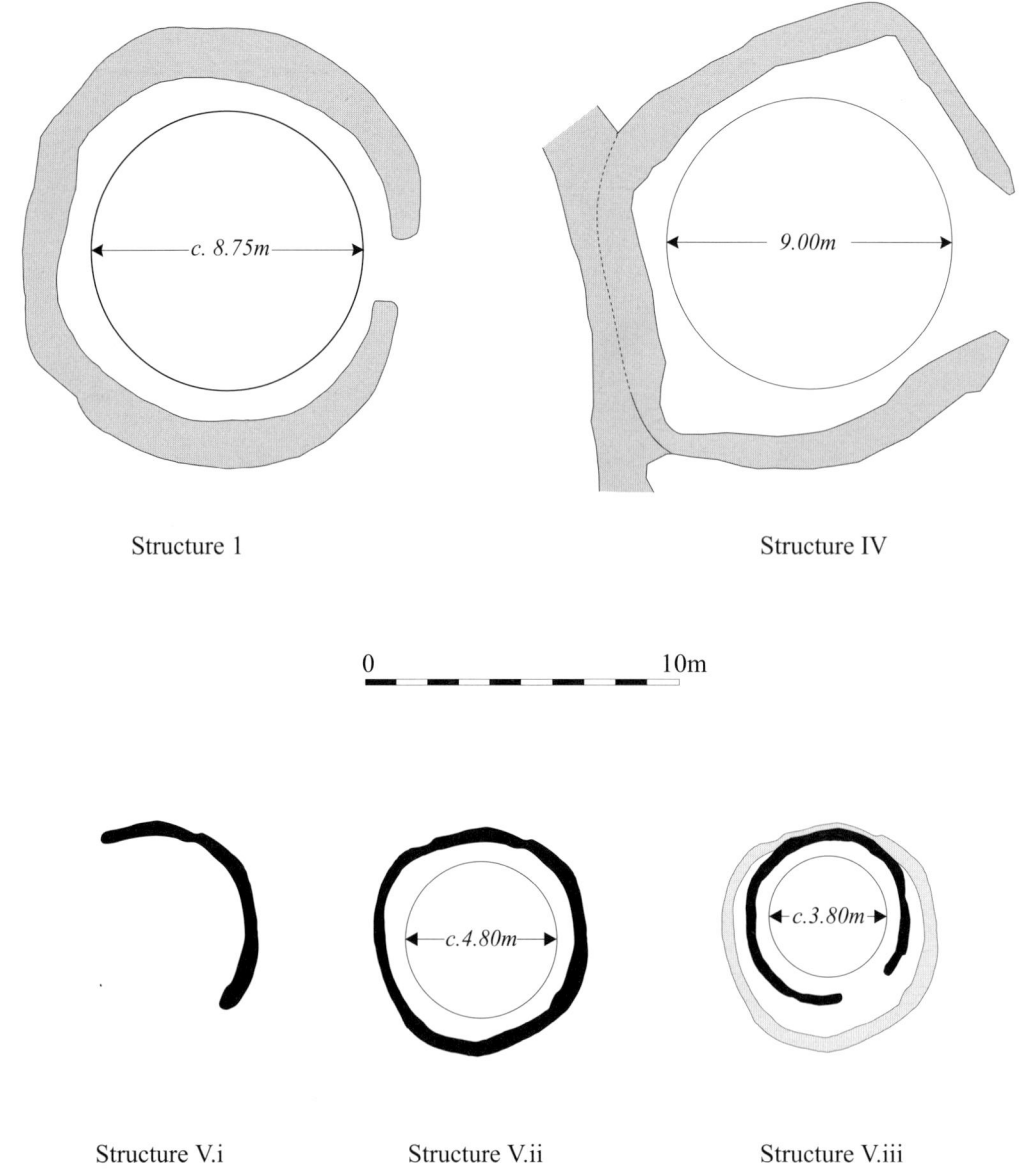

Figure 113 Building forms: Structures I and IV with wall diameters projected (top); development sequence of Structure V (bottom)

(66%; Fig. 114). It is this 'typical' range which the Wardy Hill buildings bracket, with the 'great' houses at the upper end (I and IV) and the small structures falling below. (This being said, the 7.50m diameter of Structure III obviously corresponds to the lower end of this 'peak' with 15% of all the buildings having diameters between 7.00m and 8.00m.)

There are two basic ways of envisaging the inter-relationships between the Wardy Hill buildings. The first would have all the small round structures as ancillary 'satellites' to the earliest 'great' building, I (Fig. 115). Identification of this patterning essentially arises from the regularity of the stand-off interval of Structures II, III and V in relationship to Structure I. On the same basis, the large northern building (IV) could theoretically have been constructed whilst Structure I was standing, as the interval between them matches that of the other structures (2.50–3.50m). The second building model would see a binary pairing between the two large buildings and the smaller 'middle-scale' roundhouses set immediately south-east of their entrances. Thus Structures I/III and IV/V respectively would be linked (Fig. 115). Both of these are valid readings of the buildings' spatial interrelation. It will be a matter of detailed argument, based on distributional patterning, to determine which seems the more appropriate. However, to this must also be added the logistics of time/accumulation and phasing: not surprisingly, these factors seem to erode 'ideal' model precepts.

Any discussion of the respective status of, and potential relationships between, the Ringwork's four main buildings (I and III–V) is entirely biased by the greater size of the two western structures (I and IV) and particularly the scale of their defining eaves-gullies, which results in their dominance of the site's finds assemblages. Given that Structures II and VI (judging from their negligible finds and plant macrofossil content) could not have had a residential function, the crucial issue is whether the 'medial' Structures III and V could have been of independent status, or if they were necessarily ancillary to Structure I. (Separately or together, their usage could also of course have overlapped with that of Structure IV, although their spatial relationship with the later main 'house' would have been more awkward.) The evidence relating to this question is essentially negative. Aside perhaps from the high representation of pig within Structure III (50%) — though strictly its faunal assemblage is too small to be statistically meaningful — there is nothing that points particularly to a specialised function for these smaller buildings. Those activities that are readily attested to by distinct 'type' markers — weaving and metalworking — are only really evidenced in the two larger buildings (the four loomweights associated with Structure V come from the packing of a pit on its eastern exterior, and not from within the building *per se*). Perhaps most telling is the absence of querns and grindstones from the two eastern structures (again, the grindstone from V comes from the F. 102 pit), as this could suggest that neither were loci for food production/meal preparation.

Yet even this line of argument must be qualified further. In contrast with the main buildings, the much smaller gullies surrounding Structures III and V would have been less prone to catch 'tossed' discard — the trapping of casually-thrown larger items — a category within which querns and grindstones would have to be included. Equally, it may be relevant that both of these had the highest overall mean density of cereal grains of any of the structures on the site (0.58 and 0.79 per litre), with III also having the highest density of cereal chaff. (After Structure I's density of 4.58 weed seeds per litre, III and V had the highest densities — 2.41 and 2.25 respectively, figures substantially greater than IV's 1.68.) What this definitely shows is that hearths would have been present in both structures to allow cereals and processing waste to be charred. It is, however, conceivable that cereals were also being stored in them.

Although not readily identified, it is possible that Structures III and V themselves had quite distinct functions. While producing roughly comparable finds totals (541 and 276 pieces of pottery and bone respectively) the mean densities within the southern 'half-arc', though less than in the main buildings, were substantially greater than Structure V's. When factored according to volume, Structure III has far and away the highest cubic density on site. Aside from the reasons outlined, in many respects its assemblages seem comparable to the main buildings': this extends to the recovery of bird bone, which Structure V lacked altogether. While the outer gully of Structure V, with a diameter of *c.* 6.40m, is similar to that of III (7.50m), at only *c.* 5.00m its inner ring seems too small to have defined a house as such. Yet the fact that it was definitely interrupted on its south-south-east side to provide threshold access would indicate that it enclosed a building of some description. As suggested by size alone, the inner-gully phase of V may have had a specific function (the wall-enclosed floor area could not exceed 3.80–4.00m dia.): that its gully was the only one associated with any of the four main buildings in which the density of pottery was greater than that of bone may be relevant here. Therefore an interpretation as some kind of small shrine — essentially on the basis of its plan and in the absence of other evidence — seems plausible. However, no specific depositional evidence would corroborate this.

Whilst recognising *caveats* relating to the representational biases of the buildings, pottery seems to provide clear insights concerning their sequence. As indicated in Table 66, in terms of coarse and fine/table ware distinctions — potentially denoting the locus of where food was served — in Structures III and V burnished wares only account for 2% of the assemblages, compared to 8% and 9% respectively for Structures I and IV. This could further point to the ancillary status of the smaller buildings in relation to the 'great' houses. Yet, possibly relevant for their chronology, the wheelmade wares suggest a different basis of association. Structures I and III's assemblages respectively had only 2% and 3%, whereas the percentage of wheelmade pottery was substantially higher in the two northern buildings (13% in V and 33% in IV). From this it is reasonable to propose greater duration and/or later date for the latter two. (This presupposes that the single small sherd of Samian found in the gully of Structure III is intrusive.) Further support for this interpretation could also be provided by the different ratio of pottery to bone amongst them. At 36% and 48%, a much greater frequency of pottery was present in Structures IV and V than in I and III (20% and 25% respectively). Possibly reflecting different patterns of use, this certainly indicates that the processes or 'matrices' of their closure and infilling differed from those of the two southern buildings.

It is the status of the second 'great' building that must, finally, be considered. It seems outstanding on a number of counts, particularly its range of its artefacts and its quasi-polygonal plan. Yet, concerning the latter, there is evidence that this building form is a distinctly later Iron Age type: rather than indicating a 'special' design it may reflect the wider adoption of straight wall-plate/-panel construction (Carter 1998, 120–1, fig. 77; Flitcroft 2001, 16, figs 8 and 9; Evans and Hodder forthcoming). As has been shown, the irregularities in the plan of Structure IV are largely attributable to its accommodation with the enclosure's inner circuit, and the *ad hoc* character of its eaves-gullies need not necessary reflect the layout of its walls. Equally, that building's 'extraordinary' finds must relate in part to the Phase 4 entranceway deposition; otherwise its closure marks the Ringwork's abandonment, and may have prompted a general sorting and discard of its associated goods. There is, however, one category of material that it unique to this portion of the site and which may denote a special function for that building: human bone. This is reported upon by Dodwell (below).

In recent years the recovery, or at least the recognition, of 'loose' human bone on Iron Age settlements has become increasingly commonplace (Hill 1995). In a regional context, at HAD V they were recovered only in association with the main building and the enclosure's entranceway (Evans and Hodder forthcoming); cut skulls have also been found in the circuits of Stonea Camp

	% Pottery to bone	% Burnished	% Wheelmade
St. I	20	8	2
St. III	25	2	3
St. IV	36	9	33
St. V	48	2	13

Table 66 Comparative frequency of pottery assemblages and finds matrices by Structure

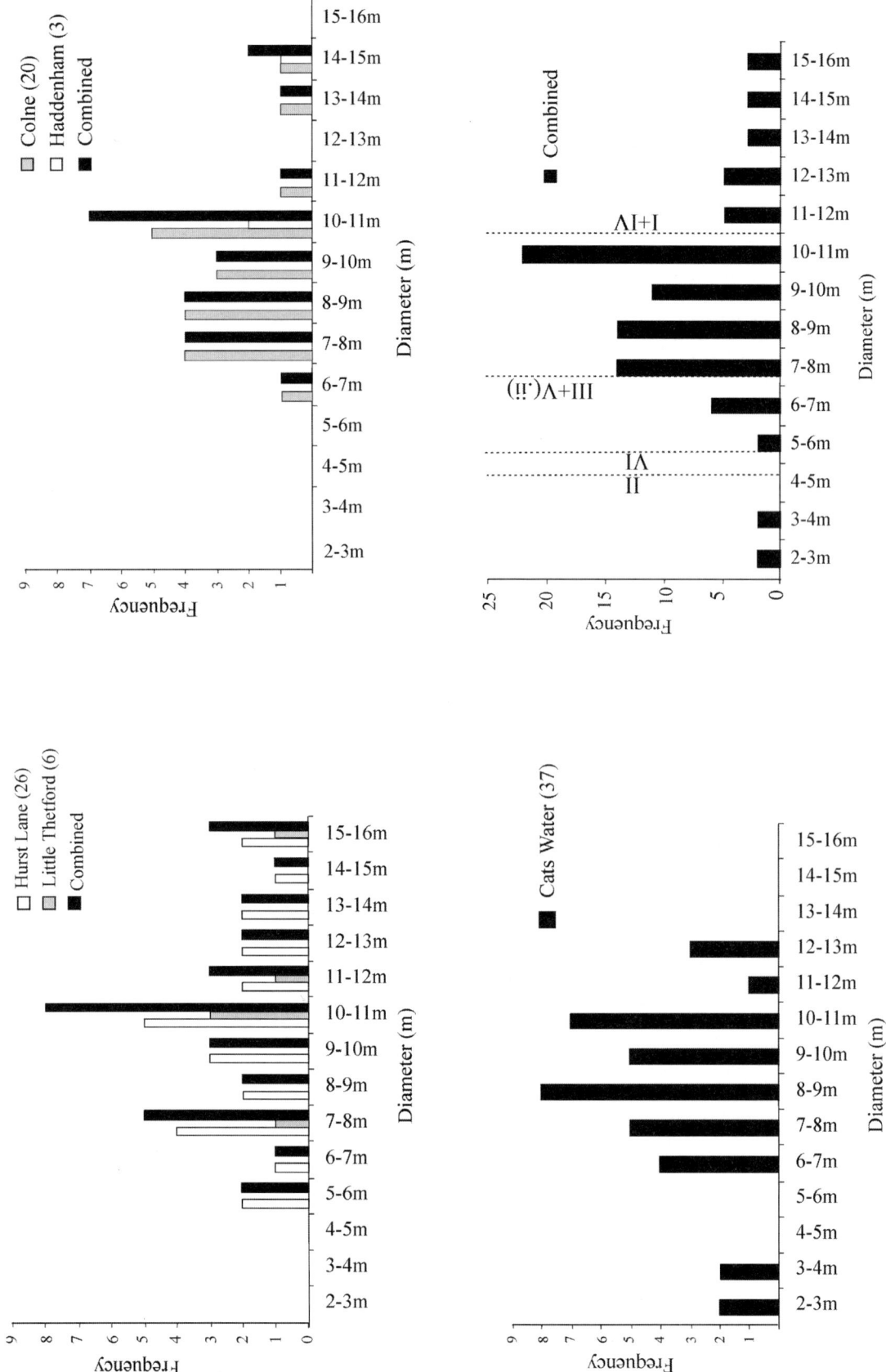

Figure 114 Frequency of roundhouse diameters (mid points of building eaves-gullies): top left, Isle of Ely series; upper right, lower Ouse sites; bottom left, Cats Water, Fengate; lower right, combined series with Wardy Hill structures indicated

228

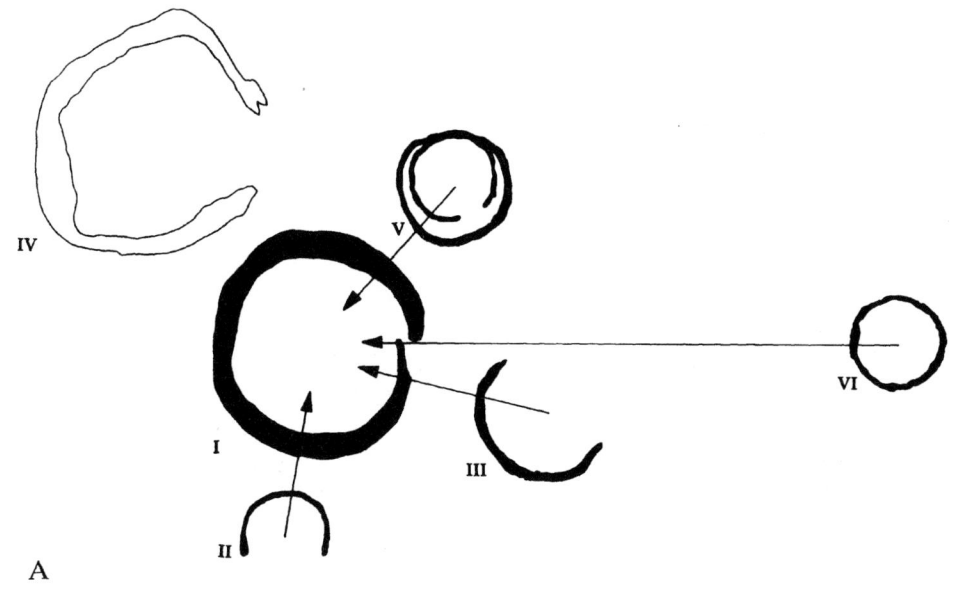

A

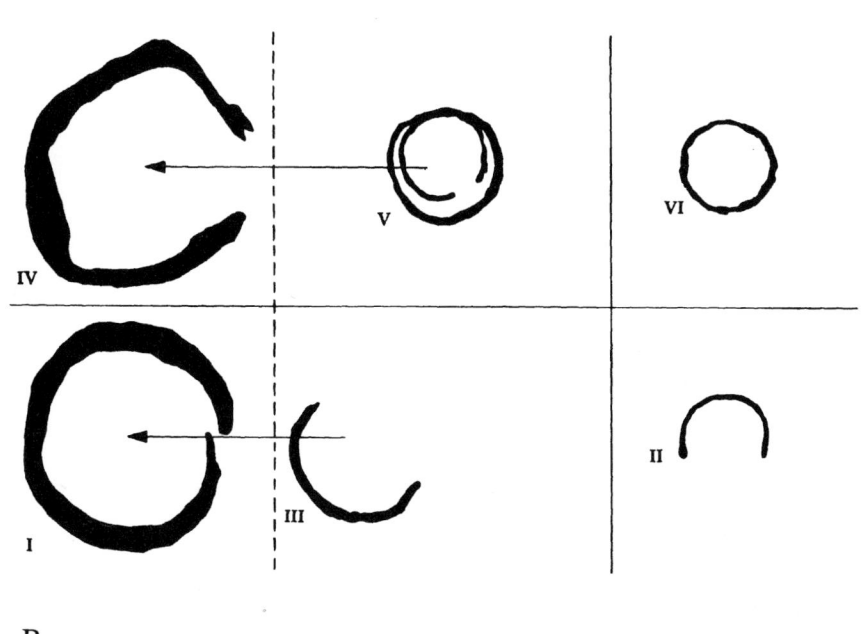

B

Figure 115 Building inter-relationship models: (A) 'satellite'; (B) binary pairing

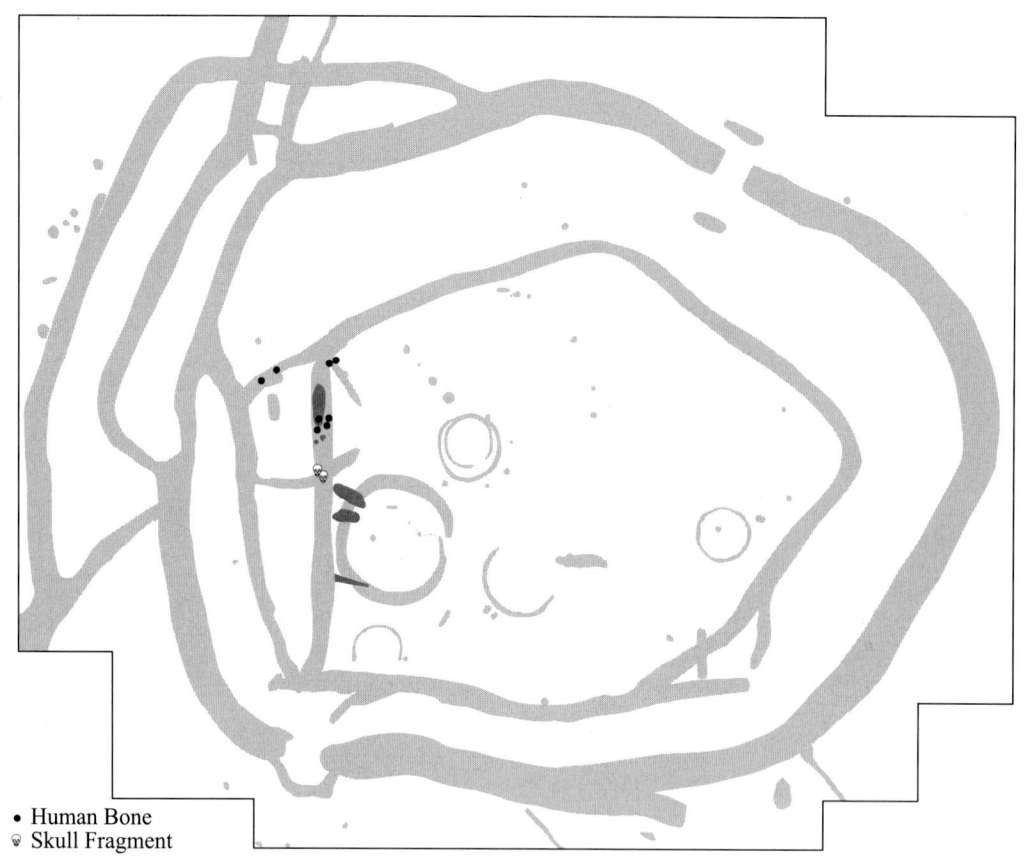

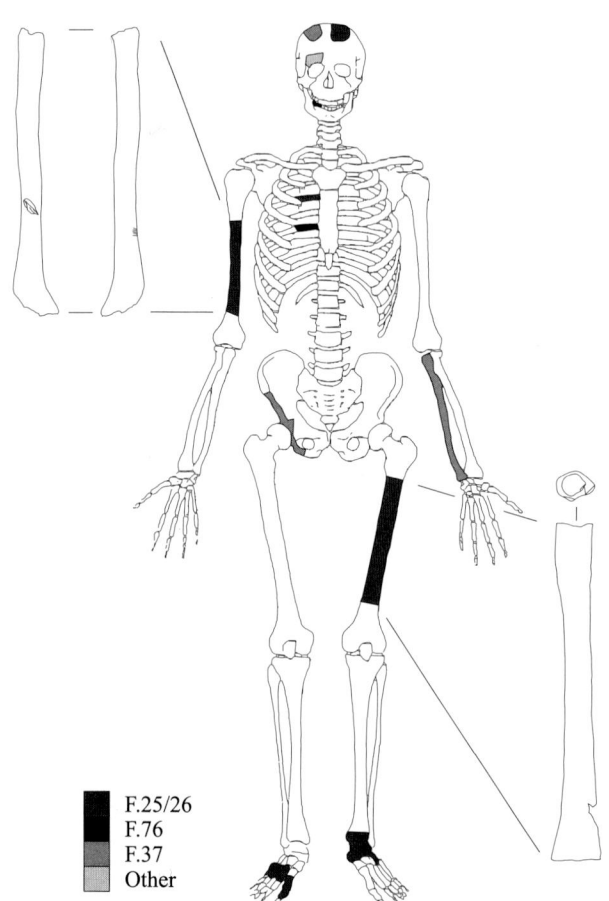

Figure 116 Human bone: Structure IV distribution (top); bodily part distribution (below)

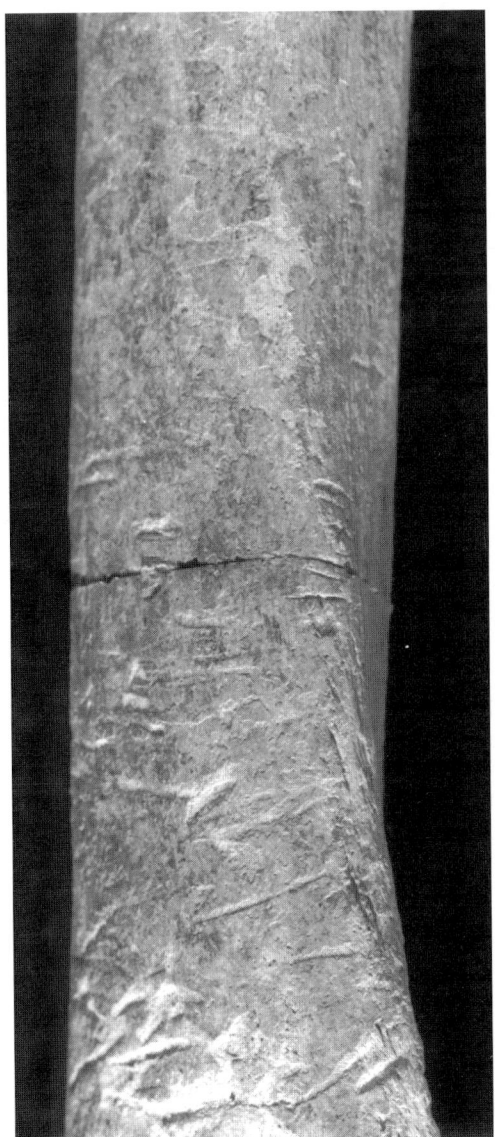
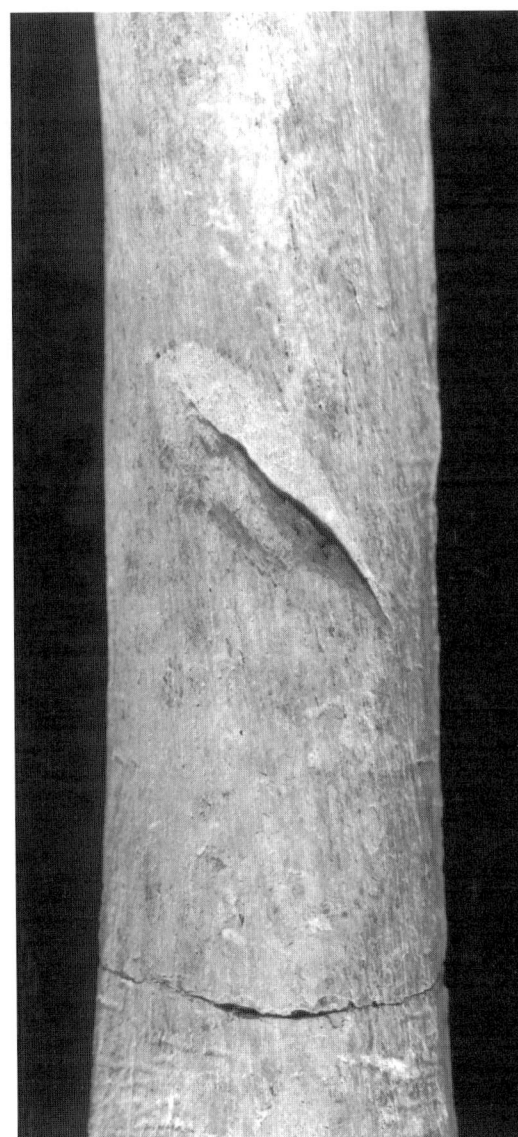
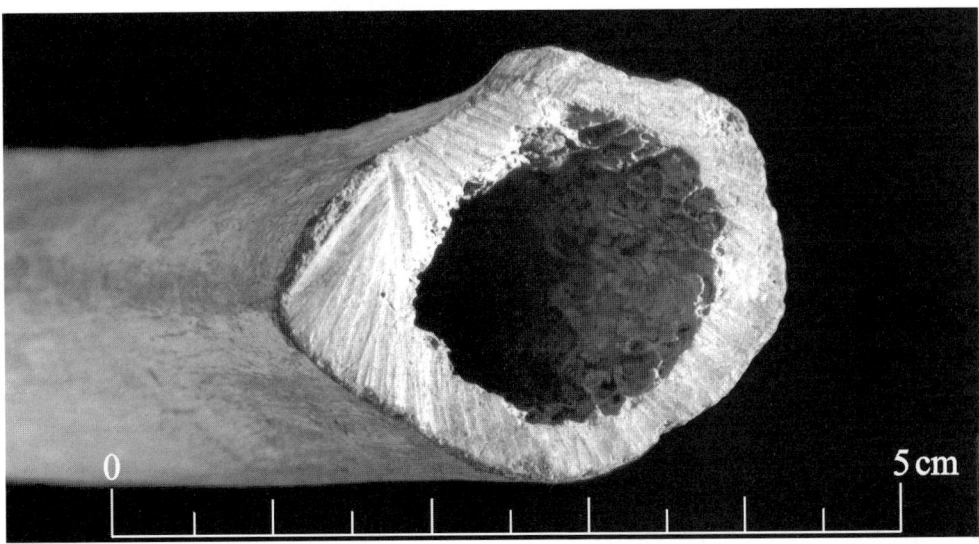

Plate XVII Details of cut marks and sawing on human bone (see Fig. 116 for location; photo G. Owen, University of Cambridge Museum of Archaeology and Anthropology)

(Malim 1992; see below for discussion of the Hurst Lane site remains). It is not, therefore, so much the occurrence of human bones at Wardy Hill that is remarkable but rather their frequency and tight clustering within the vicinity of only the final building (Fig. 116), and the extensive evidence for their 'modification' (cutting, chopping and sawing). As to the former, the terminal status of Structure IV may be relevant. This could suggest either that graves had been dug out upon the site's abandonment — perhaps with the intention of carrying parts of ancestors away to a new 'home' — or that the building saw a distinct usage (*e.g.* as a mortuary house or shrine). There is evidence that could support both of these interpretations. Of the first, it has been considered that the troughs associated with the proceeding Phase 4 gateway might have been graves, since a human tooth was found in F. 76. Equally, that the recovery of both left and right foot bones from F. 25 coincided with the recovery of a spiral finger ring (within a post-medieval ditch cutting this area) could also suggest the location of a disturbed grave.

Despite having only a minimal representation of one individual (based on the absence of sexing data and bone duplication) this seems an unlikely 'population estimate', given that both 'green' and 'dry' bone modification is attested to and the over-representation of skull fragments in relation to other skeletal parts. Given this, while not ruling out the possibility of excarnation, it is understood that the deposition of this bone relates to the final Ringwork phase of *usage* (and not just to abandonment procedures) and reflects upon the distinct status of Structure IV (*e.g.* group-related rituals) as opposed to the site's earlier buildings.

VII. Human bone
by N. Dodwell
(Plate XVII; Fig. 116)

Disarticulated human bone was retrieved from three adjacent features (F.37, 76 and F.25/6); in addition, a single skeletal element was recovered nearby during machining. The bones are all adult-sized and represent a minimum of one individual.

F.37   *368*: left ulna (length = 258mm); left distal tibia.
369: refitting fragments of a right ilium and acetabulum (pelvis); costal end of right rib.
     The size of the acetabulum and flare of the iliac blade are characteristically male, although it must be stressed that using only two diagnostic traits is not sufficient to determine sex.
384: two refitting fragments (modern break) of right parietal.
     The outer surface of the vault exhibits slight porosity. These fragments do not refit with *355*.

F. 25/26   *310*: right humerus shaft with cut marks; left femur shaft with cut marks.
     Both the proximal and distal ends of the humerus are missing and there is evidence of gnawing at each end of the shaft. A deep (*c.* 4mm) chop mark measuring *c.* 22 x 8mm is located on the anterior of the shaft *c.* 90mm superior to the surviving distal end. The chop mark slopes down across the bone from the lateral to the medial aspect of the shaft, and the blow would seem to have been struck from the medio-superior end of the bone/body. There are five deep cut marks located just above the lateral supracondylar ridge.
     Only the femur shaft survives; both ends have been sawn. The proximal end has been sawn through, although not completely, just below the lesser trochanter. A small tab of bone remains along the posterior-medial edge and the bone appears to have been snapped at this point. At the distal end, despite several recent breaks, it is possible to identify saw marks along the entire posterior edge.
316: costal end of right rib.
334: left calcaneus and talus; right metatarsals (MT I–V) and 1st proximal phalanx.
     The left calcaneus and the talus articulate, as do the right MT II–V (and most probably also the MT I and the phalanx). These bones are from two different feet, although they may possibly be from the same individual. The distal ends of MT II–IV and the proximal end of MT I are missing; the breaks are clean but are not recent.
355: two refitting fragments of the left parietal bone.
     The outer surface of the vault exhibits slight porosity. These fragments do not refit with those from *384*.

F.76   *379*: 2nd mandibular molar (unsided).
     Almost all the dentine is exposed on the occlusal surface of the tooth and the remaining enamel has recently been damaged and chipped. Whilst it is unwise to etiolate the age of an individual from the attrition of a single tooth, the severe wear suggests an age of death of middle/mature adult. Calculus was recorded on all sides of the tooth at the junction of the crown and the root. The presence of bone between the roots suggests that this tooth was not 'lost' ante-mortem.

Surface find   *016* (from 10 x 10m machined area vicinity F.32, F.33, F.37, Structure I): fragment of right frontal bone, including part of the orbit (rounded supra-orbital margin).

The disarticulated human bone derives from a minimum of one individual (there are no duplicated skeletal parts and no obvious age/sex differences). All the elements are adult-sized and fairly robust. The chop marks recorded on the humerus appear to be from heavy blows with a sharp-edged instrument (axe, cleaver or sword: Plate XVII), while the five cut marks are most likely from a metal knife or from lighter blows of any of the above sharp-edged instruments. There is no evidence of bone remodelling around the cut marks, implying that these wounds occurred at the time of death or shortly after. All were probably made while the bone was still fresh/wet; however there is nothing about the placement and/or morphology of the marks to indicate whether the body was fleshed or defleshed when the wounds were inflicted.

The breaks on the metatarsals appear to have been on dry bone and to have occurred post-deposition. The breakage patterns suggest that the MT II–IV may have still been in articulation when broken, although the fracture position on MT I indicates that the foot was not completely articulated.

VIII. The 'rhythm' of buildings
(Figs 117 and 119)

While the building sequence need not reflect the development of the larger enclosure system directly, it would not have been entirely independent of it. Having already outlined the phasing of the latter, in order to avoid unnecessary repetition and allow for wider discussion of their context the building sequence will here be linked to the main phasing outline presented in Chapter 2 (Figs 117 and 119). This need not, however, imply any one-to-one co-relationship. The construction of Structure IV, for example, probably post-dated the initiation of this phase's alterations to the Ringwork (*i.e.* after the closure of the West Central Entrance), when the Phase 4 'shrine' probably still stood. Yet the character of the latter's pottery assemblage makes it unlikely that it was still standing at the time of the Ringwork's abandonment. Given this, though it is here so phased by convenience, it is equally unlikely that the tripartite Structure V alterations would have related directed to the Ringwork's phased development in any way.

Phase 1
Although certainty is not possible, it would appear that the two 'half-gully' buildings lapping upon the Period I bank stood alone, and initiated the structural sequence (Structure III and V.i). There is no obvious spatial factor that would determine their bank-side location unless simply to facilitate drainage around their doorways (see Evans 1997a, appendix, concerning putative 'half buildings'). The orientation of their 'C's need not necessarily have correlated with the location of the doorways; both could have been beside their southern terminals and, for example, have been to the south-east.

Phases 2/3
This is marked by the construction of the first 'great' building, Structure I. Oriented eastward, the flattening of its western sector in relationship to the western rectilinear ditch (F. 37) could suggest either that it somewhat post-dates the boundary system and/or that a 'design' error occurred. If having been laid out somewhat after the enclosure system and if this building was to be sited in the south-western half of its system then, after erection of the extant bank and Phase 1 buildings, this would have been the only open ground area of sufficient size. Therefore, siting a building of this scale would necessitate compromise. Given that it would have impeded the view from the threshold of Structure I, its relationship to Structure III lying immediately to the west is less comfortable (see Evans and Hodder forthcoming concerning the importance of threshold views). This implies that their construction was not contemporaneous but there are no obvious grounds to determine which was first, I or III. The proposal here that the latter was primary is based only upon an *inferred* logic of the development of the larger enclosure system. For the same reasons it is presumed that the eastern hayrick (VI) also dates to this period. The completion of Structure V's circuit (V.ii) is also tentatively phased to this time. Implying localised levelling of the Period I bank, its resultant flattened-ovoid plan is superficially similar to that of Structure I.

Phase 4
The re-working of Structure V by the insertion of the small inner ring could well have occurred independent of the development of any of the site's other buildings. In this case it is assigned to this phase essentially because of its diminutive size and since, perhaps appropriately if it was a shrine, it would have then fallen on the central axis of the West Central entrance. Its form certainly suggests that it marks the demise of Structure V as a residential/ancillary building; there is no evidence as to whether or not Structures I and III (and VI) were still standing at this time.

Phase 5
Some time after the closure of the West Central entrance, Structure IV was inserted into what had been its gap in the north-western corner of the Ringwork's interior. Its accommodation is what must have determined the straightening of its north-eastern gully in relation to the Period I bank which, though locally levelled, must still have survived over much of its length. Given that this structure may have included functions relating to the Structure V 'shrine' — as suggested by their pottery assemblages — their usage may have overlapped, with the latter situated immediately before the eastern doorway of Structure IV.

The ditch-side location of Structure II would have only been feasible following the western extension of the inner circuit blocking off the Landward entrance. Judging from its relationship to the ditch this can only have been a 'half-circle', and probably little more than a screened partition (though its drip-gully does pre-suppose some form of roofing). Possible interpretations of its function include as an animal pen or even as a toilet, though a 'watch' facility to control enclosure access remains another possibility in the light of its proximity to the re-modelled south-western entrance.

IX. Enclosure categorisation
(Figs 118–121)

As outlined, the Ringwork's sequence raises an important question: at what point did the enclosure complex become a fort? Was it with the establishment of the Phase 3 inner circuit, with the Phase 5 outworks, or with the construction of the outer circuit? It must, of course, be marked most significantly by the latter — the intervening Phase 4, of which the Phase 5 developments are an elaboration. While the Phase 3 plan clearly influenced the subsequent layout, and the inner circuit is certainly ancestral to, and integrated with, the outer circuit, it is the Phase 4 developments that mark the 'sea-change' in the site's sequence (Fig. 121). Not only is this attested to by its much heavier perimeter (presumably also reflecting the scale of its accompanying banks/ramparts), but also by the integration of the enclosure with, and the complete 'closure' of, the larger western boundary system running from the Wardy Hill-top down to the North Field circuit. Perhaps most telling is that each of the three entrances into the Ringwork — the Watergate, the Landward and West Central entrances — were all defended, or, at least 'elaborated', at this time by the addition of access-control 'structures' (*i.e.* pit-and-trough configurations with timber settings; Fig. 118).

If the Phase 4 Ringwork is to be considered a fort, how are the forms of the preceding enclosures to be characterised? Open across the north and along most of its eastern side, the layout of the Phase 2 rectilinear system is most unusual. Its formal 'axiality' seems without obvious interconnection with the earlier embanked landscape system. Especially noteworthy are the two short ditch lengths that lie parallel at its eastern end (Fig. 37). Whilst it is suspected that the westernmost of these at least represents an eaves run-off trench flanking a rectangular structure, no direct evidence corroborated this. Whatever the formal intent of this system as a whole, some degree of north-eastward closure would have been provided by the diagonally-oriented bank thought to lie across that side.

With the subsequent enclosure of this area by the establishment of the F. 2 circuit in Phase 3, the site took on a more recognisable form: a quasi-horse-shoe-shaped/polygonal compound that, as discussed, has local parallels in the main Hurst Lane enclosure. Regardless of whether first constructed in Phase 2 or Phase 3, the addition of the ditches radiating east and north-west from the enclosure's south-western entrance is without regional parallels. It would, however, have affinities in the

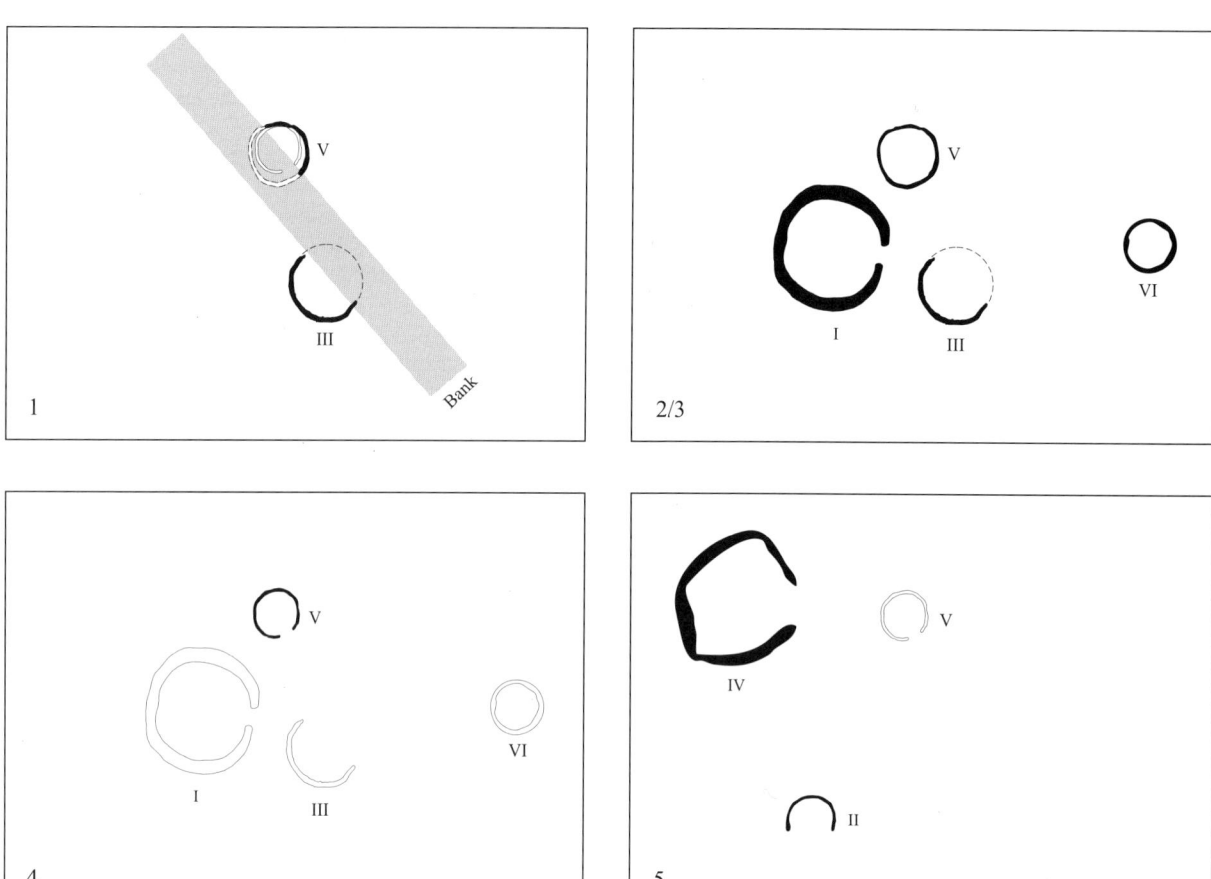

Figure 117 Building sequence phasing

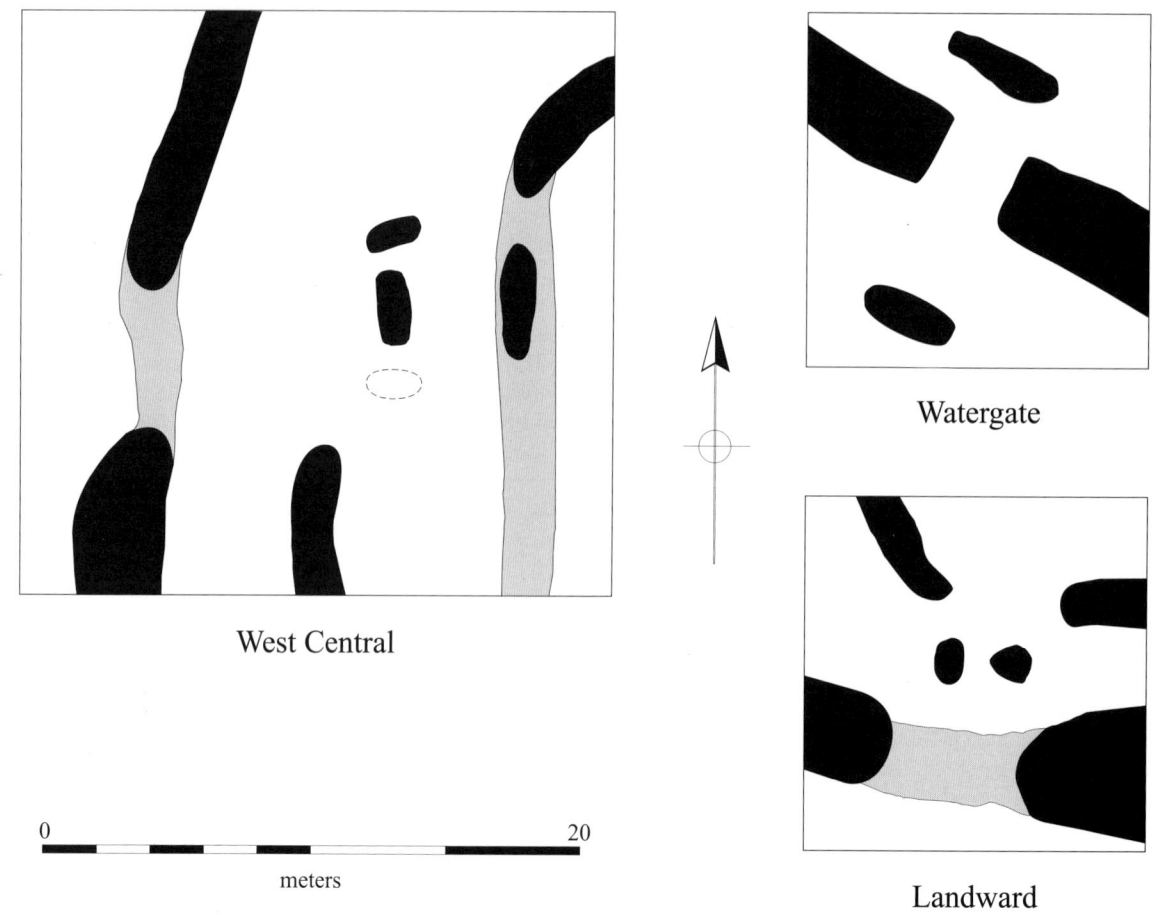

Figure 118 Controlled access: the Phase 4 entrances

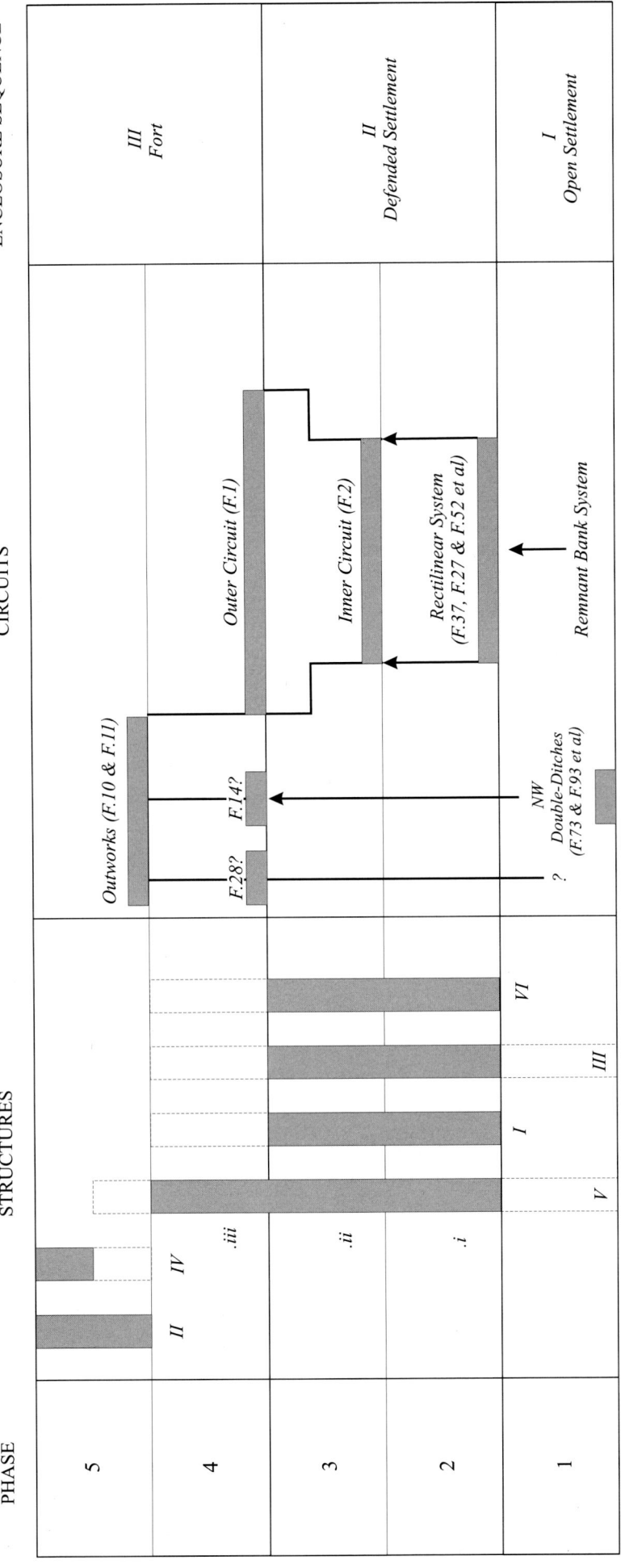

Figure 119 Ringwork phasing sequence

'antenna' ditch systems of enclosed farmsteads of the period in Wessex (*e.g.* Gussage or Little Woodbury) and the Oxford Region (Mingies Ditches), often considered, at least in Wessex, as 'defended farmsteads'. The addition of this entrance-related system at Wardy Hill, reinforcing its predominant south-western 'front', raises the issue of the attribution and categorisation of enclosure form within a gradient of different degrees of control, defence and fortification. In contrast to Hurst Lane, the combination of an antenna-like system with the Phase 3 compound, at least, at Wardy Hill probably does make it warrant the title of *defended* settlement. However, it is only with the creation of the completely surrounding 'heavy' circuit of the Phase 4 enclosure — a *Ringwork* with an internally concentric circuit and elaborate entranceway structures — that the term 'fort' seems appropriate. Recognising the ancestry of the Ringwork fort in a defended compound to some extent re-casts the context of the Phase 5 outworks system. Rather than necessarily having affinities with developed 'Wessex hillfort-type' entrance systems, it may represent more immediately an elaboration of antenna-line perimeters.

Continuing to work backwards through sequence and site 'type', the relationship between what seems to be an open settlement in Phase 1 (including Structures III and V) and the ensuing defended settlement is equally important (Figs 120 and 121). The key issue that this raises is whether the Phase 2/3 layout originated in the Phase 1 settlement, or just relates to the vagaries of long-term 'place' sequence. Given that the buildings established within Phase 1 continued to be utilised at least until Phase 3, this does seem to attest to direct residential continuity.

What the site's sequence therefore charts is a transformation from an open settlement to a defended settlement to a fort. The use of terminology in this way is, of course, always inadequate, and should not imply exclusivity of function. The 'fort' may well still have been a defended settlement but with a much greater emphasis given to its defensive capability. Yet surely it was also 'something more': another issue that these developments reflect upon is to what extent the increased complexity of the site's plan, and the greater pool of labour they necessitated, also related to changes in the relationship between its inhabitants and the broader community. In this context, it becomes relevant to question whether the fort was just intended for defensive purposes or if it also hosted larger group assemblies. These issues will be further addressed within Chapter 6.

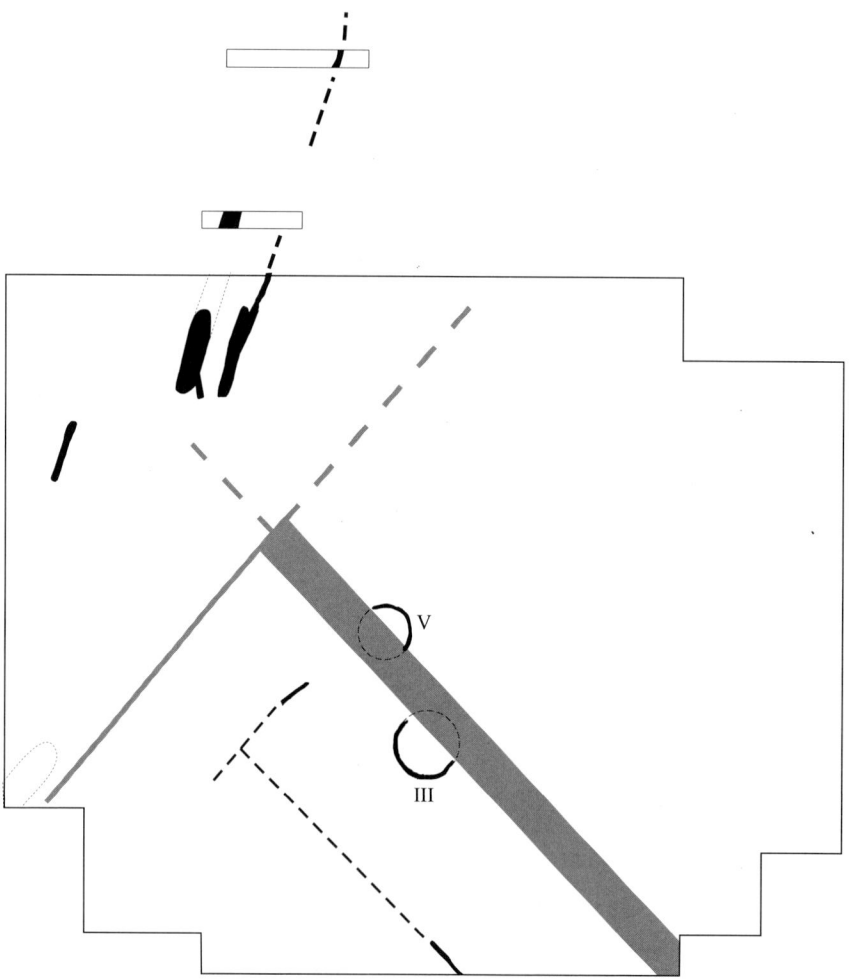

The Open Settlement (Phase 1)

Figure 120 Enclosure sequence (Phase 1)

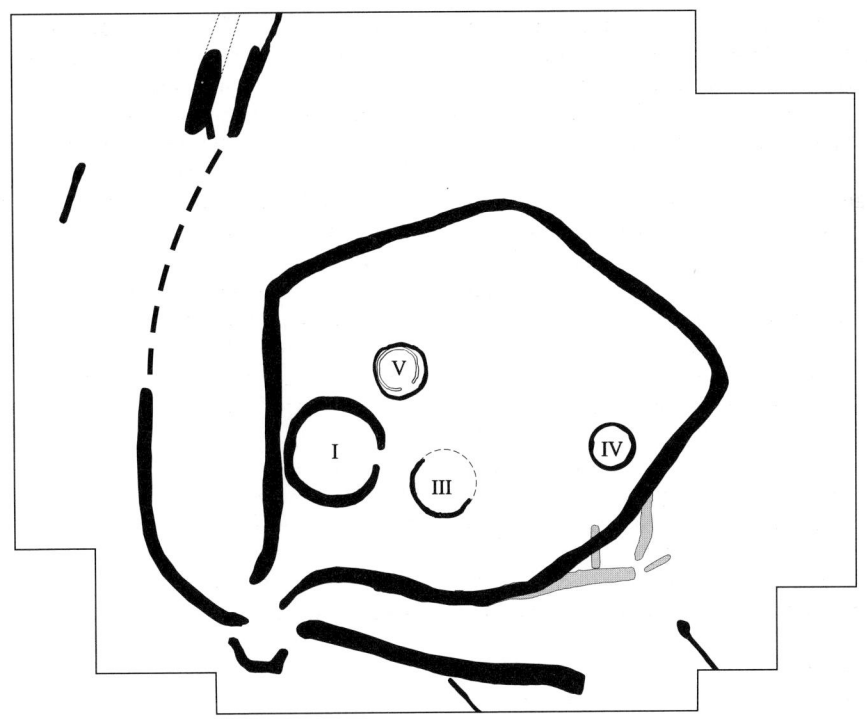

The Defended Settlement (Phases 2 & 3)

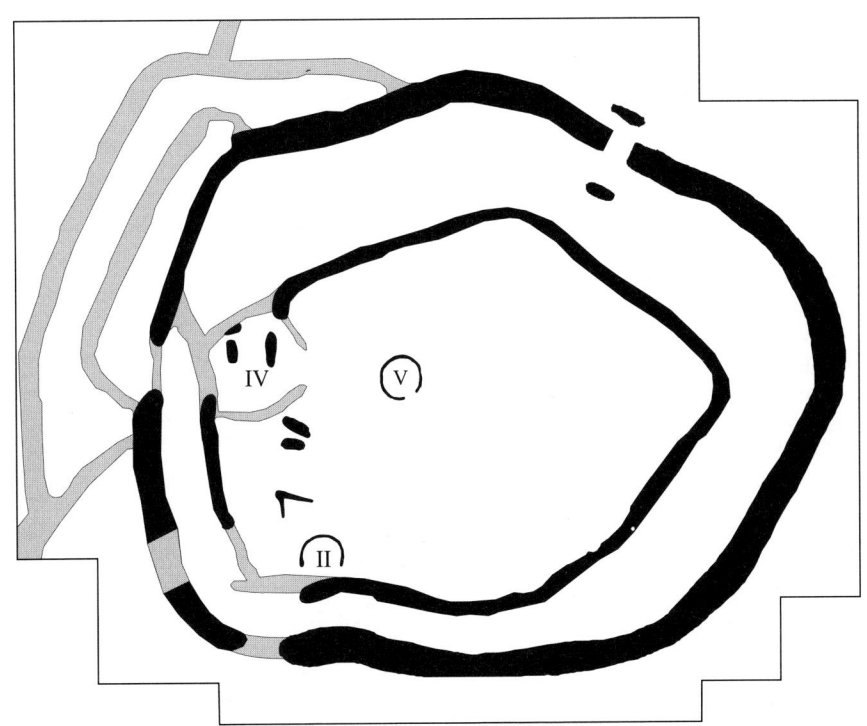

The Fort (Phases 4 & 5)

Figure 121 Enclosure sequence (Phases 2–5)

X. Absolute chronology

by A. Bayliss, C. Evans, F.G. McCormac and C. Bronk Ramsey
(Figs 122–4; Table 67)

Nine radiocarbon measurements have been obtained. Eight were processed by the Radiocarbon Dating Laboratory of the Queen's University, Belfast between 1999 and 2001, with another processed by the Oxford Radiocarbon Accelerator Unit in 2001. One further sample failed to produce sufficient collagen for radiometric dating (F. 1, *606* <2670>B), and three other samples which were submitted for dating by Accelerator Mass Spectrometry also failed to produce results (F. 58, *243* <1952>A and B; F. 56, *220* <1818>A).

General approach

The radiocarbon dating programme was attempted because there have been significant technical and methodological developments over the past decade which, for the first time, make it feasible to design a strategy to tackle many of the chronological problems raised by this Iron Age site. Foremost among these have been the application of a Bayesian approach to the interpretation of archaeological data (Buck *et al.* 1996) and the achievement of considerable reductions in the quoted errors on AMS measurements (Bayliss 1998, fig 11.9).

The approach to chronology adopted here is unashamedly interpretative. The simple calibrated age ranges of the radiocarbon measurements are accurate estimates of the dates of the samples and are presented in Table 67 and in outline in Fig. 122, but it is the dates of the archaeological events represented by those samples which are significant. Methodology is now available which allows us to combine the results of the radiocarbon analyses with other information, such as stratigraphy, to produce realistic estimates of dates of archaeological interest. It should be emphasised that these posterior density estimates are not absolute: they are interpretative estimates, which can and will change as further data become available and as other researchers choose to model the existing data from different perspectives.

The technique used is a form of Markov Chain Monte Carlo sampling, and has been applied using the program OxCal v3.5 (http://www.rlaha.ox.ac.uk/), which uses a mixture of the Metropolis-Hastings algorithm and the more specific Gibbs sampler (Gilks *et al.* 1996; Gelfand and Smith 1990). Details of the algorithms employed by this program are available from the on-line manual or in Bronk Ramsey (1995; 1998; 2000), and fully-worked examples are given in the series of papers by Buck *et al.* 1991 and 1992, Buck, Litton *et al.* 1994 and Buck, Christen *et al.* 1994. The algorithms used in the models described below can be derived either from the structure shown in Fig. 122 or from the chronological query language files which are contained in the project archive. Replicate radiocarbon measurements on the same sample have been combined before calibration by taking a weighted mean, and the consistency of groups of results which are, or may be, of the same actual age has been tested using methods outlined by Ward and Wilson (1978).

This section concentrates on the archaeology, and particularly on the reasoning behind the interpretative choices made in producing the models presented. These archaeological decisions fundamentally underpin the choice of statistical model.

Objectives and sampling

The principal aims of the dating programme were:

1. To determine when the later Iron Age Ringwork was built, when it was abandoned, and for how long it was in use;
2. To determine the relative chronology of different elements of the Ringwork complex;
3. To provide absolute dating for the ceramic phases, particularly for the introduction of wheelmade wares;
4. To test the presumption of a 'short chronology' (based on the immediate succession of the two main buildings within the Ringwork: Structures I and IV) for the occupation.

The initial step in sample selection was to identify short-lived material which was demonstrably not residual in the context from which it was recovered. The taphonomic relationship between a sample and its context is the most hazardous link in this process, since the route by which a sample came to be in its context is a matter of interpretative decision rather than certainty. Extreme rigour was attempted at this stage. All samples consisted of single entities (Ashmore 1999). Material was selected only where there was evidence that a sample had been put fresh into its context, or where there was an apparent functional relationship between sample and context. The main categories of material which met these taphonomic criteria were:

1. Articulated animal bone deposits: these must have been buried with tendons attached or they would not have remained in articulation, and so were almost certainly less than six months old when buried (Mant 1987, 71);
2. Complete examples of fragile bones which would probably have not survived extensive redeposition (*e.g.* skulls and pelvises);
3. Substantial bones from 'toss-zone deposits' (*i.e.* fresh bone from contexts adjacent to entranceways whose deposition is presumed to reflect primary activity).

Once a pool of potentially suitable samples had been identified, a number of models were built simulating the results of the dating programme (*e.g.* Fig. 123). These models included the stratigraphic order of samples and phases, and archaeological estimates of the likely age of the site. Radiocarbon results were simulated using the R_Simulate function in OxCal, with error terms estimated on the basis of the material available and the type of measurement to be commissioned (*e.g.* high-precision, single-run AMS or multiple-run AMS). The models were largely determined by the availability of articulated bone samples. Once constructed, they were used to determine how many measurements would be needed from those parts of the sequence where suitable material was relatively abundant. In particular, how many repeat single-entity samples should be dated from charred deposits? Where would possibly residual samples from lower down in a sequence helpfully constrain articulated material above? Which parts of the stratigraphic sequence would benefit sufficiently from high-precision measurements to justify the additional destruction required?

Radiocarbon analysis and quality assurance

Samples handled at the Queen's University, Belfast Radiocarbon Laboratory were processed according to methods outlined in Longin 1971, Pearson 1984 and McCormac *et al.* 1993, and measured using Liquid Scintillation Counting (Noakes *et al.* 1965). The sample dated at the Oxford Radiocarbon Accelerator Unit was prepared and measured using methods outlined in Hedges *et al.* 1989 and Bronk Ramsey and Hedges 1997. The pre-treatment method used for the bone was collagen extraction (Hedges and Law 1989; Hedges *et al.* 1989) followed by gelatinisation and separation by filtration (Bronk Ramsey *et al.* 2000). Both laboratories maintain continual programmes of quality assurance procedures, in addition to participation in international inter-comparisons (Rozanski *et al.* 1992; Scott *et al.* 1998). These tests indicated no laboratory offsets, and demonstrate the validity of the precision quoted.

Results and calibration

The results are given in Table 67, and are quoted in accordance with the international standard known as the Trondheim convention (Stuiver and Kra 1986). They are conventional radiocarbon ages (Stuiver and Polach 1977).

The calibrations of these results, which relate the radiocarbon measurements directly to the calendrical time scale, are given in Table 67 and in outline in Figure 122. All have been calculated using the datasets published by Stuiver *et al.* (1998) and the computer program OxCal (v3.5) (Bronk Ramsey 1995; 1998; 2000). The calibrated date ranges cited in the text are those for 95% confidence. They are quoted in the form recommended by Mook (1986), with the end-points rounded outwards to ten years if the error term is greater than or equal to 25 radiocarbon years, or to five years if it is less. The ranges in Table 67 have been calculated according to the maximum intercept method (Stuiver and Reimer 1986); all other ranges are derived from the probability method (Stuiver and Reimer 1993). Those ranges printed in italics in the text and tables are posterior density estimates and have been derived from the mathematical modelling of archaeological problems.

Analysis and interpretation

The model for the chronology of Wardy Hill is shown in Figure 122.

Stage I: the samples and the sequence
Three samples of articulated animal bone were recovered from the basal fills of the Ringwork circuits. UB-4448 relates to the primary use of the outer circuit by the north-eastern (Watergate) entrance. This access point showed no evidence of redefinition, in contrast to the main Landward entrance. Accordingly, UB-4446 from the basal fill of the re-cut terminal of the primary Landward entrance should be later in the archaeological sequence. UB-4453 is from the inner circuit (F. 2) along its south-eastern sector.

UB-4448 and UB-4453 are statistically consistent and may be precisely contemporary (T'=1.2; T'(5%)=3.8; v=1). The relationship between the primary construction of the outer and inner circuits is equivocal and has already been discussed in this chapter. In the model shown in Figure 122, no sequence has been assumed between the circuits. However, if the suggestion that the inner circuit is earlier than the outer is included, the model still shows good overall agreement (Overall A=124.1%; UB-4453 A=112.6%; Bronk Ramsey 1995). These three samples must relate closely to the digging of the ditches from which they were recovered, because they were all articulated bone samples from their respective bases.

Three samples of disarticulated bone were dated from what was initially interpreted as the toss zone of the secondary Landward Entrance. Statistically the three results are significantly inconsistent (T'=29.1; T'(5%)=6.0; v=3). This suggests that the bones were not precisely contemporary. The model which constrains all these dates to be later than UB-4446 shows poor agreement (Overall A = 25.2%; UB-4446, A=1.5%). However, given the structural sequence, the inter-relationship between the two entranceways does seem justified. Rather, it is the identification of these bones as relating to entranceway-specific toss zone deposition that must be at fault. Either UB-4450 is residual and the statistical consistent measurements on the other two bones relate to the toss zone (UB-4451 and UB-4452; T'=3.0; T'(5%)=3.8; v=1), or all these bones derive from activity earlier than the construction of the entranceway. The limited area of excavation makes both options tenable.

The model shown in Fig. 122 presumes the latter, and suggests that UB-4451 and UB-4452 are not redeposited, and do not relate to entranceway deposition but rather to the earlier re-cutting of the ditch at the same time as the primary Landward entrance was established. This may be supported by the fact that these measurements are statistically indistinguishable from UB-4446 which dates this event (T'=3.9; T'(5%)=6.0; v=2). It should be noted that the other bone from this deposit (UB-4450) is statistically indistinguishable from the bones relating to the primary construction of the Ringwork circuits (UB-4448 and UB-4453; T'=1.4; T'(5%)=6.0; v=2). This may mean that there we have dated material from two major episodes in the development of the Ringwork circuit. The third, the establishment of the secondary Landward Entrance, has no absolute dating.

A single determination is available from an articulating sheep/goat femur and tibia from the fill of the eaves-gully of Structure I. This provides a date for the use of Structure I of *510–380 cal BC (95% probability; OxA-10735)*.

UB-4449 was a disarticulated bone from the toss zone of Structure IV, and was intended to date its use. However, the result suggests that it must have been a residual piece from the underlying ditch (F. 37). This is because Structure IV is associated with both wheelmade Iron Age wares and early Roman ceramics.

UB-4454 is a equid skull from the base of the inner Ringwork circuit on its southern side. On the assumption that the fragility of this bone means it is unlikely to have been redeposited, it suggests a later localised re-cutting of the ditch. This may be related to the construction of Structure IV.

Stage II: objectives of the dating programme
The model shown in Fig. 122 estimates the date of the primary construction of the defended farmstead (Phases 2 and 3). This dates from *700–390 cal BC (95% probability; 'start')*. This is rather earlier than the estimate of *510–380 cal BC (95% probability)* for OxA-10735, which is the only dated sample from these phases of activity. This suggests that there are insufficient age determinations

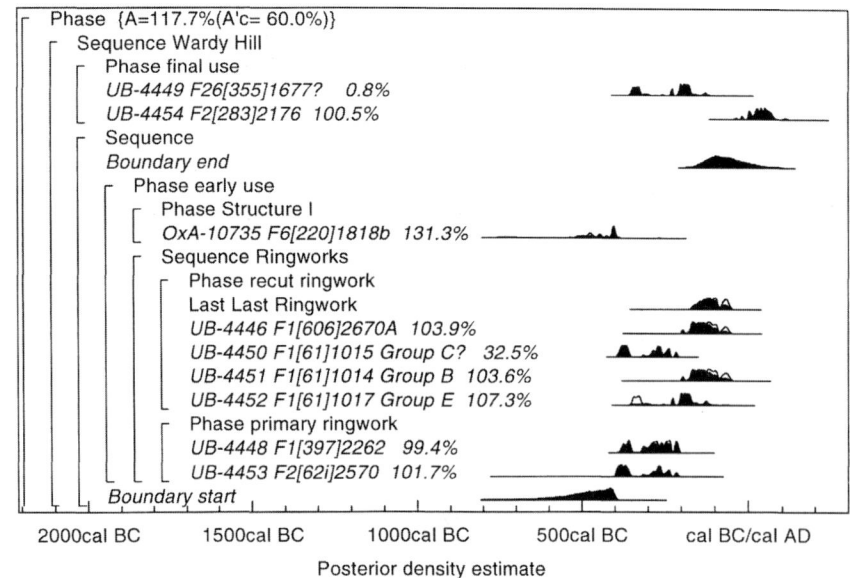

Each distribution represents the relative probability that an event occurred at a particular time. For each of the radiocarbon dates two distributions have been plotted, one in outline (which is the result of simple radiocarbon calibration) and a solid one (based on the chronological model used). The other distributions correspond to aspects of the model. For example, the distribution *start* is the estimated date for the primary construction of the defended farmstead. This graph shows the actual radiocarbon results in the model defined in the simulation shown in Figure 123, which has been modified in the way described in the *Analysis and Interpretation* section above. The large square brackets down the left hand side, along with the OxCal keywords, define the overall model exactly.

Figure 122 Probability distributions of radiocarbon dates from Wardy Hill.

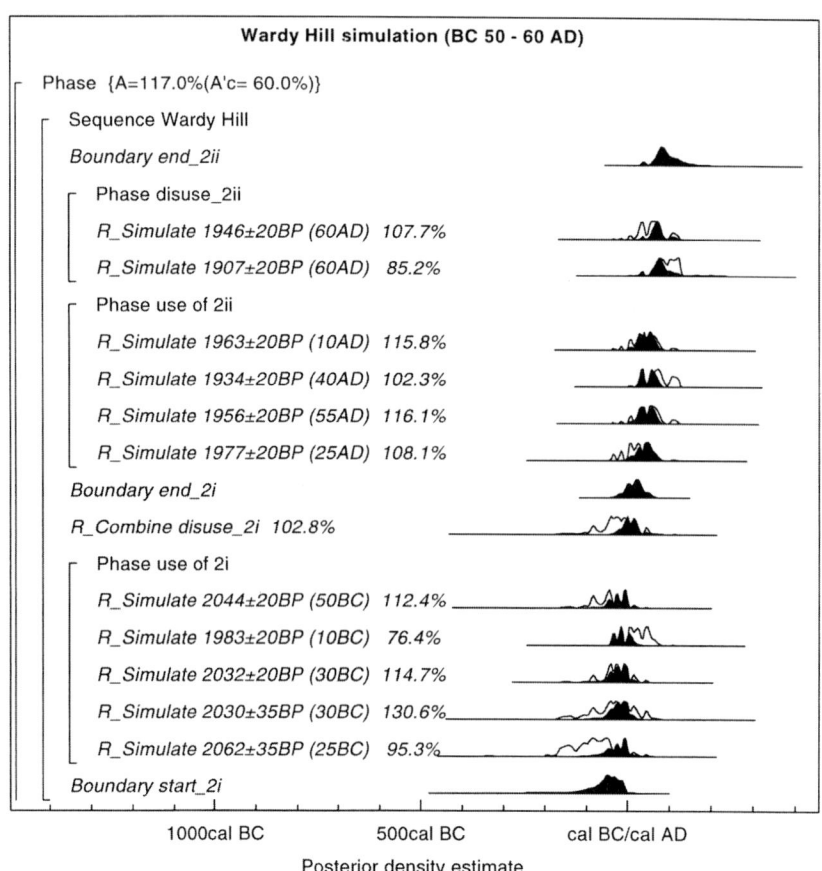

The format is identical to that of Figure 122. In this simulation, the sequence is assumed to have accumulated between 50 BC and AD 50. The large square brackets down the left hand side, along with the OxCal keywords, define the overall model exactly.

Fig. 123 Probability distributions of simulated dates from Wardy Hill.

Laboratory number	Feature/context	Sampled material	Radiocarbon Age (BP)	δ13C (‰)	Calibrated date range (95% confidence)	Posterior density estimate (95% probability)
OxA-10735	F6 220 1818b	Sheep/goat femur, probably articulating with tibia from the fill of the eaves-gully of Structure 1	2370±29	−21.5	Cal BC 520–390	Cal BC 510–380
UB-4446	F1 606 2670 A	Articulated cattle metacarpal and proximal phalanges from the primary fill of the landward entrance of the outer circuit	2107±17	−21.5±0.2	Cal BC 200–50	Cal BC 200–60
UB-4448	F1 397 2262	Articulated cattle left metatarsal and proximal phalanges from the primary fill of the fenward entrance of the outer circuit	2236±19	−21.9±0.2	Cal BC 390–200	Cal BC 390–340 (26.1%) or cal BC 320–200 (69.3%)
UB-4449	F26 355 1677	Horse metatarsal from the toss zone of structure IV	2157±19	−22.2±0.2	Cal BC 360–120	Cal BC 360–290 (33.3%) or cal BC 240–110 (62.0%)
UB-4450	F1 61 1015 Group C	Cow radius from the toss zone of the secondary landward entranceway	2259±21	−20.8±0.2	Cal BC 400–200	Cal BC 400–350 (41.1%) or cal BC 320–230 (49.7%) or cal BC 220–200 (4.5%)
UB-4451	F1 61 1014 Group B	Cattle mandible from the toss zone of the secondary landward entranceway	2105±20	−21.6±0.2	Cal BC 200–40	Cal BC 200–50
UB-4452	F1 61 1017 Group E	Equids pelvis from the toss zone of the secondary landward entranceway	2155±21	−21.7±0.2	Cal BC 360–110	Cal BC 350–320 (4.2%) or cal BC 240–110 (91.2%)
UB-4453	F2 621 2570	Articulated cattle right metatarsal and cubonavicular from the primary fill of the inner ditch circuit	2277±32	−22.2±0.2	Cal BC 400–200	Cal BC 400–350 (50.5%) or cal BC 320–230 (41.5%) or cal BC 220–200 (3.4%)
UB-4454	F2 283 2176	Equid skull from the primary fill of the inner ditch circuit	1966±19	−21.8±0.2	Cal BC 20–80 cal AD	Cal BC 20–10 (2.2%) or cal AD 1–90 (91.5%) or cal AD 100–120 (1.7%)

Table 67 Radiocarbon age determinations

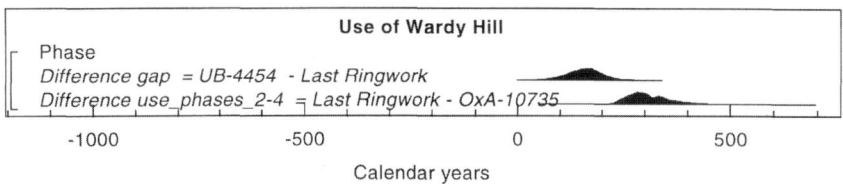

Figure 124 Probability distribution showing the duration of Iron Age activity at Wardy Hill. The distribution is derived from the model defined in Figure 122.

within this phase to counteract the inevitable statistical scatter on the radiocarbon measurements. In default of further data, the single date from Structure I probably provides the best estimate for the start of the Iron Age settlement at the site — rather earlier than expected.

The construction of the Phase 4 Ringwork is dated by an articulated bone samples from the base of the ditch F. 1 (*UB-4448; 390–340 cal BC (25.8% probability)* or *320–200 cal BC (69.6% probability)*). Another sample of articulated bone comes from the primary fill of the inner Ringwork circuit, F. 2. This sample may provide a date for Phase 3, unless it comes from a portion of ditch which had been subsequently re-cut (*UB-4453; 400–350 cal BC (50.5% probability)* or *320–230 cal BC (41.5% probability)*). It appears that Structure I was built before the Ringwork proper (*98.2% probability*), which may belong to the 3rd century cal. BC.

The remaining dates from the F. 1 circuit form a coherent group, which suggests that active deposition within the ditches continued until *170–50 cal BC (95% probability; 'Last Ringwork')*. This estimate is to be preferred to the estimate for the end of the farmstead (*160 cal BC–cal AD 30; 'end'*) because, again, there are too few radiocarbon determinations to counteract the scatter on the measurements. Comparing this estimate with that for the use of Structure I suggests that this period of use of the site *lasted between 230 and 410 years* (*95% probability*; Fig. 124).

The other sample from the inner Ringwork circuit, F. 2, is considerably later than all other radiocarbon samples from the site (Fig. 122), and is interpreted as associated with the final use of the site (Phase 5). This activity is dated to *cal AD 1–90* (*92% probability; UB-4454*): it must relate to a localised re-cutting of this ditch, and may be associated with re-use of the site relating to Structure IV.

There appears to be a gap between the two major phases of activity on the site, lasting between *70 and 240 years* (*95% probability*; Fig. 124).

The first and last of the aims of the dating programme, as outlined above, have been achieved: there is now a basic chronology for the use of the Ringwork and its associated structures. The possibility of a short chronology for activity at the site can also now be dismissed. The dating programme has been less successful in providing absolute dating for the ceramic phases and in disentangling the relative sequence of different elements in the complex. This is at least partially because there are insufficient measurements to tackle such questions, which require refined dating resolution. It is not possible to obtain sufficient measurements, firstly because the collagen preservation means that a number of samples have failed to produce results, and secondly because the 'open'

character of the Ringwork's circuits and the paucity of closed contexts means that material suitable for dating is scarce. Nevertheless, the limited number of radiocarbon dates which could be obtained has significantly altered the interpretation of the site.

XI. Sequence and chronology

Aside from the difficulties of phasing arising from the open, organic character of the Ringwork's features, its dating is not clarified by the scale of developmental change and maintenance of its basic structure. There are few sealed earlier features and none producing substantial finds assemblages. What the sequence documents is the impact of immediate changes: for example, the alteration of an entrance or the establishment of a new circuit. These were not of a scale that are likely to have coincided with changes in lifestyles or correlate with developments in the manufacture of ceramics.

Based on the ceramic chronology alone, both short and long sequences would be feasible. Associated with early Roman wares, the infilling of Structure IV anchors the end of the sequence to the last decades of the 1st century AD (*c.* AD 70–80). Yet from this *terminus ante quem*, given the generic date range of later Iron Age wares, the Ringwork sequence *per se* could theoretically have lasted from anywhere between 450 years to less than a century. In other words, it could potentially begin as early as *c.* 350–300 BC or as late as the final decades of the 1st century BC. In trying to refine this span, the status of Structure I and the implications of its low percentage of wheelmade pottery are crucial. Does the latter reflect a low currency of such wares at the time of the building's usage, or has it been subsequently introduced as the house circle was later utilised as a midden?

In many respects the key issue concerning the duration of the Ringwork's sequence is whether there was continuity of occupation between its two 'great' round buildings: did the Phase 2/3 buildings stand through Phase 4? If there was direct succession then this would limit the main Ringwork sequence to between 60 and 100 years, given a 30–50 year life expectancy for such buildings (plus perhaps up to 20 years if Structures III and V proceeded Phase 2). Given that the later building, Structure IV, cannot have been constructed until some time after the Phase 4 West Central entrance was closed, this would have to imply that Structure I stood through Phases 2–4. Can this only represent 30–50 years of development or was there a hiatus in the occupation of the Ringwork? If so, this *interregnum* would have to fall throughout Phase 4 and perhaps during the first part of Phase 5. This is an unfortunate ambiguity. On it hangs the question of whether there was a resident family within, and probably responsible for the construction of, the enclosure when it was transformed into a fort and, from this, whether the 'work' is to be considered an expression of communal co-operation or of personal/familial power.

The radiocarbon dates support a long chronology for the site's sequence. Not only is its duration evidently much greater than was originally thought but the Ringwork's main usage, instead of being rooted in the succession of two 'great' roundhouses (I and IV), becomes bracketed by them. While the main Phase 2/3 building, Structure I, may well have still stood during the earlier usage of the Phase 4 Ringwork, realistically it cannot have functioned for more than 25 to 50 years of the 300–400 years of this phase. Taken at face value, they suggest that Phase 2/3 should probably be assigned to the 5th century, with the Ringwork probably established in the 4th. Although Structure IV, at the other end of the sequence, was not itself dated (the UB-4449 attribution being considered residual), its pottery indicates that it must date to at least the late 1st century BC; more probably it is of 1st century AD attribution alone. This could imply that the immediate enclosure was without interior settlement for some three to four centuries. Yet this does not mean that it did not see active usage/deposition during this time. If by nothing else, this is attested to by the series of radiocarbon determinations from bone within its main circuit (UB-4446, UB-4451 and UB-4452).

The radiocarbon determinations suggest a much more 'gapped' sequence (*viz.* settlement *per se*) than expected, and their greater-than-anticipated span further highlights the importance of Wardy Hill as a major 'place' within the 1st millennium BC landscape. The dates essentially confirm the site's ceramic chronology: a Middle Iron Age Ringwork hosting Late Iron Age activity. One discrepancy, however, is the early dating of Structure I (*OxA-10735; 520–390 cal BC*). On this basis, Phases 2 and 3 would have to be assigned to at least the 5th century cal BC. Yet Structure I produced a 'classic' Middle Iron Age assemblage and, therefore, this date would seem too early by as much as a century in relation to the established 350–300 BC divide between 'Early' and 'Middle' ceramic traditions. Rather than trying to dismiss this result it is perhaps best to let the discrepancy stand, for the 'Early'–'Middle' transition cannot at this time be said to be dated within the immediate region. The nearest site of relevance, Lingwood Farm, Cottenham (COT 5; Evans 1999), produced 7th–6th century BC dates for its Early Iron Age assemblages that calibrate to *c.* 800–400 BC (GU-5731, 2490±60BP and GU-5732, 2480±50BP). By typological parallels, Pryor noted that the Early Iron Age pottery (Group 1) from Fengate should date to the same period. However, their associated calibrated dates would indicate a 4th- or 5th-century date (Pryor 1984, 153: 790–1 cal BC, UB-822, 2290±125BP; 520–200 cal. BC, HAR-3199, 2310±60BP; 410–200 cal BC, GaK-4198m 2300±46BP).

The more thorough dating of the Wardy Hill complex, when compared to other major enclosures of the period within the region (see below), raises crucial questions concerning continuity of settlement and the long-term 'structuration' provided by substantial ditch/enclosure systems. In dated sequences with only one or two elements, settlement 'gaps' are not apparent. Direct continuity is usually presumed of building sequences, whereas the lingering framework provided by major ditch earthworks may itself have been what drew subsequent usage, if only intermittently. Of course in the case of Wardy Hill, given the (undated) evidence of occupation within the bounds of its broader enclosure system, occupation may well have continued unabated beyond the Ringwork itself. Such occupation may then have been a source of its outer perimeter deposition.

To this extent, the radiocarbon attributions may be somewhat misleading in apparently distinguishing a cessation of the outer perimeter: *i.e.* Phase 4 marking the end of the circuits' active maintenance, after which there was a gap in the enclosure's usage. There are no dates for the Outwork ditches and, as Hill has noted, more 'classic' Aylesford-Swarling pottery assemblages were present in that vicinity (F. 11 and 13). Probably of 1st century BC date and relating to features around the site's western margin, these certainly tell of an *interregnum* settlement presence even though their relationship to the Outworks system is ambiguous (as is the dating of the portion of the ditch perimeter itself). On one hand, this material could suggest a transgression (dis-use) of the Outwork's perimeter, in which case the closure of the West Central entrance and the establishment of the Outworks must be a late Phase 4 development. Yet, alternatively, this activity could pre-date the Outworks and relate to the north-western access. Under this scenario this pottery in these features would be residual; further support for this interpretation may come from the fact that a number of the west-side features appeared truncated by the outermost Outworks line (F. 10).

Another consequence of the site's longer duration is, in effect, to lessen the intensity of its artefact densities, especially the non-building associated, midden-derived ploughsoil assemblages. As detailed above, although artefacts are still occurring in high numbers and attributable to non-daily/'domestic' accumulation, a greater span must impact upon how their attendant activities are envisaged (*i.e.* either fewer mass gatherings or a reduced number of participants 'meeting' over a longer period).

As opposed to the building and pottery sequences, what the dates ultimately highlight is the sheer complexity of settlement sequences. There can be few 'simple' sites, and interpretation is made all the more difficult through 'erasure' by plough damage, de-watering, curation and off-site deposition of objects *etc*. Whilst broad patterns can be distinguished, the writing of 'history' from prehistory may ultimately lie beyond our grasp.

XII. The Cove Environs/Ely excavations
(Figs 125–9; Tables 68 and 69)

The constraints of volume size and the different stages of analyses reached by various other projects means that there is no scope here to include full presentation of the results of the other recent Iron Age excavations within the area. However, before proceeding to the concluding Discussion, some more detailed reference to them is necessary in order to provide a measure of context for the Ringwork findings. Therefore, the following summaries emphasise aspects of particular relevance.

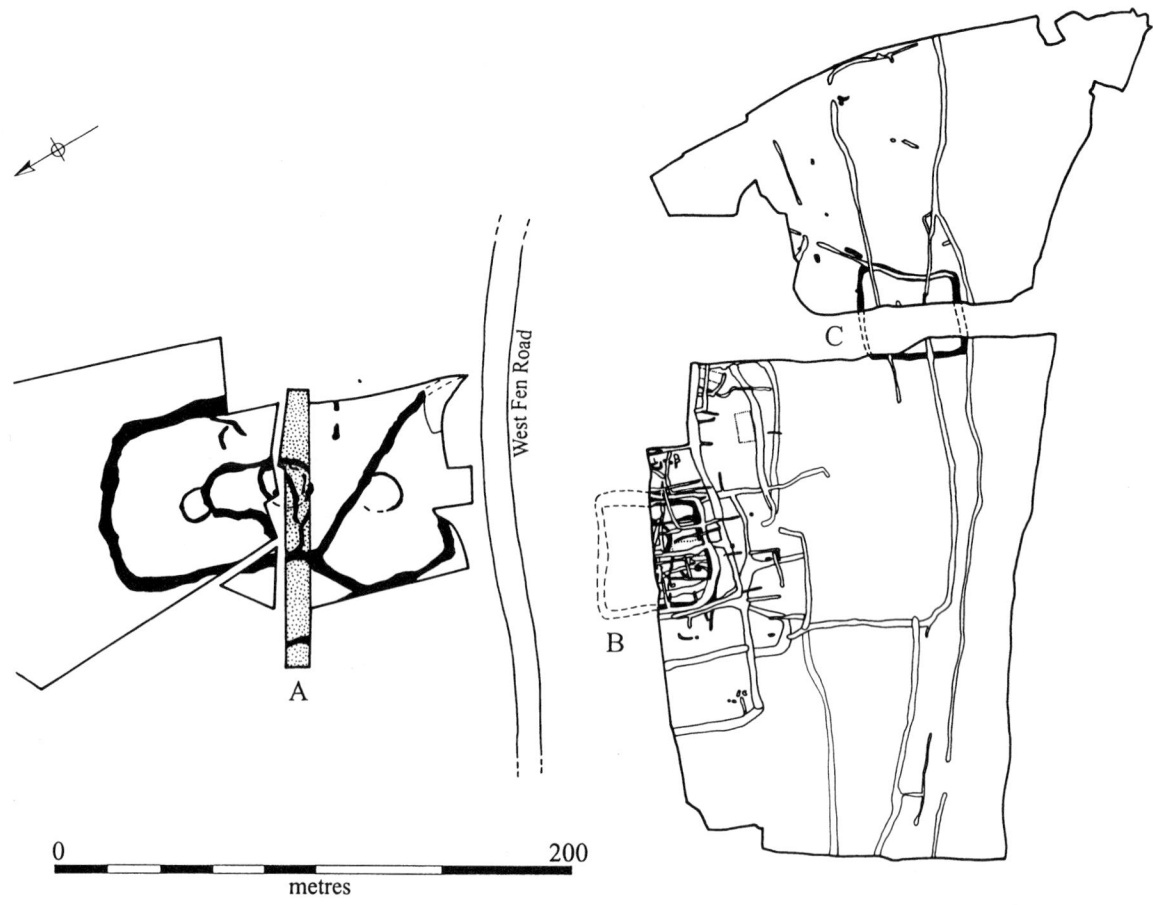

Figure 125 West Fen Road, Ely: Iron Age features black, with Roman features left open (Saxon and medieval systems not shown). (A) North Field site with 1995 CAU trench indicated by stippling (otherwise excavated by Northants. Unit); (B) and (C) sub-square Iron Age compounds in southern Cornwell fields (excavated by CAU).

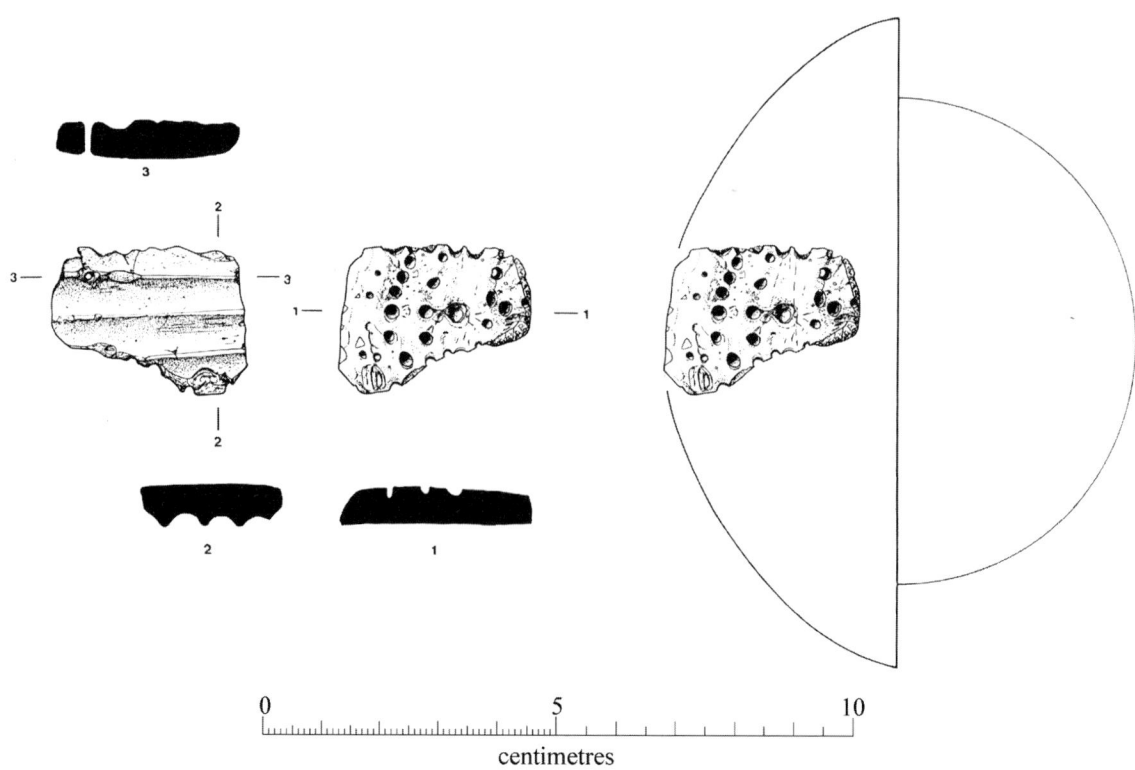

Figure 126 West Fen Road, Ely: impressed clay plaque

West Fen Road, Ely: 'decorative assemblages' and status

This later Iron Age settlement was first discovered during pipeline-related investigations in 1995. Full excavation followed over a 100m length of the 10m wide easement strip (Figs 8 and 125; Gibson 1996). Located on Kimmeridge Clay, the site lies above the Cove (at *c.* 6.50m OD) on the opposite side of the ridge on which Ely itself is located. Later, throughout 1999 and continuing into the spring of the following year, large-scale excavations occurred across both sides of West Fen Road as a result of house construction (Mortimer 2000; Regan 2001).

The later Iron Age complex (slight traces of later Bronze Age occupation were also found) was superseded first by an extensive Romano-British settlement and field system, with subsequent occupation from Middle Saxon through to early medieval times. There is not the scope here to further outline the sequence, except to note that one explanation of why such an extensive and long-term settlement complex should be located near to Ely could relate to the fact that it may have been sited at the end of a causeway running west to either Coveney or Downham. Instead, discussion here will be confined to the site's Iron Age utilisation, and primarily to the results of the 1995 excavation. (During the 1999–2000 campaigns there was relatively limited evidence of Iron Age occupation in the fields south of the road, where work was undertaken by the CAU. Rather, this account concentrates on the north side where fieldwork was conducted by Northamptonshire Archaeology; post-excavation is in progress on both projects at the time of writing.)

As chance would have it, the original 1995 trench bisected the core of the northern settlement, which seems to consist in the main of two overlapping, large sub-square/ovoid enclosures. In contrast with the nearby Hurst Lane settlement, the traces of only three definite roundhouses were recovered (along with another on the southern side). Two were within the northern compound, and the one positioned centrally in its southern end appears itself to be set within a small ovoid enclosure whose layout is roughly concentric to the main compound.

In the course of the CAU's excavations, the features within the vicinity of this central building produced an extraordinary array of small finds. Aside from a small cylindrical bone/antler object (15mm long and 10mm in diameter), this included a bone gouge or point decorated in a regular pattern of drilled dots: it is extremely rare to recover such decorated bonework within the region. The other find of note is a fragment of an impressed clay plaque (Fig. 126). Made of a shell-tempered fabric, this seems to have been either circular or lozenge-shaped (32 x 23 x 9mm) and has a bevelled exterior edge. One side is decorated in impressed dots, with the other having *parallel* lines of reeds or rods impressions (*i.e.* not basket/mat weave impression). In contrast to the dirty grey brown colouration of the latter face, the dot-decorated surface has been discoloured orange-pink through heating or contact with fire. The function of this object is unknown, though uses as some kind of lid or cooking plate, or even as a gaming piece/board, are all possible.

It is difficult to know what to make of these finds. The recovery of such an array of material from what was a very limited excavation is intriguing and, in the light of the Ringwork's assemblages, raises questions concerning material cultural and status. As opposed to the more open settlement plan of the Hurst Lane site, the West Fen enclosures seem essentially to be discrete household compounds. This raises the question of what, if any, was the relationship between these two nearby sites and whether the recovery of this material from the 1996 excavation somehow reflects the higher status of and/or different group affinities of the West Fen inhabitants. Of course, it could be the case that (aside from pottery) so little of the material culture within the region was then evidently decorated that it had little if any 'readable' meaning, as it were (see Evans 1989a and Fitzpatrick 1997 concerning the ambiguities of Iron Age decorative styles). While they are unusual findings there is no direct evidence that these pieces were imported into the area, and therefore they cannot necessary be read as markers of status.

Phase	Main structure	Ancillary structure
i	4 (10.0m)	7 (5.6m)
ii	3 (15.4m)	1 (11.3m)
iii	5 (10.8m)	8 (6.8m)
iv	2 (10.8m)	6 (5.6m)

Table 68 Watson's Lane, Little Thetford: pairing of roundhouses (bracketed figures denote diameter)

Structures ranked by size	Diameter(m)	Average Depth (m)	% of gully sampled*	Sampled total	Expected population**
Structure 6	5.4	0.15	15%	28	187
Structure 7	5.6	0.04	1.5%	0	-
Structure 8	6.8	0.18	9%	19	211
Structure 4	10.0	0.14	19%	268	1410
Structure 2	10.8	0.29	6%	121	2017
Structure 5	10.8	0.13	6%	14	233
Structure 1	11.3	0.22	14%	90	649
Structure 3	15.4	0.39	60%	3501	5835

Table 69 Watson's Lane, Little Thetford: Total finds densities compared with house size. *Calculated by multiplying the proportion of the circuit excavated by the proportion of depth survived (using maximum depth for size rank as standard); ** worked out by expressing the sampled total as the same percentage as that of the gully excavated. $N = \frac{n \times 100}{\%}$.

Figure 127 Watson's Lane, Little Thetford: location of roundhouses, main Iron Age features in black

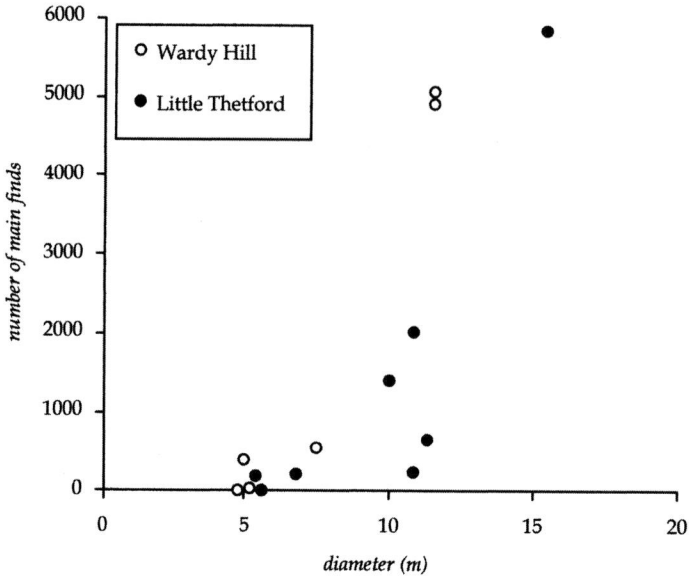

Figure 128 Frequency of finds by structure size at Wardy Hill and Little Thetford

Indirect support for this argument could, however, come from an unexpected source: the site's plant macrofossils, whose assemblage is unusual in the context of the other Ely sites (Stevens in Gibson 1996). As discussed above by Stevens with reference to Wardy Hill (Chapter 3), a marked paucity of smaller weed species would suggest that its cereals had been fine-sieved prior to final processing. This could indicate either that their initial processing occurred on another part of the settlement, or that the site's social organisation was such that there was sufficient labour to allow for initial *en masse* processing prior to storage.

A final alternative relates to the almost-complete absence of weeds of wetland habitants; from this it could be postulated that the cereals had been imported into the site. Here it is relevant that Wiltshire was able to identify a distinct calcareous component amongst the herbaceous taxa within that site's palynological analysis, which she suggests might have been brought in with animal dung. (Amongst the macrofossils there is only one weed seed that could positively attest to 'importation': Selfheal, a grassland species of neutral/calcareous soils.) Similarly, due to a lack of older animals and a high proportion of meat joints of 'high economic utility', Yannouli's study of the faunal remains also raises the possibility that this may

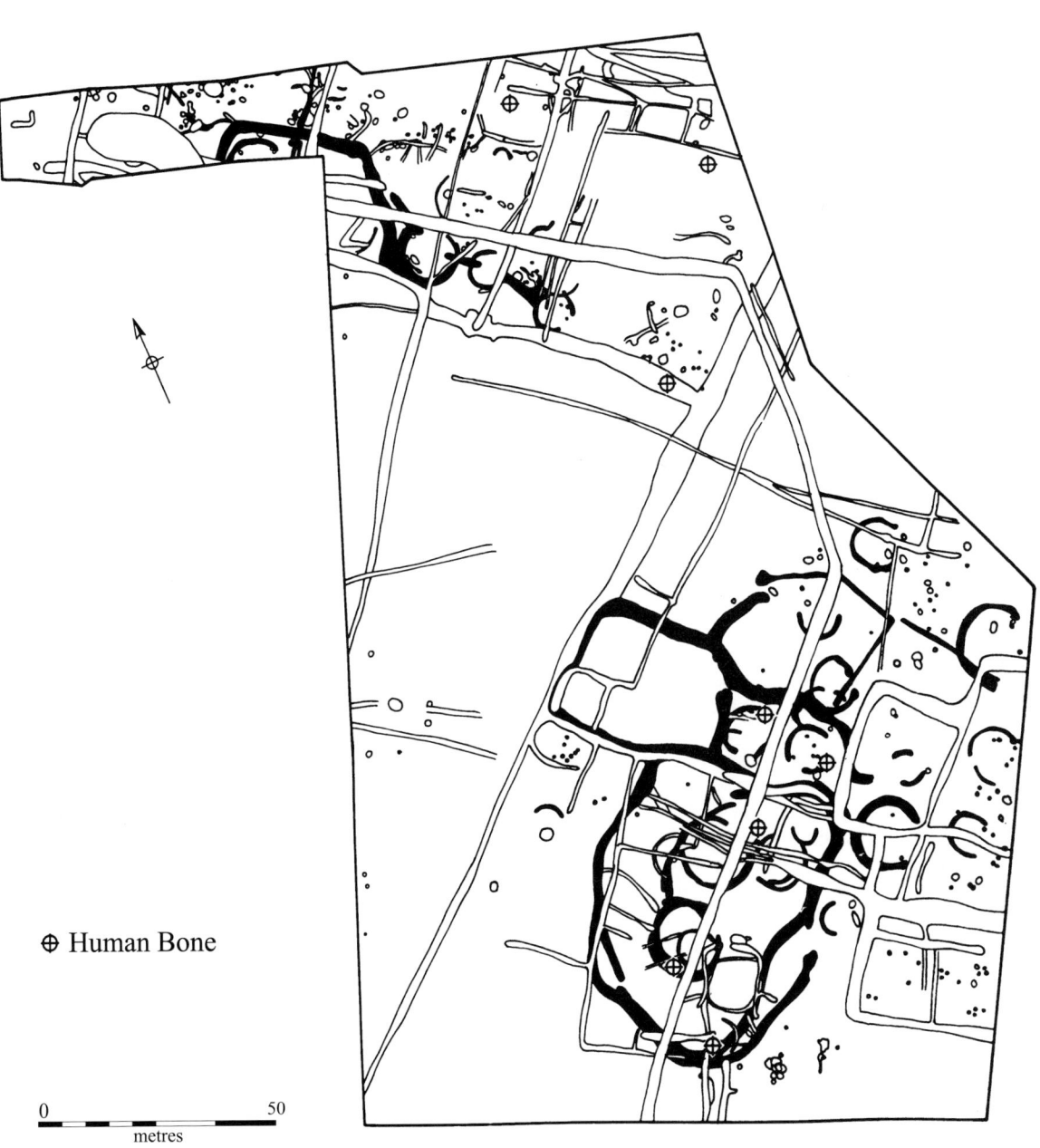

Figure 129 Hurst Lane: Iron Age features (black) with distribution of human skull fragments indicated

have been a 'consumer' rather than a 'producer' site. The site's environmental and economic evidence potentially raises key issues concerning the settlement's status, but which unfortunately cannot be confirmed or developed in advance of full analysis of the subsequent phases of its excavation.

Watson's Lane, Little Thetford: the calculation of buildings
The *c.* 4000m 'core' of this Iron Age and Roman site was excavated in advance of housing development in 1995 (Fig. 127; Lucas and Hinman 1996; Lucas 1998). The settlement evidence was extraordinarily dense and, consequently, residuality proved a major problem when trying to untangle its frequently re-cut paddocks, which in part were contemporary with the Iron Age occupation (Fig. 127). In total, the eaves-gullies of eight later Iron Age roundhouses were recovered. Due to the intensity of subsequent Roman utilisation and the impact of ploughing (ridge-and-furrow prevented aerial photographic appreciation of the settlement) many of these were only slight and fragmentary, leaving between 1.5% and 60% of their circuits available for excavation; their depth also varied greatly, from *c.* 0.05–0.40m. Based on the reconstruction of their circles, the house gullies would fall into two distinct size ranges: 5.4–6.8m (Structures 6–8) and 10–11.3m diameter (1, 2, 4 and 5), with Structure 3 being exceptionally large at 15.4m.

The buildings seem to have been laid out on two approximate north-to-south axes; generally, though not exclusively, the larger ones lay in the eastern line, with the smaller in the western cluster. Although it is conceivable that their different sizes had chronological implications, when considered alongside what is really the sole dating indicator — the frequency of wheelmade wares — there is no discernible distinction. Lucas in his analysis rather interpreted their inter-relationship as essentially complementary, and as one between main residual and ancillary structures. From this, based on their stratigraphic succession and the affinity of their assemblages, four successive pairings were tentatively identified (Table 68).

The relevance of this site to the study of the Ringwork lies in the frequency of finds from the respective building classes. As this was clearly determined by the size of their gully 'catchments', they have been factored according to the percentage of their survival/excavation (Table 69).

There is considerable variability within the finds-population estimates for the Watson's Lane buildings. Attempting to establish some sense of 'mean', with 2017 and 1410 finds respectively, Structures 2 and 4 can perhaps be considered as representative of the 'large-building' totals; with 187 and 211 pieces, the estimates for Structures 6 and 8 provide the same for the smaller ancillary buildings. Although approximately a third to half lower than their Wardy Hill equivalents, the ratio of finds between the respective main/ancillary pairings would be comparable — 1/7–11 at Watson's Lane and 1/9–12 at Wardy Hill (Fig. 128). That being said, Structure 3 at Watson's Lane — the diameter of whose gully was considerably greater than the largest Wardy Hill buildings — has, accordingly, an estimated finds population of 5835 pieces that is actually *c.* 15% greater than either Structure I or IV's totals at the Ringwork. Structure 3 is thought to have been paired with Structure 1, itself a large-diameter building but one that has an estimated finds total of only 649. If so interrelated, at 1/9 the ratio between their finds totals would still be consistent with the other pairings.

Otherwise, estimated totals from the remaining buildings at Watson's Lane, Structures 5 and 7, must simply be considered unaccountably low. However, this may be attributable, in part, to the overall density of the buildings on that site. Their 'packing' may have given rise to intense middening, and heaping and re-deposition of refuse could also have contributed directly to the buildings' densities. (All of the site's major features shared near-uniform dark loam upper fills with high finds densities; probably 'churned', this midden-like matrix made it impossible to establish relationships by plan alone.)

Hurst Lane Reservoir: houses and bodies
Due to planning circumstances, English Heritage-funded rescue excavations occurred across this 2.85ha(+) site over a two-month period in the summer of 1999. Divided into two distinct settlement clusters, the eaves-gullies of 30 later Iron Age roundhouses were recovered (Figs 8 and 129; Evans and Knight 2000a), making it one of the few sites of the period in the region which approaches the scale and density of the Cats Water, Fengate settlement. (Neither of the Hurst Lane settlement clusters were exposed in their entirety and they continued, respectively, east and northwards.) This may, however, be due in part to its greater duration, as the settlement would seem to have its origins in the Middle Iron Age and some elements could easily date as early as the 3rd or even the 4th century BC. If so, both this and the apparent intensity of occupation here when compared to the other Ely sites could relate to the lighter gravel subsoils on which it lay. Starting as an open settlement both its foci subsequently involved a series of interconnecting ditched compounds, with those of the main southern cluster conjoining a large horse-shoe-plan enclosure comparable to the inner circuit of the Wardy Hill Ringwork.

The site's subsequent usage in Romano-British times saw the laying out of a quasi-rectilinear field system with a network of smaller paddocks within its south-east part. Only four structures — of both sub-square and half-circular plan — were associated with this phase. Essentially dating to the 1st to the earlier–mid 2nd century AD, there is clear evidence of Iron Age/Roman continuity; the alignments of a number of the latter's boundaries were directly determined by the paddock system of the earlier phase and the 'Iron Age' roundhouse occupation actually seems to have continued until early Flavian times.

Amongst the most important findings from the excavations was a Class II potin (1st century BC), one of the few instances when a coin of this type has been found in a settlement context. While no Roman coinage was recovered, a 1st-century AD fibula was found. Also of probable Roman attribution was a fragment of a copper alloy bracelet embossed with a leaf-shaped design; a ring was also recovered.

Aside from issues of dating and settlement continuity, the main relevance of this site for the Ringwork's sequence are the various finds of 'loose' human bone. There is, unfortunately, some potential for mis-attribution as Roman burials were also present, and two probable Iron Age burials were also excavated (one an infant). This aside, however, human skull fragments (alone) were recovered from four of the Iron Age buildings within the southern settlement cluster, and from three other locations on the site (some of the latter conceivably derive from disturbed graves). Of the house-related remains, an extraordinary deposit was associated with Structure 2, the main building within the southern horseshoe-plan enclosure. There the dome of a skull, evidently polished through handling (as was also that in Structure 3), had been placed beside a paving of large sherds in the base of a rectangular pit. The skull had been severed by blows to the back and side, and cut marks were visible across the line of fracture. Possibly suggestive of violence/sacrifice, and having obvious significance for the Ringwork's interpretation, this will be further considered in the concluding Discussion (Chapter 6).

6. Discussion: Violence, Power and Place

The heretofore obscure histories of remote islands deserve a place alongside the self-contemplation of the European past — or the history of civilizations — for their own remarkable contributions to an historical understanding. We thus multiply our conceptions of history by the diversity of structures. *Suddenly, there are all kinds of new things to consider.*

Marshall Sahlins, *Islands of History* (1987, 72; emphasis added).

The Wardy Hill sequence raises the possibility of 'new things' in the past. The Sahlins citation, primarily referring to the South Seas, takes on greater resonance in the knowledge that it was Richard Taylor, former Curate of Coveney and later a 'missionary tramper' in New Zealand, who authored the Treaty of Waitangi of 1840 (P. Saunders, *pers. comm.*). Thereby forging what became in, in effect, that colony's constitution and the crown's relationship with the Maori, his involvement tells of unexpected connections, possibilities and avenues of history — appropriate concerns for any fieldwork.

Although most of themes reviewed in this section relate to the Ringwork alone (*i.e.* the Iron Age), the sequence of the site's basic periodisation will still structure this chapter. Faced with potential alternative orderings, this does not relate to any kind of facile concern with 'hard' chronology. Rather, without such period-sequential bracketing of the enclosure's usage (*i.e.* Bronze Age and post-medieval), issues pertaining to its long-term place associations would be sacrificed to the 'apparentness' of its main occupation.

I. Bronze Age: an embanked landscape
(Figs 130–2)

In the light of the evidence for Wardy Hill's utilisation during the Bronze Age, remarkably little material of pre-Iron Age attribution was recovered on Ely's clays in the course of the Fenland Survey (Hall 1996, fig. 87). While highlighting all the more Iron Age densities and perhaps suggestive of contemporary 'arrival' (*i.e.* colonisation), how real is this pattern? Here the results of the Stansted Airport surveys across some 6km on the Boulder Clays of North Essex may offer insights. When compared to only four sites of Middle Iron Age date, the seven there attributable to the Late Iron Age suggest a greater intensity of usage. These all apparently show at least locational continuity into Roman times; three new sites were then also established, taking the total number of Romano-British settlements up to ten (Brooks 1993, 46–53, figs 4.7, 4.8 and 4.10). Equally relevant, however, is that five later Bronze Age/Early Iron Age sites were also discovered. Admittedly the latter period brackets a much longer time span than either the Middle or Late Iron Age. Nevertheless they include at least one substantial

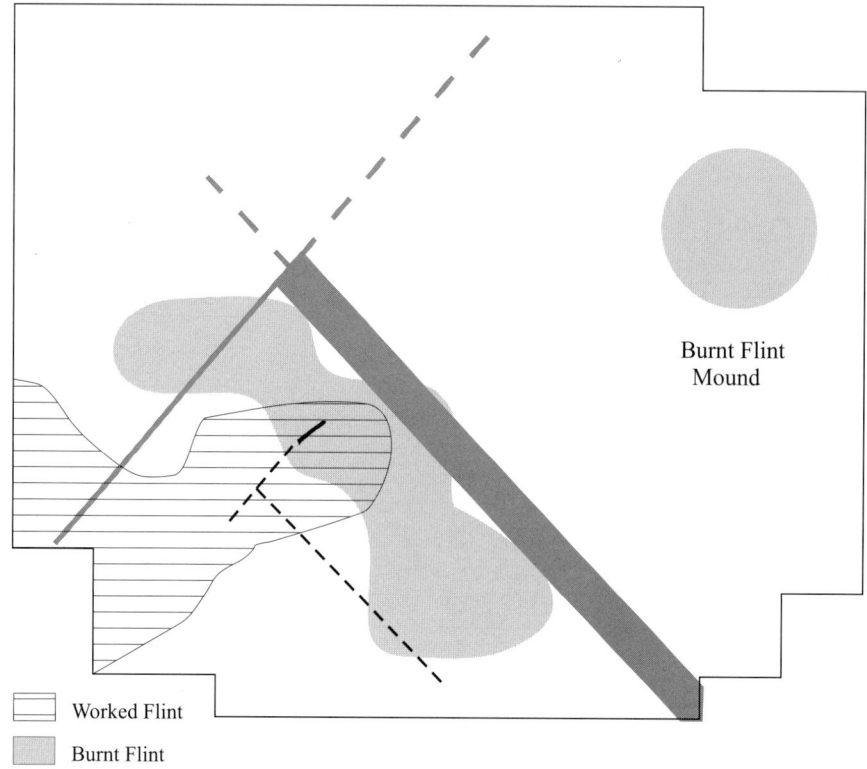

Figure 130 Wardy Hill: the Bronze Age landscape

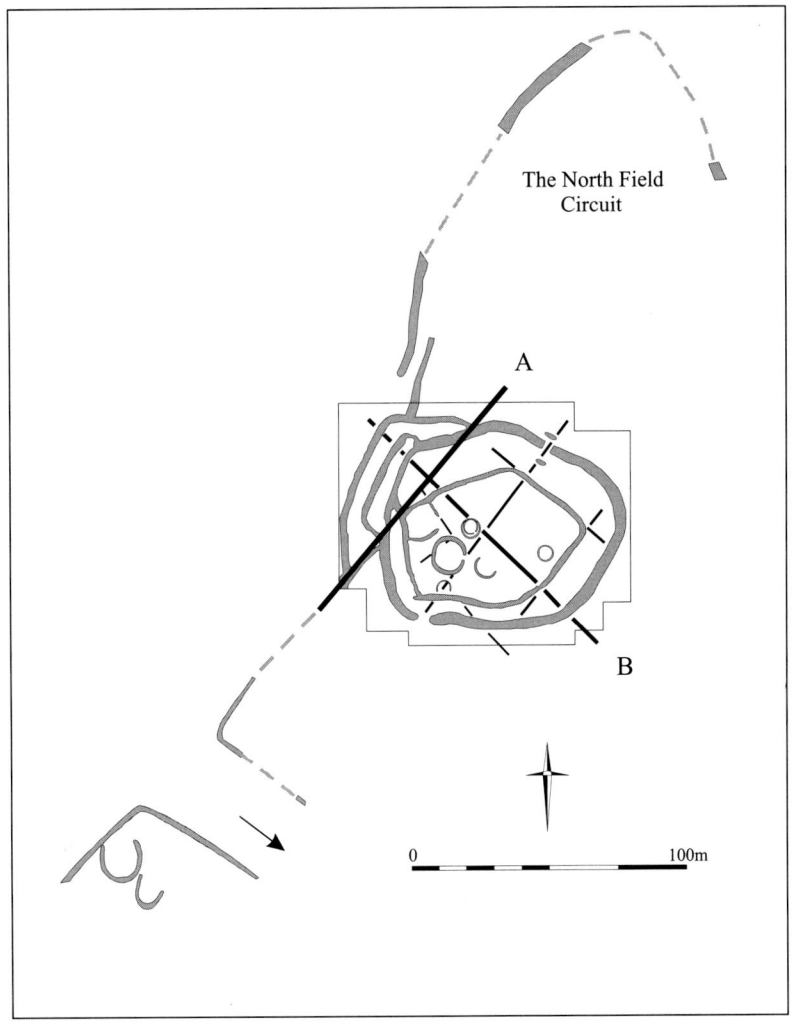

Figure 131 *Landscape axes:* A indicates the main axis of the up-hill system projected northwest across the site; B, the line of the postulated Bronze Age bank with the corresponding network of the Ringwork's 'diagonals' shown.

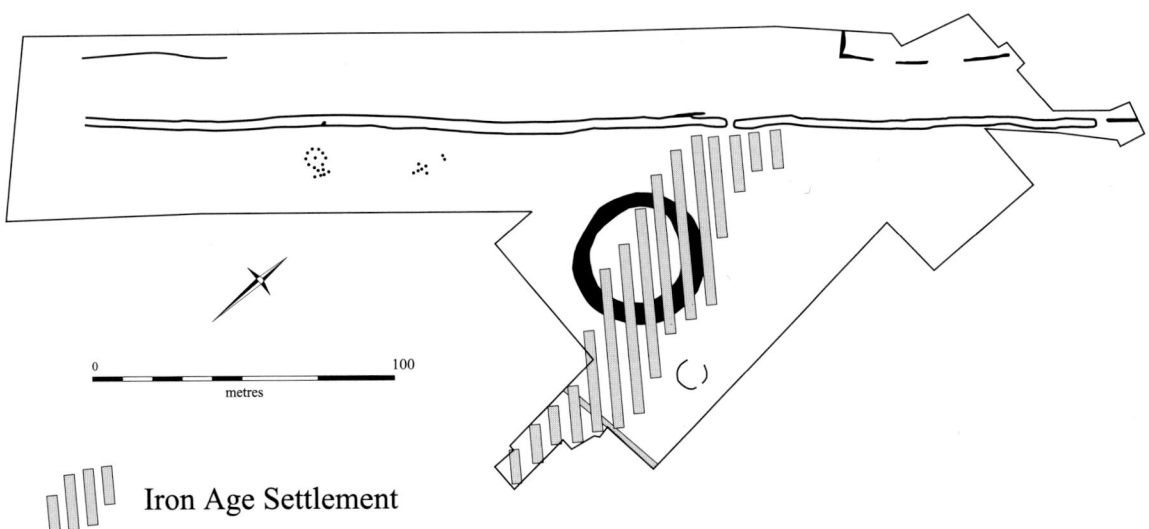

Figure 132 Broom Quarry, Bedfordshire: The relationship between the later Bronze Age double-ditch/bank system and subsequent Early–Middle Iron Age settlement (the latter overlapping an Early Bronze Age barrow)

settlement (the Social Club site; Brooks 1993, 45–6, fig. 4.5), and this indicates that while heavy clays may have discouraged pre-later Iron Age settlement, this was a matter of propensity and not exclusivity (see Knight 1984 concerning earlier Iron Age colonisation of the middle reaches of the River Great Ouse by Midland communities).

Aside from the Period I settlement at Wardy Hill, the evidence of pre-Iron Age occupation on Ely's clays thus far would suggest no more than seasonal visitation. Though no other substantive settlement has yet been recovered, this cannot yet be counted as negative evidence and has probably been biased by a combination of 'expectations' and colluvial masking. Admittedly pre-Iron Age usage is unlikely to have rivalled the intensity suggested by recent recovery rates on the gravel terraces of the region's river valleys. But unless, for example, the quantity of Bronze Age metalwork known from its environs was all imported specifically for the purposes of watery deposition or, alternatively, that the communities responsible were confined to the few localised gravel seams in the area, it is reasonable to presume some degree of occupation on the clays. This will be difficult to find, but so it is on the gravels too and its recovery demands broad, near quarry-scale exposures which have so far been few on the clays.

Given this background, the results of the Wardy Hill excavations are intriguing. As attested to by the spread of lithics and the location of the burnt flint mound, the site was occupied by the north-eastern extent of a low-density settlement. It is difficult to marry this evidence directly with the recovery of later Bronze Age pottery and the putative embanked field system — are they directly contemporary or do they represent separate horizons of Bronze Age usage? From the evidence at hand, this unfortunately cannot be resolved with any certainty. Nevertheless, it is reasonable to presume that most of the flint scatter at least is of later Bronze Age date. As indicated on Fig. 130, the 'high-value' distribution of residual worked flint within later contexts falls on the west side of the bank postulated to run north-west to south-east across the site, and this also correlates with the main west-central spread of struck flint recovered from the surface collection (Fig. 15). Even more telling of their inter-relationship is that the surface-collected burnt flint that rings the eastern end of the struck flint spread seems to have been confined by the bank. With the 'settlement-marginal' burnt flint mound lying on its north-eastern side, this major bank-line clearly structured the early occupation. (The distribution of flint-tempered pottery is equally restricted to the bank's western side. However, because of the situation of the Ringwork's settlement features, so too is the vast majority of the site's ceramics.) While the settlement's dynamics cannot be further disentangled, aside from the absence of slight house circles (although see Fig. 108), its scale and densities are generally comparable to other later Bronze Age settlements recently excavated within the region (*e.g.* Evans and Knight 2000b). Probably something more than a 'camp', to this extent it does begin to provide some degree of settlement context for the Island's wealth of contemporary metalwork.

The inferred existence of a Late Bronze Age field system upon clay subsoils must count as amongst the most significant results of these excavations. Again, its identification can only be considered tentative, and unfortunately no material was produced to provide an absolute date. Yet, given the spread of such field systems now known on the region's gravels (*e.g.* Evans 1999; Evans and Knight 2000b, 2001), surely it leaves too much to environmental determinism to pre-suppose that none would have existed on its clays. Only involving the 'ghosts' of slight ditches and inferred bank-/hedge-lines, the evidence for this system is fragmentary, and could suggest that any later Bronze Age land allotment on the clays may not have relied heavily upon ditched division and, instead, largely involved upstanding components.

The orientation of the on-site bank/field system clearly determined the boundaries that extend across the Wardy Hill-top (Fig. 131). By extrapolation, this pre-supposes that the latter also had its origins in the later Bronze Age. In much the same manner as at Flag Fen (Pryor 2001) this axis may ultimately relate to the alignment of, and the approach to, the postulated causeway to Coveney (Fig. 137). As will be further discussed below, on the basis of regional precedent it would be perfectly reasonable to attribute this crossing to the later 2nd to earlier 1st millennia BC. Given this, it would be feasible to assign the north-west ditch/bank system at least to the earlier Iron Age, if not the later Bronze Age. That the scale of its putative bank matches that of the main north-west to south-east bank raises the question of whether this just represents a very robust field system or if it should be classed as a 'dyke-type' defence. Certainly if topped by hedges it would have made a considerable barrier, impeding landscape movement and, perhaps, restricting the approach down to the causeway.

Regional parallels to such a system could be drawn with the recently-excavated later Bronze Age open stockade/fence systems at Barleycroft Farm on the lower Ouse opposite the Willingham/Over barrow cemeteries (Evans and Knight 2001) or, more specifically, to a double-ditch system at Broom, Bedfordshire. The latter involved minor paired ditches set *c.* 4.00m apart and extended over some 450m; the manner in which the paired ditches joined to produce rounded terminals at crossing-points of the system indicates that it enclosed 'something' (Fig. 132). Presumably delineating a turf bank, its impact in the organization of the larger landscape was clearly considerable, as an Early Iron Age settlement was confined to only one side (Mortimer 1996). Alternatively, the Wardy Hill system might be compared to 'Ranch-type' divisions in Wessex (Cunliffe 1991; see also Dawson 2000 and Malim 2000b concerning large-scale earlier Iron Age boundary systems within the region).

Finally, the scale and later impact of Wardy Hill's later Bronze Age/earlier Iron Age landscape system potentially reflects upon the sense of 'arrival' in the Island's later Iron Age record. While within the confines of the site itself there seems no evidence of direct settlement continuity, this need not imply that Early Iron Age settlement does not lie elsewhere within the larger Wardy Hill-top complex (*e.g.* the southern hill-side spread). Although at a general Island-wide level the marked intensity of the later Iron Age findings may suggest colonisation, Wardy Hill, at the very least, shows re-occupation of a later Bronze Age locale. Unfortunately, the extent of settlement continuity on the Island, and the degree to which it may have been colonised, cannot be resolved until pre-/Early Iron Age usage of its clay soils is investigated more thoroughly.

II. Iron Age
(Figs 133–44; Tables 70–72)

Obviously, understanding of the site during this period is much more detailed and nuanced than for its pre- and post-Ringwork usage, and this raises a number of key points that warrant further development. Having already considered the enclosure sequence at length, discussion here will be confined to major issues: primarily, the inter-relationship of defence, war and social status, and the Ringwork's affinities, usage and role within the larger Cove system. These, in turn, reflect upon broader themes ranging from the period's spatial structures, tenancy and 'landedness', and the character of regionality and cultural 'imprinting'.

Assembly and the translation of space
Having had four major entranceways at various times — of which up to three at one time were contemporary — access into the Ringwork was clearly determined by a number of variables which changed over time (Fig. 133). Paramount was the Landward Entrance in the south-west. Once re-fashioned and thereafter shifting immediately westwards (the II.5 West Crossing), its consistency tells of the importance of southern access from the internal eastern side of the larger Wardy Hill/North Field system.

It is in the later fort phases that the entrances multiplied, and the Ringwork clearly then acted as a nodal point channelling cross-terrace movement. Aside from the Landward Entrance there was the Watergate, which provided access to the North Field Circuit lands via a through-enclosure passage. Beyond this, its original focus was clearly the entrance centrally located along its western 'front' (II.4). Given the earlier (and continued) existence of the Landward Entrance, another western entrance would have only been necessary had the south-western F. 28 boundary already linked the up-Wardy Hill-top system to the main perimeter, necessitating additional 'exterior' access. Thereafter, in the terminal phase, western access could only have been achieved through the pre-existing south-western approach via the larger Wardy Hill-top system. It must indicate the Ringwork's perceived vulnerability that it was when this West Central entrance was closed, in the final phase, that the outworks perimeter was added to this side. Cutting off the 'out-system-side', not only does this blocking attest to a greater sense of westward closure and the perceived direction of vulnerability, but also reflects upon the dynamics of 'back' and 'front' space. Whereas the situation of the former seems to have been constant within the north-eastern half of the Ringwork, 'front space' seems to have shifted from the south-west to the west and then back again. What does seem rather contradictory within the spatial logistics of its 'design' is that western access was obviously thought necessary when the fort was first laid out (II.4). From the distribution of wheelmade wares across its projected axis in that direction, and the evidence for contemporary settlement along the western margins of the site, this approach was clearly much utilised. Closure of this western access, supplemented by the establishment of the Outworks — whilst involving a 'design' compromise — emphasised the Ringwork's role as a fort and must either represent a reduction in, and/or a re-routing of, through-enclosure movement.

Spatially successive, concentrically bounded units of space, like those present at Wardy Hill, lend themselves both to ritual and defensive enclosure layouts (see Evans 1989b for further discussion; Fig. 140). Whereas for the latter it is a matter of delineating zones of exclusion, in the case of ritual usage staged progression inwards is sympathetic to rites of initiation. For each it is 'membership' that allows interior progression: permitting 'insiders' to 'get in', as it were. In this context, the closure of the Ringwork's western entrance must ultimately relate to fear and to perceptions that the 'outside' could penetrate the western axis.

The complex translation from 'bounded settlement' to 'fortified space' involved in the Ringwork's sequence — the change of 'types' — belies the inadequacy of simple enclosure categorisation. Here a line of transition between the two has been drawn at Phase 4. While no doubt marking a significant change, such a hard-edged distinction does seem arbitrary. Is this 'change' only a matter of scale and within a gradient of spatial 'control' (Fig. 134)? In both of its main phases 'fronts' are emphasised and entranceways elaborated to control access. Yet, at the same time, the fort — especially during Phase 4 — saw a much greater formality of layout, and a different balance between the site's domestic components (if it was then occupied at all) and the 'weight' of its *complete* defensive perimeter.

Though presuming some degree of contemporaneity between the Phase 2/3 structures and the Phase 4 fort, at a most basic level the spatial organisation of the Ringwork's interior seems straightforward. All the residential buildings were situated within the western half, with open space in the east (including the Structure VI haystack). The changing ratio of enclosed 'open' space to built space can be measured between its two main episodes of its enclosure (2/3 and 4/5). At 2065m, the secondary area of the inner circuit is approximately a tenth larger that its primary layout (c. 1840m). This difference becomes all the more marked when the area respectively covered by buildings is taken into account:

Primary (Phases 2/3): Structures I, III, V, and VI (c. 250m) — c. 1590m open space;
Secondary (Phase 4/5): Structures IV and II (c. 142m) — c. 1925m open space.

By this measure the secondary open space (not including the inter-circuit 'annex' of c. 375m) would be 20% greater. This was largely because the main building of the site's terminal phase was awkwardly tucked into the corner of the Ringwork, perhaps with the specific intention of creating more open ground. However, this would not account for the area taken up by the interior midden (c. 400m). Essentially a 'late' phenomenon, this would imply that the secondary open space was actually less than in its early layout: c. 1525m vs. 1590m. Yet this qualification might be missing the point altogether. Aside from a handful of pits, in both phases a c. 600m area of the enclosure north of Structure VI and east of Structure V seems consistently to have been left open. It is, in fact, possible that the definition of 'built' and open space was actually formally demarcated by the F. 118 fence and the 'four-pit group' — the main north-west to south-east bank line. If so, this would imply that in both phases an area of c. 1010m (albeit including Structure VI) was reserved as open space. While such a diagonal division of the interior might seem uncomfortable given the circular layout of the

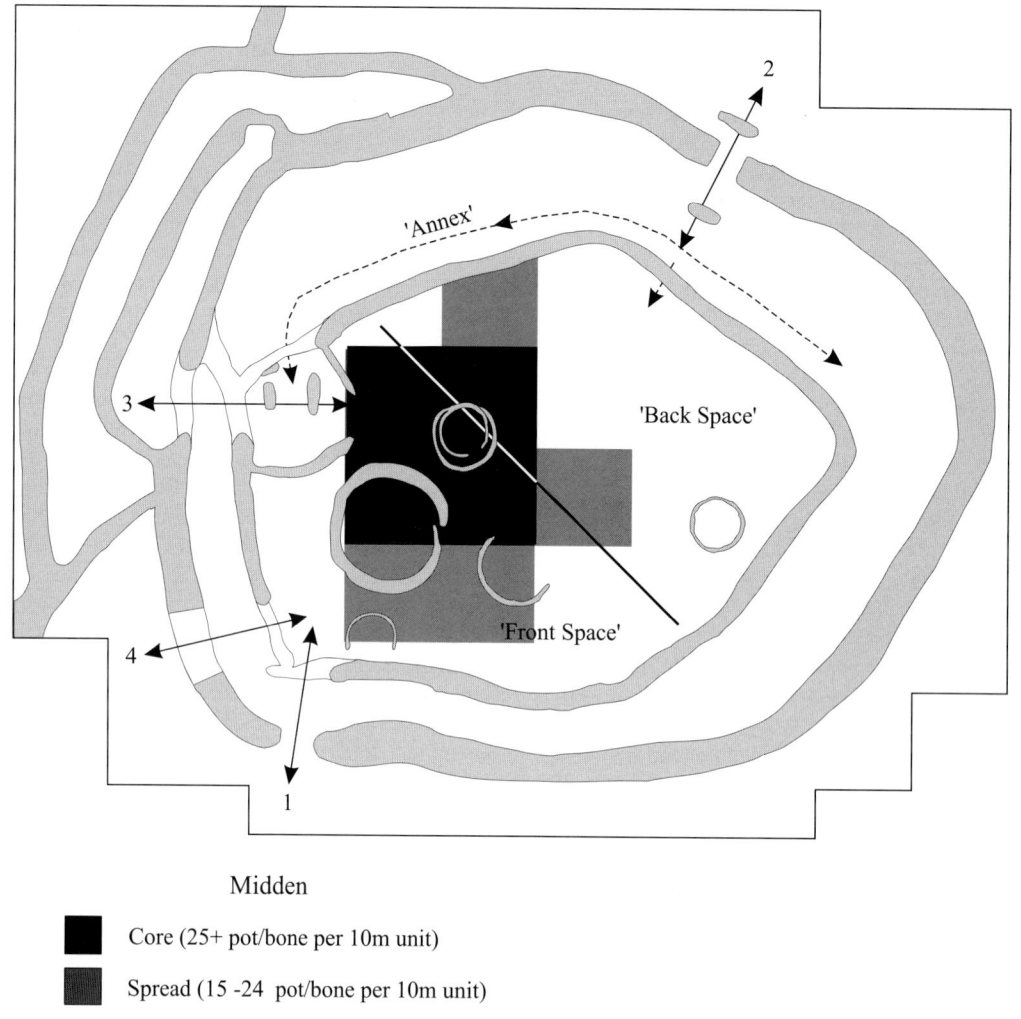

Figure 133 *Ringwork dynamics*. (1)–(4): enclosure entrances, with the dashed lines from the Watergate (2) indicating potential access to behind-bank annex space. Note that the situation of the midden — in front of Structure IV — transgresses the diagonal axial division between 'front' and 'back' space.

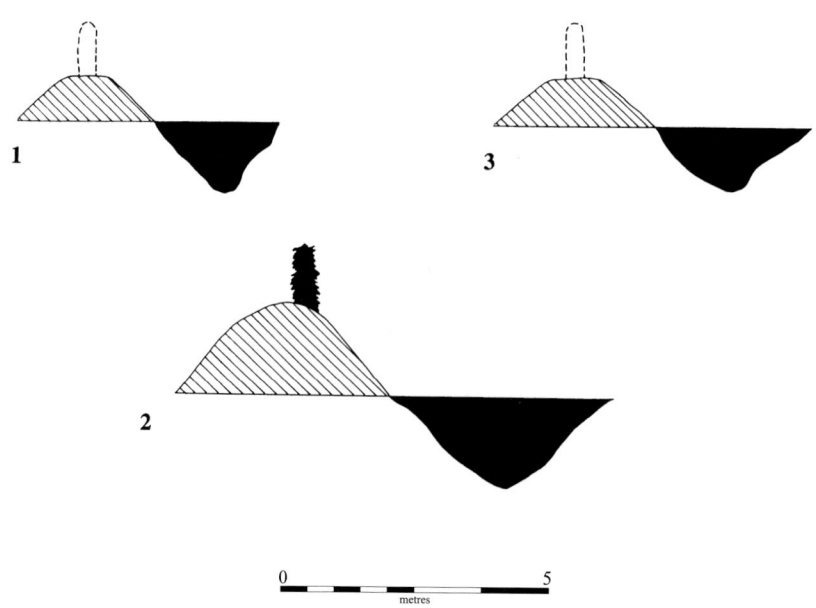

Figure 134 *A gradient of 'control'*. Reconstruction of the ditch and bank system at Wardy Hill: (1) inner circuit; (2) outer, the latter with a 'hedge-work' upon its bank. This is shown in relationship to the circuit of the main Hurst Lane enclosure (3); in both (1) and (3) a hedged barrier comparable to (2) is shown dashed.

Ringwork as a whole, it has already been argued that it would have been complemented by the location of the main entrances, and be consistent with the accumulative/dual spatial principles of its 'design'. However, that the midden appears to transgress this diagonal element could suggest a westward extension of this open swathe in the final period, at least, of the Ringwork's usage.

Aside from its defensive capability, it is the long-term provision of enclosed open space that most clearly distinguishes the Ringwork, and this characteristic becomes even more marked if it was without interior settlement for much of its life-span. The layout of most domestic compounds of the period in the region basically situates the main roundhouse(s) somewhere near their approximate centres, effectively reducing the functional capability of open ground by making it equally peripheral to/around the building (*e.g.* HAD V, Colne Fen A or Werrington: Evans and Hodder forthcoming; Mackreth 1988). The Hurst Lane enclosure, for example, is 'crowded'. Similarly at Mingies Ditches, while in any one of its phases the area of its interior open is comparable to that of Wardy Hill, processes of lateral building shift meant that at one time or another most of its interior was built over (Allen and Robinson 1993) — there clearly was *no space held in reserve*. While Wardy Hill may never have seen the intensity of the Mingies Ditches or Hurst Lane structural sequence, the manner in which all its residential buildings were packed into the western end would suggest the intentional creation (and maintenance) of open ground.

How is this essentially 'empty' bounded space to be understood? Having ruled out its potential usage for corralling, we are left with two possible modes of explanation. The first is that of a *refuge*: a place where stock, and possibly a larger populace, could be harboured at times of conflict. Of course, if this need never actually arose this activity would leave no tangible trace. The alternative explanation would relate this instead to *social assembly*, and where a larger community met: effectively an arena where social rights and duties were negotiated and which saw the 'performance' of tithe and tribute (see Pantos and Semple forthcoming for general discussion of assembly practices). In many respects the latter explanation would better complement the evidence of the site's dense surface midden-type deposits, to which group feasting may have contributed. Nevertheless, it is within the capacity of bounded open space that both of these interpretations may have simultaneously operated. The one — a defended refuge — was perhaps never required, but would have provided the *raison d'être* for the assembled enactment of social obligations (*i.e.* the possibility of defence came at the cost of tributed tithes).

Although the two sites differ greatly in scale and the geometric regularity of their formal planning, given these arguments there are basic affinities between the Ringwork's layout (*i.e.* 'sidedness') and that of the extraordinary Late Iron Age complex at Fison Way, Thetford (Gregory 1992), probably an Iceni shrine complex. In the final, much-bounded form of that site, three round buildings faced onto a large enclosed ground that presumably also hosted large group gatherings (see Table 75). This analogy with the Thetford complex takes on greater resonance in relationship to the 'special' qualities of Structure IV, and especially the recovery of human bone only within its vicinity. Of course its situation, set in the north-eastern corner of the Ringwork, is in marked contrast to the formal centring of the great roundhouses/shrines at Fison Way. Pushed tightly as it is against the rampart, it could be argued that the building compromised the Ringwork's defensive integrity, and that the provision of meeting space was thus held to be more important than defensive considerations. This inference cannot, however, be sustained given that its construction correlated with the closure of the West Central entrance and the establishment of the Outworks System on that side; Structure IV lay well within the defensive 'depth', and if anything the Ringwork's defensive capability was then at its greatest.

The recovery of pattern lies at the heart of archaeology: the establishment of norms and repetitive 'building blocks' that provide re-assurance against the fallibility of excavation practice. As discussed at the start in this volume the 'alien' or regionally non-analogous quality of the Ringwork, especially its Outworks System, seems inescapable. The only obvious comparison for its western defences lies in the organically radiating, entrance-related earthworks of Wessex hillforts (*e.g.* Cunliffe 1991, fig. 14.13). The potential implications of this are extraordinary: the fact that visitors to our site were at pains to evoke more 'domesticated' modes of analogy (*e.g.* 'surely it must relate to stock sorting', *etc.*) reflects just how deeply ingrained are concepts of regionality and 'expectation'. Having duly weighed and dismissed alternative interpretations, it remains — much as it was upon initial encounter in the field — without direct regional parallel. The Outworks, therefore, raise questions concerning the character of independent invention and displaced or 'foreign' influence.

Figure 135 shows the Ringwork's developed form in relation to its neighbouring Iron Age 'forts' (the attribution of Narborough and Thetford being tentative; Davies *et al.* 1991). Whereas Narborough, by its size, provides the closest parallel (1.5ha) it would also have affinities to the organic plan of Stonea (though their scales differ vastly). Given these criteria (*i.e.* size and plan form), the Ringwork would certainly contrast with Belsar's Hill, which could be seen as an outlier of the group of univallate circular forts in southern Cambridgeshire: Arbury, Wandlebury and, possibly, the War Ditches (Evans 2000c). (There is also a cluster of circular enclosures of probable Iron Age attribution in Norfolk such as Warham Camp and South Creake; Rickett in Davies *et al.* 1991, 59–61, 66–8; Evans 1992; Evans and Knight forthcoming). There is not the scope here to review all the region's 'great' Iron Age enclosures and outline the extent of their variability. The Ringwork's basic concentric plan (Phase 4) is perhaps most reminiscent of the enclosure at Tattershall Thorpe: this is almost six times larger than the Ringwork, however (Chowne *et al.* 1986), and would seem to offer no obvious parallel for the Wardy Hill complex (see Davies, *et al.* 1991; Gregory and Gurney 1986; Martin 1988; Morris and Buckley 1978; Evans 1992; Evans and Knight forthcoming for overviews). That being said, it does have other distant affinities to Stonea Camp. Apart from sharing the deposition of cut human skulls (Malim 1992a and b) the minor settlement component of Stonea, in contrast for example to the bivallate Borough Fen enclosure (French and Pryor 1993; Malim and McKenna 1993), neither justifies its scale nor the complexity of its enclosure sequence. Due largely to the occurrence of coin hoards and other

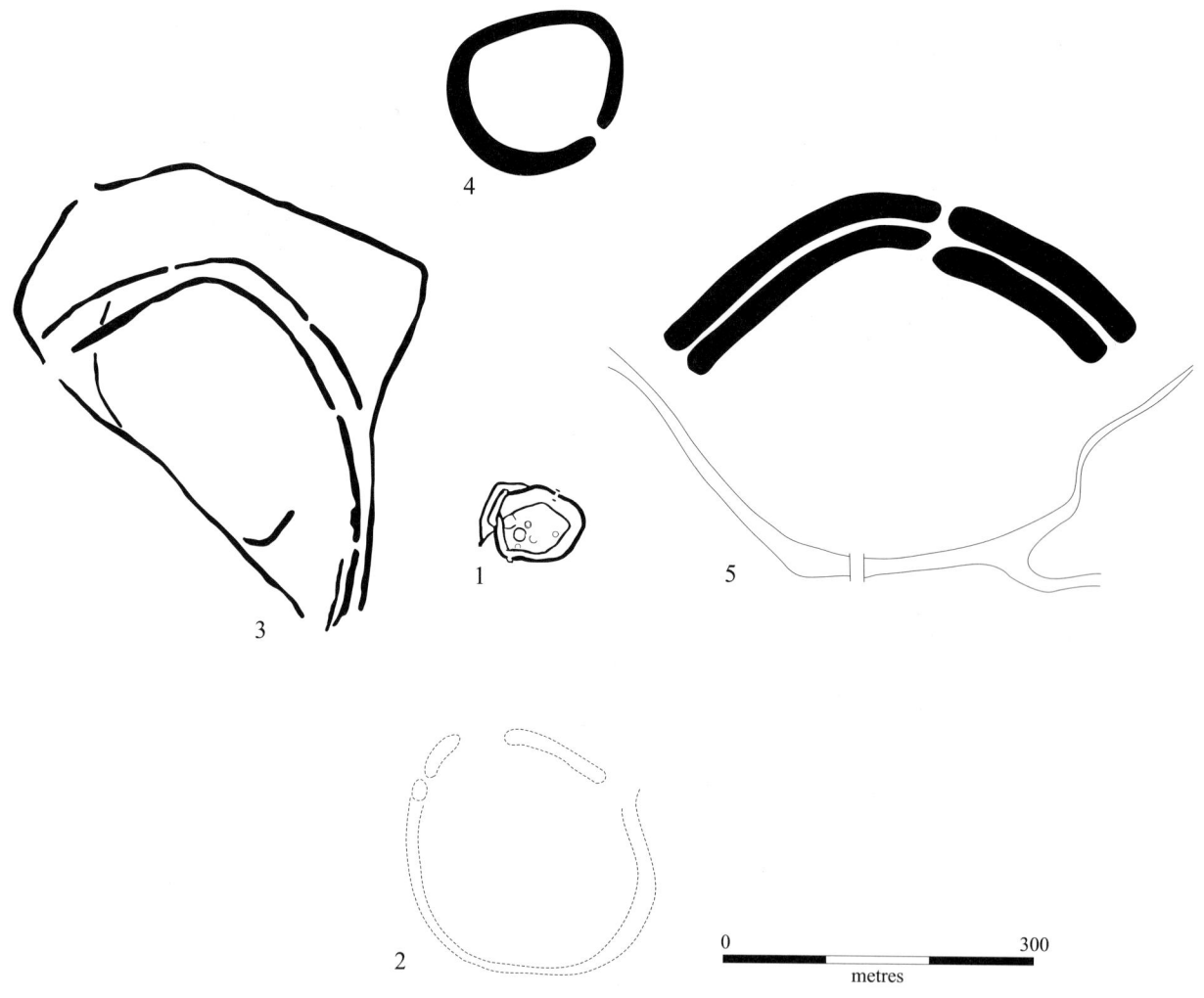

Figure 135 Iron Age 'forts'. Wardy Hill (1) and its neighbouring enclosures by directional proximity: (2) Belsar's Hill, Cambs. (after Hall 1996, fig. 79); (3) Stonea Camp, Cambs (Jackson and Potter 1996, fig. 4; Malim 1992 a and b); (4) Narborough, Norfolk (after Davies *et al*. 1991, fig. 43); (5) Thetford Castle, Norfolk (after Davies *et al*. 1991, fig. 43).

metalwork of the period within its vicinity (and in relation to its essentially empty interior), it has been characterised as a trade/exchange and ritual 'centre' (Jackson and Potter 1996). Similarly Arbury, through its paucity of occupation remains, has been envisaged as a 'commanding gesture': effectively a 'false-front' fort staking a claim to land (Evans 1992; Evans and Knight forthcoming). Like Wardy Hill — which may also have been essentially 'empty' through much of its sequence — their role as assembly places may have been crucial, first in their actual construction and subsequently as places of group gathering.

Given the marked differences in scale, form and function between the Ringwork and the other known defended enclosures of the period in the region, while the site was being excavated general parallels had to be sought further afield: primarily Mingies Ditches (Figs 136.2 and 135.8.4; Allen and Robinson 1993), Gussage All Saints (SU 005115; Barrett *et al*. 1991, fig. 6.4e) and Orsett Cock (Fig. 136.3; Toller 1980; Carter 1998). (In terms of enclosed, sub-ovoid Iron Age settlements the Little Waltham complex would also provide a comparison, and there are undated crop-mark sites in Essex that have vague affinities: Drury 1978a and b; Buckley *et al*. 1987, fig. 35). Since that time, however, fieldwork along the western margin of Ely has greatly expanded our knowledge of the later Iron Age occupation on the Island. The horseshoe-shaped enclosure excavated at the Hurst Lane Reservoir provides a close parallel to the interior circuit of Wardy Hill (Figs 137 and 143; Evans and Knight 2000a). Of the same later Iron Age date, and with four roundhouses (two very substantial) within its interior, its recovery re-casts the context of the Ringwork. Instead of seeing it as some kind of regional variant on 'grand' hillfort models, it seems more a matter of a defensive elaboration of a basic settlement form. What then becomes crucial, of course, is the nature of this elaboration — the *translation* of a 'domestic module' (see *eg*. Taylor 1997 concerning spatial transformation). As already discussed, paramount here is the absence of open space within the Hurst Lane enclosure. Its buildings are centrally placed and its interior also eventually became 'packed', suggesting that it had little or no capacity for assembly. Another major difference with the Ringwork — whose

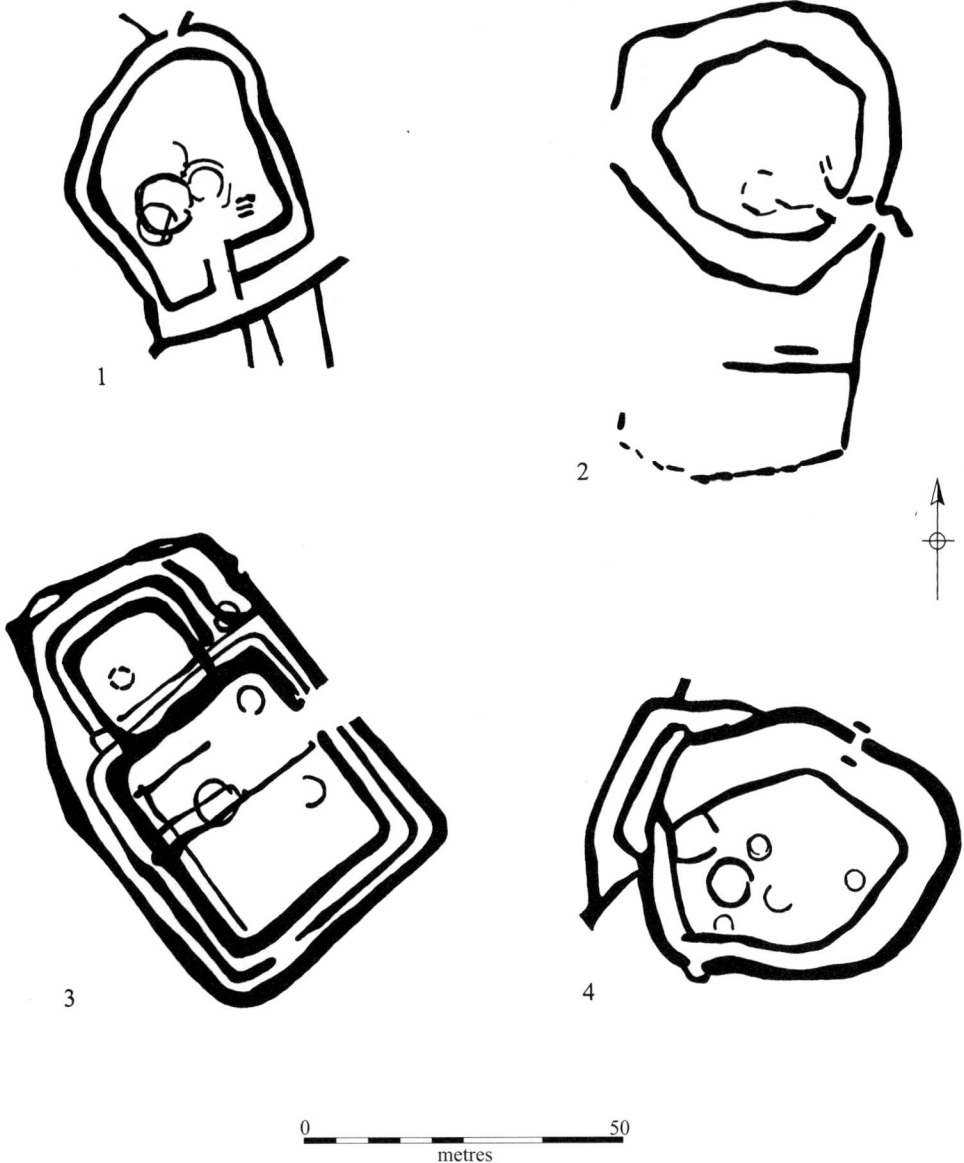

Figure 136 'Elaborated' concentric enclosures (extra-regional affinities): (1) Groundwell Farm, Wilts (Gingell 1982); (2) Mingies Ditches, Oxon (Allen and Robinson 1993); (3) Orsett Cock, Essex (Toller 1980); (4) Wardy Hill.

basic layout, once the 'horseshoe' was established, continued relatively 'pristine' — is the compounding at Hurst Lane. Involving the re-modelling of its circuit and the addition of small paddocks to its north-eastern side, this degree of re-working is both telling of the greater intensity of its settlement components (*i.e.* population and number of houses) and of the fact that compromise/alteration may be characteristic of prolonged and more exclusively domestic usage: the 'messy' fabric of daily life.

The discovery of a local parallel to the 'core' of the Ringwork is somehow reassuring, as it helps to root the seemingly 'alien' quality of its plan as a whole. Nevertheless, still entirely without regional precedent is the ripple-like layout of the site's western Outworks. Although general affinities could be sought in the elaboration of antennae-like ditch systems such as at Gussage All Saints (Wainwright 1979), Mingies Ditches (Fig. 136.2; Allen and Robinson 1993) or Groundwell Farm (Fig. 136.1; Gingell 1982), these seem without any direct parallel within Eastern England and are evocative, though at a much reduced scale, of Wessex models of fortification. Of course, in Wessex itself such layouts are essentially a Middle Iron Age phenomenon. Here, the dating of the Wardy Hill Outworks becomes a moot point. Although not without some element of ambiguity, they seem to relate directly to Phase 5 developments — the closure of the West Central Entrance and the establishment of Structure IV — and, accordingly, must be 'late' (2nd–1st century BC). How are we, therefore, to account for the Outworks in the light of the earlier associations of comparable systems elsewhere? Is this just a matter of the fens being 'late again', or does it reflect subsequent exposure to earthwork defences? The issue of what could have inspired this must remain open, along with consideration of whether it is just a 'sided' elaboration of concentric perimeter (*i.e.* 'invention') or reflects a displaced individual's familiarity with distant modes of defensive layout (*i.e.* grafting something seen elsewhere onto a local enclosure form). Pots and other elements of material culture evidently moved: why not people? In this manner, the Ringwork's sequence raises key questions concerning the transmission of knowledge and 'style'.

Defensive architectures, status and the labour of others

By way of introducing this section, a personal aside is relevant. Whilst excavating in Kurdistan, Iran, in 1978 our host village was subjected to a sheep raid. Occurring in the middle of the night, it engendered great fear and mayhem as an up-mountain tribe descended upon us. (Inspired by anti-revolutionary sympathies, this same group had slaughtered 25 merchants in a neighbouring town the day before.) Though the arrival of the horsemen provoked consternation and alarm, the ultimate outcome was only a broken arm and a few sheep taken. The threat and the fear was genuine but the outcome was minimal, and would certainly have left no discernible material traces. Offering a more immediate correlate is the World War II pill box which still commands the crown of Wardy Hill proper. Highly symbolic in the brutal modernism of its geometric design and a manifestly concrete testimony to war/defence, nonetheless it never saw action.

When trying to strike a balance the poles of current Iron Age hillfort studies — between war and symbolism — perhaps the real problem is understanding the linkage between defence and warfare, and whether one must necessarily determine the other. The need to command a strategic locale cannot by any means be weighed in terms of the presence/absence of the evidence of conflict. Rather, defensive architecture implies possible threat and/or a need to control, but not necessarily war. If 'peaceful communities' are the only alternative lacking direct evidence of war *per se* then this is an unequal equation, and relegates most archaeology to being only a record of quasi-utopian communities. It is the *perceived* need to dominate landscape and the perception of vulnerability that must be the determining factors, with the latter involving the risk of raiding, the theft of stock and the potential for intimidation, abduction or violence against individuals and/or families. This is quite a different matter from war as practised today. While leaving few material 'signatures' (*e.g.* burnt stockades) the social impact of this threat in prehistory, and its correlate in the impetus to control, should not be underestimated: both imply alliance and closure (see Carman and Harding 1999 concerning the 'archaeology of war'). The performance of war is, of course, itself highly ritualised and physical enclosure will always have symbolic implications (Evans 1997a; Hingley 1984). The problem here, given the flavour of so much recent interpretation, is whether the absence of evidence of mass destruction of defences now must *de facto* imply only symbolic behaviour. If so, it implies that symbolism cannot have content rooted within the 'active world'.

While there is no direct evidence of war at Wardy Hill, the degree of manipulation of the human remains certainly suggests violence to bodies. Crucial, of course, is whether this was inflicted on corpses or reflects the causes of death. In other words, does it actually constitute the elaborate burial rituals of the Ringwork's inhabitants or the 'sacrifice' of others? Unfortunately, this cannot be resolved with certainty. However, the deep chop mark on the humerus shaft from Structure IV was probably the result of a heavy blow from a sharp-edged instrument (*e.g.* sword, axe or cleaver) and may well have been a wound inflicted in combat. Equally at the Hurst Lane settlement, aside from the recovery of polished (*i.e.* much handled) human skull fragments, there is the extraordinary pit deposit associated with the main roundhouse within the horseshoe-plan enclosure. The dome of a skull within it had been severed by heavy blows to the back and side of the head; cut marks were also visible across the main fracture lines (Dodwell in Evans and Knight 2000a). While the recognition of 'loose' human bone has recently proved widespread on Iron Age settlements (*e.g.* Hill 1995), these pieces rarely show such an extreme degree of intentional 'dissection' (see however Bayley 2001 concerning the perforated skulls and skull vault 'bowls' at Billingborough). Although we must be wary of judging the past by normative standards of behaviour, nor should we be blind to potential terror in the record. These remains only occur in the final phase of the Ringwork's sequence; within the rhetoric of more systematic modes of analysis they could be seen as indicative of 'stress' in response to the marked changes then occurring within Late(st) Iron Age societies in southern England. Whatever terminology is adopted, this does not seem to reflect any manner of 'friendly' group ritual (*i.e.* 'playing' with the dead). It is difficult to imagine that these actions could be performed on the body of a close relative, and some element of sacrifice seems likely.

When exploring Iron Age settlement systems, and particularly the issue of defence, the ethos of a 'Celtic society' cannot be avoided. Due critique has been made of its 'warrior spirit' (Champion 1997; Fitzpatrick 1995); the period's much-evident weaponry may have often ended in being ritually deposited, and largely relate to the display of status. Yet there is no escaping that this was, at least in part, an armed society and that its 'displays' were of a certain kind — one whose implied threat would have structured social relations and fostered obligation (*eg.* Randsborg 1999; see also Treherne 1995). Otherwise those models that have most thoroughly explored the potentially hierarchical nature of Iron Age settlement and ranked systems of land-use draw upon the textual evidence for contemporary social relations: as if one must have a direct correlate in the other (Clarke 1972; Cunliffe 1984). Given this, are (for example) the main buildings at Wardy Hill to be considered the 'halls' of chieftains or 'knights'? (see Evans 1998b for further discussion.) Whilst not accepting any kind of simplistic 'one-to-one' linkage, it would be naive to deny (proto-)historical sources and, in the face of their stratified world of serfs, vassals and slaves, only espouse a vision of a 'free peasantry'. (Admitting to the potential existence of 'lesser-order inhabitants' could affect the evaluation of domestic space *vs.* occupation within very small buildings.)

In his paper 'Warfare in the Iron Age of Wessex', Sharples (1991) explored differences in the character of defence, group identity and individual status throughout the Iron Age. Relating the developed hillforts of its Middle phase to a broadly-based control of agricultural resources and land, he argued that it had a corollary in group definition through the construction, maintenance and subsequent expansion of these great earthwork enclosures. In contrast, the Late Iron Age saw a marked rise in weaponry and a decline in hillfort construction, with wealth becoming more mobile and tied to long-distance trade: something individuals could steal and kill for. Although this is not a model arising from the 'Eastern' English sequence (though the impact of trade and contact was equally significant there during the later Iron Age), it is relevant that the final elaboration of the Wardy Hill Ringwork — though having its origins in, and seeing its main development during, the Middle Iron Age — appears to correspond with the latter, *Late* horizon.

Given that the radiocarbon dating of other fort-type enclosures within the region has been restricted to only one or two samples, and considering the problems of calibration in this period, it is difficult to compare the Wardy Hill sequence with them. Variously spanning the 5th–4th to the 2nd centuries BC, and when combined with the evidence of their pottery sequences, the dating of Stonea (2070±65BP, 360 cal BC–80 cal AD; OxA-3620; Malim 1992b), Borough Fen (2090±80BP, 370 cal BC–80 cal AD; Har-8512; French and Pryor 1993), Tattershall Thorpe (2350±90BP, 770–200 cal BC; Har-4315; Chowne *et al.* 1986) and Arbury (2160±50BP, 380–40 cal BC; OxA-6582 and 2250±60BP, 410–160 cal BC; Beta-142340; Evans and Knight forthcoming) would suggest that they had their origins during the Middle Iron Age. Yet these date assignments that rest on only one or two measurements must must conceal considerable complexity in the re-use and modification of these enclosures. This problem may be typified by Tattershall Thorpe. Its single date, obtained from primary ditch fills — 770–200 cal BC (Har-4315) — is the earliest of any of these, yet it would seem to correlate with only one of the sherds recovered, with the remainder of its pottery apparently 'Late' and attributable to the first half of the 1st century AD (Chowne *et al.* 1986, 183). To this extent, and as is possibly the case at Wardy Hill, it is essential to remember that these were monumental earthwork constructions, and the impetus for their subsequent usage/re-investment may have been quite different from the social processes that led to their construction in the first place.

Comparing the Ringwork with the contemporary settlements west of Ely — especially given the density of buildings at Hurst Lane — it is imperative that the settlement swathe discovered along the southern side of Wardy Hill is borne in mind, as it may have been quite extensive. The location of what are obviously two quite substantial building eaves-gullies detected in the geophysical survey clearly correlates with the surface spread found at the foot of the spur (Fig. 137). Together, the evidence suggests that the settlement there extends over an area of *c.* 0.5ha, and could well continue much further to the south along the gravel terrace beds. (The Wardy Hill environs could have readily sustained upwards of fifteen households: see *Landscape resources and carrying capacity* above.) From the geophysical plots the house gullies seem bounded by the opposed 'L'-shaped alignment of ditches that define one side of the 'great' drove running down to the fen and the putative causeway crossing. The settlement appears contemporary with the spur-top dyke system, and therefore with the Ringwork itself. Presuming that at least two contemporary household groups, and possibly many more, are represented the nature of their relationship with the Ringwork's sometime inhabitants is crucial — separate but equal (*i.e.* co-operative affiliation), or hierarchical and possibly one of clientage? Given that these respective settlement clusters were 'knitted' within the broader enclosure system, the spatial remove and extraordinary

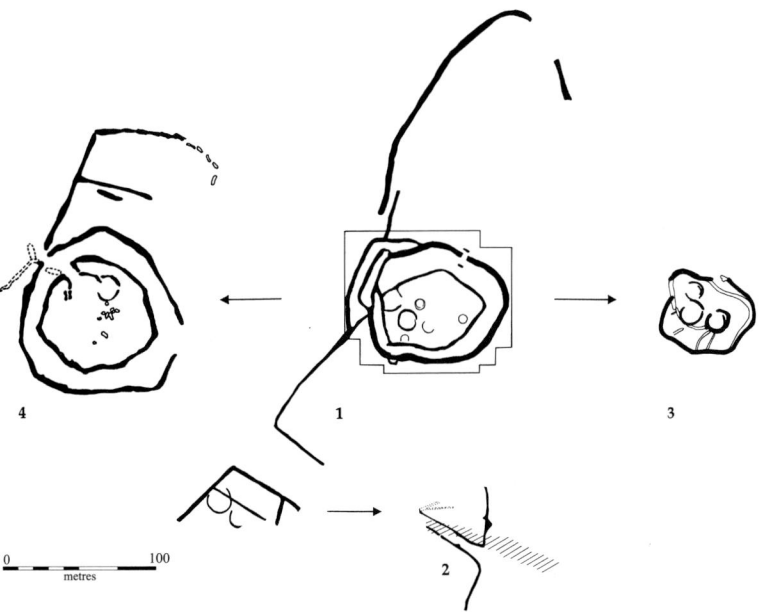

Figure 137 Comparable Iron Age enclosures and components: (1) The Wardy Hill System; (2) Fengate Power Station, showing junction of 'post alignment' (shaded) and droveway system (after Pryor 1991, figs. 85 and 89); (3) the 'horseshoe-plan' enclosure at Hurst Lane, Ely (Evans and Knight 2000a); (4) Mingies Ditches, Oxon (Allen and Robinson 1993). (Note that, whilst shown to the same scale, the orientations of (3) and (4) have been adjusted from north).

bounding of the Ringwork settlement — evidently a residence to only one household — the latter certainly seems the more likely proposition, suggesting that their relationship was hierarchical. Whether or not this fulfilled any of the abstract criteria of formal chieftainship seems irrelevant given the nature of the immediate evidence. All that can be said is that it does not appear to be a matter of equality but an *expression of power*.

Once it is accepted that such items as swords or shields were evidently only deposited off settlements — whether in graves or watery votive deposits — it does not advance study of the period that the recognition of social differentiation within the settlement record rarely amounts to more than an expression of 'first amongst equals' (*e.g.* Pryor 1984). Beyond, perhaps, a certain threshold of house size (*c.* 8.00m+ diameter; Fig. 138) elite display need not necessarily have any immediate correlates within the domestic record. Should we really expect that having a sword would directly result in an increase in, for example, the numbers of loomweights *etc.*? Given what now appears to be the insensitivity of the domestic record to such representation — beyond, perhaps, having achieved the status of a metalworking site (however broadly based this distinction might be) — is, for example, the recovery of the site's decorated wooden container *or* the Samian platter *or* the La Tène-style vessels sufficient to tip the balance of status-related 'distinction'? (It is a salient lesson from the remarkable preservation of the HAD V enclosure, which allowed for near-total artefact recovery, how little of the material collected — considerably less than 1% — 'spoke' directly of status, and how much of this derived from the site's surface deposits: Evans and Hodder forthcoming.) The other side of this issue is, of course, the possibly limited scale of any such social hierarchies: the restriction of their social distance and the degree to which élite households may have been grounded in their local communities. A lamb, for example, received from (or, alternatively, given to) five to ten households might account for the entire material expression of these social relations. If so, our detailing of the record may simply be insufficiently subtle to distinguish such traces.

Ultimately none of the recovered artefacts necessarily reflect, by type or density, an elevated status for the Ringwork's inhabitants. What is more compelling, however, is the scale of the workforce required for the site's construction. By whatever means — élite command, coercion or group co-operation — the Ringwork itself, let alone the associated 'landscape' systems, obviously involved a considerable expenditure of labour and, as already argued, participants were probably drawn from further afield than the immediate settlement(s) itself.

As evidenced by the radiocarbon dates, the enclosure's interrupted or 'gapped' settlement sequence raises the problem of labour, and by what means the Ringwork was constructed. Seen as a defended enclosure without interior settlement for most of its lifespan, it might be considered as a quasi-communal group project. Though organisational direction is, of course, implied by its scale and the co-ordination of its execution, this need not have entailed the hand of a formal social hierarchy. Alternatively, Structure I may well have stood during the Ringwork's early usage, and the social organisation responsible for the defended farmstead could also have lain behind the construction of the larger enclosure complex. This is an issue without easy resolution, which essentially hinges upon how we envisage or 'want' the past to be. Yet spatial correlates between the Phase 2/3 and Phase 4/5 enclosures seem ancestral (*e.g.* locational continuity of the Landward Entrance, determination and 'rippling' of the outer perimeter off the earlier F. 2 circuit, and the core situation of Structure I in both). From this, support could be drawn for the latter argument: that the origins of the Phase 4 Ringwork lay in the earlier defended farmstead and its social relations. If so, what then remains unanswered is whether the subsequent demise of that building reflects a change within immediate social relations (*e.g.* decline of a particular family *vs.* 'the group') or simply a shift of the household exterior to the Ringwork proper.

It is difficult to locate the Wardy Hill Ringwork between the household compounds and 'great' enclosures of the period within the region. Table 70 indicates the inter-relationship between the occupied space and cubic capacity of their ditched perimeters of 'domestic-scale', later Iron Age fen-edge enclosures in comparison to the Ringwork. While the interior of the HAD V enclosure, at *c.* 1220m, is relatively small and densely packed, the bounded 'living zones' of the Colne Fen (A) and Hurst Lane enclosures (respectively extending over 1656 and 1850m) are roughly comparable with the area of the inner circuit at Wardy Hill (2065m); the compound at Plants Farm, Maxey, was approximately a quarter larger in area (Gurney, Neve and Pryor in Simpson *et al.* 1993; the Werrington enclosure is discussed below). There is, however, considerable variability in the cubic capacity of their ditched surrounds. Ultimately concerning the 'heaviness' of boundaries, this of course becomes greatly exaggerated in the case of the multiple circuits at Wardy Hill. It is what truly distinguishes the enclosure within this grouping: the boundaries that delineate the area of almost 3,000m between the 'lived' interior and its total area (5036 m).

Although the average dimensions of the Hurst Lane enclosure, aside from length, are greater than those of the inner circuit at Wardy Hill (despite their comparable plans), within this group of enclosures only the circuit at the HAD V enclosure is comparable to the profile of the outer Wardy Hill boundary. While there is some risk of circular argument, the HAD V compound is also thought to have had a defensive capacity (Evans and Hodder forthcoming). The relative 'weight' of that enclosure's boundary and the Ringwork is expressed in their shared ratio between the area of their enclosed space and the cubic capacity of their perimeters. Both have values of 3.8:1 — significantly lower than for the other enclosures. Otherwise, ditches of this size are almost exclusively found only in the great enclosures (*i.e.* 'forts') within the region — Arbury, Stonea, Borough Fen and Tattershall Thorpe — where they are *c.* 4–9.00m across and *c.* 1–2.00m deep (Table 71; see Evans and Knight forthcoming b). Although the Haddenham compound demonstrates that there need not be a relationship between enclosure size and circuit profile, this may be a matter of an exception proving the rule. (Pryor 1982 discusses the possibility of timber-only defensive enclosures within the region; see also Dix and Jackson 1989 concerning defence and ditch capacity.)

Using Startin's estimate that a gang of four workers would dig between 5.43m and 8.15m per day (Startin 1982), creating the Wardy Hill Ringwork in its totality would have entailed four to eight times greater investment

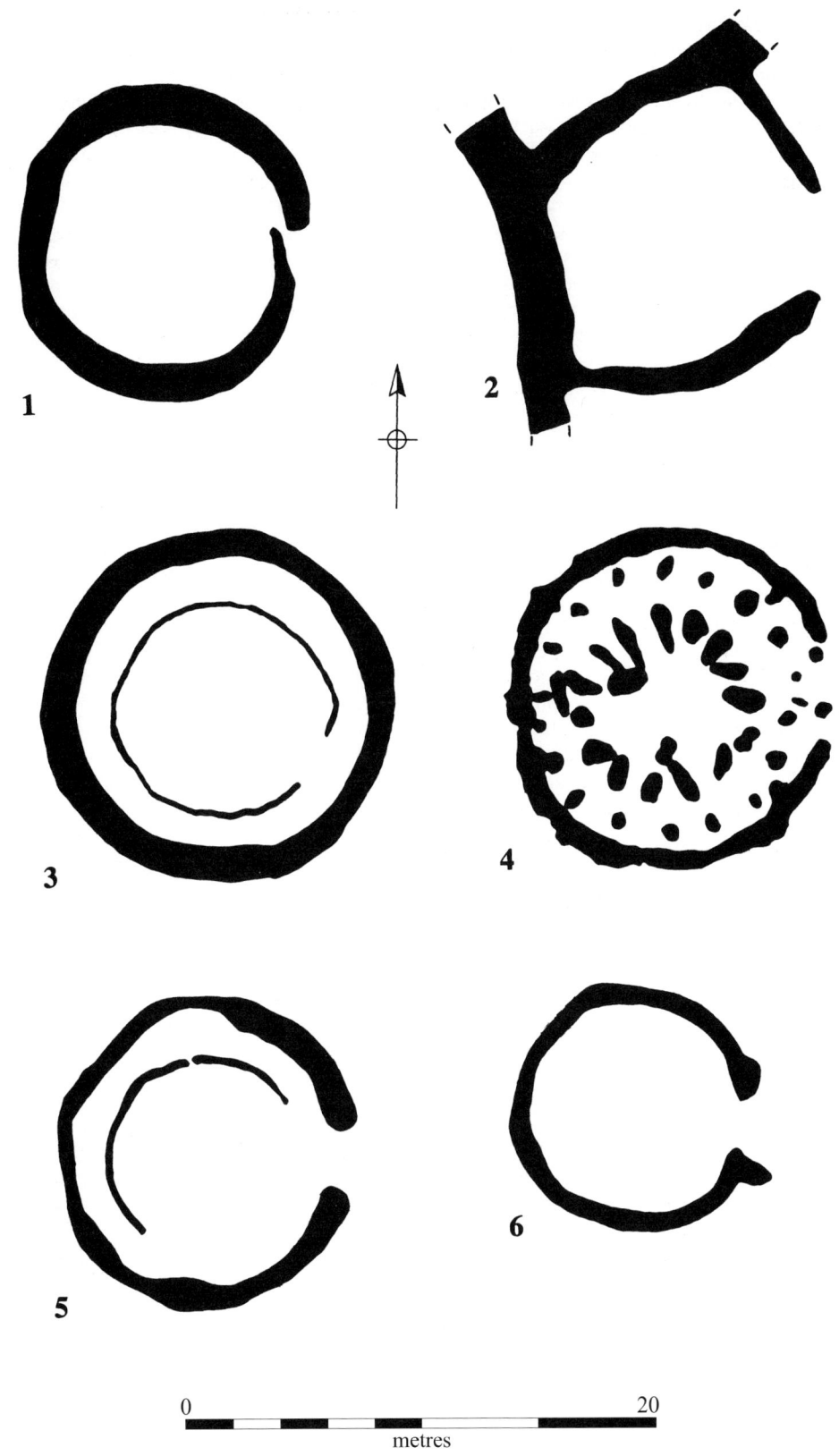

Figure 138 *Great houses:* (1) and (2) Wardy Hill Structures I and IV; (3) HAD V, Building 4 (Evans and Serjeantson 1988; Evans and Hodder forthcoming); (4) Fison Way, Thetford, Building 2 (Gregory 1992); (5) Structure I, Colne Fen, Earith (Regan and Evans 1988); (6) Structure 20, Cats Water, Fengate (Pryor 1984).

in labour than these other 'domestic' enclosures. These estimates are based on excavating gravel, and not clays such as those at Wardy Hill: these would have involved much heavier work, and therefore only the lower of these figures may be employed. Even then, all of these figures are probably still too low. It is unlikely that work would have occurred in an uninterrupted, regular eight-hour regime over such a span, and they take no account of bank construction (*i.e.* 'grooming' and transportation of spoil; Fig. 134). Nevertheless, they provide a basis for relative measure, and the *c.* 240-day, four-person team estimate for Wardy Hill indeed represents a substantially greater investment than the one to two months estimated for the other enclosures, which could be readily accommodated within the span of perhaps a winter. No manner how the Wardy Hill figures are calculated (*e.g.* ten people over 96 days, or 88 days if the inner perimeter was not dug at the same time), it clearly involved more labour than one extended family could reasonably have provided. Labour may, for example, have been tithed, and it could be envisaged that 5–10 family groups may have provided one or two members for a period of 3–4 months during the Ringwork's construction.

Thus far these arguments have only involved the Ringwork itself, and not the larger Wardy Hill system across the North Field lands and the spur-top itself. Extending in total over 2ha, their inclusion represents more than a threefold increase in the area of the Ringwork alone (and probably greater, as surely not all of its components have been detected to their full extent). If these are incorporated with the Ringwork, this would entail some 1600 person days' labour (4.4 years for an individual, or some 400 days for a gang of four). Yet, while massively greater than the figures for the domestic enclosures (Table 71; Fig. 139), this is still substantially less than the labour input/perimeter capacity of the 'great' fenland enclosures of this period (by a factor of two to four) — a discrepancy which tells of the 'betwixt' status of the Ringwork.

The Wardy Hill system differs greatly from these other 'great' enclosures, which essentially seem organised as single unified entities. It instead saw a series of *components*: the Ringwork fort on the lower spur appended to a large dyke system laid out to control access down to the causeway approach and, in the south of the system, evidently another settlement swathe (Fig. 137). Strung out in this manner, in some ways it is almost oppidum-like in having a number of distinct foci (and seemingly also enclosed 'open' space). Yet, ultimately, its layout is probably based on neither of these models — neither an oppidum nor a great 'single' enclosure — and its strongest affinities probably lie with defended farmsteads. Elaborating upon the architectural grammar of domestic compounds, it is basically a modest-sized Ringwork fort connected with a larger dyke system.

To provide a further sense of perspective, in Table 72 what can be considered 'medial-scale' enclosures are compared to the Ringwork in terms of their size and labour demands. Ranging from large enclosed settlements (Little Waltham) to the Fison Way shrine complex, in terms of morphology alone Mingies Ditches certainly provides the

	Ditch length (m)	*Area (m)*	*Perimeter (m)*	*Ratio*	*Labour*
Had V	143	1221	322	3.8/1	39–59
Colne Fen (A)	156	1656	153	10.8/1	19–28
Hurst Lane (Main Enclosure)	156	1850	247	7.5/1	30–45
Plants Farm, Maxey	199	2756	268	10.3/1	33–49
Wardy Hill					
Inner Circuit (F.2/38)	177	2065	179	11.5/1	33*
Total Ringwork	574	5036	1311	3.8/1	241*

Table 70 Comparison of the cubic capacity of enclosure perimeters and estimated labour required (after Startin's figures of 5.43–8.15m for a four person team per day; * indicates lower figure for clay working); 'Ratio' indicates co-relationship of interior area and ditch capacity.

	Ditch length (m)	*Area (ha)*	*Perimeter (m)*	*Ratio (m/m)*	*Labour (4 x days)*
Wardy Hill					
Total Ringwork	574	0.50	1311	3.8/1	241*
Total System	1001	2.16	2185	9.9/1	402*
Tattershall Thorpe	1156	2.93	4195	6.9/1	515–772
Arbury Camp	872	5.94	4231	14/1	779*
Stonea Camp (III)	1207	6.35	5720	11/1	702–1053
Borough Fen	1767	7.51	9430	8/1	1157–1737

Table 71 Cubic capacity/estimated labour comparison between the Wardy Hill Ringwork and its larger system and the other 'great' fenland Iron Age enclosures (* indicates lower estimate based on working in clayey subsoils). While each of the circuits of Tattershall Thorpe, Borough Fen and Stonea (Phase III only: Jackson and Potter 1996, fig. 5) may have been built separately, like the Arbury circuit they appear unto themselves as if constructed in one episode. Therefore their scale, variously involving 224–1309 days for a four-person team (3.12–14 single-person years), would certainly have required a substantial 'dedicated' workforce raised by a social mechanism of some kind.

closest parallel. This even extends to the area of its bounded 'core', which at 2054m is only some 10m less than the Ringwork's. However, its perimeter was much less substantial and would have only required approximately a third to half the same construction labour. While of totally different, sub-square/-rectangular layout, in terms of construction demands the primary enclosure complex at Fison Way (Gregory 1992) and the Werrington compound (Mackreth 1988) are both more closely comparable, with the area of the latter more closely matching that of the Ringwork (Fig. 140). A sub-square compound with a large central roundhouse (very much akin to an enlarged version of the HAD V site), the layout of the Werrington enclosure is relatively simple and is generally typical of a 'class' of household compounds within the region (Evans and Hodder forthcoming). What distinguishes it however, aside from its overall size, is the massive scale of its ditches. At 1.60–2.10m depth and 4–5.00m across, these compare with those of both the other defended compounds and the 'great' enclosures within the region. Interestingly, the ratio between its area and the cubic capacity of its perimeter is also in the same 3–4:1 range as the Ringwork and HAD V, which could suggest that it, too, had a defensive capacity.

In the face of ambiguities concerning defensive attribution and its relationship to the character of concentric spaces, attention should be drawn to the basic similarities in centrally-focused layout and scale that exist between the primary Fison Way complex and the Werrington compound. Rather than displaying a distinct suite of 'ritually-related' characteristics, the former is only really interpreted as a shrine on the basis of its subsequent elaboration. The concentricity of its circuits cannot be held to be its sole determining attribute since, as already discussed, this is equally applicable to defensive space. In this context the primary Fison Way enclosure may conceivably have been a defended farmstead; given the dynamics of group assembly, the subsequent transformation of defended space into ritual space would have been a sympathetic one.

Figure 140 is therefore intended to express ambiguities which underlie simple enclosure classification — is Werrington to be considered as a domestic compound, and/or did it have a defensive component? Equally, given its lack of 'hard' non-domestic evidence and the logistics of concentric depth (and if Wardy Hill was basically a fort), then what makes Fison Way a shrine? If it is only the latter's central great building (albeit possibly one with a clerestory — much as Woodbury's was first reconstructed: Gregory 1992; Bersu 1940), then we also know this to be characteristic of a range of domestic enclosures of the period (*e.g.* Werrington, Colne Fen *etc.*). What this highlights, quite simply, is the impossibility of drawing any absolute distinction between domestic, ritual and defended space. None of them would have been exclusive and ritualised behaviours would surely have occurred whenever people meet *en masse,* sanctioning authority and binding the group. Although essentially a fort in its later phases, the possibly 'shrine-suggestive' plan of the inner ring of Structure V within the Ringwork, and the deposition associated with Structure IV, surely indicates that activity at Wardy Hill, too, had a ritual component.

Before broadening discussion to encompass the Cove environs, the inter-relationship between compounded settlements and concentric spatial structures warrants further comment, as both can represent a 'doubling' of a basic enclosure form. Yet, whereas it is in the nature of concentric construction to respect and effectively mirror an original core, 'domestic' compounding is inherently additive: projecting something new (though related), be it a stockyard or household compound, off from a primary unit (or units). It may be intrinsic to the nature of domestic life that such processes of expansion generally result in more organic forms, and effectively erode 'pristine' spatial structures. Compounding may equally reflect upon the issue of tenancy and the long-term investment of labour within plots (both fields and their associated compounds) — the decision to re-build and expand at one locale rather than shift to a new site. This would seem distinctive of later 1st millennium BC settlement and is something that did not occur previously (see Dawson 2000 and Hill 1999 concerning enclosure compounding and settlement shift). What is irresolvable is to what extent this was a matter of *choice* — perhaps telling of different patterns of familial bounding and residence (*i.e.* inheritance and the accumulation of the domestic 'surround') — or whether *tenancy*, at least locally, was proscribed through a hierarchical control of land (*i.e.* social obligations tying communities to land).

This discussion returns us squarely to the moot point of the Ringwork's phasing: specifically its transformation into a fort in Phase 4 with the addition of the concentric outer circuit. It is conceivable that at the end of the Phase 3 defended settlement's usage, the decision could have instead been made to add secondary compounds onto (perhaps) its western side. Whatever the reason(s) why this was not done — immediate threat, an enhancement of the authority of its residents and/or familial or larger group population dynamics — it was this choice that determined the enclosure's formal spatial structure and its predominant attribution as a fort, distancing it from the 'purely' domestic. (The addition of the western Outworks, while a major development, was not such a turning-point since it only further emphasised its defensive capacity, and was not a 're-direction' as such.)

Causeway approaches and marshland networks

The proposal that the greater Wardy Hill system controlled access to a causeway leading to Coveney calls for an appraisal of such routes across the southern fen. Within the immediate Ely area only that at Little Thetford/Stuntney has been excavated, and that summarily by Lethbridge in the 1930s (1934 and 1936). Consisting of large driven posts, this was assigned to the later Bronze Age. A similar date can also be proposed for the Aldreth causeway approaching the island from the south. On the 'landward' side it is commanded by Belsar's Hill, a univallate ring fort (Fig. 135.2). Although associated with Hereward's defence of the Island against the Normans (as indeed was also the Stuntney crossing), based on its relationship to the surviving relic field system, and by the recent recovery of Iron Age pottery eroded from its ramparts, this fort must also be of Iron Age date (C. Evans and D. Hall *pers. obser.*; Hall 1996).

The most renowned causeway system within the region is, of course, that approaching Flag Fen, which seems of the same later Bronze Age date as the well-known timber platform itself. With much accompanying metalwork, it has been ambiguously termed a 'timber alignment' and its ritual significance emphasised

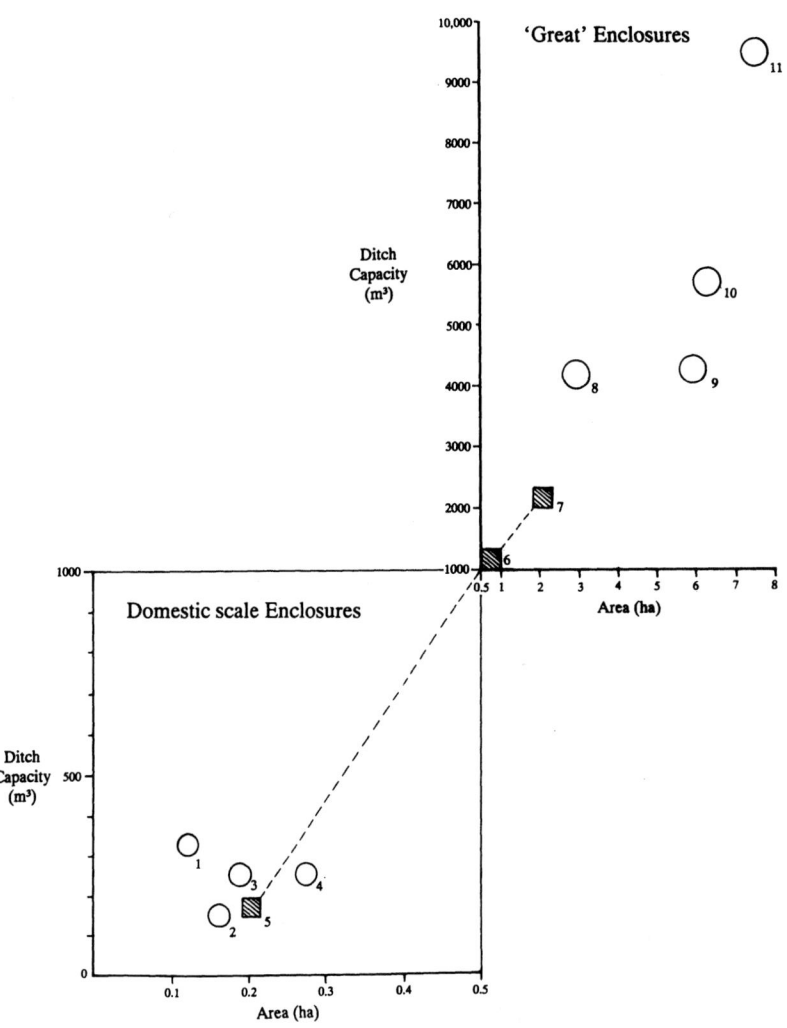

Figure 139 Plot of ditch capacity against area of both domestic-scale and 'great' regional enclosures: (1) HAD V; (2) Colne Fen (A); (3) Hurst Lane enclosure; (4) Plants Farm, Maxey; (5) Wardy Hill inner circuit (F. 2 only); (6) Wardy Hill Ringwork (with F.1 and outworks); (7) Wardy Hill total system (with spur-top and northern circuits); (8) Tattershall Thorpe, Lincs; (9) Arbury Camp; (10) Stonea Camp (III); (11) Borough Fen.

	Ditch Length (m)	Area (ha)	Perimeter (m3)	Ratio (m2/m3)	Labour (4 x days)
Werrington	268	0.47	1331	3.5/1	204**
Little Waltham	327	0.76	481	15.8/1	59–81
Mingies Ditches	410	0.45	715	6.3/1	88–132
Gussage All Saints	510	1.03	928	11.1/1	171*
Wardy Hill, *Ringwork*	574	0.50	1311	3.8/1	241*
Fison Way					
Phase II, Enclosure	653	0.95	1651	5.8/1	203–304
Phase III, Enclosure	1240	3.62	3182	11.4/1	390–586

Table 72 Comparison between the Wardy Hill Ringwork and 'medium-scale' enclosures (* indicates lower four-person working estimate based on working in clayey subsoils; ** denotes averaged day-rate range as Werrington's perimeter cut through gravel upon clay deposits)

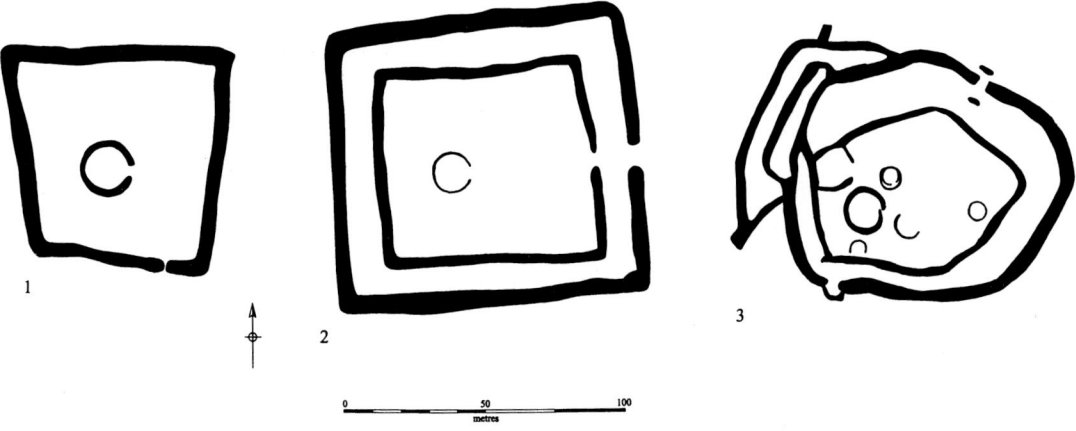

Figure 140 *A spectrum of ambiguity:* concentricity and enclosure. (1) Werrington, Peterborough (Period I; Mackreth 1988); (2) Fison Way, Norfolk (Phase II, Enclosure I; Gregory 1991); 3) Wardy Hill.

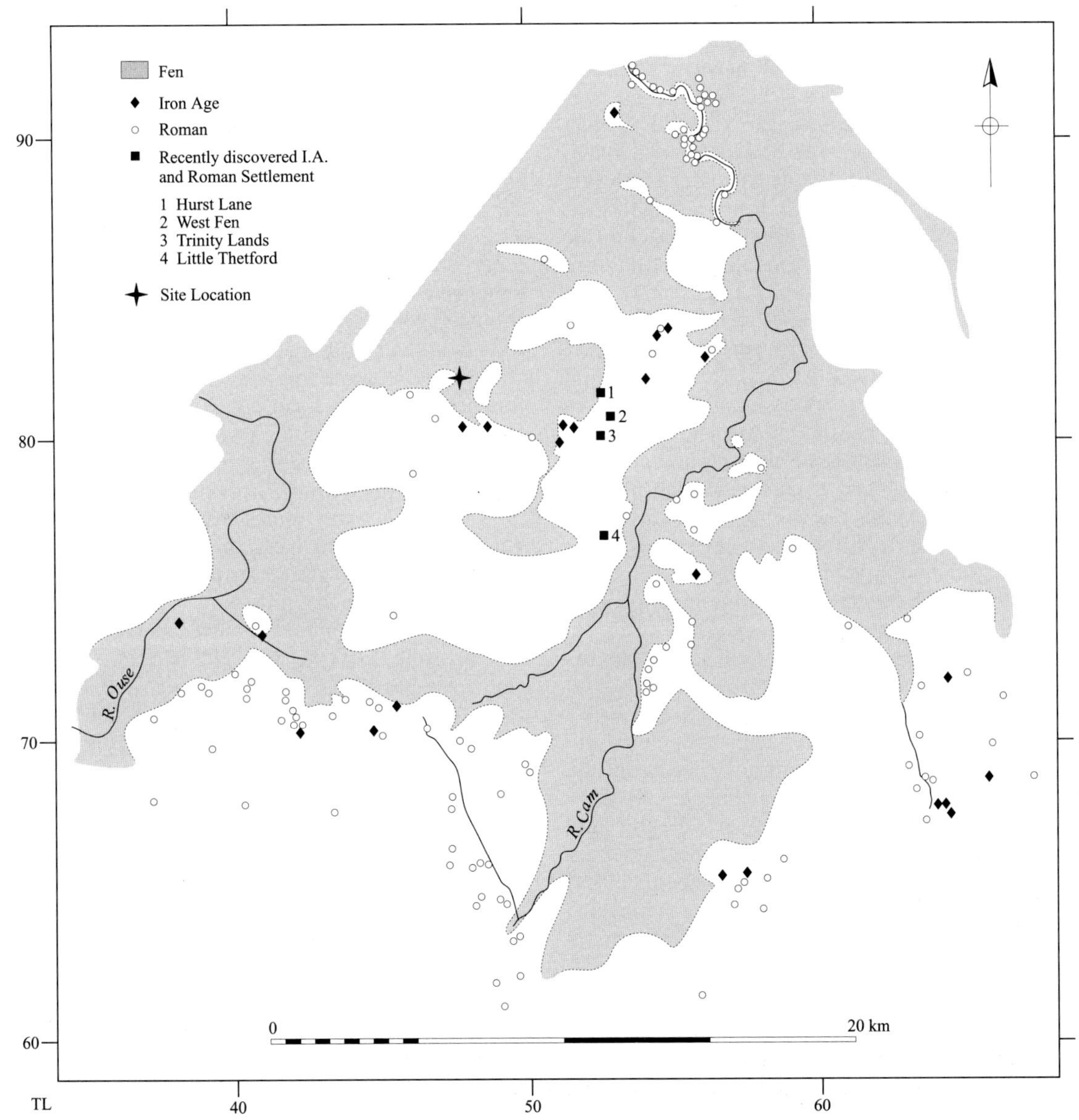

Figure 141 Iron Age and Roman distributions in the south-western Fenlands (after Hall 1996, fig. 88)

(Fig. 137.2; Pryor 1991 and 2001). However, the pattern/interval of its post-settings leaves little doubt that these relate to the re-establishment of a raised causeway comparable to that at Stuntney (Evans and Knight 2001). Further north in the southern Lincolnshire fens the construction of such routes continued into the Iron Age, as evidenced by the Fiskerton causeway, which also saw much 'in-wet' metalwork deposition (Field 1986; Field and Parker Pearson forthcoming).

In terms of the definition of strategic landscape locales and routeways, the importance of this means of cross-fen transportation should not be underestimated. With continuous occupation from Iron Age to earlier medieval times, the larger West Fen Road site was clearly a long-term 'place' (Mortimer 2000; Regan 2001) and was possibly related to a causeway crossing, leading either to Coveney Island or, more likely, Downham (Fig. 142). With dense Saxon settlement remains extending over at least 6ha, all beyond the bounds of the present-day limits of Ely — *i.e.* early settlement may extend right across the width of the saddleback ridge on which the town sits — its recovery may therefore demonstrate the primary role of trans-fen causeway communication prior to the 12th–13th centuries AD. Only thereafter, perhaps, was the nature of social organisation (and the impetus of foreign trade) sufficient to permit riverside reclamation on a scale which allowed rivers to become the predominant means of fenland transport.

Based on geographic factors, the existence of other early fenland causeways have also been proposed (Malim 2000a). Within the context of Wardy Hill, what is relevant (aside from their later Bronze and Iron Age dating) is their accompanying votive deposition and, based on the example of Belsar's Hill (and possibly an Iron Age precursor to Ely Castle itself: Baggs nd), the ringworks/forts that commanded them. Ritual and defence, or at least *control*, are things go that hand in hand. Crossing these rickety and much-rebuilt causeways would probably have been perilous: appeasing the gods beforehand may well have been considered auspicious. Equally, tolls may have been demanded for the passage.

Apart from the fact that it commands the putative causeway route to Coveney, there is nothing in the immediate landscape of Wardy Hill that need have given rise in itself to such an elaborate defensive system. This, and the evidence from the subsequent Ely environs investigations, may call for a re-situation of the Wardy Hill complex. Perhaps more than a centre in its own right, rather it seems to command the north-western access into the Cove, which itself may have encompassed a 'settlement system'. While we must be wary of confusing topography and cultural geography, since these are not necessarily the same, here the importance of causeway linkages — effectively communication corridors — comes to the fore, and are what provided broader direct connections with the site (Fig. 142). In relation to the West Fen complex and cross-Cove causeway routes, the question of what once lay on Coveney Island itself (potentially undetected under the present village) arises. Its dramatic locale would certainly have recommended it as a natural marshland fortress. Equally, the importance of interconnection between the Cove and Grunty Fen to the south, commanded by Witchford — 'The Watch on the Ford' — must be acknowledged, and the siting of Iron Age sites there may have been equally strategic.

The group of western Ely sites seems to form part of a distinct system. Aside from what seems to be their regular spacing, at approximately 400–500m intervals, all share a common chronology. Established in the Middle/Late Iron Age, each apparently continued without interruption into early Roman times. It is the latter which is perhaps their most distinctive trait, as work in the region would otherwise lead us to expect discontinuity as the norm. There seems every reason to think that the sites discovered by survey around the southern side of the Cove are part of this same network and, with them, the Wardy Hill complex.

Certainly, the clustering of sites around the Cove is very marked when considering the broader distribution of sites of the period in the southern fenlands (Fig. 141). This is further emphasised by the lack of such sites across the southern two-thirds of the Isle of Ely itself. (Although unlikely to have then been entirely uninhabited, this paucity of settlement there must reflect some 'reality' as it was subject to the same intensity of field survey as the northern part: this was, after all, how the vast majority of the Cove's sites were found in the first place.) This is clearly not a matter of an island-wide distribution pattern but of one focused upon the Cove's marshes. An attractive 'niche' environment, it would have offered the immediate provision of seasonal wetland resources (including pasture) from the raised flanks of the Island, where arable farming could have been practised free from the risk of winter floods. Yet there can be no specific environmental determinants for this settlement pattern. Ely's other embayments, and those elsewhere along the southern fen-edge, would have presented the same resource potential but were evidently not utilised to this extent.

Socio-cultural and 'historical' factors must have contributed to the character and establishment of this settlement network. Here two approaches are possible, ultimately relating to the respective roles that either continuity or colonisation are thought to have played. In terms of the latter, a larger community 'coming into land' may have been able to assess its potential relatively coldly and, if wishing to maintain the (sub-) groupings with which they arrived, may have settled in close proximity. Alternatively, if settlement continuity is stressed, then the putative cross-Cove causeway routes may have been the critical factor. Perhaps established in part in relationship to broader communication/transportation linkages (*e.g.* extra-Cove/off-Island), if dating to the later Bronze Age then they may have attracted subsequent occupation. (It is also possible that the loss of skirtland through the encroachment of marsh during the later 2nd/earlier 1st millennia BC may have resulted in a retreat of settlement to more elevated locations, and consequently to higher local settlement densities. This, however, would have been a widespread phenomenon and cannot itself account for the Cove's settlement densities.) Although there are linkages between the later Bronze Age and Iron Age usage of Wardy Hill, it is not presently possible to determine whether this is a matter of direct continuity or if it simply reflects the re-use of a favoured locale. Nevertheless — and when taking recovery bias into account — given the broader patterns of Ely's settlement sequence in the 1st millennium BC (*i.e.* paucity of Early Iron Age occupation) the density of its later Iron Age settlement is unlikely simply to reflect population growth within local communities. It probably indicates some degree of colonisation of the Island's clays. This would be consistent with the

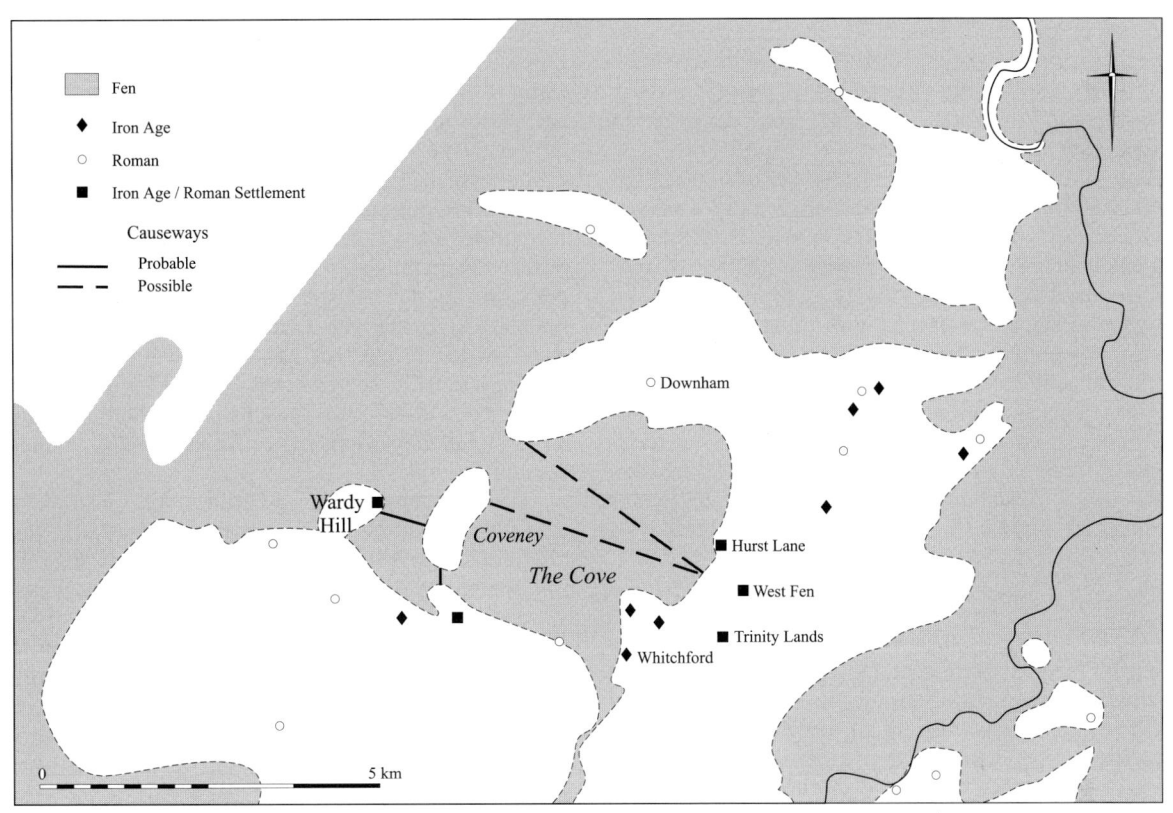

Figure 142 The Cove settlement system

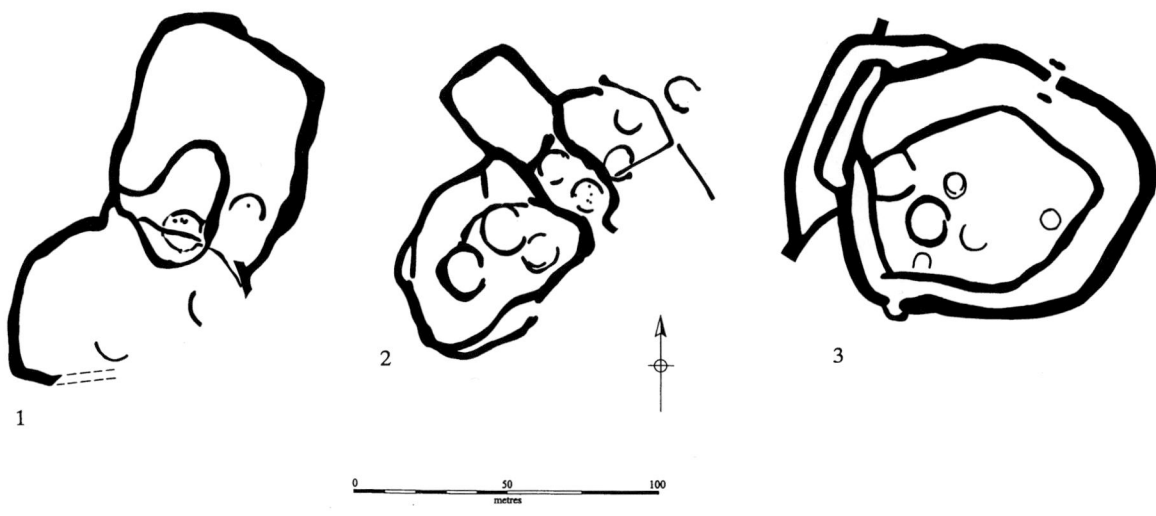

Figure 143 *Compounded enclosure.* The Cove network sites. (1) West Fen Road; (2) Hurst Lane (southern settlement cluster); (3) Wardy Hill.

evidence of trade and these sites' off-Island connections since these groups would probably have had, at least occasional, access to the Romanised 'world' through down-the-line exchange, perhaps *via* their parent communities.

Fostered by a spirit of maximal resource exploitation, the study of settlement systems has tended to focus upon economic carrying capacity. Yet here it is argued — consistent with the theme of *assembly* — that the maintenance of social life and the binding of extra-site relations are equally important factors that must be taken into account when modelling settlement. Recently far too much archaeological analysis has envisaged sites as if they were closed entities, with only scant attention given to their larger social ties. Here a tiered imprint of 'place' is proposed for the cultural landscape of the Wardy Hill environs, which equally reflects the levels at which 'community' resides:

1. The Wardy Hill rise;
2. The Cove Embayment;
3. The Isle of Ely.

Given the paucity of contemporary settlement across most of the Island during the later Iron Age, the second and third of these points essentially conflate. (Beyond this level may also lie higher-level affiliations — perhaps encompassing 'tribal' sub-sets — that could also have had topographic roots, such as the lower Cam reaches. No group identity above this level is likely to have had direct, or at least appreciable, geographical linkages.) Although a distinct place, Wardy Hill itself could never have constituted an enclosed 'world' for its populace; it simply would have been too small. By comparison the Cove network — involving perhaps 7–10 settlements, each with an estimated population of 15–40 — with a total population of some 100–400 persons, would have constituted a viable socio-reproductive community, though one probably featuring exogamous marriage by its elite members. While there is no obvious major centre to this grouping comparable to Stonea, for example, within the Cove's environs, there would seem to be at least three 'significant' complexes: Wardy Hill, Witchford and Hurst Lane/West Fen (Fig. 143). Each of these may have had their own higher-status families. Although at this time it is not possible to say definitely which, if any, of these was paramount, the latter site is suspected. (Should, of course, Ely Castle ever prove conclusively to have its origins in an Iron Age fort this could re-cast the context of any Cove-based settlement system.)

While it is possible, with a wide degree of error, to model the Ringwork's economic range (175ha), short of purely arbitrary means there is no basis of determining the size of any territory that it, or any of the other major Ely complexes, may have commanded (*i.e.* the extent of cliented households). Providing no more than a sense of scale, the entire area of the Isle of Ely as indicated in Fig. 144 would have fitted within Cunliffe's hypothetical Danebury territory (1984, fig. 10.1). Yet the fenland is certainly not a 'regular' land-surface in the manner of Wessex, and the distribution of its great enclosures is sporadic. What is more, the evidence of its 'islanded' landscape would erode any direct relationship between the size of (defended) enclosures and their potential territory. This is also demonstrated in Fig. 144, where the situation of Stonea Camp is shown on the island of its namesake at the same scale as Ely/Wardy Hill superimposed with Danebury and its environs. Although at *c.* 9ha, the size of Stonea is just above half that of the total area of Danebury's earthworks (*c.* 16ha), its 'home' island only extends over 340ha, less than a twentieth of Danebury's territory. This must, however, amount to little more than a cautionary tale. Unlike Danebury, Stonea only saw limited occupation (Jackson and Potter 1996). Serving as a centre for sub-regional assembly and exchange, it may have drawn its membership from much further afield and perhaps commanded the entire area of all the central fenland islands (Stonea, Chatteris and March). Nevertheless, within such an 'interrupted' landscape the inter-relationship between territory and enclosure scale could not have been 'mechanical', and what was commanded may not have been land so much as lines of communication.

The immediate Ely environs falls just beyond Cunliffe's 'Cambridge' socio-economic zone and within his 'Woodcock Hill/Saham Toney' group (1991, fig. 7.2). Ely is marked by a paucity of contemporary coinage, although the larger area sees the overlap of both Catuvellaunian/Trinovantian and Icenian issues (*e.g.* Evans 1890; Cunliffe 1991) and this makes it difficult to establish the cultural group affinities of this network. The organic character of Ely's Iron Age enclosures contrasts with the more formal rectangular plans of distinctly Iceni-associated enclosures of the period (Gregory and Gurney 1986, 32–5), and there seems no reason to evoke an eastward linkage with Norfolk and Suffolk. (The area of the Island, in fact, represents a major gap in the distribution of Icenian coin hoards between the eastern Breckland cluster and those on the central fenland islands: Gregory 1992, fig. 155; Evans forthcoming b.) Similarly, obviously not forming part of the Scored Ware ceramic tradition, its relations are unlikely to lie with western and northern groups with ties to the Midlands (*e.g.* the lower Ouse Valley groups: Hill in Evans and Hodder forthcoming). Therefore, it is logical to postulate a southward orientation for this Ely 'network'. This may equally have been directed westwards towards the Cam Valley — the Cambridge area was clearly a significant centre during the 1st century BC (Hill *et al.* 1999) — or into northern Essex.

If adopting a historicist perspective and seeing the Ely settlements, at least in part, as an 'arrival', they could be related to northward expansion by the Catuvellauni in the 1st century BC (*e.g.* Gregory and Rogerson in Davies *et al.* 1991, 69). However, given the nature of the site's 'continuities', such a declaration would be premature awaiting full analysis of the other Cove excavations. Indeed it may always remain so given that 'tribal' affinities, again, only seem expressed through off-site deposition and, if without direct proto-historical reference, essentially lack domestic correlates. It is, nevertheless, necessary to see the Ely grouping as existing very much on the frontier of the Late Iron Age Aylesford-Swarling core, and immediately beyond the range of direct Gallo-Belgic/Romanised influence. While a part of this sphere of 'foreign' influence in terms of the reception of wheelmade pottery and the occasional imported trade good (*e.g.* Samian), they seem to lie just beyond the geographical extent of the Late Iron Age cremation rite (Hill *et al.* 1999, fig. 15). This picture would, of course, change radically if the small crop-mark circles on the west side of Wardy Hill proved to be cremation enclosures comparable to those recently excavated at Hinxton, south of Cambridge. Be this as it may, the

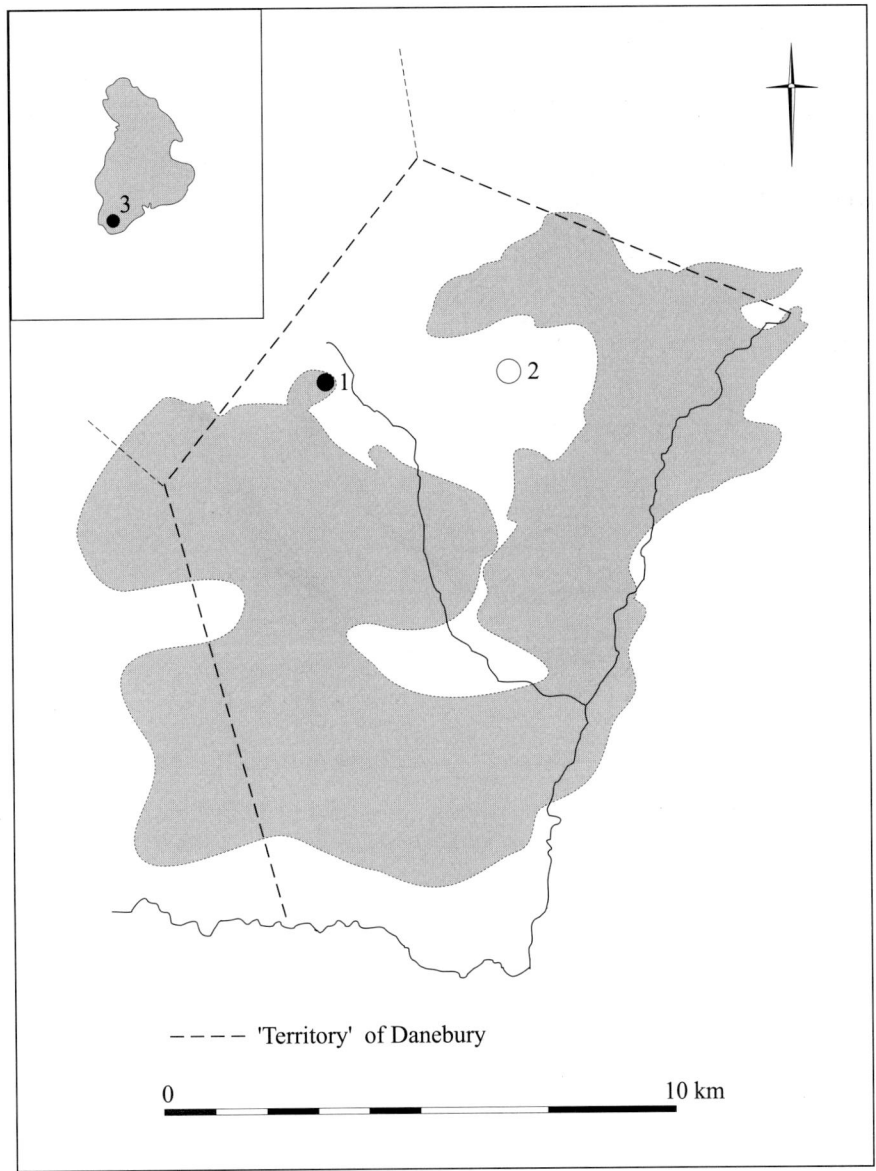

Figure 144 *Landscape polities.* Superimposed upon the Isle of Ely (grey toned, with Wardy Hill indicated as '1') is Cunliffe's postulated Danebury territory (with the hillfort's position relative to it marked as '2'). With regard to arguments about enclosures' sizes/locations in relationship to their 'domains', the inset figure shows Stonea Camp ('3') upon its island. Covering only 340ha, this latter site's landed/island 'territory' must have been much smaller than Danebury's.

Island's situation, reminiscent of the character of the Ringwork itself, is also *betwixt* since it straddles the Aylesford-Swarling 'core' and its northern 'periphery'.

Throughout this section the term 'network' has been applied to the Ely/Cove group of sites. In order to circumvent long-standing debates concerning the constitution of 'archaeological cultures', this is an intentionally neutral term. Nevertheless we must now finally consider what the nature of this grouping may have been. Firstly, the settlements seem to have been contemporaneous; lying in some proximity to each other, they share locational propensities *vis-a-via* access to marshland water meadows. Beyond this, they evidently had in common certain trade/exchange relations, pottery styles, and a basic settlement architecture (*e.g.* ditched roundhouses in household compounds), although the distribution of the latter two features is, of course, much more widespread. We can *presume* that they shared language and a suite of religious beliefs and ritual practices, and that they were probably bound by kinship and obligational ties. Ultimately the key criterion that may have determined their potential grouping is simply whether or not their inhabitants conceived of themselves as a social unit. Although they *may* have occasionally met *en masse* for fairs and ceremonies, even this is not a prerequisite for their potential self-identification as a larger community.

As has been demonstrated, here it is crucial that much of the domestic record of the period essentially seems insensitive to more broadly distributed 'higher-level' socio-cultural expression, perhaps expressed by decorated

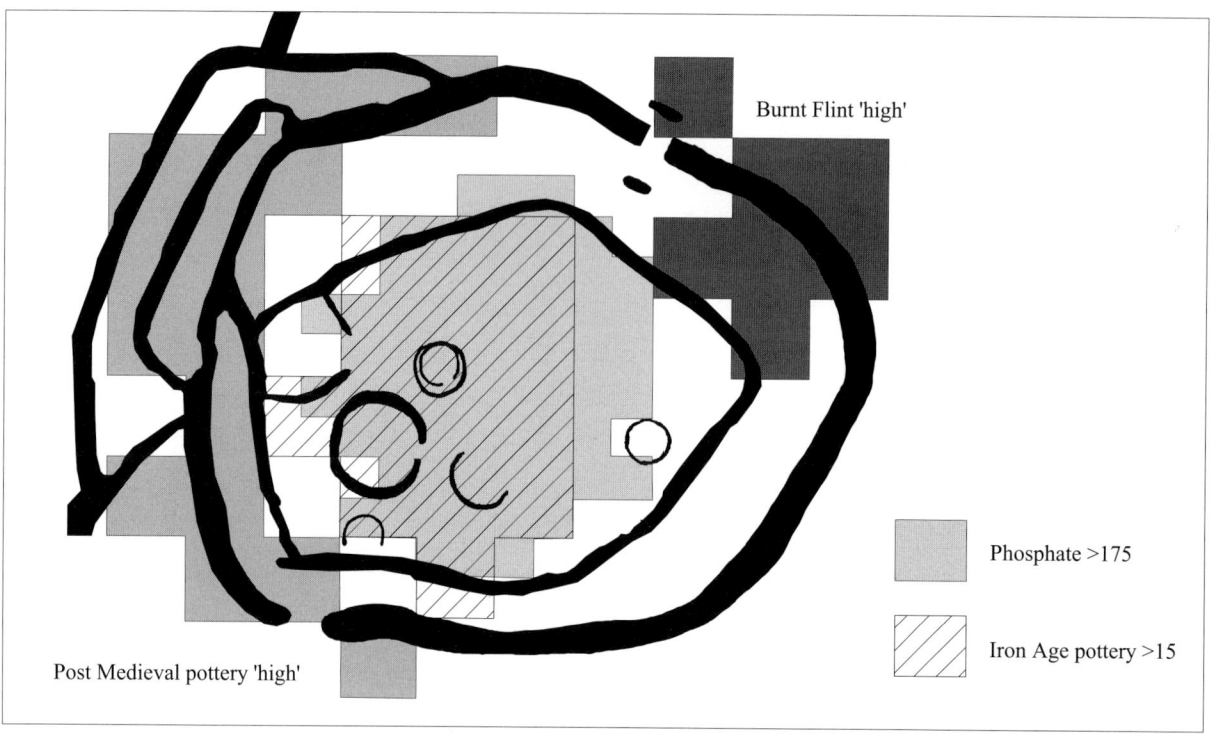

Figure 145 *The cumulative imprint.* The long-term structure of surface finds distributions at Wardy Hill. Effectively amounting to a caricature, the site's ploughsoil distributions could be interpreted as representative of shifting foci and a retreat upslope in the face of rising marsh levels. A more appropriate reading would, however, relate this to its changes as a place: variously marked as a distinct locale in the Bronze and Iron Ages (*i.e.* the burnt flint mound and Ringwork respectively), the later dumping of village-derive refuse suggests it was more marginal in post-medieval times. Yet, despite this apparent relegation, the distribution of the 'late' pottery attests to the Ringwork's lingering presence as an earthwork. The very fact that the site was accessible for this deposition indicates the continuity of the causeway route — the *Short Causeway* road — from Wardy Hill to Coveney.

metalwork ('La Tène style') or 'tribal' coinage. This has significant ramifications for our understanding of regionality. Relevant here are also our attempts to 'read' settlements and social space culturally — the idea that constructions somehow bear a *cultural imprint* directly reflective of group expression, as if enclosure must involve some kind of group-specific cultural mapping or classificatory 'blueprint'. Such concepts underpin Fig. 135, all of them negatively. If these great enclosures did share a classification (*e.g.* 'fort assemblies') and arose from similar social circumstances, then they should share criteria and, in effect, look alike. Obviously, they do not. In *some* specific instances *some* enclosures do seem to reflect a clear sense of group-type. The 'pairing' of Arbury and Wandlebury suggests such direct interconnection (Evans and Knight forthcoming), as might also the rectangular Iceni-associated enclosures of Norfolk (Gregory and Gurney 1986; Gregory 1992), but these seem to be exceptions to the rule. Yet this is equally applicable to the Cove network's enclosures themselves: beyond principles of 'compounding' (again a widespread phenomenon) and the horseshoe plans of Wardy Hill and Hurst Lane, they seem to share few obvious characteristics. What this erodes is the concept of a direct relationship between material culture and 'cultural content'. Social space need not bear the explicit imprint of specific groupings and, rather, may only express basic principles of communal social reproduction (*i.e.* compounded household expansion and the ditched emphasis of houses: Evans 1997a).

III. Roman(isation): 'archaic' communities?

Given that usage of the Wardy Hill Ringwork clearly continued until the last quarter of the 1st century AD, the absence of coinage from the site warrants comment. Yet this absence is not uncommon on early Roman sites: for example, the recent excavation of a Conquest-period kiln complex at Cambridge Airport also produced none (Gibson and Lucas forthcoming). Unless in contact with the military (such as at Langwood Farm, Chatteris: Evans forthcoming b), the rural economy then was simply not moneyed. Having more significant implications, however, is the absence of personal grooming and dress equipment at Wardy Hill (*e.g.* brooches and tweezers). Present at the Airport site, these frequently accompany the cremation burials of the period (*e.g.* Hill *et al.* 1999). Hill has argued that the occurrence of tweezers during the later Iron Age and the intensification of brooch-use during the 1st centuries BC/AD marks a major change in codes of personal appearance (1997). Although certainty is always difficult when interpreting negative evidence, the total lack of this range of material at Wardy Hill could imply that its inhabitants did not participate in this 'revolution' in grooming and dress. This may also tell of the site's wider relationship with 'things' Roman (and, earlier, Gallo-Belgic). Whilst they were evidently willing to accept 'foreign' pottery, they may not have taken a complete package: an assemblage which, with regard to bodily grooming, communities immediately to the south of this area had obviously adopted at least a half century earlier.

From the presence of early Roman pottery on the site, the question of the nature of its post-Conquest usage becomes critical. There are two main ways of interpreting this. One would see it as marking no more than surreptitious visits to what was by then an abandoned site of remnant cultural significance. Although attractive, the problem with this explanation is that the Roman pottery, such as it is, largely concentrates around the circuit of Structure IV and is obviously associated with that 'Late' building, suggesting that it then still stood. Equally, aside from the Samian platter, there is nothing distinctive within the Roman assemblage — apart, of course, from the human bone — nor in the manner of its deposition, to indicate any particularly 'special' practices. Therefore the alternative argument, that the site continued to operate (*i.e.* was occupied) throughout the third quarter of the 1st century AD, seems the more plausible. In this case the paucity of distinctly Roman pottery would relate to only sporadic access to its production (by intermittent market trade or occasional visits by itinerant potters; see Gibson and Lucas forthcoming). Given this, it would then have to be presumed that 'Iron Age' pottery continued in production until this time (see Willis 1994 and 1997a concerning the penetration of early Roman wares). Within the context of the Ringwork's sequence, the radiocarbon dates indicate that must, in effect, have been a re-occupation. Yet there is nothing to say that during the apparent *interregnum* settlement did not occur around its perimeter, and elsewhere within the bounds of the larger Wardy Hill system. Indeed, as noted by Hill, the Outwork ditches F. 11 and 13 (probably correlating with the scatter of settlement features along the site's western margin) produced more 'classic' Aylesford-Swarling assemblages (including carinated bowls) than Structure IV. This attests to a 'presence', if nothing else, during the 1st century BC and the earlier 1st century AD.

The evidence of Structure IV therefore indicates that the Ringwork continued to function for approximately two or three decades after the Boudiccan rebellion of AD 60. This evidence, implying that local élites were not then immediately ousted, is quite remarkable. Yet it is consistent with the fact that there is no evidence of razing or intentional demolition of the Ringwork's circuit, or indeed of conflict. Equally it complements what seems to be the late 1st/early 2nd century AD date of 'full' Romanisation, in terms of landscape re-organisation, within the southern fenlands. Civic works here, such as the layout of Stonea (Jackson and Potter 1996), the Car Dyke canal and, locally, the Snow's Farm shrine at Haddenham (Evans and Hodder forthcoming) all date to the early–mid 2nd century. Even at Cats Water, Fengate (Hayes in Pryor 1984), it is then that the fabric of the Roman landscape was established, and the impact of full Romanisation felt in the countryside.

Within a strictly local context, the later 1st century AD auxiliary helmet from Witcham has — not surprisingly given the local persistence of 'event-led' interpretation — been directly associated with the Boudiccan rebellion (*i.e.* battle loss). Alternative explanations may, however, be equally valid. As proposed by Roymans in relation to similar deposits of early Roman arms and armour amongst the Batavians (1995 and 1996), it may reflect the 'barbaric' composition of the Roman army. Upon returning home, portions of their equipment may well have been sacrificed in what was essentially a pre-Roman tradition of watery votive placement. The depositional context of the Witcham helmet may therefore have differed little from that of the later Iron Age swords at Isleham, ultimately attesting to a tradition that had its roots in later Bronze Age practices (*e.g.* Bradley 1990). Against this strand of long-term continuity, and the fact that the Ringwork seems only to have been abandoned in the final decades of the 1st century AD, it may tell of the *subsequent* impact of Romanisation — especially in the light of the possible ritual associations of the Ringwork's final usage — that, judging from the paucity of later Roman depositional activity, the fort seems not to have been visited, or at least further utilised, after this date. (The absence of 'wet' votive deposits and of 'loose' human remains on settlements after this time also indicates disruption in ritual practices.)

It must surely reflect upon the Ringwork's status as a fort that it is the only site amongst the five Iron Age complexes recently investigated on Ely that has not produced evidence of later (2nd-century) Roman settlement *per se*. This suggests the intentional 'unseating' of its inhabitants, probably through enforced displacement and/or the erosion of the social network within which they were maintained (*i.e.* tithe *vs.* taxation; see Millett 1990). Otherwise, this indicates a high degree of Iron Age/Roman settlement continuity on the remaining Cove sites and suggests that Romanisation was a staged process which, at least within the fen margins, occurred over a span of one or two generations. Although it is beyond the scope of this discussion to review in detail the later 1st century AD occupation from the other Ely settlements, these also seem to reflect a similar sequence. This is most apparent at Hurst Lane, where there is evidence that its 'Iron Age' roundhouses were occupied until early Flavian times (*c.* AD 70–80); only in the later decades of that century was the Roman (*per se*) enclosure system laid out (Evans and Knight 2000a). The other sites also show evidence of a 'lingering' Iron Age, with mixed early Roman and Iron Age assemblages.

Rather than reflecting any manner of Roman/Iron Age continuity, the Wardy Hill sequence essentially attests to the processes of *contact* and *acculturation*. It reflects an eventual access to Roman(ised) pottery that need not imply that its inhabitants were then necessarily becoming 'Romans', as it were. Prior to the end of the 1st century AD the receipt of 'imports' may have differed little from, and can even be seen as an extension to, what occurred in the century before the Conquest within the more southerly Aylesford-Swarling 'contact core'. Should this Ely grouping then be considered as some kind of archaic backwater community, maintaining Iron Age traditions while (full) Romanisation continued apace elsewhere? Such a judgement can only be supported by the known outcome or trajectory of history, and involves pre-determining the past. In response to this is what appears to have been their exercise of choice of what elements of the Roman 'package' they adopted, and also their actual visibility within the record at this time. Lying just beyond the

Aylesford-Swarling core (and, subsequently, more fully Romanised communities to the south), the situation of Ely is quite unique and this may have been what provided the exchange networks that permitted them any access to early Roman goods in the first place. Without this and these imported 'markers', such groups — if maintaining an 'Iron Age' lifestyle throughout much of the later 1st century — would otherwise effectively be archaeologically invisible. This kind of sequence may well eventually prove to hold true elsewhere in the fen, and at other 'margins' where there is a marked paucity of recorded settlements during the half-century following the Conquest. Is this due, at least in part, to our failure to detect what in effect are post-mid 1st century AD Iron Age communities?

IV. Post-medieval: naming and ends
(Fig. 145)

Aside from the fact that the Ringwork's late earthwork survival is demonstrated by the sensitivity of the post-medieval features and distributions to its circuits (Fig. 145), the site's terminal usage warrants little comment apart from its apparent lack of recognition as such. Albeit surely only a subtle monument by this time — without, for example, the obvious landscape impact of Belsar's Hill guarding the Island's southern approach — the fact that it was not named may reflect the biases and limited coverage of the region's 19th-century antiquarians. Whilst arguably reflective of true breaks in direct settlement continuity (*i.e.* Romanisation and subsequent fenland inundation), its 'loss from history' should caution against the over-backdating of 'living' fenland traditions (see Evans 1997b).

This negative evidence equally reflects upon the constitution of Ely's broader past. Resting as this does in Saxon times, compared to the rest of southern Cambridgeshire in general it has a vibrant historical identity whilst still sharing a wider fenland ethos of rebelliousness. This is somewhat ironic. Although there is no obvious evidence of participation in the Boudiccan Rebellion of *c.* AD 60, the Island, as defined by its pattern of settlement, does seem to have been a distinct 'place' in the later Iron Age. However, without key individuals to enliven this much more distant past (particularly Boudicca herself), this has been overlooked in favour of the drama of its Saxon 'ancestors'. These processes of constructing pasts — staking ancestry at the expense of some precursors and variously characterising others — would have surely been as relevant in the making of the cultural landscape of the Iron Age as they are today. Yet Ely's topographical rise would always have been a landmark and a distinct locale, and the Iron Age Ringwork itself incorporated, and was structured by, previous Bronze Age landscape components. From the character of the Island's later 2nd millennium BC votive metalwork, the argument could be advanced that the Isle was even then a 'place' that attracted distinct ritual expression (Evans forthcoming a).

Albeit with a *caveat* that sites are not necessarily representative of the gamut of social dynamics (*e.g.* status or individual action/displacement), the 'missing' finally warrants mention: in other words, what this text and the record omit. Apart from that the Island was probably the hunting and foraging hills of the Mesolithic and Neolithic, and that the clutch of medieval coins found on site are perhaps the remnants of a purse dropped whilst *en route* to Ely, the portion of the road running from Wardy Hill west towards Witcham — near where the Roman helmet was found — is named *Jerusalem*. That this deep-fen village should reference a locale in another part of the globe obviously relates to the Chapel movement, and conveys a utopian vision of earthly social relations. The resultant juxtaposition of cultural geography has parallels in the region's colonial-derived place-names (*e.g. The America* or *Australia Farm*), which themselves reflect upon the character of post-medieval plantation, the evaluation of 'wastes' and the in-take of new land. Though the grid-iron of the site's field systems attest to this ethos of 'improvement', just as the recovery of clay pipes and Blue Willow wares hints of distant influences (respectively tobacco and 'china'), in this case it is really only at the level of metaphor and allusion that its environs resonate within a broader context of world relations. More tangible, testifying to international conflict and the defence of the nation, is the pill box atop Wardy Hill.

The site's traces are not themselves closed totalities and have connections that lead outwards — beyond the immediate hill-top, the Cove's marshes and the Island. Telling of the vagaries of place-association and the impact of history, this is an appropriate note on which to conclude: to draw to an end, as it were, with both first and last things. Whereas the forging of identities within landscape will always be interrupted and arbitrary, the cumulative roots of local 'place-value' simultaneously recede and expand, and are ultimately open-ended.

Appendix: bone measurements

Measurements in tenths of a millimetre of mammal bones and teeth and bird bones, arranged by part of skeleton and taxon. Measurements are as in von den Driesch (1976), Payne and Bull (1988) for pig teeth and Davis (1996) for artiodactyl metapodials; approximate values are in parentheses.

Key
Box: The animals bones box number
Elem: Bones are coded as follows:

HU	humerus	CA	calcaneum
UL	ulna	AST	astragalus
MC	metacarpal	MT	metatarsal
CmC	carpometacarpal	TmT	tarsometatarsal
FE	femur	P1	proximal (first) phalanx
TI	tibia		

Tax: Sh/G are sheep or goat (probable sheep)
Fus: The state of fusion of the epiphysis is coded as follows:
F   fused
UE   epiphysis unfused

Pig
Teeth

Box	Feature	Context	Cat No.	Tax	DP4l	Dp4w	M1l	M1wa	M1wp	M2l	M2wa	M2wp	M3l	M3wa	M3wc	M12l	M12wa	M12wp
1	2	20	869	Pig												198	121	118
5	41	110	1222	Pig												207	126	127
14	6	204	1257	Pig				106										
18	21	169	1473	Pig													98	
20	13	336	2422	Pig														98
20	25	333	1646	Pig													133	131
21	26	354	1672	Pig												172	105	109
18	21	174	1490	Pig									317	156	147			
6	39	124	2118	Pig									325	150	136			
6	12	146	1325	Pig									330	151	145			
22	26	357	1733	Pig									352	158	146			
6	34	188	2028	Pig									357	155	147			
21	26	355	1677	Pig									374	154	154			
14	6	207	1177	Pig				96		181	126	131	332	145	146			
12	38	605	2446	Pig				97		187	124	131		131	137			
22	26	359	1681	Pig						202	126	126	310	147	137			
16	6	222	1824	Pig						202	122	128	327	141	139			
20	13	336	2422	Pig					104	210	135	135		150				
20	13	347	1653	Pig						214	142	153	386	167	168			
14	6	205	1717	Pig			143	94	98	197	121	120						
16	6	221	1665	Pig			146	90	94									
13	2	624	2636	Pig			147	89	95									
14	6	203	1156	Pig			152		103	204	118	134						
20	25	332	1630	Pig			155	92	100	207	126	132						
9	32	294	1985	Pig			156	102	102	203	127	129	327	150	140			
6	2	148	1607	Pig			156	104	108	208	128	140						
22	26	358	2133	Pig			156	100	103	209	125	125						
19	25	310	1547	Pig			164	103	110									
14	6	204	1257	Pig			165		111	217	131	142						
23	20	436	1372	Pig			166	105	111	216	135	133						
16	6	223	1830	Pig			179	97	101	211	122	126						
14	6	206	1726	Pig	176	84	166	97	106									

Table 73 Bone measurements: pig teeth

Box	Feature	Context	Cat No.	Tax	M3I	M3wa
99	26	356	1769	Cattle	352	
99	6	221	1665	Cattle	300	137
22	26	358	2133	Cattle		138
99	1	404	2160	Cattle	351	143
99	49	179	2046	Cattle	343	145
5	38	119	1312	Cattle	341	149
99	6	253	1879	Cattle	356	150
99	25	306	1450	Cattle	336	150
99	6	206	1726	Cattle	340	151
99	67	219	1813	Cattle	347	151
99	12	553	2458	Cattle	362	152
99	37	239	2151	Cattle		152
99	12	553	2458	Cattle	356	153
3	1	53	1081	Cattle	352	154
099	6	206	1726	Cattle	342	154
99	6	225	1842	Cattle	345	154
99	1	61	1014	Cattle	362	155
99	37	630	2685	Cattle	352	156
99	37	666	2342	Cattle	377	160
99	6	204	2102	Cattle		161
99	61	268	1881	Cattle	380	161
99	6	269	1900	Cattle	364	162
20	13	336	2422	Cattle		163
21	26	356	1764	Cattle	364	164
99	6	202	1708	Cattle	366	178

Table 74 Bone measurements: cattle teeth

Box	Feature	Context	Cat No.	Tax	Elem	Fus	GI	Bd	BT	HTC
2	2	33	1110	Cattle	HU	F				300
6	37	154	1624	Cattle	HU	F				272
7	37	239	2151	Cattle	HU	F				278
10	12	393	2244	Cattle	HU	F				296
16	6	221	1665	Cattle	HU	F			649	319
17	61	268	1881	Cattle	HU	F			654	295
19	25	310	1547	Cattle	HU	F				292
6	46	158	1330	Equid	HU	F				338
10	1	413	2252	Equid	HU	F			632	322
12	1	606	2670	Equid	HU	F				335
12	1	606	2670	Equid	HU	F			683	344
7	37	239	2151	Sh/G	HU	F				122
20	25	333	1646	Sh/G	HU	F				119
1	2	31	974	Sheep	HU	F			253	127
1	2	31	974	Sheep	HU	F			266	126
4	2	85	1210	Sheep	HU	F			286	137
6	43	152	1118	Sheep	HU	F			262	119
10	1	411	1986	Sheep	HU	F			251	122
11	76	576	2461	Sheep	HU	F				124
13	130	662	2524	Sheep	HU	F				120
16	6	233	1748	Sheep	HU	F			238	120

Box	Feature	Context	Cat No.	Tax	Elem	Fus	Gl	Bd	BT	HTC
21	26	356	1764	Sheep	HU	F			258	130
22	26	357	1733	Sheep	HU	F			249	122
22	26	357	1733	Sheep	HU	F			252	123
6	12	146	1325	Pig	HU	F			258	183
6	34	188	2028	Pig	HU	F			274	175
7	52	230	2079	Pig	HU	F			274	182
19	25	308	1454	Pig	HU	F			285	182
20	13	347	1653	Pig	HU	F				190
22	26	357	1733	Pig	HU	F			274	181
18	21	170	1477	Dog	HU	F		312		118
11	121	582	2462	Dog	HU	F	(.1670.)	317		132

Table 75 Bone measurements: humerus

Box	Feature	Context	Cat No.	Elem	Tax	Fus	Gl	Bd
18	21	163	1399	TI	Cattle	F		496
6	52	194	2017	TI	Cattle	F		514
8	2	279	2156	TI	Cattle	F		523
2	2	32	978	TI	Cattle	F		534
14	6	203	1156	TI	Cattle	F		535
5	38	118	1309	TI	Cattle	F		542
1	2	30	968	TI	Cattle	F		546
11	1	495	2258	TI	Cattle	F		566
8	1	271	1945	TI	Cattle	F		620
12	1	606	2670	TI	Cattle	F	3054	554
4	29	69	983	TI	Equid	F		690
21	26	356	1764	TI	Sh/G	F		200
22	26	357	1733	TI	Sh/G	F		210
20	13	331	1601	TI	Sh/G	F		214
14	6	202	1708	TI	Sh/G	F		216
18	6	418	1998	TI	Sh/G	F		223
7	27	215	2129	TI	Sh/G	F		226
17	63	267	1848	TI	Sh/G	F		229
10	1	412	2204	TI	Sh/G	F		230
18	21	163	1399	TI	Sh/G	F		236
15	6	220	1818	TI	Sh/G	F	1853	215
6	10	198	1114	TI	Dog	F		229

Table 76 Bone measurements: tibia

Box	Feature	Context	Cat No.	Elem	Tax	Gl	Bd	Dd
5	45	116	1300	AST	Cattle		411	
7	58	214	2102	AST	Cattle	527	328	
16	6	225	1842	AST	Cattle	541	327	295
4	31	71	1282	AST	Cattle	551	348	314
13	13	680	2557	AST	Cattle	571	368	317
12	2	621	2570	AST	Cattle	584	392	331
12	1	606	2670	AST	Cattle	589	(.358.)	323
13	13	680	2557	AST	Cattle	589	361	324
22	26	357	1733	AST	Cattle	598		331
19	13	330	1594	AST	Cattle	613	363	343
20	13	336	2422	AST	Sh/G	232	149	(.124.)
21	26	349	1637	AST	Sh/G	267	166	143
2	2	34	937	AST	Sheep	217	139	123
22	26	357	1733	AST	Sheep	230	149	123
22	26	357	1733	AST	Sheep	239	155	
6	2	148	1607	AST	Pig	387		
19	25	312	1353	AST	Pig	415		
20	13	336	2422	AST	Pig	417		
8	2	281	2186	AST	Pig	435		
20	25	332	1630	AST	Equid		451	
						Gh= 510	LmT= 517	
6	10	198	1114	AST	Dog	267		

Table 77 Bone measurements: astragalus

Box	Feature	Context	Cat No.	Tax	Elem	Fus	Gl
21	26	356	1764	Sh/G	CA	F	443
21	26	356	1764	Sh/G	CA	F	457
5	3	122	1318	Sh/G	CA	F	480

Table 78 Bone measurements: calcaneum

Box	Feature	Context	Cat No.	Tax	Elem	Fus	Gl	Bd	Dd	SD	Bp	Dp*
1	2	28	940	Equid	P1	F				312		
8	2	279	2156	Equid	P2	F				274		
4	29	69	983	Equid	P3	F	774	449		359	526	333
15	6	220	1818	Equid	P4	F	729	403	214	343	502	325

Table 79 Bone measurements: proximal phalanx

Box	Feature	Context	Cat No.	Tax	Elem	Fus	Gl	Bd	SD	Bat F	A	B	1	2	3	4	5	6
17	63	267	1848	Cattle	MC	F		478		422	233	225	212	282	245	197	275	252
12	1	606	2670	Cattle	MC	F	1685	546	272	527	267	258	227	297	264	211	286	264
12	2	621	2570	Cattle	MC	F	1777	572	294	499	276	269	236	306	270	214	295	267
9	37	293	2146	Cattle	MC	F	1844	518	276	466	250	244				202		254
17	6	268	1884	Cattle	MC	F	1767		278		258		219	288	252			
18	21	174	1490	Sheep	MC	F		215			98	104	86		93			
19	25	306	1450	Sheep	MC	F	1091	215	108		103	100	95		88			
13	13	680	2557	Sheep	MC	F	1111	213	104		100	96	93		89			
21	26	354	1672	Sheep	MC	F	1164	222	(.107.)		109	106	94		89			

Table 80 Bone measurements: metacarpal

Box	Feature	Context	Cat No.	Tax	Elem	Fus	Gl	Bd	Dd	SD	Bat F	A	B	1	2	3	4	5	6
12	2	621	2570	Cattle	MT	F	2027	562		247	514	281	257	219	298	263			256*
12	2	616	2626	Cattle	MT	F	(2110.)	(.458.)		(.226.)	423	221	206	205	285	254	194	278	260
5	1	90	985	Cattle	MT	F	2270	516		255	497	246	228	218	306	272			266
10	1	397	2262	Cattle	MT	UE		528				257	242	217	295	258	199	284	258
15	6	209	1723	Cattle	MT	F	2018						218				184	281	254
7	37	239	2151	Sheep	MT	F		207	139										
21	26	356	1764	Sheep	MT	F		217	146										
13	13	680	2557	Sheep	MT	F	1196	206	141	91									
6	2	150	1613	Sheep	MT	F	1238	209	142	97									
11	1	495	2258	Sheep	MT	F	1349			95									
12	38	605	2446	Equid	MT	F	2247	411	310										
12	1	603	2410	Equid	MT	F	2250			238									
21	26	355	1677	Equid	MT	F	2407			257									
10	1	404	2160	Equid	MT	F	2528	458	(.364.)	260									

* Slightly assymetric

Table 81 Bone measurements: (metatarsal)

Box	Feature	Context	Cat No.	Tax	M1l	M1w	M1–M3l	P2l	P2w	P3–M1l	P3l	P3w	P4l	P4w	P2–P4l	P1–P4	Ramus depth behind M1
2	2	34	937	Dog	215	85											
10	1	404	2160	Dog	232	90					112	58	121	67	372	433	274
5	10	109	1253	Dog	232	91	370	97	49		112	54	123	68			248
99	1	412	2204	Dog	213	83	354										220
3	2	60	25041	Cat	84	36					223	60	28	71	34		113
18	32	290	2287	Otter		69											148
19	13	329	2431	Otter	137	74											153

Table 82 Bone measurements: carnivores mandibles/teeth

Box	Feature	Context	Cat No.	Tax	Elem	Gl	Bd	Dd	Bp	Dp	DiP
20	13	331	1601	cf Anas	HU		135				
1	2	27	1004	Corvus corax	HU		200				
9	38	344	2222	Corvus corax	HU		209				
19	13	328	1591	Gallus/Numida/Phasianus	HU		147				
19	25	316	1534	Scolopax rusticola	HU		103				
19	25	306	1450	Gallus/Numida/Phasianus	UL	673			673		130
19	25	305	1444	Anas cf platyrrhnchos	CmC	531			124		
19	13	327	1588	Anas cf platyrrhnchos	CmC	538					
21	26	354	1672	Anas cf platyrrhnchos	CmC	563					
22	25	377	1686	Cygnus cf cygnus	CmC	1345					
1	2	26	918	Corvus corone	FE	516	(.106.)	81	105	58	
5	38	117	1303	Gallus/Numida/Phasianus	Ti		94	98			
5	38	117	1303	Gallus/Numida/Phasianus	Ti		99	98			
10	1	413	2252	Corvus cf corone	TmT		74				
9	38	344	2222	Corvus corax	TmT		97				

Table 83 Bone measurements: bird bones

Bibliography

Abrams, J., 2000 — *Iron Age Settlement and Post-Medieval Features at 36b St Johns Road, Ely: An Archaeological Evaluation*, Cambridgeshire County Council Archaeological Field Unit (Cambridge)

Albarella, U., 1997 — *The Iron Age Animal Bone Excavated in 1991 from Outgang Road, Market Deeping, Lincolnshire* (HBMC AM Lab. report 5/97, London)

Albarella, U. and Davis, S.J.M., 1994 — *The Saxon and Medieval Animal Bones Excavated 1985–1989 from West Cotton, Northamptonshire* (HBMC AM Laboratory report 17/94, London)

Albarella, U. and Davis, S.J.M., 1996 — 'Mammals and birds from Launceston Castle, Cornwall: decline in status and the rise of agriculture', *Circaea* 12, 1–156

Albarella, U. and Payne, S., forthcoming — *The Pigs from Durrington Walls, a Neolithic Data Base*

Alexander, J. and Pullinger, J., 1999 — 'Roman Cambridge: Excavations on Castle Hill 1956–1988', *Proceedings of the Cambridge Antiquarian Society* 86, 1–255

Allen, T.G. and Robinson, M.A., 1993 — *The Prehistoric Landscape and Iron Age Enclosed Settlement at Mingies Ditch, Hardwick-with-Yelford, Oxon* (Oxford Archaeological Unit, Oxford)

Arnold, D., 1985 — *Ceramic Theory and Cultural Process* (Cambridge University Press, Cambridge)

Arnold, E.N. and Burton, J.A., 1978 — *A Field Guide to the Reptiles and Amphibians of Britain and Europe* (Collins, London)

Ashmore, P., 1999 — 'Radiocarbon dating: avoiding errors by avoiding mixed samples', *Antiquity* 73, 124–30

Baggs, A., n.d. — A note concerning Ely Castle, unpublished

Bagyaraj, D.J. and Varma, A., 1995 — 'Interaction between arbuscular mycorrhizal fungi and plants: their importance in sustainable agriculture in arid and semiarid tropics', in Gwynfryn Jones, J. (ed.), *Advances in Microbial Ecology* (14), 119–42 (Plenum Press, New York)

Bailey, G.N., Levine, M. and Rogers, S.J.Q., 1981 — 'Animal remains', in Orme, B.J., Coles, J.M., Caseldine, A.E. and Bailey, G.N., *Meare Village West 1979*, Somerset Levels Papers 7, 38–45

Barrett, J.C., Bradley, R. and Green, M., 1991 — *Landscape, Monuments and Society: The Prehistory of Cranborne Chase* (Cambridge University Press, Cambridge)

Bate, D.M.A., 1934 — 'The domestic fowl in pre-Roman Britain', *Ibis*, 390–5

Bayley, J., 1985 — 'What's what in ancient technology: an introduction to high-temperature processes', in Phillips, P. (ed.), *The Archaeologist and the Laboratory*, CBA Research Report 58, 41–4

Bayley, J., 1992 — *Non-ferrous Metalworking in England: Late Iron Age to Early Medieval*, unpublished Ph.D thesis, University of London

Bayley, J., 2001 — 'Human Skeletal Material', in Chowne, P., Cleal, R.M.J. and Fitzpatrick, A.P., *Excavations at Billingborough, Lincolnshire, 1975–8: A Bronze–Iron Age Settlement and Salt-working Site*, 73–8, East Anglian Archaeology Report No. 94

Bayliss, A., 1998 — 'Some thoughts on using scientific dating in English archaeology and buildings analysis for the next decade', in Bayley, J. (ed.), *Science in Archaeology: An Agenda for the Future*, 95–108 (English Heritage, London)

Bell, T., 1837 — *A History of British Quadrupeds Including the Cetacea* (van Voorst, London)

Bennett, K.D., Whittington, G. and Edwards, K.J., 1994 — 'Recent Plant Nomenclatural Changes and Pollen Morphology in the British Isles', *Quaternary Newsletter* 73, 1–6

Benninghof, W.S., 1962 — 'Calculations of pollen and spore density in sediments by addition of exotic pollen in known quantities', *Pollen et Spores* 4, 332–3

Bersu, G., 1940 — 'Excavations at Little Woodbury, Wiltshire. Part I, the settlement as revealed by excavation', *Proceedings of the Prehistoric Society* 6, 30–111

Bewley, R., 1994 — *Prehistoric Settlements* (Batsford/English Heritage, London)

Biddick, K., 1984 — 'Animal bones from the Cat's Water Subsite, Fengate', in Pryor, F.M.M., *Excavations at Fengate, Peterborough, England: the Fourth Report*, Northamptonshire Archaeological Society Monograph 2/Royal Ontario Society Museum Archaeological Monograph 7, fiche 245–75 (Leicester/Toronto)

Boardman, S. and Jones, G., 1990 — 'Experiments on the effects of charring cereal plant components', *Journal of Archaeological Science* 17, 1–11

Boessneck, J., 1969 — 'Osteological differences between sheep (*Ovis aries* Linne) and goat (*Capra hircus* Linne)', in Brothwell, D. and Higgs, E.S. (eds), *Science in Archaeology* (2nd ed.), 331–58 (Thames and Hudson, London)

Bonny, A.P., 1972 — 'A method for determining absolute pollen frequencies in lake sediments', *New Phytologist* 71, 393–405

Boon, J.A., 1982 — *Other Tribes, Other Scribes: Symbolic Anthropology in the Comparative Study of Cultures, Histories, Religions, and Texts* (Cambridge University Press, Cambridge)

Bowden, M. and McOmish, D., 1987 — 'The required barrier', *Scottish Archaeological Review* 4, 76–84

Boycott, A.E., 1936 — 'The habitats of freshwater mollusca in Britain', *Journal of Animal Ecology* 5, 166–86

Bradley, R., 1990 — *The Passage of Arms: An Archaeological Analysis of Prehistoric Hoards and Votive Deposits* (Cambridge University Press, Cambridge)

Brain, C.K., 1967 — 'Hottentot food remains and their bearing on the interpretation of fossil bone assemblages', *Scientific papers of the Namibia Desert Research Institute* 32, 1–11

British Museum, 1922 — *A Guide to the Antiquities of Roman Britain in the Dept. of British and Medieval Antiquities* (London)

Bronk Ramsey, C., 1995 — 'Radiocarbon calibration and analysis of stratigraphy', *Radiocarbon* 36, 425–30

Bronk Ramsey, C., 1998 — 'Probability and dating', *Radiocarbon* 40, 461–74

Bronk Ramsey, C., 2000 — 'Comment on "The use of Bayesian statistics for C dates of chronological ordered samples: a critical analysis"', *Radiocarbon* 42, 199–202

Bronk Ramsey, C. and Hedges, R.E.M., 1997 — 'Hybrid ion sources: radiocarbon measurements from microgram to milligram', *Nuclear Instruments and Methods in Physics Research* (B) 123, 539–45

Bronk Ramsey, C., Pettitt, P.B., Hedges, R.E.M., Hodgins, G.W.L. and Owen, D.C., 2000 — 'Radiocarbon dates from the Oxford AMS system: Archaeometry Datelist 29', *Archaeometry* 42, 243–54

Brooks, H., 1993 — 'Fieldwalking and Excavation at Stansted Airport', in Gardiner, J.P. and Williamson, T. (eds), *Flatlands and Wetlands: Current Themes in East Anglian Archaeology*, 40–57, East Anglian Archaeology 50

Brown, L., 1991 — 'The Iron Age pottery', In Cunliffe, B. and Poole, C. (eds), *Danebury: An Iron Age Hillfort in Hampshire. Vol 5, The Excavations 1979–1988: The Finds*, 277–319, Council for British Archaeology Research Report 73

Brown, N. and Glazebrook, J. (eds), 2000 — *Research and Archaeology: A Framework for the Eastern Counties (2) Research Agenda and Strategy*, East Anglian Archaeology Occasional Paper No. 8

Buck, C.E., Cavanagh, W.G. and Litton, C.D., 1996 — *Bayesian Approach to Interpreting Archaeological Data* (Wiley, Chichester)

Buck, C.E., Christen, J.A., Kenworthy, J.B. and Litton, C.D., 1994 — 'Estimating the duration of archaeological activity using C determinations', *Oxford Journal of Archaeology* 13, 229–40

Buck, C.E., Kenworthy, J.B., Litton, C.D. and Smith, A.F.M., 1991 — 'Combining archaeological and radiocarbon information: a Bayesian approach to calibration', *Antiquity* 65, 808–21

Buck, C.E., Litton, C.D. and Scott, E.M., 1994 — 'Making the most of radiocarbon dating: some statistical considerations', *Antiquity* 68, 252–63

Buck, C.E., Litton, C.D. and Smith, A.F.M., 1992 — 'Calibration of radiocarbon results pertaining to related archaeological events', *Journal of Archaeological Science* 19, 497–512

Buckley, D.G., Hedges, J.D. and Priddy, D., 1987 — *Excavation of a Cropmark Enclosure at Woodham Walter, Essex, 1976 and An Assessment of Excavated Enclosures in Essex*, East Anglian Archaeology Report 33

Bull, G. and Payne, S., 1982 — 'Tooth eruption and epiphysial fusion in pigs and wild boar', in Wilson, B., Grigson, C. and Payne, S. (eds), *Ageing and Sexing Animal Bones from Archaeological Sites*, 55–71, British Archaeological Reports, British Series 109

Bullock, P., Fedoroff, N., Jongerius, A., Stoops, G. and Tursina, T., 1985 — *Handbook for Soil Thin Section Description* (Wolverhampton)

Calcote, R., 1998 — 'Identifying forest stand types using pollen from forest hollows', *The Holocene* 8 (4), 423–32

Cameron, R.A.D. and Pannett, D.J., 1980 — 'Hedgerow shrubs and landscape history: some Shropshire examples', in Crothers, J. (ed.), *Field Studies* (London)

Carman, J. and Harding, A., 1999 — 'Introduction', in Carman, J. and Harding, A. (eds), *Ancient Warfare*, 1–9 (Sutton, Stroud)

Carter, G.A., 1998 — *Excavations at the Orsett 'Cock' Enclosure, 1976*, East Anglian Archaeological Reports 86

Champion, T., 1997 — 'The power of the picture: the image of the ancient Gaul', in Molyneaux, B. (ed.), *The Cultural Life of Images: Visual Representation in Archaeology*, 213–29 (Routledge, London)

Chaplin, R.E. and McCormick, F., 1986 — 'The animal bones', in Stead, J.M. and Rigby, V., *Baldock, The Excavation of a Roman and Pre-Roman Settlement, 1968–1972*, 396–415, Britannia Monograph Series 7 (Society for the Promotion of Roman Studies, London)

Chatwin, C.P., 1961 — *British Region Geology: East Anglia and Adjoining Areas* (London)

Chowne, P., Girling, M. and Greig, J., 1986 — 'The excavation of an Iron Age defended enclosure at Tattershall Thorpe, Lincolnshire', *Proceedings of the Prehistoric Society* 52, 159–88

Clark, J.G.D. and Godwin, H., 1940 — 'A Late Bronze Age find near Stuntney, Isle of Ely', *Antiquaries Journal* 20, 52–71

Clarke, D.L., 1972 — 'A provisional model of an Iron Age society and its settlement system', in Clarke, D.L. (ed.), *Models in Archaeology*, 801–85 (Methuen, London)

Cole, M., 1993 — *Wardy Hill, Cambridgeshire: Report on Geophysical Survey, 1993* (HBMC AM Lab. Report 43/93, London)

Coles, J. and Minnitt, S. 1995 — *'Industrious and Fairly Civilized': The Glastonbury Lake Village* (Somerset Levels Project, Taunton)

Collis, J., 1977 — 'An approach to the Iron Age', in Collis, J. (ed.), *The Iron Age in Britain: A Review*, 1–7 (University of Sheffield, Dept. of Prehistory and Archaeology, Sheffield)

Connell, B. and Davis, S.J.M., in prep — *Animal Bones from Roman Carlisle, Cumbria: The Lanes (2) Excavations, 1978–1982* (HBMC AM Lab. Report, London)

Cooper, M.R. and Johnson, A.W. 1984 — *Poisonous Plants in Britain and their Effects on Animals and Man* (London: HMSO)

Corcoran, J.X.W.P., 1952 — 'Tankards and tankard handles in the British Early Iron Age', *Proceedings of the Prehistoric Society* 18, 85–102

Coy, J. and Maltby, M., 1987 — 'Archaeozoology in Wessex: vertebrate remains and marine molluscs and their relevance to archaeology', in Keeley, H.C.M. (ed.), *Environmental Archaeology: A Regional Review* (2), 294–351 (English Heritage, London)

Cra'aster, M., 1961 — 'The Aldwick Iron Age settlement, Barley, Hertfordshire', *Proceedings of the Cambridge Antiquarian Society* 54, 22–46

Cra'aster, M., 1969 — 'The New Addenbrokes Iron Age site, Long Road, Cambridge', *Proceedings of the Cambridge Antiquarian Society* 62, 21–8

Crawford, R.D., 1984 — 'Domestic fowl', in Mason, I.L. (ed.), *Evolution of Domesticated Animals*, 298–311, (Longman, London)

Crowther, D., 1983 'Old land surfaces and modern ploughsoil: implications of recent work at Maxey, Cambs.', *Scottish Archaeological Review* 2, 31–44

Cunliffe, B.W., 1971 'Some aspects of hill-forts and their cultural environments', in Jesson, M. and Hill, D. (eds), *The Iron Age and its Hill-Forts*, 53–70 (Southampton)

Cunliffe, B., 1974 *Iron Age Communities in Britain* (Routledge, London)

Cunliffe, B., 1984 *Danebury: An Iron Age Hillfort in Hampshire. Vol. 1: The Excavations 1969–1978*, Council for British Archaeology Research Report 52

Cunliffe, B., 1984 *Danebury Excavations 1969–78. Vol. 2: The Finds*, Council for British Archaeology Research Report 52

Cunliffe, B., 1991 *Iron Age Communities in Britain* (3rd ed.) (Routledge, London)

Curtis, L.P. Jr., 1968 *Anglo-Saxons and Celts: A Study of Anti-Irish Prejudice in Victorian England* (University of Bridgeport, Connecticut)

Darby, H.C., 1940 *The Medieval Fenland* (Cambridge University Press, Cambridge)

Davies, J.A., Gregory, T.A., Lawson, A.J., Rickett, R. and Rogerson, A., 1991 *The Iron Age Forts of Norfolk*, East Anglian Archaeology Report 54

Davis, S.J.M., 1992 *A Rapid Method for Recording Information about Mammal Bones from archaeological Sites* (HBMC AM Lab. Report 19/92, London)

Davis, S.J.M., 1995 *Animal Bones from the Iron Age Site at Edix Hill, Barrington, Cambridgeshire, 1989–91 Excavations* (HBMC AM Lab. report 54/95, London).

Davis, S.J.M., 1996 'Measurements of a group of adult female shetland sheep skeletons from a single flock: a baseline for zooarchaeologists', *Journal of Archaeological Science* 23, 593–612

Davis, S.J.M., 1998 'Faunal remains', in Malim, T., 'Prehistoric and Roman Remains at Edix Hill, Barrington, Cambridgeshire', *Proceedings of the Cambridge Antiquarian Society* 86, 13–56

Dawson, M., 2000 'The Iron Age and Romano-British period: a landscape in transition', in Dawson, M. (ed.), *Prehistoric, Roman and Post-Roman Landscapes of the Great Ouse Valley*, 107–30, Council for British Archaeology Research Report 119

Deniz, E. and Payne, S. 1982 'Eruption and wear in the mandibular dentition as a guide to ageing Turkish Angora Goats', in Wilson, B., Grigson, C. and Payne, S. (eds), *Ageing and Sexing Animal Bones from Archaeological Sites*, British Archaeological Reports, British Series 109, 155–205

Dimbleby, G.W., 1985 *The Palynology of Archaeological Sites* (Academic Press, London)

Dix, B. and Jackson, D., 1989 'Some Late Iron Age defended enclosures in Northamptonshire', in Gibson, A. (ed.), *Midlands Prehistory: Some Recent and Current Researches into the Prehistory of Central England*, British Archaeological Reports, British Series 204, 158–79

Dowdeswell, W.H., 1987 *Hedgerows and Verges* (Allen and Unwin, London)

Driesch, A. von den., 1976 *A Guide to the Measurement of Animal Bones from Archaeological Sites*, Peabody Museum Bulletin 1 (Harvard University, Cambridge, Mass.)

Driesch, A. von den and Boessneck, J., 1974 'Kritische Anmerkungen zur Widerristhohenberechnung aus Langenmassen vor- und Fruhgeschichtlicher Tierknochen', *Saugetierkundliche Mitteilungen* 22, 325–48

Drury, P., 1978a 'Little Waltham and pre-Belgic Iron Age settlement in Essex', in Cunliffe, B. and Rowley, T. (eds), *Lowland Iron Age Communities in Europe*, British Archaeological Reports International Series 48, 43–76

Drury, P., 1978b *Excavations at Little Waltham 1970–71*, Council for British Archaeology Research Report 26

Earwood, C., 1988 'Wooden containers and other wooden artefacts from the Glastonbury Lake Village', *Somerset Levels Papers* 14, 83–90

Edmonds, M. and Evans, C., 1991 'The place of the past: art and archaeology in Britain', *Excavating the Present* (2) (Kettle's Yard, Cambridge)

Edmonds, M., Evans, C. and Gibson, D., 1999 'Assembly and collection: lithic complexes in the Cambridgeshire Fenlands', *Proceedings of the Prehistoric Society* 65, 47–87

Edwards, K.J., 1989 'The cereal pollen record and early agriculture', in Milles, A., Williams, D. and Eisenmann, V., 1981. 'Etudes des Dents Jugales Inferieures des Equus (Mammalia. Perissodactyla) Actuels et Fossiles', *Palaeovertebrata* 10, 127–226

Elsdon, S., 1975 *Stamped Iron Age Pottery*, British Archaeological Reports, British Series 10

Elsdon, S., 1992 'East Midlands scored ware', *The Leicestershire Archaeological and Historical Society* 44, 83–91

Elsdon, S., 1997 *Old Sleaford Revealed* (Oxford)

Evans, C. 1987 'Nomads in "Waterland"? Prehistoric transhumance and fenland archaeology', *Proceedings of the Cambridge Antiquarian Society* 76, 27–39

Evans, C., 1989a 'Perishables and worldly goods: artefact decoration and classification in the light of recent wetlands research', *Oxford Journal of Archaeology* 8, 179–201

Evans, C., 1989b 'Acts of enclosure: a consideration of concentrically organised causewayed enclosures', in Barrett, J. and Kinnes, I. (eds), *The Archaeology of Context* (University of Sheffield, Dept. of Prehistory and Archaeology, Sheffield)

Evans, C., 1989c 'Archaeology and modern times: Bersu's Woodbury 1938/39', *Antiquity* 63, 436–50

Evans, C., 1992 'Commanding gestures in lowland: the investigation of two Iron Age ringworks', *Fenland Research* 2, 16–26

Evans, C., 1997a 'Hydraulic communities: Iron Age Enclosure in the East Anglian Fenlands', in Gwilt, A. and Haselgrove, C. (eds), *Re-Constructing the Iron Age*, 216–27, Oxbow Monograph 71

Evans, C., 1997b 'Sentimental prehistories: the construction of the fenland past', *Journal of European Archaeology* 5, 105–36

Evans, C., 1997c *The Wardy Hill Ringwork Excavations, Assessment Report*, Cambridge Archaeological Unit (Cambridge)

Evans, C., 1998a 'Historicism, chronology and straw men: situating Hawkes' Ladder of Inference', *Antiquity* 72, 398–404

Evans, C., 1998b 'Constructing houses and building context: Bersu's Manx roundhouse campaign', *Proceedings of the Prehistoric Society* 64, 183–201

Evans, C., 1999 'The Lingwood wells: a waterlogged first millennium BC settlement at Cottenham, Cambridgeshire', *Proceedings of the Cambridge Antiquarian Society* 87, 11–30

Evans, C., 2000a 'Testing the ground: sampling strategies', in Crowson, A., Lane, T. and Reeve, J. (eds), *The Fenland Management Project: Summary Volume*, 15–21, Lincolnshire Archaeology and Heritage Reports Series No. 3

Evans, C., 2000b 'Wardy Hill, Coveney', in Crowson, A., Lane, T. and Reeve, J. (eds), *The Fenland Management Project: Summary Volume*, 44–51, Lincolnshire Archaeology and Heritage Reports Series No. 3

Evans, C., 2000c 'Iron Age forts and defences (#12)', in Kirby, T. and Oosthuizen, S. (eds), *An Atlas of Cambridgeshire and Huntingdonshire History* (Centre for Regional Studies, Cambridge)

Evans, C., forthcoming a. 'Metalwork and "cold claylands": pre-Iron Age occupation on the Isle of Ely', in Lane, T. and Coles, J. (eds), *Through Wet and Dry: Proceedings of a Conference In Honour of David Hall*, Lincolnshire Archaeology and Heritage Reports Series No. 5/WARP Occasional Paper 17

Evans, C., forthcoming b. 'Britons and Romans at Chatteris: investigations at Langwood Farm, Cambridgeshire'

Evans, C. and Serjeantson, D., 1988 'The backwater economy of a fen-edge community in the Iron Age: the Upper Delphs, Haddenham', *Antiquity* 62, 360–70

Evans, C. and Knight, M., 2000a. *Investigations at Hurst Lane, Ely, Cambridgeshire: Integrated Assessment and Updated Project Design*, English Heritage/Cambridge Archaeological Unit (Cambridge)

Evans, C. and Knight, M., 2000b 'A fenland delta: later prehistoric land-use in the Lower Ouse Reaches', in Dawson, M. (ed.), *Prehistoric, Roman and Saxon Landscape Studies in the Great Ouse Valley*, 89–106, Council for British Archaeology Research Report 119

Evans, C. and Knight, M., 2001 'The 'community of builders': the Barleycroft post alignments', in Brück, J. (ed.), *Bronze Age Landscapes: Tradition and Transformation*, 83–98 (Oxbow, Oxford)

Evans, C. and Hodder, I., forthcoming *The Haddenham Project II: Marshland Communities and Cultural Landscape.* McDonald Institute Research Series (Cambridge)

Evans, C. and Knight, M., forthcoming 'A great circle: investigations at Arbury Camp, Cambridge', *Proceedings of the Cambridge Antiquarian Society*

Evans, J. 1881 *Ancient Bronze Implements, Weapons and Ornaments of Great Britain and Ireland* (London)

Evans, J., 1890 *The Coins of the Ancient Britons* (supplement) (London)

Evans, J. 1993 'Function and finewares in the Roman North', *Journal of Roman Pottery Studies* 6, 95–118

Farwell, D. and Molleson, T.L., 1993 *Excavations at Poundbury 1966-80. Vol II: The Cemeteries*, Dorset Natural History and Archaeological Society

Fens Exhibition Project 1990 *The Vanishing Fens: Report to Sponsors*, Fens Exhibition Project

Field. N., 1986 'An Iron Age timber causeway at Fiskerton, Lincolnshire', *Fenland Research* 3, 49–53

Field, N. and Parker Pearson, M., forthcoming *Fiskerton: An Iron Age Timber Causeway with Iron Age and Roman Votive Offerings*

Feinman, G., Upham, S. and Lightfoot, K., 1981 'The production step measure: an ordinal index of labor input in ceramic manufacture', *American Antiquity* 46, 871–84

Fitzpatrick, A.P., 1995 '"Celtic" Iron Age Europe: the theoretical basis', in Graves-Brown, P., Jones, S. and Gamble, C. (eds), *Cultural Identity and Archaeology: the Construction of European Communities*, 238–55 (Routledge, London)

Fitzpatrick, A.P., 1997 'Everyday life in Iron Age Wessex', in Gwilt, A. and Haselgrove, C. (eds), *Reconstructing the Iron Age*, 73–86, Oxbow Monograph 71

Flitcroft, M., 2001 *Excavation of a Romano-British Settlement on the A149 Snettisham Bypass, 1989*, East Anglia Archaeology Reports 93

Fox, C., 1923 *The Archaeology of the Cambridge Region* (Cambridge University Press, Cambridge)

Frazer, Sir J.G., 1890 *The Golden Bough: A Study in Comparative Religion* (Macmillan, London)

French, C. and Pryor, F. 1993 *The South-West Fen Dyke Survey Project 1982–86*, East Anglia Archaeology Reports 59

Gallois, R.W., 1988 *Geology of the Country Around Ely*, British Geological Survey (HMSO, London)

Gelfand, A.E. and Smith, A.F.M., 1990 'Sampling approaches to calculating marginal densities', *Journal of the American Statisical Association* 85, 398–409

Gell, A.S.R., 1949 'An Early Iron Age site at Lakenheath, Suffolk', *Proceedings of the Cambridge Antiquarian Society* 42, 112–16

Gibson, D., 1996 *Excavations at West Fen Road, Ely*, Cambridge Archaeological Unit (Cambridge)

Gibson, D. and Lucas, G., forthcoming 'Pre-Flavian kilns at Greenhouse Farm and the social context of Early Roman pottery production in Cambridgeshire', *Britannia*

Gilks, W.R., Richardson, S. and Spiegelhalthe, D.J., 1996 *Markov Chain Monte Carlo In Practice* (Chapman and Hall, London)

Gingell, C., 1982 'Excavation of an Iron Age enclosure at Groundwell Farm, Blundon St Andrew, 1976–7', *Wiltshire Archaeological Magazine* 76, 33–75

Gleed-Owen, C.P., 1998 *Quaternary Herpetofaunas of the British Isles: Taxonomic Descriptions, Palaeoenvironmental Reconstructions and Biostratigraphic Implications*, unpublished Ph.D. thesis, Coventry University

Gleed-Owen, C.P., 1999 *Archaeozoological Investigations into the Possible Native Status of the Pool Frog* (Rana lessonae) *in England: Final Report*, Report for English Nature (Peterborough)

Grant, A., 1982 'The use of tooth wear as a guide to the age of domestic ungulates', in Wilson, B., Grigson, C. and Payne, S. (eds), *Ageing and Sexing Animal Bones from Archaeological Sites*, 91–108, British Archaelogical Reports British Series 109

Grant, A., 1984a 'Animal husbandry in Wessex and the Thames Valley', in Cunliffe, B. and Miles, D. (eds), *Aspects of the Iron Age in Central Southern Britain*, 102–19, University of Oxford Committee for Archaeology

Grant, A., 1984b 'Animal husbandry', in Cunliffe, B., *Danebury: An Iron Age Hillfort in Hampshire, Vol. 2: The Excavations 1969–78: The Finds*, 496–548, Council for British Archaeology Research Report 52

Grant, A., 1991 'Animal husbandry', in Cunliffe, B. and Poole, C., *Danebury: An Iron Age Hillfort In Hampshire, Vol 5: The Excavations 1979–88: The Finds*, 447–87, Council for British Archaeology Research Report 73

Grant, A., in press 'Diet, economy and ritual: evidence from the faunal remains', in Fulford, M. (ed.), *Iron Age and Roman Silchester: Excavations on the Site of the Forum-Basilica at Silchester* (Society for the Promotion of Roman Studies, London)

Gregory, A.K., 1992 *Excavations in Thetford, 1980–1982: Fison Way*, East Anglian Archaeology Reports 53

Gregory, A.K. and Gurney, D., 1986 *Excavations at Thornham, Warham, Wighton and Caistor St Edmund, Norfolk*, East Anglian Archaeology Reports 30

Grime, J.P., Hodgson, J.G. and Hunt, R., 1988 *Comparative Plant Ecology: A Functional Approach to Common British Species* (Urwin Hyman, London)

Grimm, E.C., 1991 *TILIA and TILIA-GRAPH* (Illinois State Museum, Springfield)

Grove, R.H., 1995 *Green Imperialism: Colonial Expansion, Tropical Island Edens and the Origins of Environmentalism, 1600–1860* (Cambridge University Press, Cambridge)

Guilday, J.E., 1977 'Animal remains from archaeological excavations at Fort Ligonier', in Ingersoll, D., Yellwn, J.E. and MacDonald, W. (eds), *Experimental Archaeology* (Columbia Press, New York)

Gwilt, A., 1997 'Popular practices from material culture: a case study of the Iron Age settlement at Wakerley', in Gwilt, A. and Haselgrove, C. (eds), *Reconstructing the Iron Age*, 153–66, Oxbow Monograph 71

Hall, D.N., 1996 *The Fenland Project, Number 10: Cambridgeshire Survey, The Isle of Ely and Wisbech*, East Anglian Archaeology Report 79

Hall, D.N. and Coles, J., 1994 *The Fenland Survey: An Essay in Landscape and Persistence* (English Heritage, London)

Hancock, A., Evans, J. and Woodward, A., 1998 'The prehistoric and Roman pottery', in Ellis, P., *Excavations Alongside Roman Ermine Street, Cambridgeshire*, 34–113, British Archaeological Reports, British Series 276

Harcourt, R.A., 1974 'The dog in prehistoric and early historic Britain', *Journal of Archaeological Science* 1, 151–75

Harting, J.E., 1880 *British Animals Extinct Within Historic Times with Some Account of British Wild White Cattle* (Trubner, London)

Hayden, B. and Cannon, A., 1983 'Where all the garbage goes: refuse disposal in the Maya Highlands', *Journal of Anthropological Archaeology* 2, 117–163

Hedges, R.E.M., Bronk Ramsey, C. and Housley, R.A., 1989 'The Oxford Accelerator Mass Spectrometry facility: technical developments in routine dating', *Archaeometry* 31, 99–113

Hedges, R.E.M. and Law, I. 1989 'The radiocarbon dating of bone', *Applied Geochemistry* 4, 249–54

Hill, J.D., 1995 *Ritual and Rubbish in the Iron Age of Wessex: A Study on the Formation of a Specific Archaeological Record*, British Archaeological Reports, British Series 242

Hill, J.D., 1996 'Hill-Forts and the Iron Age of Wessex', in Champion, T.C. and Collis, J.R. (eds), *The Iron Age in Britain and Ireland: Recent Trends*, 95–116 (J.R. Collis Publications, Department of Archaeology and Prehistory, University of Sheffield, Sheffield)

Hill, J.D., 1997 'The end of one kind of body and the beginning of another kind of body? Toilet instruments and 'Romanization' in the 1st century AD in Southern England', in Gwilt, A. and Haselgrove, C. (eds), *Reconstructing the Iron Age,* 96–107, Oxbow Monograph 71

Hill, J.D., 1999 'Settlement, landscape and regionality: Norfolk and Suffolk in the Pre-Roman Iron Age of Britain and beyond', in Davies, J. and Williamson, T. (eds), *Land of the Iceni: The Iron Age in Northern East Anglia*, 185–207, (Centre of East Anglian Studies, Norwich)

Hill, J.D., forthcoming 'Not just about the potter's wheel: making, using and depositing pottery in later Iron Age East Anglia', in Woodward, A. and Hill, J.D. (eds), *Prehistoric Britain: The Ceramic Basis* (Oxbow, Oxford)

Hill, J.D. and Braddock, P., 1998 *The Iron Age Pottery from Watson's Lane, Little Thetford, Ely, Cambridge*. Report for the Cambridge Archaeological Unit

Hill, J.D. and Braddock, P. 1999 *The Iron Age Pottery from Excavations at Greenhouse Farm, Fen Ditton, Cambridge*. Report for Archaeological Field Unit, Cambridgeshire County Council

Hill, J.D., Evans, C. and Alexander, M. 1999 'The Hinxton Rings: a Late Iron Age cemetery at Hinxton, Cambridgeshire, with a reconsideration of Northern Aylesford-Swarling distributions', *Proceedings of the Prehistoric Society* 65, 243–74

Hill, J.D. and Braddock, P., forthcoming 'The Iron Age Pottery', in Evans, C. and Hodder, I., *The Haddenham Project II: Marshland Communities and Cultural Landscape*, McDonald Institute Research Series (Cambridge)

Hillman, G.C., 1981 'Reconstructing crop husbandry practices from charred remains of crops', in Mercer, R.J. (ed.), *Farming Practice in British Prehistory*, 123–62 (Edinburgh University Press, Edinburgh)

Hillman, G.C., 1984 'Interpretation of archaeological plant remains: the application of ethnographic models from Turkey', in Van Zeist, W. and Casparie, W.A. (eds), *Plants and Ancient Man: Studies in Palaeoethnobotany*, 1–42, Proceedings of the 6th Symposium of the International Work Group for Palaeobotanists (A.A. Balkema, Rotterdam)

Hingley, R., 1984 'Towards social analysis in archaeology: Celtic society in the Iron Age of the Upper Thames Valley', in Cunliffe, B. and Miles, D. (eds), *Aspects of the Iron Age in Central Southern*

	Britain, 72–88, Oxford Committee for Archaeology Monograph 2	Knight, D., 1984	*Late Bronze Age and Iron Age Settlement in the Nene and Great Ouse Basins*, British Archaeological Reports, British Series 130
Hodder, I., 1978	*The Archaeology of the M11: Excavations at Wendon Ambo* (London)	Lethbridge, T.C., 1934	'Investigation of the ancient causeway in the fen between Fordey and Little Thetford', *Proceedings of the Cambridge Antiquarian Society* 35, 85–9
Hooper, H.D., 1971	'Hedges and history', in *Hedges and Local History* (National Council for Social Service, London)	Lethbridge, T.C., 1936	'Fen Causeways', *Proceedings of the Cambridge Antiquarian Society* 36, 161–2
Hunter, J., 1992a	*Archaeological Investigations at Brays Lane, Ely, 1991*, Cambridge Archaeological Unit, (Cambridge)	Longin, R., 1971	'New method of collagen extraction for radiocarbon dating', *Nature* 230, 241–2
Hunter, J., 1992b	*Archaeological Investigations at Walsingham House, Ely, 1991*, Cambridge Archaeological Unit (Cambridge)	Lucas, G., 1998	*The Iron Age Settlement at Watson's Lane, Little Thetford*, Cambridge Archaeological Unit (Cambridge)
Jackson, R.P.J. and Potter, T.W., 1996	*Excavations at Stonea, Cambridgeshire, 1980–85* (British Museum, London)	Lucas, G. and Hinman, M., 1996	*Archaeological Excavations of an Iron Age Settlement and Romano-British Enclosures at Watson's Lane, Little Thetford, Ely, Cambridgeshire*, Cambridge Archaeological Unit, (Cambridge)
Jecock, H.M., 1985	'The querns', in Fasham, P.J., *The Prehistoric Settlement at Winnall Down, Winchester*, Hampshire Field Club Monograph 2 (Gloucester)		
Jones, A., 1994	'Little Paxton Quarry, Diddington, Cambridgeshire: archaeological excavations, 1992–3, 2nd Interim Report', *Proceedings of the Cambridge Antiquarian Society* 83, 7–22	MacFarlane, C., 1897	*The Camp of Refuge* (first published 1844: edited by, and with an introduction by, G.L. Gomme) (London)
		Mackreth, D.F., 1988	'Excavations at an Iron Age and Roman enclosure at Werrington', *Britannia* 19, 107–19
Jones, G.E.M., 1984	'Interpretation of plant remains: ethnographic models from Greece', in Zeist, W. van. and Casparie, W.A. (eds), *Plants and Ancient Man, Studies in Palaeoethnobotany*, 43–61, Proceedings of the 6th Symposium of the International Work Group for Palaeoethnobotany (A.A. Balkema, Rotterdam)	Mant, A.K., 1987	'Knowledge acquired from post-war exhumations', in Boddington, A., Garland, A.N. and Jannaway, R.C. (eds), *Death, Decay, and Reconstruction: Approaches to Archaeology and Forensic Science*, 65–78 (Manchester University Press, Manchester)
Jones, G.E.M., 1987	'A statistical approach to the archaeological identification of crop processing', *Journal of Archaeological Science* 14, 311–23	Malim, T., 1992a	*Stonea Camp, Wimblington, An Iron Age Fort in the Fens: Interim Report*, Cambridgeshire County Council Archaeology Field Section (Cambridge)
Jones, G.E.M., forthcoming	'Cereal processing, household space and crop husbandry', in Evans, C. and Hodder, I., *The Haddenham Project II: Marshland Communities and Cultural Landscape*, McDonald Institute Research Series (Cambridge)	Malim, T., 1992b	'Excavation and site management at Stonea Camp, Wimblington 1990–1992', *Fenland Research* 7, 27–34
		Malim, T., 2000a	'Prehistoric trackways' (#11), in Kirby, T. and Oosthuizen, S. (eds), *An Atlas of Cambridgeshire and Huntingdonshire History* (Centre for Regional Studies, Cambridge)
Jones, M., 1978	'The plant remains', in Parrington, M. (ed.), *The Excavation of an Iron Age Settlement, Bronze Age Ring-Ditch and Roman Features at Ashville Trading Estate, Abingdon, Oxfordshire, 1974–6*, Council for British Archaeology Research Report No. 28	Malim, T., 2000b	'The ritual landscape of the Neolithic and Bronze Age along the Middle and Lower Ouse Valley', in Dawson, M. (ed.), *Prehistoric, Roman and Saxon Landscape Studies in the Great Ouse Valley*, 57–88, Council for British Archaeology Research Report 119
Jones, M.U., Kent, J.P.C., Musty, J. and Biek, L., 1976	'Celtic coin moulds from Old Sleaford, Lincolnshire', *Antiquaries Journal* 56, 238–40		
Kenward, H.K., Hall, A.R. and Jones, A.K.G., 1980	'A tested set of techniques for the extraction of plant macrofossils from waterlogged archaeological deposits', *Science and Archaeology* 22, 3–15	Malim, T. and McKenna, R., 1993	'Borough Fen Ringwork: Iron Age fort, Newborough, Cambridgeshire', *Fenland Research* 8, 53–62
King, A., 1978	'A comparative survey of bone assemblages from Roman sites in Britain', *Bulletin of the Institute of Archaeology* 15, 207–32	Maltby, M., 1987	*The Animal Bones from the Excavations at Owslebury, Hants, An Iron Age and Early Romano-British Settlement* (HBMC AM Lab. report 6/87, London)
Kingsley, C., 1866	*Hereward the Wake* (Cambridge)	Maltby, M., 1993	'Animal bones', in Woodward, P.J., *Excavations at the Old Methodist Chapel and Greyhound Yard, Dorchester, 1981–1984*, 315–40 (Dorchester)
Kirch, P., 1986	'Introduction: the archaeology of island societies', in Kirch, P. (ed.), *Island Societies: Archaeological Approaches to Evolution and Transformation*, 1–5 (Cambridge University Press, Cambridge)		
		Martin, E., 1988	*Burgh: The Iron Age and Roman Enclosure*, East Anglian Archaeology Report 40
Kloet, G.S. and Hincks, W.D., 1977	*A Check List of British Insects: Coleoptera and Strepsiptera* (revised 2nd ed.), Royal Entomological Society of London, Handbook for the Identification of British Insects (11, pt. 3)	Masser, P. and Evans. C. 1999	*West Fen and St Johns Roads, Ely, Cambridgeshire: An Archaeological Evaluation: The Trinity, Carter and Runciman Lands*, Cambridge Archaeological Unit (Cambridge)

May, J., 1995 — *Dragonby: Report on Excavations at an Iron Age and Romano-British Settlement in North Lincolnshire* (Oxford)

McCormac, F.G., Kalin, R.M. and Long, A., 1993 — 'Radiocarbon dating beyond 50,000 years by liquid scintillation counting', in Noakes, J.E., Schnhofer, F. and Polach H. (eds), *Liquid Scintillation Spectrometry*, 125–33 (Radiocarbon, Tucson, Arizona)

McFadyen, L., 2000 — *Archaeological Excavations at Eye Quarry, Peterborough* (Phase 2), Cambridge Archaeological Unit (Cambridge)

Medlycott, M., 1994 — 'Iron Age and Roman material from Birchanger, Near Bishops Stortford: excavations at Woodside Industrial Park, 1992', *Essex Archaeology and History* 25, 28–45

Mills, B., 1989 — 'Integrating functional analyses of vessels and sherds through models of ceramic assemblage formation', *World Archaeology* 21, 133–47

Millett, M., 1990 — *The Romanisation of Britain: An Essay in Archaeological Interpretation* (Cambridge University Press, Cambridge)

Molyneaux, B., (ed.) 1997 — *The Cultural Life of Images: Visual Representation in Archaeology* (Routledge, London)

Mook, W.G., 1986 — 'Business meeting: recommendations/resolutions adopted by the Twelfth International Radiocarbon Conference', *Radiocarbon* 28, 799

Moore P.D., Webb, J.A. and Collinson, M.E., 1991 — *Pollen Analysis* (2nd ed.) (Blackwell Scientific Publications, Oxford)

Morris, E.L., 1994 — 'Production and Distribution of Pottery and Salt in Iron Age Britain: A Review', *Proceedings of the Prehistoric Society* 60, 371–93

Morris, E.L., 1996 — 'Iron Age artefact production and exchange', in Champion, T.C. and Collis, J.R. (eds), *The Iron Age in Britain and Ireland: Recent Trends*, 41–65 (J.R. Collis Publications, Department of Archaeology and Prehistory, University of Sheffield, Sheffield)

Morris, E.L., 2001 — 'Briquetage and salt production and distribution systems: a comparative study', in Lane, T. and Morris, E.L. (eds), *A Millennium of Saltmaking: Prehistoric and Romano-British Salt Production in the Fenland*, 389–404, Lincolnshire Archaeology and Heritage Reports Series No. 4

Morris, S. and Buckley, D.G., 1978 — 'Excavations at Danebury Camp, Essex, 1974 and 1977', *Essex Archaeology and History* 10, 1–28

Mortimer, C., 1991 — *Technical Analysis of Metalworking Debris from Snettisham Bypass, Norfolk* (AM Lab. Report 80/91, London)

Mortimer, R. 1996 — *Investigations of the Archaeological Landscape at Broom, Bedfordshire: The Plant Site and Phases 1 and 2.* Cambridge Archaeological Unit Report 202

Mortimer, R., 2000 — *The Cotmist Field, West Fen Road, Ely: Assessment Report*, Cambridge Archaeological Unit (Cambridge)

Mudd, A., 2000 — *West Fen Road, Ely, Cambs: Interim Progress Report*, Northamptonshire Archaeology Report

Murphy, C.P., 1986 — *Thin Section Preparation of Soils and Sediments* (A.B. Academic, Berkhamsted)

Needham, S.P. and Sorensen, M.L.S., 1988 — 'Runnymede Refuse Tip: a consideration of midden deposits and their formation', in Barrett, J.C. and Kinnes, I.A. (eds), *The Archaeology of Context in the Neolithic and Bronze Age: Recent Trends*, 113–26 (Department of Archaeology and Prehistory, University of Sheffield, Sheffield)

Needham, S.P. and Spence, T., 1997 — 'Refuse and the formation of middens', *Antiquity* 71, 77–90

Nelson, B., 1991 — 'Ceramic frequency and use-life: a Highlands Mayan case in cross-cultural perspective', in Longacre, W.A. (ed.), *Ceramic Ethnoarchaeology*, 162–181 (Tucson)

Noakes, J.E., Kim, S.M. and Stipp, J.J., 1965 — 'Chemical and counting advances in liquid scintillation age dating', in Olsson, E.A. and Chatters, R.M. (eds), *Proceedings of the Sixth International Conference on Radiocarbon and Tritium Dating*, 68–92 (Washington D.C.)

Northover, J.P., 1984 — 'Iron Age bronze metallurgy in central Southern Britain', in Cunliffe, B. and Miles, D. (eds), *Aspects of the Iron Age in Central Southern Britain*, 126–45, Oxford University Committee for Archaeology Monograph 2

O'Connor, T.P., 1988 — 'Slums, puddles and ditches: are molluscs useful indicators?', in Murphy, P. and French, C. (eds), *The Exploitation of Wetlands*, 61–8, British Archaeological Reports British Series 186

Orton, C., 1980 — *Mathematics in Archaeology* (Cambridge University Press, Cambridge)

Orton, C., 1989 — 'An introduction to the quantification of assemblages of pottery', *Journal of Roman Pottery Studies* 2, 94–7

Orton C., Tyers, P. and Vince, A., 1993 — *Pottery in Archaeology* (Cambridge University Press, Cambridge)

Pantos, A. and Semple, S. (eds), forthcoming — *Assembly Places and Practices in Medieval Europe* (Four Courts Press, Dublin)

Parker, C. and Corrin, L.G., 1998 — 'Up, Down, Charm, Strange (Truth and Beauty): a conversation with Cornelia Parker and Lisa G. Corrin', in *Cornelia Parker* (Serpentine Gallery, London)

Parker Pearson, M., 1996 — 'Food, fertility and front doors in the first millennium B.C.', in Champion, T.C. and Collis, J.R. (eds), *The Iron Age in Britain and Ireland: Recent Trends*, 117–37 (J.R. Collis Publications, Department of Archaeology and Prehistory, University of Sheffield, Sheffield)

Parker Pearson, M., 1999 — 'Food, sex and death: cosmologies in the British Iron Age with particular reference to East Yorkshire', *Cambridge Archaeological Journal* 9, 43–69

Parker Pearson, M. and Richards, C., 1994 — 'Architecture and order: spatial representation and archaeology', in Parker Pearson, M. and Richards, C. (eds), *Architecture and Order: Approaches to Social Space* (Routledge, London)

Payne, S., 1969 — 'A metrical distinction between sheep and goat metacarpals', in Ucko, P.J. and Dimbleby, G.W. (eds), *The Domestication and Exploitation of Plants and Animals*, 295–305 (Duckworth, London)

Payne, S., 1973 — 'Kill-off patterns in sheep and goats: the mandibles from Asvan Kale', *Anatolian Studies* 23, 281–303

Payne, S., 1975 — 'Partial recovery and sample bias', in Clason, A.T. (ed.), *Archaeozoological Studies*, 120–31 (Amsterdam).

Payne, S., 1985 — 'Morphological distinctions between the mandibular teeth of young sheep, ovis and goats, capra', *Journal of Archaeological Science* 12, 331–58

Payne, S., 1987 — 'Reference codes for wear states in the mandibular cheek teeth of sheep and goats', *Journal of Archaeological Science* 14, 609–14

Payne, S. and Bull, G., 1988 — 'Components of variation in measurements of pig bones and teeth, and the use of measurements to distinguish wild from domestic pig remains', *Archaeozoologia* 2, 27–65

Payne, S. and Munson, P.J., 1985 — 'Ruby and how many squirrels? The destruction of bones by dogs', in Fieller, N.R.J., Gilbertson, D.D. and Ralph, N.G.A. (eds), *Palaeobiological Investigations; Research Design, Methods and Data Analysis*, 31–9, British Archaeological Reports, International Series 266

PCRG, 1997 — *The Study of Later Prehistoric Pottery: General Policies and Guidelines for Analysis and Publication*, Prehistoric Ceramics Research Group Occasional Paper 2 and 3 (revised edition, Oxford)

Pearson, G.W., 1984 — *The Development of High-Precision C Measurement and its Application to Archaeological Time-Scale Problems*, unpublished Ph.D. thesis, Queens University, Belfast

Percival, S., 1999 — 'Iron Age pottery in Norfolk', in Davies, J. and Williamson, T. (eds), *Land of the Iceni*, 173–84 (Centre for East Anglian Studies, Norwich)

Phillips, C.W. (ed.), 1970 — *The Fenland in Roman Times*, Royal Geographical Research Series 5 (Royal Geographical Society, London)

Potter, T., 1981 — 'The Roman occupation of the central fenland', *Britannia* 12, 79–133

Pollard, J., 1996 — 'Iron Age riverside pit alignments at St Ives, Cambridgeshire', *Proceedings of the Prehistoric Society* 62, 93–115

Pryor, F.M.M., 1982 — 'Problems of survival: later prehistoric settlement in the southern East Anglian fenlands', *Analecta Praehistorica Leidensia* 15, 125–43

Pryor, F.M.M., 1983 — 'Gone, but still respected: some evidence for Iron Age house platforms in lowland England', *Oxford Journal of Archaeology* 2, 189–98

Pryor, F.M.M., 1984 — *Excavation at Fengate, Peterborough, England: The Fourth Report*, Northamptonshire Archaeological Monograph 2/Royal Ontario Museum of Archaeology Monograph 7 (Leicester/Toronto)

Pryor, F.M.M., 1991 — *Flag Fen* (Batsford, London)

Pryor, F.M.M., 1996 — 'Sheep, stockyards and field systems: Bronze Age livestock populations in the Fenlands of Eastern England', *Antiquity* 70, 313–24

Pryor, F.M.M., 2001 — *The Flag Fen Basin: Archaeology and Environment of a Fenland Landscape*, English Heritage Archaeological Report (London)

Pryor, F.M.M. and French, C.A.I., 1985 — *Archaeology and Environment in the Lower Welland Valley*, East Anglian Archaeology Report 27

Randsborg, K., 1999 — 'Into the Iron Age: a discourse on war and society', in Carman, J. and Harding, A. (eds), *Ancient Warfare*, 191–202 (Sutton, Stroud)

Reaney, P.H., 1943 — *The Place-Names of Cambridgeshire and the Isle of Ely*, English Place-Name Society 19 (Cambridge)

Rees, S.E., 1979 — 'The Roman scythe blade', in Lambrick, G. and Robinson, M., *Iron Age and Roman Riverside Settlements at Farmoor, Oxfordshire*, 61–4, Oxford Archaeological Unit Report 2/Council for British Archaeology Research Report 32

Regan, R., 2001 — *West Fen Road, Ely. Cornwell Field: Assessment Report*, Cambridge Archaeological Unit, (Cambridge)

Regan, R. and Evans, C., 1998 — *The Archaeology of Colne Fen: Site I*, Cambridge Archaeological Unit, (Cambridge)

Regan, R. and Evans, C., 2000 — *The Archaeology of Colne Fen: Sites III and IV*, Cambridge Archaeological Unit (Cambridge)

Robbins, K.A., forthcoming — *Metalworking Debris from Old Sleaford*, HBMC AM Lab. Report, London

Robinson, M.A., 1991 — 'The Neolithic and Late Bronze Age insect assemblages', in Needham, S.P., *Excavation and Salvage at Runnymede Bridge, 1978: The Late Bronze Age Waterfront Site*, 277–326 (British Museum Press, London)

Robinson, M. and Wilson, R., 1987 — 'A survey of environmental archaeology in the South Midlands', in Keeley, H.C.M. (ed.), *Environmental Archaeology; A Regional Review, Vol 2*, 16–100 (English Heritage, London)

Ross, A., 1967 — *Pagan Celtic Britain: Studies in Iconography and Tradition* (Routledge and Kegan Paul, London)

Round, F.E., 1981 — *The Ecology of Algae* (Cambridge University Press, Cambridge)

Roymans, N., 1995 — 'Romanisation, cultural identity and the ethnic discussion. the integration of Lower Rhine populations in the Roman Empire', in Metzler, J., Millett, M., Roymans, N. and Slofstra, J., *Integration in the Early Roman West: The Role of Culture and Ideology*, 47–64 (Luxembourg)

Roymans, N., 1996 — 'The sword of the plough: regional dynamics in the Romanisation of Belgic Gaul in the Rhineland', in Roymans, N. (ed.), *From Sword to Plough: Three Studies on the Earliest Romanisation of Northern Gaul*, 9–126, Amsterdam Archaeological Studies 1

Rozanski, K., Stichler, W., Gonfiantini, R., Scott, E.M., Beukens, R.P., Kromer, B. and van der Plicht, J., 1992 — 'The IAEA C intercomparison exercise 1990', *Radiocarbon* 34, 506–19

Russell Robinson, H. 1975 — *The Armour of Imperial Rome* (London)

Ryder, M.L., 1983 — 'A re-assessment of Bronze Age wool', *Journal of Archaeological Science* 10, 327–31

Sahlins, M., 1987 — *Islands of History* (Chicago)

Scott, E.M., Harkness, D.D. and Cook, G.T., 1998 — 'Inter-laboratory comparisons: lessons learned', *Radiocarbon* 40, 331–40

Seale, R.S., 1975 — *Soils of the Ely District* (Sheet 173), Soil Survey of England and Wales

Seale, R.S., 1979 — 'Ancient courses of the Great and Little Ouse in Fenland', *Proceedings of the Cambridge Archaeological Society* 69, 1–19

Sealey, P., 1997 — 'The Iron Age', in Bedwin, O. (ed.), *The Archaeology of Essex. Proceedings of the 1993 Writtle Conference*, 26–68 (Chelmsford)

Senior, L., 1995 — 'The estimation of prehistoric values: cracked pot ideas in archaeology', in Skibo, J., Walker, W. and Nielson, A. (eds), *Expanding Archaeology*, 111–25 (University of Utah Press, Salt Lake City)

Serjeantson, D., Wales, S. and Evans, J., 1994 — 'Fish in later Prehistoric Britain', in D. Heinrich (ed.), *Archaeo-Ichthyological Studies, Paper Presented at the 6th Meeting of the I.C.A.Z Fish Remains Working Group*, 332–39, Offa 51 (Wachholz, Neumunster)

Shanks, M., 1992 — *Experiencing the Past: On the Character of Archaeology* (Routledge, London)

Sharples, N., 1991 — 'Warfare in the Iron Age of Wessex', *Scottish Archaeological Review* 8, 79–89

Shott, M., 1996 — 'Mortal pots: on use life and vessel size in the formation of ceramic assemblages', *American Antiquity* 61, 463–82

Simpson, W.G., Gurney, D.A., Neve, J. and Pryor, F.M.M., 1993 — *The Fenland Project Number 7: Excavations in Peterborough and the Lower Welland Valley, 1960–1969*, East Anglian Archaeology Report 61

Stace, C., 1991 — *A New Flora of the British Isles* (Cambridge University Press, Cambridge)

Startin, W., 1982 — 'Prehistoric earthmoving', in Case, H. and Whittle, A. (eds), *Settlement Patterns in the Oxford Region*, 153–6, Council for British Archaeology (London)

Stead, I.M., 1971 — 'The reconstruction of the Iron Age buckets from Aylesford and Baldock', in Sieveking, G. de G. (ed.), *Prehistoric and Roman Studies*, 250–82 (British Museum, London)

Stead, I.M., 1985 — *Celtic Art in Britain Before the Roman Conquest* (London)

Stevens, C.J., 1996 — *Iron Age and Roman Agriculture in the Upper Thames Valley: Archaeobotanical and Social Perspectives*, unpublished Ph.D. thesis, Cambridge University

Stevens, C.J., in press — 'An investigation of agricultural consumption and production models for prehistoric and Roman Britain', *Environmental Archaeology*

Stockmarr J., 1972 — 'Tablets with spores used in absolute pollen analysis', *Pollen et Spores* 13, 615–21

Stuiver, M. and Kra, R.S., 1986 — 'Editorial comment', *Radiocarbon* 28 (2B), ii

Stuiver, M. and Polach, H.J., 1977 — 'Discussion: reporting of C data', *Radiocarbon* 19, 355–63

Stuiver, M. and Reimer, P.J., 1986 — 'A computer program for radiocarbon age calculation', *Radiocarbon* 28, 1022–30

Stuiver, M. and Reimer, P.J., 1993 — 'Extended C data base and revised CALIB 3.0 C Age calibration program', *Radiocarbon* 35, 215–30

Stuiver, M., Reimer, P.J., Bard, E., Beck, J.W., Burr, G.S., Hughen, K.A., Kromer, B., McCormac, F.G., van der Plicht, J. and Spurk, M., 1998 — 'INTCAL98 radiocarbon age calibration, 24,000–0 cal BP', *Radiocarbon* 40, 1041–84

Taylor, M., 1996 — 'Worked wood', in Pollard, J., 'Iron Age riverside pit alignments at St Ives, Cambridgeshire', *Proceedings of the Prehistoric Society* 62, 93–115

Taylor, J., 1997 — 'Space and place: some thoughts on Iron Age and Romano-British landscapes', in Gwilt, A. and Haselgrove, C. (eds), *Reconstructing the Iron Age*, 192–204, Oxbow Monograph 71

Tebbutt, C.F., 1961 — 'Celtic linch-pin heads from Colne Fen Huntingdonshire', *Antiquaries Journal* 41, 235–38

Thompson, I., 1982 — *Grog-Tempered 'Belgic' Pottery of South-Eastern England*, British Archaeological Reports British Series 108

Toller, H.S., 1980 — 'Orsett Cock', *Britannia* 11, 35–42

Treherne, P., 1995 — 'The warrior's beauty: the masculine body and self-identity in Bronze-Age Europe', *Journal of European Archaeology* 3, 105–44

van der Veen, M., 1992 — *Crop Husbandry Regimes: An Archaeobotanical Study of Farming in Northern England 1000 BC–AD 500*, Sheffield Archaeological Monographs 3 (Sheffield)

van der Veen, M., in press — 'The economic value of chaff and straw in arid and temperate zones', *Vegetation History and Archaeobotany*

Wacher, J.S., 1964 — 'Excavation on Breedon-on-the-Hill, Leicestershire, 1957', *Antiquaries Journal* 44, 122–42

Wainwright, G.J., 1979 — *Gussage All Saints: An Iron Age Settlement in Dorset* (HMSO, London)

Wait, G.A., 1985 — *Ritual and Religion in Iron Age Britain*, British Archaeological Reports, British Series 149

Waller, M., 1994 — *The Fenland Project, Number 9: Flandrian Environmental Change in Fenland*, East Anglian Archaeology Report 70

Ward, G.K. and Wilson, S.R., 1978 — 'Procedures for comparing and combining radiocarbon age determinations: a critique', *Archaeometry* 20, 19–31

West, S., 1990 — *West Stow: The Prehistoric and Roman-British Occupations*, East Anglian Archaeology Report 48

Williams, D., 1986/7 — 'Weekley, Northamptonshire: petrological examination of Iron Age pottery', in Jackson, D.A. and Dix, B., 'Late Iron Age and Roman settlement at Weekley, Northants', *Northamptonshire Archaeology* 21 (microfiche, 124–6)

Williams, P., 1979 — 'Waterlogged wood remains', in Smith, C.A., *Fisherwick: The Reconstruction of an Iron Age Landscape*, 71–7, British Archaeological Reports, British Series 61

Willis, S., 1994 — 'Roman imports into Late Iron Age British societies: towards a critique of existing models', in Cottam, S., Dungworth, D., Scott, S. and Taylor, J. (eds), *TRAC 94: Proceedings of the Fourth Theoretical Roman Archaeology Conference, Durham 1994*, 141–50 (Oxbow, Oxford)

Willis, S., 1997a — 'The Romanization of pottery assemblages in the East and North-East of England during the First Century A.D.: a comparative analysis', *Britannia* 27, 179–221

Willis, S., 1997b — 'Samian: beyond dating', in Meadows, K., Lemke, C. and Heron, J. (eds), *TRAC 96: Proceedings of the Sixth Theoretical Roman Archaeology Conference*, 38–54 (Oxbow, Oxford)

Willis, S., 1998 — 'Samian pottery in Britain: exploring its distribution and archaeological potential', *Archaeological Journal* 155, 82–133

Wilson, B., 1992 — 'Consideration for the identification of ritual deposits of animal bones in Iron Age pits', *International Journal of Osteoarchaeology* 2, 341–9

Wilthew, P., Bayley, J. and Linton, R., 1991 — 'Analysis of the metalworking debris', in Gregory, A.K., *Excavations in Thetford, 1980–82: Fison Way*, 141–3, East Anglian Archaeology Report 53

Wiltshire P.E.J., 1999 — *Forensic Palynological Analysis of Exhibits Associated with Operation Gratis*, unpublished report for Hertfordshire Constabulary

Wiltshire P.E.J., 2000 — *Palynological Assessment of Ditch Sediments at Zionshill Copse Enclosure (ZCE/99), Chandlers Ford, Hampshire*, unpublished report for Berkshire Archaeological Services

Wiltshire P.E.J., Edwards, K.J. and Bond, S., 1994 — 'Microbially-derived metallic sulphide spherules, pollen and the waterlogging of archaeological sites', in Davis, O.K. (ed.), *Aspects of Archaeological Palynology: Methodology and Applications*, 206–21, American Association of Stratigraphic Palynologists Contributions Series 29

Wiltshire, P.E.J. and Murphy, P.L, in prep. — *New Evidence for the History of Norway Spruce in England*

Woodward, A., 1995 — 'Vessel size and social identity in the Bronze Age of Southern England', in Kinnes, I. and Varndell, G. (eds), *Unbaked Urns of Rudely Shape*, 195–202, Oxbow Monograph 55

Woodward, A., 1997 — 'Size and style: an alternative study of some Iron Age Pottery in Southern England', in Gwilt, A. and Haselgrove, C. (eds), *Reconstructing the Iron Age*, 153–66, Oxbow Monograph 71

Woodward, A, and Blinkhorn, P., 1997 — 'Size is important: Iron Age vessel capacities in Central and Southern England', in Cumberpatch, C. and Blinkhorn, P. (eds), *Not So Much A Pot, More A Way Of Life*, 153–62, Oxbow Monograph 83

Worssam, B.C. and Taylor, J.H., 1969 — *Geology of the Country around Cambridge* (London)

Yarrell, W., 1836 — *A History of British Fishes* (van Voorst, London)

Young, R. and Humphrey, J., 1999 — 'Flint use in England after the Bronze Age: time for re-evaluation?', *Proceedings of the Prehistoric Society* 65, 231–42

Index

Illustrations are denoted by page numbers in *italics* or by *illus* where figures are scattered throughout the text.

abandonment, modelling, 215
access *see* entrances
agriculture
    agricultural processing, an overview, 138–43
    land-use model, *143*, 144
    location, 136
    see also animal bones; plant macrofossils
Akerman, Jeremy, 22
Aldreth causeway, 18, 67, 263
animal bedding, 112, 136
animal bones
    age distribution, 129, 130
    body parts, 127, 128
    butchery, 128, 130
    carnivore activity, 127, 128
    discussion/summary, 131, 136–8
    distributions
        buildings, 134, *135*, 208, *209–11*, 212
        ploughsoil, 203, *204*, 206
        Ringwork, 212–16
        test-pits, 206, *207*, 208
    flotation, recovered by, 131–2, *133*, 134
    intra-site variability, 131
    measurements, 273–8
    methodology, 122
    pathology, 130
    species frequency, 127
    species size and representation
        cattle, 122, 128
        dog, 126
        equids, 122
        fish, 126–7, 131–2
        galliform, 126
        otter, 126
        pigs, 122–6
        sheep/goat, 122, 123–4
        other, 127, 131–2
animal pen, 64, 233
antler fragments, 127, 137
Arbury Camp (Cambs), 255, 256, 259, 260, 262, 264, 270
arrowhead, leaf-shaped, 24
arsenic, 197, 200
artefact distributions/densities, 18, 203, *204–5*, 206
    artefactual paths, 222–3
    feature patterning, 208, *209–11*, 212
    modelling artefact populations, 216–18
    occupation dynamics, 223
    post-medieval period, *65*, 67
    reduction dynamics, 215–16
    relative frequencies, 215
    Ringwork catchment, 212, *213*, 214–15
    test-pits, 206, *207*, 208
axes, Neolithic, 8, 24

banks, 26, 56–7, *58–9*, 63, 64, 252
Barrington (Cambs), 128, 130
barrow, 9
beads, jet, 190, 200
bees, 120, 121, 136
Belsar's Hill (Cambs), 18, 67, 255, *256*, 263
bone objects, 194, 199; *see also* animal bones; human bones
Borough Fen (Cambs), 255, 259, 260, 262, 264
Boudiccan rebellion, 271
bracelets
    Bronze Age, 7
    Roman, 248
bracken, 112, 136, 200
bridge structure, 34, 62
Bronze Age period, 23–6, *250–1*, 252
brooch, 1st century, 248
Broom Quarry (Beds), *251*, 252

bucket/tankard fragment, 18, 194, *195–6*, 197
buildings *see* structures
burials
    Hurst Lane, 248–9, 258
    Wardy Hill, 232, 258
burnt flint mound, 23, *25*, 26, 252
button, post-medieval, 184

Cambridge (Cambs)
    clay pipe maker, 65
    Kettle's Yard Gallery, 21
Catuvellauni, 268
causeways, 2, 7, 9, 245, 252, 263–6
cemeteries, 9
cereals
    crops grown, 138
    harvesting, 138–40
    macrofossils
        densities, 110
        Period I, 85, 108
        Period II, 86–108
    pollen, 74, 79, 80, 81, 82, 83, 84
    processing, 109, 140–1, 141–3
    storage, 141
    waste, 141
Chatteris (Cambs), 268
chisel, iron, 184
chronology, 238–43; *see also* phasing
clay pipes *see* tobacco pipes
claying trenches, 64
clock escapement, 184, *185*
cobbled surface, *19*, 34, *36*
coins
    Iron Age, 248
    medieval, 64, 184
Colne Fen (Hunts), 228, 255, 260, *261*, 262, 264
comb fragment, 194, 197, 199
copper alloy finds, 184, *185*, 198
The Cove
    archaeological context, *8*, 243, *244*, 245, *246–7*, 248–9
    environmental reconstruction, 10, *11–14*, 15
    location and topography, *1*, 2
    settlement system, 266, *267*, 268–9, 270
Coveney
    archaeological context, 7–10
    causeway, 263–6, *267*
    environmental reconstruction, 10, *11–14*, 15
    location, *1*
crop-processing
    evidence
        plant macrofossils, 109–11
        pollen, 82, 83, 84, 136
    overview, 138–43
crop-storage, 141
crucibles, 186, 187, *188*, 189, 197, 198
currency bar, 8

The Dams (Cambs), 67
dating *see* radiocarbon dating
daub, 194
decorative styles, *199*, 200
defence
    Bronze Age, 252
    Iron Age
        assembly and translation of space, 253, *254*, 255, *256*, 257–8
        need for, 18–21
        status and labour, 258, *259*, 260–3
distributions *see* artefact distributions/densities
ditches, Ringwork, *254*
    early, 45–6, *47–53*, 54
    circuit, 26, *27–30*, 31, *32*
    phasing, 57, *58–62*, 63–4
Downham (Cambs), 9, 245, 266
droveway, 7, 259

dyke system, 45–6, 108

eggshell, 138
Ely (Cambs)
  Castle, 21, 268
  clay pipe maker, 65
  Hurst Lane
    animal bones, 134
    buildings, 223, 225, 228, 271
    in context, 267, 268
    enclosure, *254*, 255, 256–7, *259*, 260, 262, 264
    excavations, 9–10, *247*, 248–9
    human bones, 232, 258
    plant remains, 138, 139, 140, 141, 142
    pottery, 161
  occupation, Iron Age, 10
  Trinity Lands, 8, 9
  West Fen Road
    animal bones, 134, 138
    enclosure, 266, *267*, 268
    excavations, 8, 9, *244*, 245, 247–8
    finds, *244*, 245
    plant remains, 138, 139, 140, 141, 142–3, 247
  see also Isle of Ely
enclosures, in vicinity, 9–10
entrances
  phasing, 233, *234*, 235, 239, 253
  structure and sequence, 31–2, 62, 63
    Landward, 34, *35–6*, 37
    Watergate, 32, *33*, 34, 37
    West Central Crossing, 34, *37–8*, 39
    Western Crossing, 34, 37
environment
  environmental reconstruction, 10, *11–14*, 15
  evidence, discussion of, 132–44
  sampling, 17–18, 70
  see also animal bones; insect remains; molluscs; palynology; phosphate analysis; plant macrofossils; soil micromorphology; wood fragments
Erche, Charles, 21
Excavating the Present, 21–2
excavation methodology, 17–18

feature patterning, 208, *209–11*, 212
fences, 59, 253
Fengate (Cambs)
  animal bones, 127
  buildings, 223, 228, *261*
  enclosure, *259*
  pottery, 18, 180, 243
  Romanisation, 271
fenland islands, 2, *3*, 6
Fenland Management Project, 1
Fenland Survey, 1, 8, 67
finds distributions/densities *see* artefact distributions/densities
finger ring, copper alloy, 184, *185*, 197
fired clay objects, 190, *192–3*, 194
fishing, evidence for, 126–7, 131–2, 137
Fiskerton causeway (Lincs), 266
Flag Fen (Cambs), 263–6
flax, 108
flints, 8, 23–5, 26, 252; *see also* burnt flint mound
flooring material, 112, 136, 137

gaming piece?, stone, 190
gate structure, 34, 62
Gdaniec, Kasia, 22
geology and soils *see* soils
geophysical survey, 5, 6, *7*
  magnetic susceptibility, distribution, 218, *219–20*, 221–2
  results, *205*, 206
gouge, bone, 245
grain processing, 199
grindstones *see* whetstones/grindstones
Groundwell Farm (Wilts), *257*
Grunty Fen, 1, 7, 9, 266
Gussage All Saints (Dorset), 256, *257*, 264

Haddenham (Cambs)
  IV, 146

V
  animal bones, 127, 137, 138
  artefact populations, 18, 216, 217–18, 223
  buildings, 223, 228, 260, *261*
  enclosure, 262, 264
  human bones, 227
  layout, 255
  plant macrofossils, 109
  pottery, 146, 148, 170–1, 178, 180, 181, 182, 183
  Snow's Farm shrine, 271
handle, bone, 194
harvesting, 138–40
haystack, 39, 57–9, 233, 253
hedges, 56, 57, 59, 252
  environmental evidence, 80, 83, 115, 121, 136
helmet, Roman, 8, 271
Hereward the Wake, 2–3, 67, 263
herpetofauna, 132, *133*
Hinxton (Cambs), 268
hoards, Bronze Age, 7
human bones, 227, *230–1*, 232, 258
hunting, evidence for, 127, 137

inscription, clay pipe, 65
insect remains, 114–21, 136
Iron Age period (*illus*)
  discussion, 253–70
  excavation, 26–64
iron objects, 184, *185*
Isle of Ely
  environmental reconstruction, 10, *11–12*, 15
  location and topography, *xii, 1, 2–3*
  settlement, 10, 266, *267*, 268–9, 272
Isleham (Cambs), swords, 8, 271

kiln, 9
kindling, 109, 136

labour, 260–2
land-use model, *143*, 144
latrine, 233
Little Thetford (Cambs)
  causeway, 263
  Watson's Lane
    animal bones, 134, 138
    buildings, 223, 225, 228, 245, *246*, 248
    excavation, 9
    plant remains, 138, 139, 140, 141, 142
    pottery, 146, 162, 178, 180, 181, 183
Little Waltham (Essex), 146, 256, 262, 264
locations, *xii, 1, 5*
loomweights, 192, *193*, 194, 197, 199

March (Cambs), 268
Maxey (Cambs), Plants Farm, 260, 262, 264
medieval–post-medieval period, 64–8, 272
metalwork
  description, 65, 67, 184, *185*
  discussion, 197
  distribution, *198*
  stray finds, 7, 8
metalworking, 188, 189, 197, 199, 227
metalworking debris
  analysis, 185–9
  distribution, 197, *198*
middens, 23, 208, 220, 222, 223, 253, 255
millstone fragment, 188
mineral, red, 197, 200
Mingies Ditches (Oxon), 236, 255, 256, *257*, *259*, 262–3, 264
mistletoe, 112, *113*, 136
molluscs, 106, 112–14, 136
mortuary house, 232

nails, 67, 184, *185*, 197, 198
Narborough (Norfolk), 255, *256*
non-ferrous metalworking, 188, 189

occupation dynamics, 223
Orsett Cock (Essex), 256, *257*
oven fragments, 192, 194

290

Owen, Elspeth, 22

palynology, 71
   discussion, 83–4, 136
   interpretation, 79–82
   methods, 71–4
   pollen assemblage zones, 72–3, 74–9
parasites, 79, 80, 81
Parker, Cornelia, 22, 202
path, 31, 56
phasing
   buildings, 232–3, 235
   Ringwork, 54–64
phosphate analysis, 17, 203, *205*, 206, *220*, 221–2
pigment, 197
pill box, 1, *4*, *17*, 67, 258
pins, bone, 194, 199
pits and troughs
   excavation, *37*, 38, 44–5, *46*
   four-pit group, 59, 253
   plant macrofossils, 96–8
place cognition, 21
placename, 1
plant macrofossils
   assemblage composition, 103
   F1 sections, 104–5
   frequencies, 102, 107
   overview, 138
      crops grown, 138
      harvesting, 138–40
      land-use modelling, 143–4
      processing, 140–1, 141–3
      storage, 141
   Period I and II.1, 85–7, 108
   Period II, 87–8, 108–12, *113*
      pits *etc.*, 94–6
      Ringwork ditches, 97–9
      Structures II and III, 90
      Structure IV, 100–1
      Structures V and VI, 91–3
   sampling, 84
plaque, clay, *244*, 245
plough scarring, *15*, 17, 67
point, bone, 245
population, 144, 268
pottery
   Bronze Age, 24, *150*, 161
   Iron Age and Early Roman
      assemblage, 145
      described, *149–61*
         Phase 1, 161
         Phase 2, 161–2
         Phase 3–5, 164–6
         Ringwork, 162–4
      distributions: artefactual paths, 222–3, *224*
         feature patterning, 208, *209–11*, 212
         ploughsoil, 203, *204–5*, 206
         Ringwork, 212–16
         test-pits, 206, *207*, 208
      fabrics, 166–9
      forms
         surface treatment and decoration, 171–6
         handmade, 176–7, *195*, *199*, 200
         wheelmade, 177–81, *195*
      petrology, 168, 169–70
      phasing and dating, 145–8
      production and exchange, 170–1, 200
      recovered by sieving, 184
      use, 181–4
   post-Roman, 64–5
   see also crucibles; fired clay objects
punch, iron, 184
Pymore (Cambs), 10

quernstones, 9, 189–90, *191*, 197, 199, 200

radiocarbon dating, 18, 238–42
ramparts *see* banks
rapiers, Bronze Age, 7, *8*
ring-ditches, 9

rings
   Hurst Lane, 248
   Wardy Hill, 184, *185*, 197
   see also finger ring
Ringwork
   chronology, 239–43
   discussion
      Bronze Age period, *250–1*, 252
      Iron Age period (*illus*), 253–70
      Romanisation, 270–2
      post-medieval period, 272
   excavation, *4–6*, 15–18
      Bronze Age period, 23–6
      pre/early Ringwork, 45–6, *47–53*, 54
      Iron Age period
         buildings and structures, 39, *40–3*, 44
         ditches, 26, *27–30*, 31
         entrances, 31–2, *33*, 34, *35–8*, 39
         pits and troughs, 44–5, *46*
      historical period, 64, *65–6*, 67
   phasing and structuring, 54–6
      alternatives and ambiguities, 63–4
      enclosure categorisation, 233, *234–7*
      linkages and embankment, 56–7
      outline, 57, *58–62*, 63
      spatial determinants, *55*, 56
Robinson, Ben, 22
Romanisation, 10, 270–2
roundhouses *see* structures
rubbers, 189, *191*, 199

sacrifice, 249, 258
sheep pen *see* animal pen
sheet fragment, iron, 184
Shelton, Risley, 65
shields, Bronze Age, 7
shrine, 227, 232, 233, 255, 263
Sibley, Robert, 65
slag *see* metalworking debris
smithing, 189
social status, 260
soils
   geology and soils, 10, *11–12*, 13, *14*, 15
   soil micromorphology, 18, 69–71
South Creake (Norfolk), enclosure, 255
spindle whorls
   bone, 194
   distribution, 197, *199*
   fired clay, *192*, 194
   stone, 190, *192*, *199*, 200
stave, decorated, 194, *195–6*, 197, *199*, 200
stone objects, 189–90, *191–2*, 197–9
Stonea Camp (Cambs)
   dating, 259
   enclosure, 255, *256*, 260, 262, 264, 268
   human bones, 227
   pottery, 10
   Romanisation, 271
structures
   building types and inter-relationships, 223, *225–6*, 227–8, *229*, *261*
   finds distribution, 208, *209–11*, 212
   rhythm of, 232–3
   Structure I
      animal bones, 134, 137, 138
      artefact densities, 206, 208, *211*, 212, 214, 215, 216, 218
      chemical signatures, 218, 220–1, 222
      chronology/phasing, 57, 63, 233, 239, 242, 243
      excavation, *17*, 39, *40–1*
      fired clay, 194
      metalworking debris, 185, 189
      plan/function, 225, *226*, *261*
      plant macrofossils, 89, 103, 109, 110, 111, 136
      pottery, 146, *150–2*, 162
   Structure II
      animal bones, 134
      artefact densities, 206, 208, 212, 215, 216–17, 218
      chemical signatures, 218, 220–1, 222
      chronology/phasing, 63, 233, 243
      excavation, 39, *43*, 44
      plan/function, 225, 226

    plant macrofossils, 90–2, 103, 109, 110, 111, 136
  Structure III
    animal bones, 134, 137, 138
    artefact densities, 206, 208, *211*, 212, 214, 215, 216, 217, 218
    chemical signatures, 218, 220–1, 222
    chronology/phasing, 57, 233, 242
    excavation, *17*, 39, *42*, 44
    plan/function, 225, 226–7
    plant macrofossils, 90–2, 103, 109, 110, 136
    pottery, *154*, 162, 166
  Structure IV
    animal bones, 134, 137, 138
    artefact densities, 206, 208, *211*, 212, 214, 215, 216–18
    artefact paths, 222–3
    chemical signatures, 218, 220–1, 222
    chronology/phasing, 63, 233, 239, 242, 243
    excavation, *17*, *20*, *38*, 39, *40–1*, 44
    fired clay, 194
    human bones, 227, *230–1*, 232, 255, 263
    metalwork/metalworking debris, 185, 189, 197
    plan/function, 225, *226*, 255, *261*, 263
    plant macrofossils, 101, 103, 109, 110, 111, 136
    pottery, 146, *153–4*, *155–9*, 162, 164–6
  Structure V
    animal bones, 134, 138
    artefact densities, 206, 208, *211*, 212, 214, 215, 216, 217, 218
    chemical signatures, 218, 220–1, 222
    chronology/phasing, 57, 233, 242
    excavation, *17*, 39, *42*, 44
    plan/function, 225, *226*, 227, 263
    plant macrofossils, 93–5, 103, 109, 110, 136
    pottery, 162
  Structure VI
    artefact densities, 208, 212, 215, 216–17, 218
    chemical signatures, 220–1
    chronology/phasing, 57–9, 233
    excavation, 39, *43*, 44
    plan/function, 226
    plant macrofossils, 93–5, 103, 109, 110, 111, 136
  Structure VII, 64, 67
stud, copper alloy, 184
Stuntney causeway, 263, 266
survey, 15, *16*, 17; *see also* geophysical survey

swords
  Bronze Age, 7
  Iron Age, 8, 271

tankard fragment *see* bucket/tankard fragment
tanning, 45
Tattershall Thorpe (Lincs), 255, 259, 260, 262, 264
Taylor, Richard, 250
test-pits, *16*, 17
  artefact densities, 206, *207*, 208, *210*
thatch, 81, 109, 136, 137
Thetford (Norfolk)
  Fison Way
    buildings, *261*
    enclosure, 255, 262, 263, 264, *265*
    pottery, 146
  Thetford Castle, 255, *256*
tobacco pipes, 65, 67
toggle, bone, 194
trade and exchange, 10, 259, 266, 268, 271
  artefacts, 170–1, 200
troughs *see* pits and troughs

visitor survey, 67–8
votive deposition, 7–8, 260, 266, 271

Wandlebury (Cambs), 255, 270
War Ditches (Cambs), 255
Wardeye, 1
warfare, 258–9
Warham Camp (Norfolk), 255
watch building, 233
water supply, 31, 44
weaving, 197, 199, 227
Werrington (Cambs), 146, 255, 263, 264, *265*
West Fen Row (Suffolk), sword, 8
West Stow (Suffolk), 161, 180
whetstones/grindstones, 190, *191*, 199, 200
Witcham (Cambs), 8, 9, 271
Witchford, 1, 9, 266, 268
wood fragments, 121–2, 136; *see also* stave, decorated
worked stone objects, 189–90, *191–2*, 197, 199

East Anglian Archaeology

is a serial publication sponsored by the Scole Archaeological Committee. Norfolk, Suffolk and Essex Archaeology Services, the Norwich Survey and the Fenland Project all contribute volumes to the series. It is the main vehicle for publishing final reports on archaeological excavations and surveys in the region. For information about titles in the series, visit **www.eaareports.org.uk**. Reports can be obtained from:

Phil McMichael, Essex County Council Archaeology Section
Fairfield Court, Fairfield Road, Braintree, Essex CM7 3YQ

Reports available so far:
No.1, 1975 Suffolk: various papers
No.2, 1976 Norfolk: various papers
No.3, 1977 Suffolk: various papers
No.4, 1976 Norfolk: Late Saxon town of Thetford
No.5, 1977 Norfolk: various papers on Roman sites
No.6, 1977 Norfolk: Spong Hill Anglo-Saxon cemetery, Part I
No.7, 1978 Norfolk: Bergh Apton Anglo-Saxon cemetery
No.8, 1978 Norfolk: various papers
No.9, 1980 Norfolk: North Elmham Park
No.10, 1980 Norfolk: village sites in Launditch Hundred
No.11, 1981 Norfolk: Spong Hill, Part II: Catalogue of Cremations
No.12, 1981 The barrows of East Anglia
No.13, 1981 Norwich: Eighteen centuries of pottery from Norwich
No.14, 1982 Norfolk: various papers
No.15, 1982 Norwich: Excavations in Norwich 1971–1978; Part I
No.16, 1982 Norfolk: Beaker domestic sites in the Fen-edge and East Anglia
No.17, 1983 Norfolk: Waterfront excavations and Thetford-type Ware production, Norwich
No.18, 1983 Norfolk: The archaeology of Witton
No.19, 1983 Norfolk: Two post-medieval earthenware pottery groups from Fulmodeston
No.20, 1983 Norfolk: Burgh Castle: excavation by Charles Green, 1958–61
No.21, 1984 Norfolk: Spong Hill, Part III: Catalogue of Inhumations
No.22, 1984 Norfolk: Excavations in Thetford, 1948–59 and 1973–80
No.23, 1985 Norfolk: Excavations at Brancaster 1974 and 1977
No.24, 1985 Suffolk: West Stow, the Anglo-Saxon village
No.25, 1985 Essex: Excavations by Mr H.P.Cooper on the Roman site at Hill Farm, Gestingthorpe, Essex
No.26, 1985 Norwich: Excavations in Norwich 1971–78; Part II
No.27, 1985 Cambridgeshire: The Fenland Project No.1: Archaeology and Environment in the Lower Welland Valley
No.28, 1985 Norfolk: Excavations within the north-east bailey of Norwich Castle, 1978
No.29, 1986 Norfolk: Barrow excavations in Norfolk, 1950–82
No.30, 1986 Norfolk: Excavations at Thornham, Warham, Wighton and Caistor St Edmund, Norfolk
No.31, 1986 Norfolk: Settlement, religion and industry on the Fen-edge; three Romano-British sites in Norfolk
No.32, 1987 Norfolk: Three Norman Churches in Norfolk
No.33, 1987 Essex: Excavation of a Cropmark Enclosure Complex at Woodham Walter, Essex, 1976 and An Assessment of Excavated Enclosures in Essex
No.34, 1987 Norfolk: Spong Hill, Part IV: Catalogue of Cremations
No.35, 1987 Cambridgeshire: The Fenland Project No.2: Fenland Landscapes and Settlement, Peterborough–March
No.36, 1987 Norfolk: The Anglo-Saxon Cemetery at Morningthorpe
No.37, 1987 Norfolk: Excavations at St Martin-at-Palace Plain, Norwich, 1981
No.38, 1987 Suffolk: The Anglo-Saxon Cemetery at Westgarth Gardens, Bury St Edmunds
No.39, 1988 Norfolk: Spong Hill, Part VI: Occupation during the 7th–2nd millennia BC
No.40, 1988 Suffolk: Burgh: The Iron Age and Roman Enclosure
No.41, 1988 Essex: Excavations at Great Dunmow, Essex: a Romano-British small town in the Trinovantian Civitas
No.42, 1988 Essex: Archaeology and Environment in South Essex, Rescue Archaeology along the Gray's By-pass 1979–80
No.43, 1988 Essex: Excavation at the North Ring, Mucking, Essex: A Late Bronze Age Enclosure
No.44, 1988 Norfolk: Six Deserted Villages in Norfolk
No.45, 1988 Norfolk: The Fenland Project No. 3: Marshland and the Nar Valley, Norfolk
No.46, 1989 Norfolk: The Deserted Medieval Village of Thuxton
No.47, 1989 Suffolk: West Stow: Early Anglo-Saxon Animal Husbandry
No.48, 1989 Suffolk: West Stow, Suffolk: The Prehistoric and Romano-British Occupations
No.49, 1990 Norfolk: The Evolution of Settlement in Three Parishes in South-East Norfolk
No.50, 1993 Proceedings of the Flatlands and Wetlands Conference
No.51, 1991 Norfolk: The Ruined and Disused Churches of Norfolk
No.52, 1991 Norfolk: The Fenland Project No. 4, The Wissey Embayment and Fen Causeway
No.53, 1992 Norfolk: Excavations in Thetford, 1980–82, Fison Way
No.54, 1992 Norfolk: The Iron Age Forts of Norfolk
No.55, 1992 Lincolnshire: The Fenland Project No.5: Lincolnshire Survey, The South-West Fens
No.56, 1992 Cambridgeshire: The Fenland Project No.6: The South-Western Cambridgeshire Fens
No.57, 1993 Norfolk and Lincolnshire: Excavations at Redgate Hill Hunstanton; and Tattershall Thorpe
No.58, 1993 Norwich: Households: The Medieval and Post-Medieval Finds from Norwich Survey Excavations 1971–1978
No.59, 1993 Fenland: The South-West Fen Dyke Survey Project 1982–86
No.60, 1993 Norfolk: Caister-on-Sea: Excavations by Charles Green, 1951–55
No.61, 1993 Fenland: The Fenland Project No.7: Excavations in Peterborough and the Lower Welland Valley 1960–1969
No.62, 1993 Norfolk: Excavations in Thetford by B.K. Davison, between 1964 and 1970
No.63, 1993 Norfolk: Illington: A Study of a Breckland Parish and its Anglo-Saxon Cemetery
No.64, 1994 Norfolk: The Late Saxon and Medieval Pottery Industry of Grimston: Excavations 1962–92
No.65, 1993 Suffolk: Settlements on Hill-tops: Seven Prehistoric Sites in Suffolk
No.66, 1993 Lincolnshire: The Fenland Project No.8: Lincolnshire Survey, the Northern Fen-Edge
No.67, 1994 Norfolk: Spong Hill, Part V: Catalogue of Cremations
No.68, 1994 Norfolk: Excavations at Fishergate, Norwich 1985
No.69, 1994 Norfolk: Spong Hill, Part VIII: The Cremations
No.70, 1994 Fenland: The Fenland Project No.9: Flandrian Environmental Change in Fenland
No.71, 1995 Essex: The Archaeology of the Essex Coast Vol.I: The Hullbridge Survey Project
No.72, 1995 Norfolk: Excavations at Redcastle Furze, Thetford, 1988–9
No.73, 1995 Norfolk: Spong Hill, Part VII: Iron Age, Roman and Early Saxon Settlement
No.74, 1995 Norfolk: A Late Neolithic, Saxon and Medieval Site at Middle Harling
No.75, 1995 Essex: North Shoebury: Settlement and Economy in South-east Essex 1500–AD1500
No.76, 1996 Nene Valley: Orton Hall Farm: A Roman and Early Anglo-Saxon Farmstead
No.77, 1996 Norfolk: Barrow Excavations in Norfolk, 1984–88
No.78, 1996 Norfolk:The Fenland Project No.11: The Wissey Embayment: Evidence for pre-Iron Age Occupation
No.79, 1996 Cambridgeshire: The Fenland Project No.10: Cambridgeshire Survey, the Isle of Ely and Wisbech
No.80, 1997 Norfolk: Barton Bendish and Caldecote: fieldwork in south-west Norfolk
No.81, 1997 Norfolk: Castle Rising Castle
No.82, 1998 Essex: Archaeology and the Landscape in the Lower Blackwater Valley
No.83, 1998 Essex: Excavations south of Chignall Roman Villa 1977–81
No.84, 1998 Suffolk: A Corpus of Anglo-Saxon Material
No.85, 1998 Suffolk: Towards a Landscape History of Walsham le Willows
No.86, 1998 Essex: Excavations at the Orsett 'Cock' Enclosure
No.87, 1999 Norfolk: Excavations in Thetford, North of the River, 1989–90
No.88, 1999 Essex: Excavations at Ivy Chimneys, Witham 1978–83
No.89, 1999 Lincolnshire: Salterns: Excavations at Helpringham, Holbeach St Johns and Bicker Haven
No.90, 1999 Essex:The Archaeology of Ardleigh, Excavations 1955–80

No.91, 2000 Norfolk: Excavations on the Norwich Southern Bypass, 1989–91 Part I Bixley, Caistor St Edmund, Trowse
No.92, 2000 Norfolk: Excavations on the Norwich Southern Bypass, 1989–91 Part II Harford Farm Anglo-Saxon Cemetery
No.93, 2001 Norfolk: Excavations on the Snettisham Bypass, 1989
No.94, 2001 Lincolnshire: Excavations at Billingborough, 1975–8
No.95, 2001 Suffolk: Snape Anglo-Saxon Cemetery: Excavations and Surveys
No.96, 2001 Norfolk: Two Medieval Churches in Norfolk
No.97, 2001 Cambridgeshire: Monument 97, Orton Longueville
No.98, 2002 Essex: Excavations at Little Oakley, 1951–78
No.99, 2002 Norfolk: Excavations at Melford Meadows, Brettenham, 1994
No.100, 2002 Norwich: Excavations in Norwich 1971–78, Part III
No.101, 2002 Norfolk: Medieval Armorial Horse Furniture in Norfolk
No.102, 2002 Norfolk: Baconsthorpe Castle, Excavations and Finds, 1951–1972
No.103, 2003 Cambridgeshire: Excavations at the Wardy Hill Ringwork, Coveney, Ely